"Deborah Lee is a masterful storyteller who reminds u▮
while we are plunged into her own. I clutched my heart as ▮
SARA ALFAGEEH, illustrat▮

"Deb Lee's beautifully delicate gray landscapes are a fitting backdrop
for this coming-of-age tale that encompasses so many of the liminal spaces of life:
between cultures, past and future, childhood and independence."
HARMONY BECKER, creator of *Himawari House*

"With breathtaking art and poignant storytelling,
In Limbo is a masterpiece in expressing one's truth as a queer Asian American."
LAURA GAO, creator of *Messy Roots*

"Deb JJ Lee's *In Limbo* is a stunning study in mood and detail. Her poetic black-and-white
illustrations bring you into her world as a lonely high school student, struggling to communicate with
her parents and few friends about her frustrations with fitting in as a Korean-born immigrant."
MALAKA GHARIB, creator of *It Won't Always Be Like This*

"A gorgeous and vital coming-of-age story full of raw, diasporic feeling.
Lee's writing breaks your heart even while her stunning ink washes soothe your soul."
KIKU HUGHES, creator of *Displacement*

"While the challenges faced in her story are starkly serious,
the virtuosity with which Lee shuffles together evocative images is unapologetically joyful."
R. KIKUO JOHNSON, creator of *No One Else*

"Deb JJ Lee's *In Limbo* is spectacular in its synthesis of visual storytelling and gripping tone;
a coming-of-age story with truth and heart. It takes the reader to the places where breathing is hard;
where I know my own breath was absolutely taken away by this incredible comic."
MOLLY MENDOZA, creator of *Skip*

"*In Limbo* lifts the comic memoir to new heights. At once heartrending and triumphant,
with sumptuous artwork, this story will take your breath away."
REBECCA MOCK, illustrator of *Salt Magic*

"An achingly beautiful and masterfully lyrical work of art by an illustrator at the top of both their creative and
technical form. Deb Lee takes the illustrated memoir to intimately personal heights and complex, sublime depths.
Lee's visual language is breathtaking, unlike anything I've seen before. I feel changed by this deeply moving work."
JONNY SUN, *creator of Goodbye, again*

"Deborah Lee's memoir stuns with its inky dreamlike illustrations and gut punch of emotion.
In Limbo is a masterpiece, a tale of the real highs and lows of growing up."
VICTORIA YING, creator of *Hungry Ghost*

"A stunningly rendered, emotionally raw memoir encompassing all the best
and worst of one's teen self. A must-read for high schoolers."
WENDY XU, co-creator of *Mooncakes*

For 장은주, 이성원, and 이동헌

First Second

Published by First Second
First Second is an imprint of Roaring Brook Press,
a division of Holtzbrinck Publishing Holdings Limited Partnership
120 Broadway, New York, NY 10271
firstsecondbooks.com
fiercereads.com

Library of Congress Control Number: 2022908541

Our books may be purchased in bulk for promotional, educational, or business use.
Please contact your local bookseller or the Macmillan Corporate and Premium Sales Department
at (800) 221-7945 ext. 5442 or by email at MacmillanSpecialMarkets@macmillan.com.

First edition, 2023
Edited by Connie Hsu
Cover design by Kirk Benshoff
Interior book design by Sunny Lee and Yan L. Moy

The names and identifying characteristics of some persons described in this book have been changed,
as have dates, places and other details of events depicted in the book.

The art in this book was created on an IPad and IPhone using Procreate, Adobe Photoshop,
and photos taken by a Canon DSLR and Photobooth.

Printed in the United States of America.

ISBN 978-1-250-25266-1 (paperback)
10 9 8 7 6 5 4

ISBN 978-1-250-25265-4 (hardcover)
10 9 8 7 6 5 4 3 2

Don't miss your next favorite book from First Second!
For the latest updates go to firstsecondnewsletter.com and sign up for our enewsletter.

IN LIMBO

deb jj lee

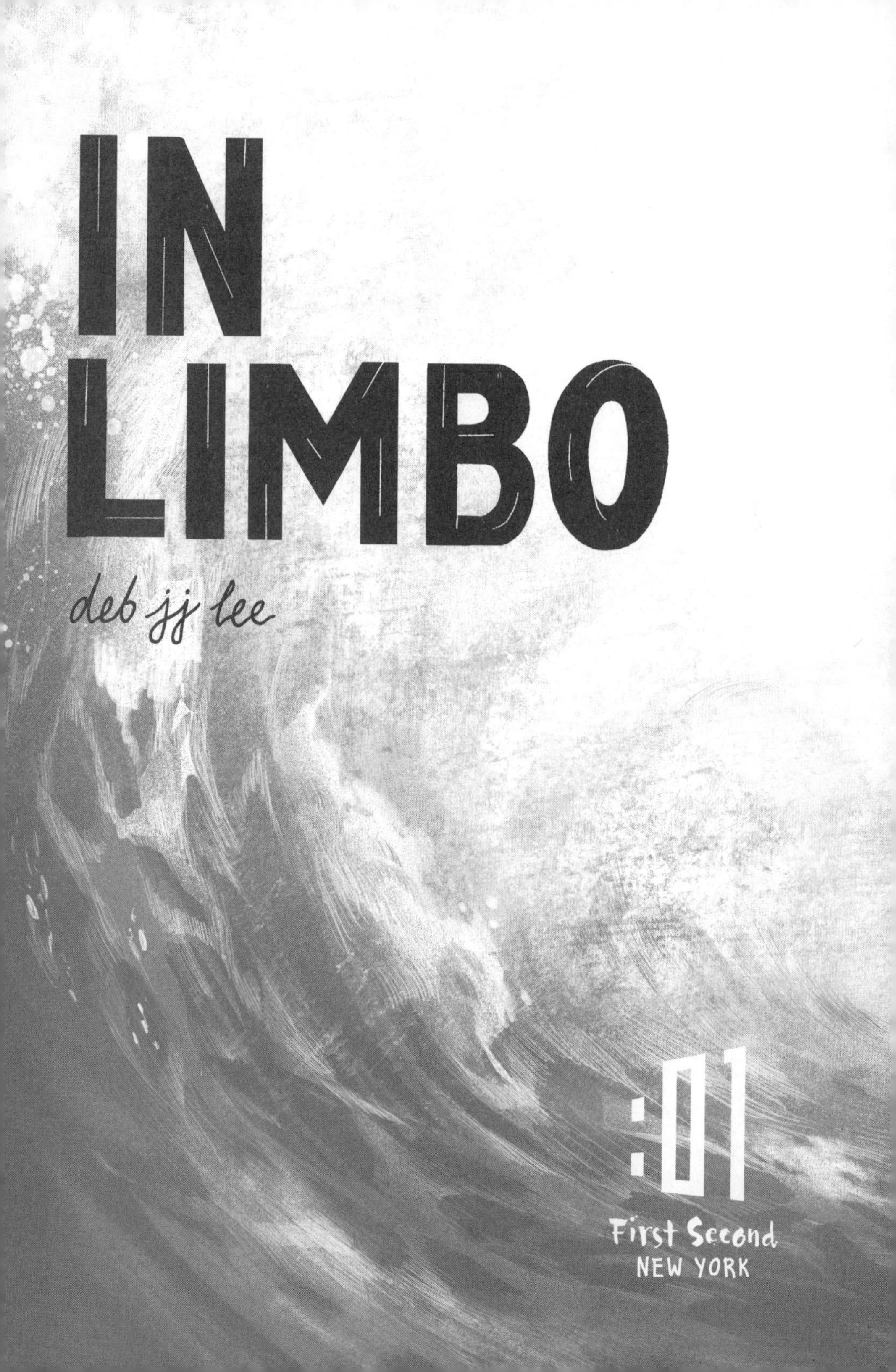

:01 First Second
NEW YORK

일

Part 1

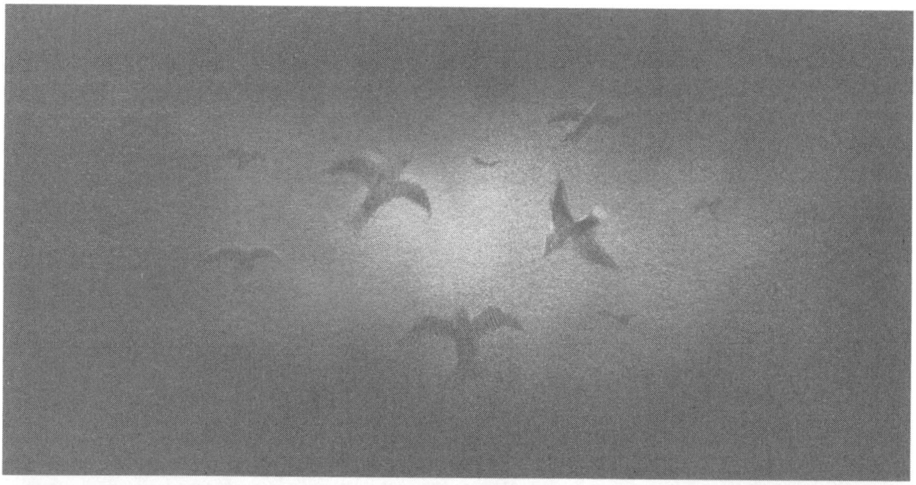
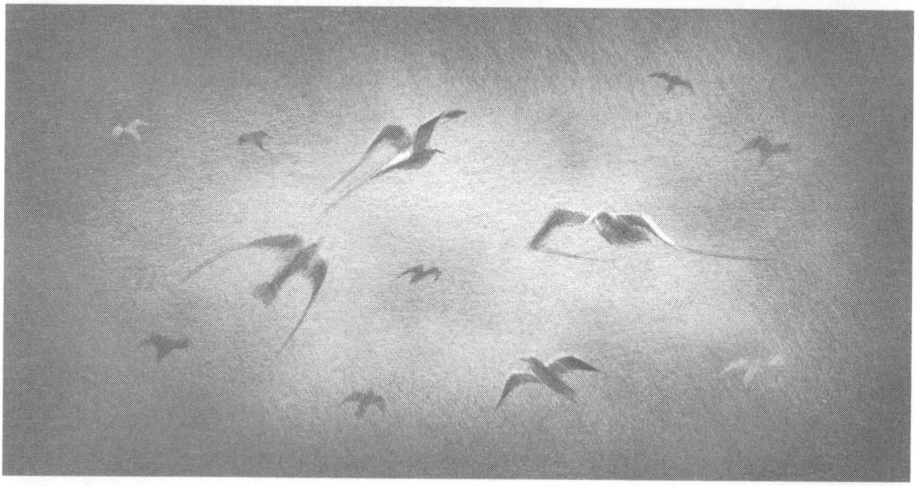
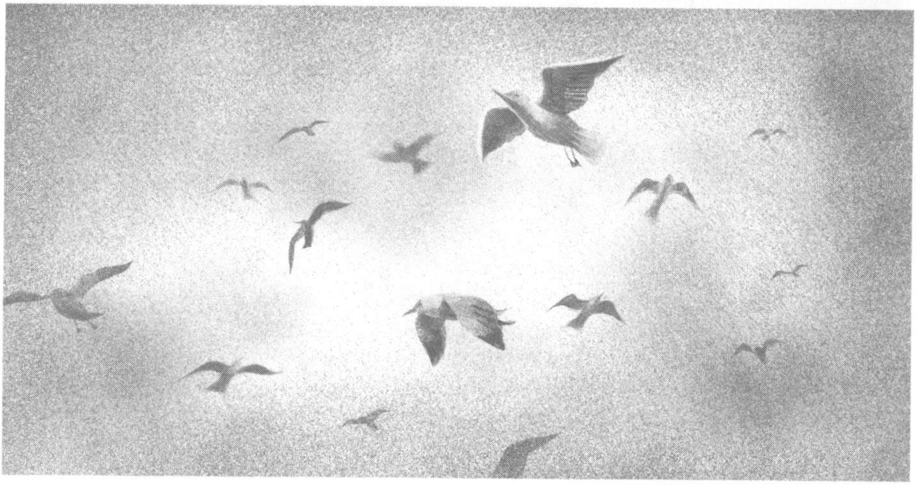

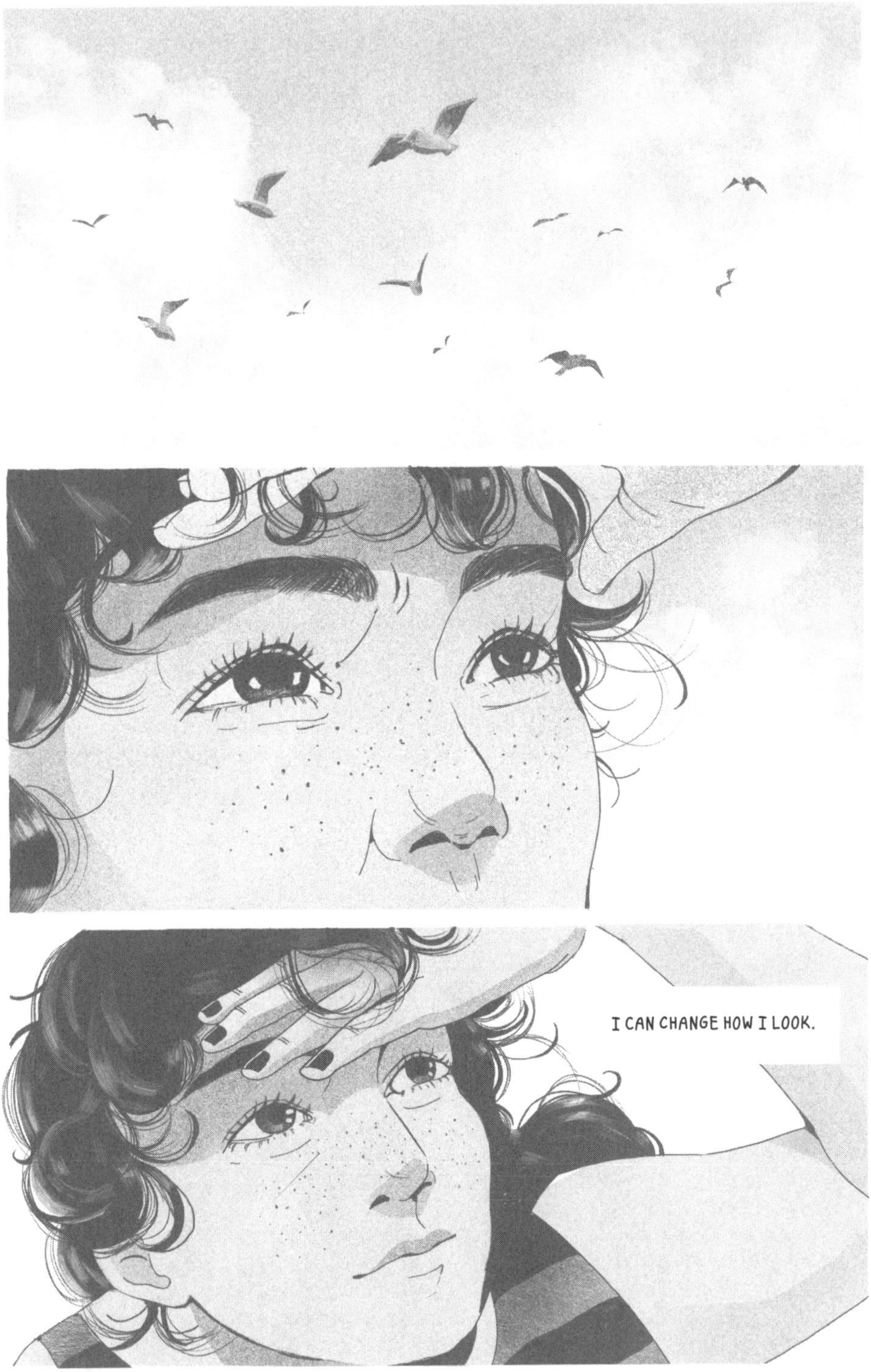
I CAN CHANGE HOW I LOOK.

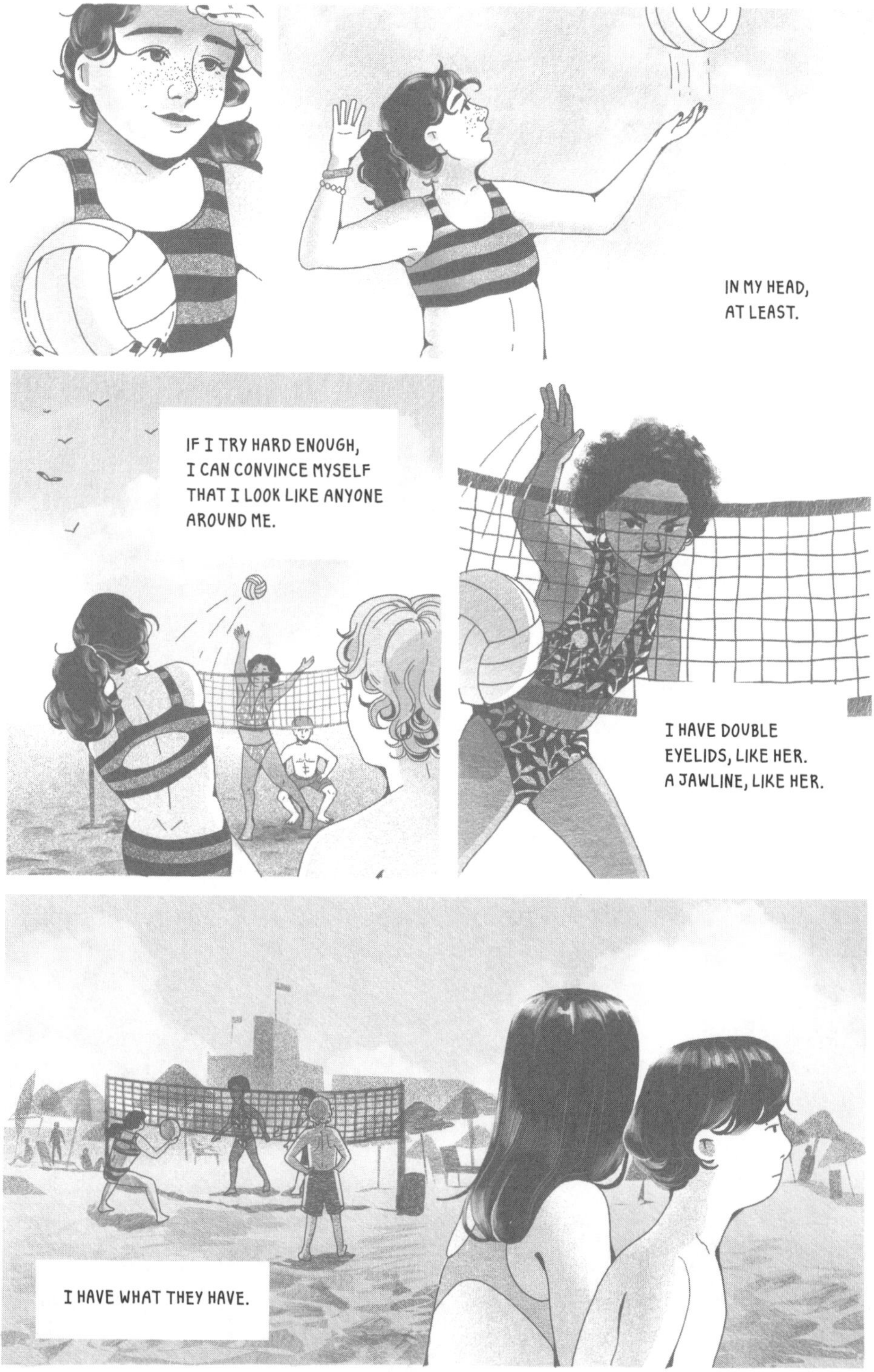
IN MY HEAD, AT LEAST.
IF I TRY HARD ENOUGH, I CAN CONVINCE MYSELF THAT I LOOK LIKE ANYONE AROUND ME.
I HAVE DOUBLE EYELIDS, LIKE HER. A JAWLINE, LIKE HER.
I HAVE WHAT THEY HAVE.

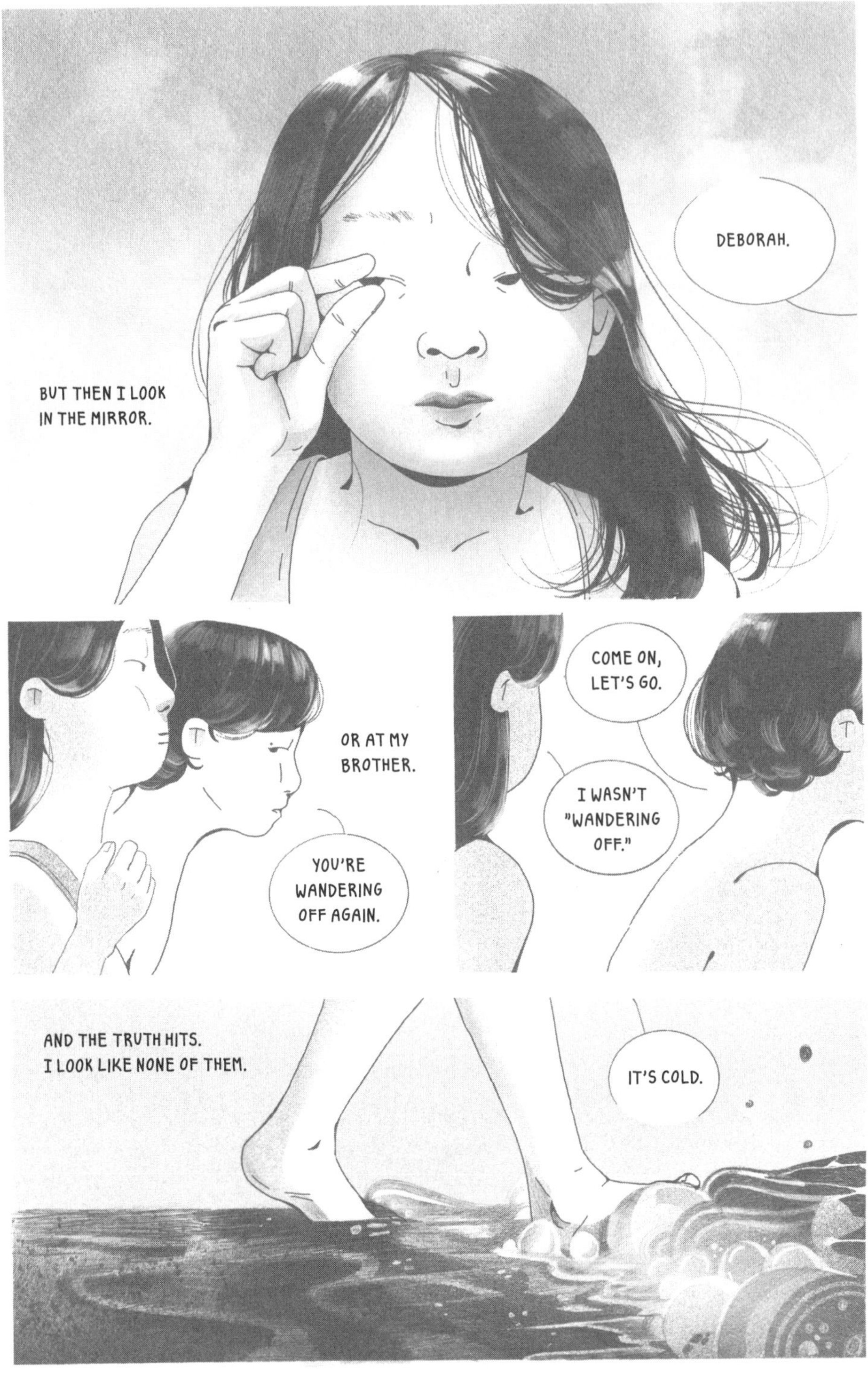
DEBORAH.
BUT THEN I LOOK IN THE MIRROR.
OR AT MY BROTHER.
YOU'RE WANDERING OFF AGAIN.
COME ON, LET'S GO.
I WASN'T "WANDERING OFF."
AND THE TRUTH HITS.
I LOOK LIKE NONE OF THEM.
IT'S COLD.

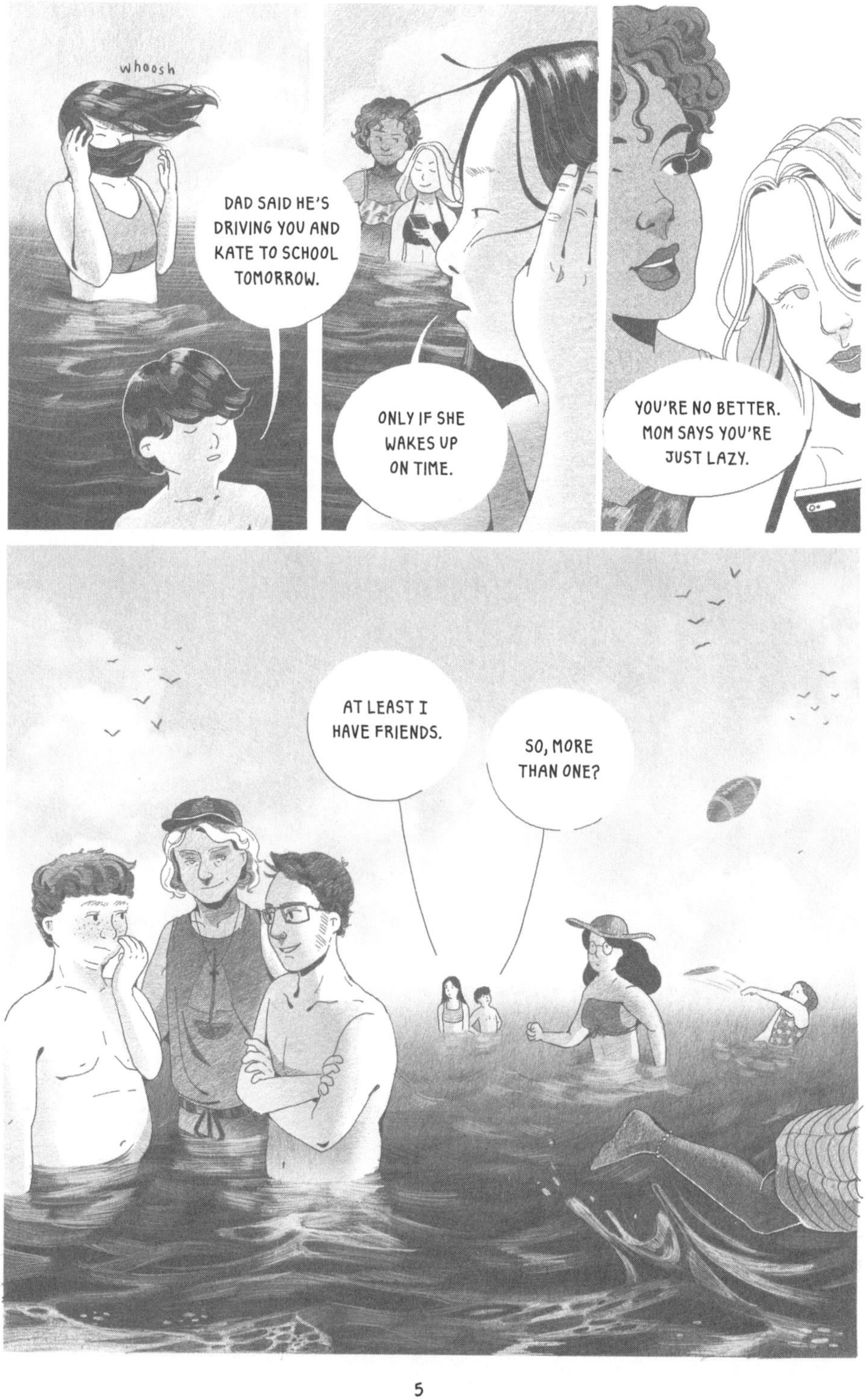
whoosh
DAD SAID HE'S DRIVING YOU AND KATE TO SCHOOL TOMORROW.
ONLY IF SHE WAKES UP ON TIME.
YOU'RE NO BETTER. MOM SAYS YOU'RE JUST LAZY.
AT LEAST I HAVE FRIENDS.
SO, MORE THAN ONE?

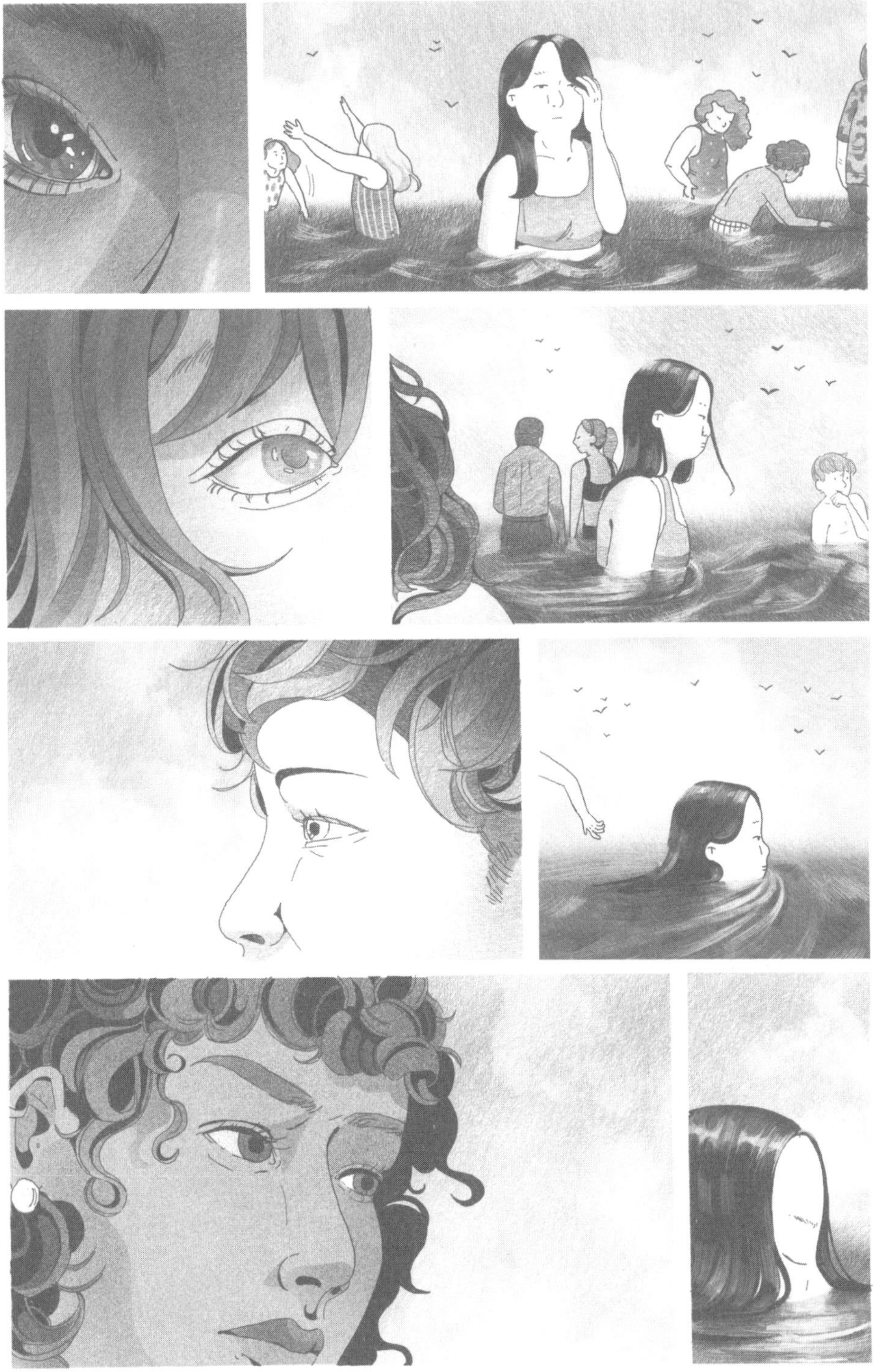

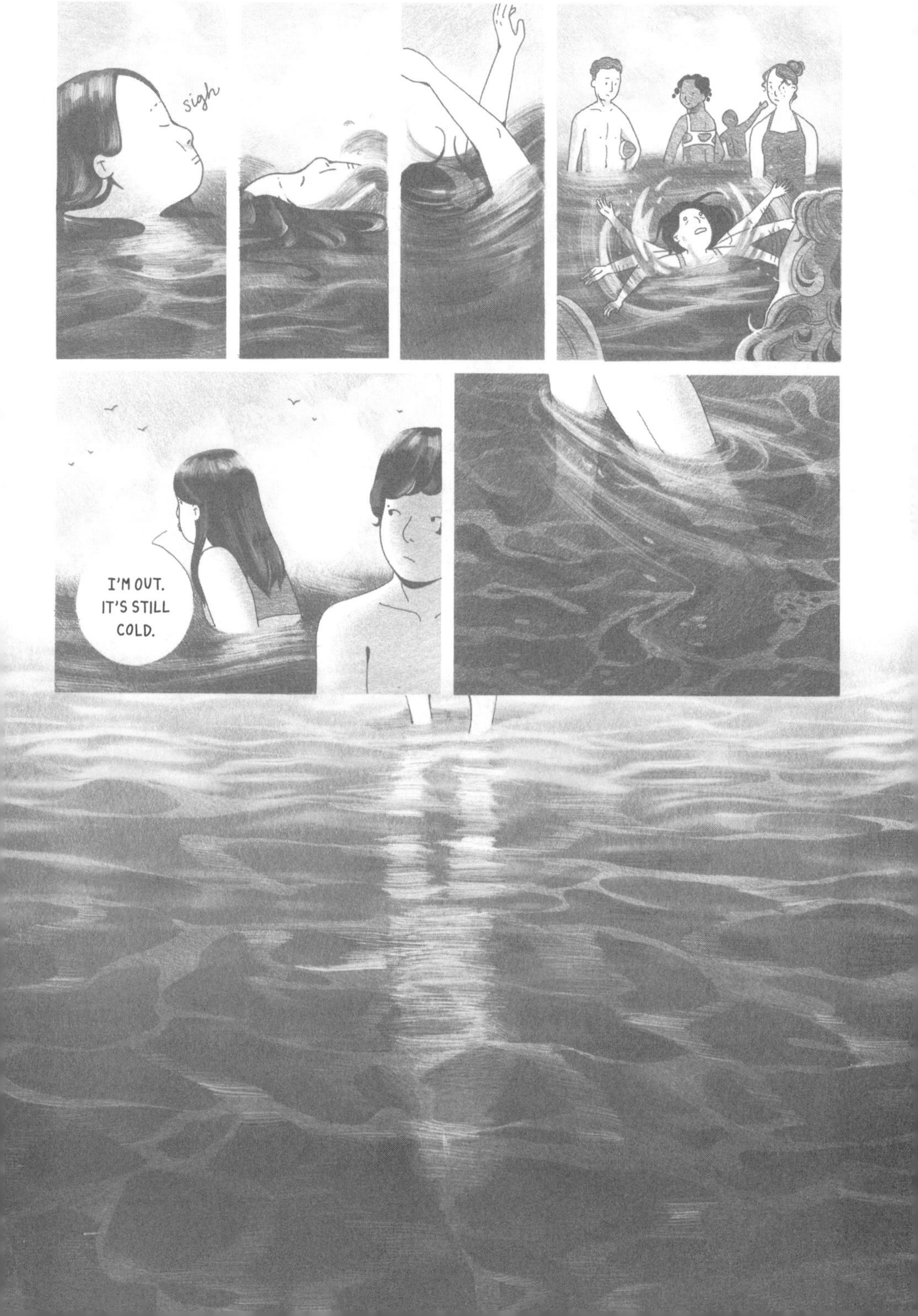
sigh
I'M OUT. IT'S STILL COLD.

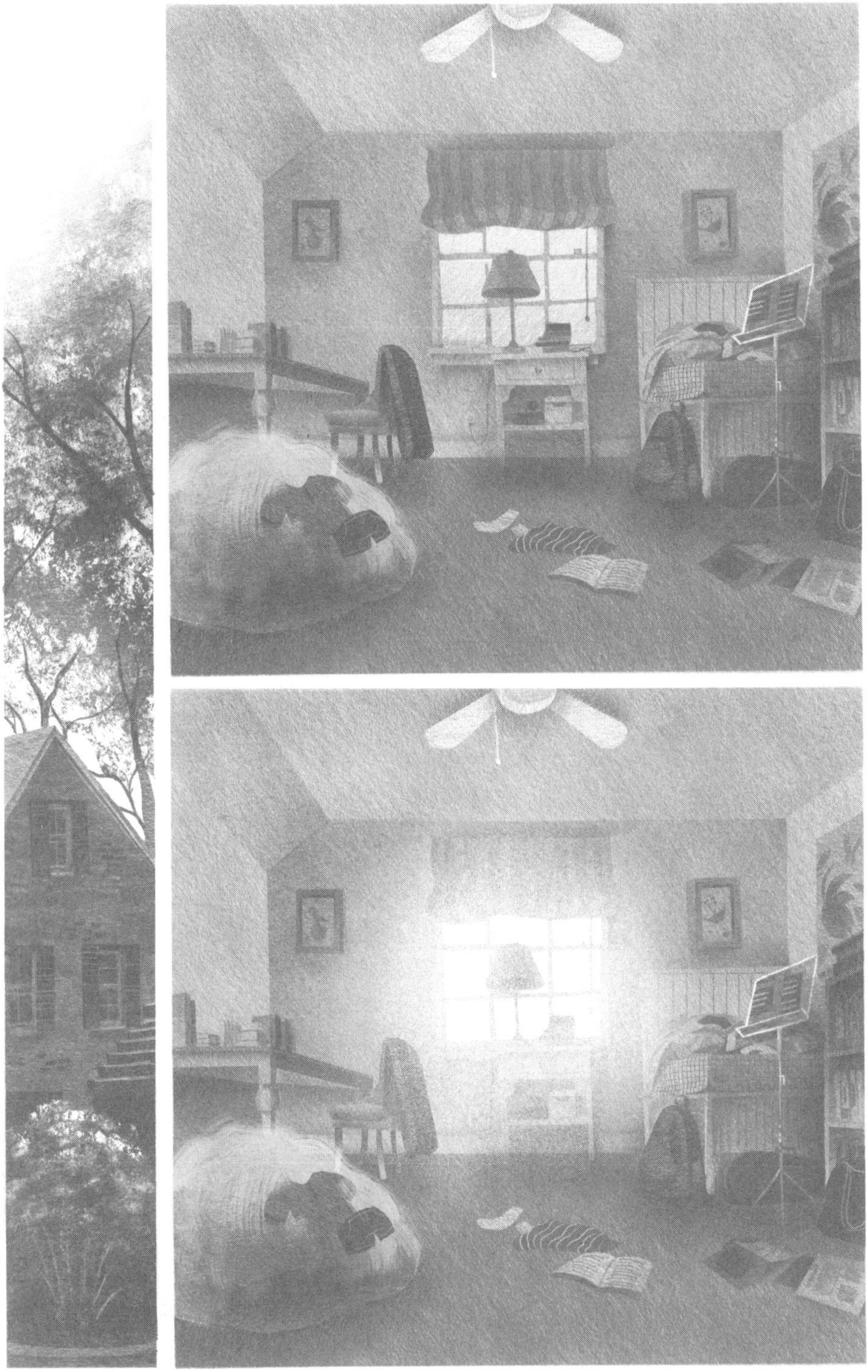

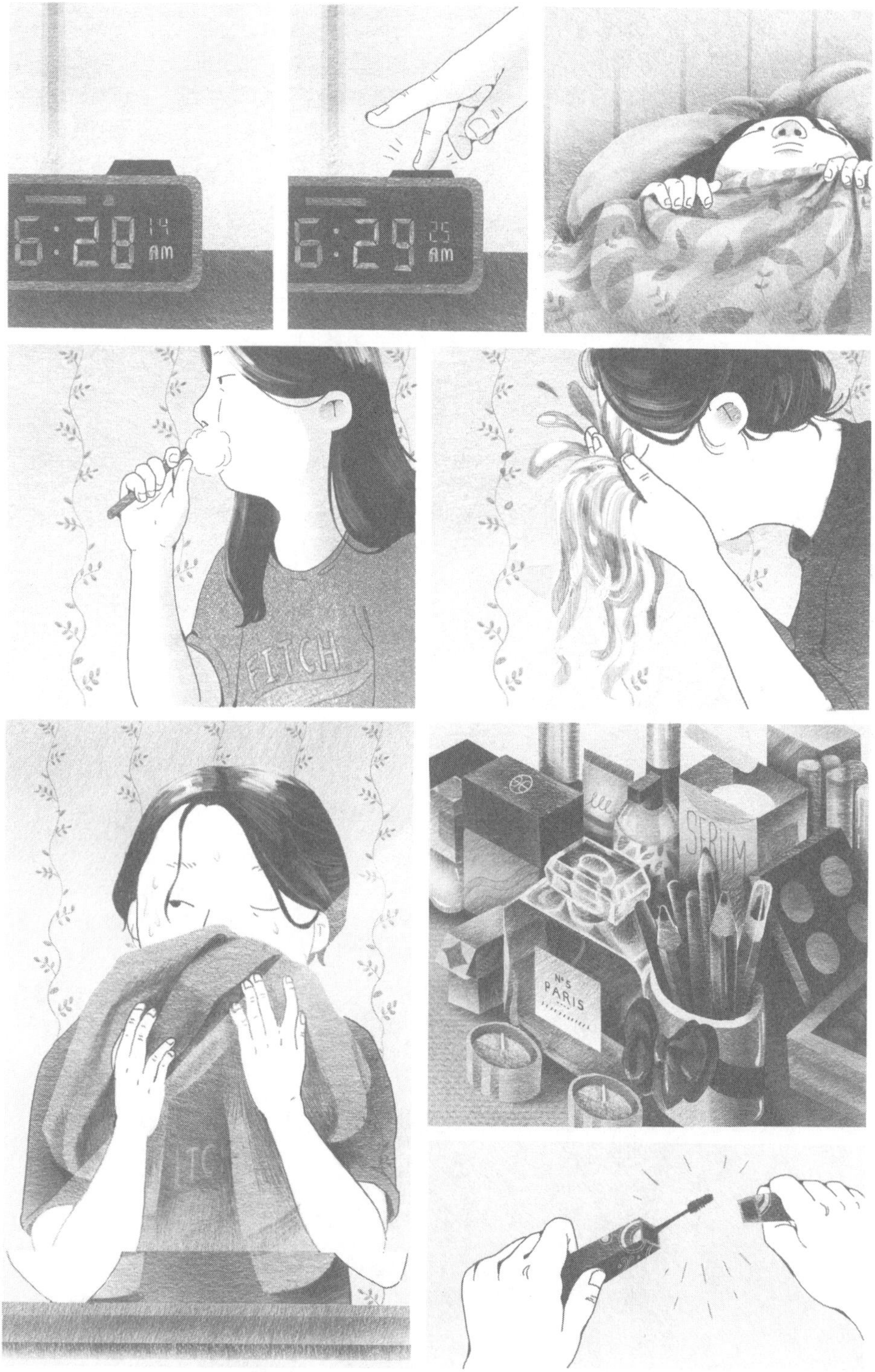
6:28
14
AM
6:29
25
AM
FITCH
SERUM
N°5
PARIS

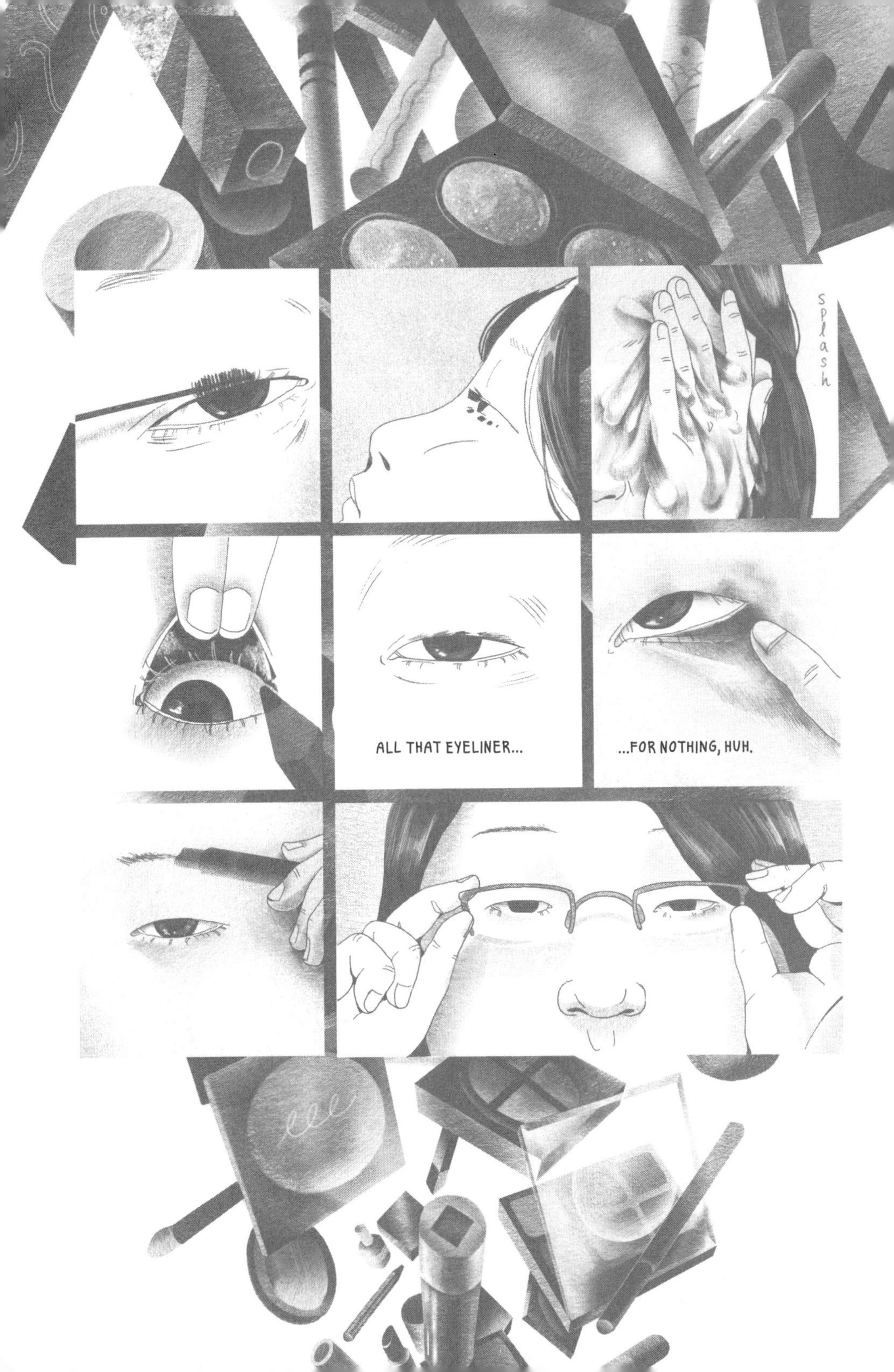
splash
ALL THAT EYELINER...
...FOR NOTHING, HUH.

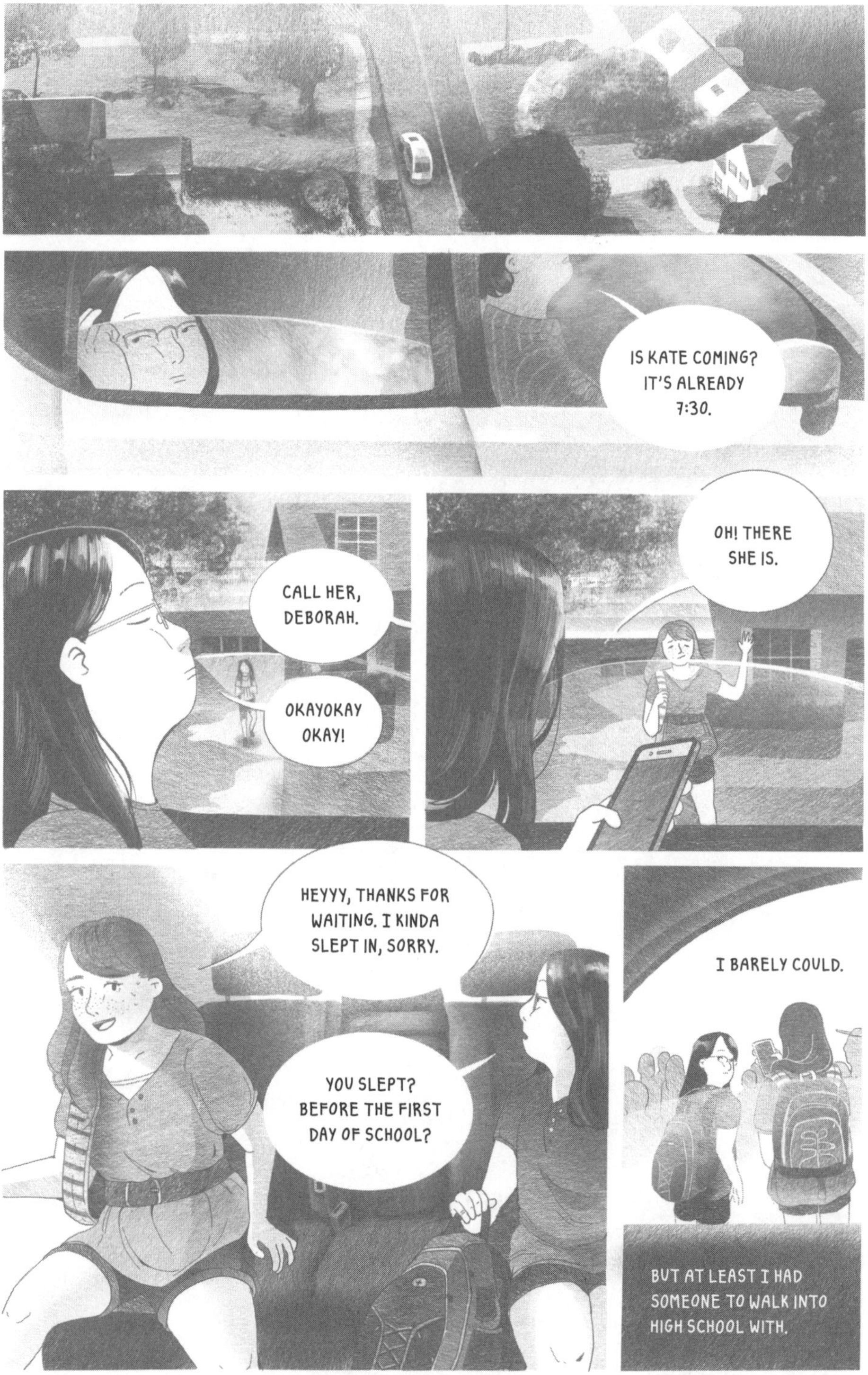
IS KATE COMING? IT'S ALREADY 7:30.
CALL HER, DEBORAH.
OKAYOKAY OKAY!
OH! THERE SHE IS.
HEYYY, THANKS FOR WAITING. I KINDA SLEPT IN, SORRY.
YOU SLEPT? BEFORE THE FIRST DAY OF SCHOOL?
I BARELY COULD.
BUT AT LEAST I HAD SOMEONE TO WALK INTO HIGH SCHOOL WITH.

IMAGINE GOING IN ALONE.

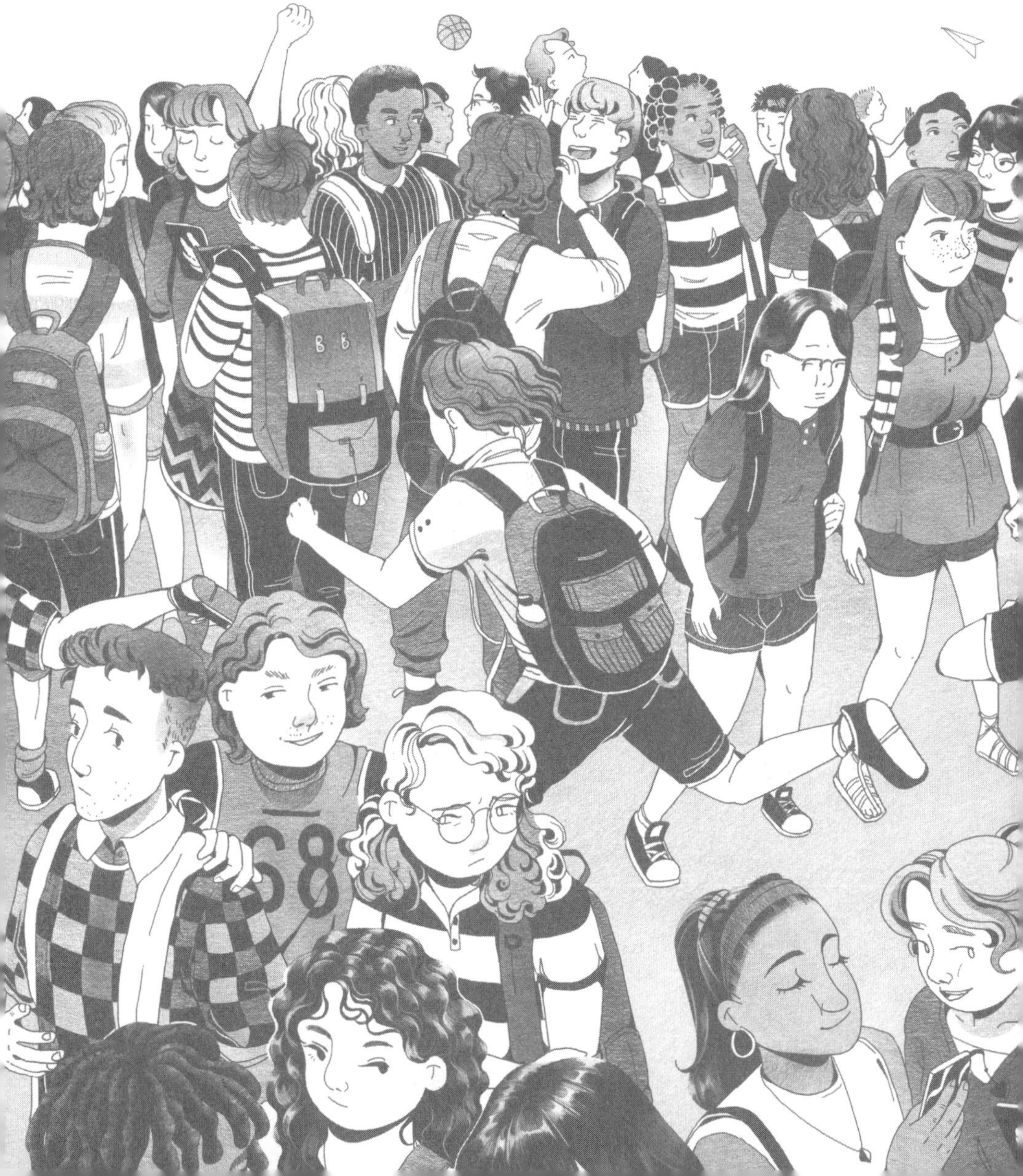
68

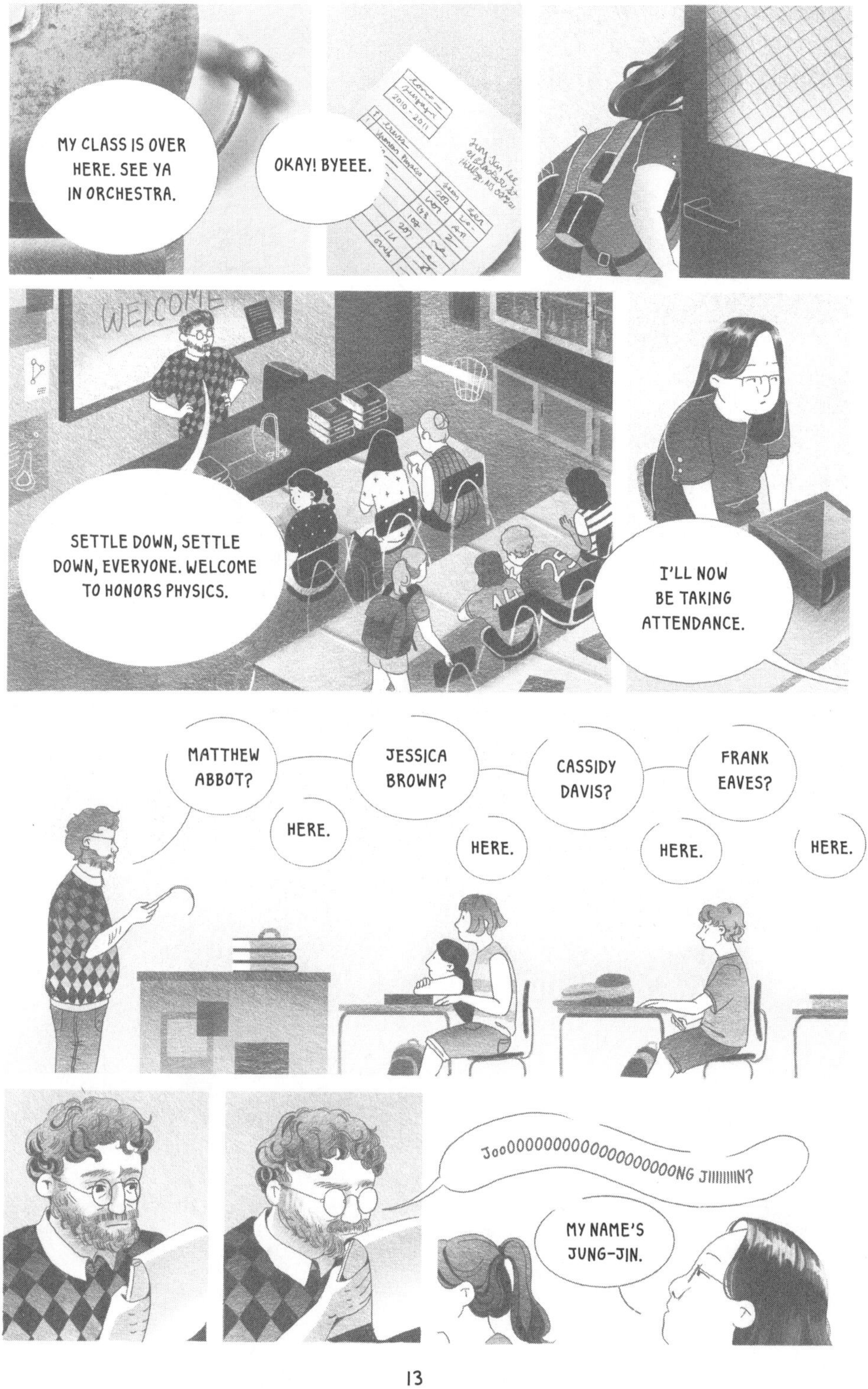
MY CLASS IS OVER HERE. SEE YA IN ORCHESTRA.
OKAY! BYEEE.
WELCOME
SETTLE DOWN, SETTLE DOWN, EVERYONE. WELCOME TO HONORS PHYSICS.
I'LL NOW BE TAKING ATTENDANCE.
MATTHEW ABBOT?
HERE.
JESSICA BROWN?
HERE.
CASSIDY DAVIS?
HERE.
FRANK EAVES?
HERE.
JooOOOOOOOOOOOOOOOOOOOOONG JIIIIIIIIN?
MY NAME'S JUNG-JIN.

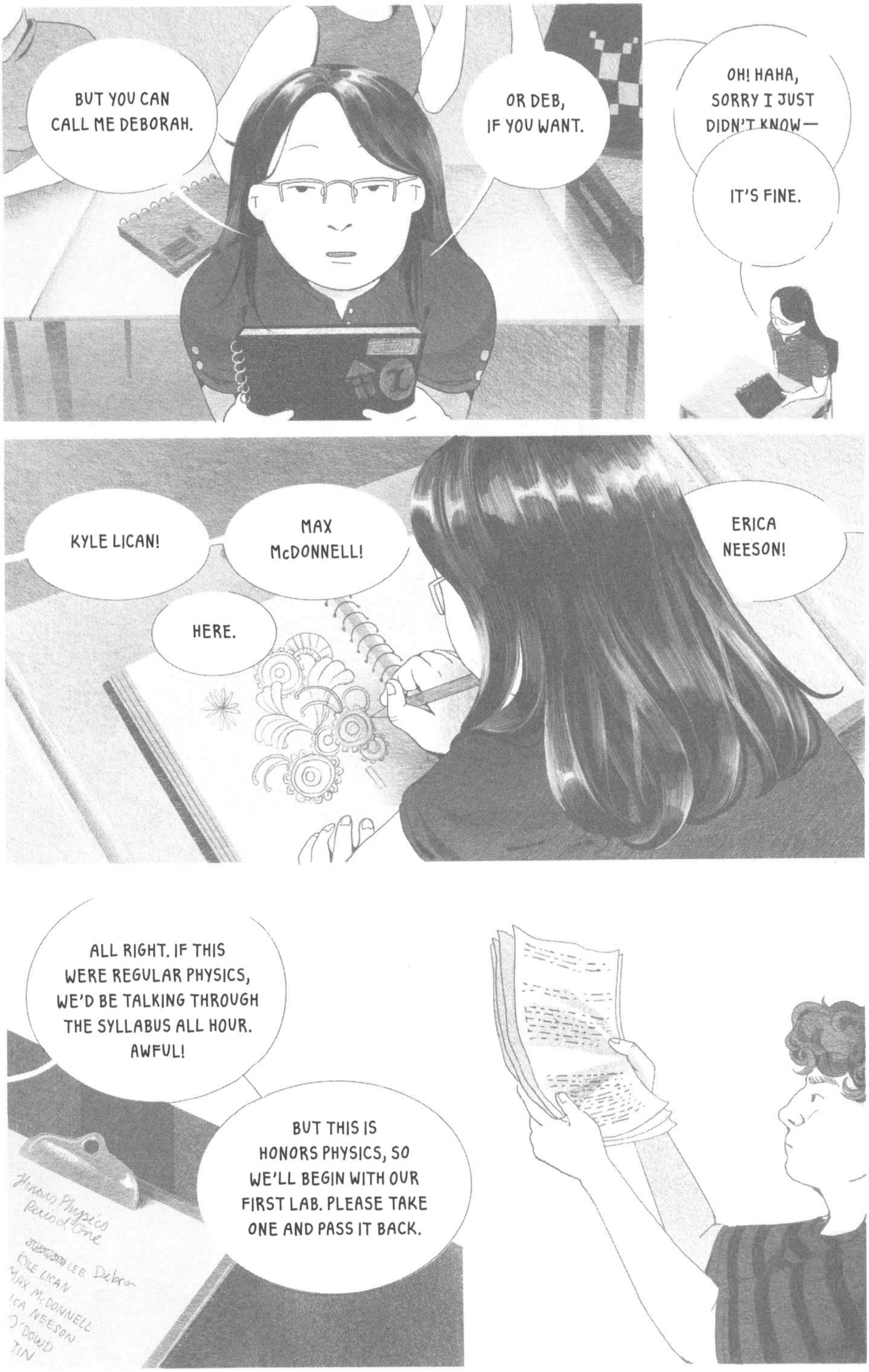
BUT YOU CAN CALL ME DEBORAH.
OR DEB, IF YOU WANT.
OH! HAHA, SORRY I JUST DIDN'T KNOW—
IT'S FINE.
KYLE LICAN!
MAX McDONNELL!
HERE.
ERICA NEESON!
ALL RIGHT. IF THIS WERE REGULAR PHYSICS, WE'D BE TALKING THROUGH THE SYLLABUS ALL HOUR. AWFUL!
BUT THIS IS HONORS PHYSICS, SO WE'LL BEGIN WITH OUR FIRST LAB. PLEASE TAKE ONE AND PASS IT BACK.
Honors Physics
Period One
KYLE LICAN
MAX McDONNELL

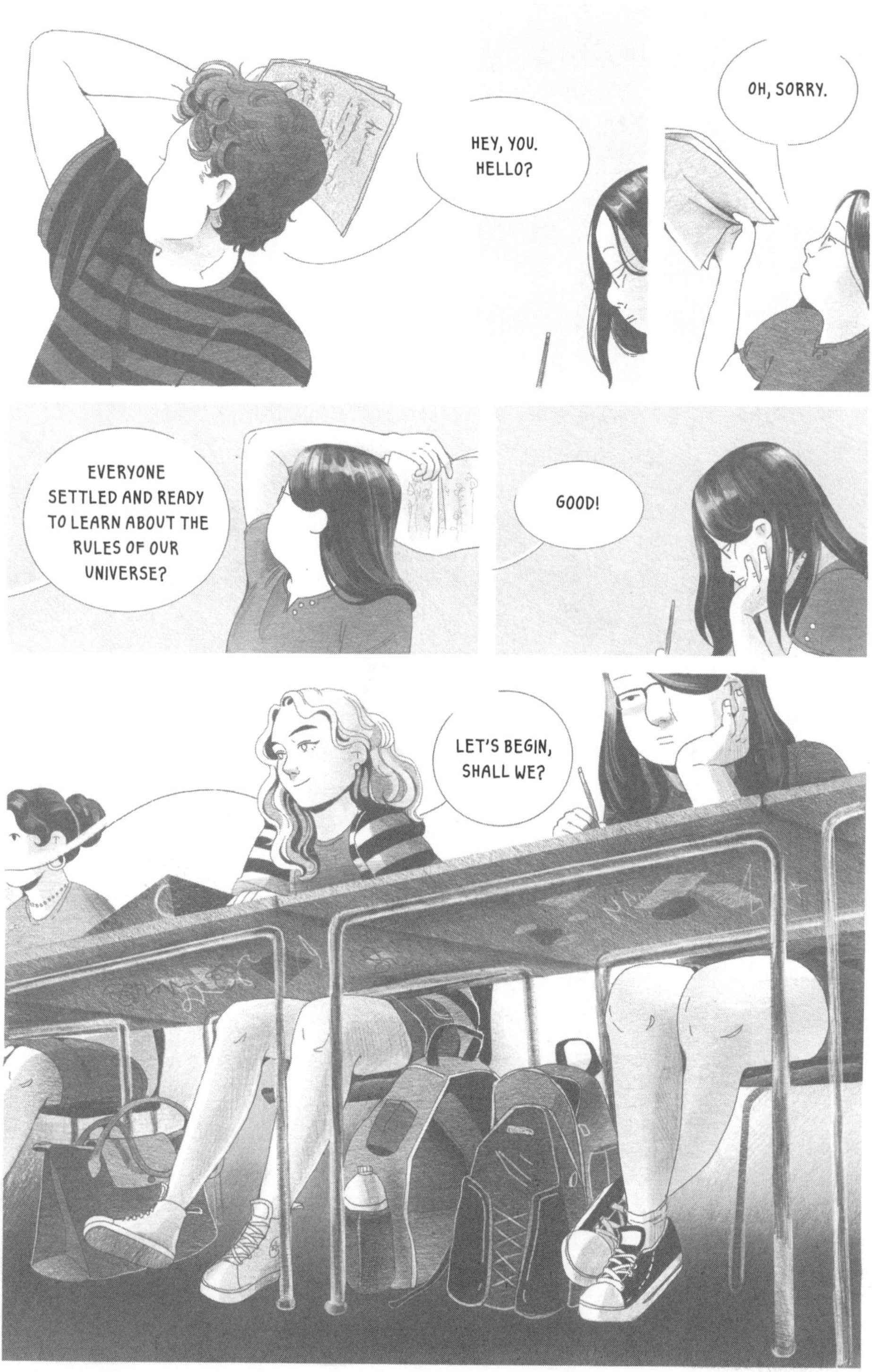
HEY, YOU.
HELLO?
OH, SORRY.
EVERYONE SETTLED AND READY TO LEARN ABOUT THE RULES OF OUR UNIVERSE?
GOOD!
LET'S BEGIN, SHALL WE?

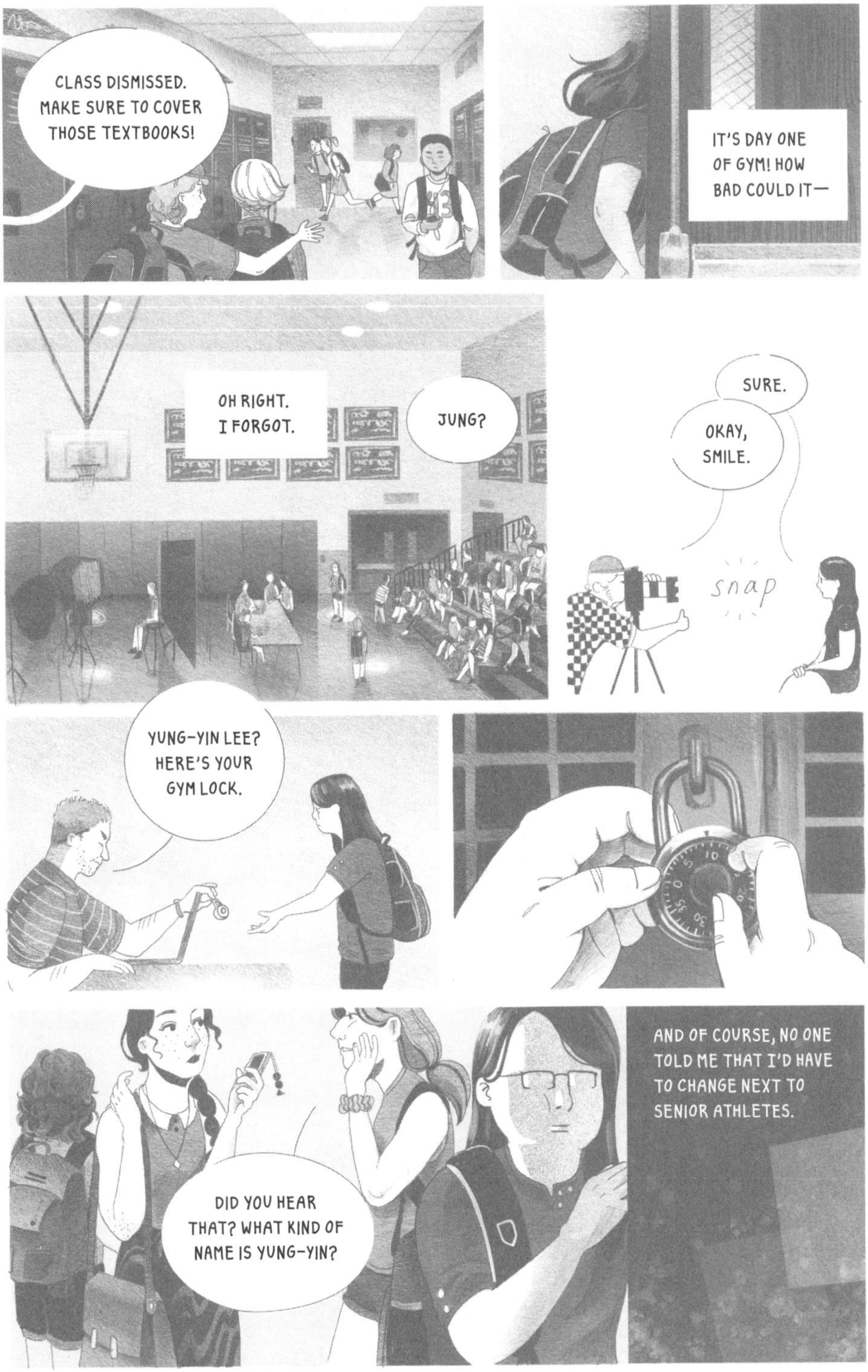
CLASS DISMISSED. MAKE SURE TO COVER THOSE TEXTBOOKS!
IT'S DAY ONE OF GYM! HOW BAD COULD IT—
OH RIGHT. I FORGOT.
JUNG?
OKAY, SMILE.
SURE.
snap
YUNG-YIN LEE? HERE'S YOUR GYM LOCK.
AND OF COURSE, NO ONE TOLD ME THAT I'D HAVE TO CHANGE NEXT TO SENIOR ATHLETES.
DID YOU HEAR THAT? WHAT KIND OF NAME IS YUNG-YIN?

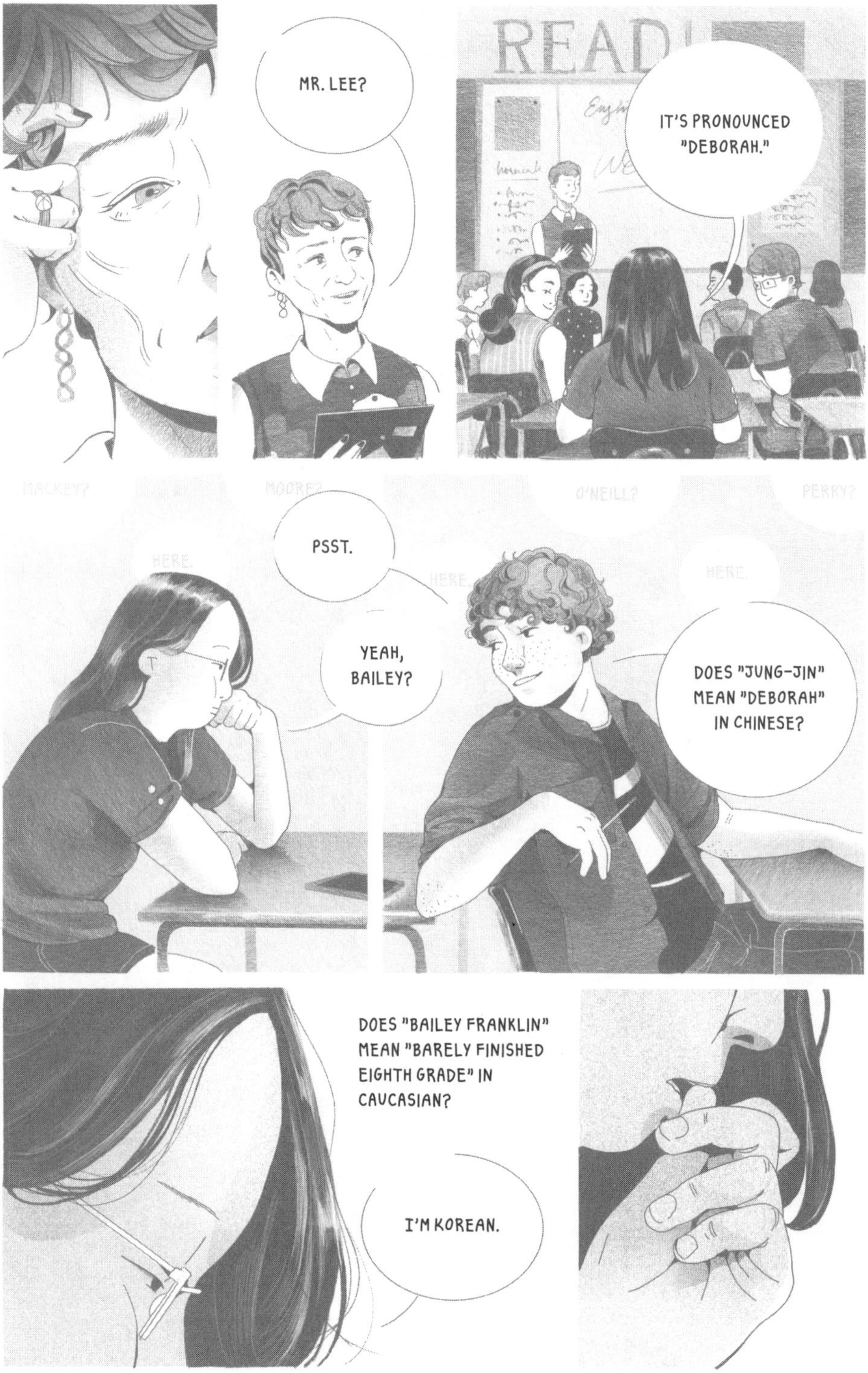
MR. LEE?
READ!
IT'S PRONOUNCED "DEBORAH."
MACKEY?
MOORE?
O'NEILL?
PERRY?
HERE.
PSST.
HERE.
HERE.
YEAH, BAILEY?
DOES "JUNG-JIN" MEAN "DEBORAH" IN CHINESE?
DOES "BAILEY FRANKLIN" MEAN "BARELY FINISHED EIGHTH GRADE" IN CAUCASIAN?
I'M KOREAN.

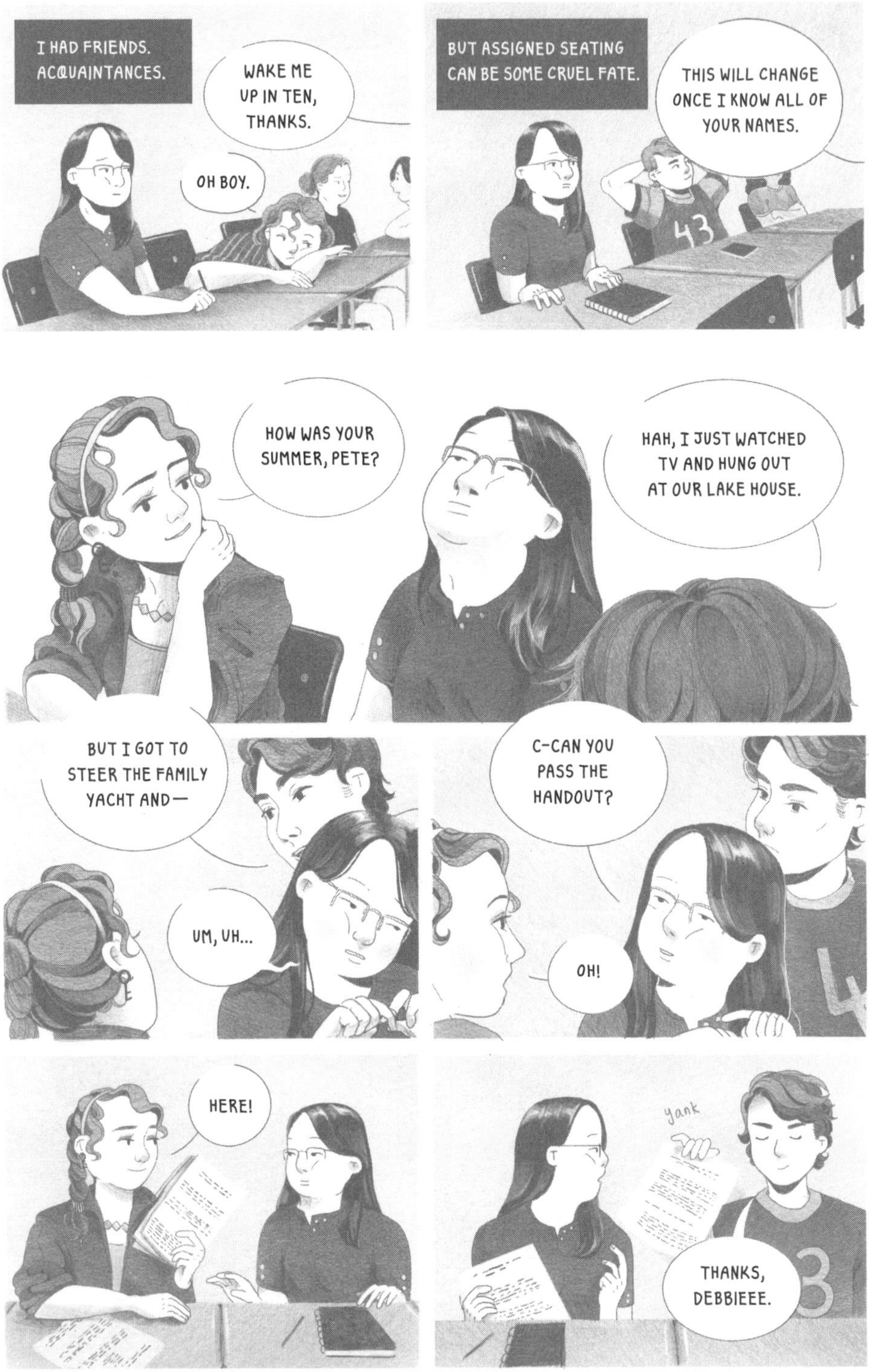
I HAD FRIENDS. ACQUAINTANCES.
WAKE ME UP IN TEN, THANKS.
OH BOY.
BUT ASSIGNED SEATING CAN BE SOME CRUEL FATE.
THIS WILL CHANGE ONCE I KNOW ALL OF YOUR NAMES.
HOW WAS YOUR SUMMER, PETE?
HAH, I JUST WATCHED TV AND HUNG OUT AT OUR LAKE HOUSE.
BUT I GOT TO STEER THE FAMILY YACHT AND—
UM, UH...
C-CAN YOU PASS THE HANDOUT?
OH!
HERE!
yank
THANKS, DEBBIEEE.

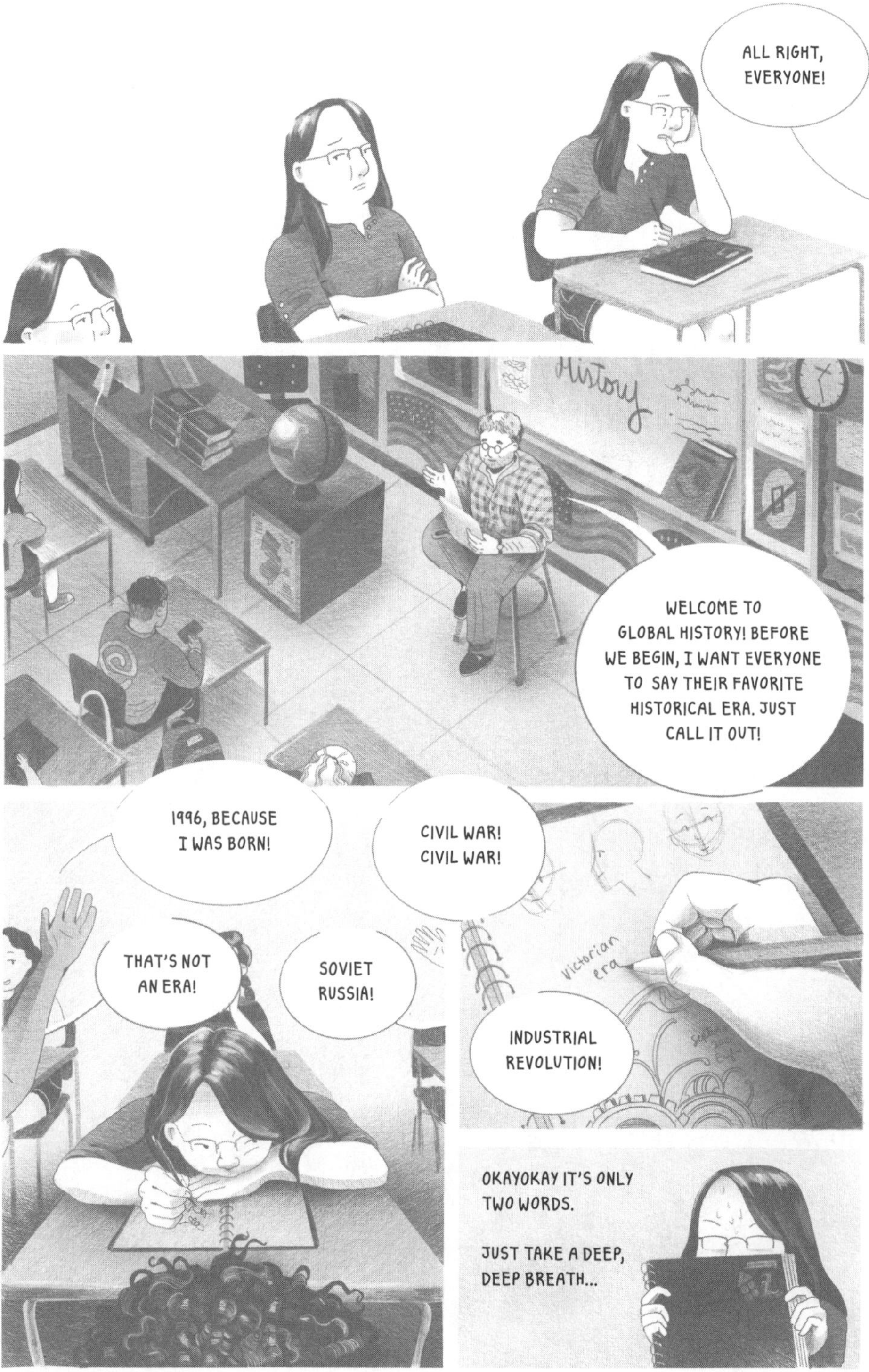
ALL RIGHT, EVERYONE!
History
WELCOME TO GLOBAL HISTORY! BEFORE WE BEGIN, I WANT EVERYONE TO SAY THEIR FAVORITE HISTORICAL ERA. JUST CALL IT OUT!
1996, BECAUSE I WAS BORN!
CIVIL WAR! CIVIL WAR!
THAT'S NOT AN ERA!
SOVIET RUSSIA!
Victorian era
INDUSTRIAL REVOLUTION!
OKAYOKAY IT'S ONLY TWO WORDS.
JUST TAKE A DEEP, DEEP BREATH...

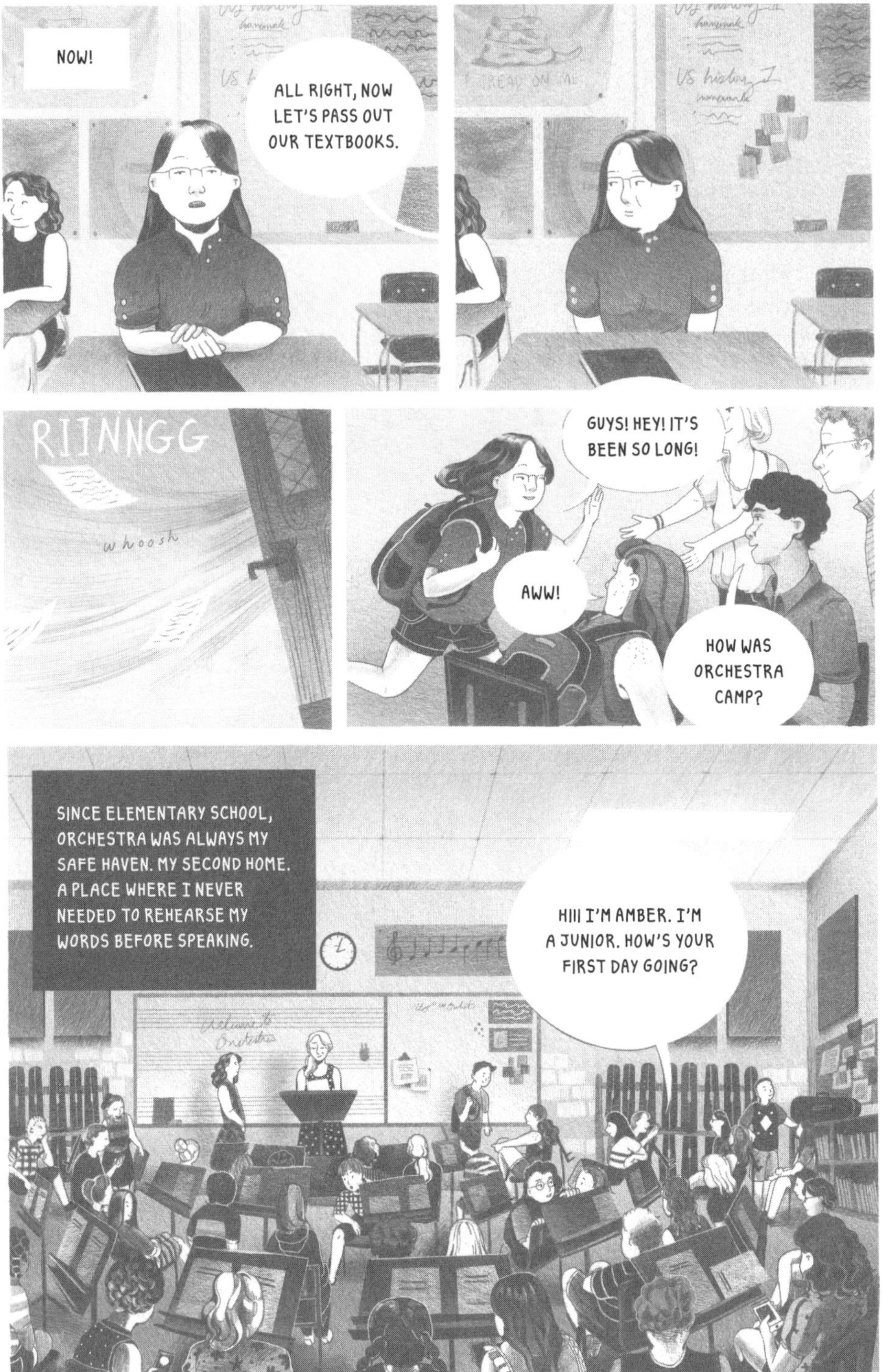
NOW!
ALL RIGHT, NOW LET'S PASS OUT OUR TEXTBOOKS.
RIINNGG
whoosh
GUYS! HEY! IT'S BEEN SO LONG!
AWW!
HOW WAS ORCHESTRA CAMP?
SINCE ELEMENTARY SCHOOL, ORCHESTRA WAS ALWAYS MY SAFE HAVEN. MY SECOND HOME. A PLACE WHERE I NEVER NEEDED TO REHEARSE MY WORDS BEFORE SPEAKING.
HIII I'M AMBER. I'M A JUNIOR. HOW'S YOUR FIRST DAY GOING?

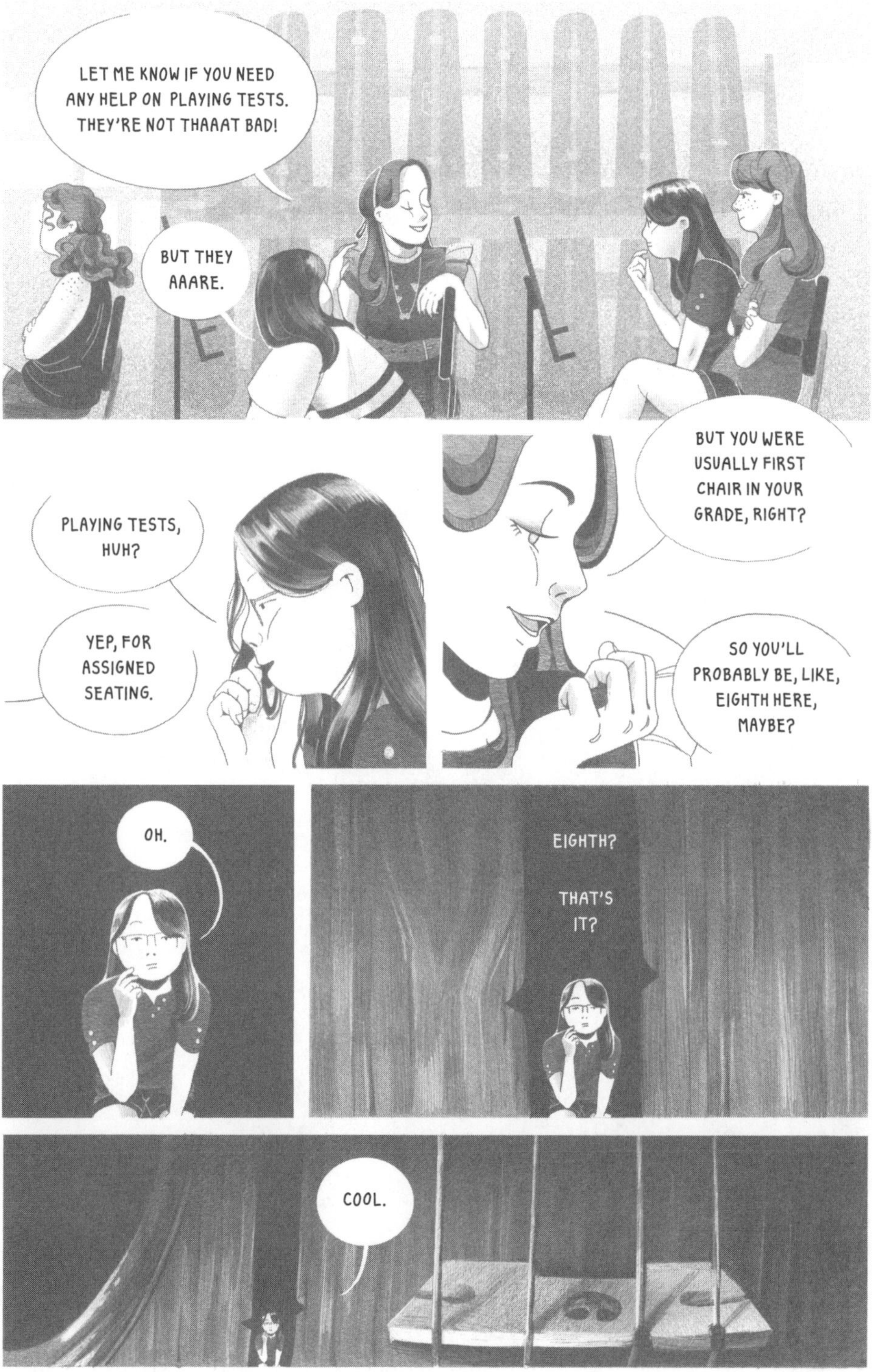
LET ME KNOW IF YOU NEED ANY HELP ON PLAYING TESTS. THEY'RE NOT THAAAT BAD!
BUT THEY AAARE.
PLAYING TESTS, HUH?
YEP, FOR ASSIGNED SEATING.
BUT YOU WERE USUALLY FIRST CHAIR IN YOUR GRADE, RIGHT?
SO YOU'LL PROBABLY BE, LIKE, EIGHTH HERE, MAYBE?
OH.
EIGHTH?
THAT'S IT?
COOL.

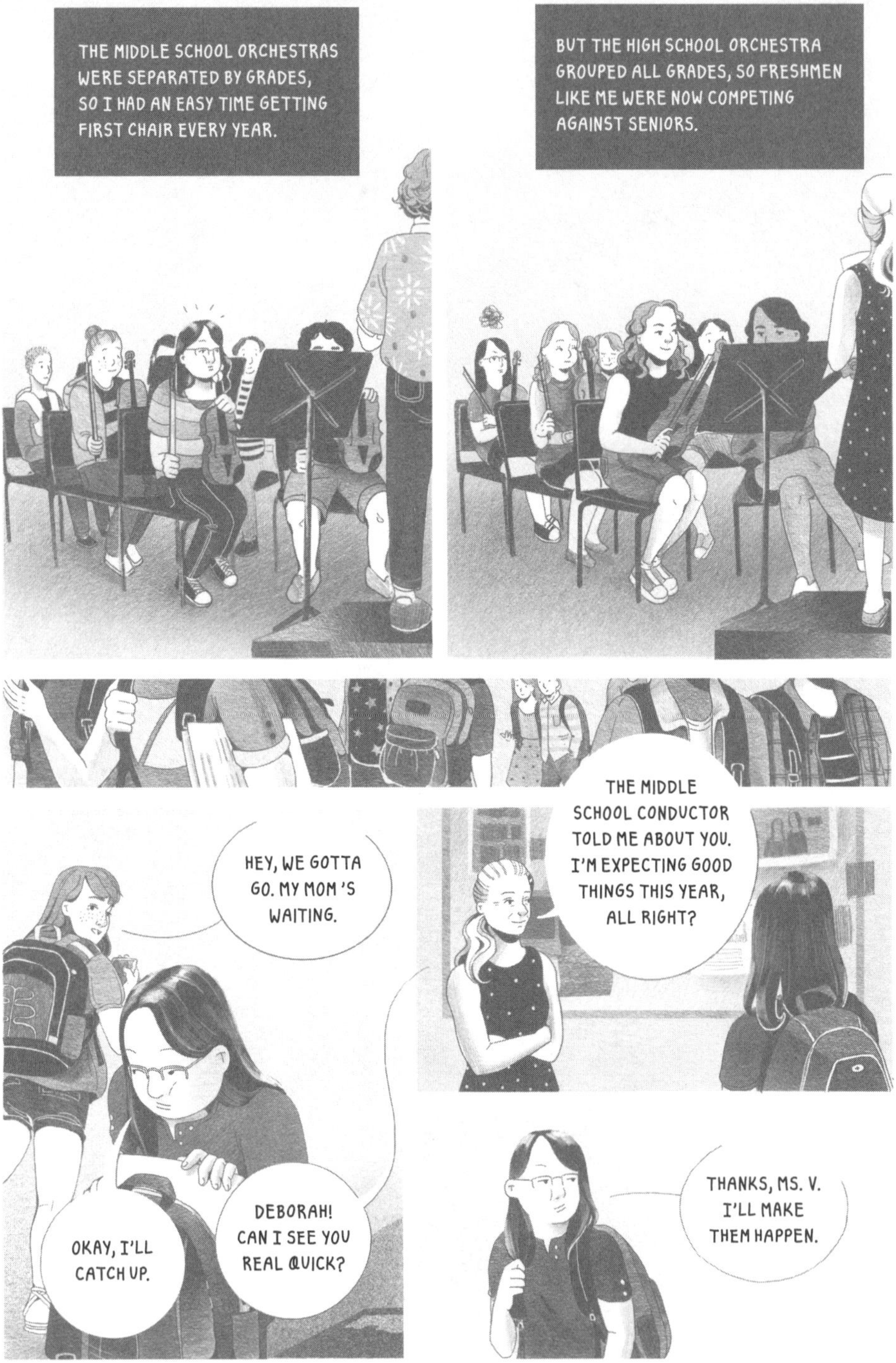
THE MIDDLE SCHOOL ORCHESTRAS WERE SEPARATED BY GRADES, SO I HAD AN EASY TIME GETTING FIRST CHAIR EVERY YEAR.
BUT THE HIGH SCHOOL ORCHESTRA GROUPED ALL GRADES, SO FRESHMEN LIKE ME WERE NOW COMPETING AGAINST SENIORS.
HEY, WE GOTTA GO. MY MOM'S WAITING.
OKAY, I'LL CATCH UP.
DEBORAH! CAN I SEE YOU REAL QUICK?
THE MIDDLE SCHOOL CONDUCTOR TOLD ME ABOUT YOU. I'M EXPECTING GOOD THINGS THIS YEAR, ALL RIGHT?
THANKS, MS. V. I'LL MAKE THEM HAPPEN.

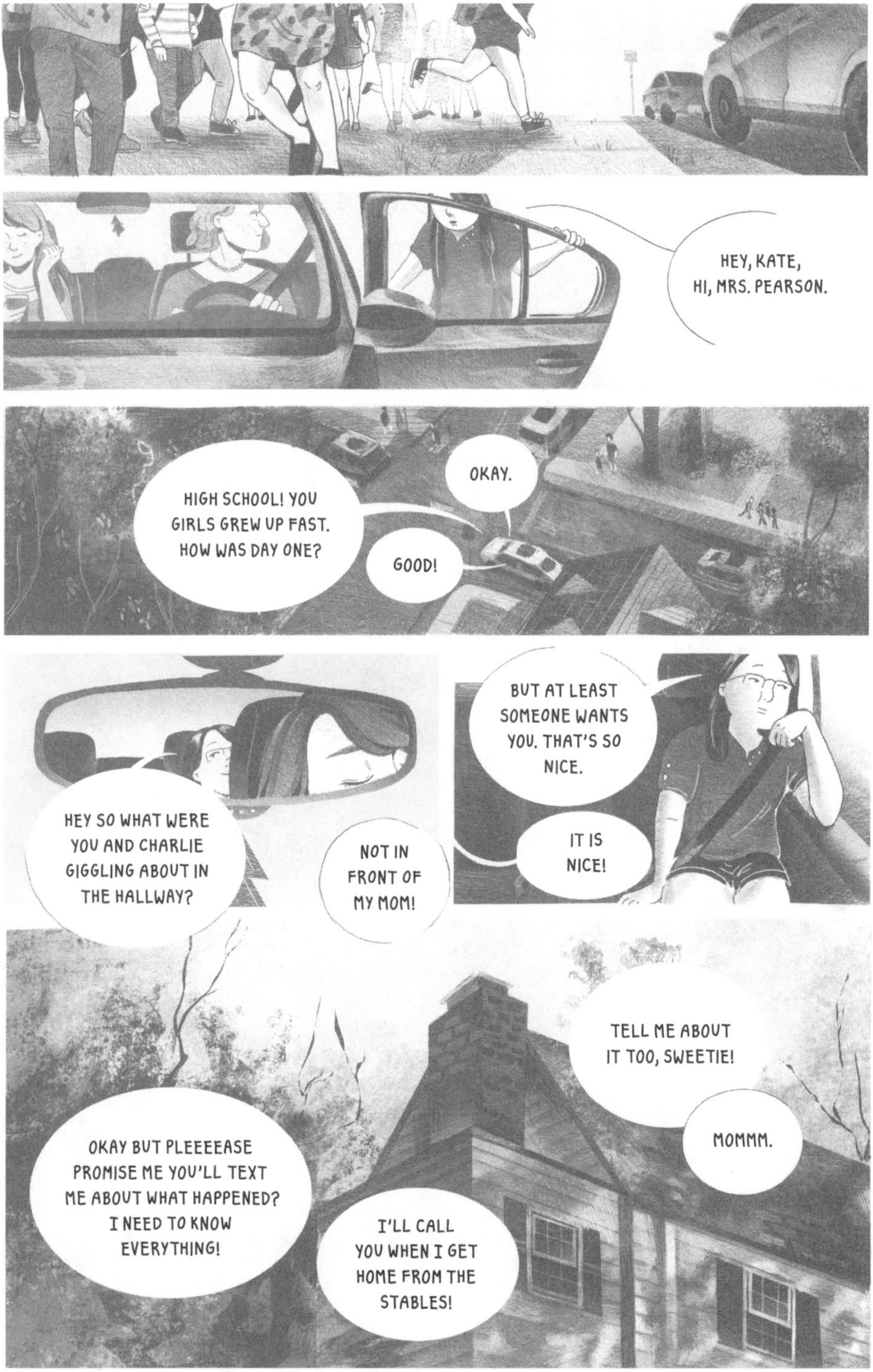
HEY, KATE,
HI, MRS. PEARSON.
HIGH SCHOOL! YOU GIRLS GREW UP FAST. HOW WAS DAY ONE?
OKAY.
GOOD!
HEY SO WHAT WERE YOU AND CHARLIE GIGGLING ABOUT IN THE HALLWAY?
NOT IN FRONT OF MY MOM!
BUT AT LEAST SOMEONE WANTS YOU. THAT'S SO NICE.
IT IS NICE!
TELL ME ABOUT IT TOO, SWEETIE!
MOMMM.
OKAY BUT PLEEEEASE PROMISE ME YOU'LL TEXT ME ABOUT WHAT HAPPENED? I NEED TO KNOW EVERYTHING!
I'LL CALL YOU WHEN I GET HOME FROM THE STABLES!

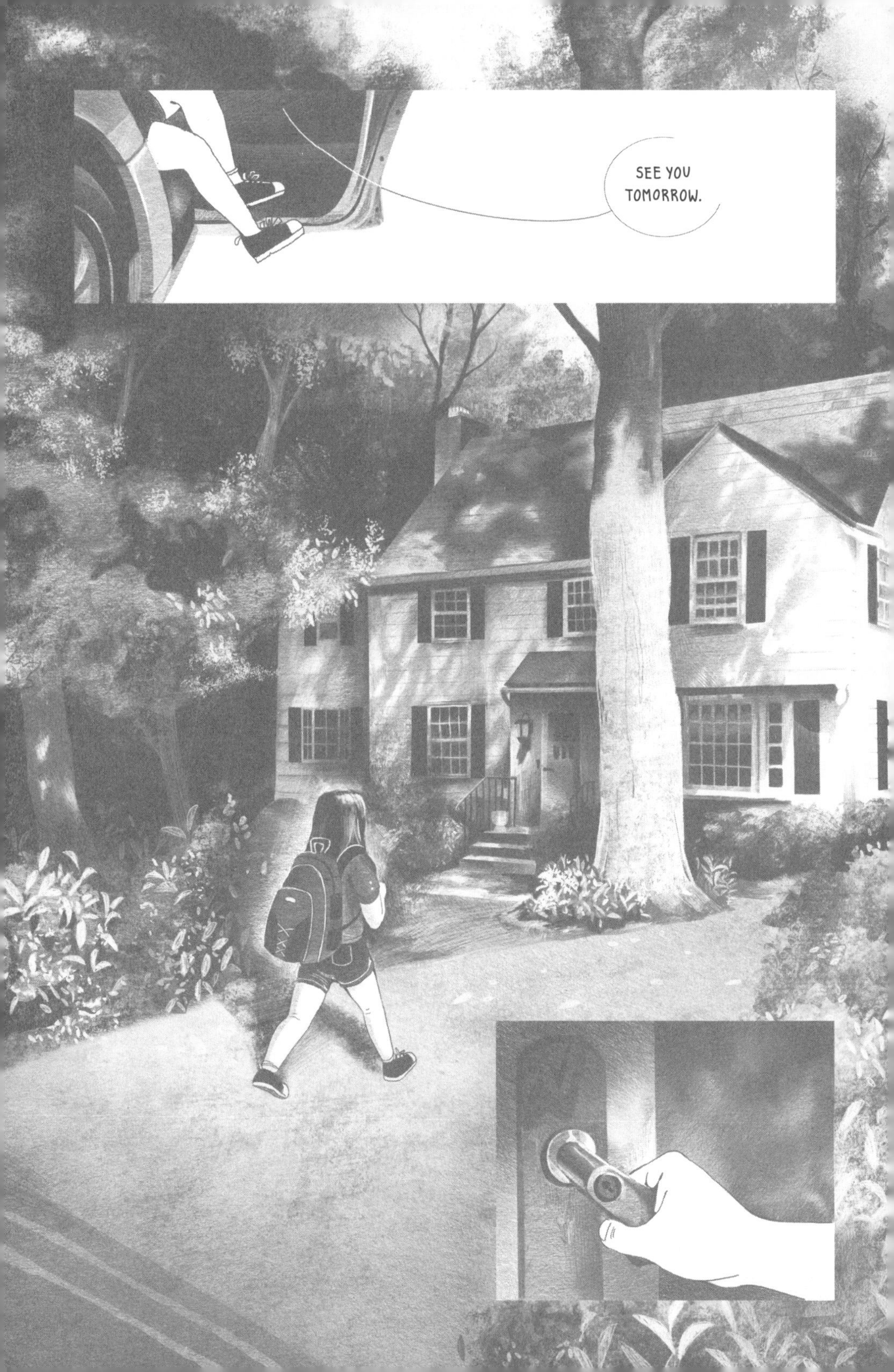
SEE YOU TOMORROW.

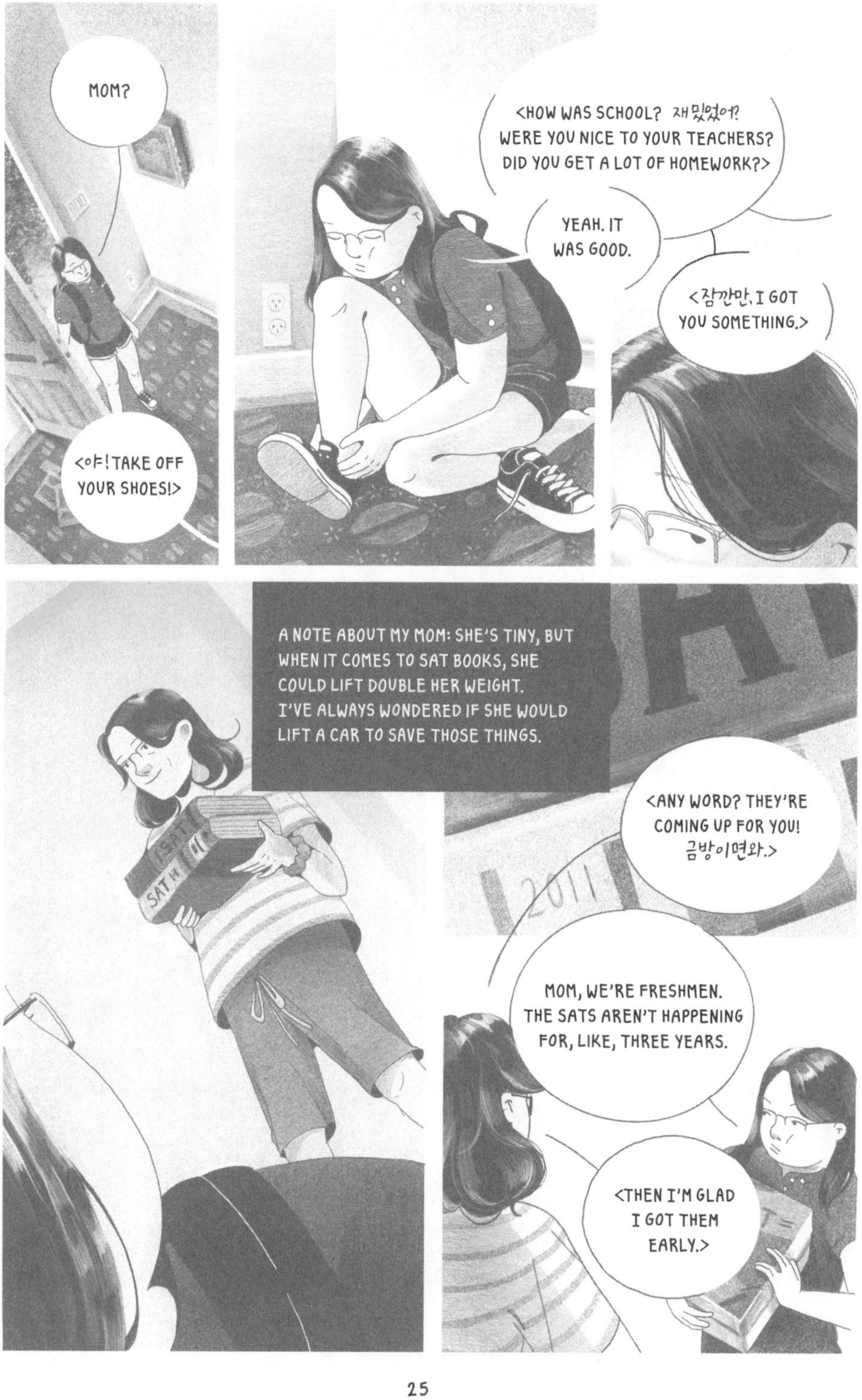
MOM?
<야! TAKE OFF YOUR SHOES!>
<HOW WAS SCHOOL? 재밌었어? WERE YOU NICE TO YOUR TEACHERS? DID YOU GET A LOT OF HOMEWORK?>
YEAH. IT WAS GOOD.
<잠깐만, I GOT YOU SOMETHING.>
A NOTE ABOUT MY MOM: SHE'S TINY, BUT WHEN IT COMES TO SAT BOOKS, SHE COULD LIFT DOUBLE HER WEIGHT. I'VE ALWAYS WONDERED IF SHE WOULD LIFT A CAR TO SAVE THOSE THINGS.
SAT
SAT
2011
<ANY WORD? THEY'RE COMING UP FOR YOU! 금방이면와.>
MOM, WE'RE FRESHMEN. THE SATS AREN'T HAPPENING FOR, LIKE, THREE YEARS.
<THEN I'M GLAD I GOT THEM EARLY.>

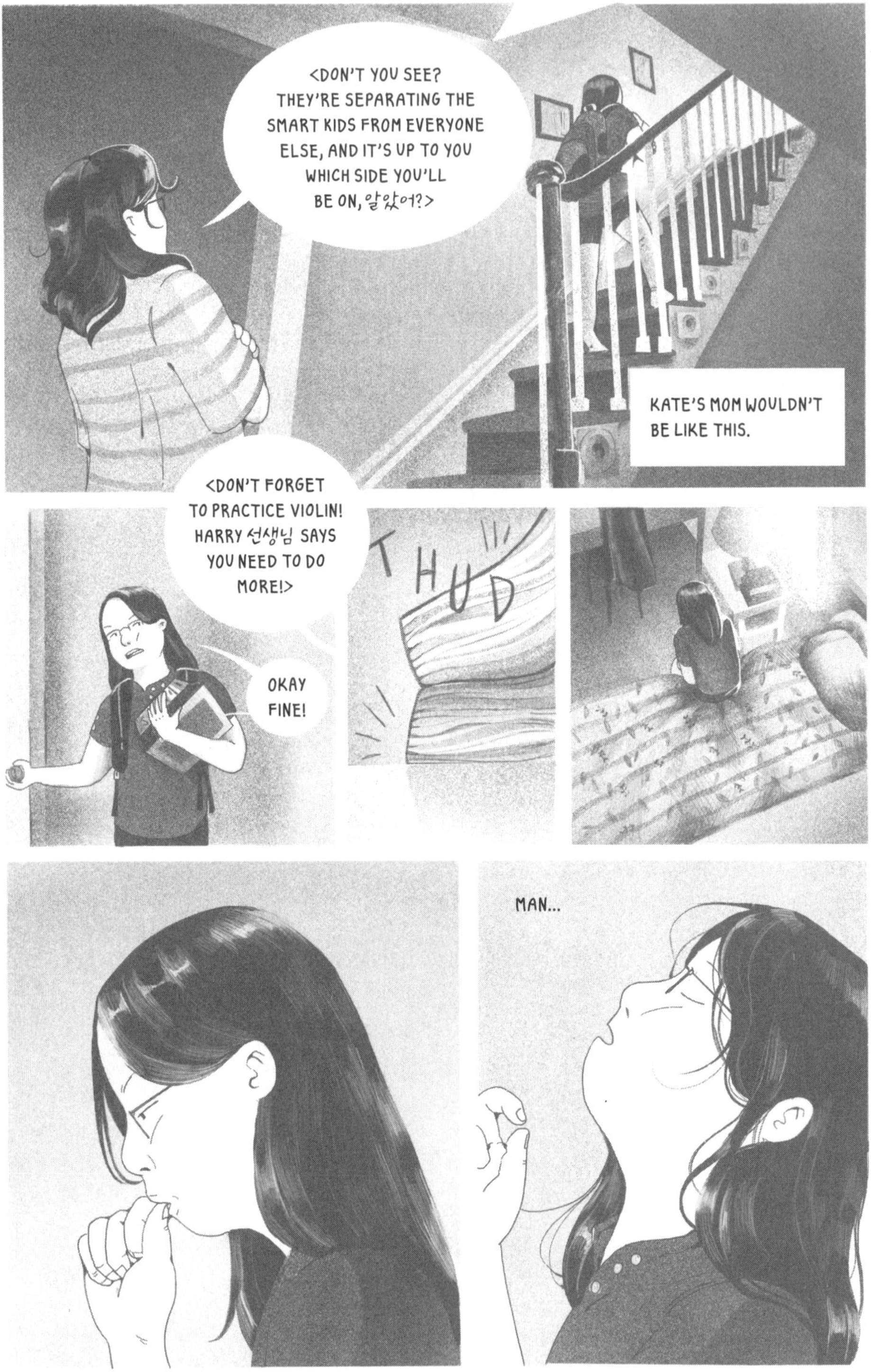
<DON'T YOU SEE? THEY'RE SEPARATING THE SMART KIDS FROM EVERYONE ELSE, AND IT'S UP TO YOU WHICH SIDE YOU'LL BE ON, 알았어?>
KATE'S MOM WOULDN'T BE LIKE THIS.
<DON'T FORGET TO PRACTICE VIOLIN! HARRY 선생님 SAYS YOU NEED TO DO MORE!>
OKAY FINE!
THUD
MAN...

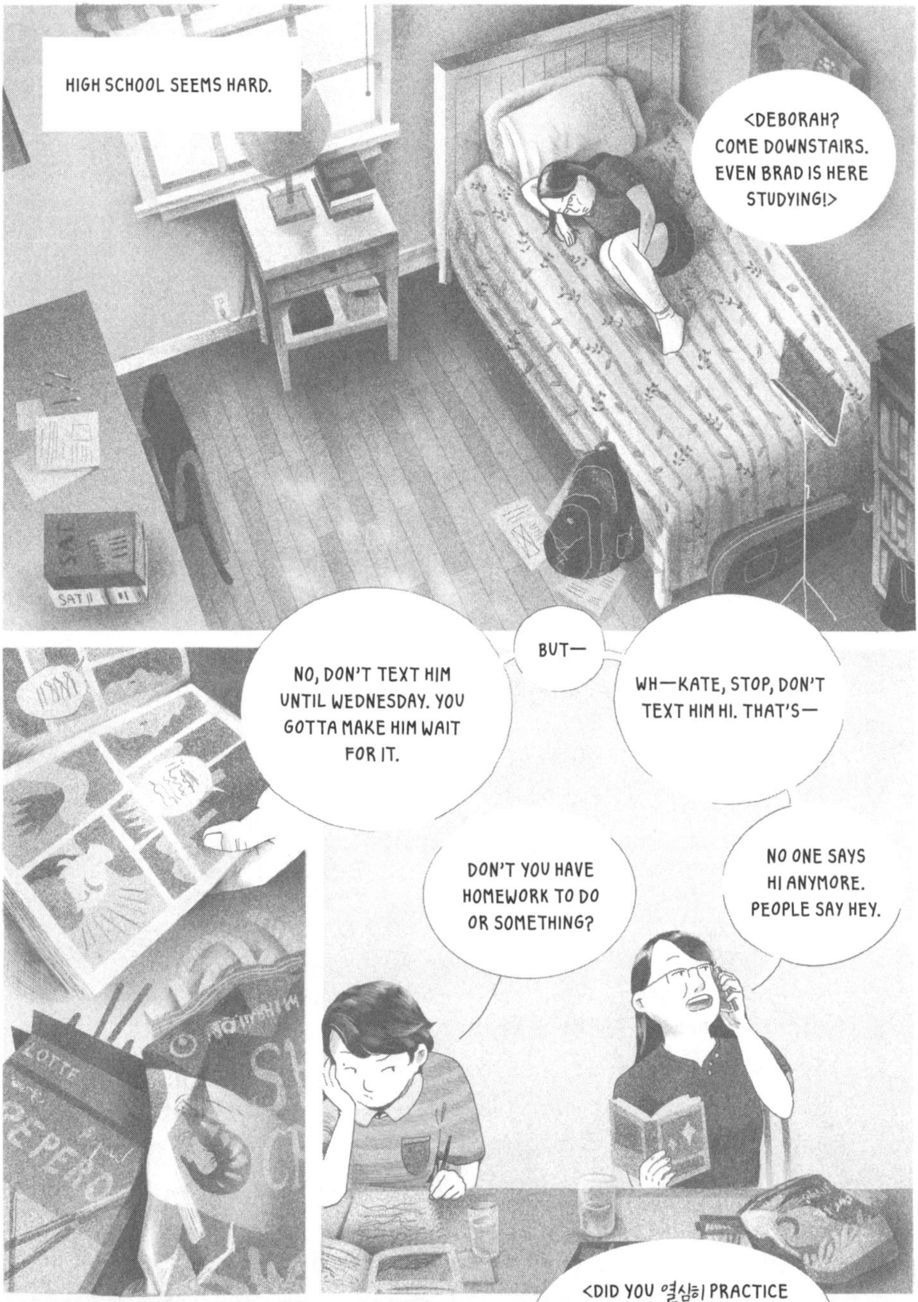
HIGH SCHOOL SEEMS HARD.
<DEBORAH? COME DOWNSTAIRS. EVEN BRAD IS HERE STUDYING!>
NO, DON'T TEXT HIM UNTIL WEDNESDAY. YOU GOTTA MAKE HIM WAIT FOR IT.
BUT—
WH—KATE, STOP, DON'T TEXT HIM HI. THAT'S—
DON'T YOU HAVE HOMEWORK TO DO OR SOMETHING?
NO ONE SAYS HI ANYMORE. PEOPLE SAY HEY.
<DID YOU 열심히 PRACTICE FOR YOUR VIOLIN LESSON TOMORROW? I BETTER NOT GET A CALL FROM HARRY AGAIN.>

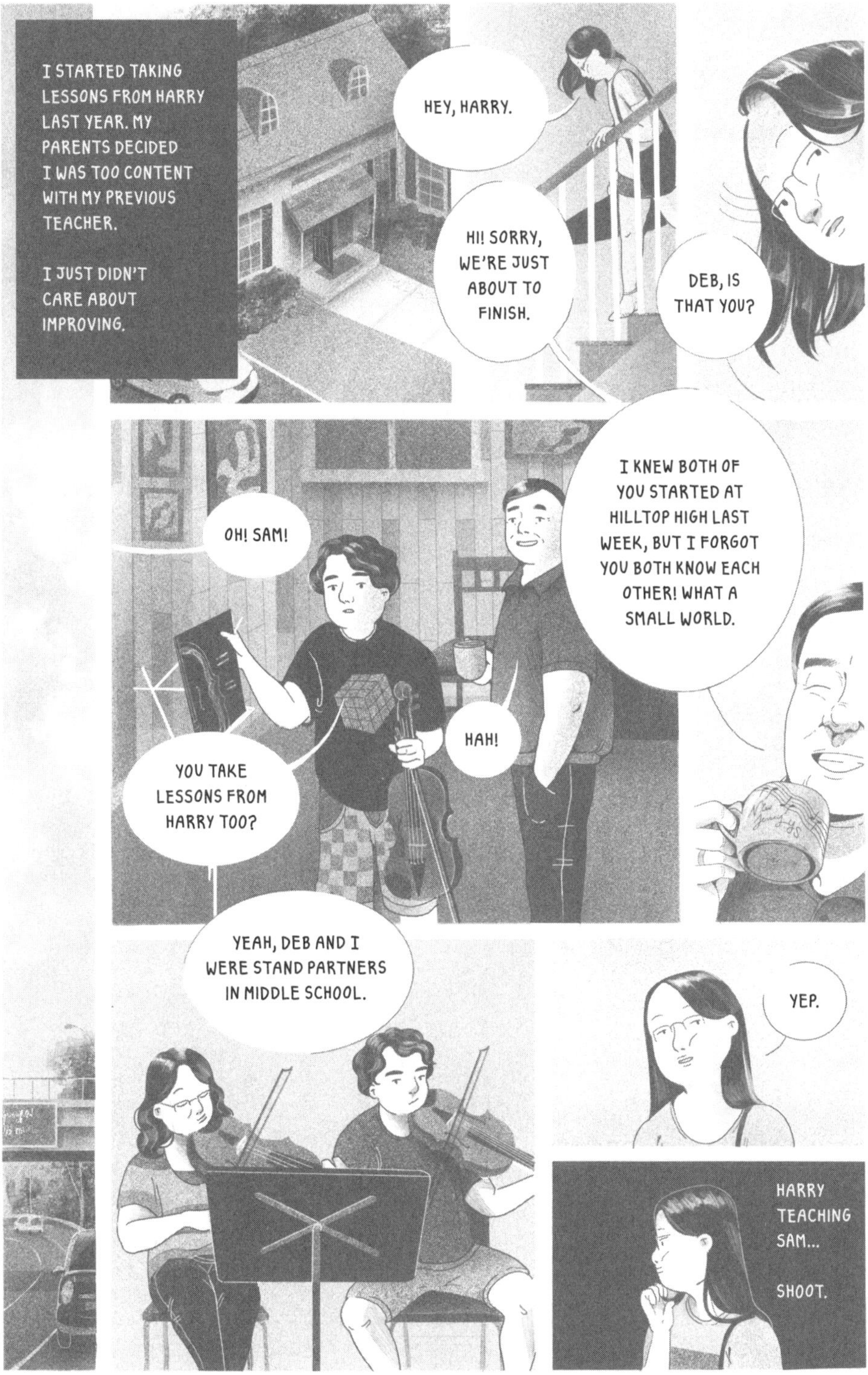
I STARTED TAKING LESSONS FROM HARRY LAST YEAR. MY PARENTS DECIDED I WAS TOO CONTENT WITH MY PREVIOUS TEACHER.
I JUST DIDN'T CARE ABOUT IMPROVING.
HEY, HARRY.
HI! SORRY, WE'RE JUST ABOUT TO FINISH.
DEB, IS THAT YOU?
OH! SAM!
I KNEW BOTH OF YOU STARTED AT HILLTOP HIGH LAST WEEK, BUT I FORGOT YOU BOTH KNOW EACH OTHER! WHAT A SMALL WORLD.
HAH!
YOU TAKE LESSONS FROM HARRY TOO?
YEAH, DEB AND I WERE STAND PARTNERS IN MIDDLE SCHOOL.
YEP.
HARRY TEACHING SAM...
SHOOT.

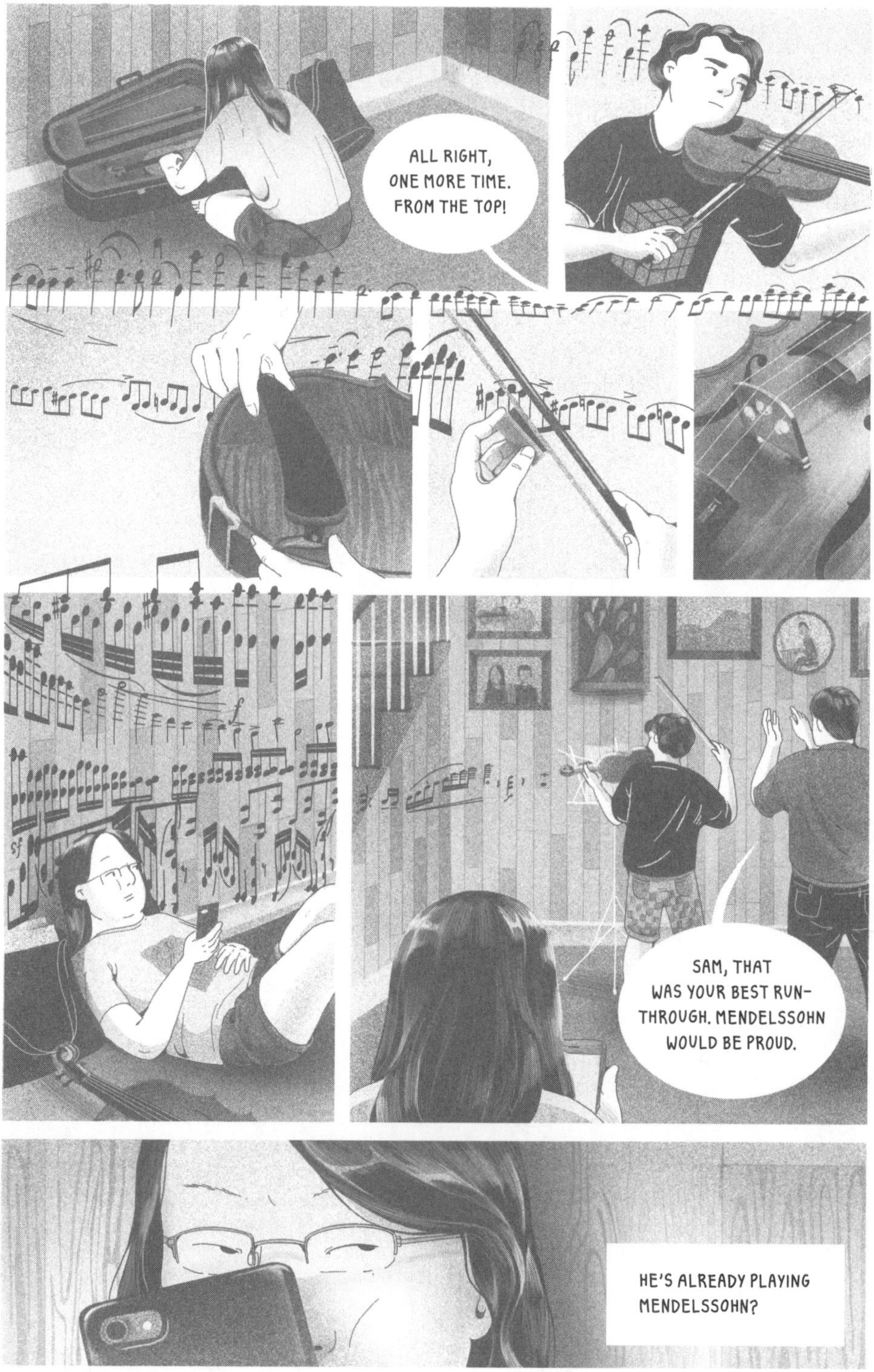
ALL RIGHT,
ONE MORE TIME.
FROM THE TOP!
SAM, THAT
WAS YOUR BEST RUN-
THROUGH. MENDELSSOHN
WOULD BE PROUD.
HE'S ALREADY PLAYING
MENDELSSOHN?

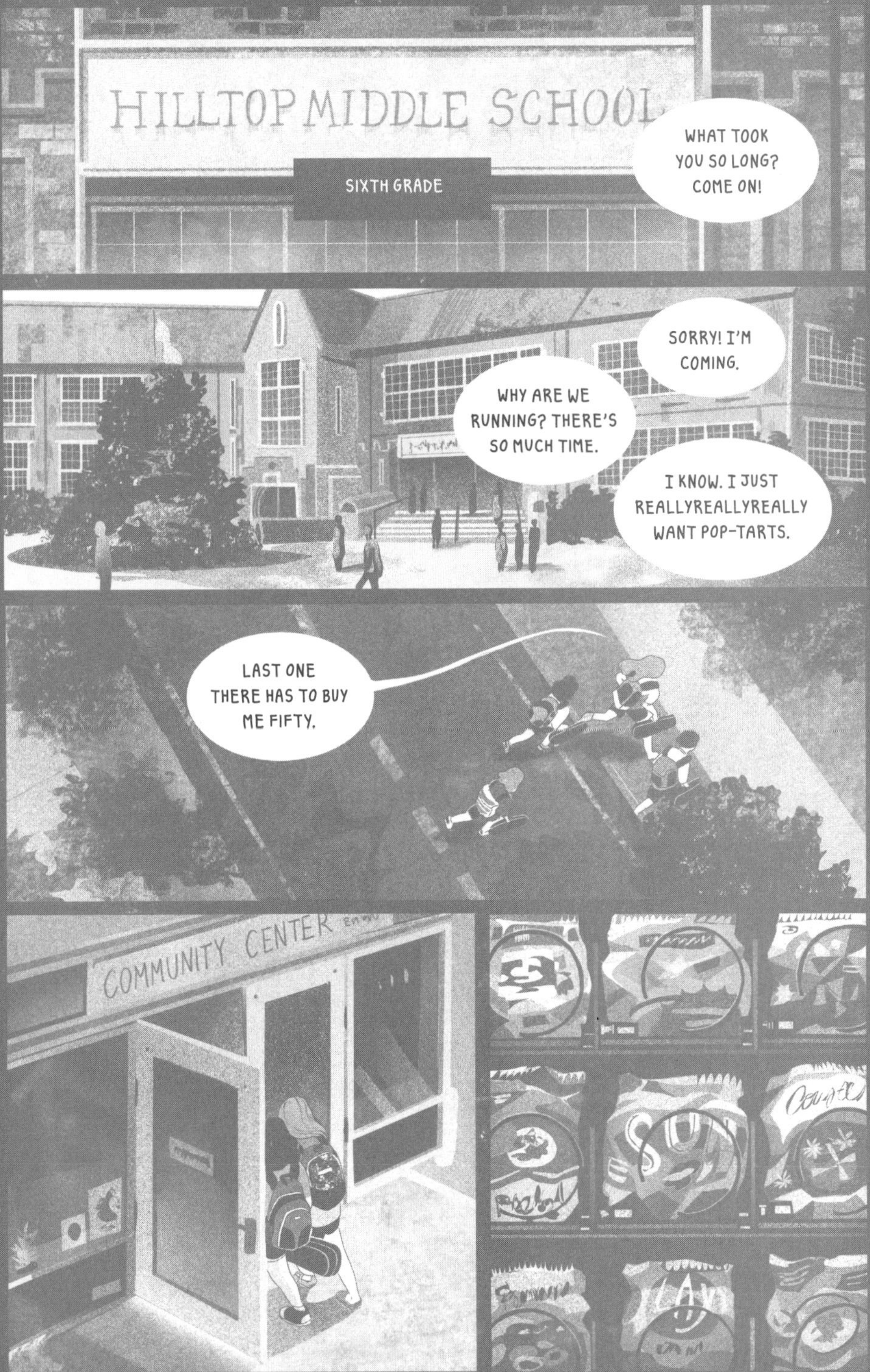
HILLTOP MIDDLE SCHOOL
SIXTH GRADE
WHAT TOOK YOU SO LONG? COME ON!
SORRY! I'M COMING.
WHY ARE WE RUNNING? THERE'S SO MUCH TIME.
I KNOW. I JUST REALLYREALLYREALLY WANT POP-TARTS.
LAST ONE THERE HAS TO BUY ME FIFTY.
COMMUNITY CENTER

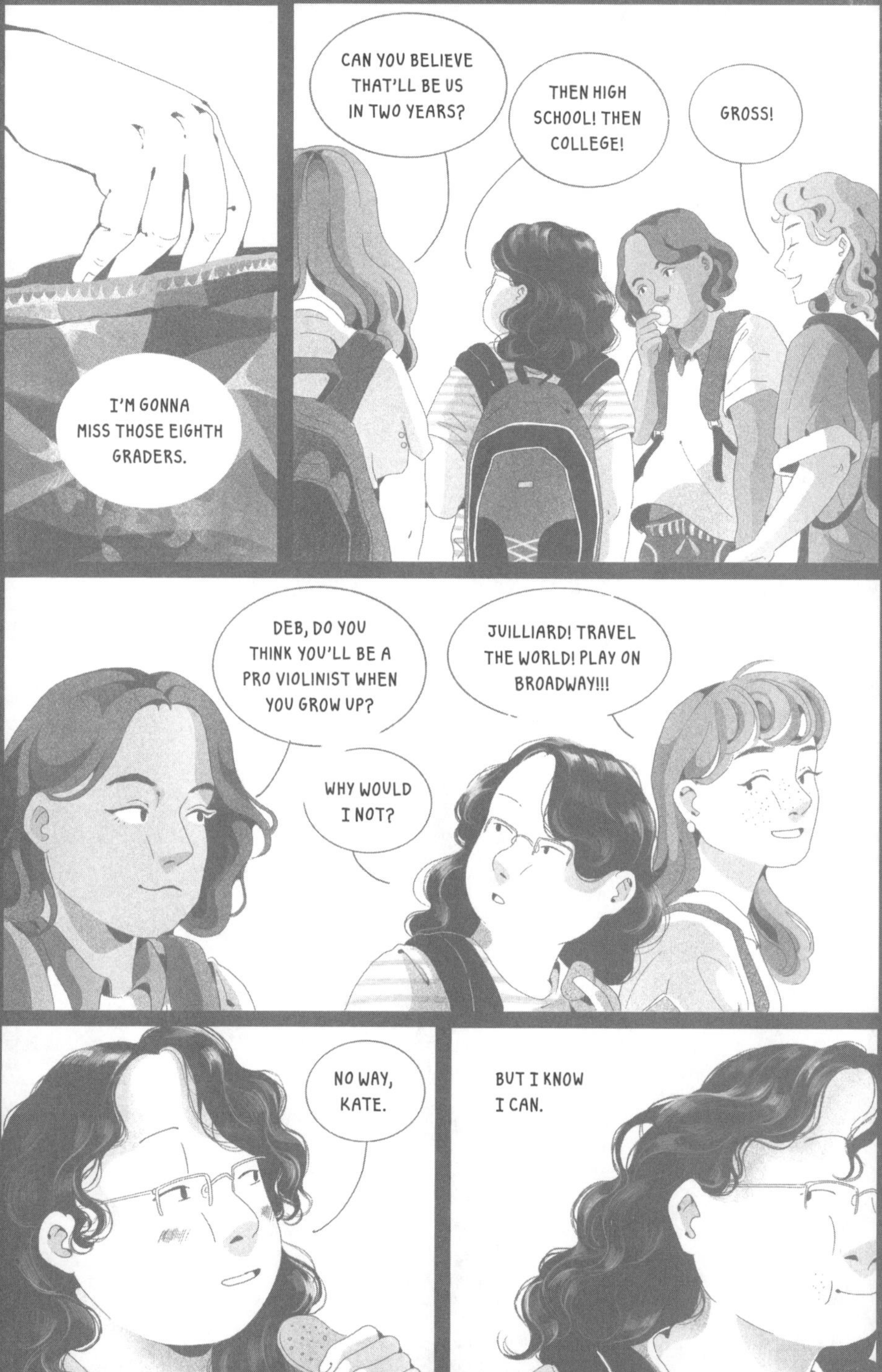
I'M GONNA MISS THOSE EIGHTH GRADERS.
CAN YOU BELIEVE THAT'LL BE US IN TWO YEARS?
THEN HIGH SCHOOL! THEN COLLEGE!
GROSS!
DEB, DO YOU THINK YOU'LL BE A PRO VIOLINIST WHEN YOU GROW UP?
JUILLIARD! TRAVEL THE WORLD! PLAY ON BROADWAY!!!
WHY WOULD I NOT?
NO WAY, KATE.
BUT I KNOW I CAN.

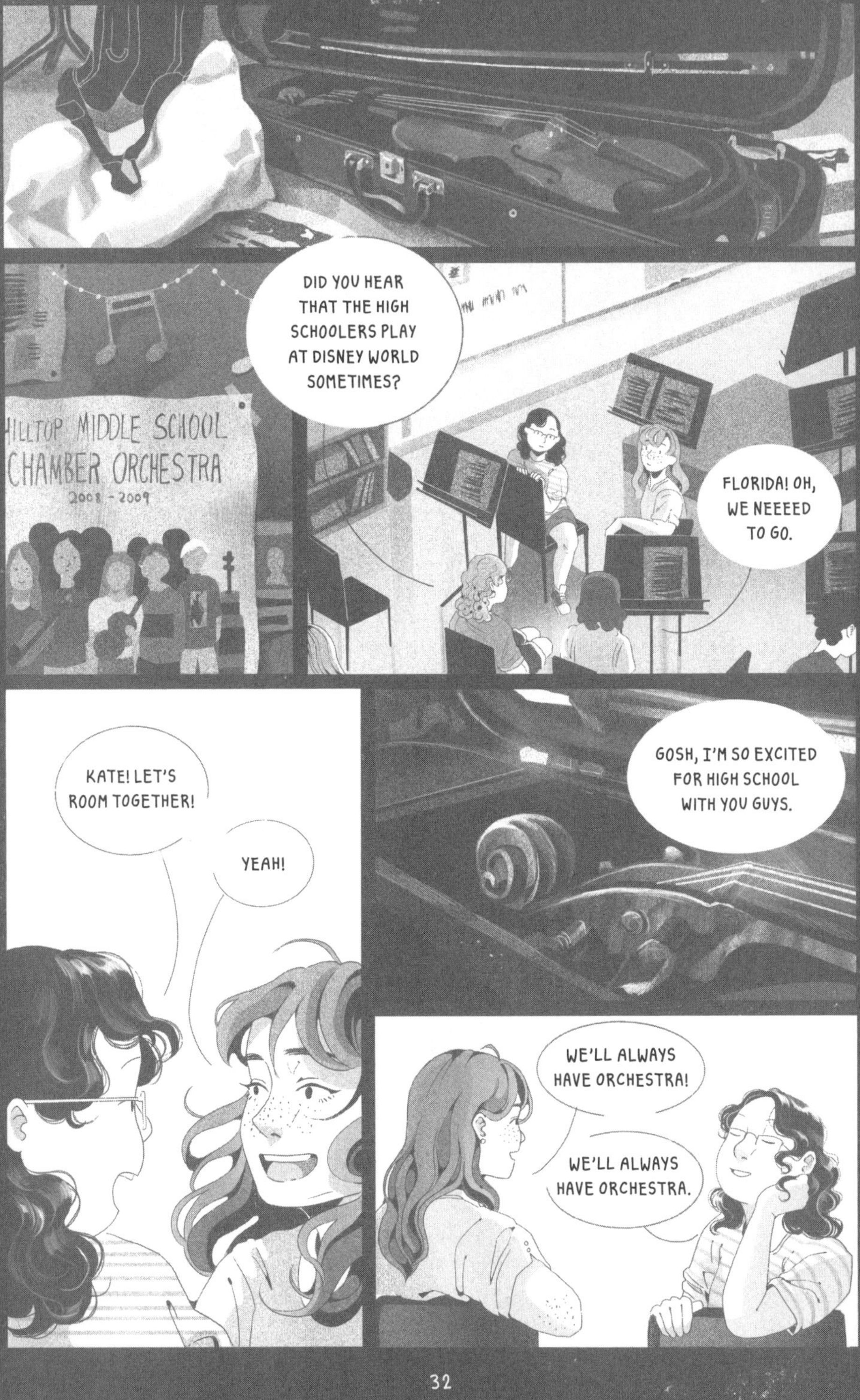

DID YOU HEAR THAT THE HIGH SCHOOLERS PLAY AT DISNEY WORLD SOMETIMES?
HILLTOP MIDDLE SCHOOL CHAMBER ORCHESTRA 2008 - 2009
FLORIDA! OH, WE NEEEED TO GO.
KATE! LET'S ROOM TOGETHER!
YEAH!
GOSH, I'M SO EXCITED FOR HIGH SCHOOL WITH YOU GUYS.
WE'LL ALWAYS HAVE ORCHESTRA!
WE'LL ALWAYS HAVE ORCHESTRA.

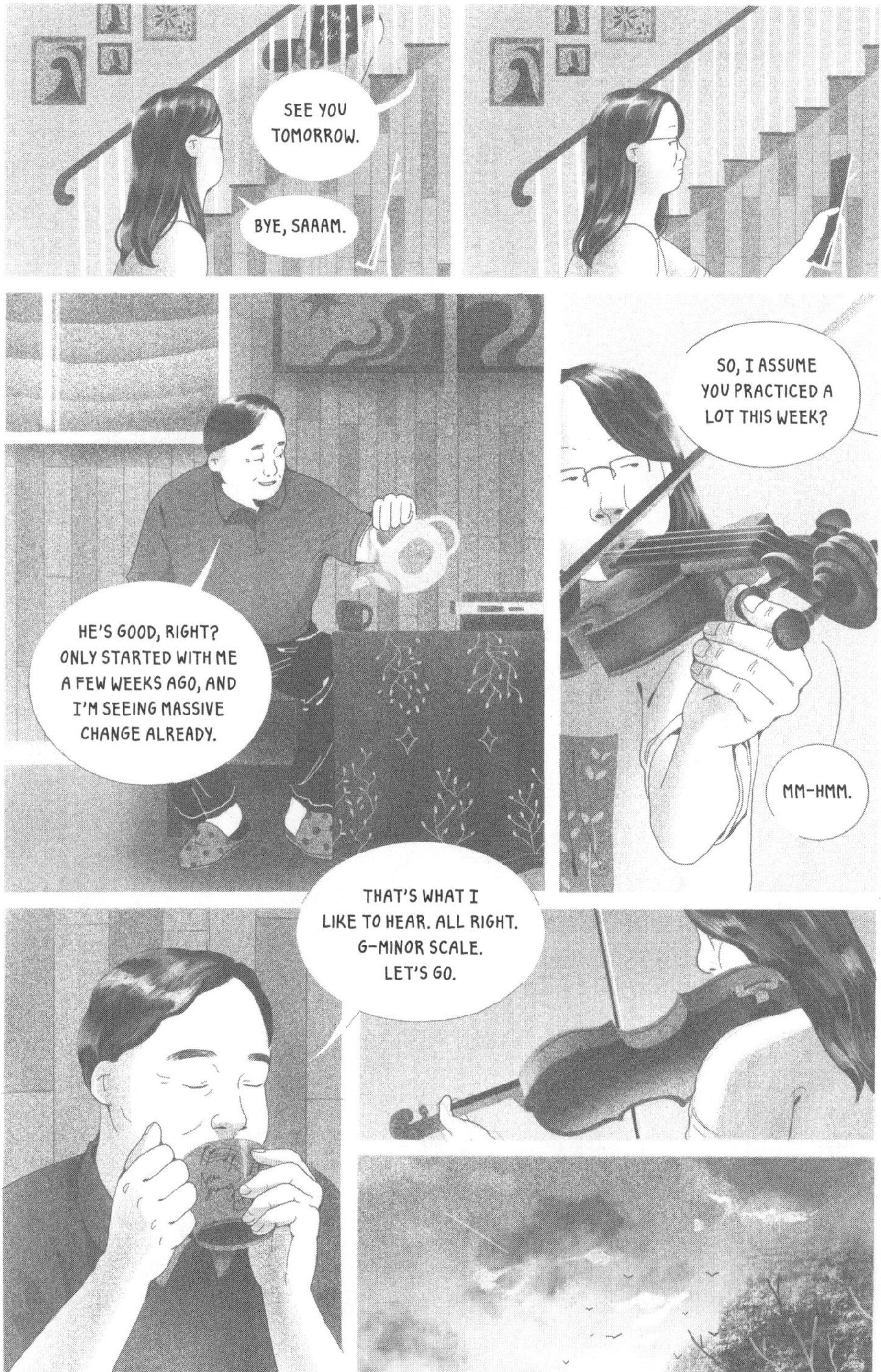
SEE YOU TOMORROW.
BYE, SAAAM.
HE'S GOOD, RIGHT? ONLY STARTED WITH ME A FEW WEEKS AGO, AND I'M SEEING MASSIVE CHANGE ALREADY.
SO, I ASSUME YOU PRACTICED A LOT THIS WEEK?
MM-HMM.
THAT'S WHAT I LIKE TO HEAR. ALL RIGHT. G-MINOR SCALE. LET'S GO.

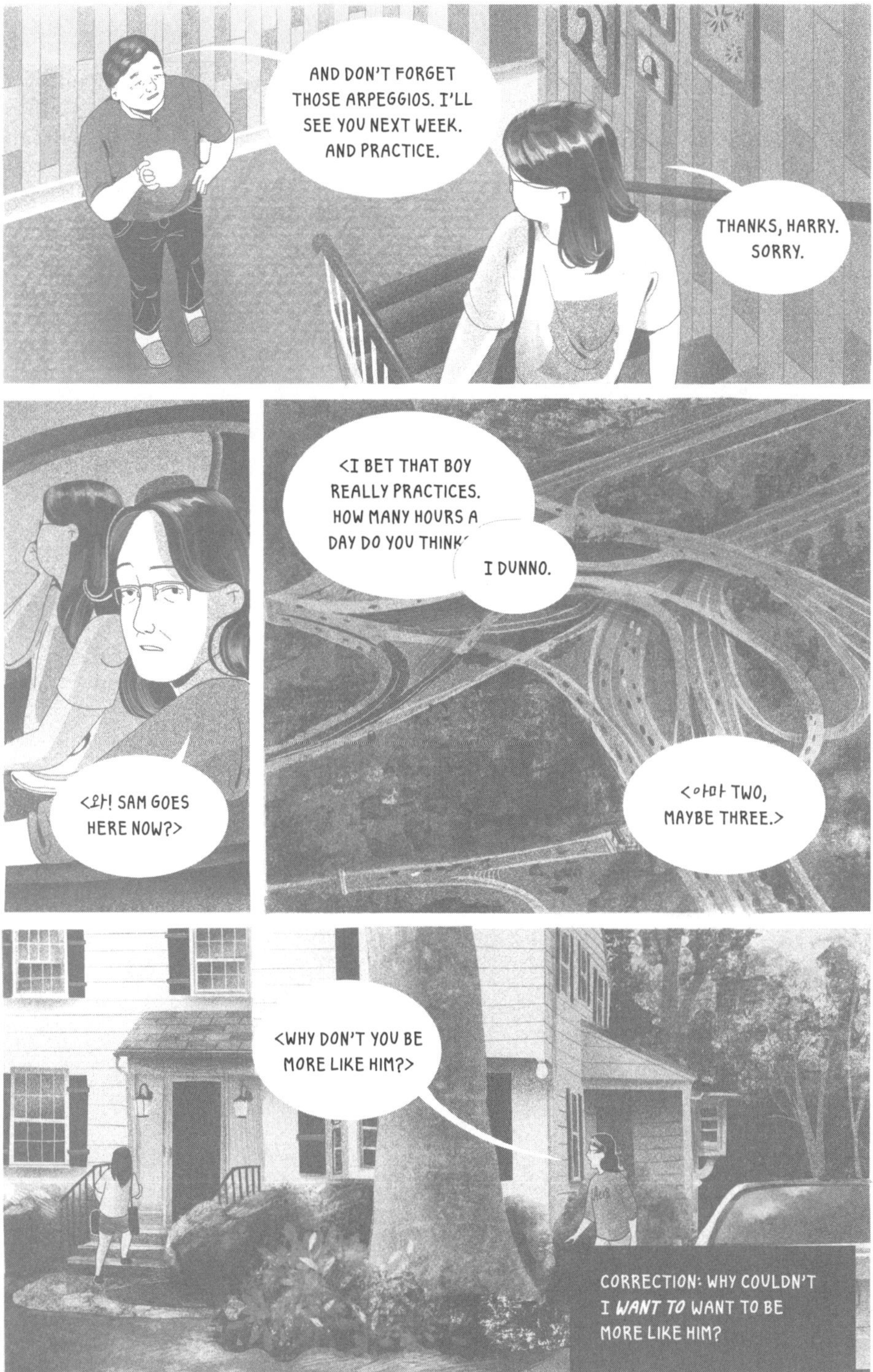
AND DON'T FORGET THOSE ARPEGGIOS. I'LL SEE YOU NEXT WEEK. AND PRACTICE.
THANKS, HARRY. SORRY.
<와! SAM GOES HERE NOW?>
<I BET THAT BOY REALLY PRACTICES. HOW MANY HOURS A DAY DO YOU THINK
I DUNNO.
<아마 TWO, MAYBE THREE.>
<WHY DON'T YOU BE MORE LIKE HIM?>
CORRECTION: WHY COULDN'T I ***WANT TO*** WANT TO BE MORE LIKE HIM?

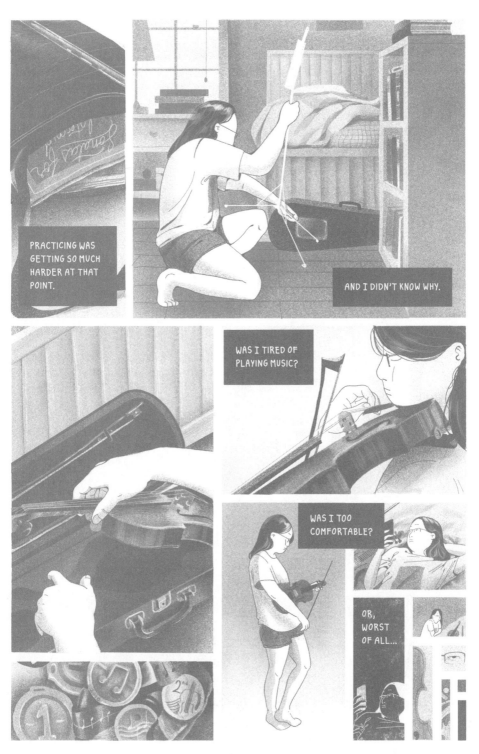

PRACTICING WAS GETTING SO MUCH HARDER AT THAT POINT.

AND I DIDN'T KNOW WHY.

WAS I TIRED OF PLAYING MUSIC?

WAS I TOO COMFORTABLE?

OR, WORST OF ALL...

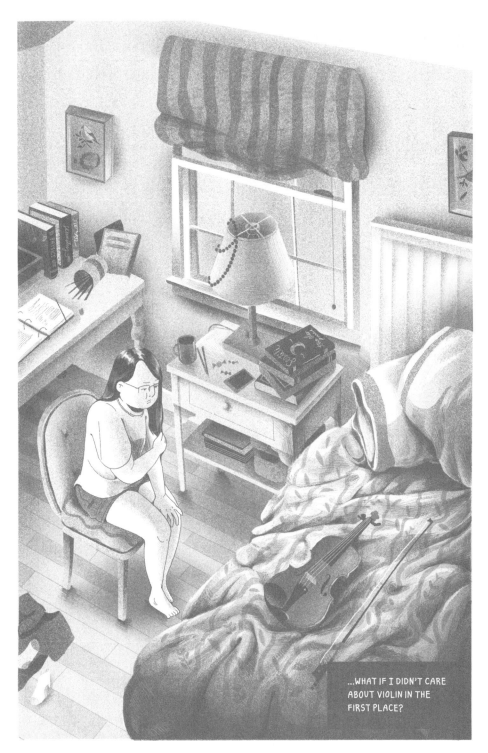

...WHAT IF I DIDN'T CARE ABOUT VIOLIN IN THE FIRST PLACE?

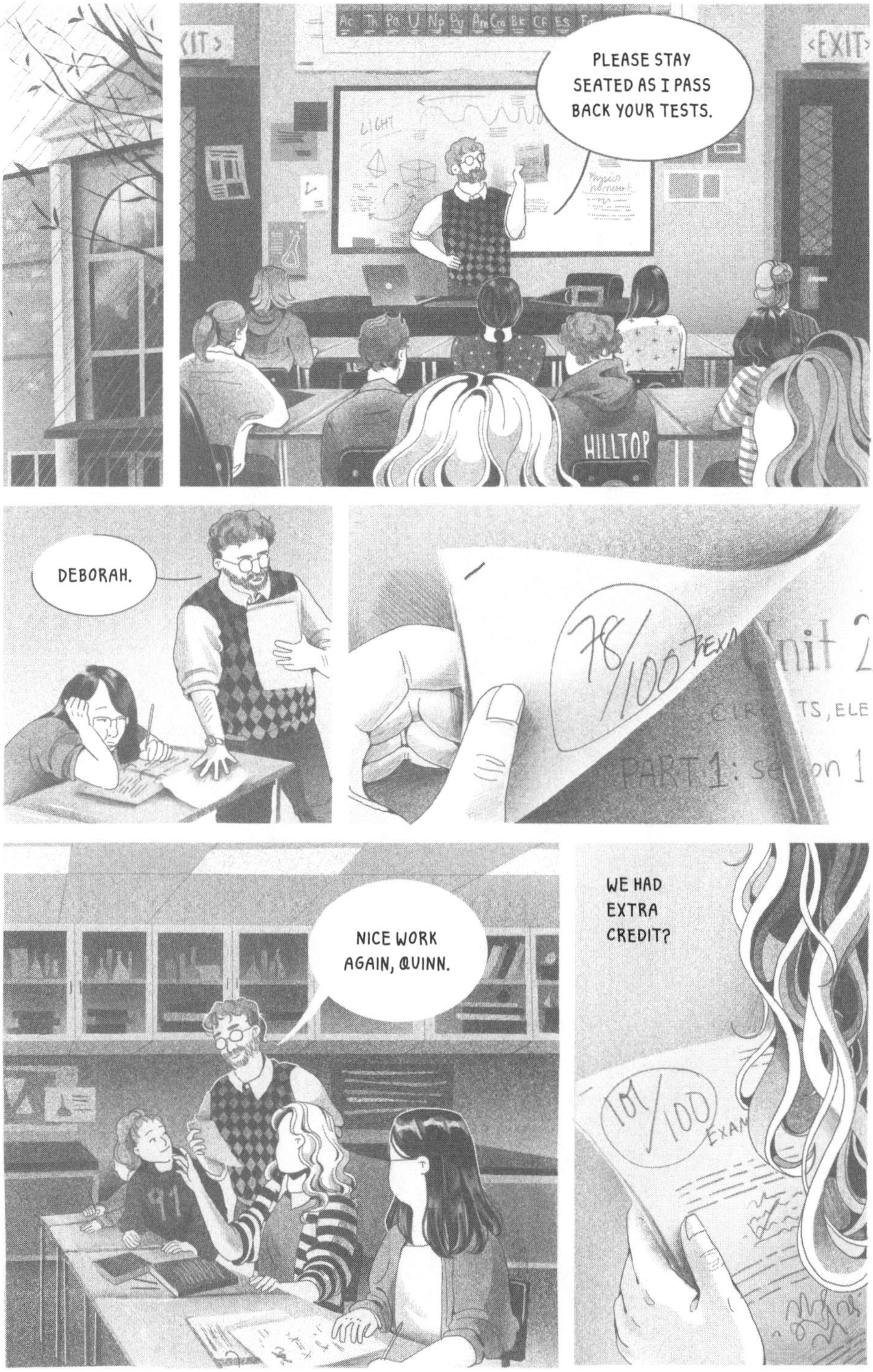
EXIT
PLEASE STAY SEATED AS I PASS BACK YOUR TESTS.
HILLTOP
DEBORAH.
78/100
CIRC TS, ELE
PART 1: se on 1
NICE WORK AGAIN, QUINN.
WE HAD EXTRA CREDIT?
101/100

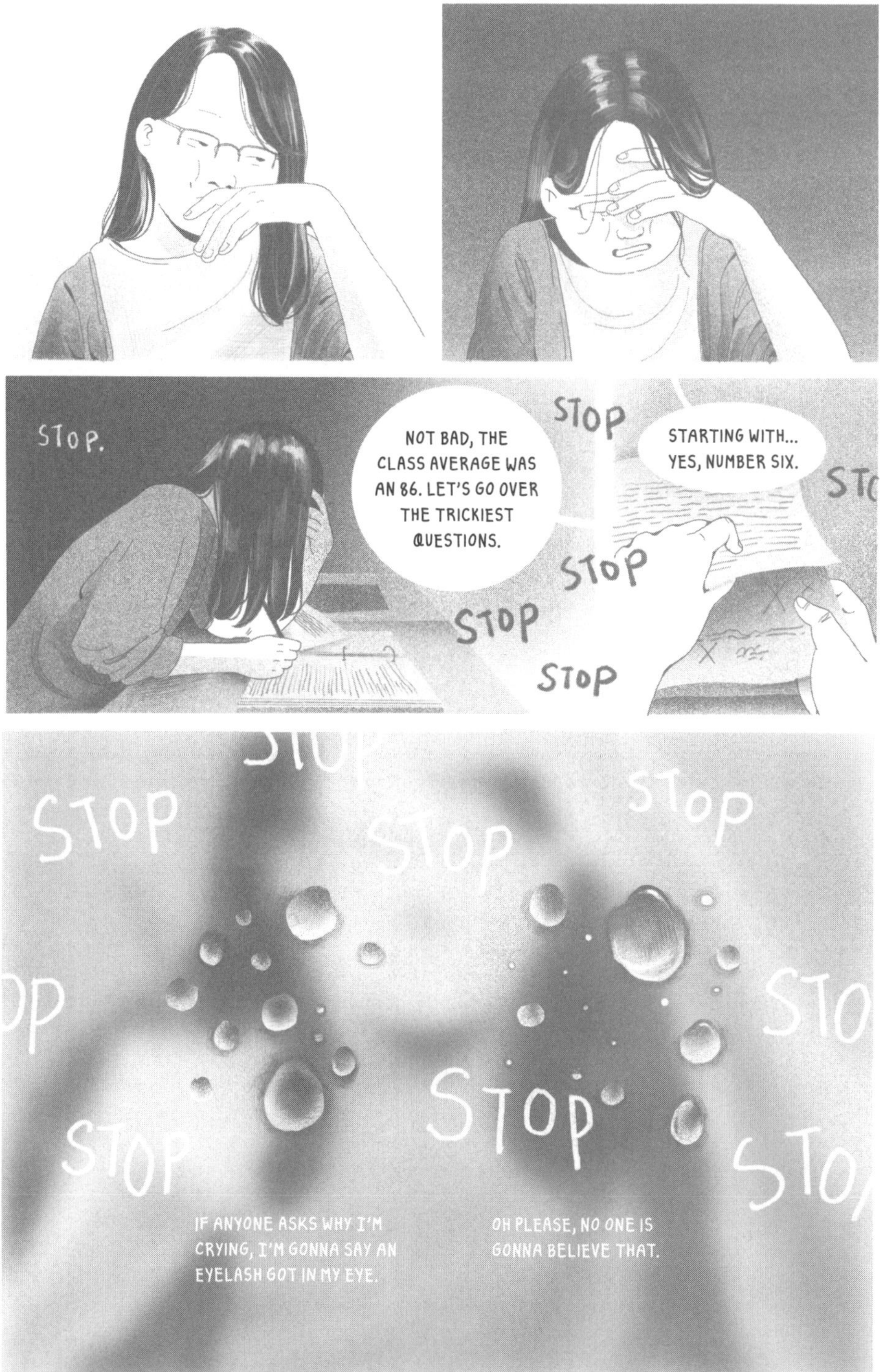

STOP.
NOT BAD, THE CLASS AVERAGE WAS AN 86. LET'S GO OVER THE TRICKIEST QUESTIONS.
STOP
STARTING WITH... YES, NUMBER SIX.
STOP
STOP
STOP
STOP
STOP
STOP
STOP
STOP
IF ANYONE ASKS WHY I'M CRYING, I'M GONNA SAY AN EYELASH GOT IN MY EYE.
OH PLEASE, NO ONE IS GONNA BELIEVE THAT.

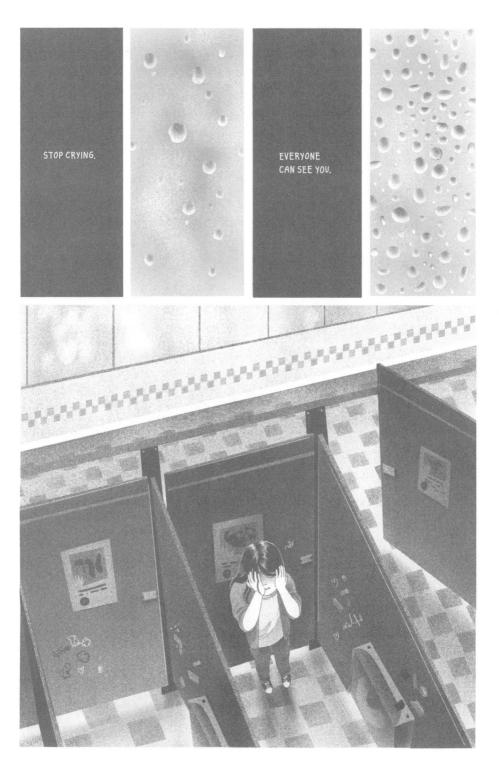

STOP CRYING.

EVERYONE
CAN SEE YOU.

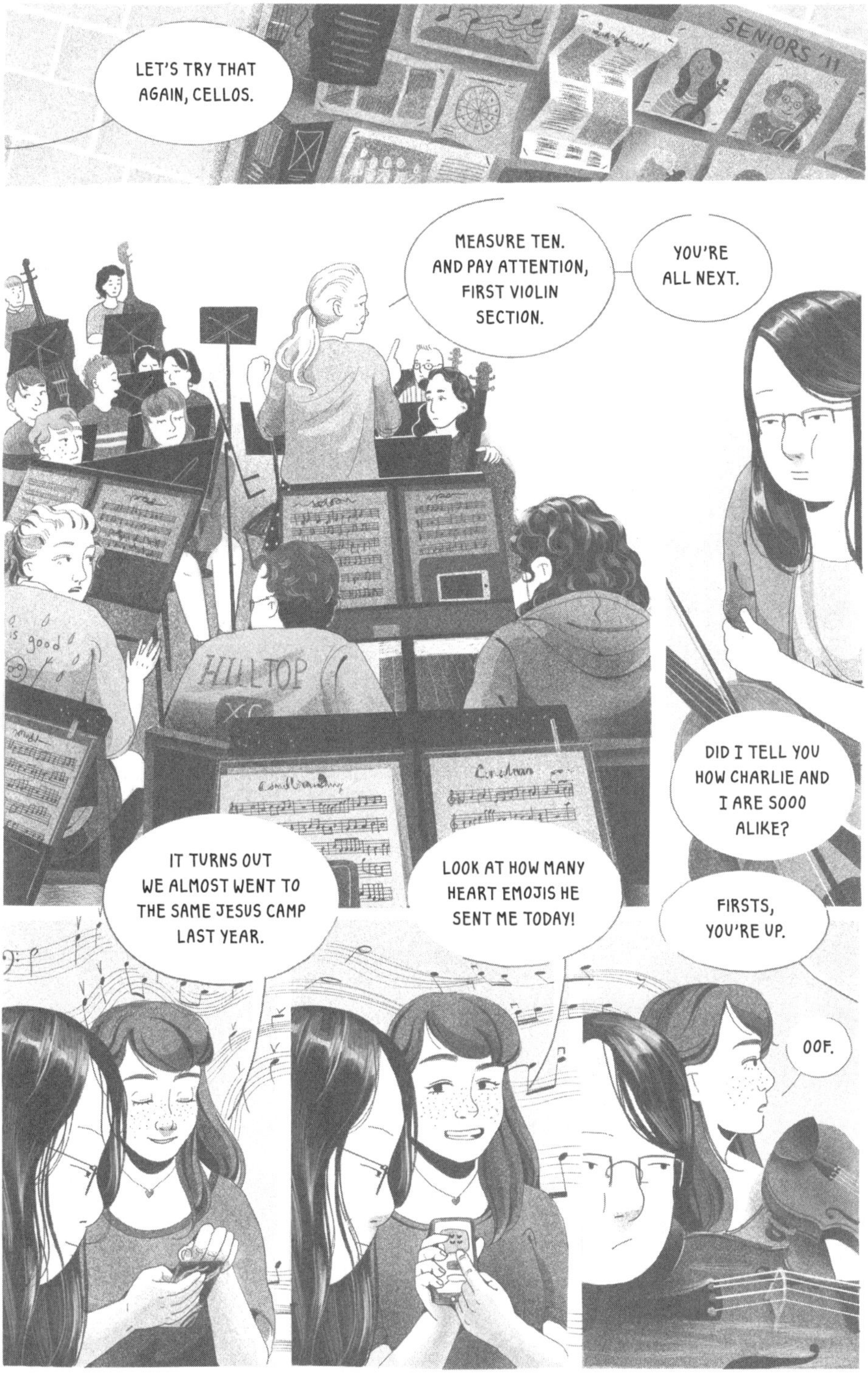
LET'S TRY THAT AGAIN, CELLOS.
SENIORS '11
MEASURE TEN. AND PAY ATTENTION, FIRST VIOLIN SECTION.
YOU'RE ALL NEXT.
HILLTOP
DID I TELL YOU HOW CHARLIE AND I ARE SOOO ALIKE?
IT TURNS OUT WE ALMOST WENT TO THE SAME JESUS CAMP LAST YEAR.
LOOK AT HOW MANY HEART EMOJIS HE SENT ME TODAY!
FIRSTS, YOU'RE UP.
OOF.

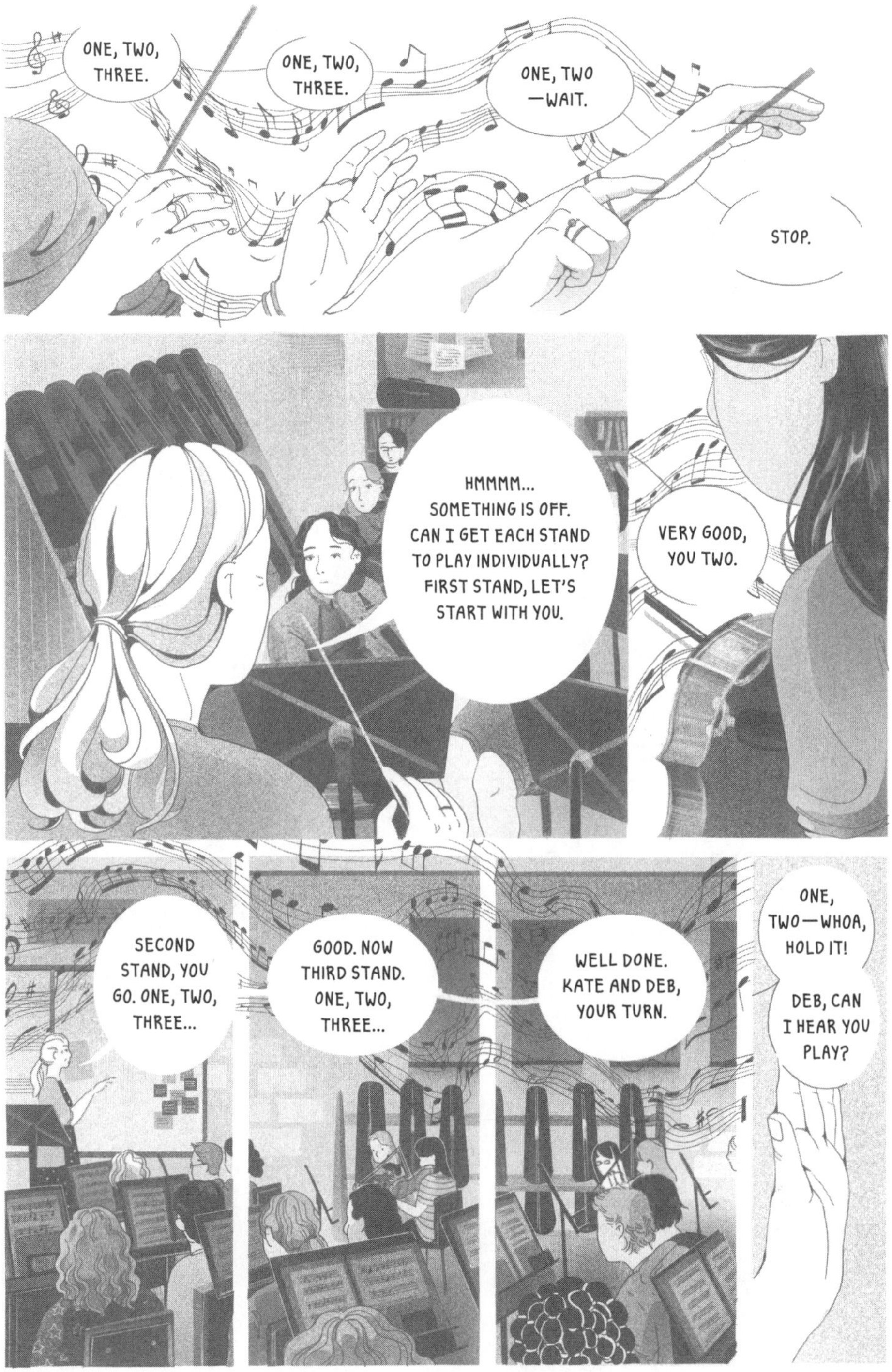
ONE, TWO, THREE.
ONE, TWO, THREE.
ONE, TWO —WAIT.
STOP.
HMMMM... SOMETHING IS OFF. CAN I GET EACH STAND TO PLAY INDIVIDUALLY? FIRST STAND, LET'S START WITH YOU.
VERY GOOD, YOU TWO.
SECOND STAND, YOU GO. ONE, TWO, THREE...
GOOD. NOW THIRD STAND. ONE, TWO, THREE...
WELL DONE. KATE AND DEB, YOUR TURN.
ONE, TWO—WHOA, HOLD IT!
DEB, CAN I HEAR YOU PLAY?

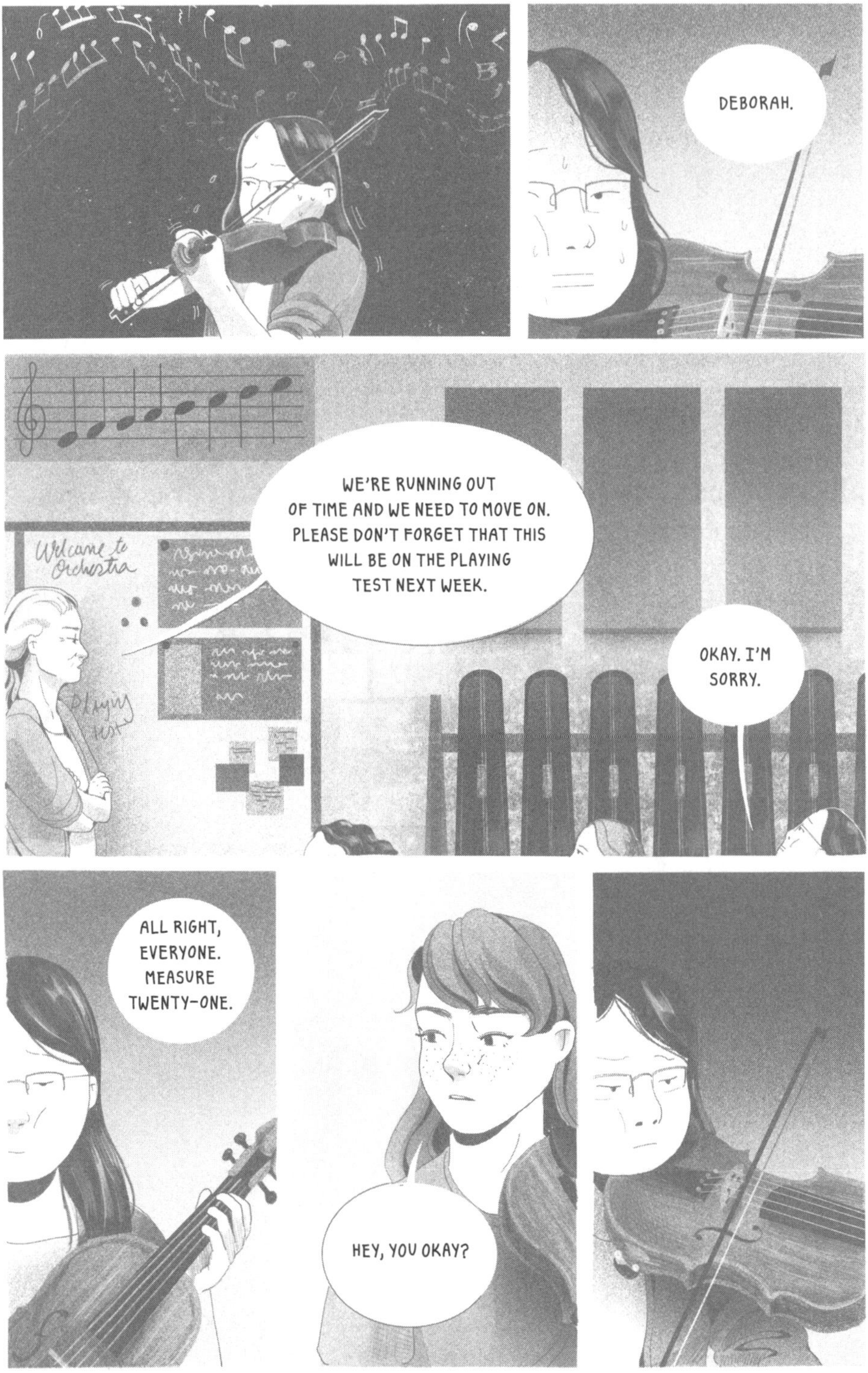
DEBORAH.
Welcome to Orchestra
WE'RE RUNNING OUT OF TIME AND WE NEED TO MOVE ON. PLEASE DON'T FORGET THAT THIS WILL BE ON THE PLAYING TEST NEXT WEEK.
Playing test
OKAY. I'M SORRY.
ALL RIGHT, EVERYONE. MEASURE TWENTY-ONE.
HEY, YOU OKAY?

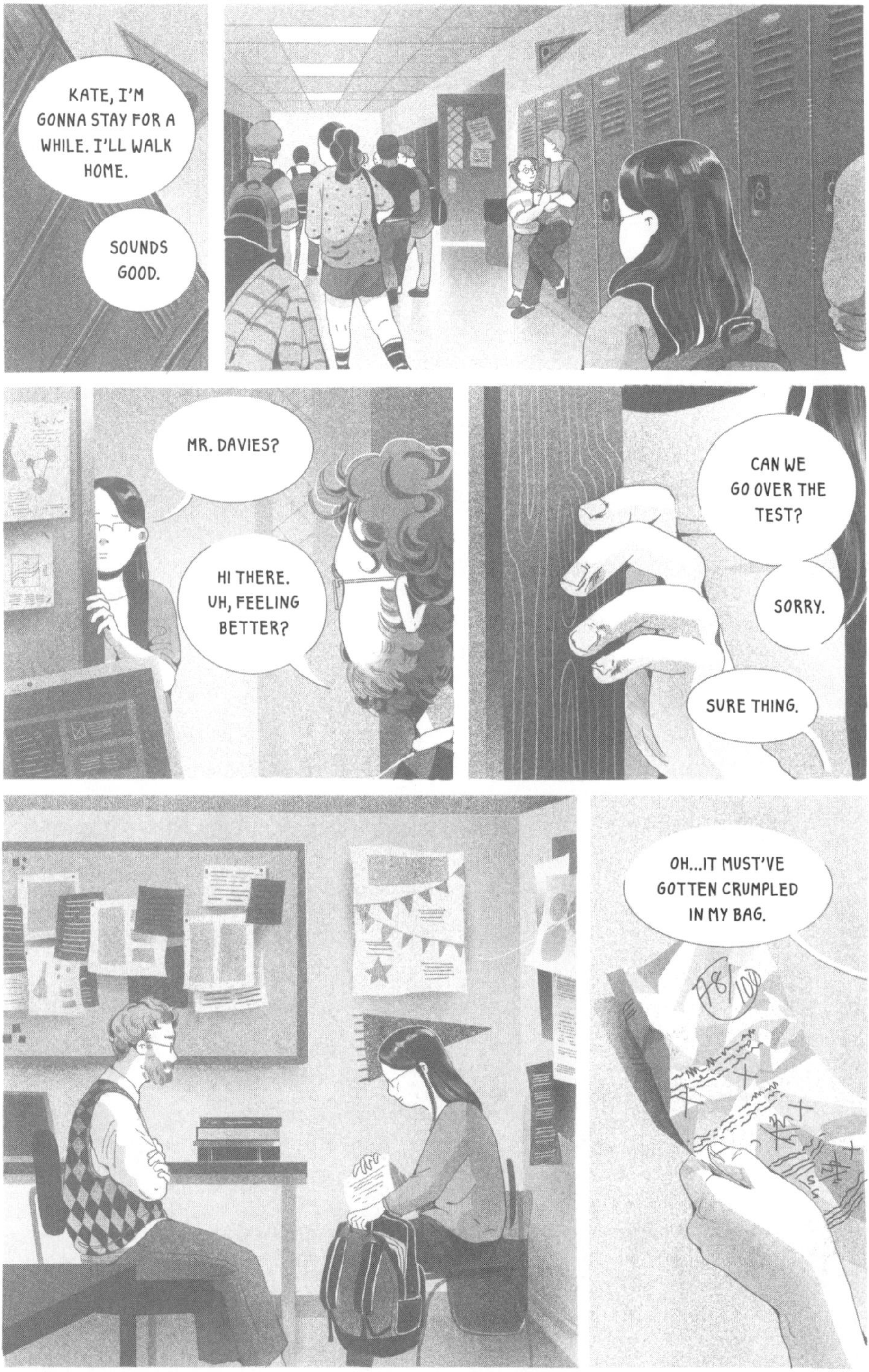
KATE, I'M GONNA STAY FOR A WHILE. I'LL WALK HOME.
SOUNDS GOOD.
MR. DAVIES?
HI THERE. UH, FEELING BETTER?
CAN WE GO OVER THE TEST?
SORRY.
SURE THING.
OH...IT MUST'VE GOTTEN CRUMPLED IN MY BAG.
78/100

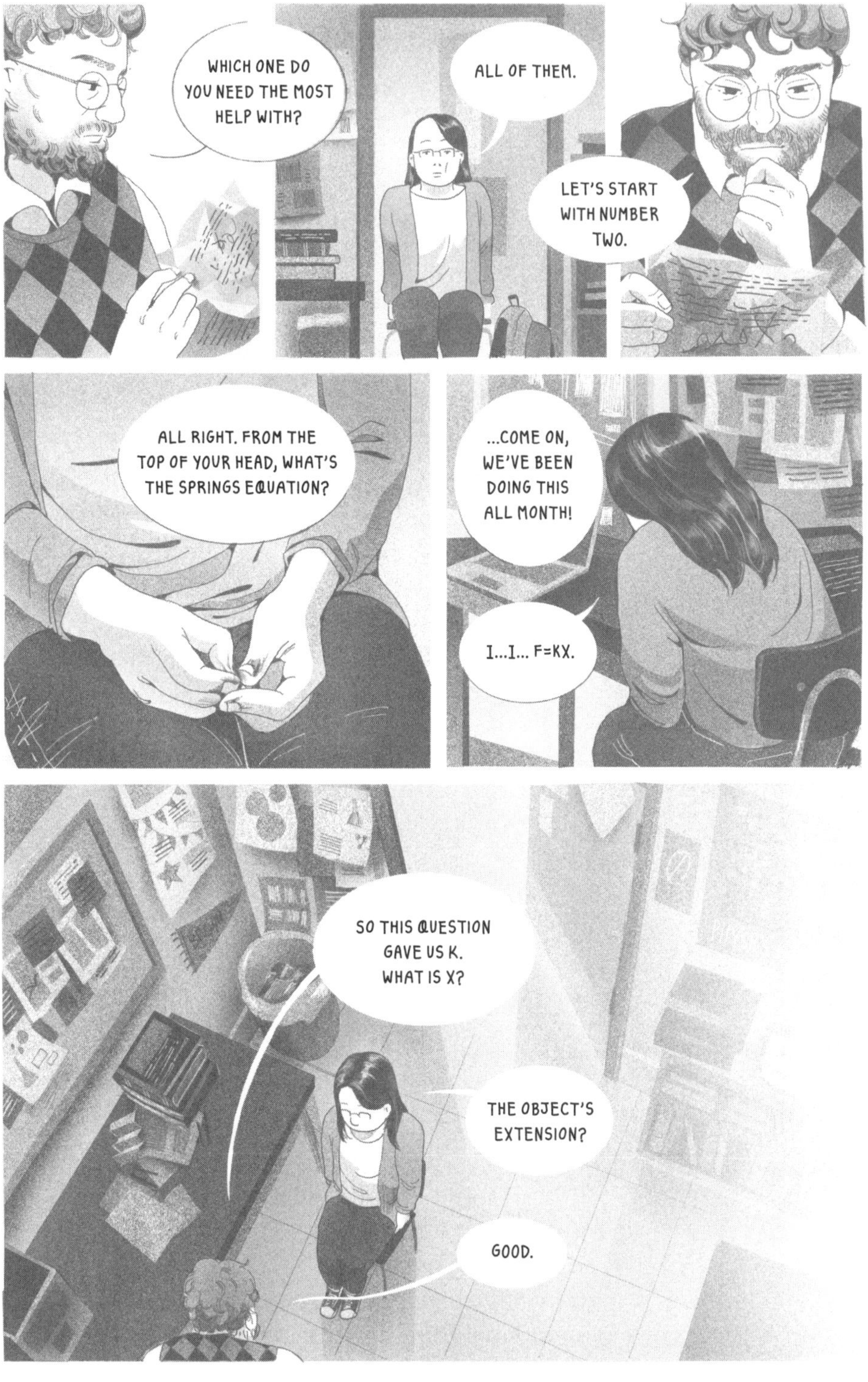
WHICH ONE DO YOU NEED THE MOST HELP WITH?
ALL OF THEM.
LET'S START WITH NUMBER TWO.
ALL RIGHT. FROM THE TOP OF YOUR HEAD, WHAT'S THE SPRINGS EQUATION?
...COME ON, WE'VE BEEN DOING THIS ALL MONTH!
I...I... F=KX.
SO THIS QUESTION GAVE US K. WHAT IS X?
THE OBJECT'S EXTENSION?
GOOD.

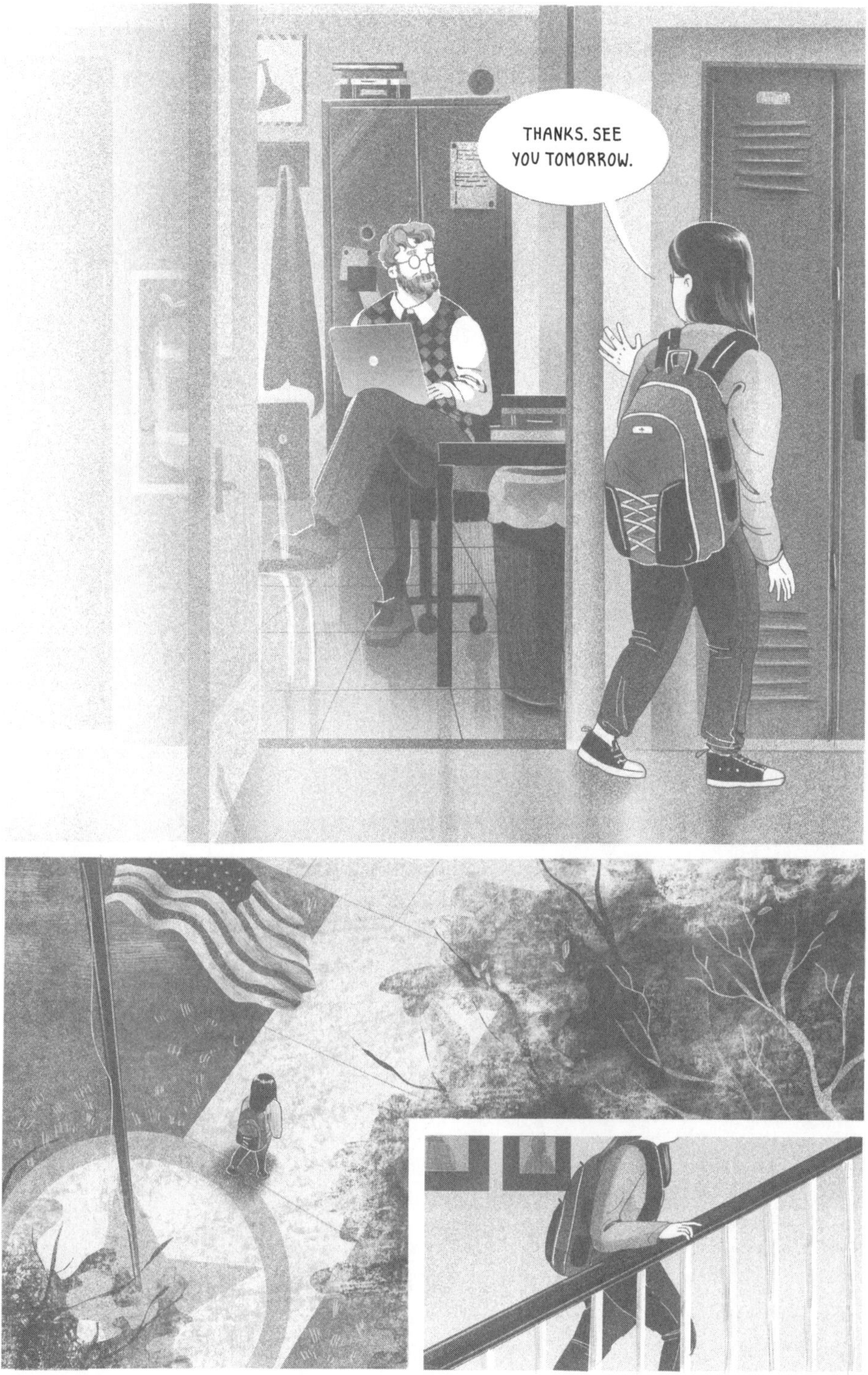
THANKS. SEE
YOU TOMORROW.

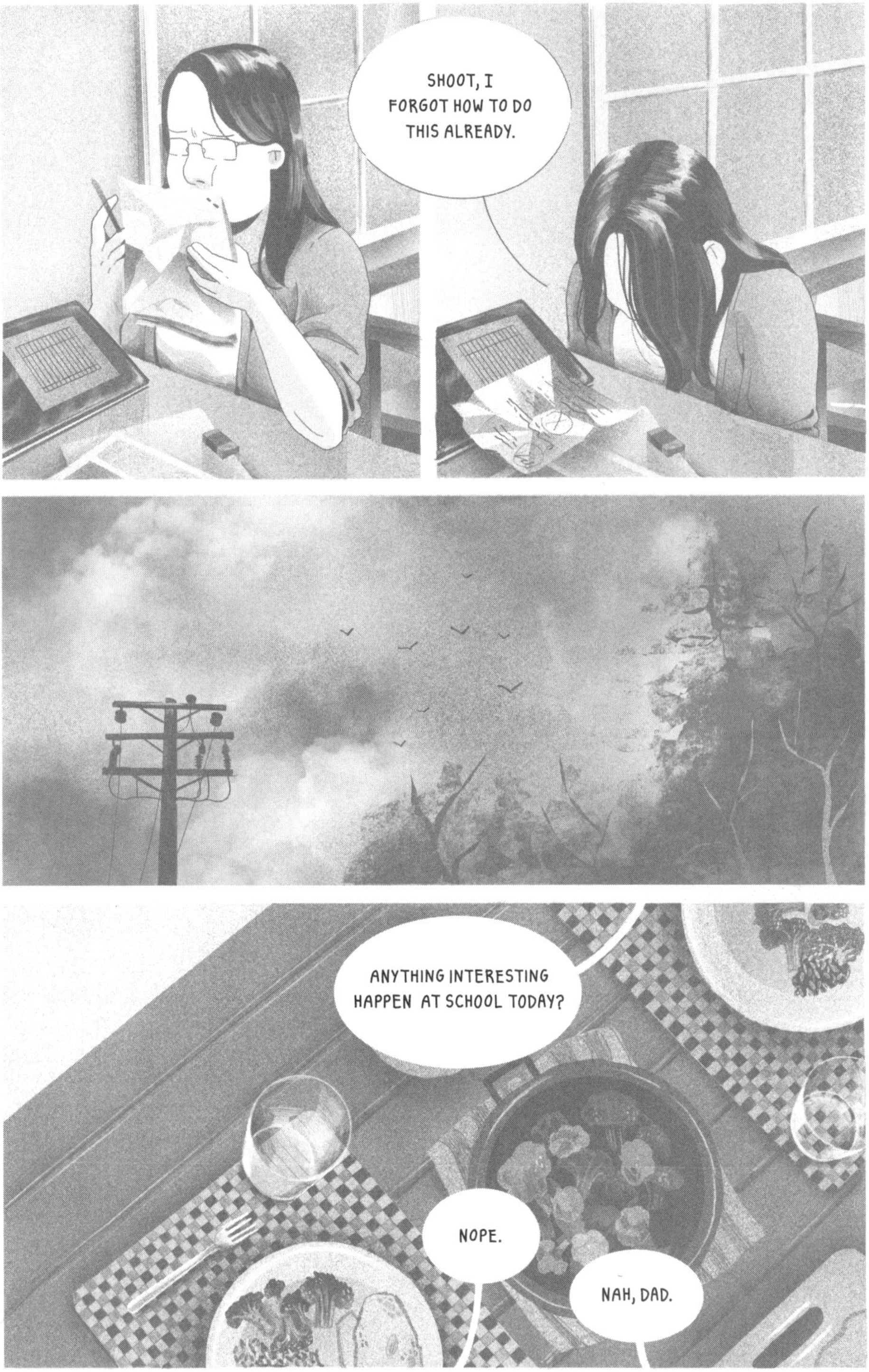
SHOOT, I FORGOT HOW TO DO THIS ALREADY.
ANYTHING INTERESTING HAPPEN AT SCHOOL TODAY?
NOPE.
NAH, DAD.

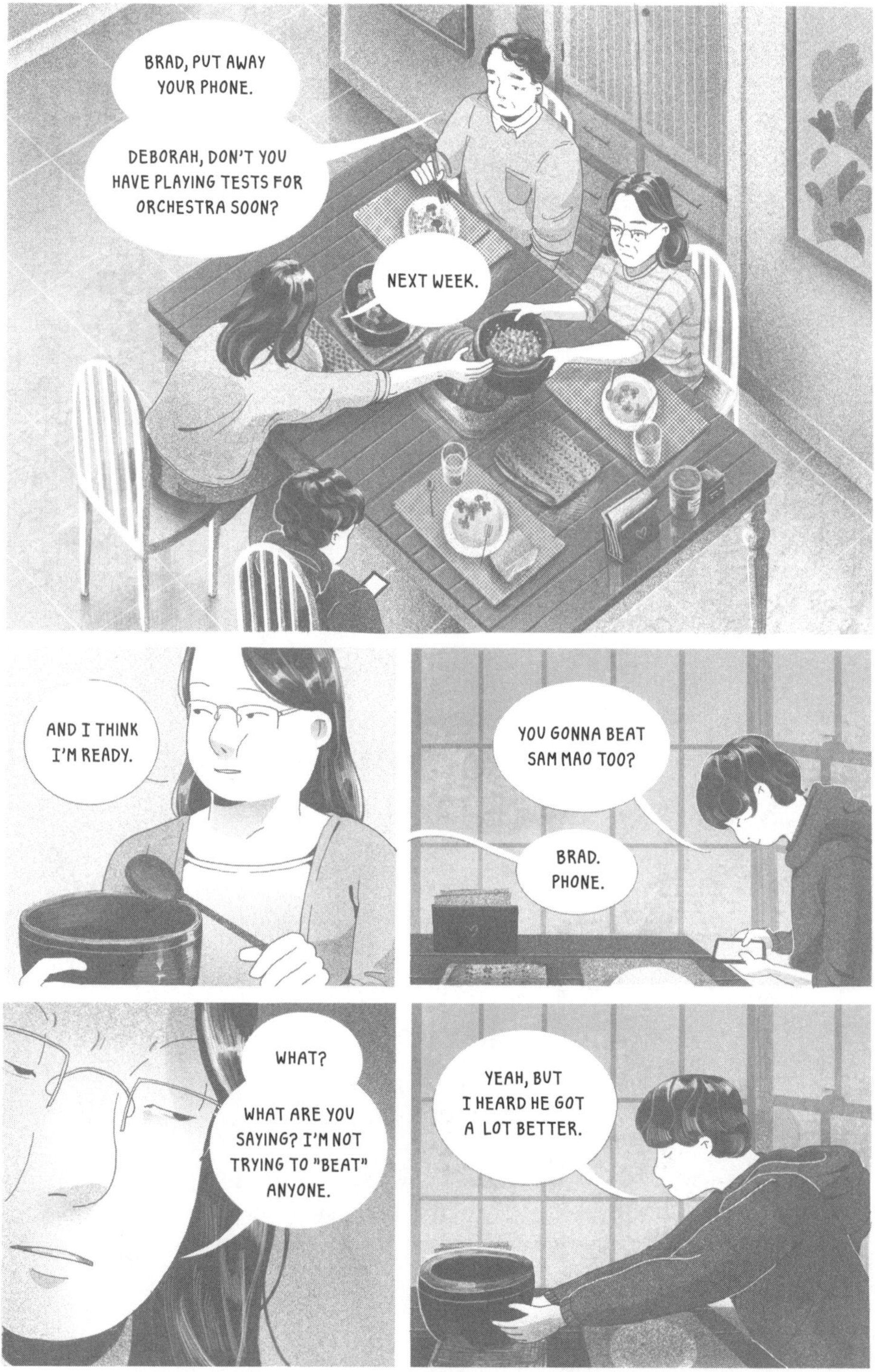
BRAD, PUT AWAY YOUR PHONE.
DEBORAH, DON'T YOU HAVE PLAYING TESTS FOR ORCHESTRA SOON?
NEXT WEEK.
AND I THINK I'M READY.
YOU GONNA BEAT SAM MAO TOO?
BRAD. PHONE.
WHAT?
WHAT ARE YOU SAYING? I'M NOT TRYING TO "BEAT" ANYONE.
YEAH, BUT I HEARD HE GOT A LOT BETTER.

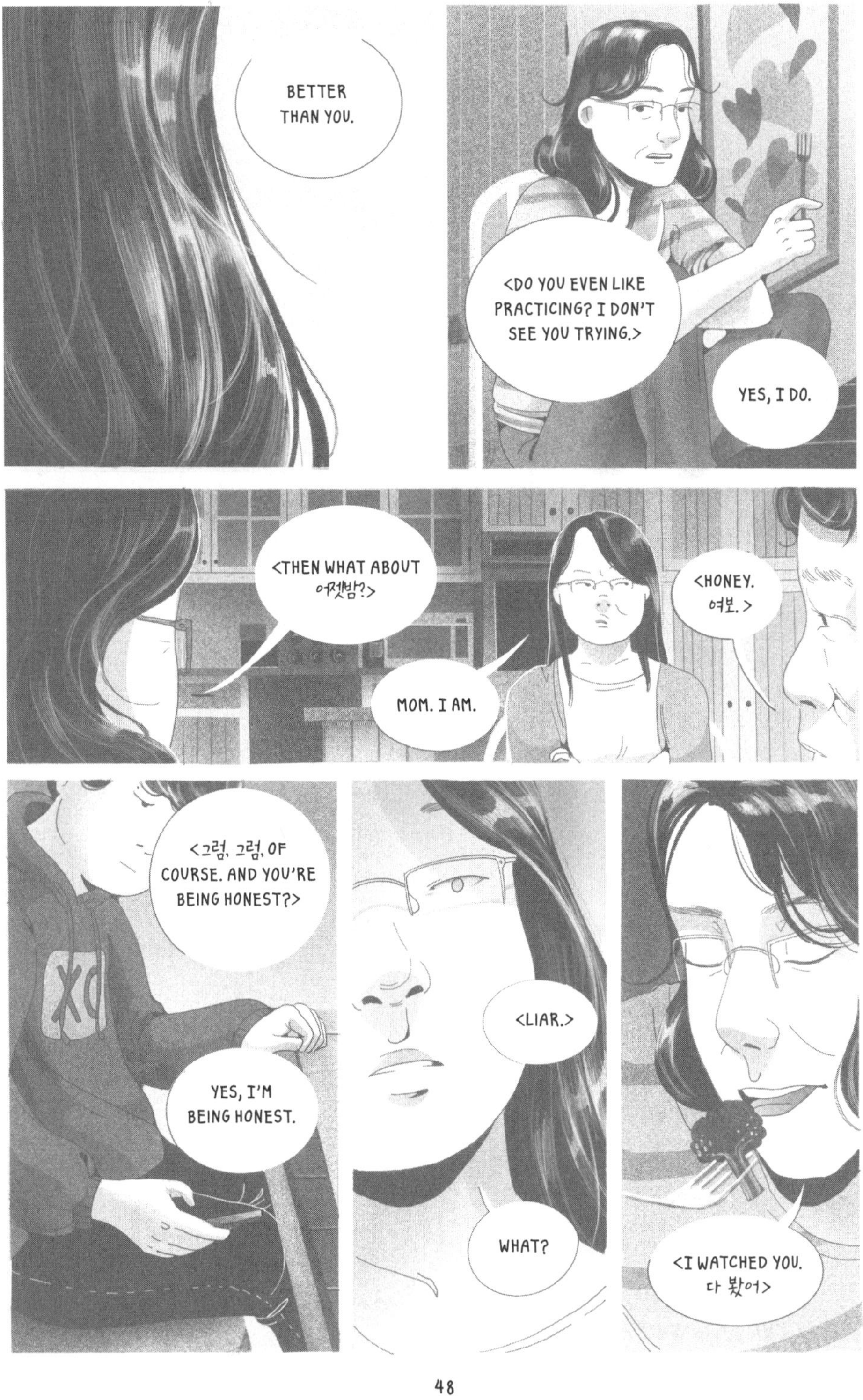
BETTER THAN YOU.
<DO YOU EVEN LIKE PRACTICING? I DON'T SEE YOU TRYING.>
YES, I DO.
<THEN WHAT ABOUT 어젯밤?>
MOM. I AM.
<HONEY. 여보.>
<그럼, 그럼, OF COURSE. AND YOU'RE BEING HONEST?>
YES, I'M BEING HONEST.
<LIAR.>
WHAT?
<I WATCHED YOU. 다 봤어>

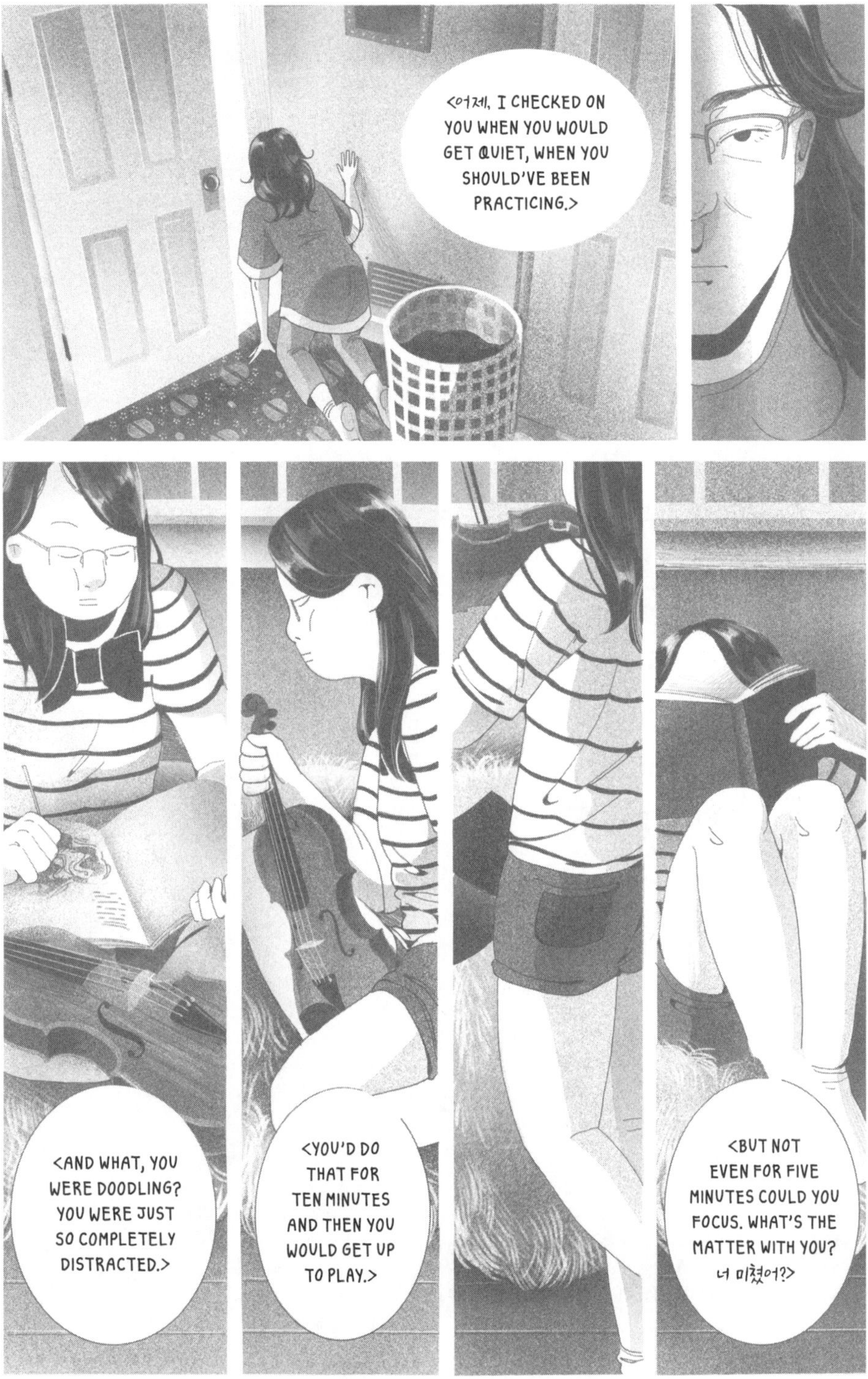
<어제, I CHECKED ON YOU WHEN YOU WOULD GET QUIET, WHEN YOU SHOULD'VE BEEN PRACTICING.>
<AND WHAT, YOU WERE DOODLING? YOU WERE JUST SO COMPLETELY DISTRACTED.>
<YOU'D DO THAT FOR TEN MINUTES AND THEN YOU WOULD GET UP TO PLAY.>
<BUT NOT EVEN FOR FIVE MINUTES COULD YOU FOCUS. WHAT'S THE MATTER WITH YOU? 너 미쳤어?>

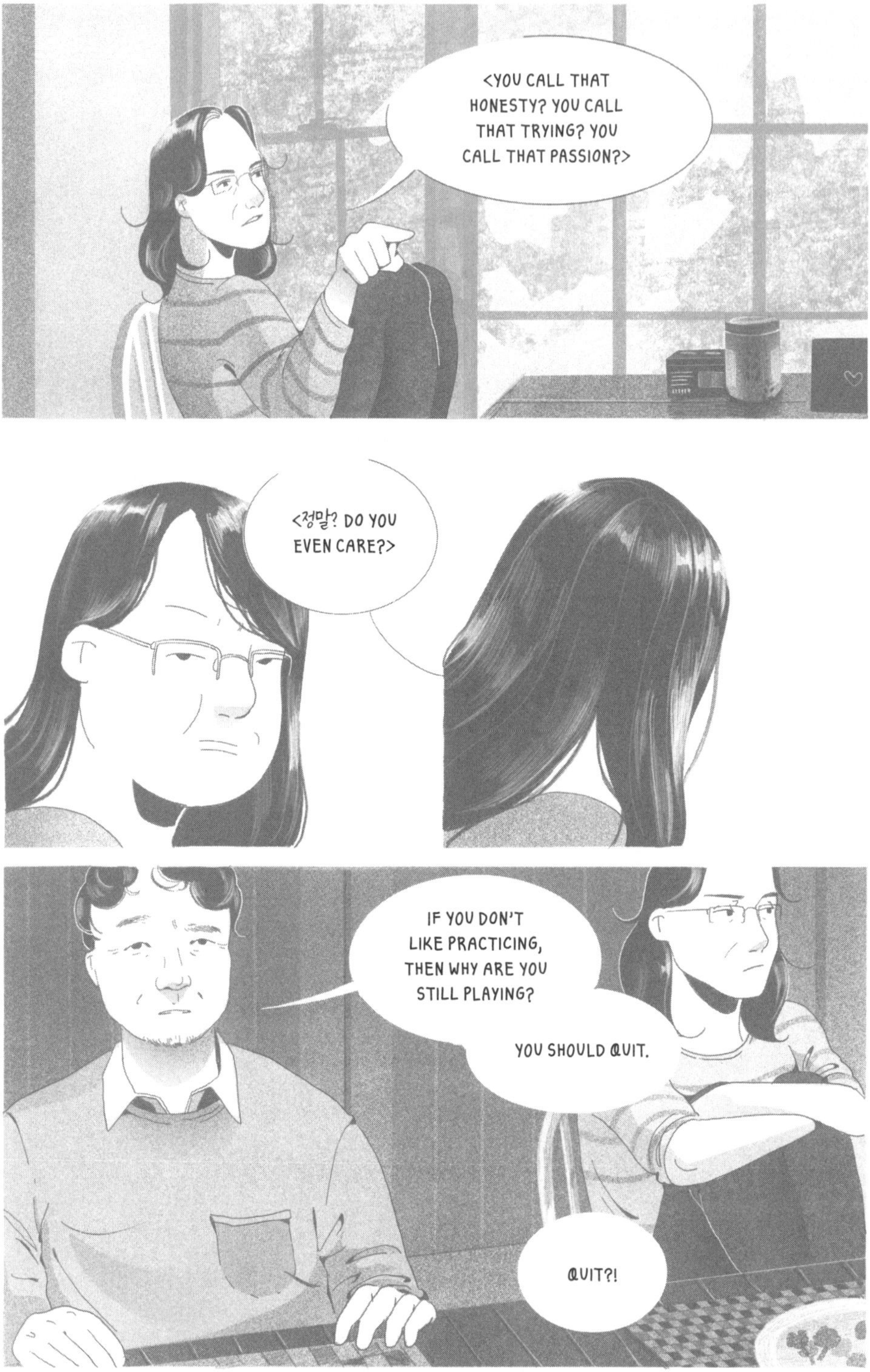
<YOU CALL THAT HONESTY? YOU CALL THAT TRYING? YOU CALL THAT PASSION?>
<정말? DO YOU EVEN CARE?>
IF YOU DON'T LIKE PRACTICING, THEN WHY ARE YOU STILL PLAYING?
YOU SHOULD QUIT.
QUIT?!

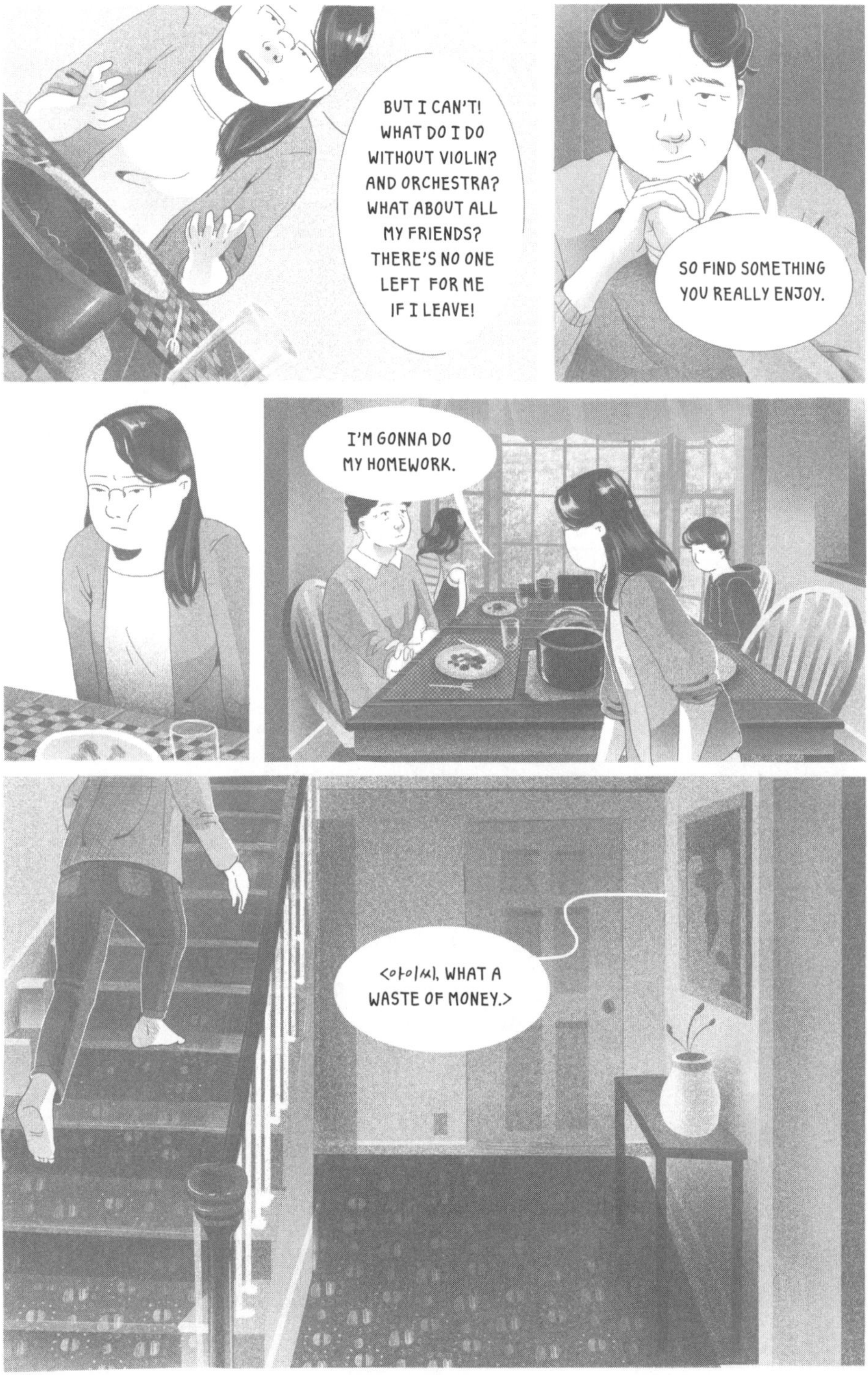
BUT I CAN'T! WHAT DO I DO WITHOUT VIOLIN? AND ORCHESTRA? WHAT ABOUT ALL MY FRIENDS? THERE'S NO ONE LEFT FOR ME IF I LEAVE!
SO FIND SOMETHING YOU REALLY ENJOY.
I'M GONNA DO MY HOMEWORK.
<아이씨, WHAT A WASTE OF MONEY.>

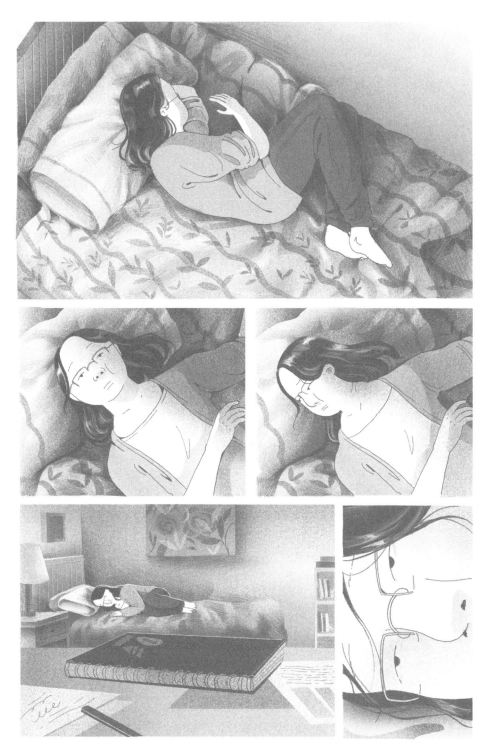

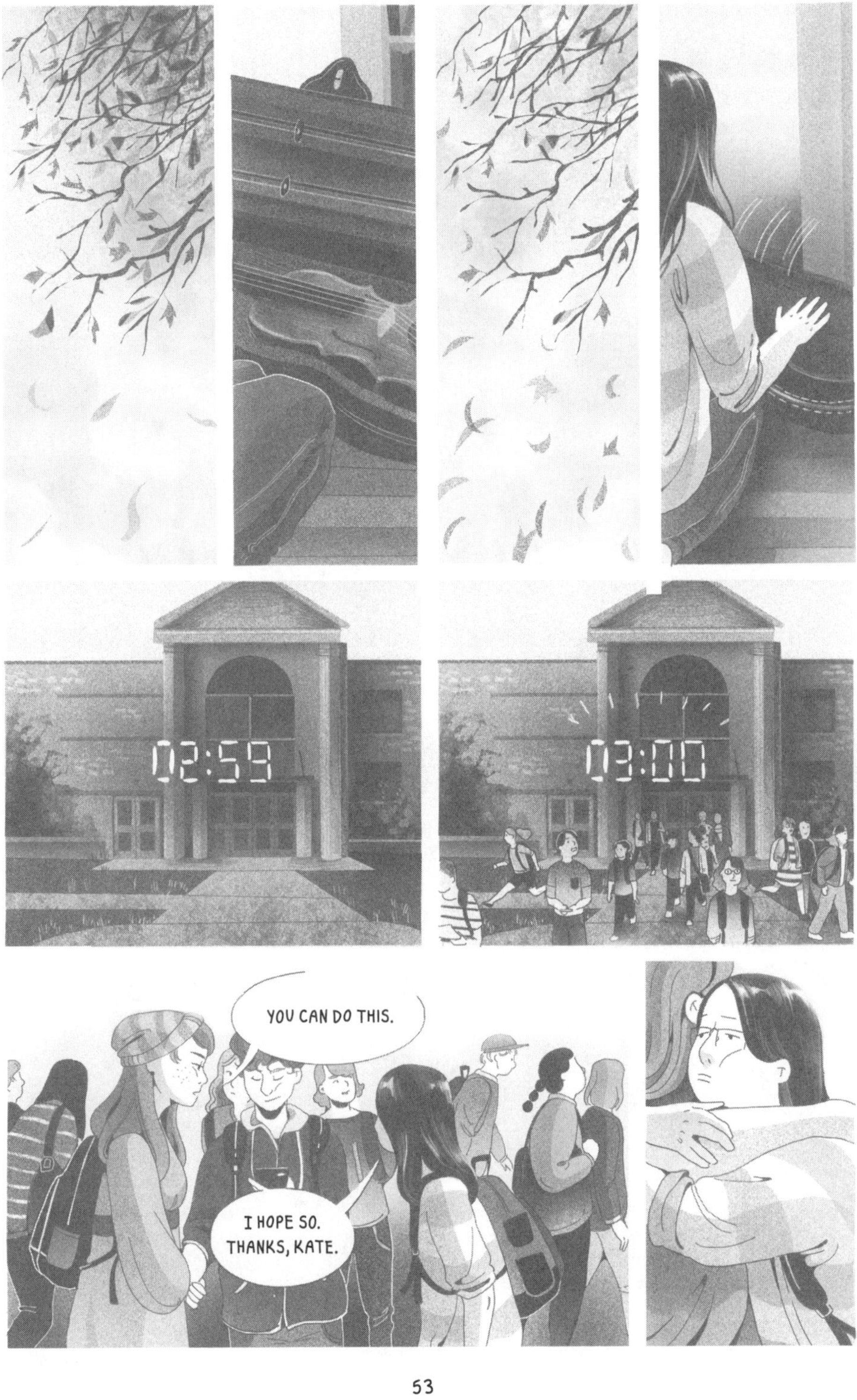
02:59
03:00
YOU CAN DO THIS.
I HOPE SO.
THANKS, KATE.

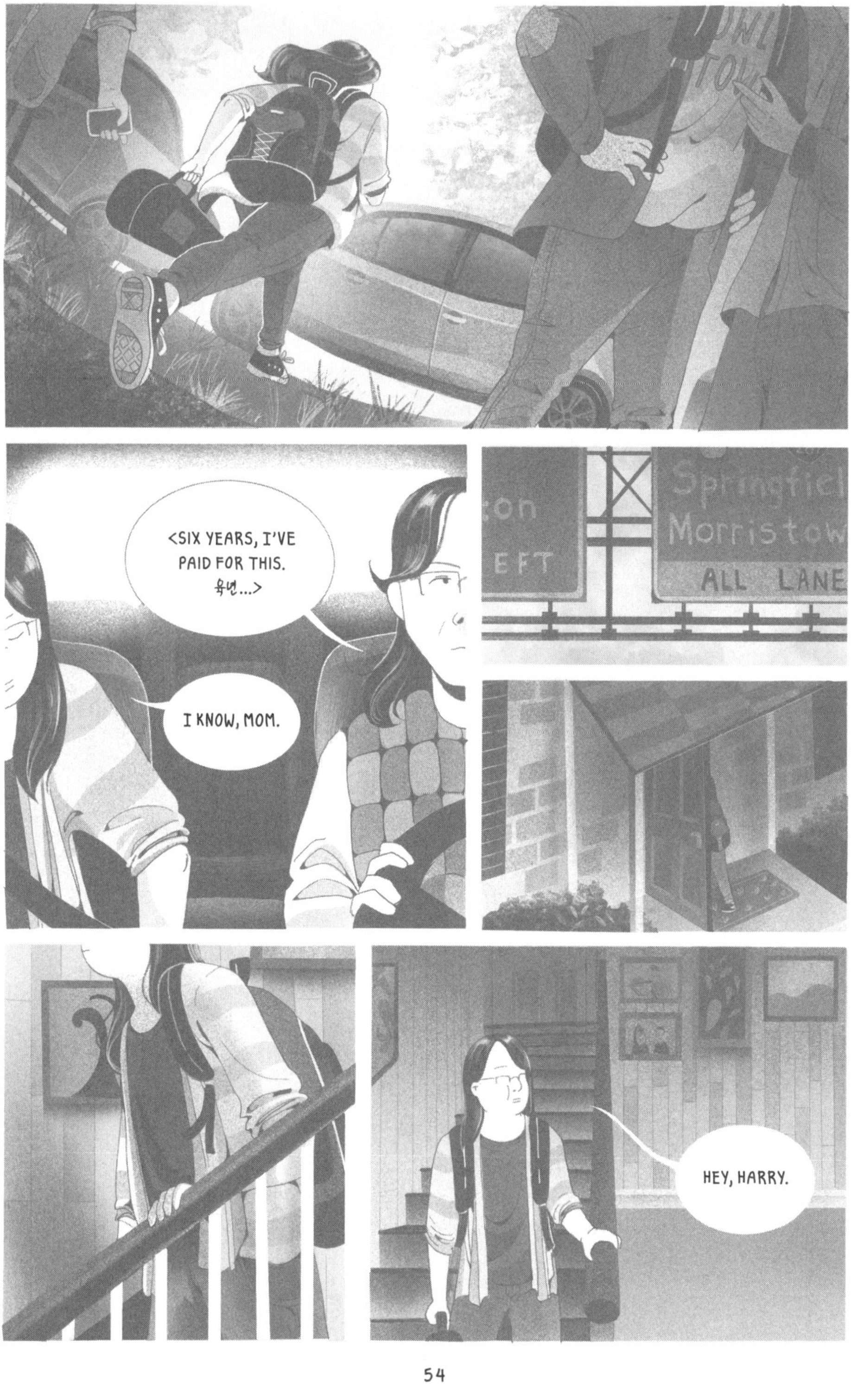
<SIX YEARS, I'VE PAID FOR THIS. 육년...>
I KNOW, MOM.
Morristow
ALL LANE
HEY, HARRY.

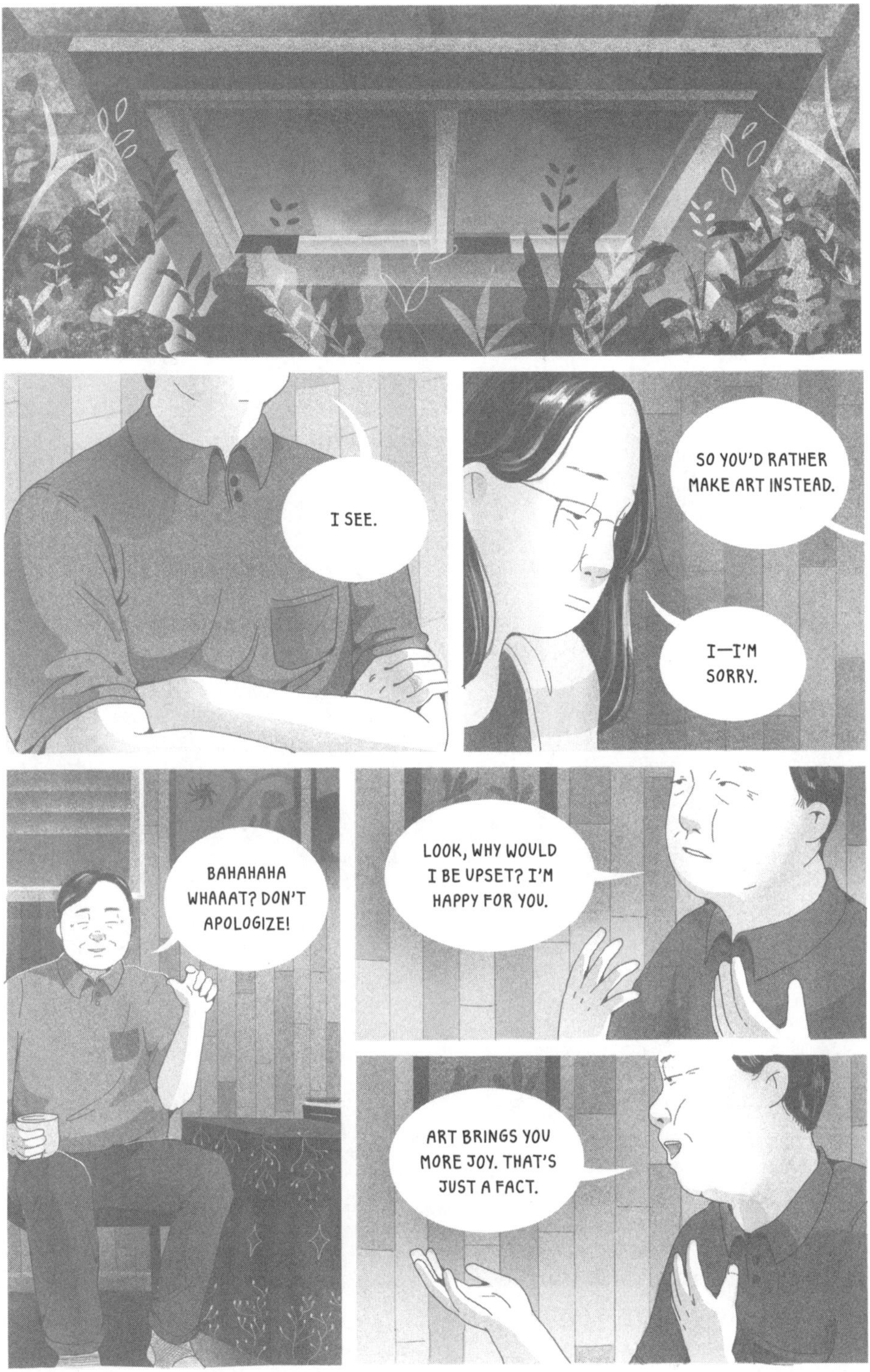
I SEE.
SO YOU'D RATHER MAKE ART INSTEAD.
I—I'M SORRY.
BAHAHAHA WHAAAT? DON'T APOLOGIZE!
LOOK, WHY WOULD I BE UPSET? I'M HAPPY FOR YOU.
ART BRINGS YOU MORE JOY. THAT'S JUST A FACT.

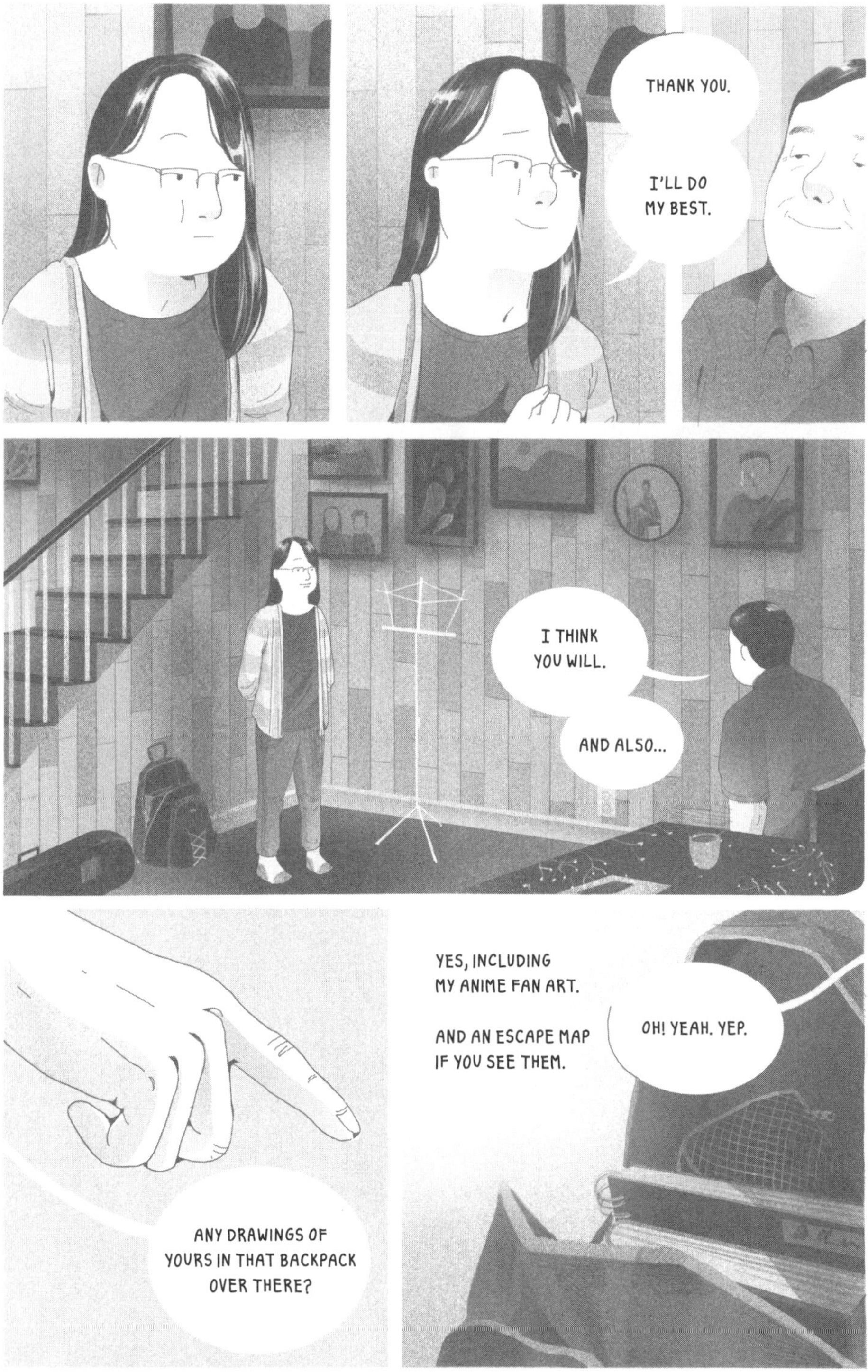
THANK YOU.
I'LL DO MY BEST.
I THINK YOU WILL.
AND ALSO...
ANY DRAWINGS OF YOURS IN THAT BACKPACK OVER THERE?
YES, INCLUDING MY ANIME FAN ART.
AND AN ESCAPE MAP IF YOU SEE THEM.
OH! YEAH. YEP.

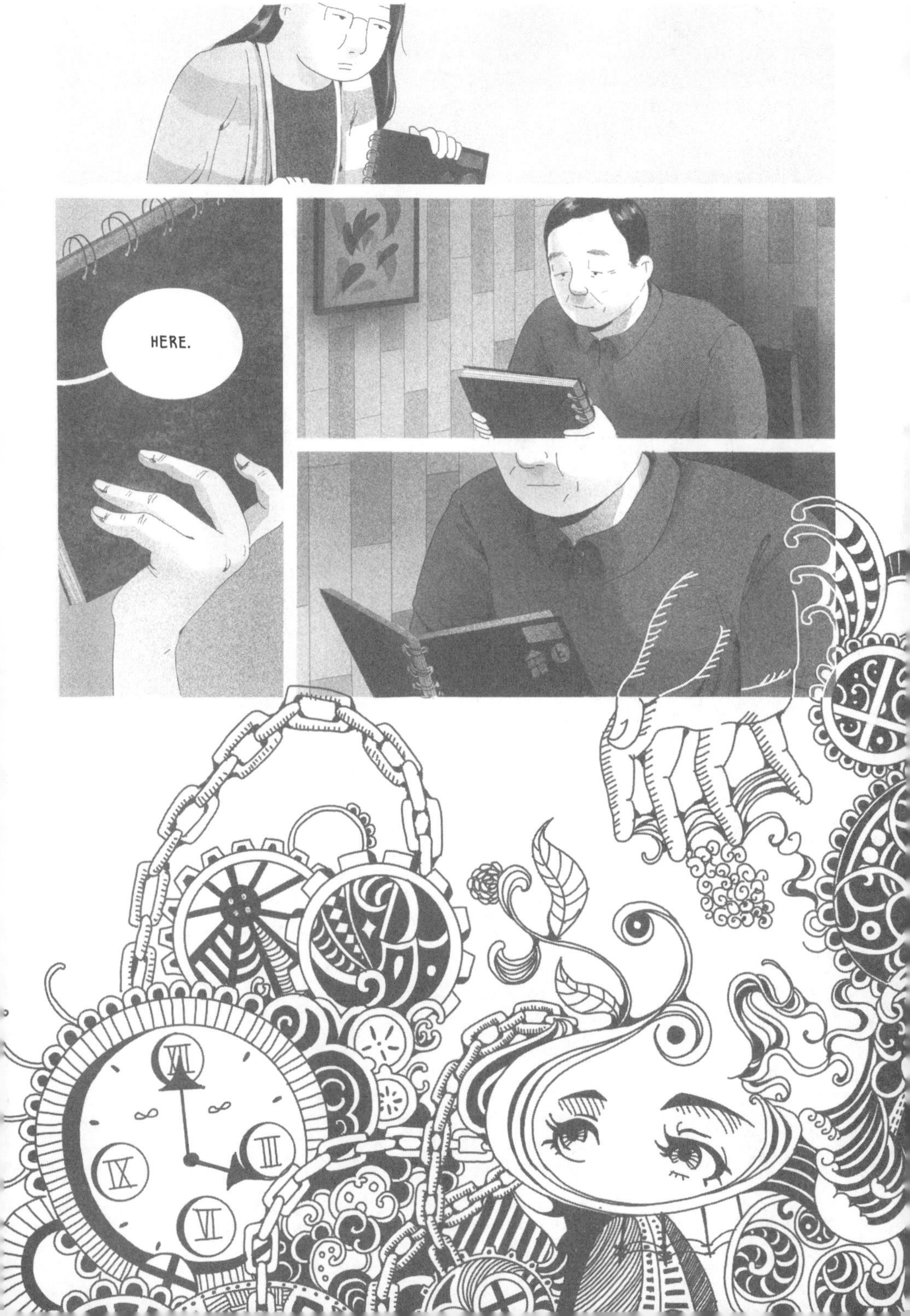
HERE.

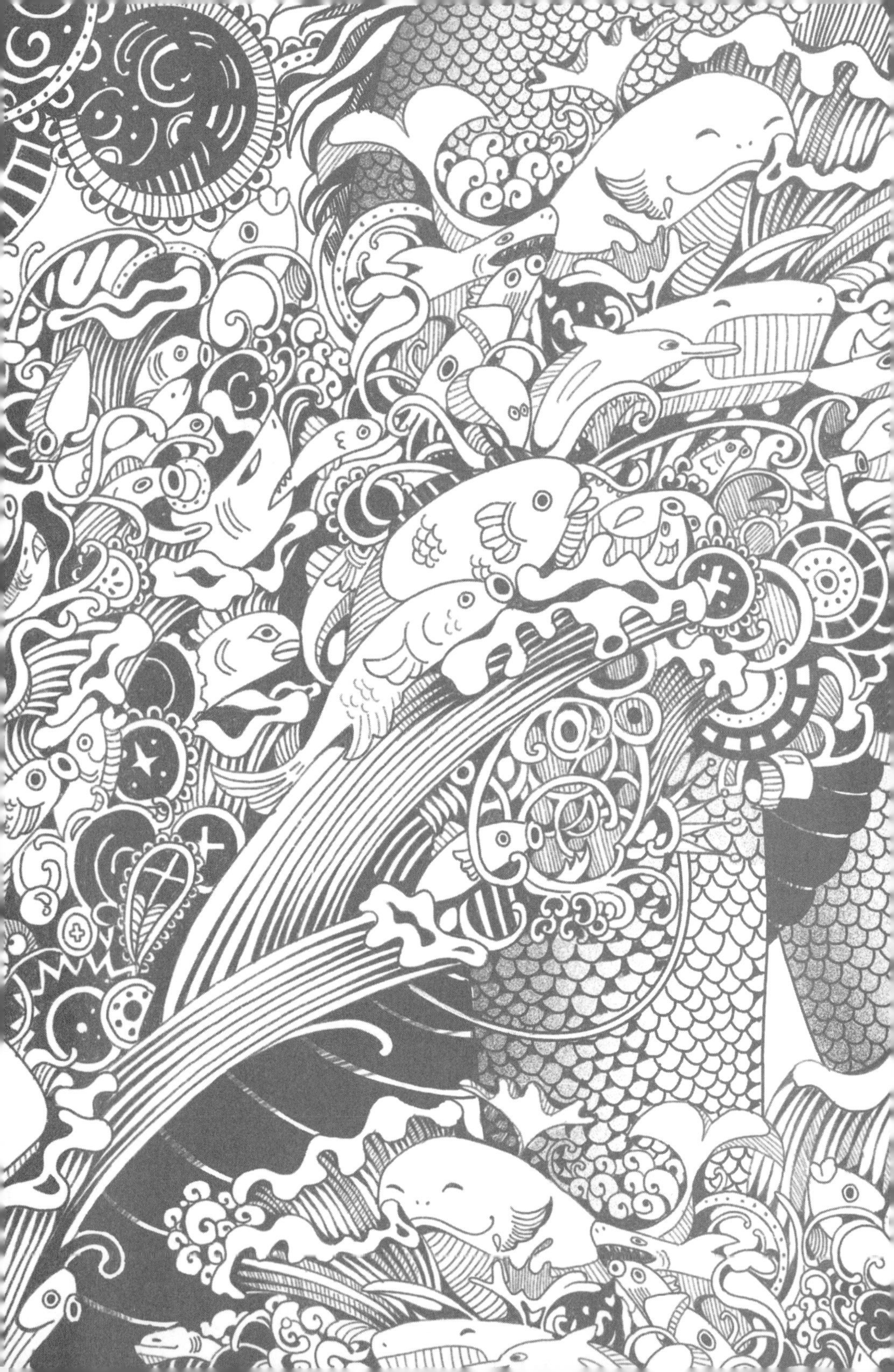

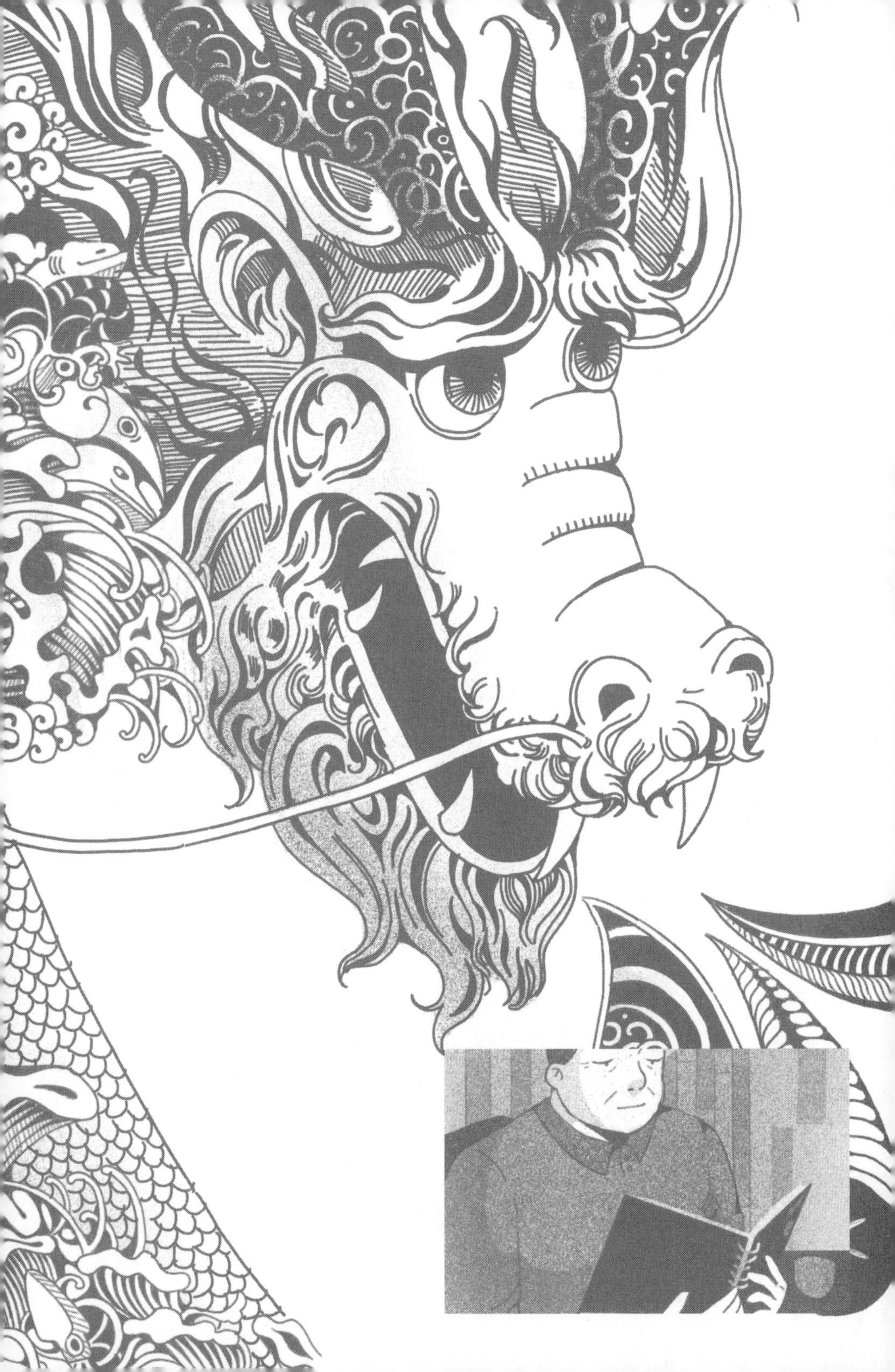

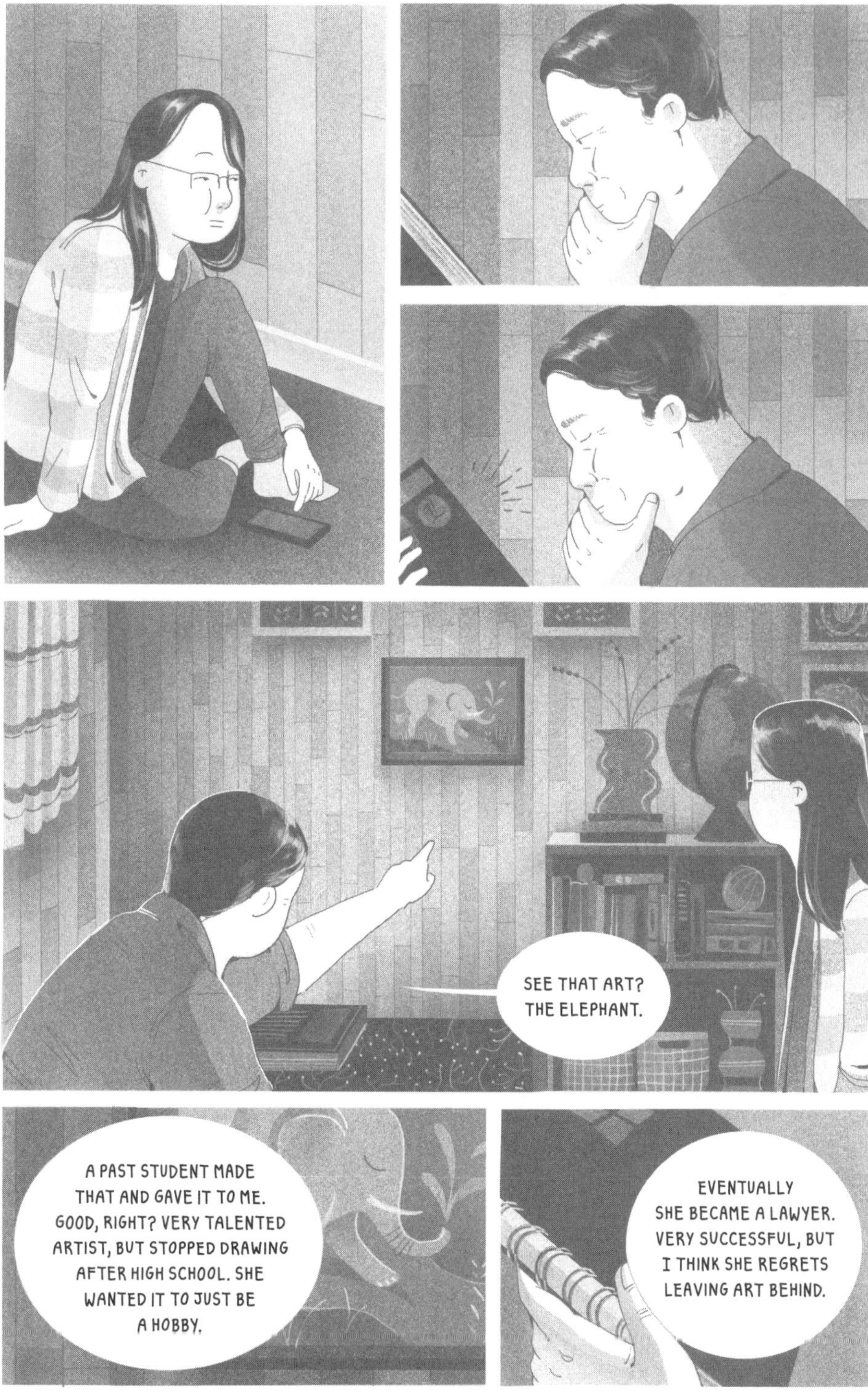
SEE THAT ART?
THE ELEPHANT.
A PAST STUDENT MADE THAT AND GAVE IT TO ME. GOOD, RIGHT? VERY TALENTED ARTIST, BUT STOPPED DRAWING AFTER HIGH SCHOOL. SHE WANTED IT TO JUST BE A HOBBY.
EVENTUALLY SHE BECAME A LAWYER. VERY SUCCESSFUL, BUT I THINK SHE REGRETS LEAVING ART BEHIND.

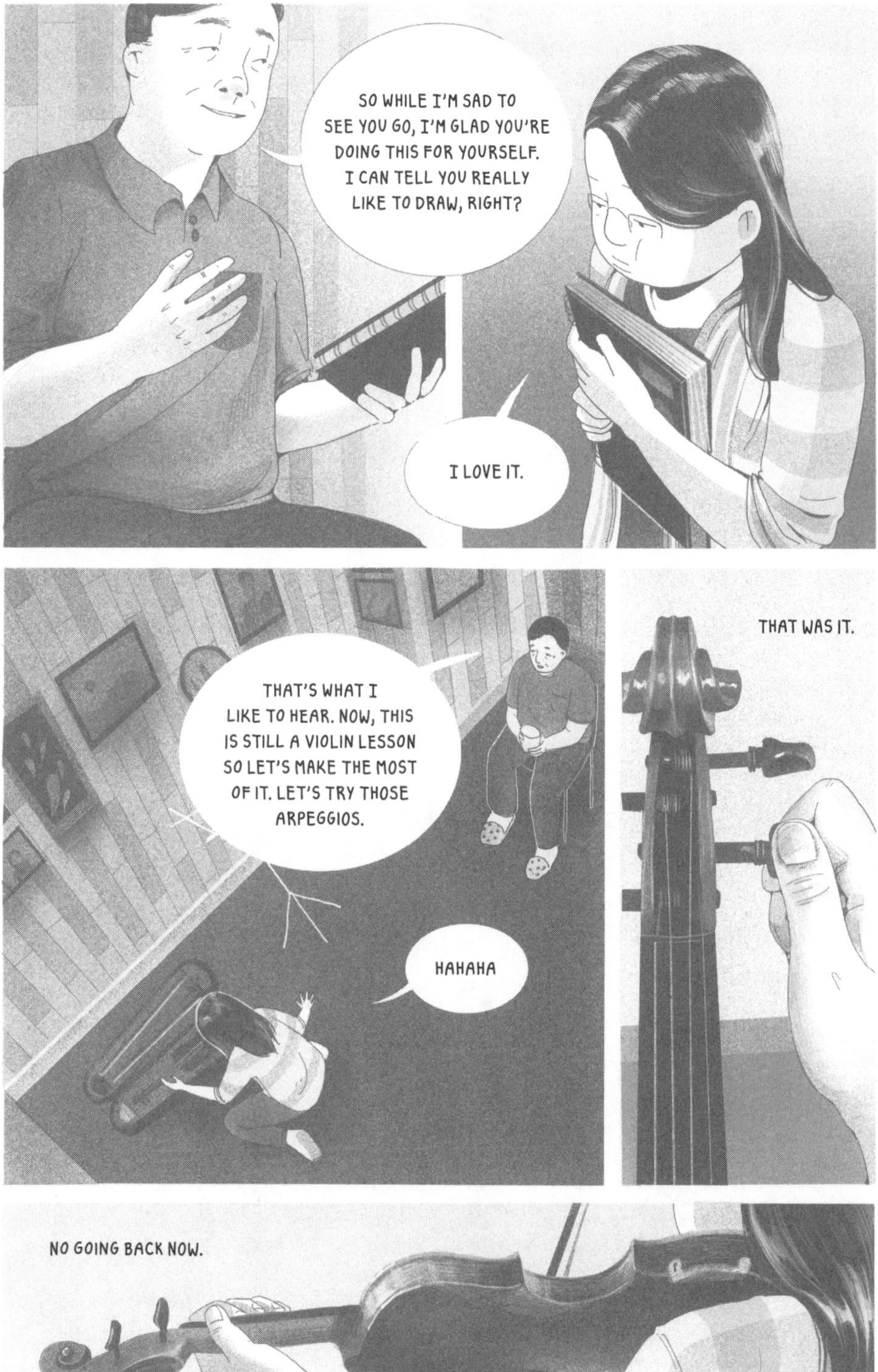
SO WHILE I'M SAD TO SEE YOU GO, I'M GLAD YOU'RE DOING THIS FOR YOURSELF. I CAN TELL YOU REALLY LIKE TO DRAW, RIGHT?
I LOVE IT.
THAT'S WHAT I LIKE TO HEAR. NOW, THIS IS STILL A VIOLIN LESSON SO LET'S MAKE THE MOST OF IT. LET'S TRY THOSE ARPEGGIOS.
HAHAHA
THAT WAS IT.
NO GOING BACK NOW.

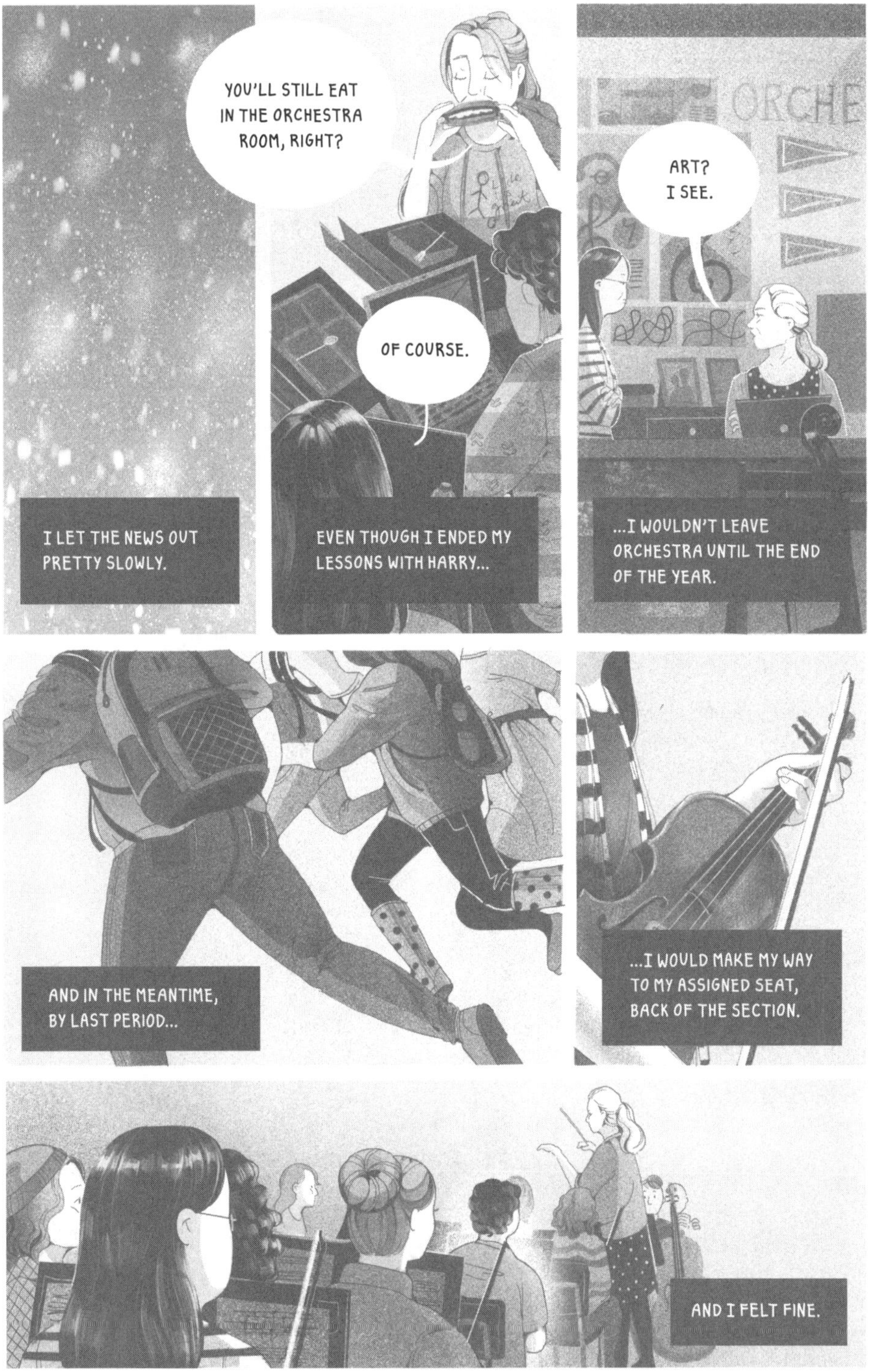
I LET THE NEWS OUT PRETTY SLOWLY.
YOU'LL STILL EAT IN THE ORCHESTRA ROOM, RIGHT?
OF COURSE.
EVEN THOUGH I ENDED MY LESSONS WITH HARRY...
ORCHE
ART? I SEE.
...I WOULDN'T LEAVE ORCHESTRA UNTIL THE END OF THE YEAR.
AND IN THE MEANTIME, BY LAST PERIOD...
...I WOULD MAKE MY WAY TO MY ASSIGNED SEAT, BACK OF THE SECTION.
AND I FELT FINE.

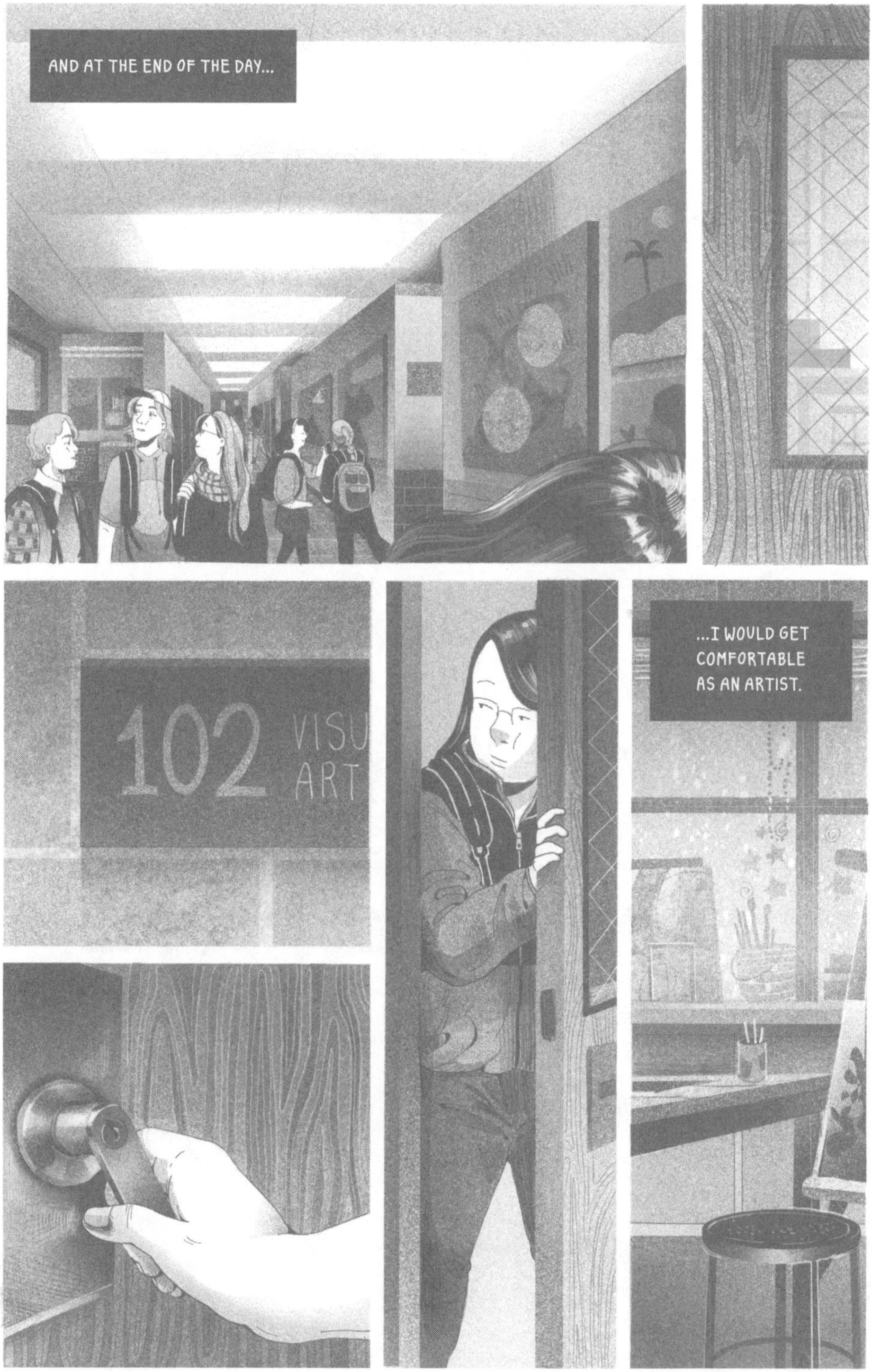
AND AT THE END OF THE DAY...
102
VISU
ART
...I WOULD GET COMFORTABLE AS AN ARTIST.

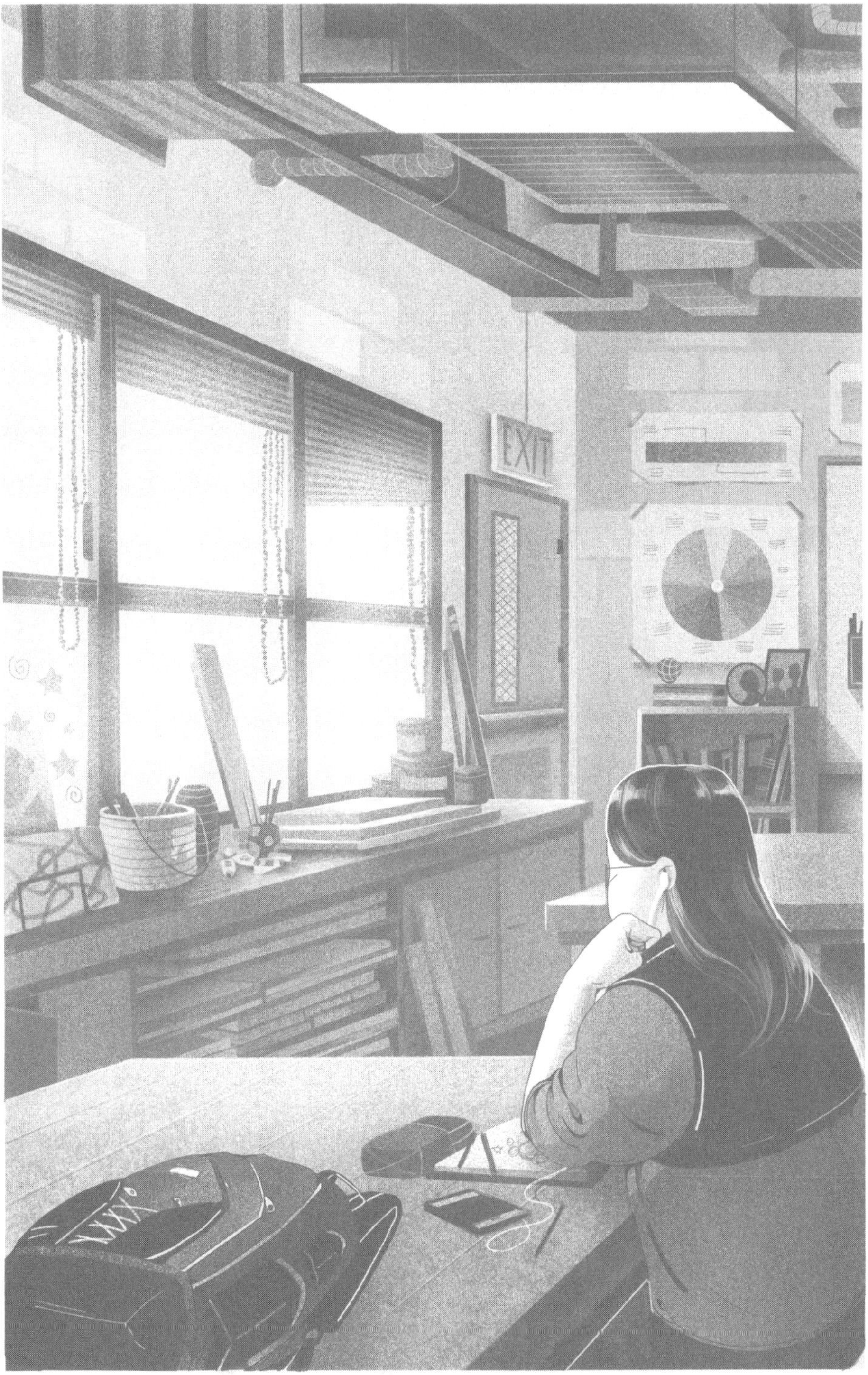
EXIT

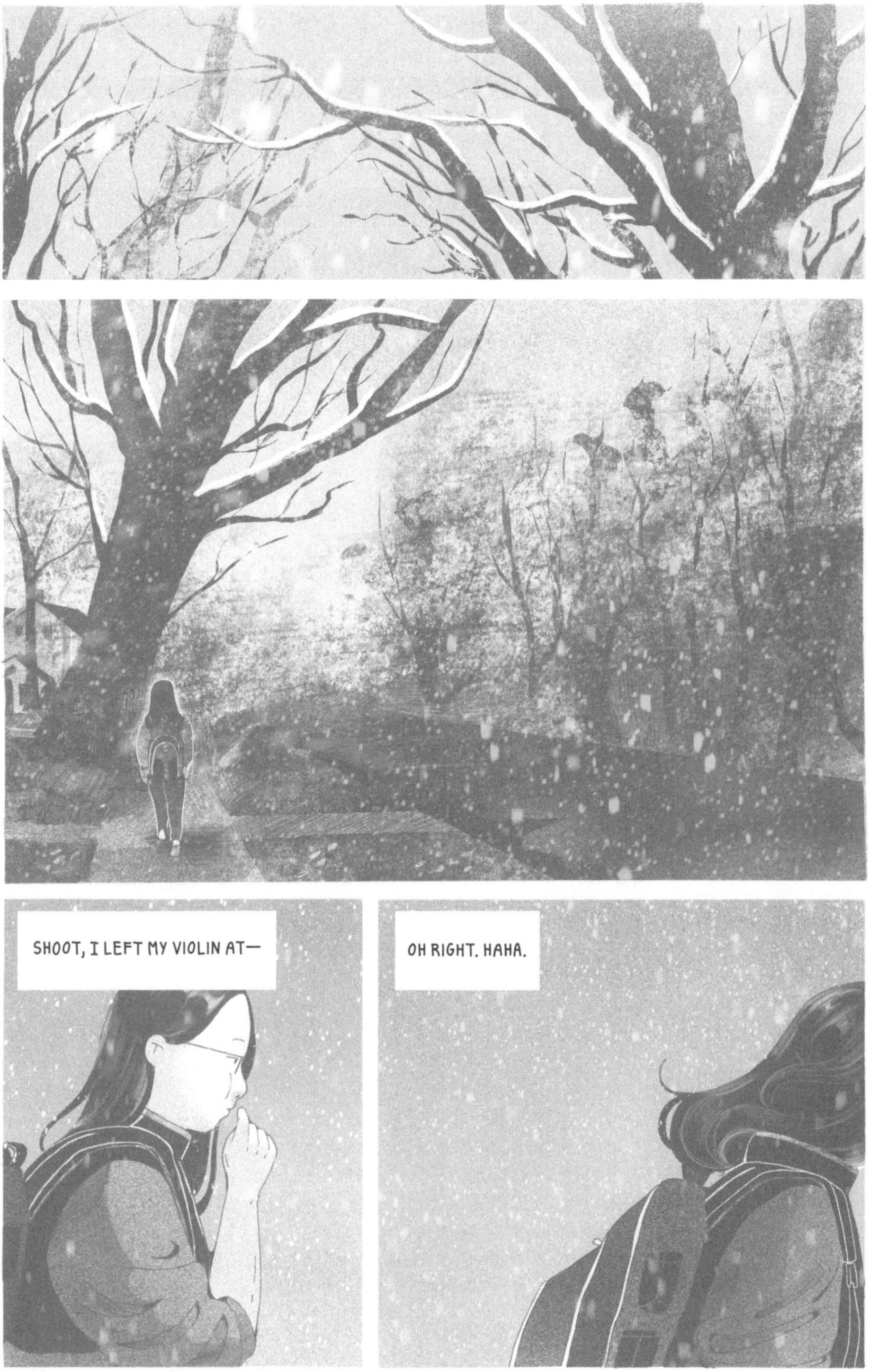
SHOOT, I LEFT MY VIOLIN AT—
OH RIGHT. HAHA.

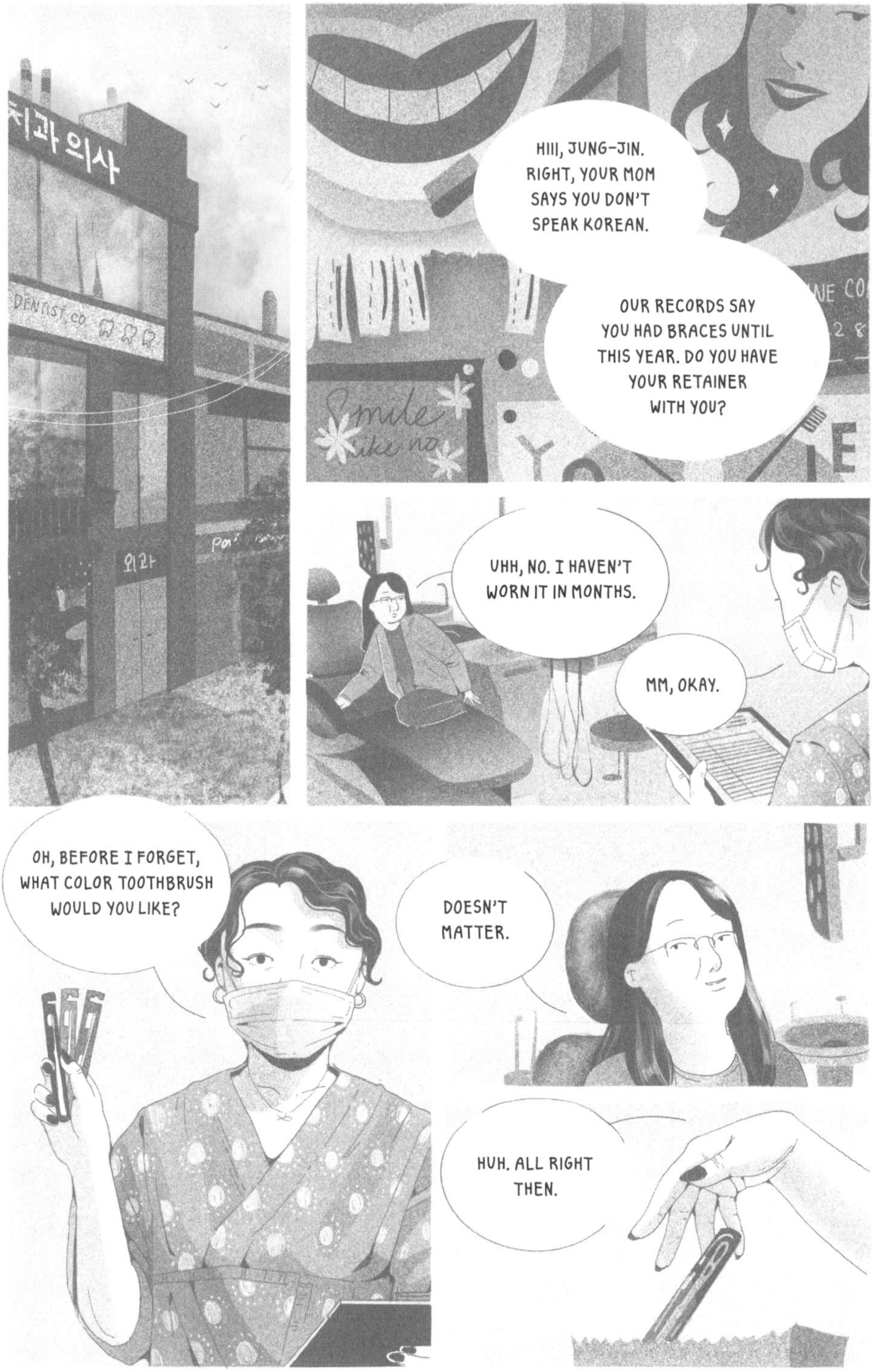

치과 의사
DENTIST. CO
외과
HIII, JUNG-JIN. RIGHT, YOUR MOM SAYS YOU DON'T SPEAK KOREAN.
OUR RECORDS SAY YOU HAD BRACES UNTIL THIS YEAR. DO YOU HAVE YOUR RETAINER WITH YOU?
UHH, NO. I HAVEN'T WORN IT IN MONTHS.
MM, OKAY.
OH, BEFORE I FORGET, WHAT COLOR TOOTHBRUSH WOULD YOU LIKE?
DOESN'T MATTER.
HUH. ALL RIGHT THEN.

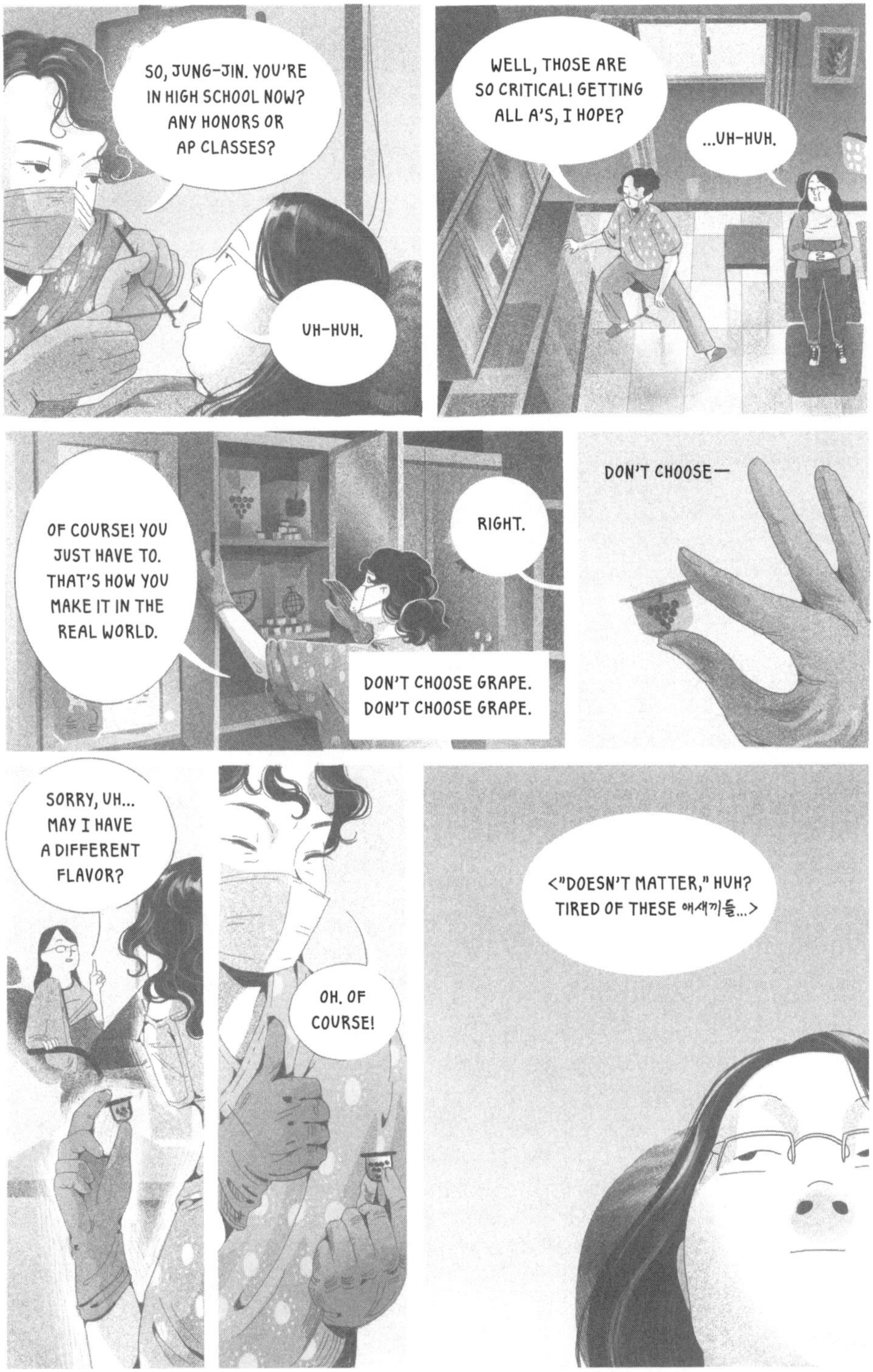
SO, JUNG-JIN. YOU'RE IN HIGH SCHOOL NOW? ANY HONORS OR AP CLASSES?
UH-HUH.
WELL, THOSE ARE SO CRITICAL! GETTING ALL A'S, I HOPE?
...UH-HUH.
OF COURSE! YOU JUST HAVE TO. THAT'S HOW YOU MAKE IT IN THE REAL WORLD.
RIGHT.
DON'T CHOOSE GRAPE. DON'T CHOOSE GRAPE.
DON'T CHOOSE—
SORRY, UH... MAY I HAVE A DIFFERENT FLAVOR?
OH. OF COURSE!
<"DOESN'T MATTER," HUH? TIRED OF THESE 애새끼들...>

<YOU KNOW THAT DENTIST'S DAUGHTER SKIPPED ANOTHER GRADE AND YALE대 MIGHT ACCEPT HER ALREADY? AND SHE'S PLAYING AT CARNEGIE HALL NEXT MONTH. 아이고...>
<TOO BAD YOU WON'T BE GOING ANYWHERE, NOT WITH THOSE GRADES. GOOD LUCK WHEN YOU'RE HOMELESS, AND TRY NOT TO COME CRYING TO ME.>
I TOLD YOU, I'M TRYING, OKAY?
<"TRYING"?>
<A C IN PHYSICS ISN'T "TRYING." WHO HAVE I BEEN RAISING? WHAT HAVE YOU DONE WITH MY CHILD? 정진이가 어떡해?>
<HONEY... 여보...>
BUT EVERYONE ELSE AT SCHOOL SAYS I'M DOING OKAY. THEY SAY I'M STILL ADJUSTING.
NO ONE ELSE'S PARENTS WOULD GET MAD AT THEM OVER A C.

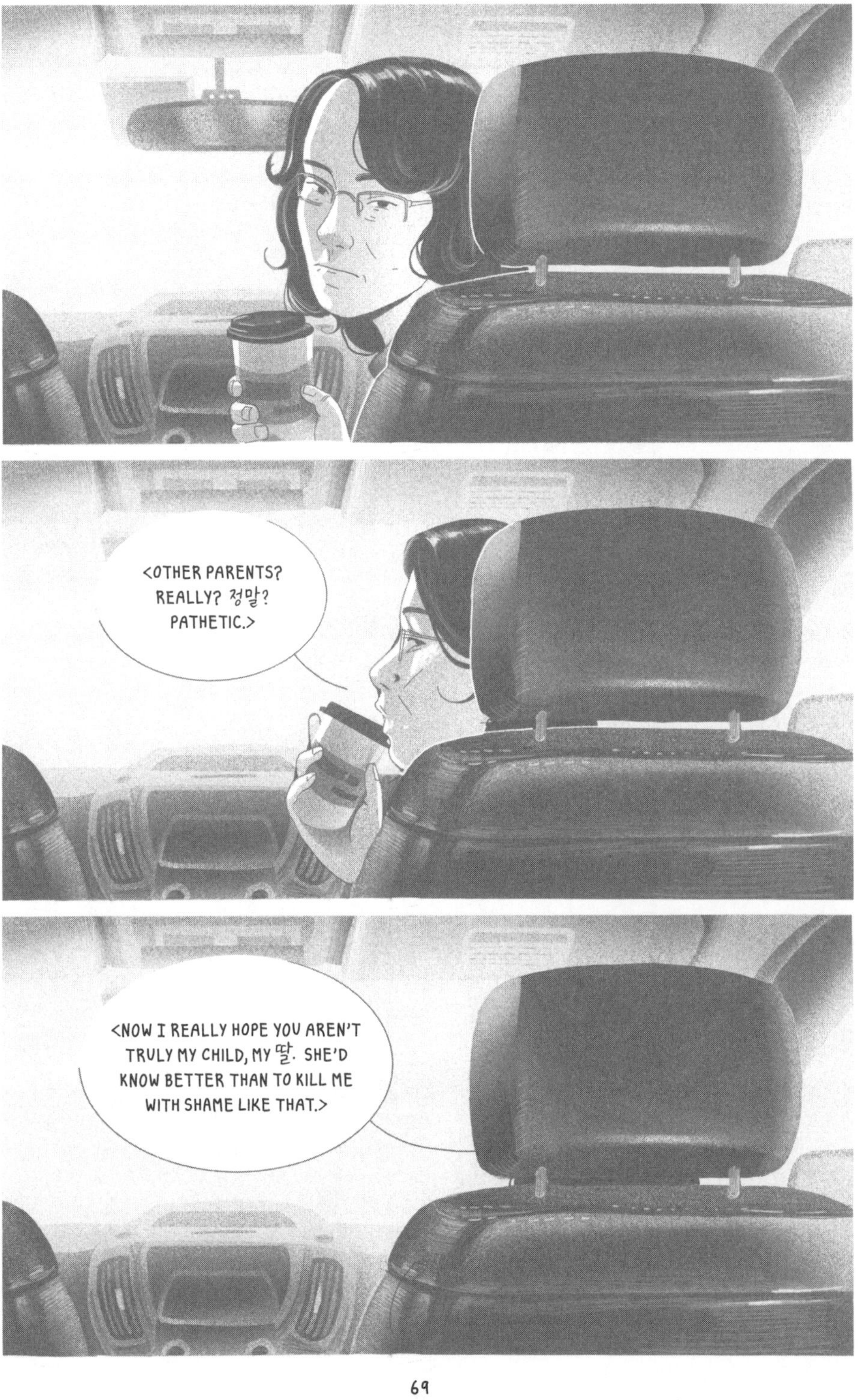
<OTHER PARENTS? REALLY? 정말? PATHETIC.>
<NOW I REALLY HOPE YOU AREN'T TRULY MY CHILD, MY 딸. SHE'D KNOW BETTER THAN TO KILL ME WITH SHAME LIKE THAT.>

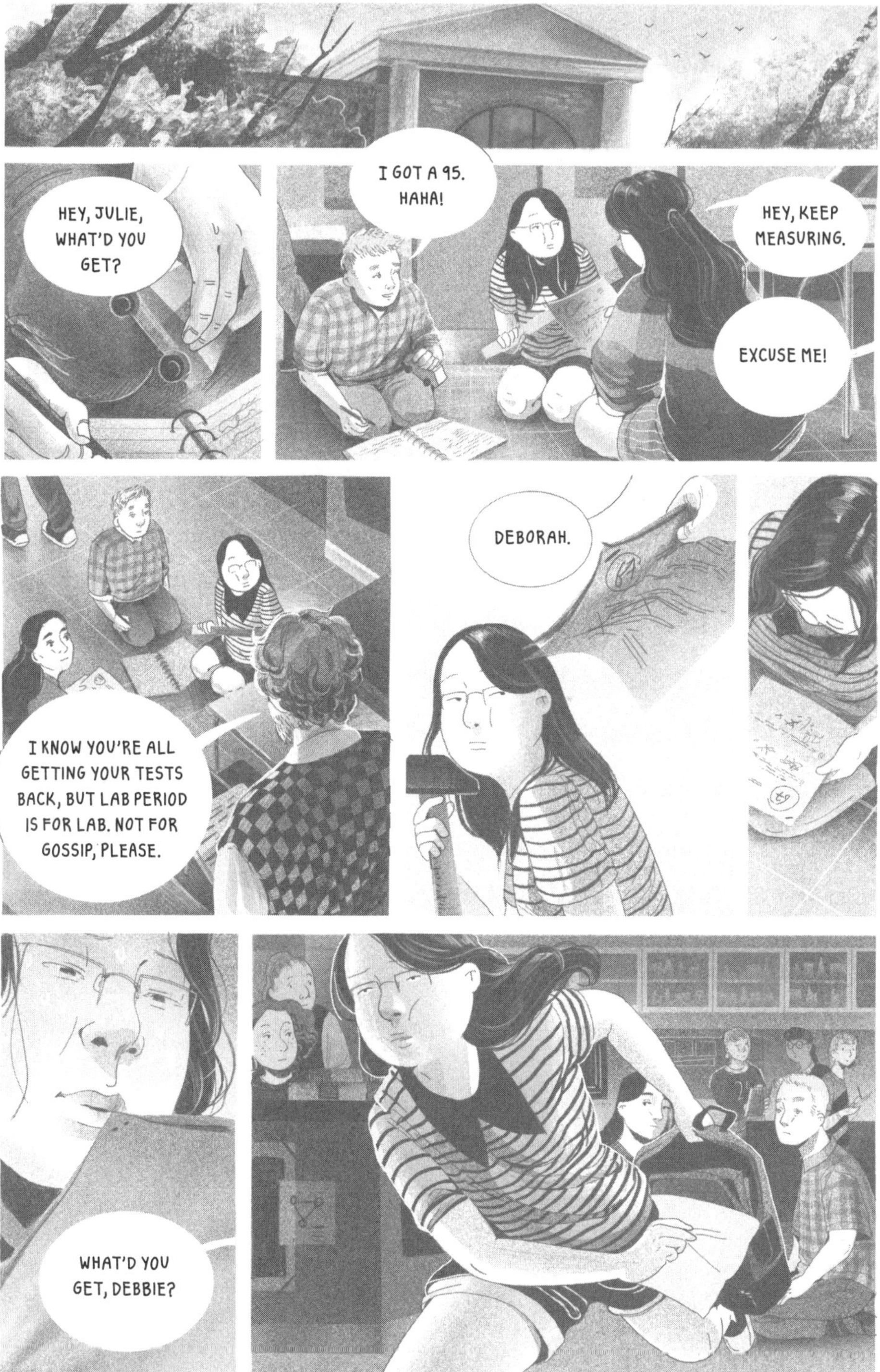
HEY, JULIE, WHAT'D YOU GET?
I GOT A 95. HAHA!
HEY, KEEP MEASURING.
EXCUSE ME!
I KNOW YOU'RE ALL GETTING YOUR TESTS BACK, BUT LAB PERIOD IS FOR LAB. NOT FOR GOSSIP, PLEASE.
DEBORAH.
WHAT'D YOU GET, DEBBIE?

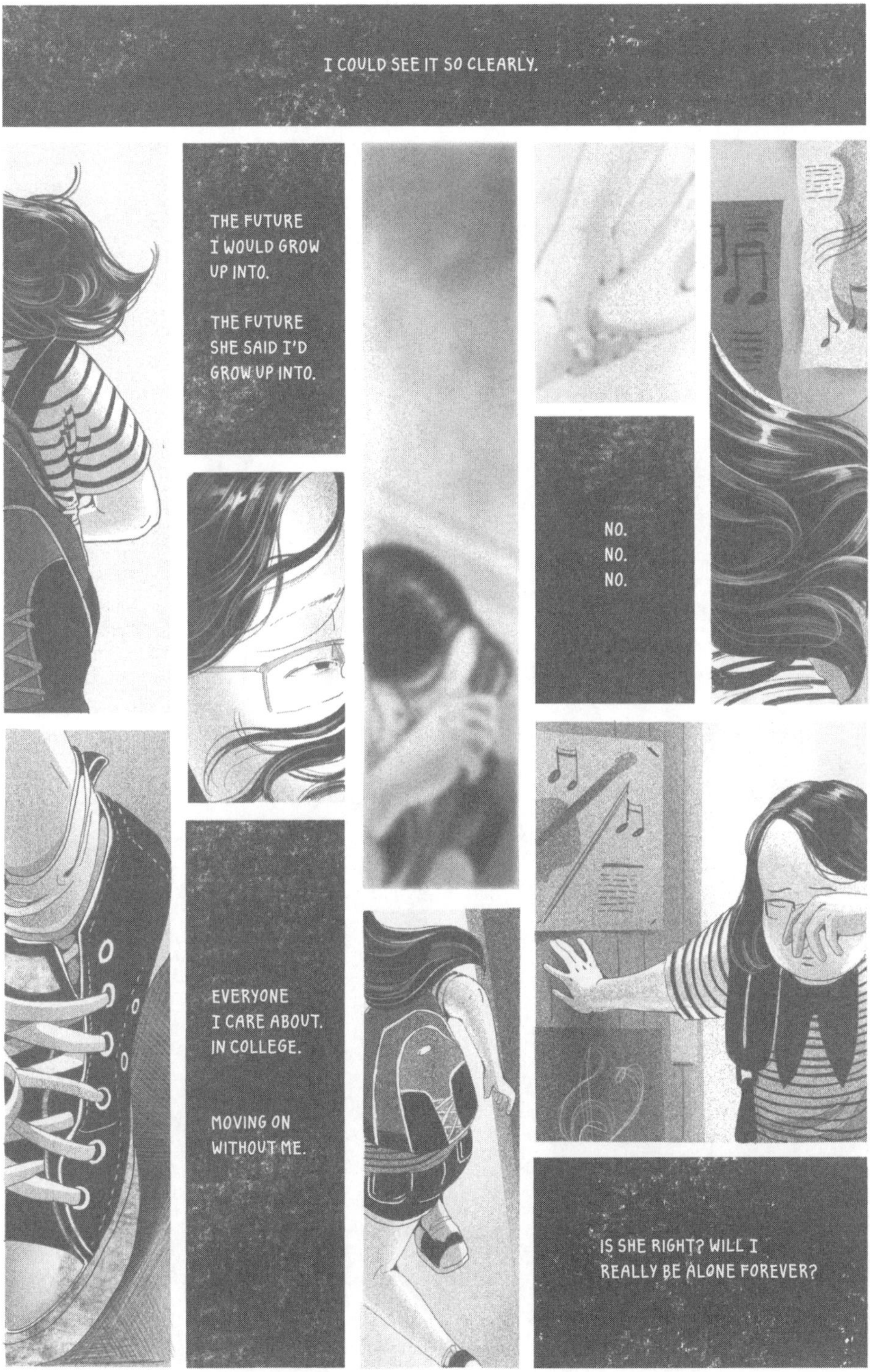
I COULD SEE IT SO CLEARLY.
THE FUTURE I WOULD GROW UP INTO.
THE FUTURE SHE SAID I'D GROW UP INTO.
NO. NO. NO.
EVERYONE I CARE ABOUT. IN COLLEGE.
MOVING ON WITHOUT ME.
IS SHE RIGHT? WILL I REALLY BE ALONE FOREVER?

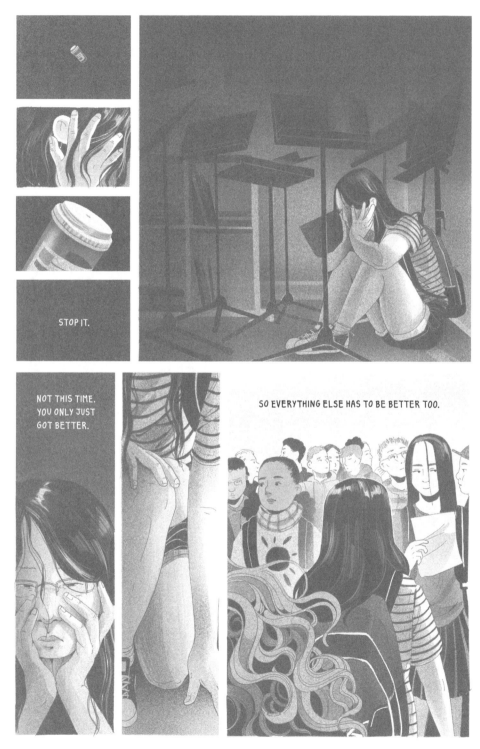

STOP IT.

NOT THIS TIME. YOU ONLY JUST GOT BETTER.

SO EVERYTHING ELSE HAS TO BE BETTER TOO.

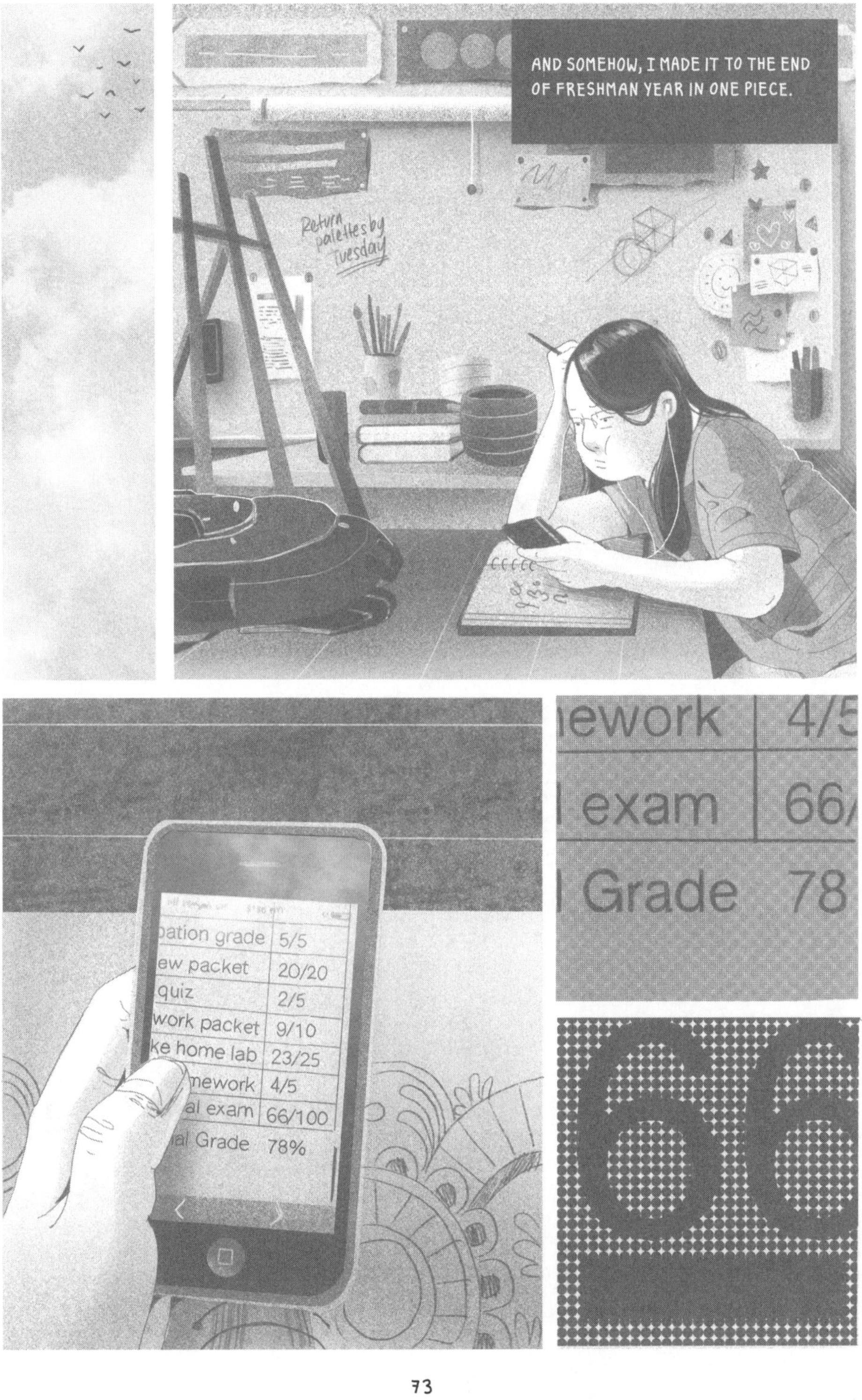
AND SOMEHOW, I MADE IT TO THE END OF FRESHMAN YEAR IN ONE PIECE.
Return palettes by Tuesday
pation grade 5/5
ew packet 20/20
quiz 2/5
work packet 9/10
ke home lab 23/25
mework 4/5
al exam 66/100
al Grade 78%
nework 4/5
l exam 66/
l Grade 78
66

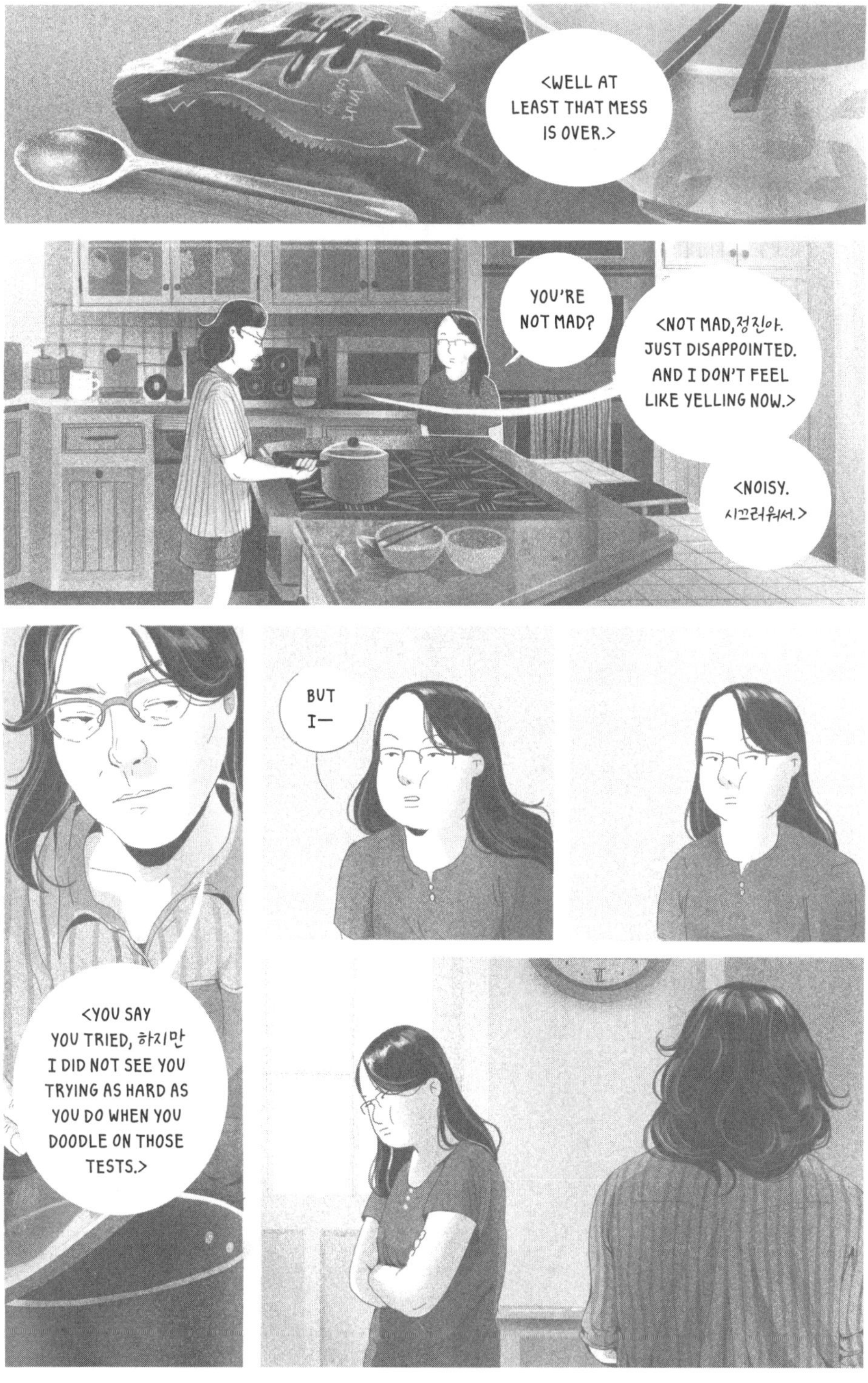
<WELL AT LEAST THAT MESS IS OVER.>
YOU'RE NOT MAD?
<NOT MAD, 정진아. JUST DISAPPOINTED. AND I DON'T FEEL LIKE YELLING NOW.>
<NOISY. 시끄러워서.>
BUT I—
<YOU SAY YOU TRIED, 하지만 I DID NOT SEE YOU TRYING AS HARD AS YOU DO WHEN YOU DOODLE ON THOSE TESTS.>

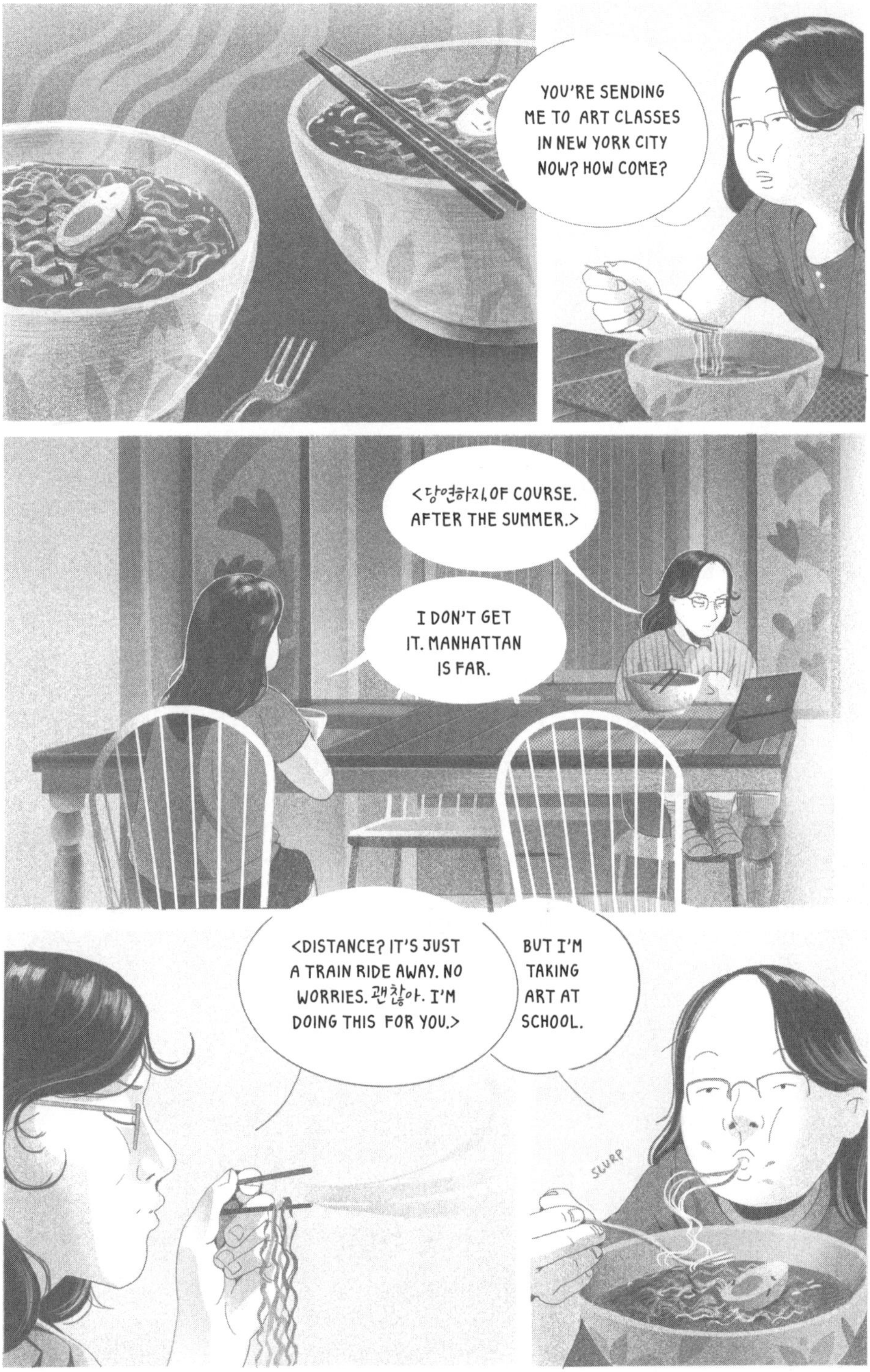

YOU'RE SENDING ME TO ART CLASSES IN NEW YORK CITY NOW? HOW COME?
<당연하지, OF COURSE. AFTER THE SUMMER.>
I DON'T GET IT. MANHATTAN IS FAR.
<DISTANCE? IT'S JUST A TRAIN RIDE AWAY. NO WORRIES. 괜찮아. I'M DOING THIS FOR YOU.>
BUT I'M TAKING ART AT SCHOOL.
SLURP

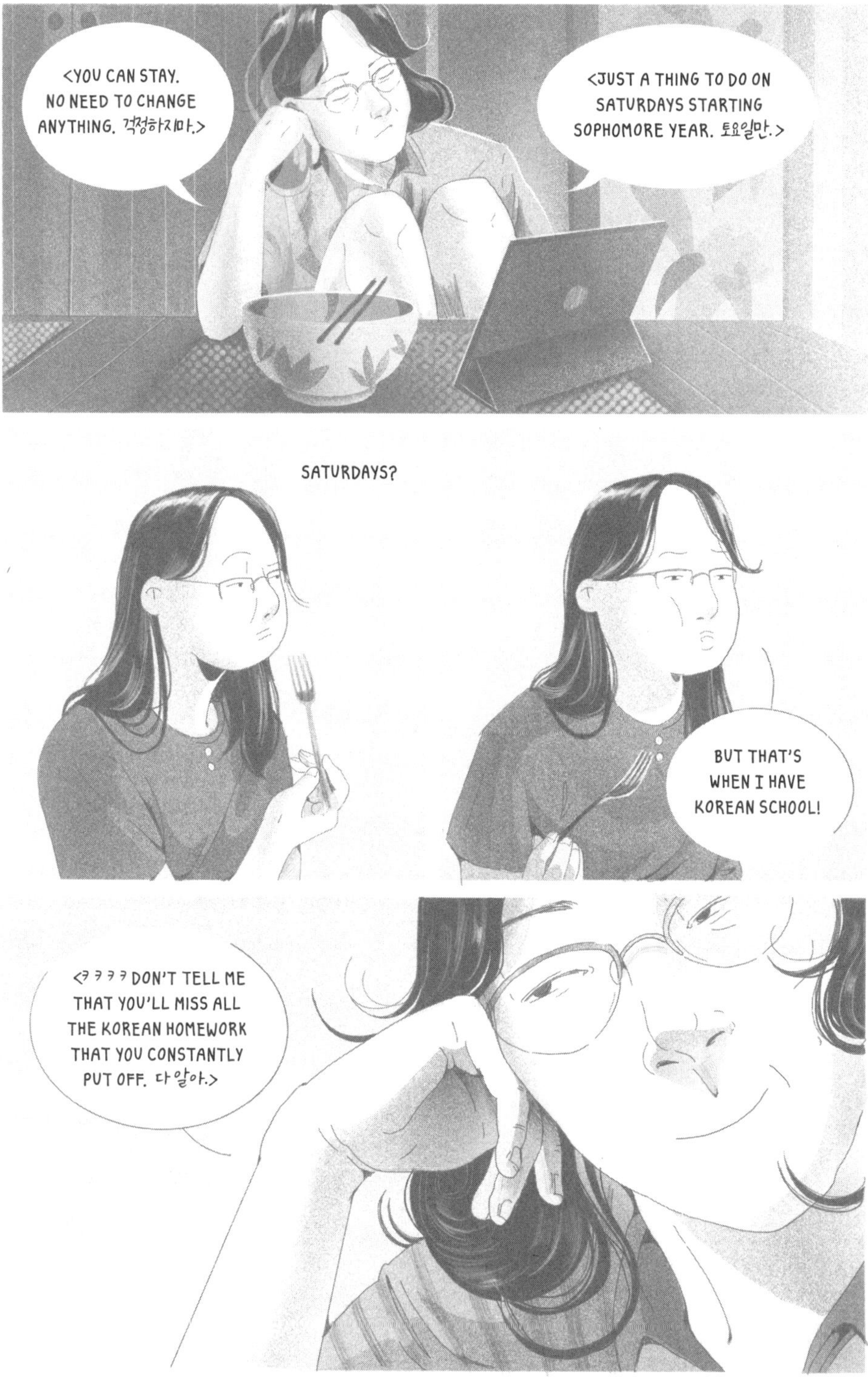
<YOU CAN STAY. NO NEED TO CHANGE ANYTHING. 걱정하지마.>
<JUST A THING TO DO ON SATURDAYS STARTING SOPHOMORE YEAR. 토요일만.>
SATURDAYS?
BUT THAT'S WHEN I HAVE KOREAN SCHOOL!
<ㅋㅋㅋ DON'T TELL ME THAT YOU'LL MISS ALL THE KOREAN HOMEWORK THAT YOU CONSTANTLY PUT OFF. 다알아.>

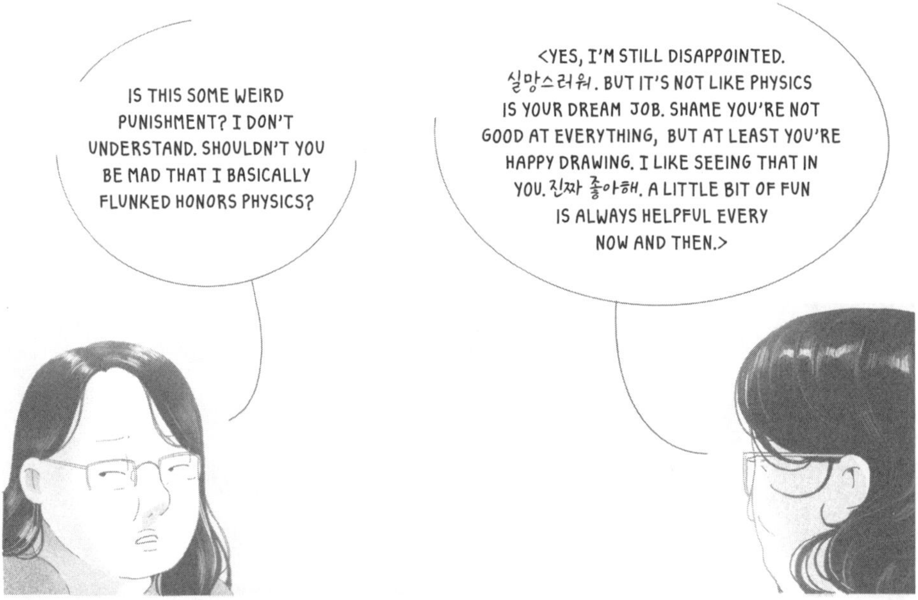
IS THIS SOME WEIRD PUNISHMENT? I DON'T UNDERSTAND. SHOULDN'T YOU BE MAD THAT I BASICALLY FLUNKED HONORS PHYSICS?
<YES, I'M STILL DISAPPOINTED. 실망스러워. BUT IT'S NOT LIKE PHYSICS IS YOUR DREAM JOB. SHAME YOU'RE NOT GOOD AT EVERYTHING, BUT AT LEAST YOU'RE HAPPY DRAWING. I LIKE SEEING THAT IN YOU. 진짜 좋아해. A LITTLE BIT OF FUN IS ALWAYS HELPFUL EVERY NOW AND THEN.>

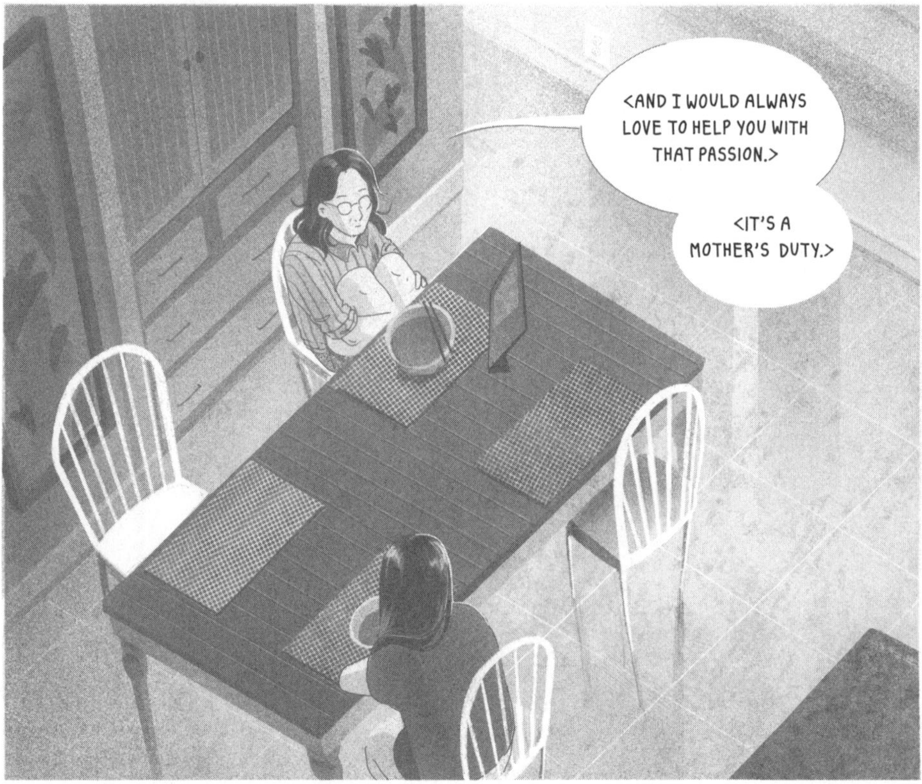
<AND I WOULD ALWAYS LOVE TO HELP YOU WITH THAT PASSION.>
<IT'S A MOTHER'S DUTY.>

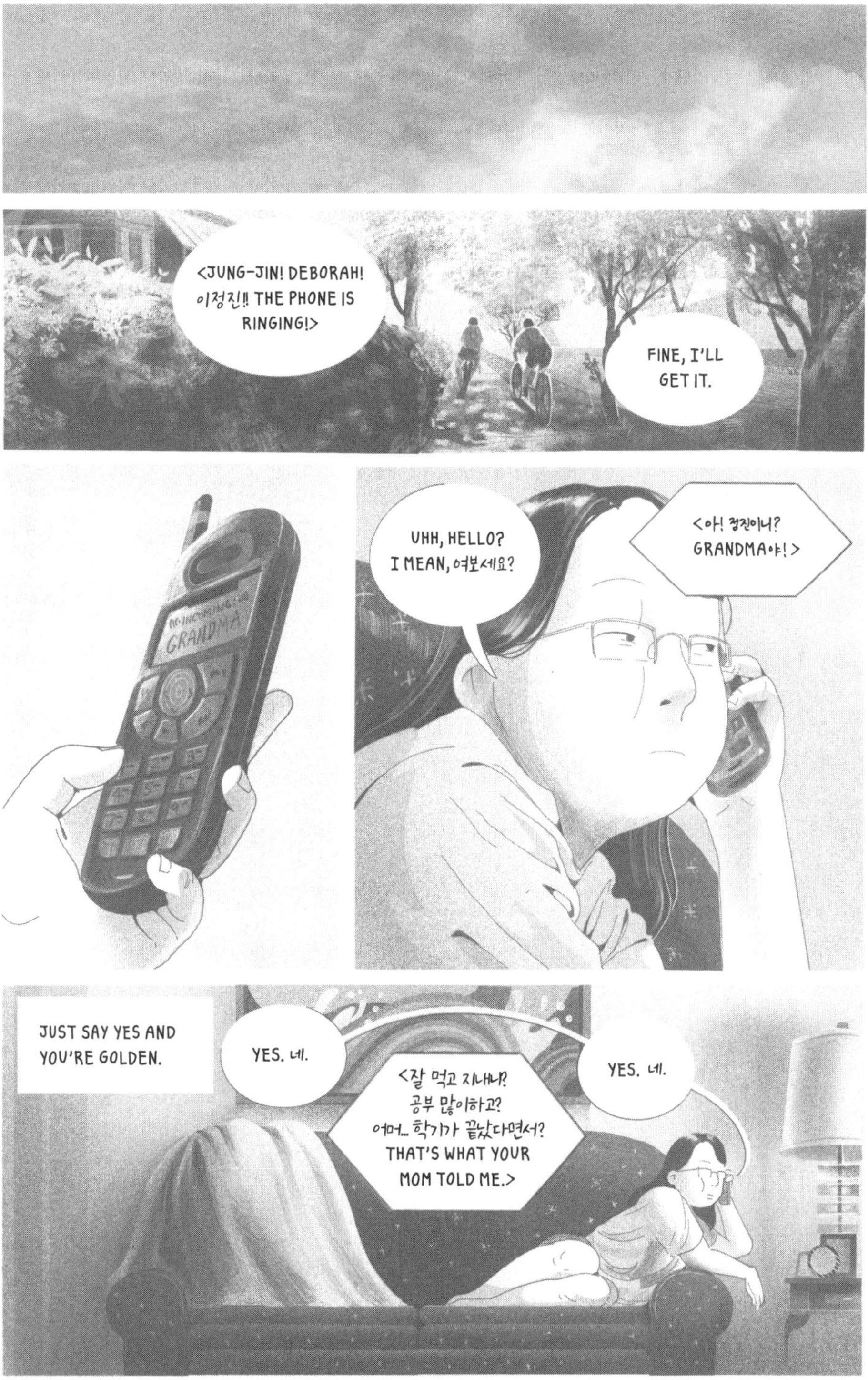
<JUNG-JIN! DEBORAH! 이정진!! THE PHONE IS RINGING!>
FINE, I'LL GET IT.
GRANDMA
UHH, HELLO? I MEAN, 여보세요?
<아! 정진이니? GRANDMA야!>
JUST SAY YES AND YOU'RE GOLDEN.
YES. 네.
<잘 먹고 지내니? 공부 많이하고? 어머... 학기가 끝났다면서? THAT'S WHAT YOUR MOM TOLD ME.>
YES. 네.

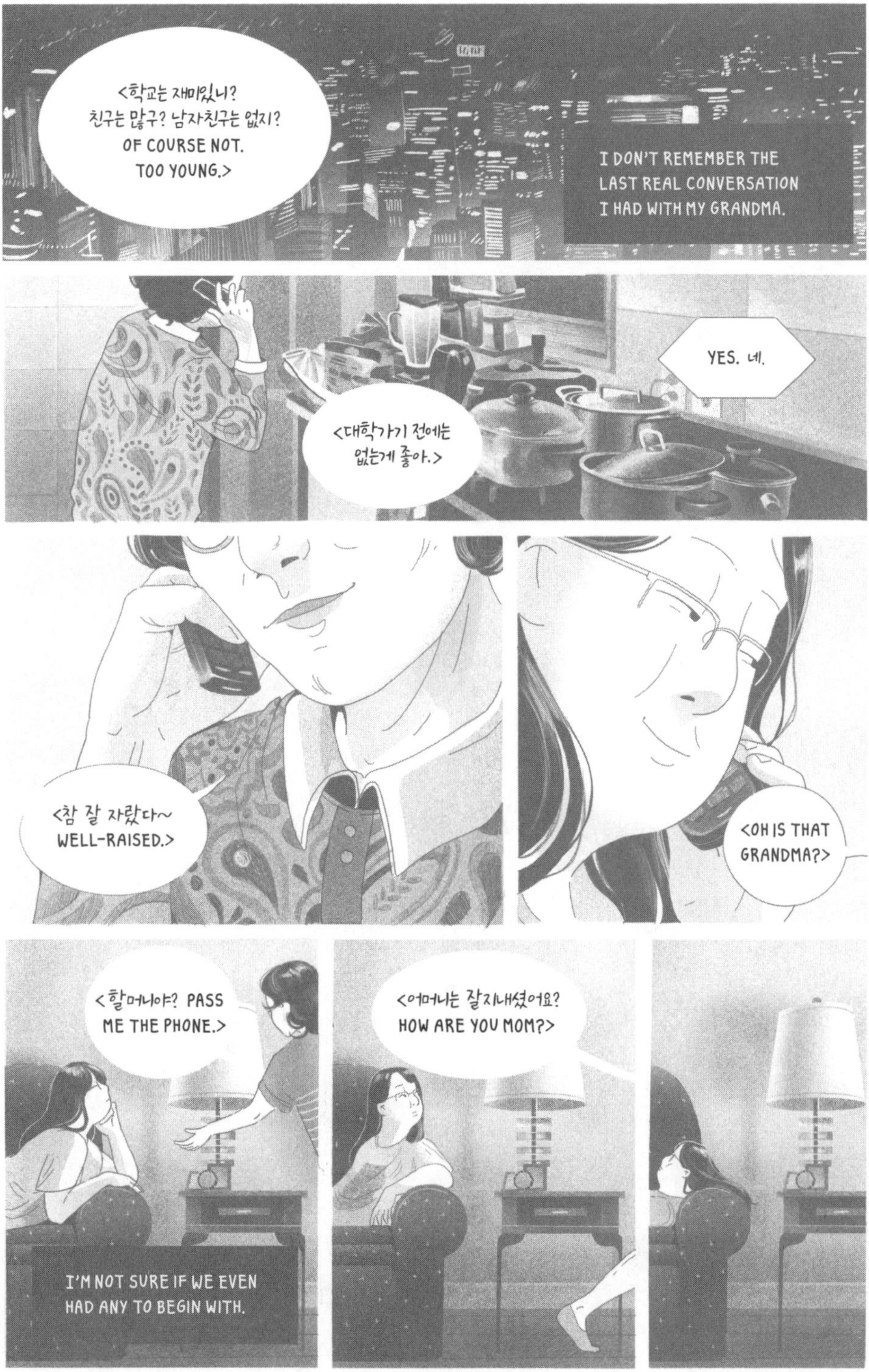
<학교는 재미있니?
친구는 많구? 남자친구는 없지?
OF COURSE NOT.
TOO YOUNG.>
I DON'T REMEMBER THE
LAST REAL CONVERSATION
I HAD WITH MY GRANDMA.
YES. 네.
<대학가기 전에는
없는게 좋아.>
<참 잘 자랐다~
WELL-RAISED.>
<OH IS THAT
GRANDMA?>
<할머니야? PASS
ME THE PHONE.>
I'M NOT SURE IF WE EVEN
HAD ANY TO BEGIN WITH.
<어머니는 잘지내셨어요?
HOW ARE YOU MOM?>

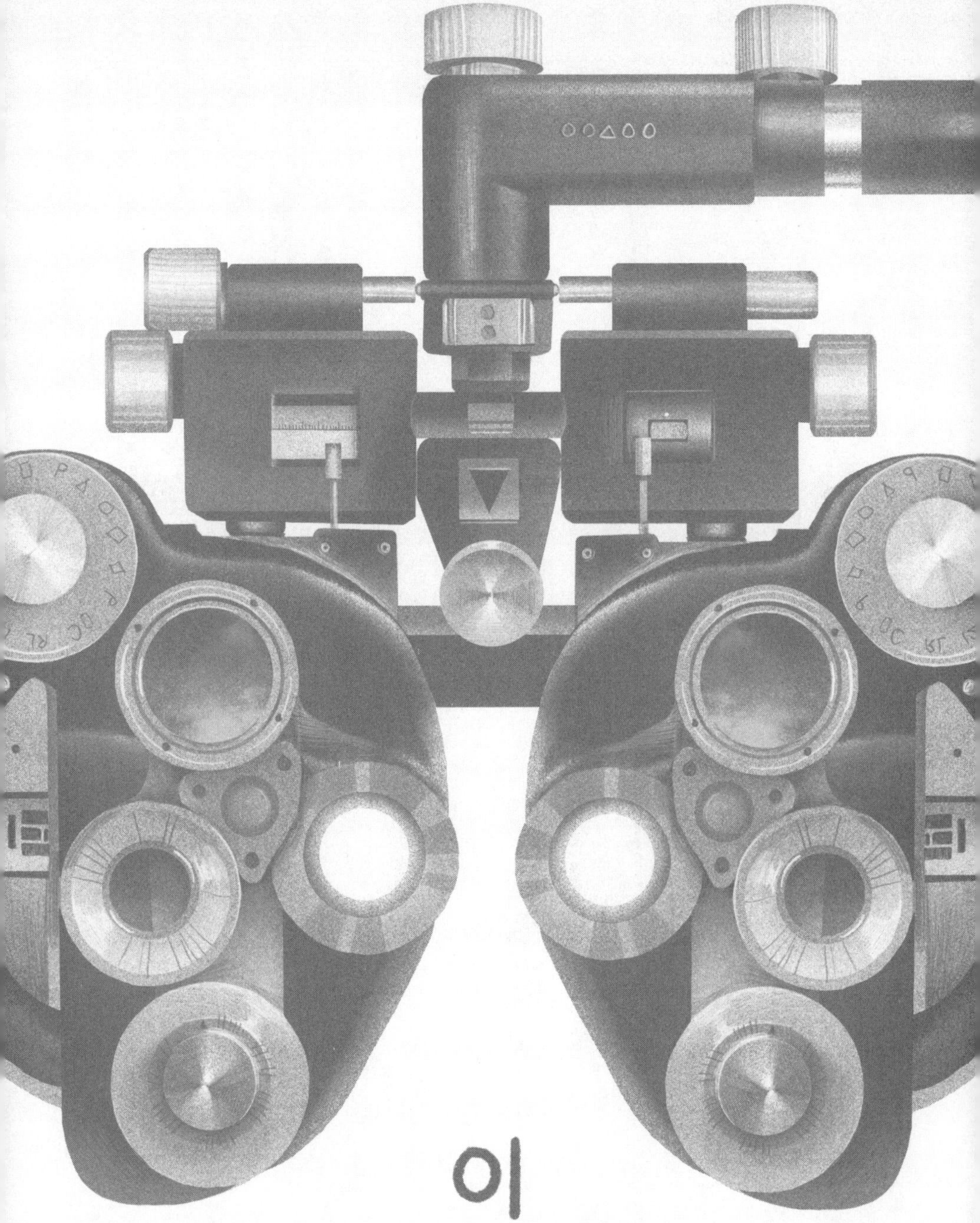

이

Part 2

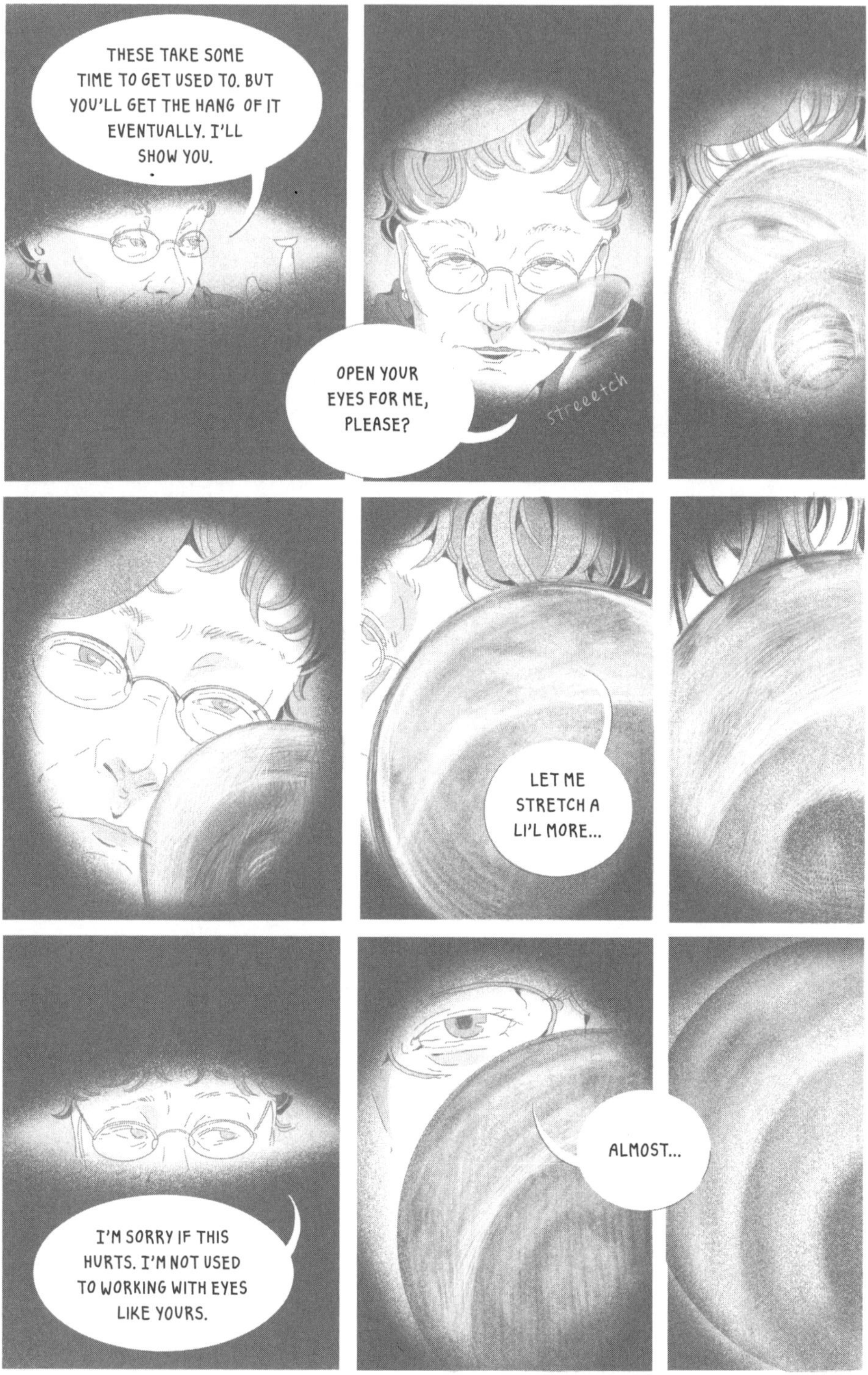
THESE TAKE SOME TIME TO GET USED TO. BUT YOU'LL GET THE HANG OF IT EVENTUALLY. I'LL SHOW YOU.
OPEN YOUR EYES FOR ME, PLEASE?
streeetch
LET ME STRETCH A LI'L MORE...
I'M SORRY IF THIS HURTS. I'M NOT USED TO WORKING WITH EYES LIKE YOURS.
ALMOST...

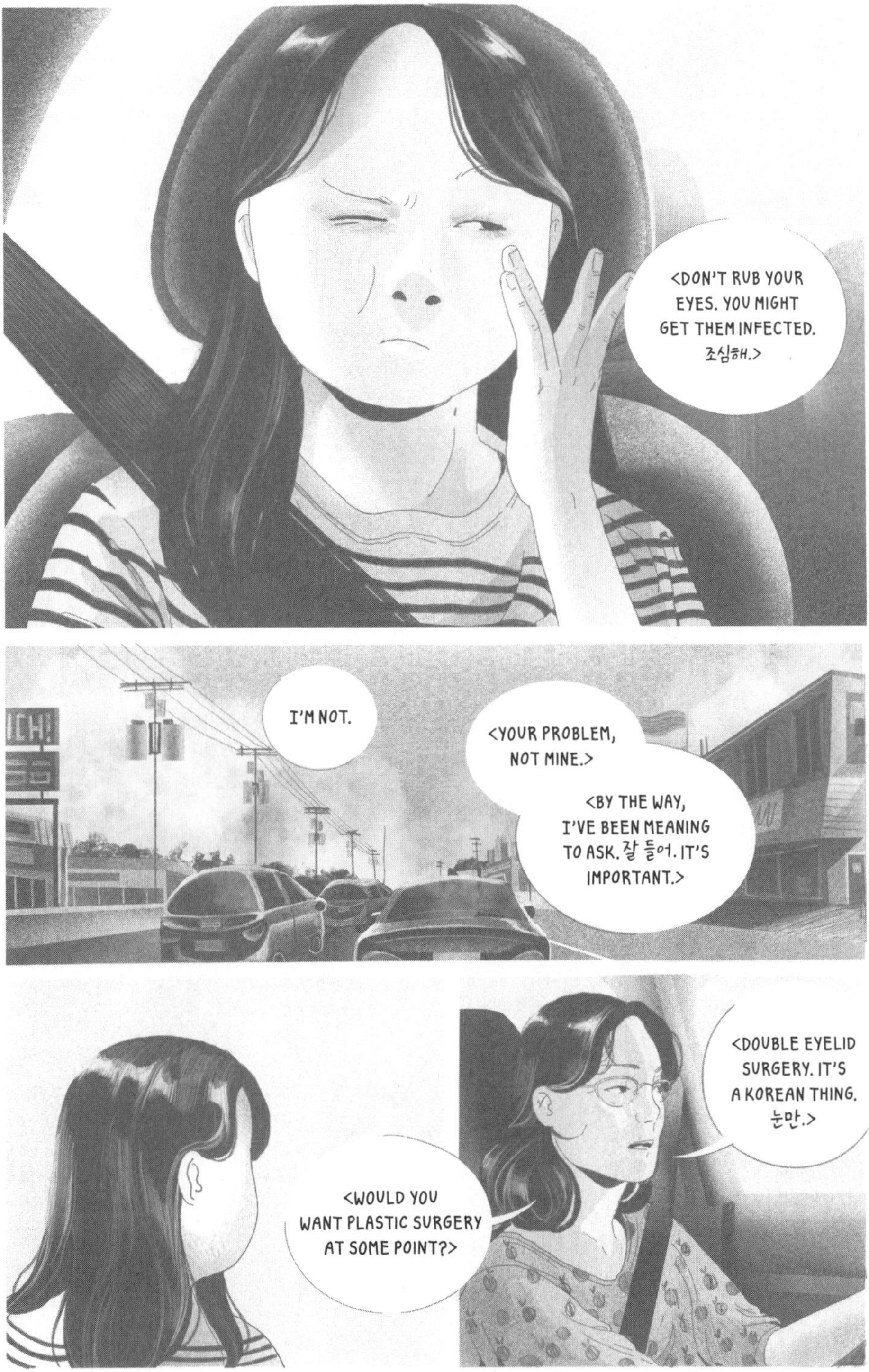
<DON'T RUB YOUR EYES. YOU MIGHT GET THEM INFECTED. 조심해.>
I'M NOT.
<YOUR PROBLEM, NOT MINE.>
<BY THE WAY, I'VE BEEN MEANING TO ASK. 잘 들어. IT'S IMPORTANT.>
<DOUBLE EYELID SURGERY. IT'S A KOREAN THING. 눈만.>
<WOULD YOU WANT PLASTIC SURGERY AT SOME POINT?>

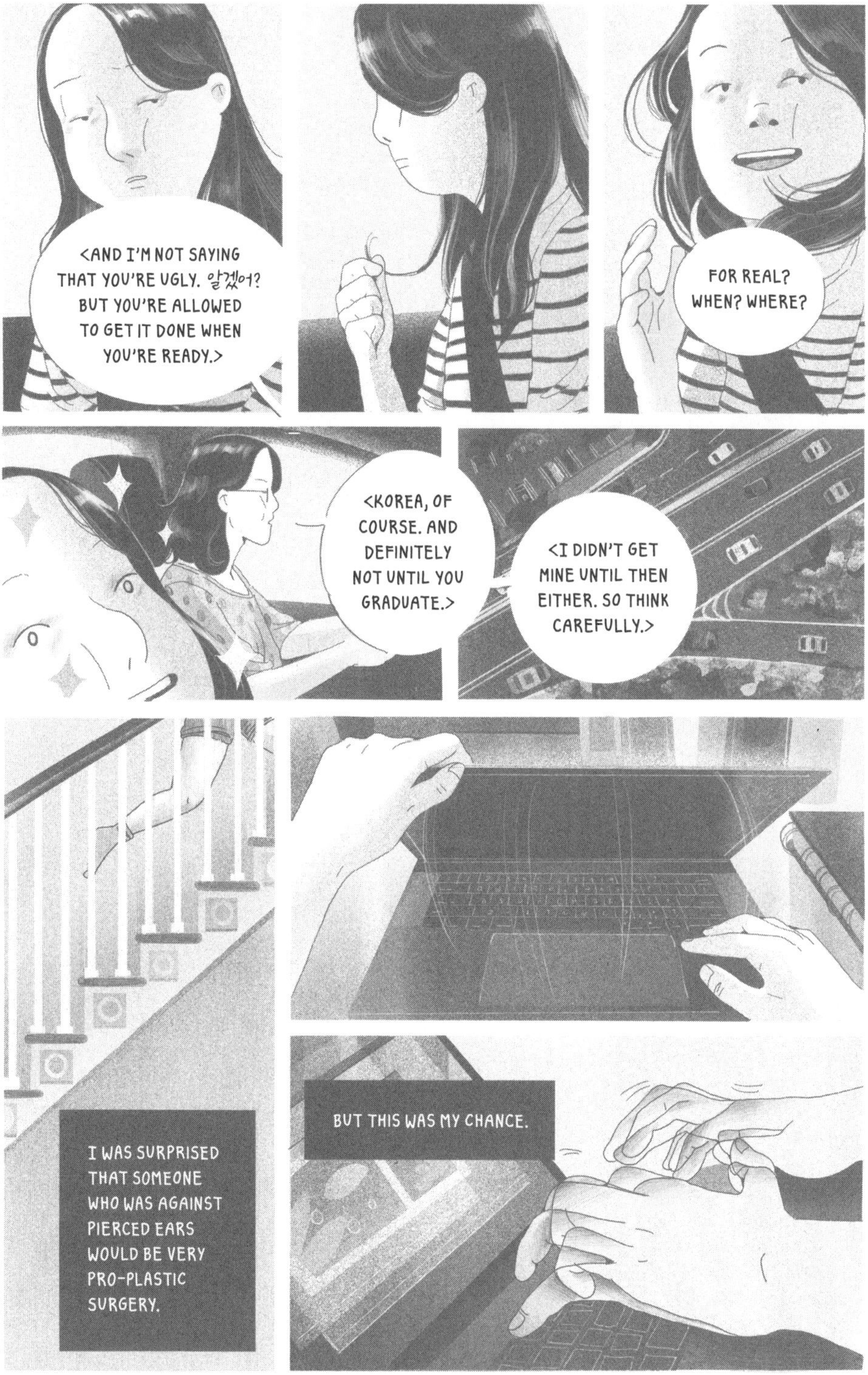
<AND I'M NOT SAYING THAT YOU'RE UGLY. 알겠어? BUT YOU'RE ALLOWED TO GET IT DONE WHEN YOU'RE READY.>
FOR REAL? WHEN? WHERE?
<KOREA, OF COURSE. AND DEFINITELY NOT UNTIL YOU GRADUATE.>
<I DIDN'T GET MINE UNTIL THEN EITHER. SO THINK CAREFULLY.>
I WAS SURPRISED THAT SOMEONE WHO WAS AGAINST PIERCED EARS WOULD BE VERY PRO-PLASTIC SURGERY.
BUT THIS WAS MY CHANCE.

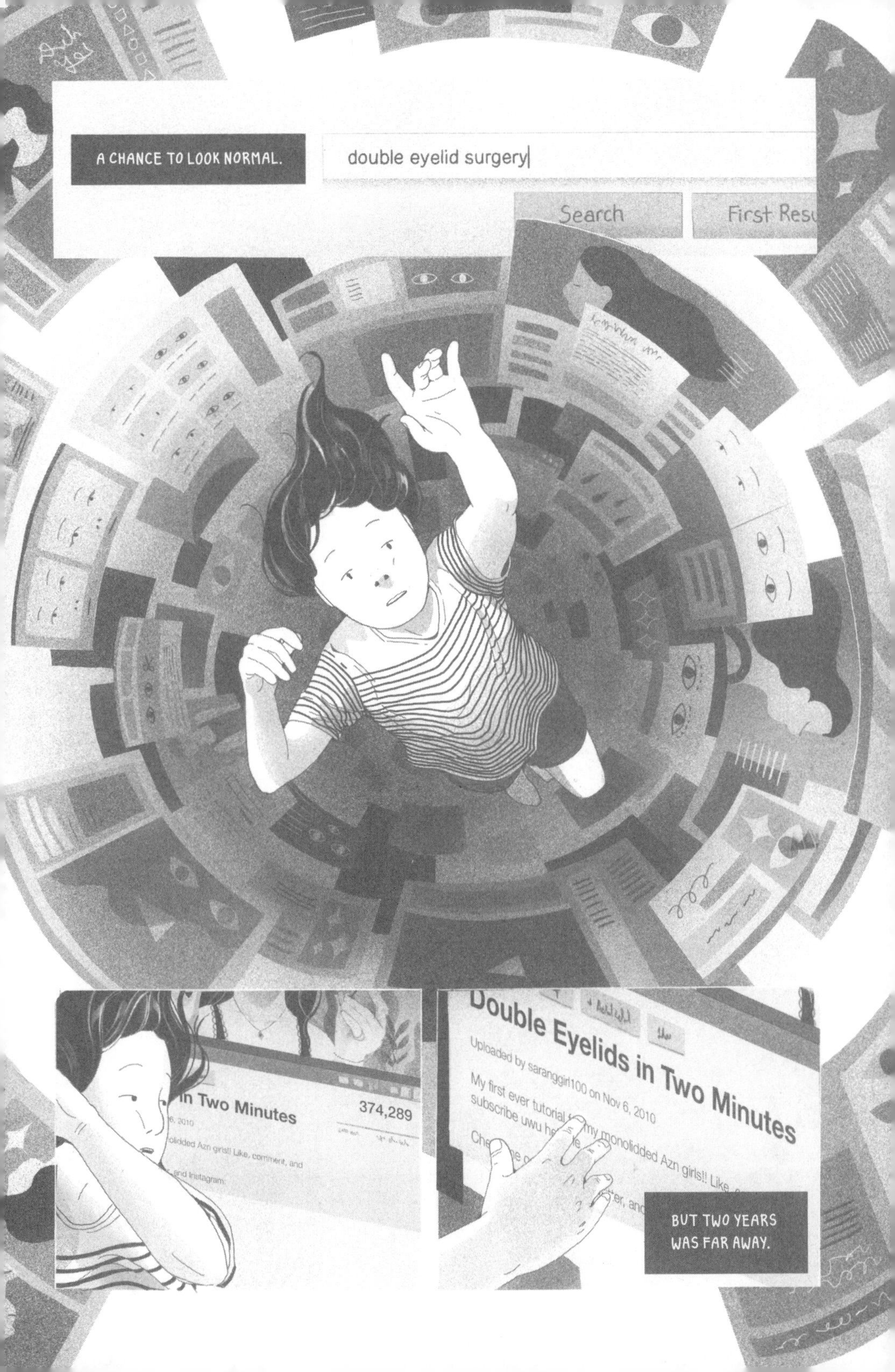
A CHANCE TO LOOK NORMAL.
double eyelid surgery
Search
in Two Minutes
374,289
Double Eyelids in Two Minutes
Uploaded by saranggirl100 on Nov 6, 2010
BUT TWO YEARS WAS FAR AWAY.

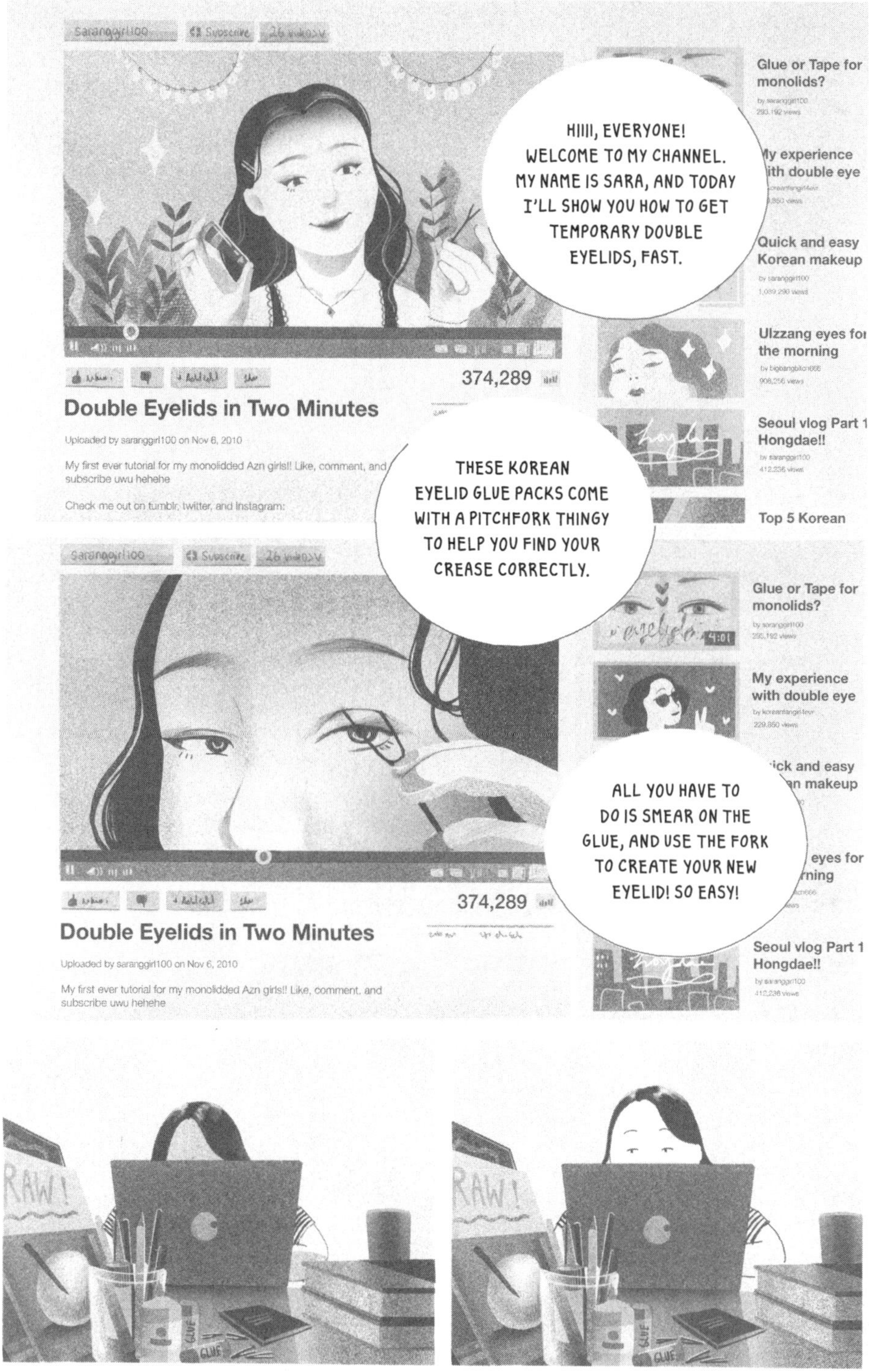
374,289
Double Eyelids in Two Minutes
Uploaded by saranggirl100 on Nov 6, 2010
My first ever tutorial for my monolidded Azn girls!! Like, comment, and subscribe uwu hehehe
Check me out on tumblr, twitter, and Instagram:
Glue or Tape for monolids?
Quick and easy Korean makeup
Ulzzang eyes for the morning
Seoul vlog Part 1 Hongdae!!
Top 5 Korean
HIIII, EVERYONE! WELCOME TO MY CHANNEL. MY NAME IS SARA, AND TODAY I'LL SHOW YOU HOW TO GET TEMPORARY DOUBLE EYELIDS, FAST.
THESE KOREAN EYELID GLUE PACKS COME WITH A PITCHFORK THINGY TO HELP YOU FIND YOUR CREASE CORRECTLY.
374,289
Double Eyelids in Two Minutes
Uploaded by saranggirl100 on Nov 6, 2010
My first ever tutorial for my monolidded Azn girls!! Like, comment, and subscribe uwu hehehe
Glue or Tape for monolids?
My experience with double eye
Seoul vlog Part 1 Hongdae!!
ALL YOU HAVE TO DO IS SMEAR ON THE GLUE, AND USE THE FORK TO CREATE YOUR NEW EYELID! SO EASY!
RAW!
GLUE
RAW!
GLUE

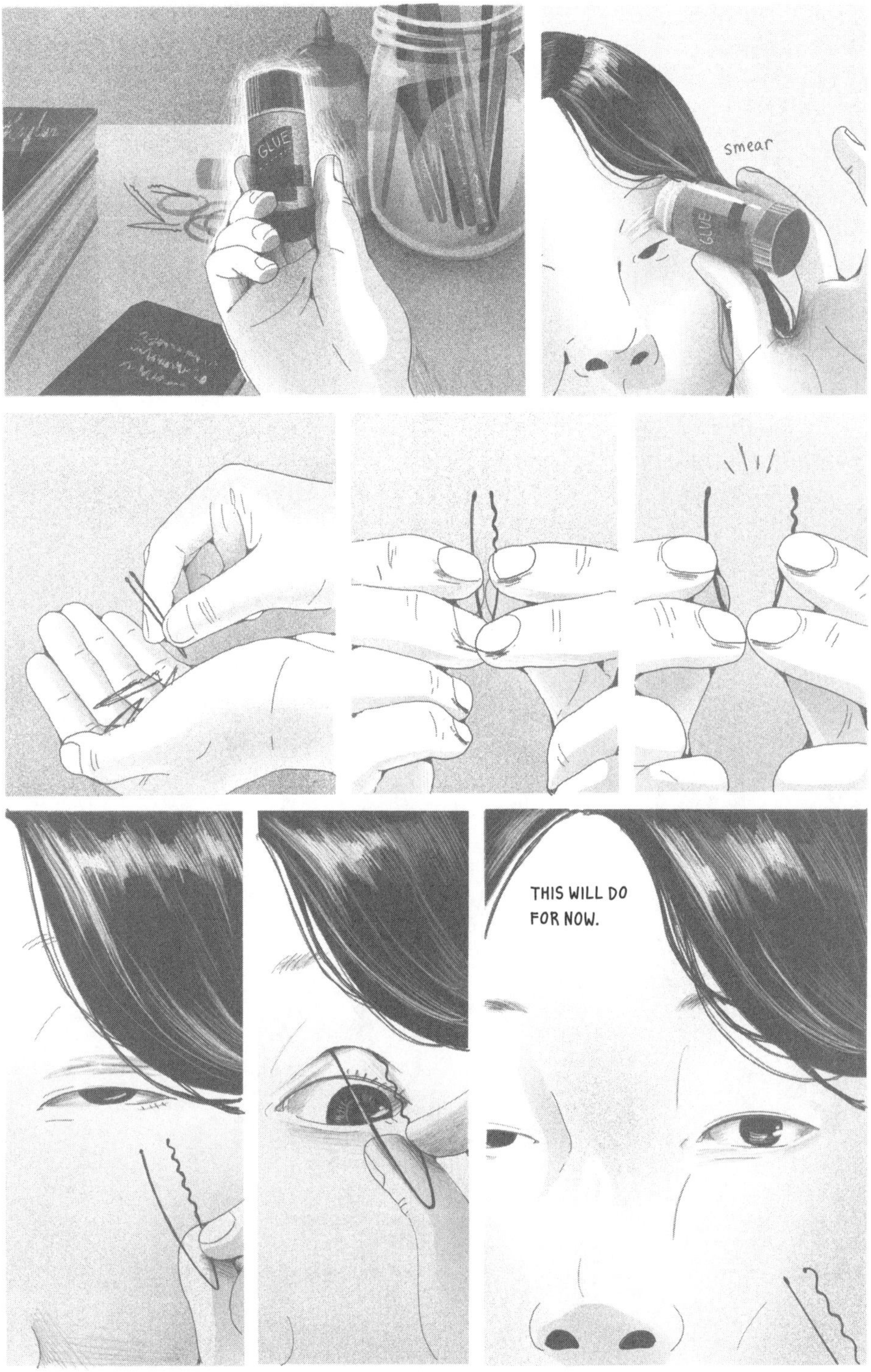
GLUE
smear
GLUE
THIS WILL DO
FOR NOW.

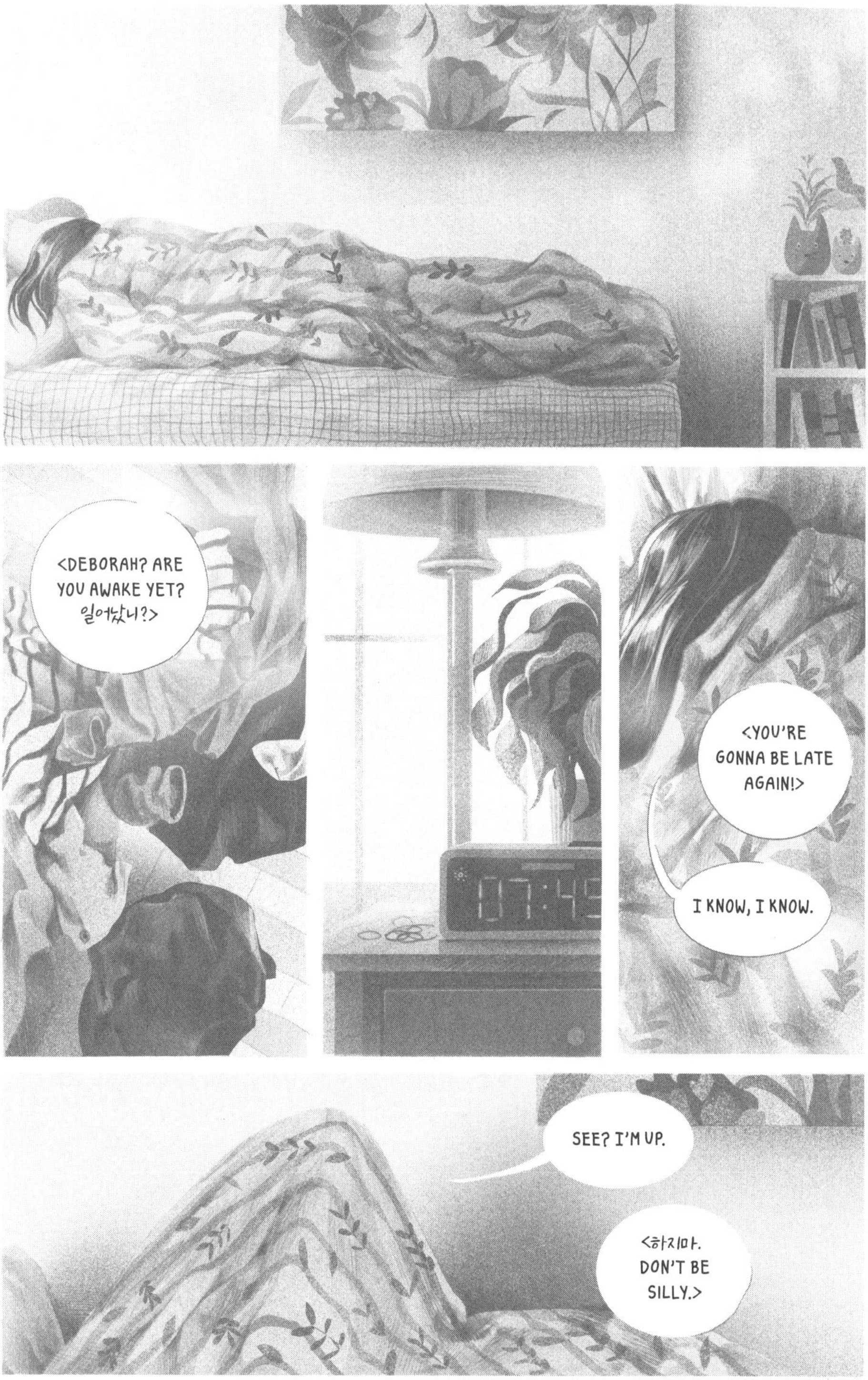
<DEBORAH? ARE YOU AWAKE YET? 일어났니?>
<YOU'RE GONNA BE LATE AGAIN!>
I KNOW, I KNOW.
SEE? I'M UP.
<하지마. DON'T BE SILLY.>

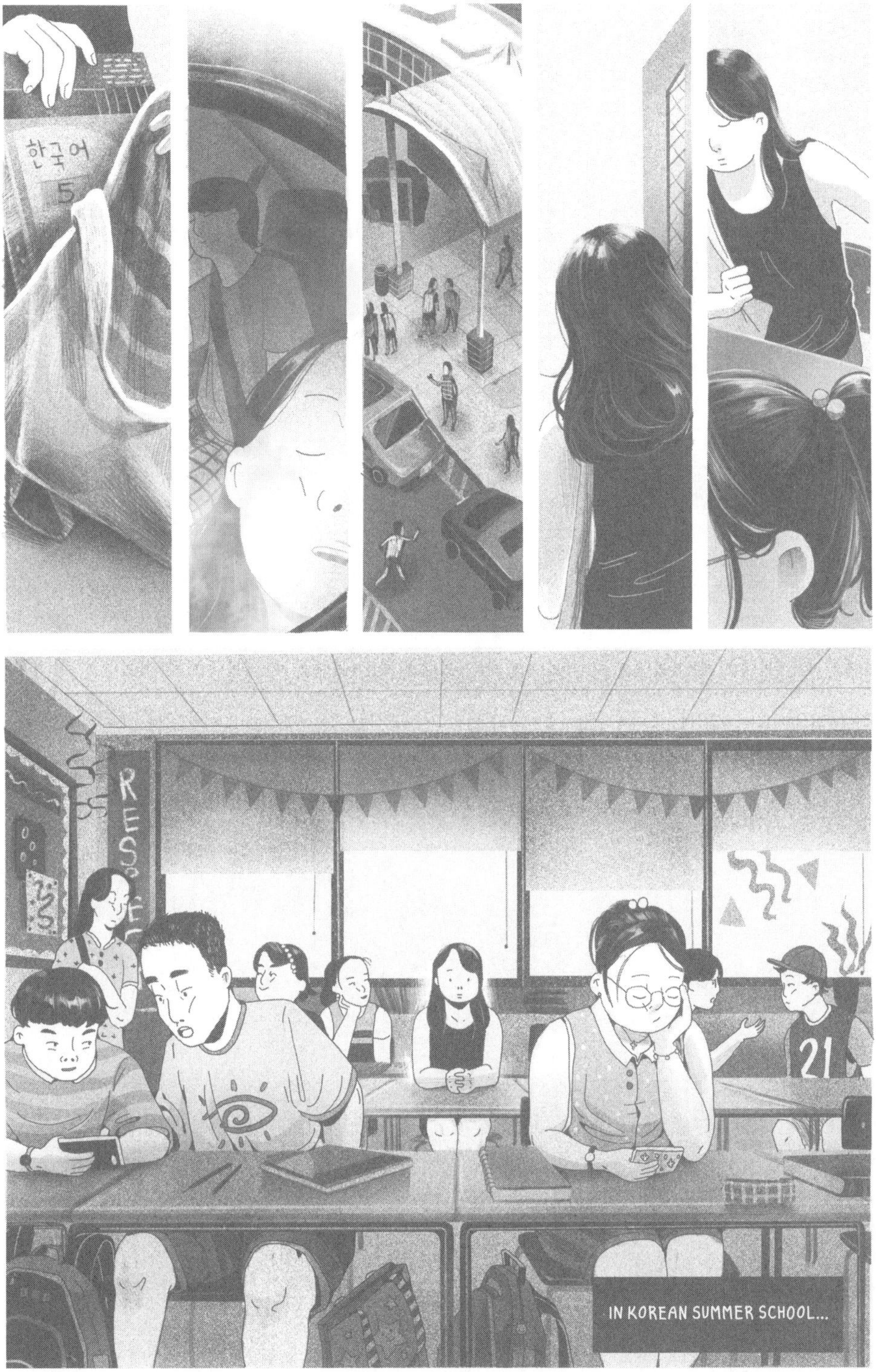
한국어
5
21
IN KOREAN SUMMER SCHOOL...

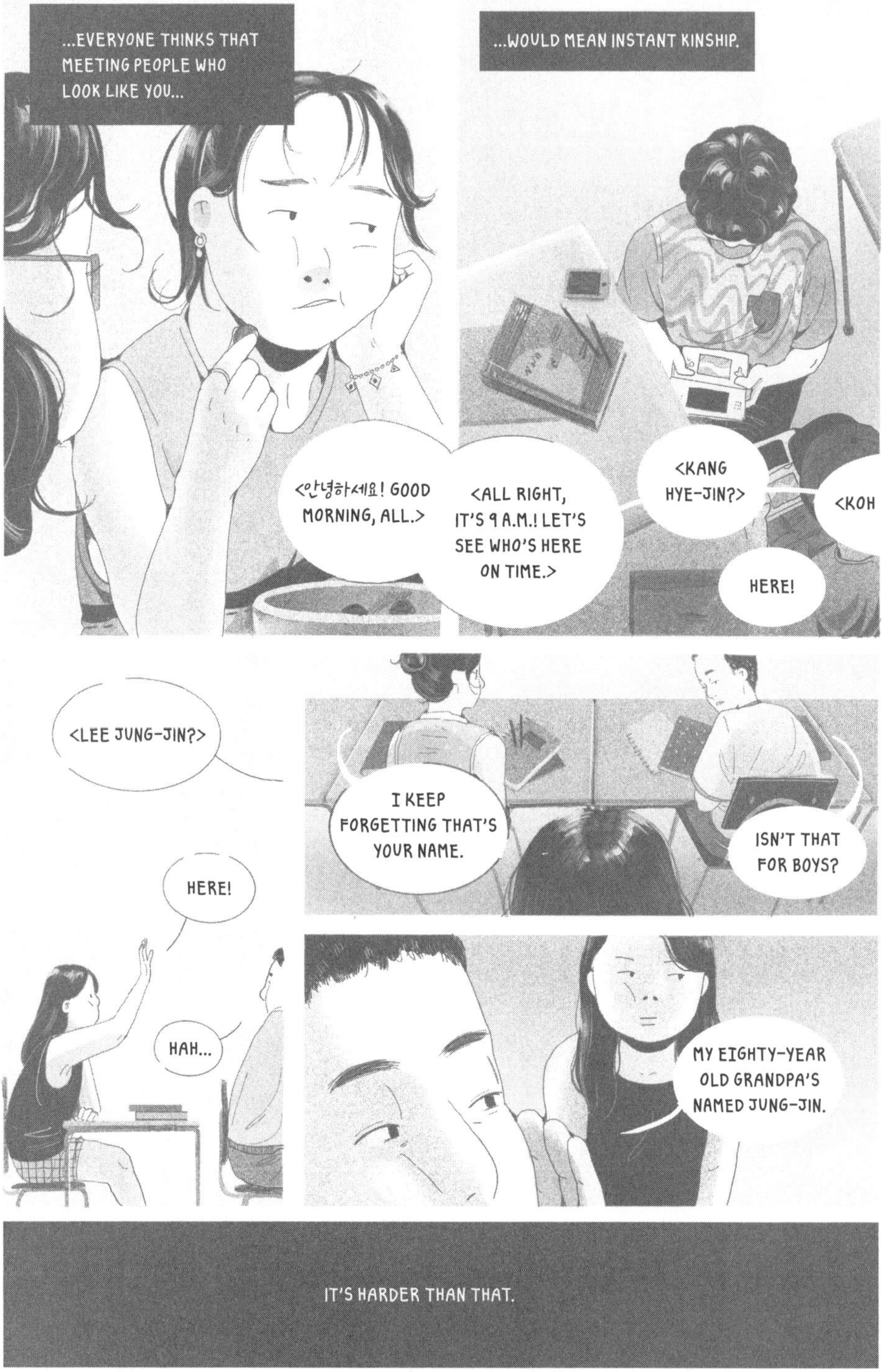
...EVERYONE THINKS THAT MEETING PEOPLE WHO LOOK LIKE YOU...
...WOULD MEAN INSTANT KINSHIP.
<안녕하세요! GOOD MORNING, ALL.>
<ALL RIGHT, IT'S 9 A.M.! LET'S SEE WHO'S HERE ON TIME.>
<KANG HYE-JIN?>
<KOH
HERE!
<LEE JUNG-JIN?>
I KEEP FORGETTING THAT'S YOUR NAME.
ISN'T THAT FOR BOYS?
HERE!
HAH...
MY EIGHTY-YEAR OLD GRANDPA'S NAMED JUNG-JIN.
IT'S HARDER THAN THAT.

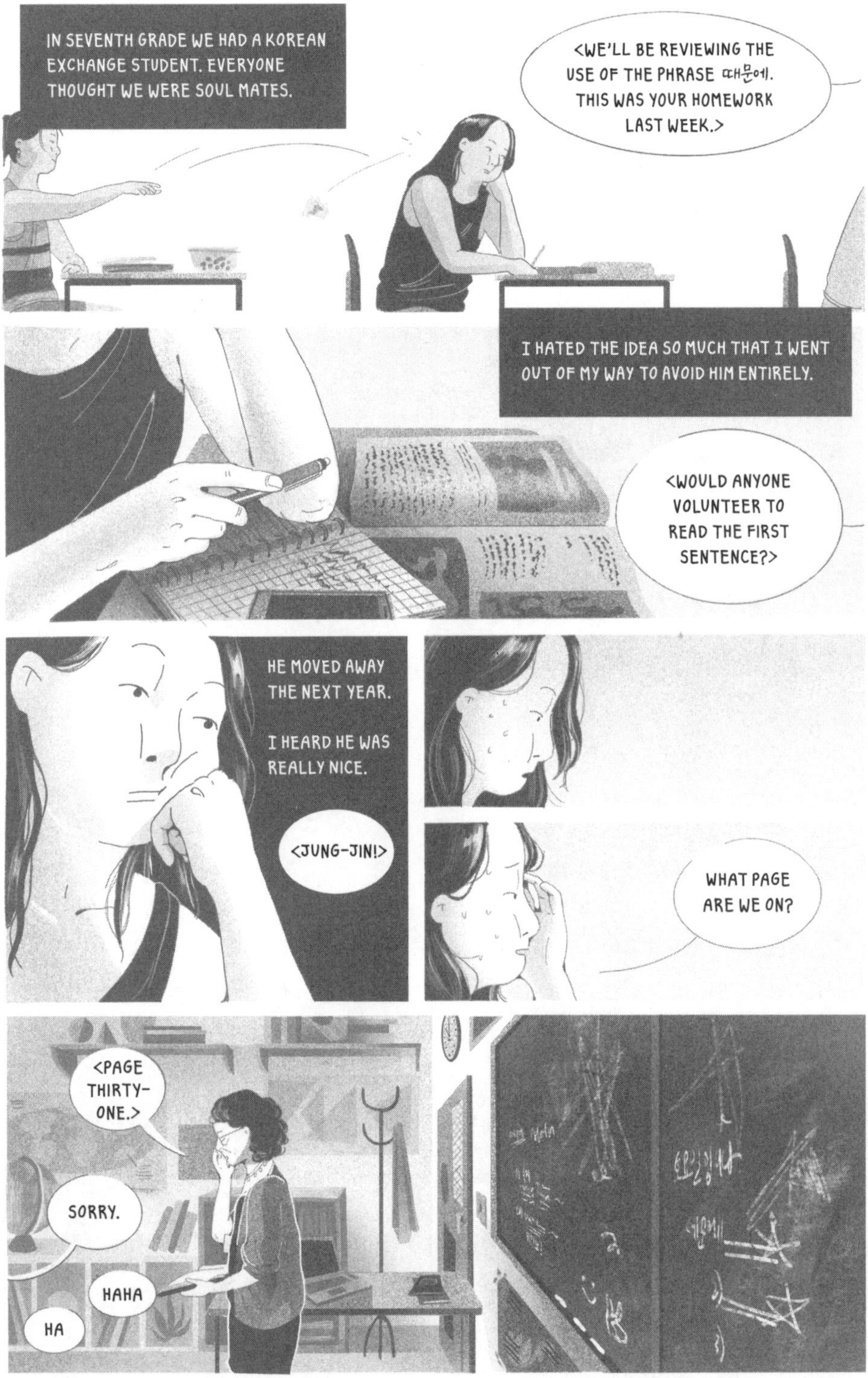
IN SEVENTH GRADE WE HAD A KOREAN EXCHANGE STUDENT. EVERYONE THOUGHT WE WERE SOUL MATES.
<WE'LL BE REVIEWING THE USE OF THE PHRASE 때문에. THIS WAS YOUR HOMEWORK LAST WEEK.>
I HATED THE IDEA SO MUCH THAT I WENT OUT OF MY WAY TO AVOID HIM ENTIRELY.
<WOULD ANYONE VOLUNTEER TO READ THE FIRST SENTENCE?>
HE MOVED AWAY THE NEXT YEAR.
I HEARD HE WAS REALLY NICE.
<JUNG-JIN!>
WHAT PAGE ARE WE ON?
<PAGE THIRTY-ONE.>
SORRY.
HAHA
HA

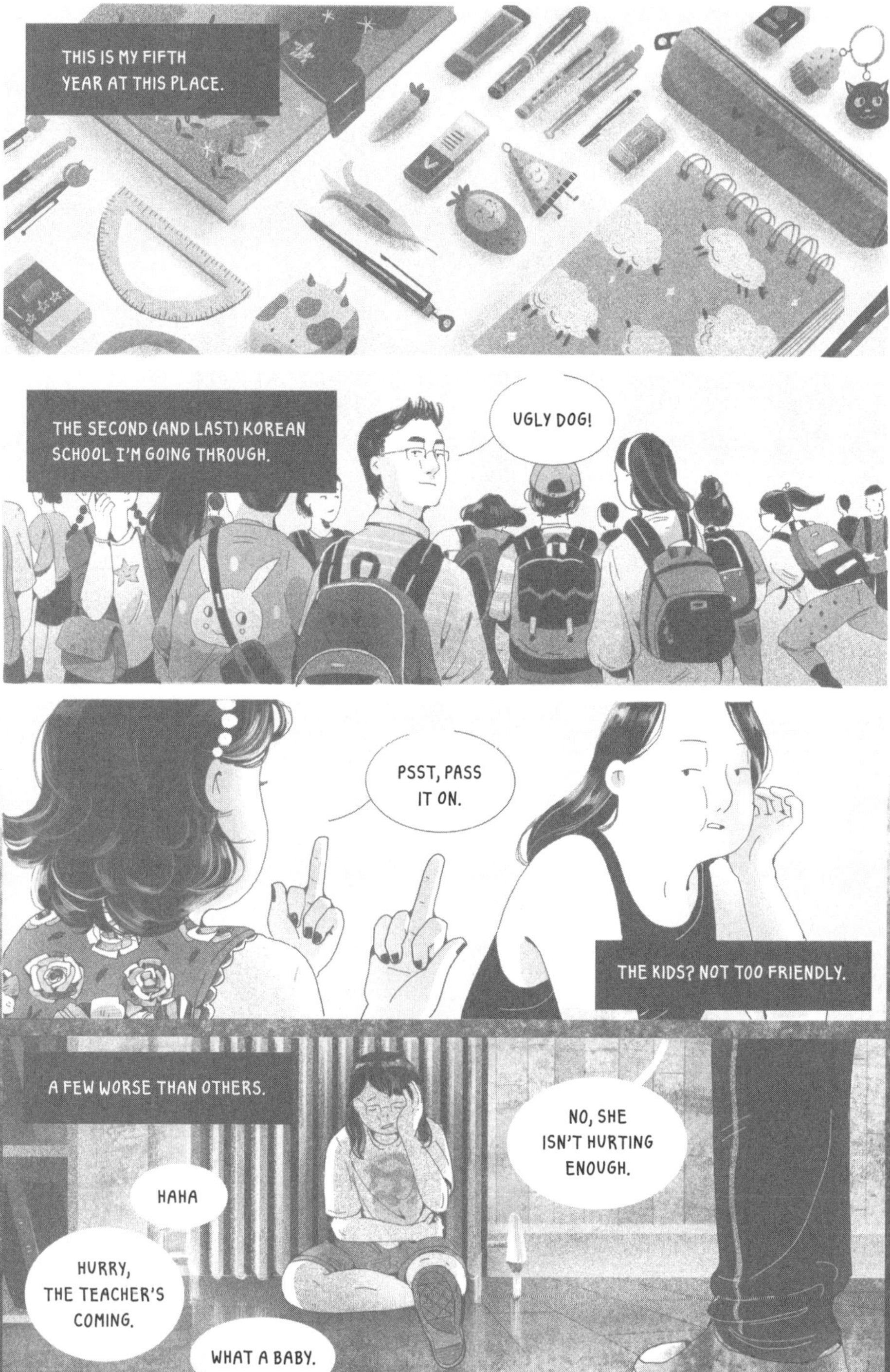
THIS IS MY FIFTH YEAR AT THIS PLACE.
THE SECOND (AND LAST) KOREAN SCHOOL I'M GOING THROUGH.
UGLY DOG!
PSST, PASS IT ON.
THE KIDS? NOT TOO FRIENDLY.
A FEW WORSE THAN OTHERS.
NO, SHE ISN'T HURTING ENOUGH.
HAHA
HURRY, THE TEACHER'S COMING.
WHAT A BABY.

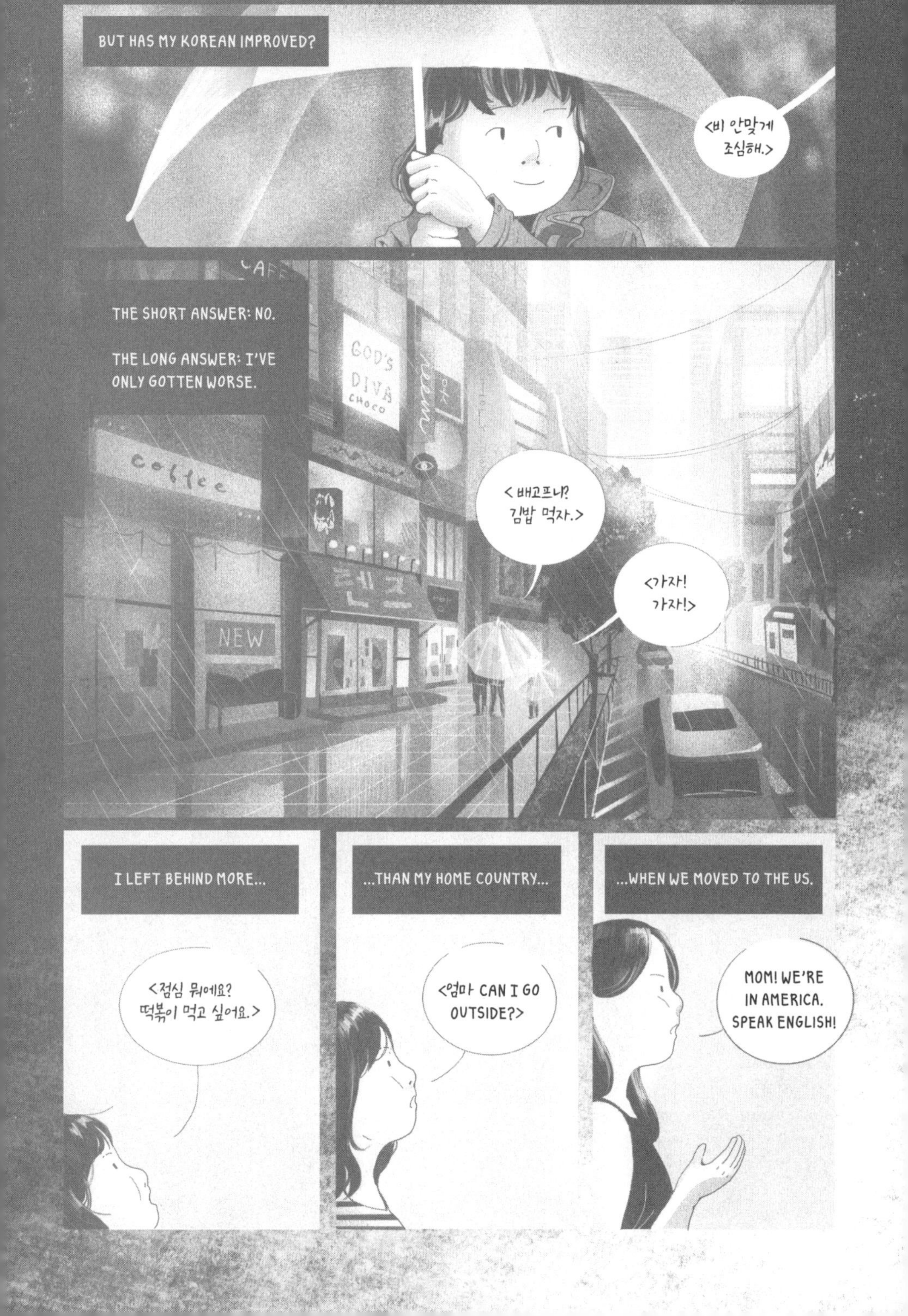
BUT HAS MY KOREAN IMPROVED?
<비 안맞게 조심해.>
THE SHORT ANSWER: NO.
THE LONG ANSWER: I'VE ONLY GOTTEN WORSE.
GOD'S DIVA CHOCO
coffee
NEW
<배고프니? 김밥 먹자.>
<가자! 가자!>
I LEFT BEHIND MORE...
<점심 뭐에요? 떡볶이 먹고 싶어요.>
...THAN MY HOME COUNTRY...
<엄마 CAN I GO OUTSIDE?>
...WHEN WE MOVED TO THE US.
MOM! WE'RE IN AMERICA. SPEAK ENGLISH!

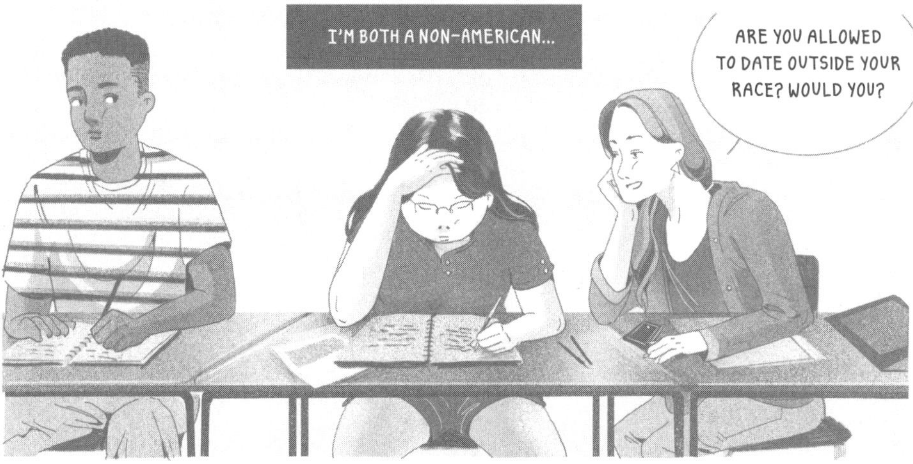
I'M BOTH A NON-AMERICAN...
ARE YOU ALLOWED TO DATE OUTSIDE YOUR RACE? WOULD YOU?

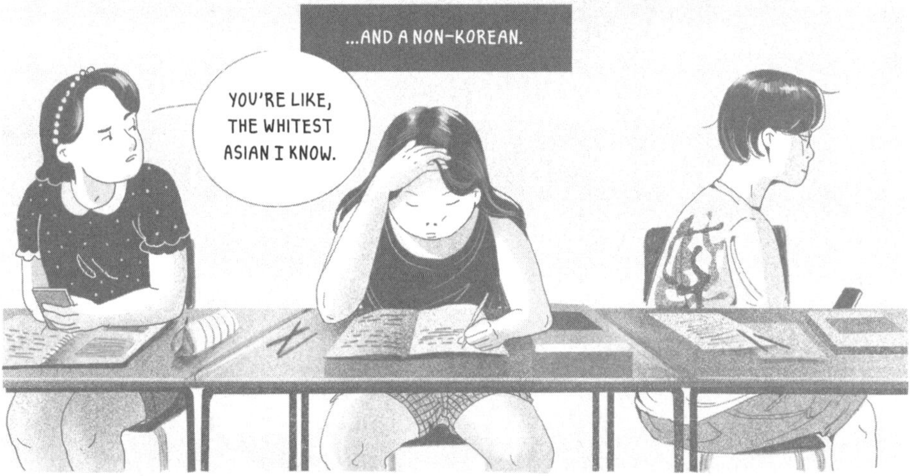
...AND A NON-KOREAN.
YOU'RE LIKE, THE WHITEST ASIAN I KNOW.

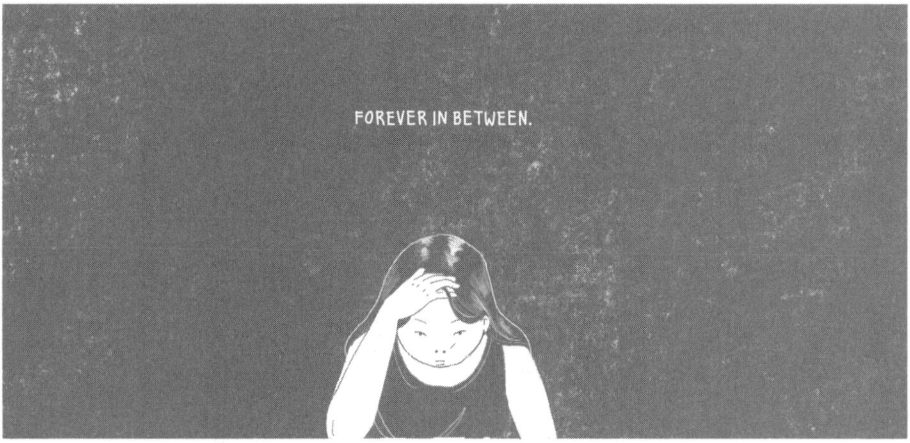
FOREVER IN BETWEEN.

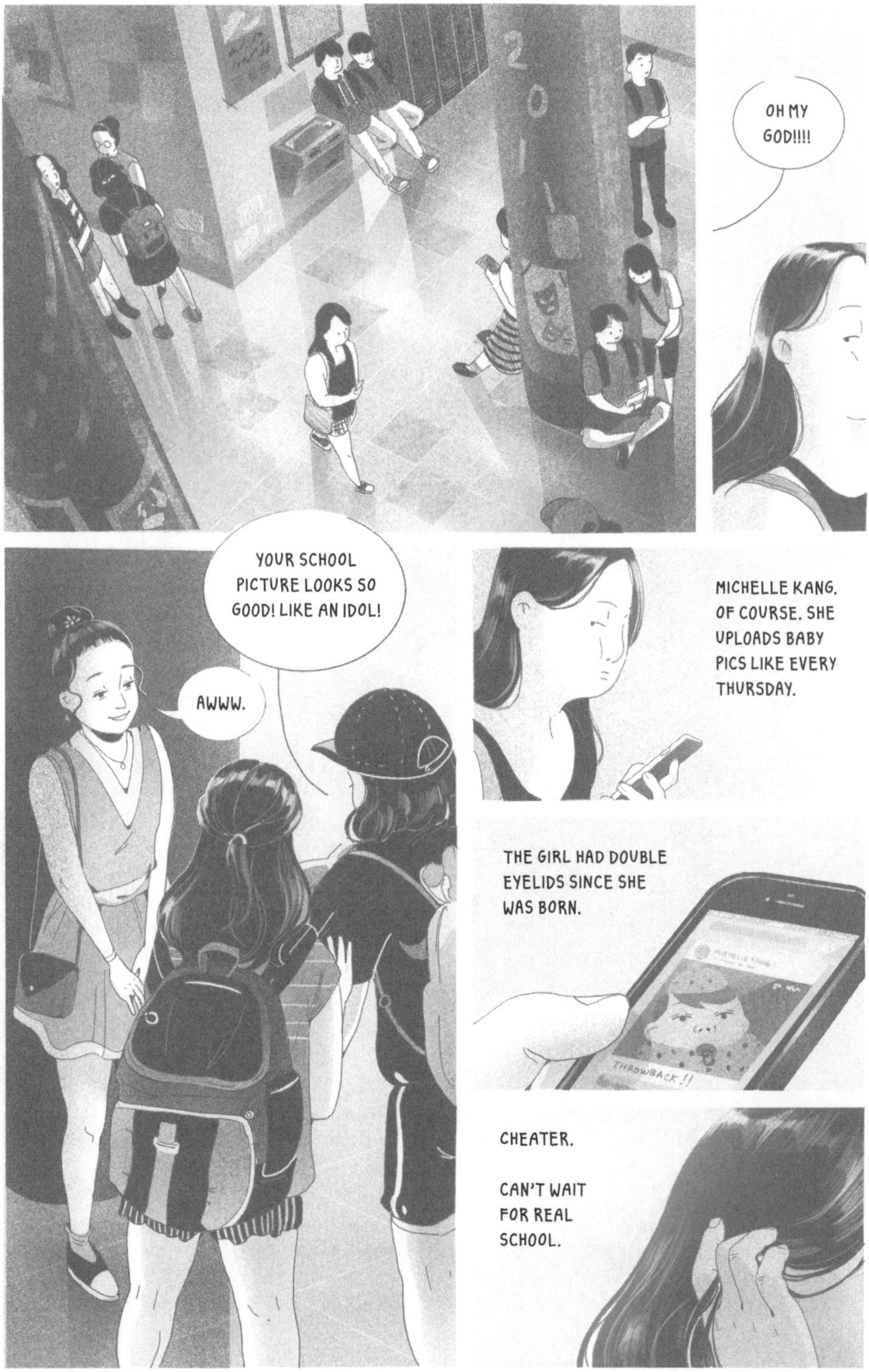
OH MY GOD!!!!
YOUR SCHOOL PICTURE LOOKS SO GOOD! LIKE AN IDOL!
AWWW.
MICHELLE KANG. OF COURSE. SHE UPLOADS BABY PICS LIKE EVERY THURSDAY.
THE GIRL HAD DOUBLE EYELIDS SINCE SHE WAS BORN.
THROWBACK !!
CHEATER.
CAN'T WAIT FOR REAL SCHOOL.

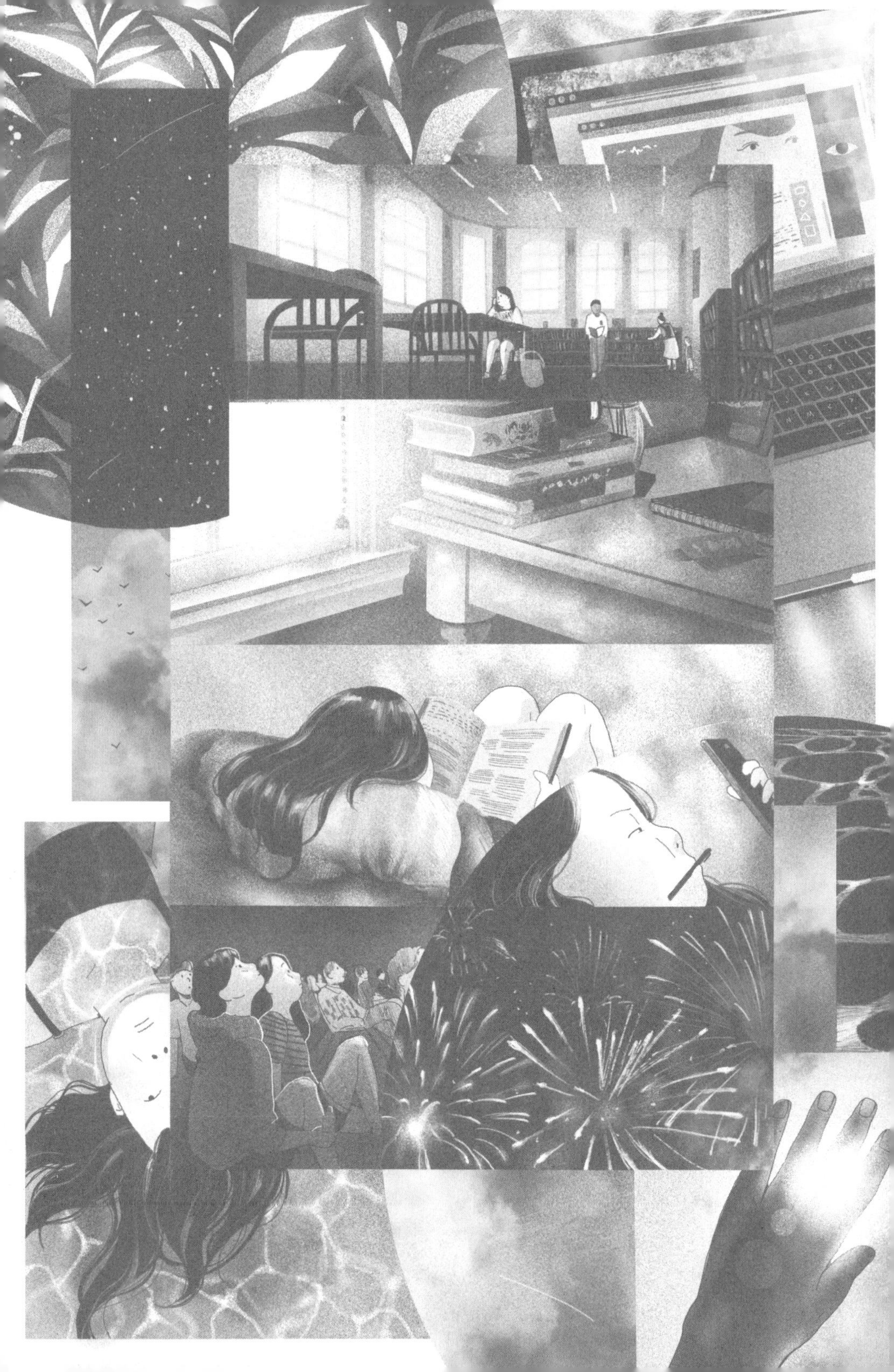

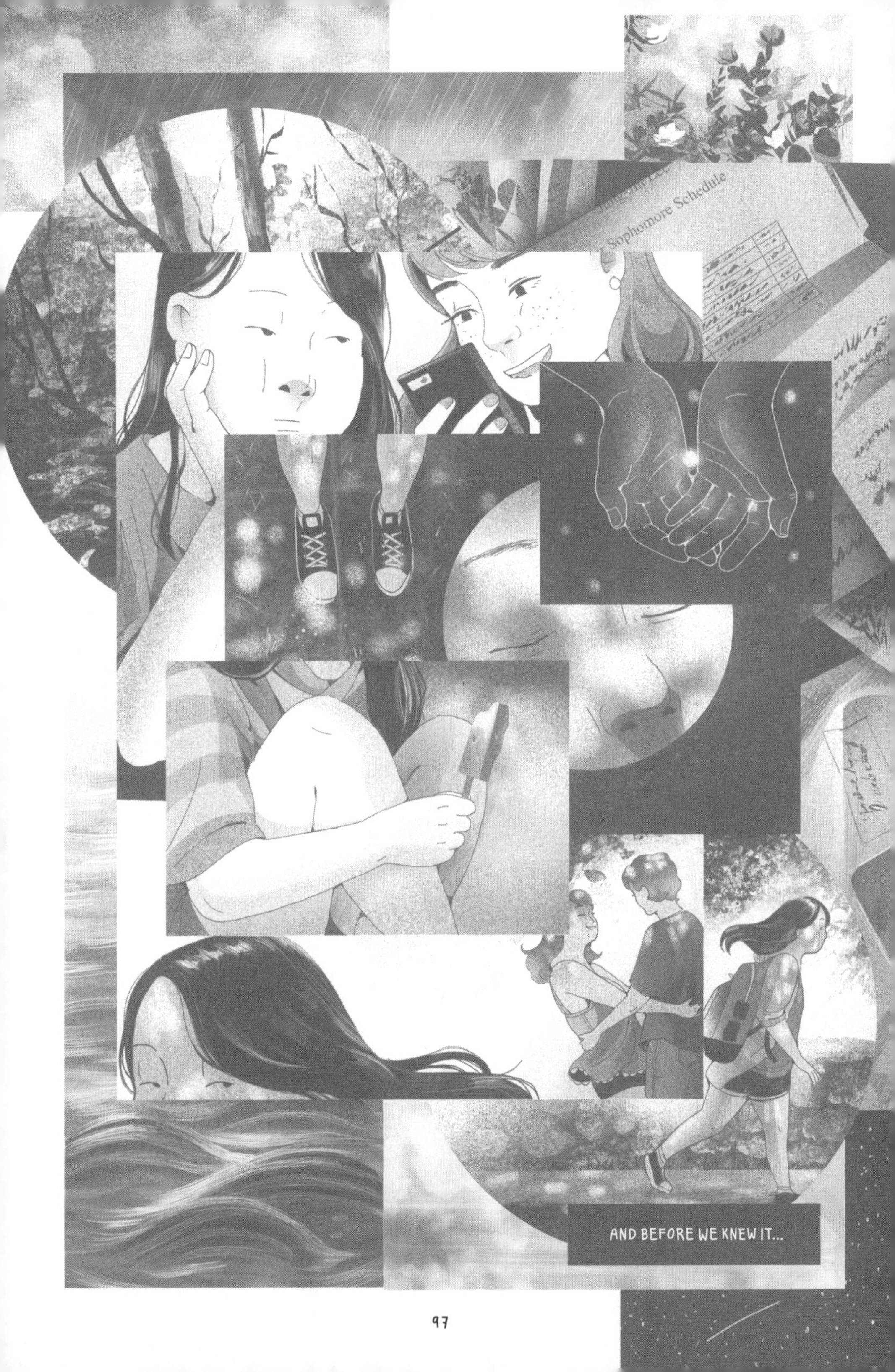
Sophomore Schedule
AND BEFORE WE KNEW IT...

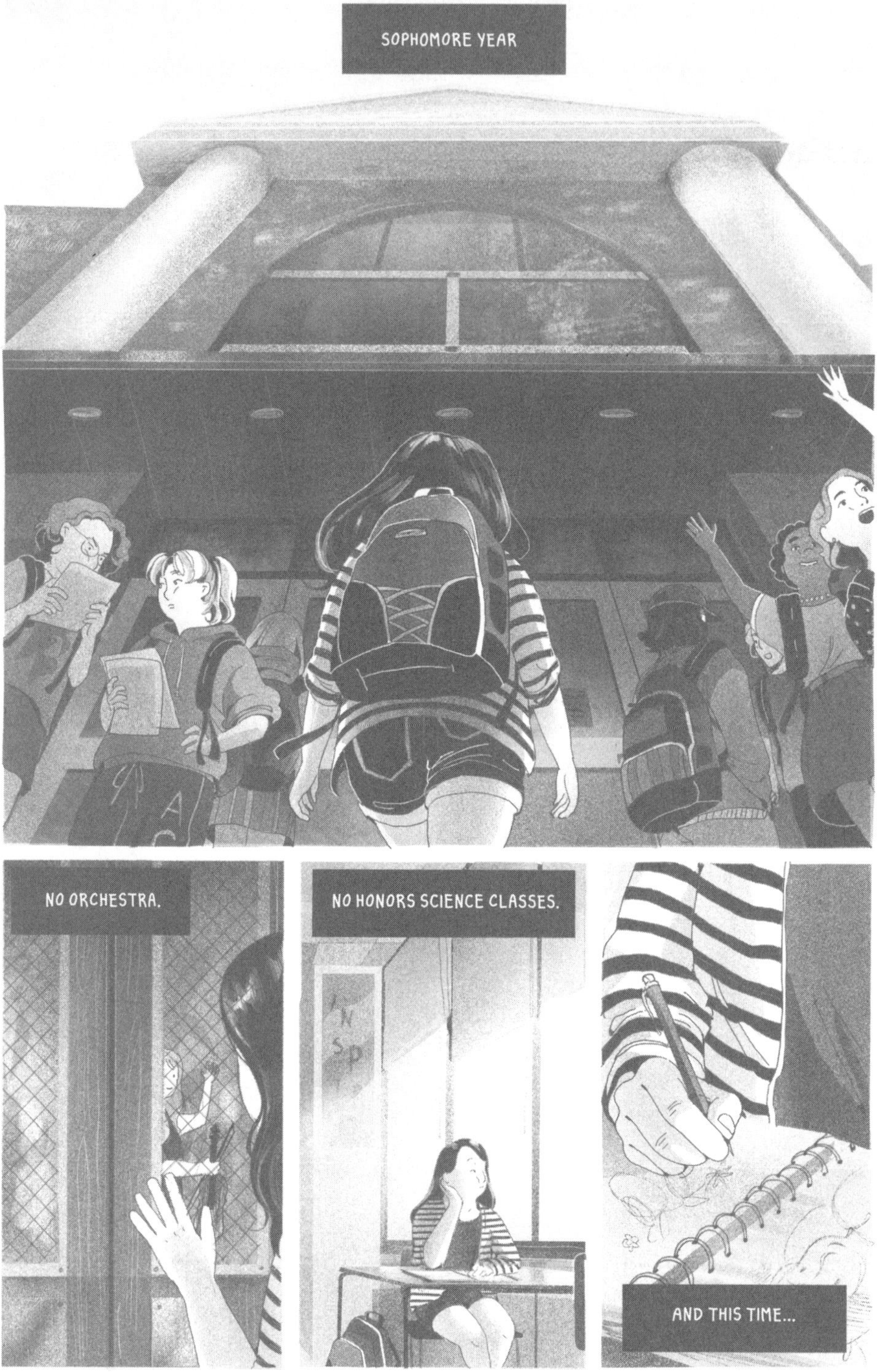
SOPHOMORE YEAR
NO ORCHESTRA.
NO HONORS SCIENCE CLASSES.
AND THIS TIME...

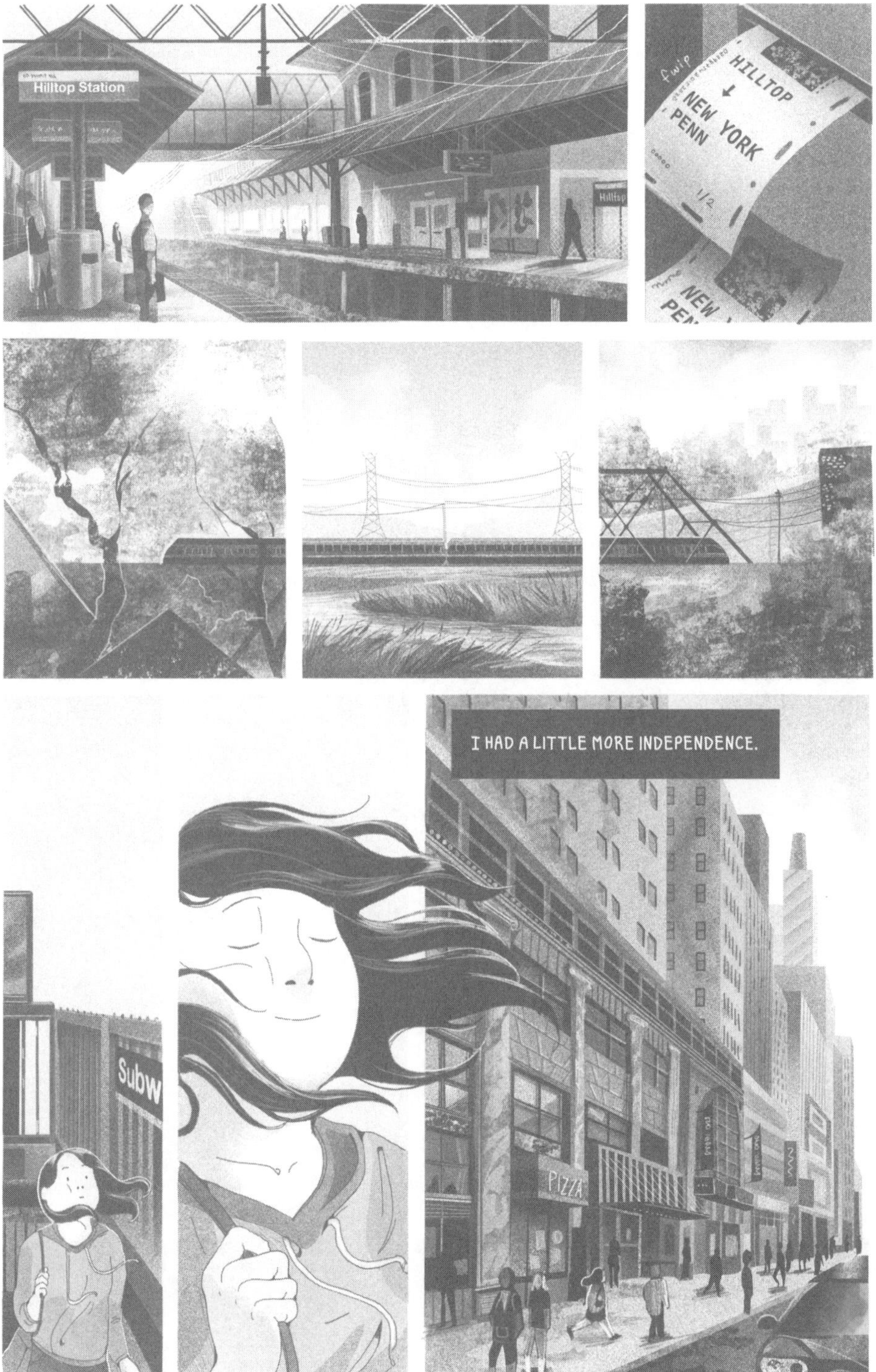
Hilltop Station
Hilltop
fwip
HILLTOP
↓
NEW YORK
PENN
1/2
NEW
I HAD A LITTLE MORE INDEPENDENCE.
Subw
PIZZA

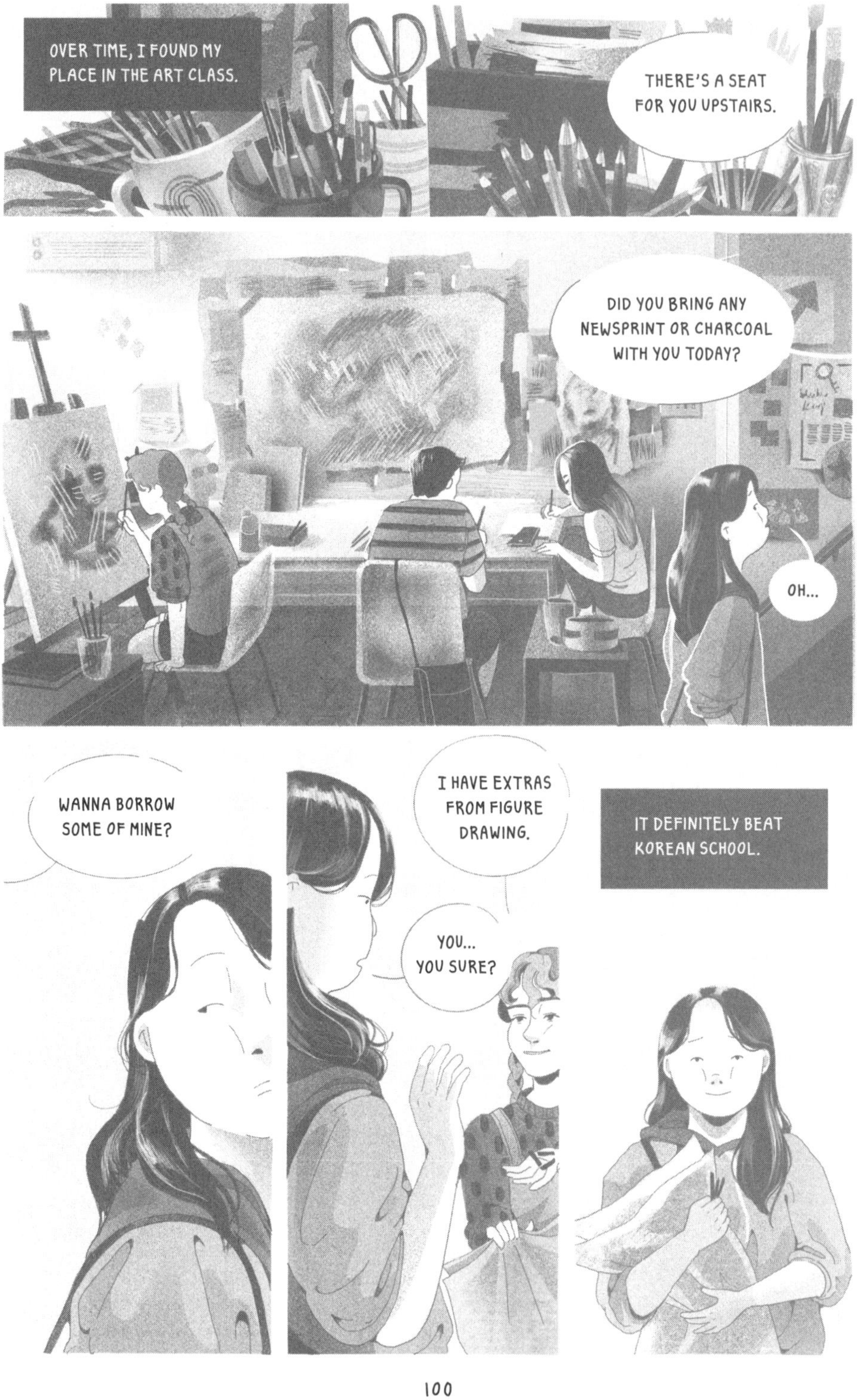
OVER TIME, I FOUND MY PLACE IN THE ART CLASS.
THERE'S A SEAT FOR YOU UPSTAIRS.
DID YOU BRING ANY NEWSPRINT OR CHARCOAL WITH YOU TODAY?
OH...
WANNA BORROW SOME OF MINE?
I HAVE EXTRAS FROM FIGURE DRAWING.
YOU... YOU SURE?
IT DEFINITELY BEAT KOREAN SCHOOL.

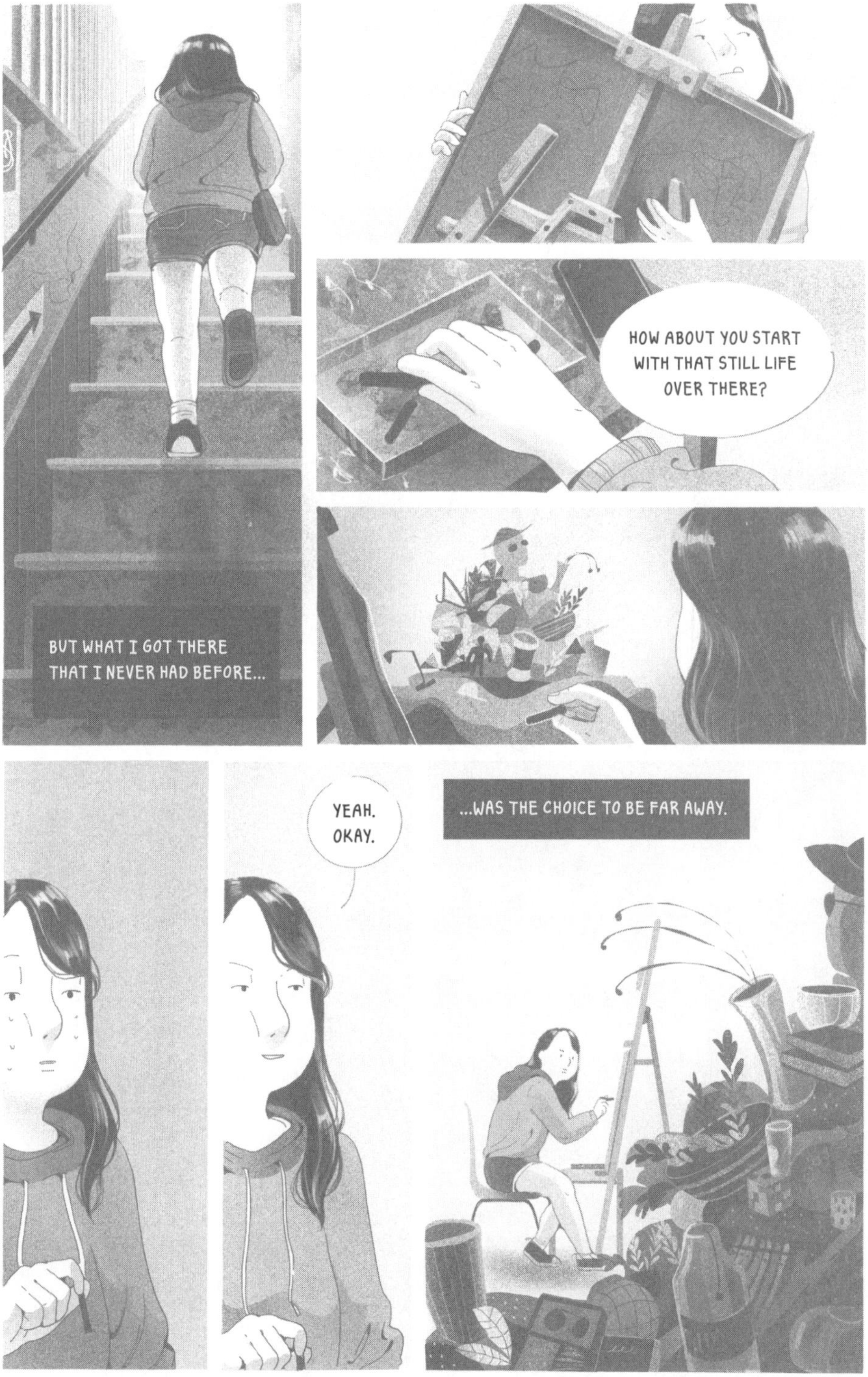
BUT WHAT I GOT THERE
THAT I NEVER HAD BEFORE...
HOW ABOUT YOU START WITH THAT STILL LIFE OVER THERE?
YEAH. OKAY.
...WAS THE CHOICE TO BE FAR AWAY.

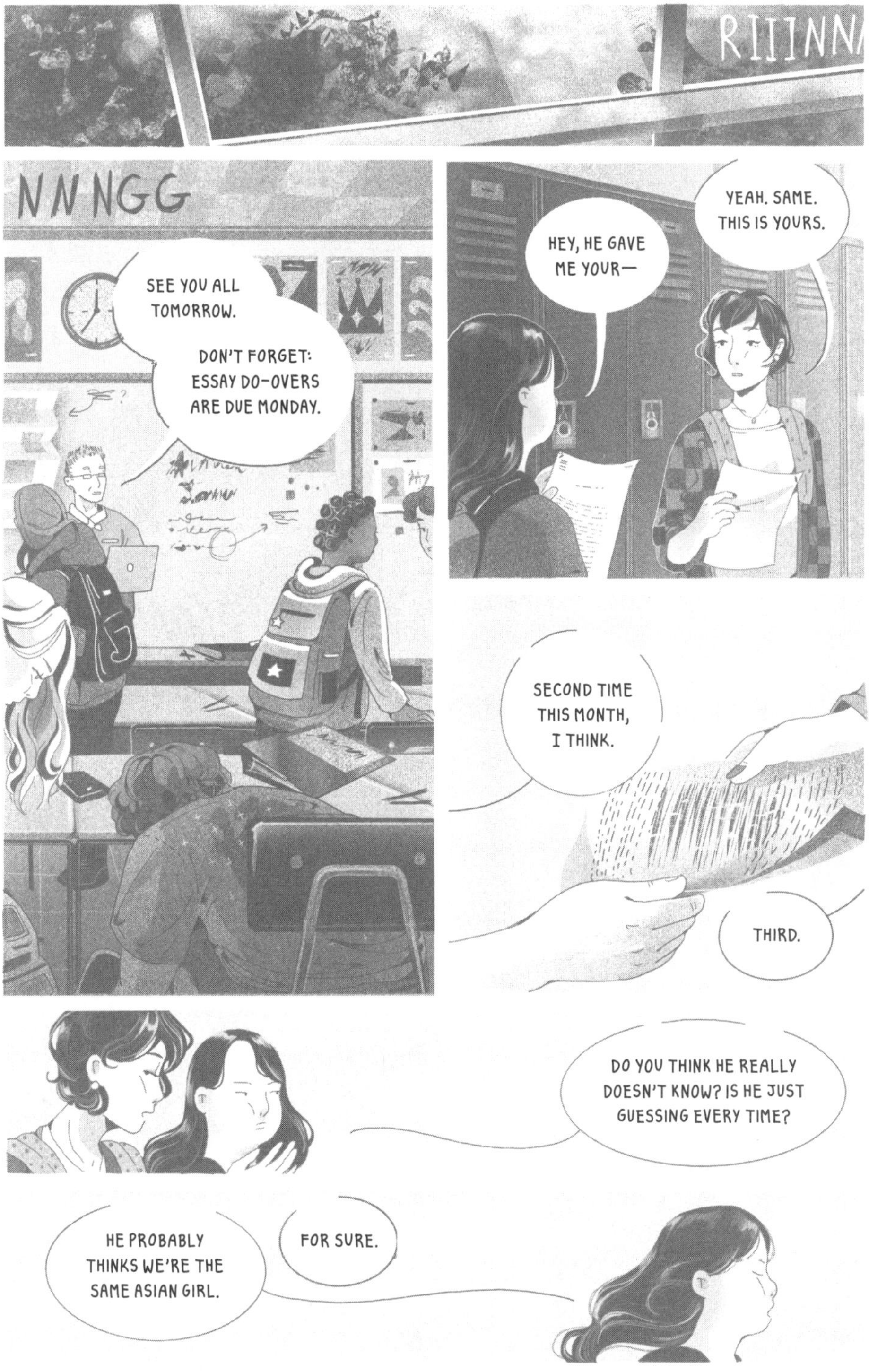
RIIINNA
NNNGG
SEE YOU ALL TOMORROW.
DON'T FORGET: ESSAY DO-OVERS ARE DUE MONDAY.
HEY, HE GAVE ME YOUR—
YEAH. SAME. THIS IS YOURS.
SECOND TIME THIS MONTH, I THINK.
THIRD.
DO YOU THINK HE REALLY DOESN'T KNOW? IS HE JUST GUESSING EVERY TIME?
HE PROBABLY THINKS WE'RE THE SAME ASIAN GIRL.
FOR SURE.

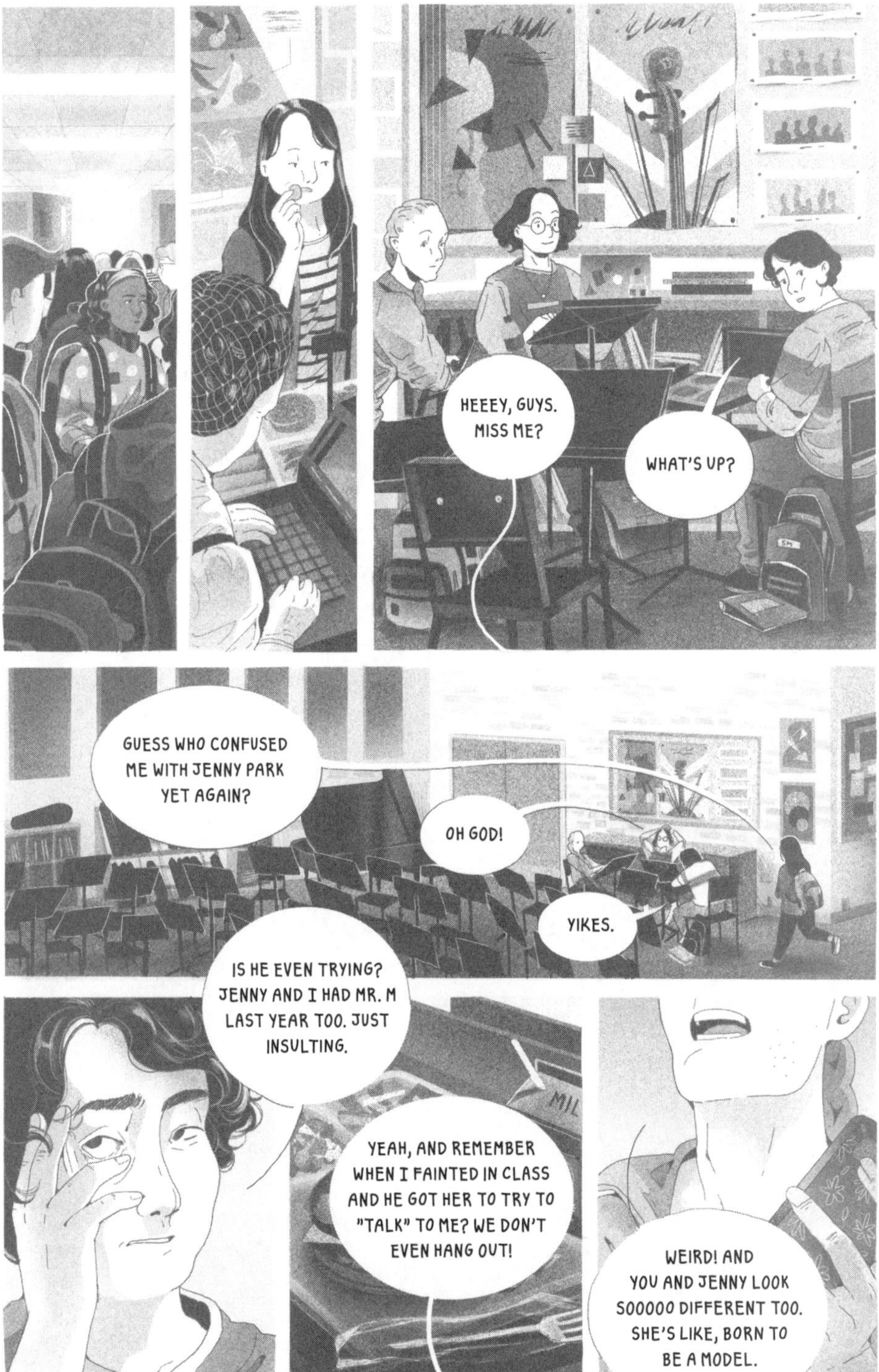
HEEEY, GUYS.
MISS ME?
WHAT'S UP?
GUESS WHO CONFUSED ME WITH JENNY PARK YET AGAIN?
OH GOD!
YIKES.
IS HE EVEN TRYING? JENNY AND I HAD MR. M LAST YEAR TOO. JUST INSULTING.
YEAH, AND REMEMBER WHEN I FAINTED IN CLASS AND HE GOT HER TO TRY TO "TALK" TO ME? WE DON'T EVEN HANG OUT!
WEIRD! AND YOU AND JENNY LOOK SOOOOO DIFFERENT TOO. SHE'S LIKE, BORN TO BE A MODEL.

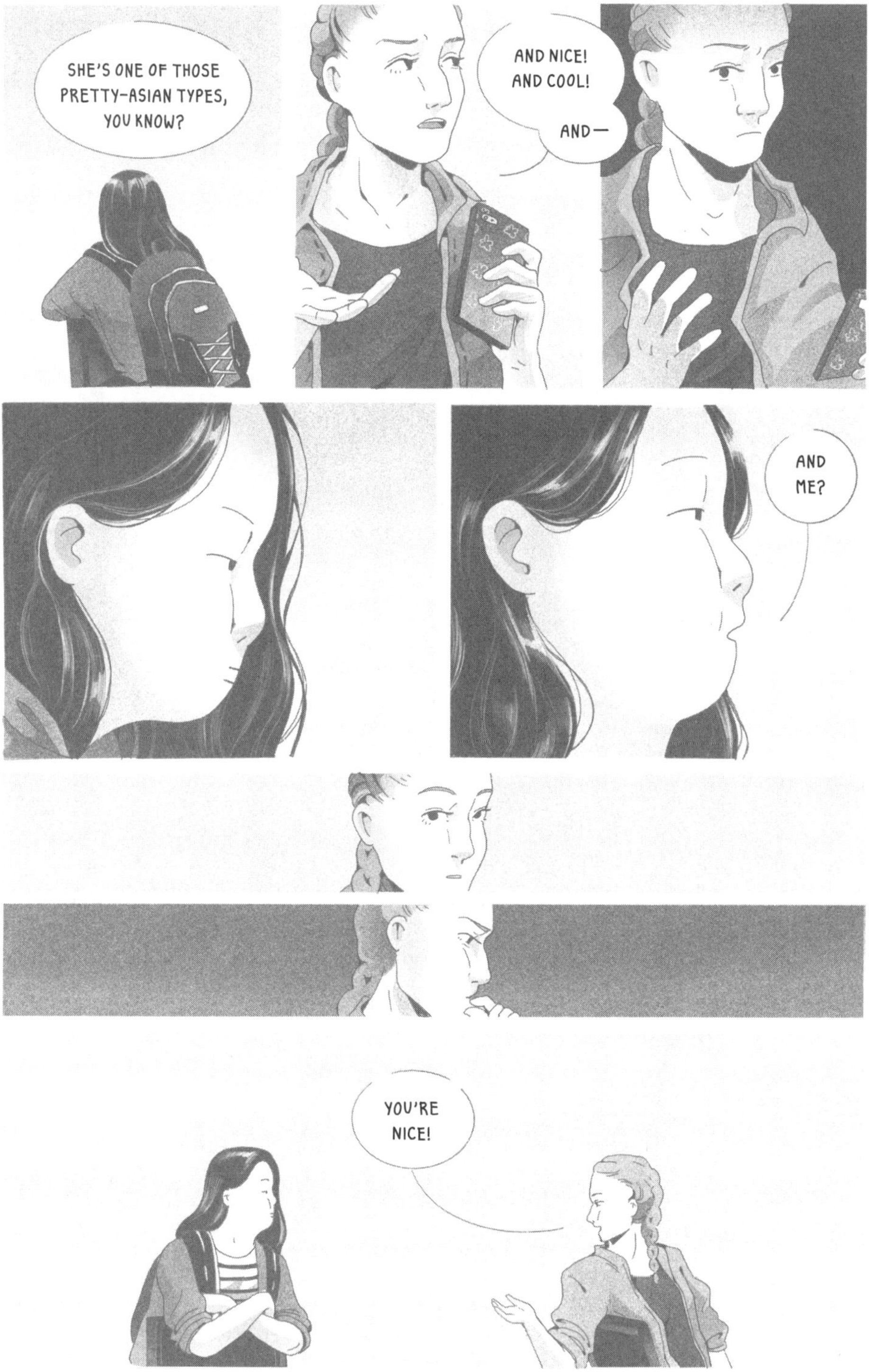
SHE'S ONE OF THOSE PRETTY-ASIAN TYPES, YOU KNOW?
AND NICE! AND COOL!
AND—
AND ME?
YOU'RE NICE!

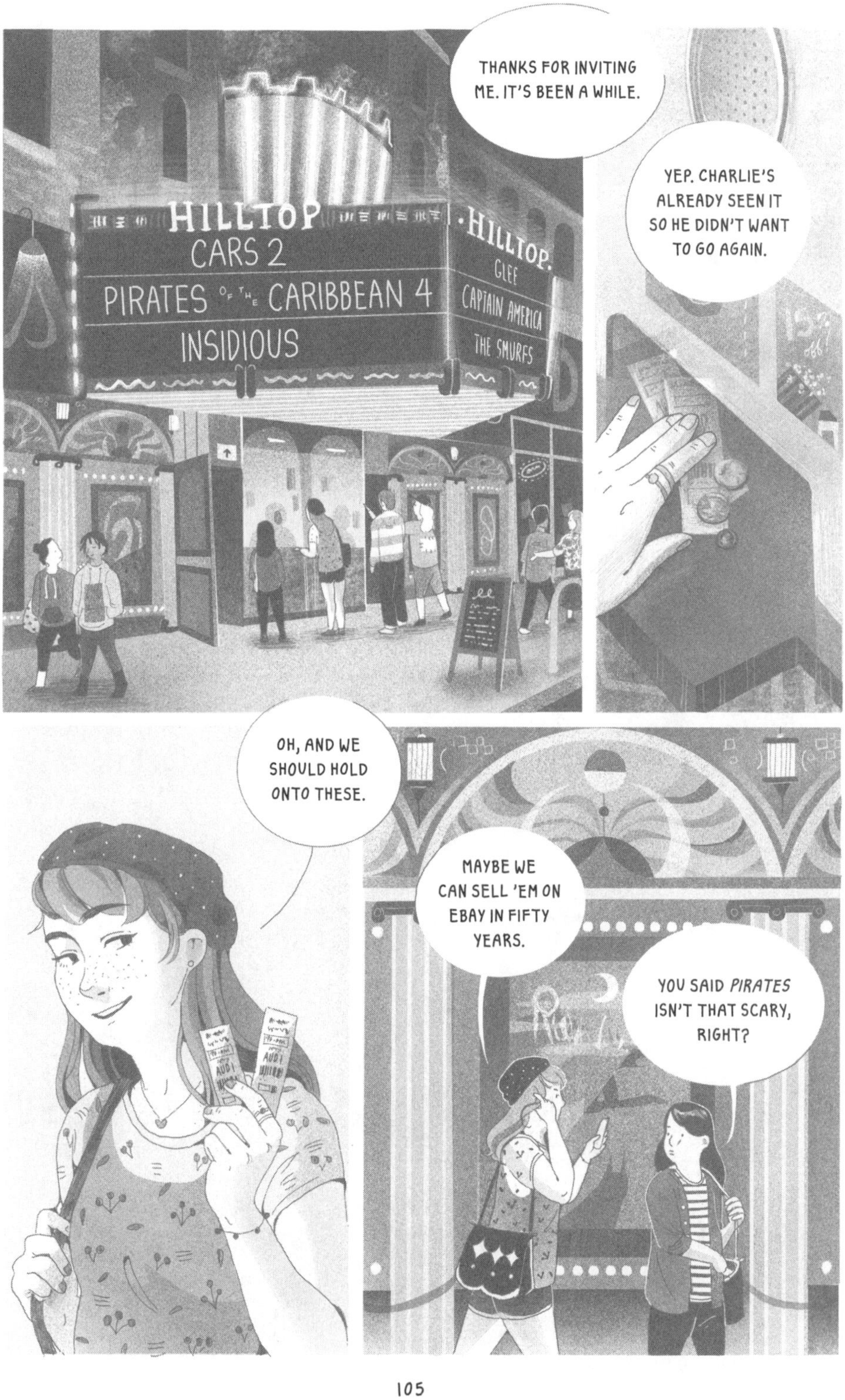
HILLTOP
CARS 2
PIRATES OF THE CARIBBEAN 4
INSIDIOUS
HILLTOP
GLEE
CAPTAIN AMERICA
THE SMURFS
THANKS FOR INVITING ME. IT'S BEEN A WHILE.
YEP. CHARLIE'S ALREADY SEEN IT SO HE DIDN'T WANT TO GO AGAIN.
OH, AND WE SHOULD HOLD ONTO THESE.
MAYBE WE CAN SELL 'EM ON EBAY IN FIFTY YEARS.
YOU SAID *PIRATES* ISN'T THAT SCARY, RIGHT?

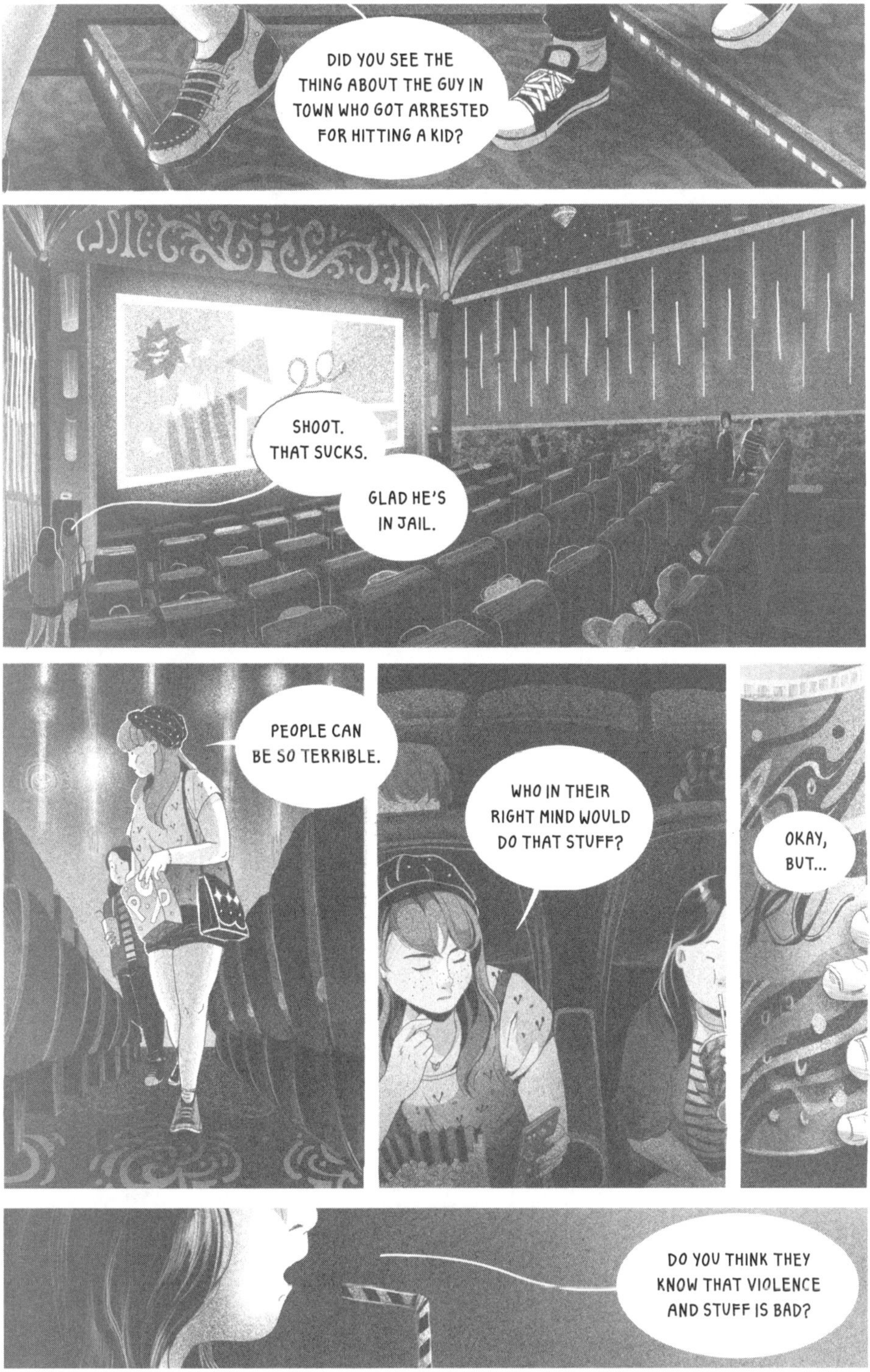
DID YOU SEE THE THING ABOUT THE GUY IN TOWN WHO GOT ARRESTED FOR HITTING A KID?
SHOOT. THAT SUCKS.
GLAD HE'S IN JAIL.
PEOPLE CAN BE SO TERRIBLE.
WHO IN THEIR RIGHT MIND WOULD DO THAT STUFF?
OKAY, BUT...
DO YOU THINK THEY KNOW THAT VIOLENCE AND STUFF IS BAD?

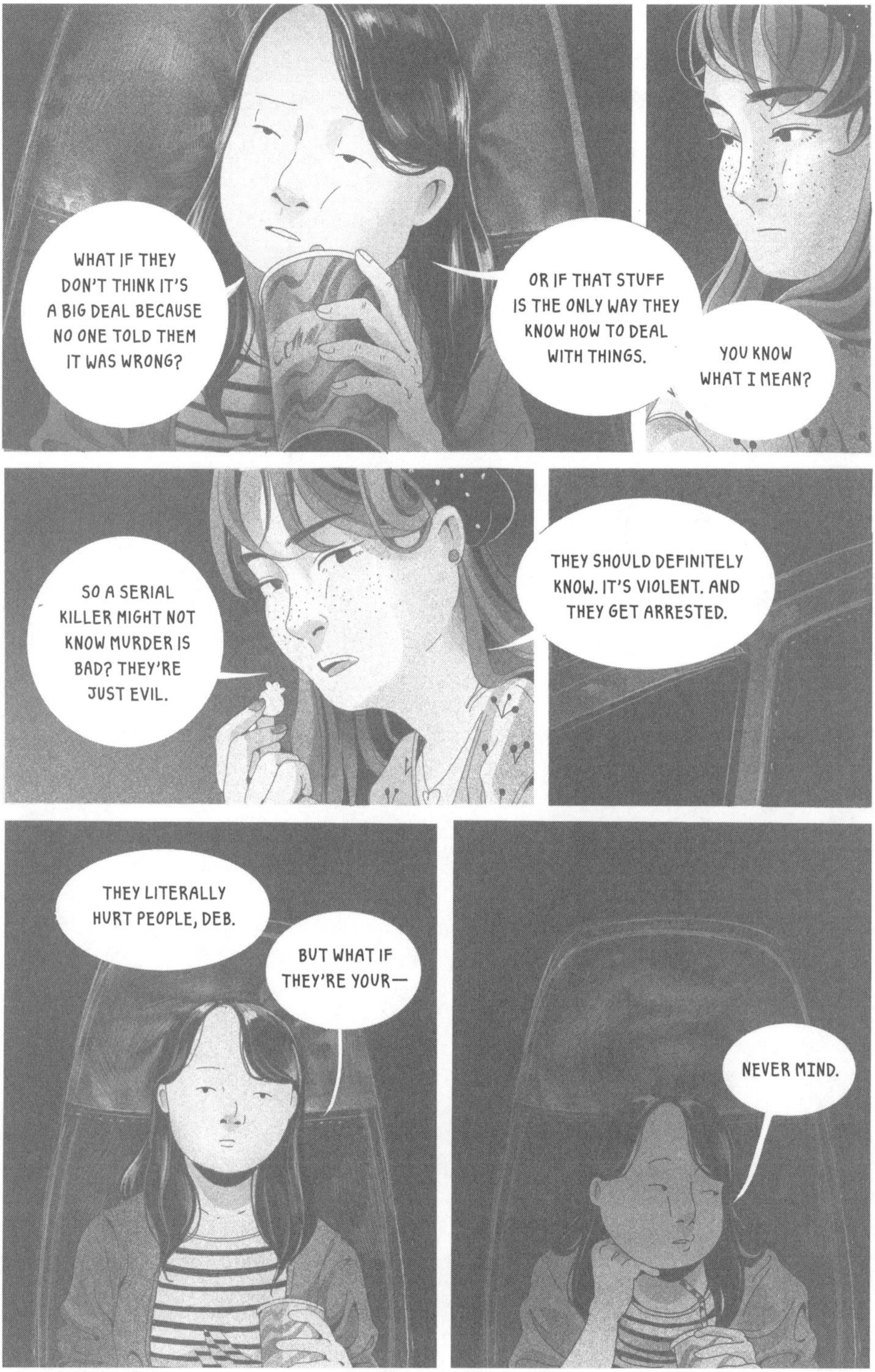
WHAT IF THEY DON'T THINK IT'S A BIG DEAL BECAUSE NO ONE TOLD THEM IT WAS WRONG?
OR IF THAT STUFF IS THE ONLY WAY THEY KNOW HOW TO DEAL WITH THINGS.
YOU KNOW WHAT I MEAN?
SO A SERIAL KILLER MIGHT NOT KNOW MURDER IS BAD? THEY'RE JUST EVIL.
THEY SHOULD DEFINITELY KNOW. IT'S VIOLENT. AND THEY GET ARRESTED.
THEY LITERALLY HURT PEOPLE, DEB.
BUT WHAT IF THEY'RE YOUR—
NEVER MIND.

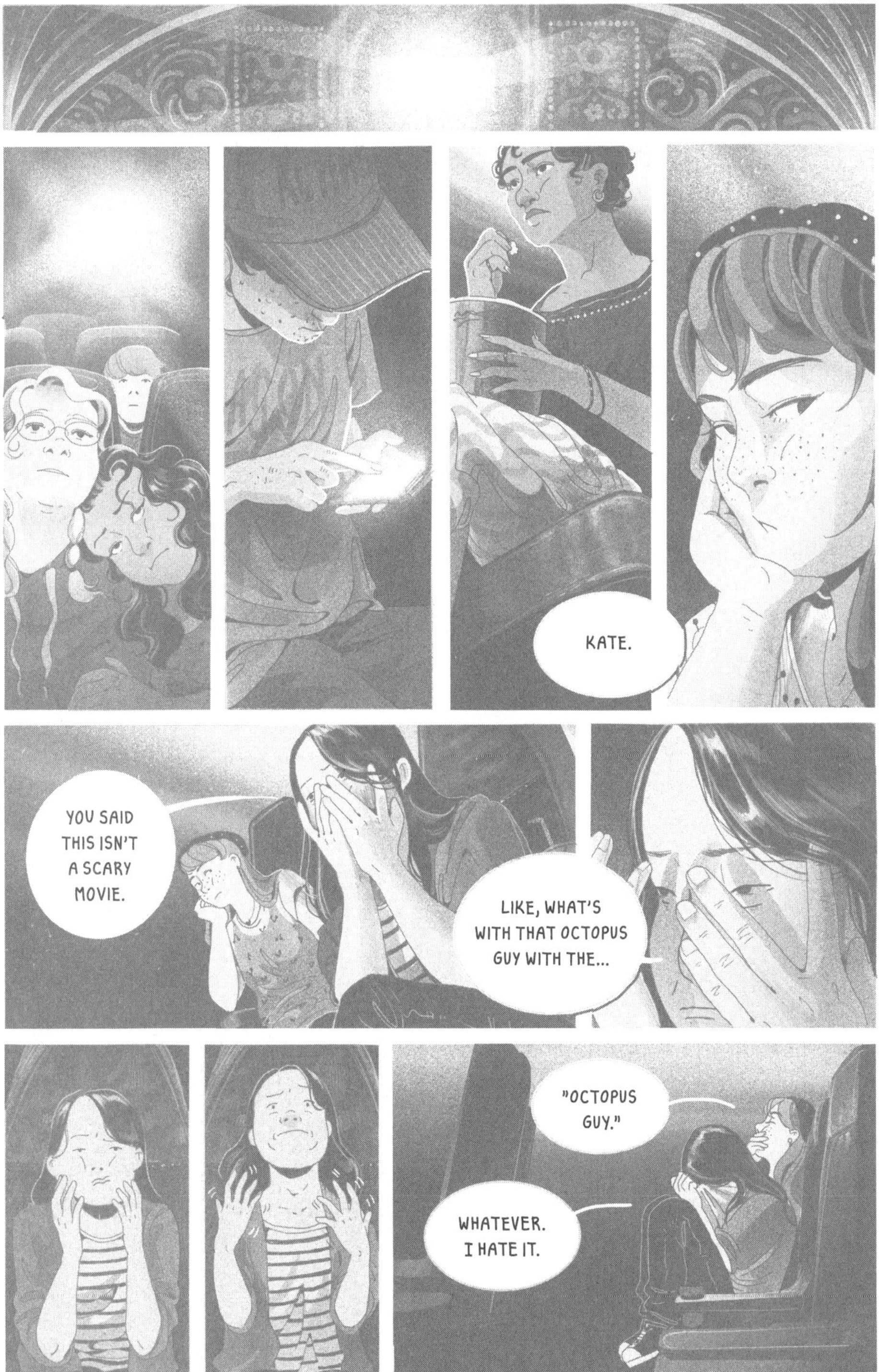
KATE.
YOU SAID THIS ISN'T A SCARY MOVIE.
LIKE, WHAT'S WITH THAT OCTOPUS GUY WITH THE...
"OCTOPUS GUY."
WHATEVER. I HATE IT.

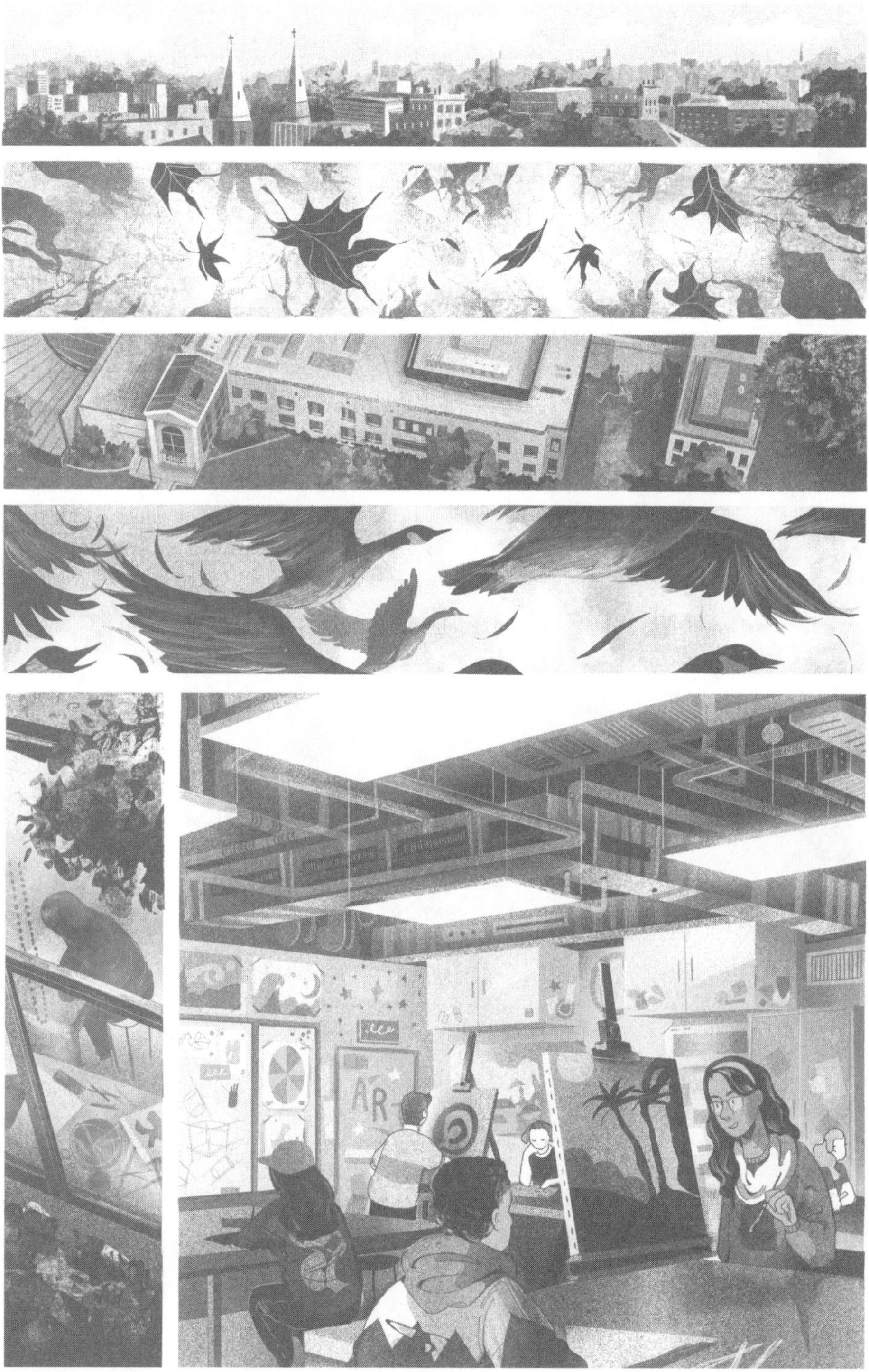
AR

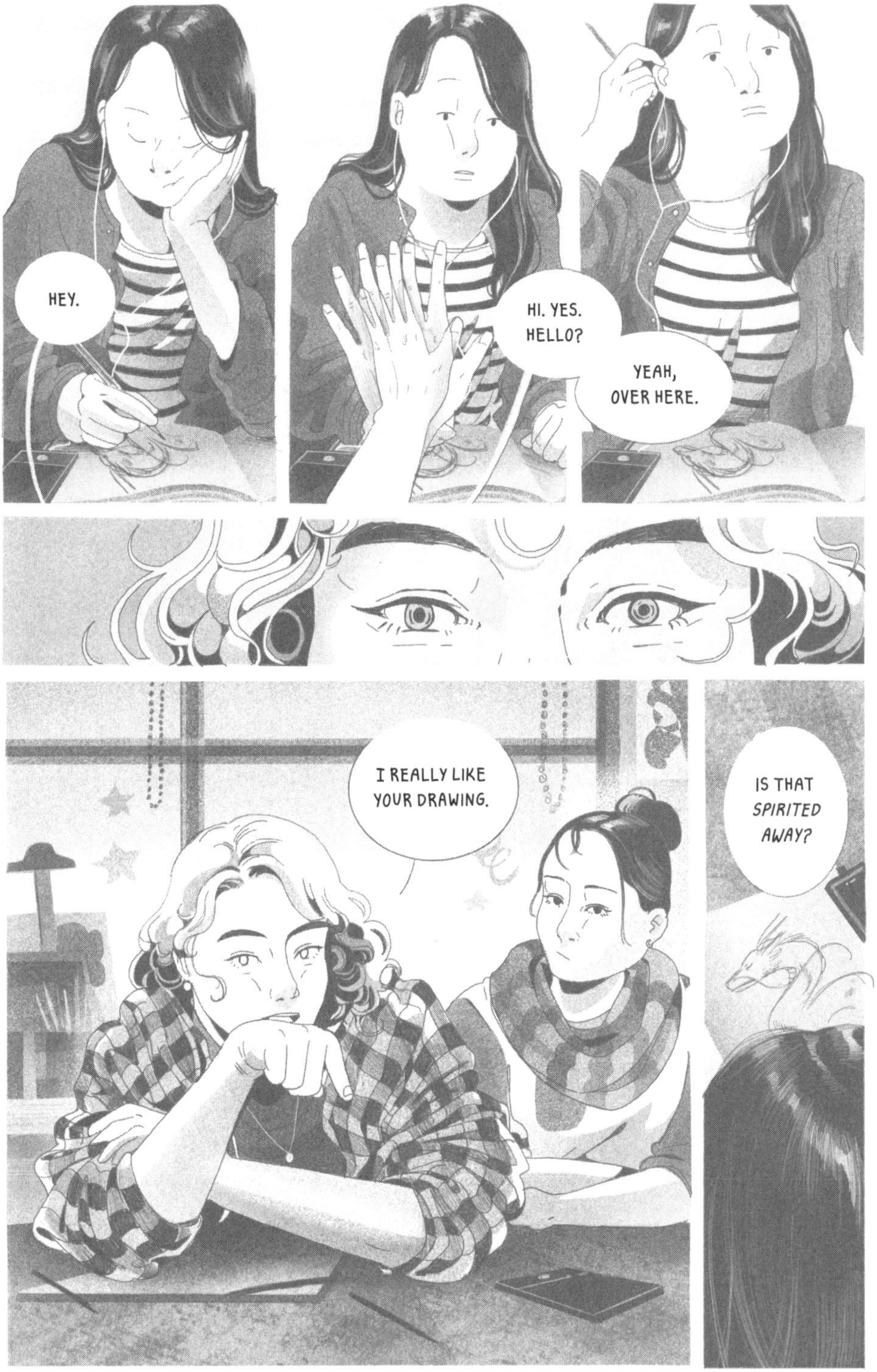
HEY.
HI. YES. HELLO?
YEAH, OVER HERE.
I REALLY LIKE YOUR DRAWING.
IS THAT *SPIRITED AWAY?*

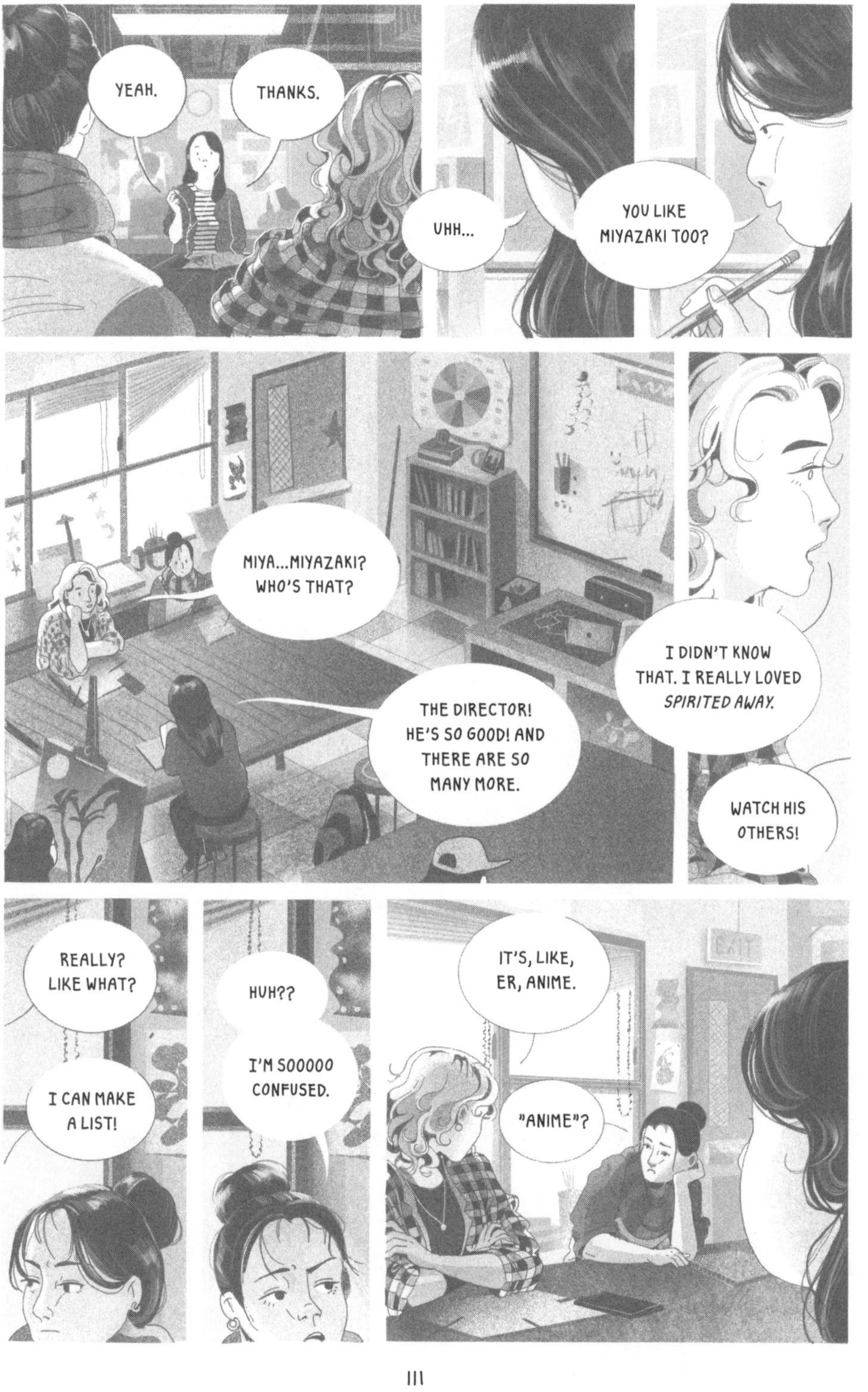
YEAH.
THANKS.
UHH...
YOU LIKE MIYAZAKI TOO?
MIYA...MIYAZAKI? WHO'S THAT?
THE DIRECTOR! HE'S SO GOOD! AND THERE ARE SO MANY MORE.
I DIDN'T KNOW THAT. I REALLY LOVED *SPIRITED AWAY.*
WATCH HIS OTHERS!
REALLY? LIKE WHAT?
I CAN MAKE A LIST!
HUH??
I'M SOOOOO CONFUSED.
IT'S, LIKE, ER, ANIME.
"ANIME"?

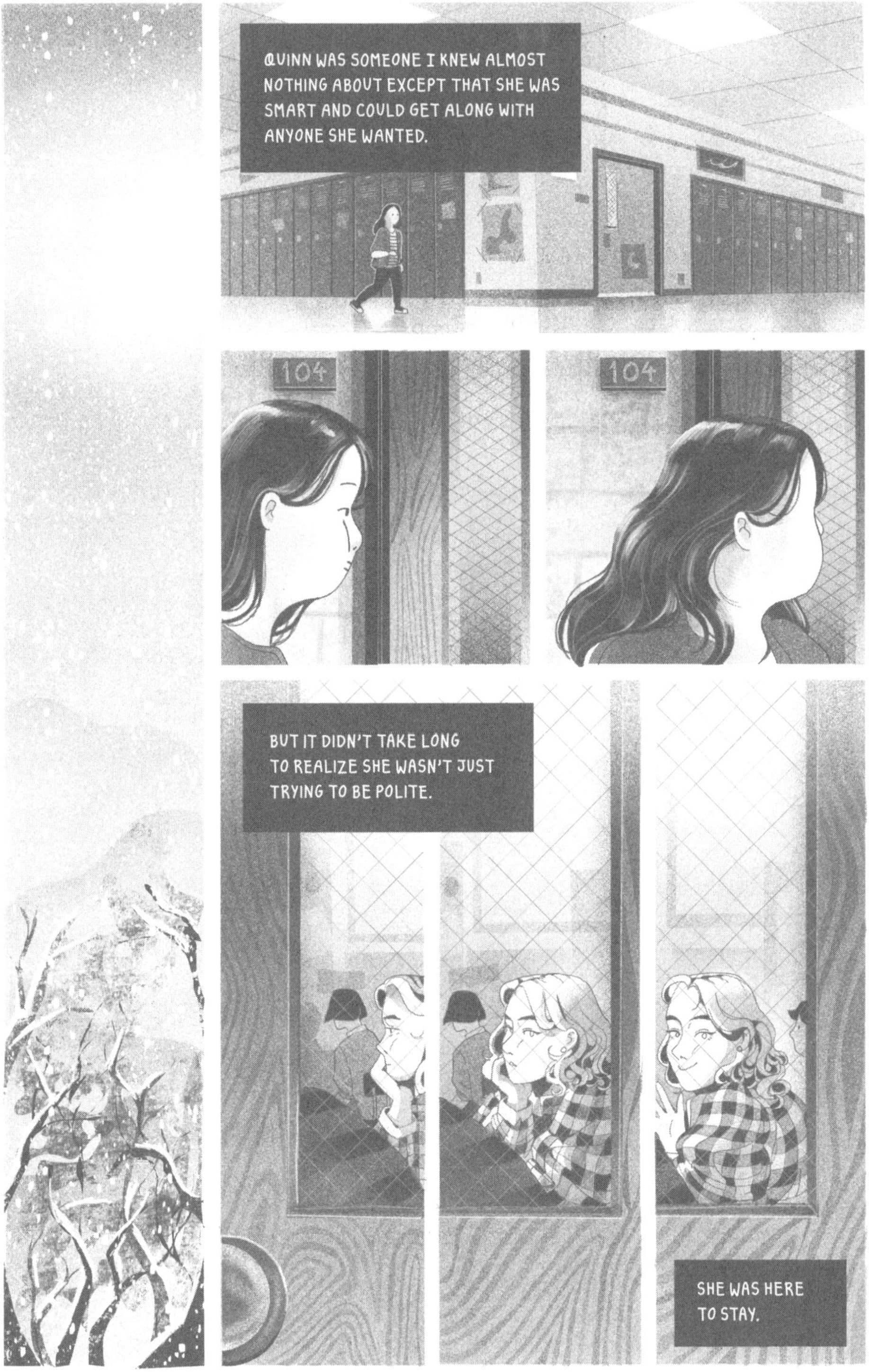
QUINN WAS SOMEONE I KNEW ALMOST NOTHING ABOUT EXCEPT THAT SHE WAS SMART AND COULD GET ALONG WITH ANYONE SHE WANTED.
104
104
BUT IT DIDN'T TAKE LONG TO REALIZE SHE WASN'T JUST TRYING TO BE POLITE.
SHE WAS HERE TO STAY.

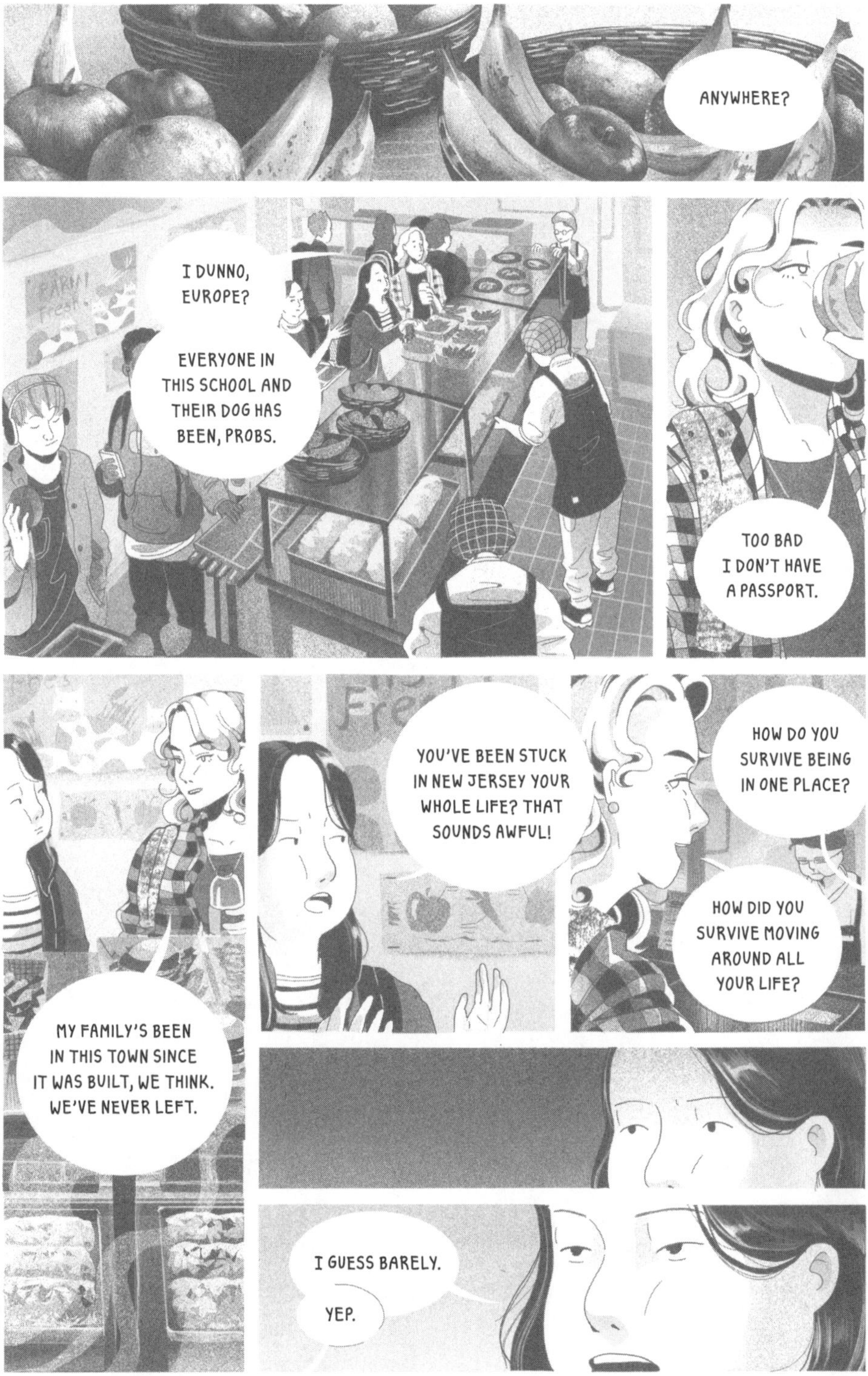
ANYWHERE?
I DUNNO, EUROPE?
EVERYONE IN THIS SCHOOL AND THEIR DOG HAS BEEN, PROBS.
TOO BAD I DON'T HAVE A PASSPORT.
MY FAMILY'S BEEN IN THIS TOWN SINCE IT WAS BUILT, WE THINK. WE'VE NEVER LEFT.
YOU'VE BEEN STUCK IN NEW JERSEY YOUR WHOLE LIFE? THAT SOUNDS AWFUL!
HOW DO YOU SURVIVE BEING IN ONE PLACE?
HOW DID YOU SURVIVE MOVING AROUND ALL YOUR LIFE?
I GUESS BARELY.
YEP.

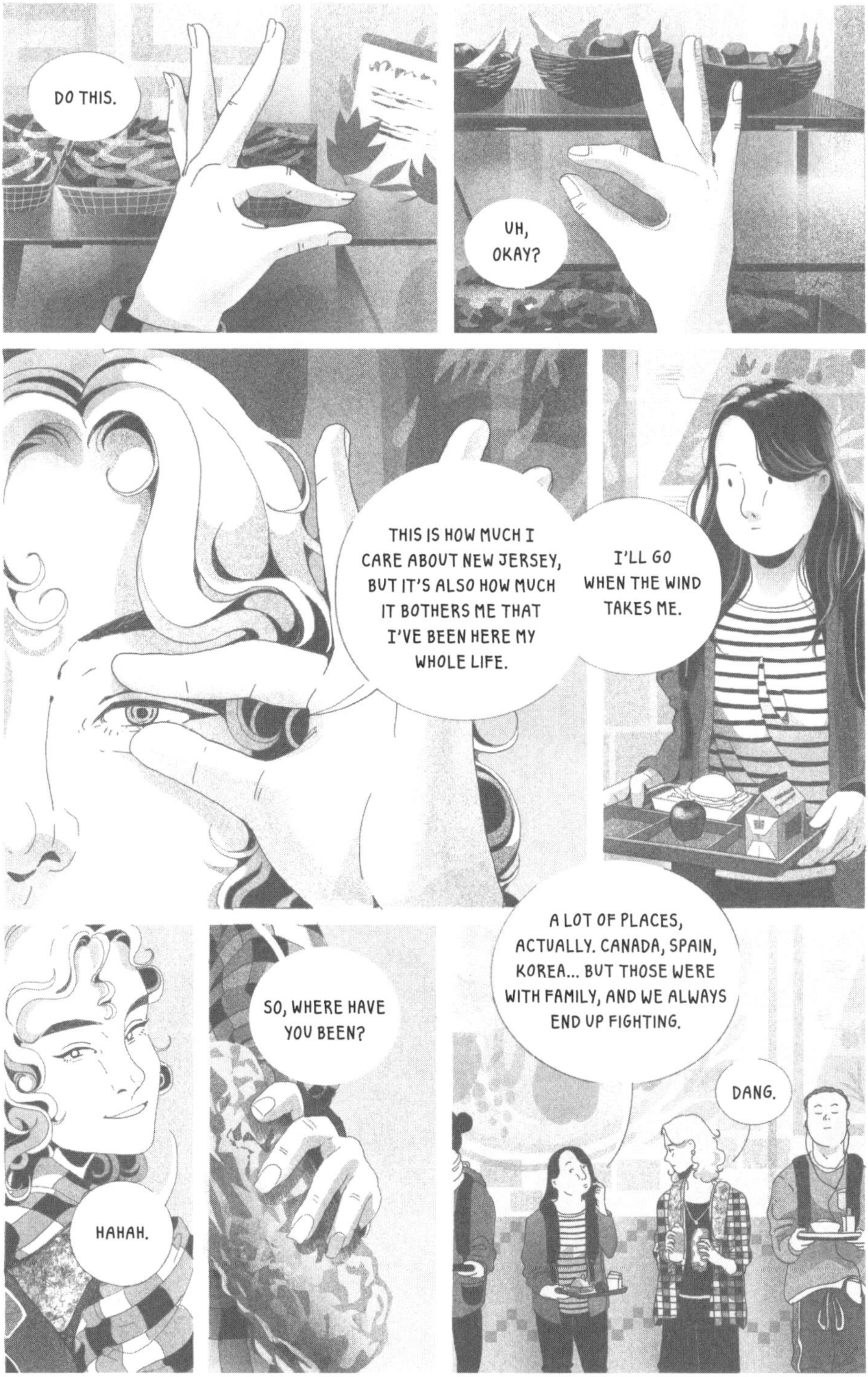
DO THIS.
UH, OKAY?
THIS IS HOW MUCH I CARE ABOUT NEW JERSEY, BUT IT'S ALSO HOW MUCH IT BOTHERS ME THAT I'VE BEEN HERE MY WHOLE LIFE.
I'LL GO WHEN THE WIND TAKES ME.
HAHAH.
SO, WHERE HAVE YOU BEEN?
A LOT OF PLACES, ACTUALLY. CANADA, SPAIN, KOREA... BUT THOSE WERE WITH FAMILY, AND WE ALWAYS END UP FIGHTING.
DANG.

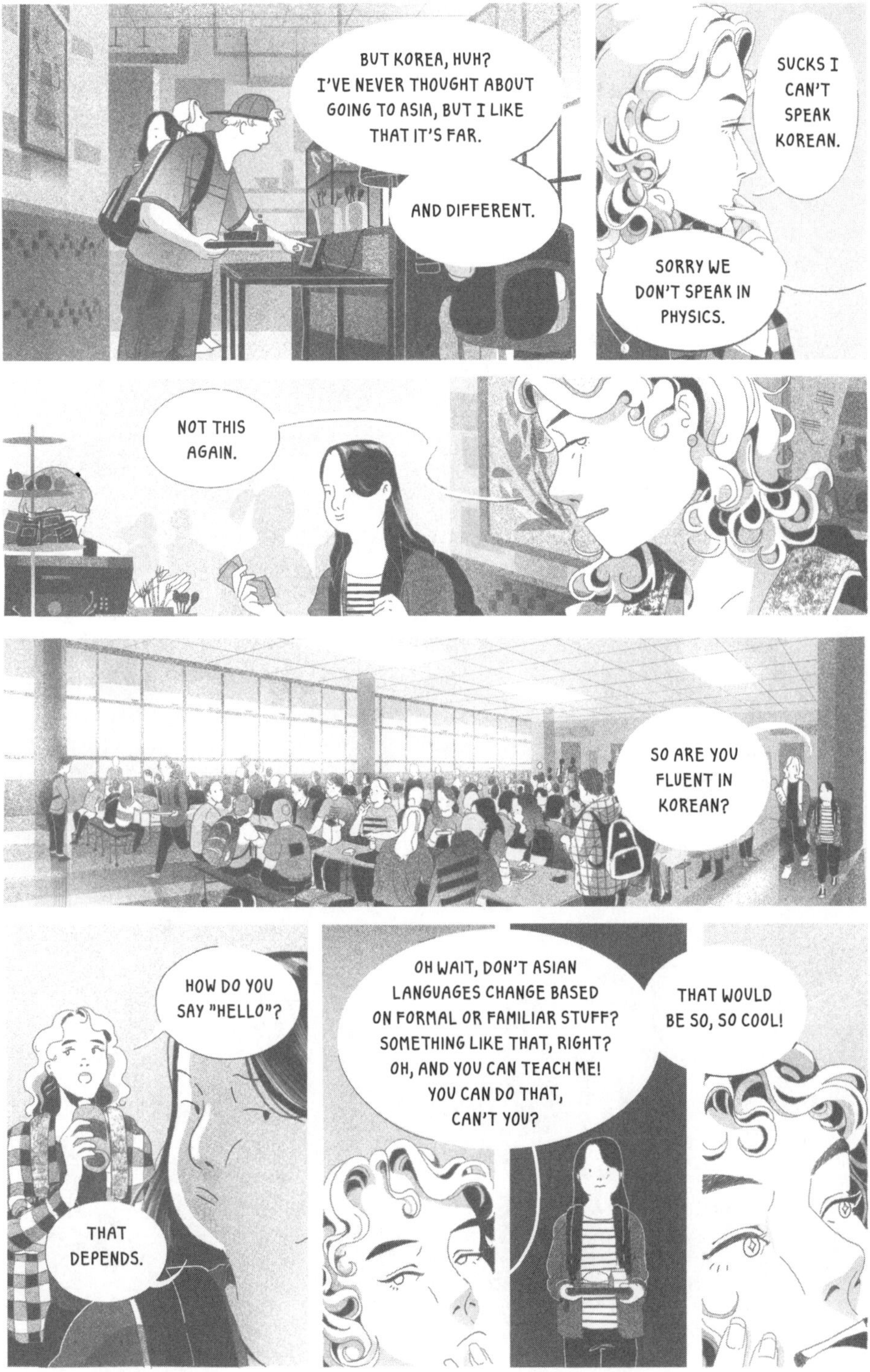
BUT KOREA, HUH? I'VE NEVER THOUGHT ABOUT GOING TO ASIA, BUT I LIKE THAT IT'S FAR.
AND DIFFERENT.
SUCKS I CAN'T SPEAK KOREAN.
SORRY WE DON'T SPEAK IN PHYSICS.
NOT THIS AGAIN.
SO ARE YOU FLUENT IN KOREAN?
HOW DO YOU SAY "HELLO"?
THAT DEPENDS.
OH WAIT, DON'T ASIAN LANGUAGES CHANGE BASED ON FORMAL OR FAMILIAR STUFF? SOMETHING LIKE THAT, RIGHT? OH, AND YOU CAN TEACH ME! YOU CAN DO THAT, CAN'T YOU?
THAT WOULD BE SO, SO COOL!

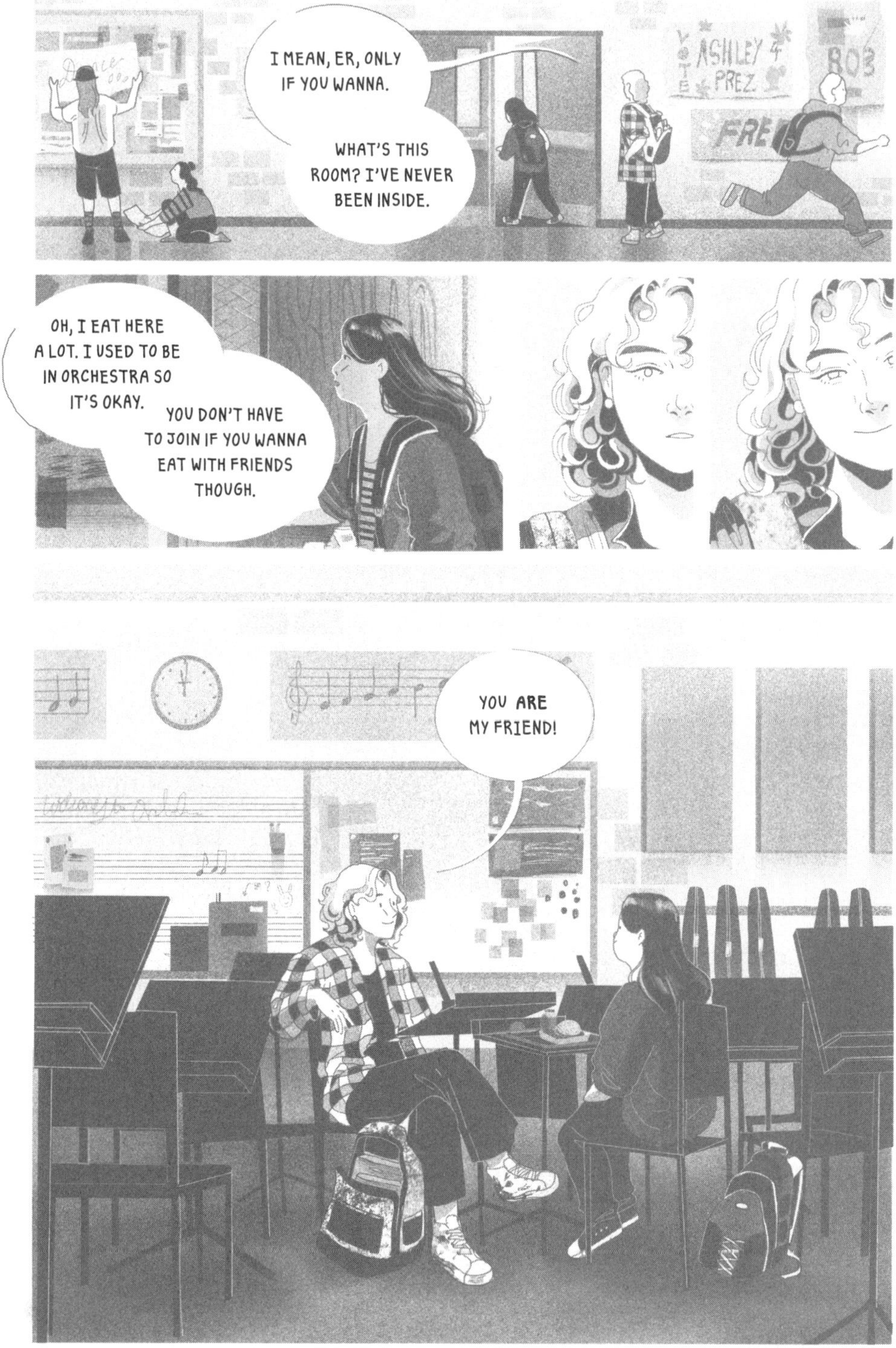
VOTE ASHLEY 4 PREZ.
I MEAN, ER, ONLY IF YOU WANNA.
WHAT'S THIS ROOM? I'VE NEVER BEEN INSIDE.
OH, I EAT HERE A LOT. I USED TO BE IN ORCHESTRA SO IT'S OKAY.
YOU DON'T HAVE TO JOIN IF YOU WANNA EAT WITH FRIENDS THOUGH.
YOU **ARE** MY FRIEND!

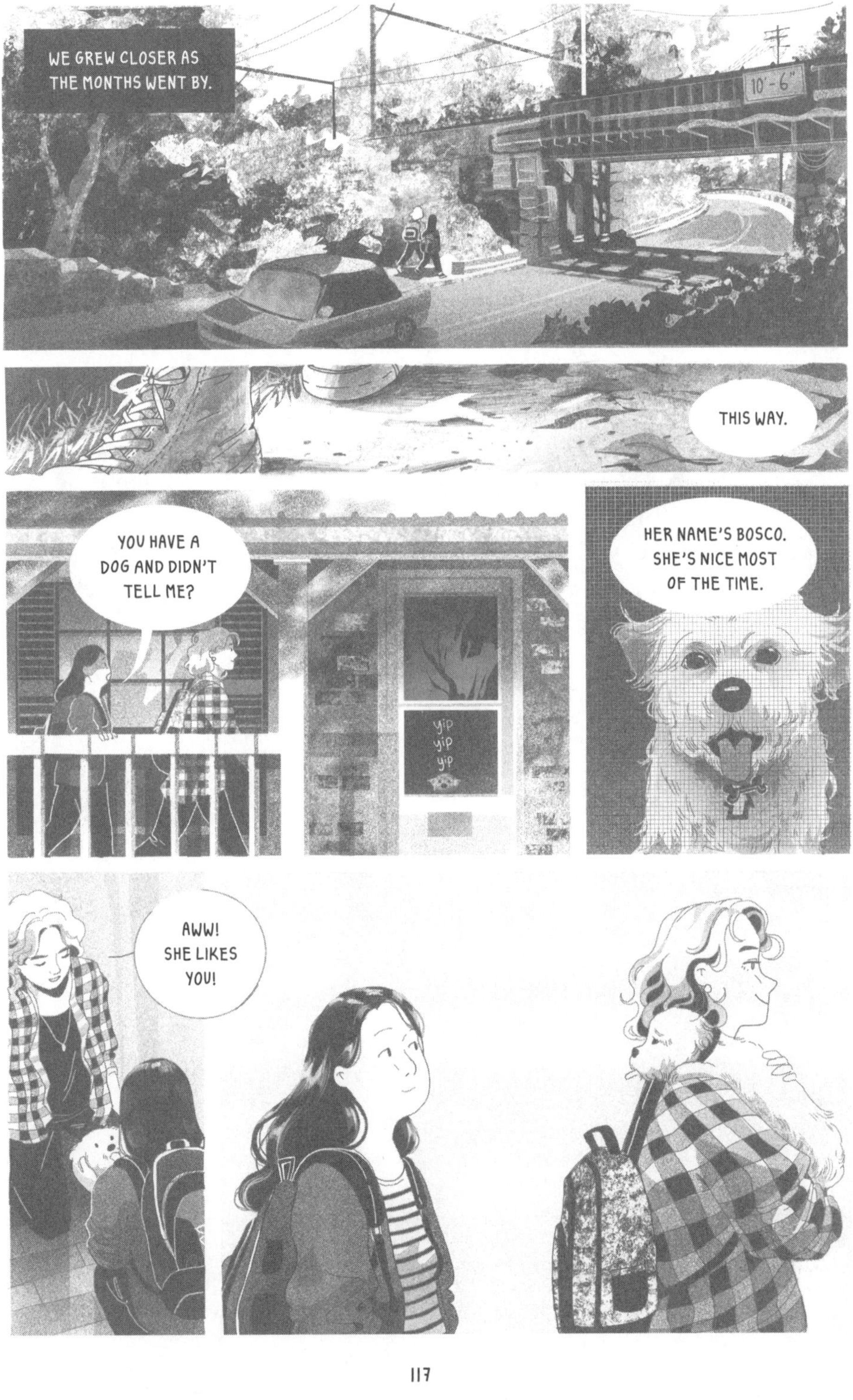
WE GREW CLOSER AS THE MONTHS WENT BY.
10'-6"
THIS WAY.
YOU HAVE A DOG AND DIDN'T TELL ME?
yip yip yip
HER NAME'S BOSCO. SHE'S NICE MOST OF THE TIME.
AWW! SHE LIKES YOU!

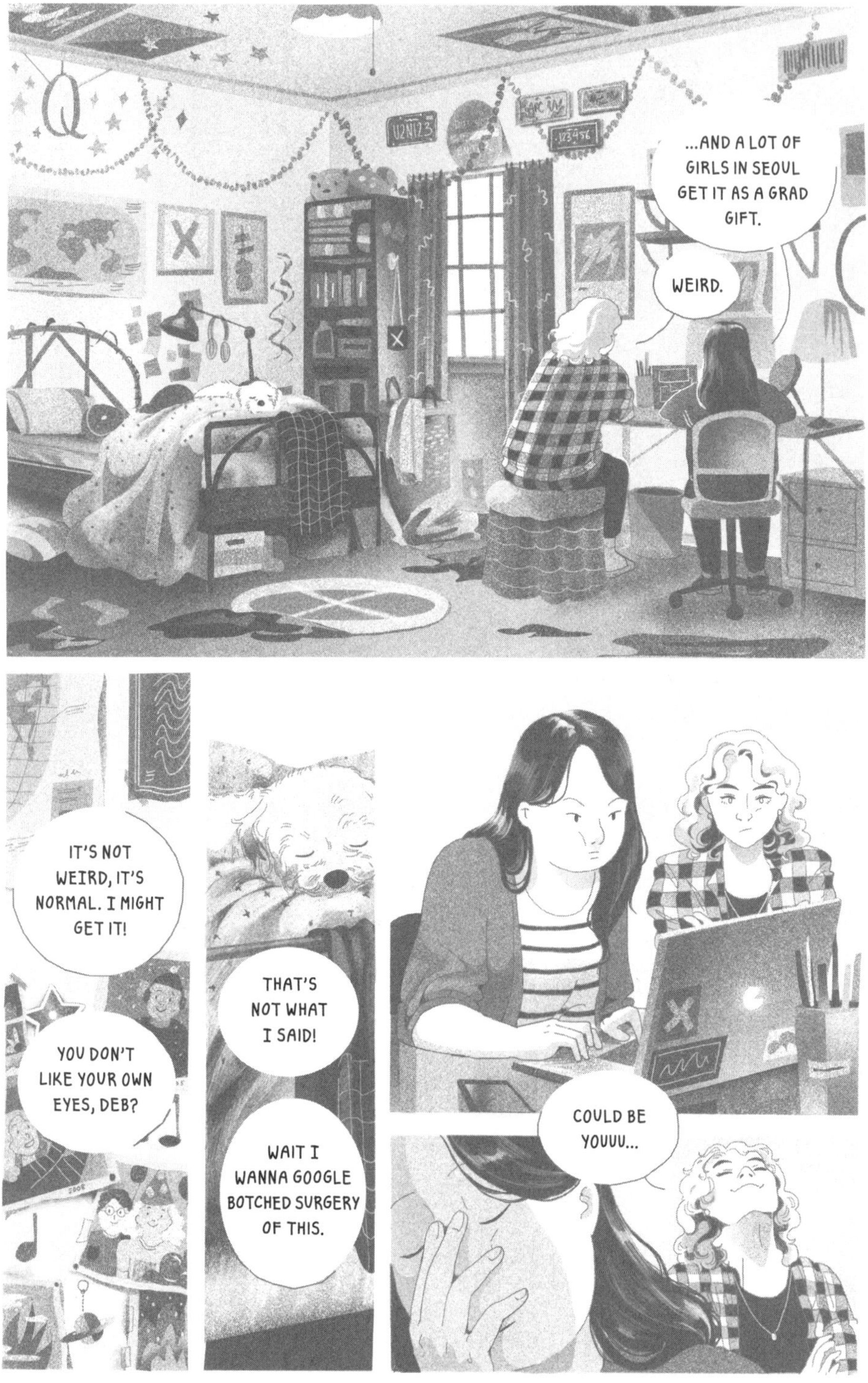
...AND A LOT OF GIRLS IN SEOUL GET IT AS A GRAD GIFT.
WEIRD.
IT'S NOT WEIRD, IT'S NORMAL. I MIGHT GET IT!
YOU DON'T LIKE YOUR OWN EYES, DEB?
THAT'S NOT WHAT I SAID!
WAIT I WANNA GOOGLE BOTCHED SURGERY OF THIS.
COULD BE YOUUU...

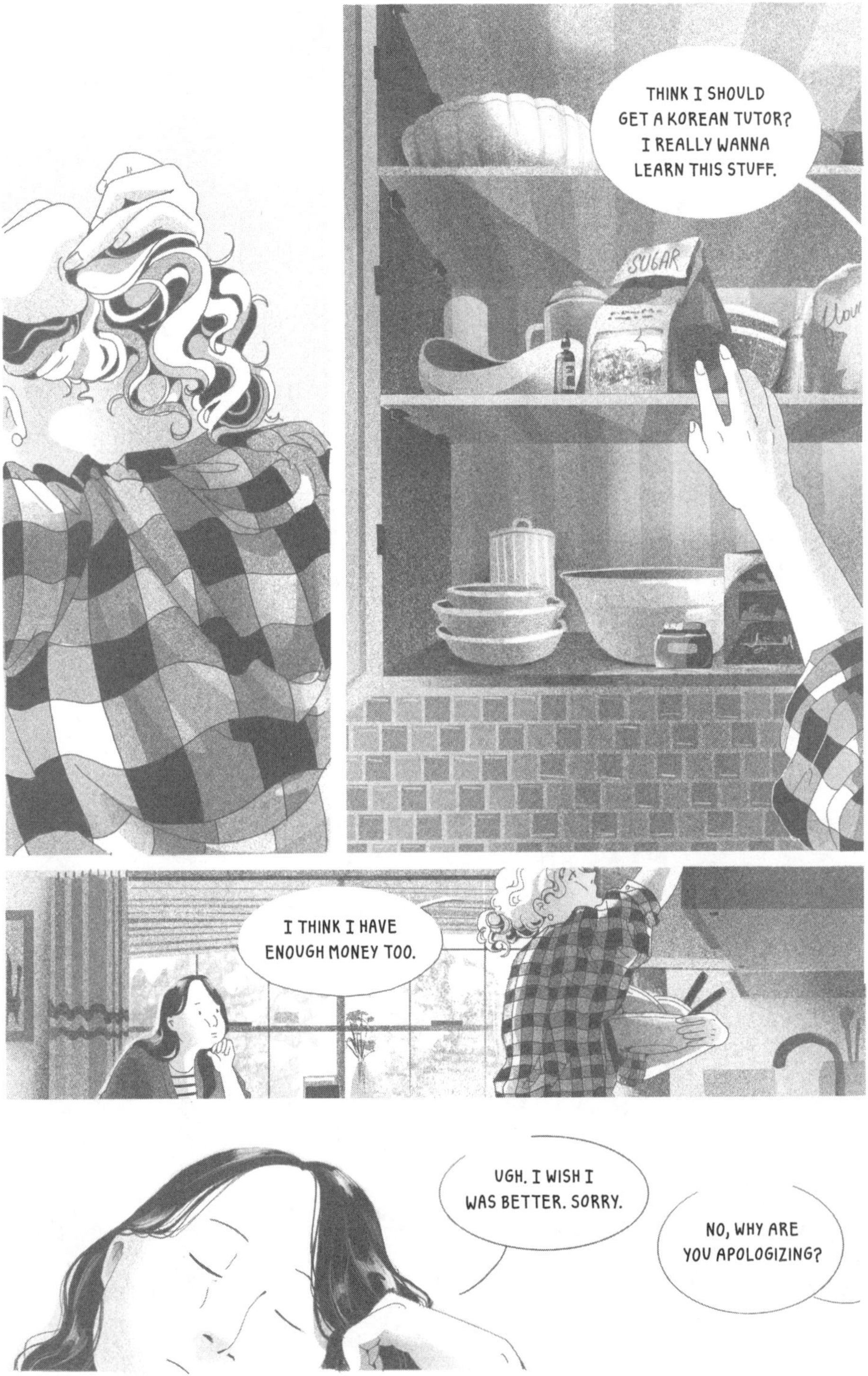
THINK I SHOULD GET A KOREAN TUTOR? I REALLY WANNA LEARN THIS STUFF.
SUGAR
I THINK I HAVE ENOUGH MONEY TOO.
UGH. I WISH I WAS BETTER. SORRY.
NO, WHY ARE YOU APOLOGIZING?

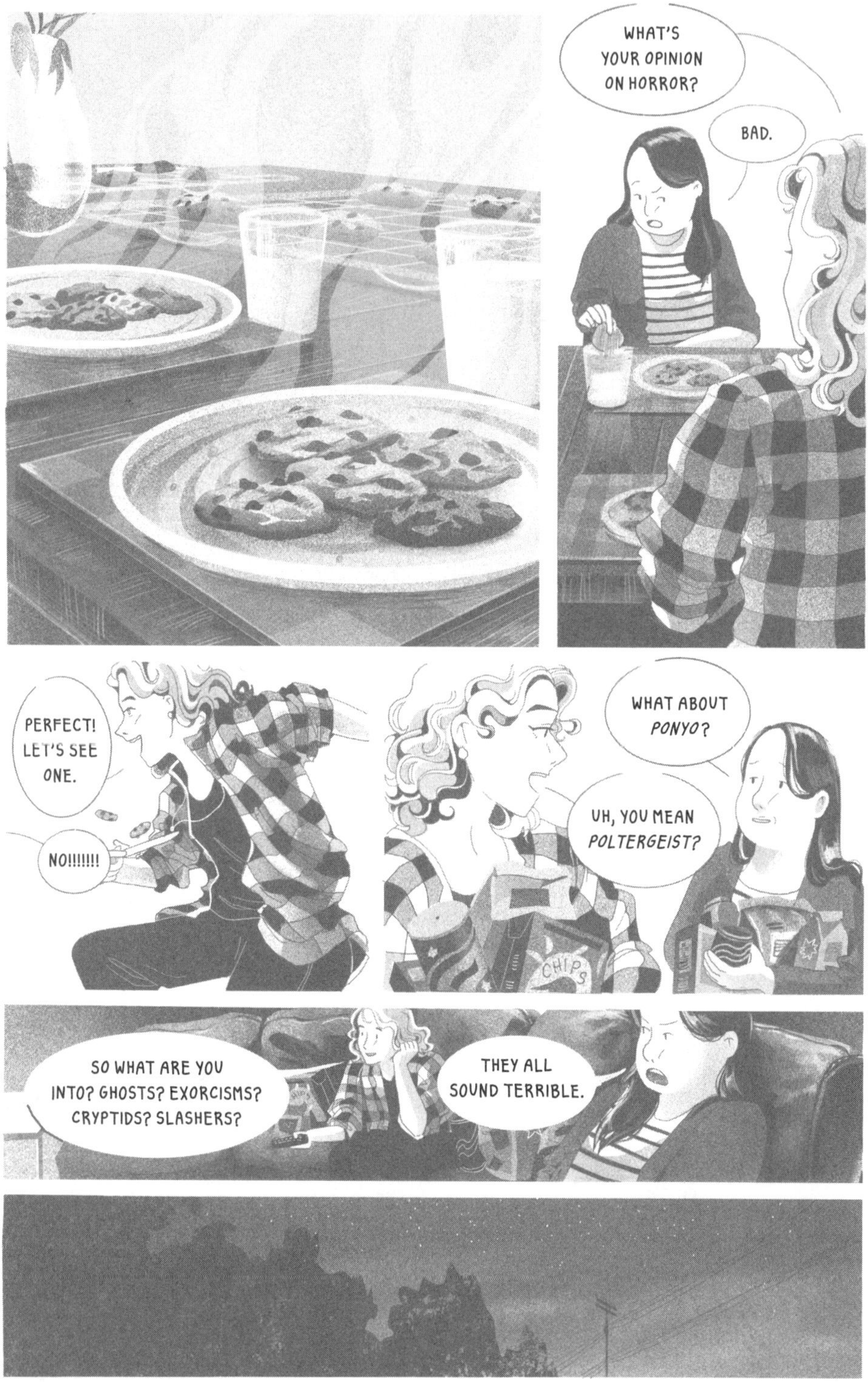
WHAT'S YOUR OPINION ON HORROR?
BAD.
PERFECT! LET'S SEE ONE.
NO!!!!!!!
WHAT ABOUT *PONYO*?
UH, YOU MEAN *POLTERGEIST*?
CHIPS
SO WHAT ARE YOU INTO? GHOSTS? EXORCISMS? CRYPTIDS? SLASHERS?
THEY ALL SOUND TERRIBLE.

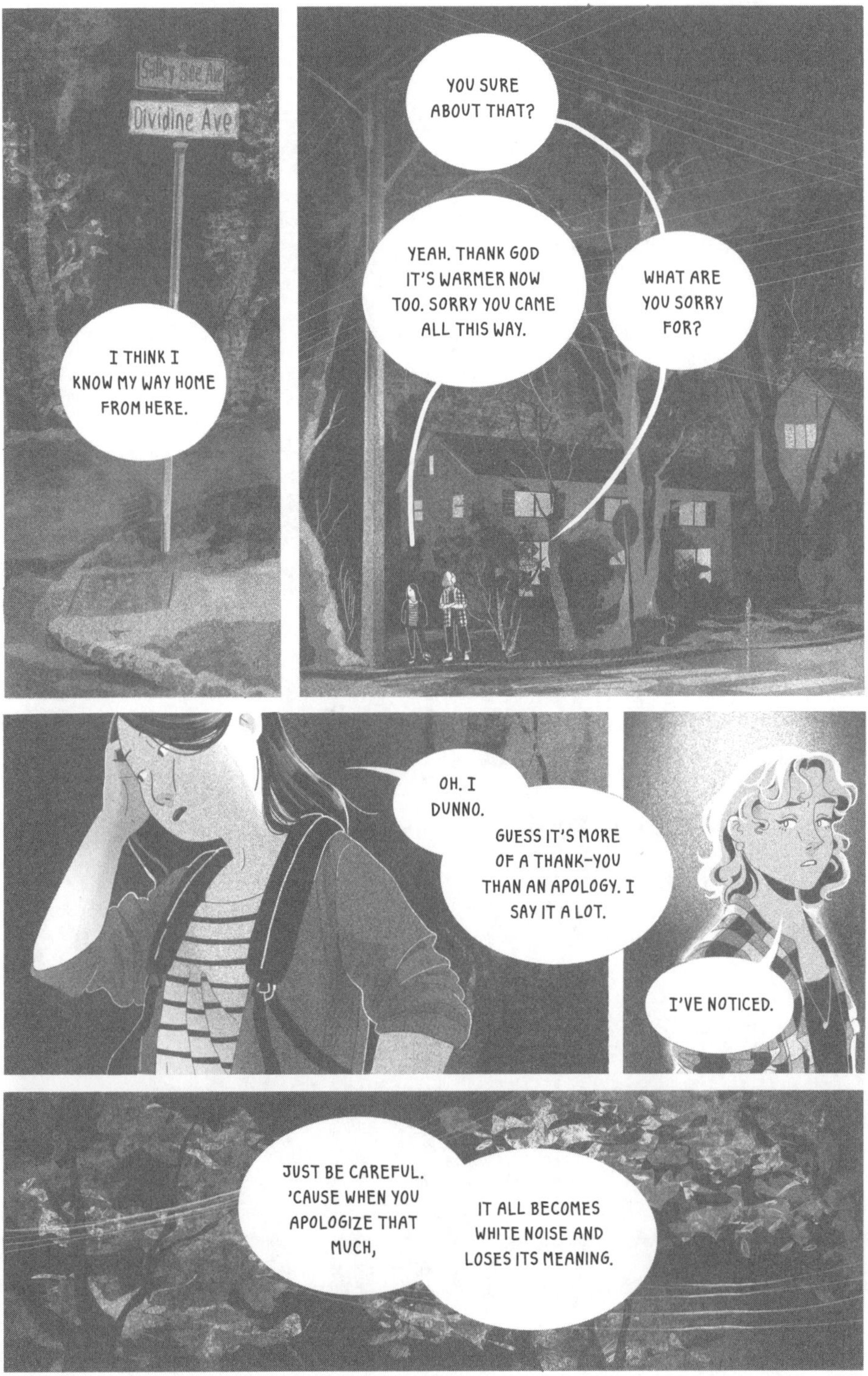
Dividine Ave
I THINK I KNOW MY WAY HOME FROM HERE.
YOU SURE ABOUT THAT?
YEAH. THANK GOD IT'S WARMER NOW TOO. SORRY YOU CAME ALL THIS WAY.
WHAT ARE YOU SORRY FOR?
OH. I DUNNO.
GUESS IT'S MORE OF A THANK-YOU THAN AN APOLOGY. I SAY IT A LOT.
I'VE NOTICED.
JUST BE CAREFUL. 'CAUSE WHEN YOU APOLOGIZE THAT MUCH,
IT ALL BECOMES WHITE NOISE AND LOSES ITS MEANING.

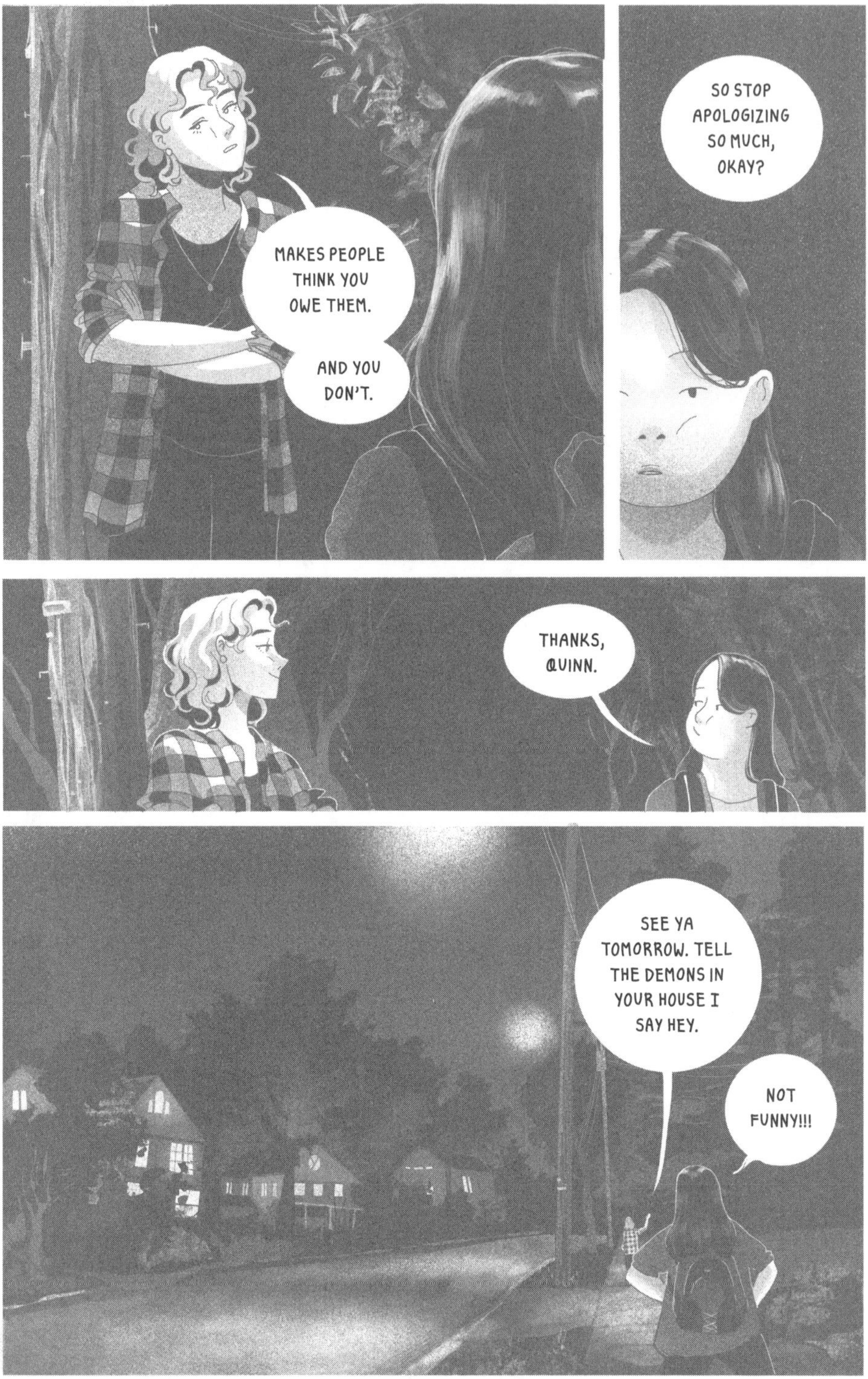
MAKES PEOPLE THINK YOU OWE THEM.
AND YOU DON'T.
SO STOP APOLOGIZING SO MUCH, OKAY?
THANKS, QUINN.
SEE YA TOMORROW. TELL THE DEMONS IN YOUR HOUSE I SAY HEY.
NOT FUNNY!!!

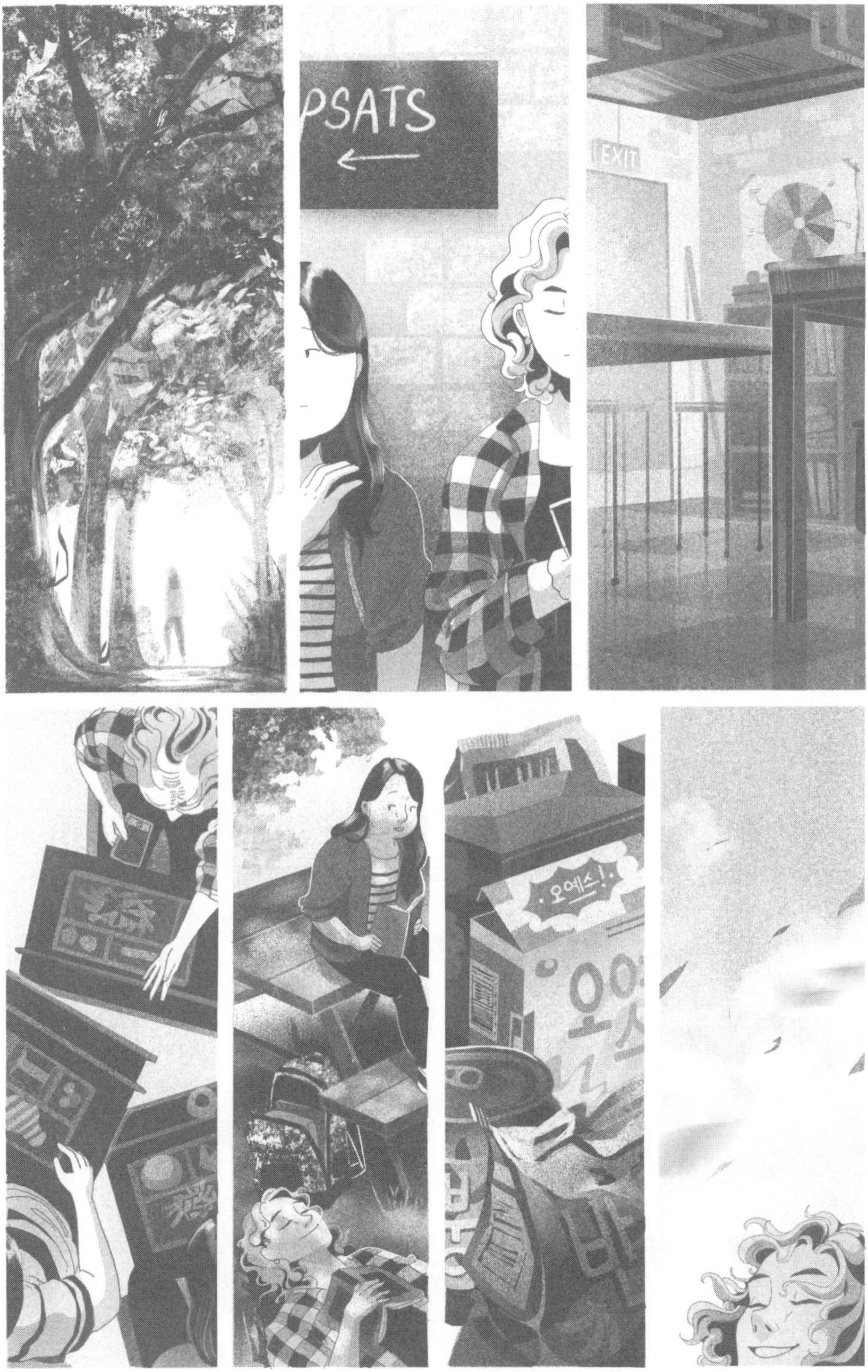
PSATS
EXIT
오예스!

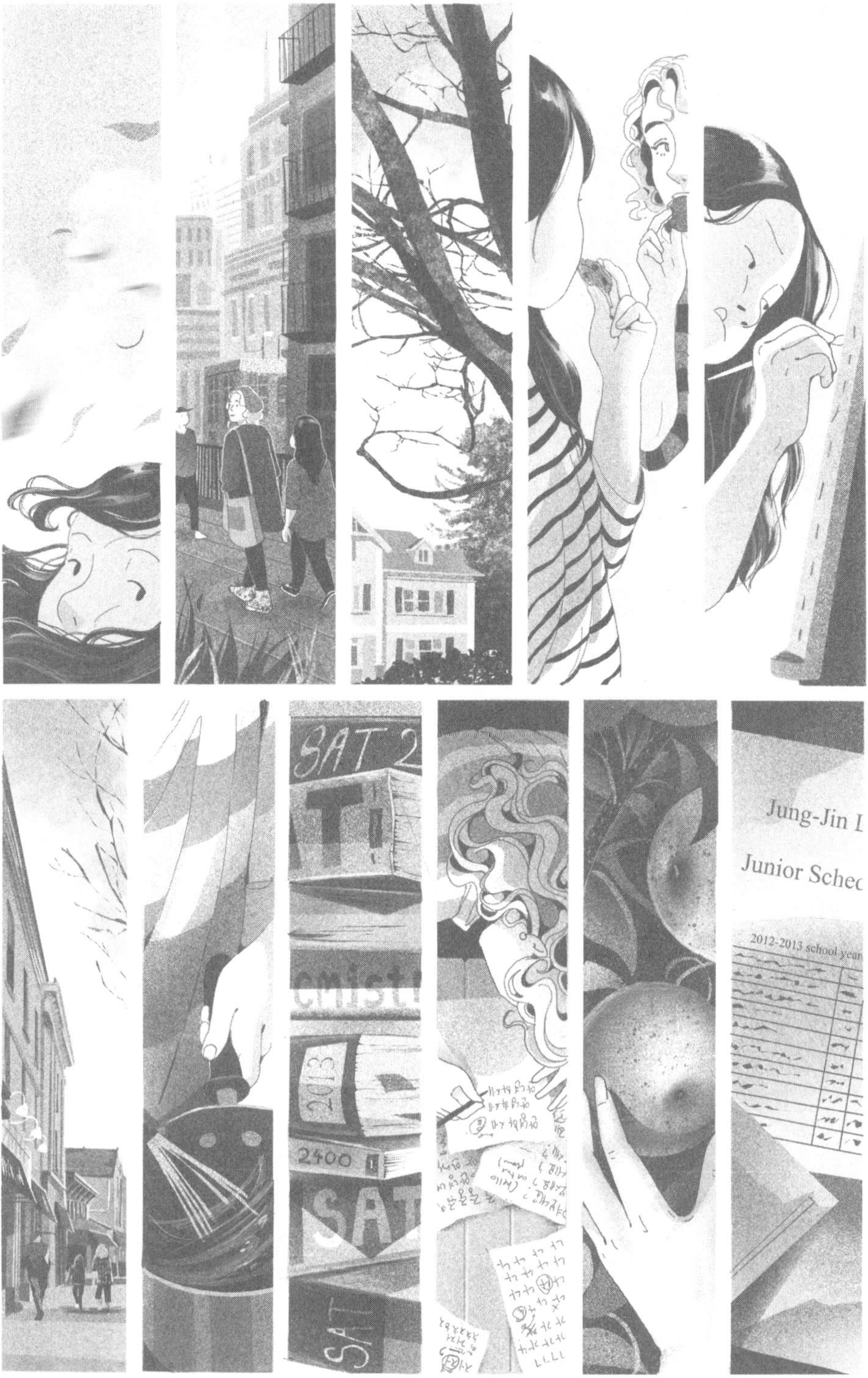
SAT 2
2013
2400
SAT
Jung-Jin
Junior Sche
2012-2013 school year

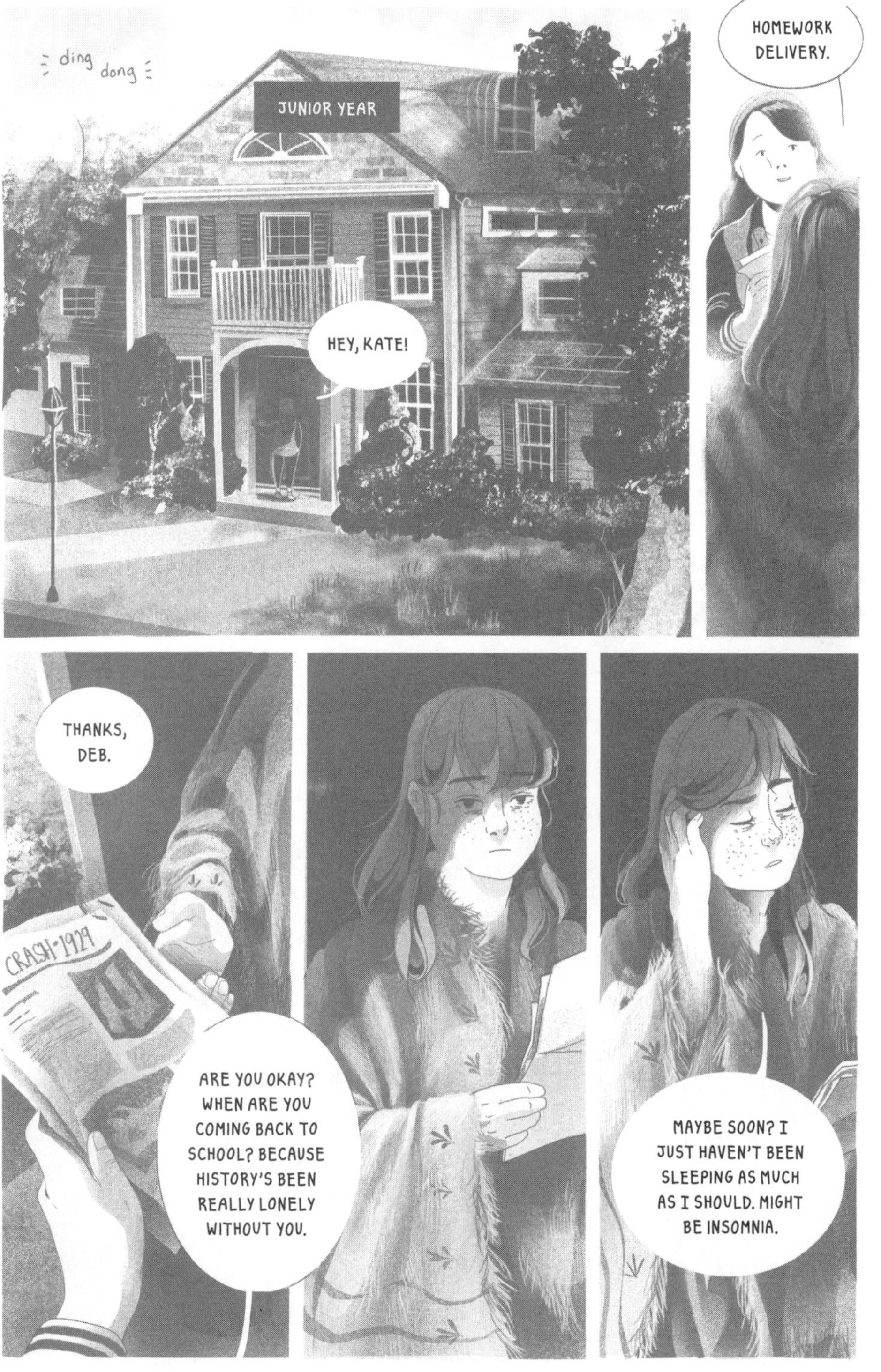

ding dong
JUNIOR YEAR
HEY, KATE!
HOMEWORK DELIVERY.
THANKS, DEB.
CRASH-1929
ARE YOU OKAY? WHEN ARE YOU COMING BACK TO SCHOOL? BECAUSE HISTORY'S BEEN REALLY LONELY WITHOUT YOU.
MAYBE SOON? I JUST HAVEN'T BEEN SLEEPING AS MUCH AS I SHOULD. MIGHT BE INSOMNIA.

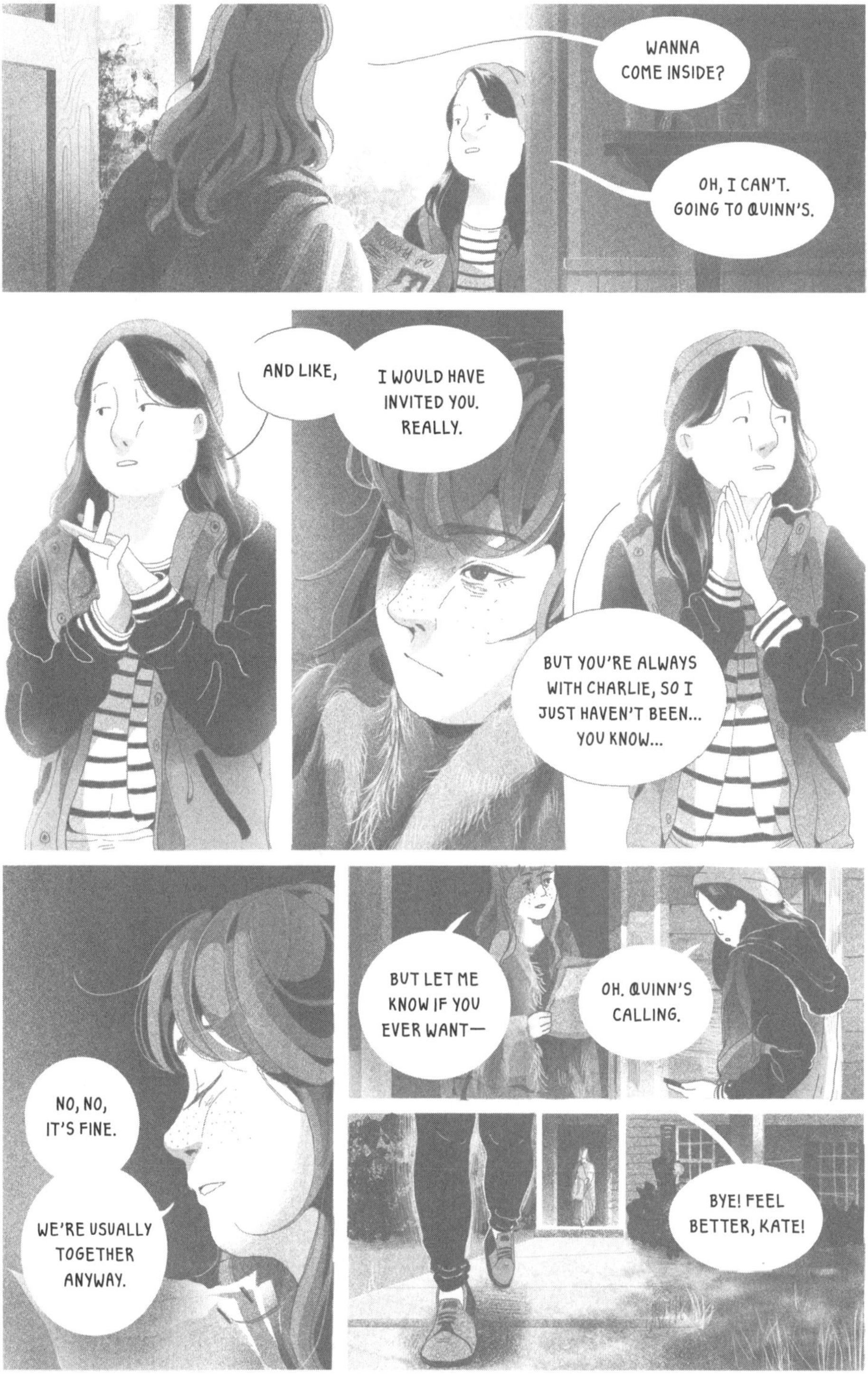
WANNA COME INSIDE?
OH, I CAN'T. GOING TO QUINN'S.
AND LIKE,
I WOULD HAVE INVITED YOU. REALLY.
BUT YOU'RE ALWAYS WITH CHARLIE, SO I JUST HAVEN'T BEEN... YOU KNOW...
NO, NO, IT'S FINE.
WE'RE USUALLY TOGETHER ANYWAY.
BUT LET ME KNOW IF YOU EVER WANT—
OH. QUINN'S CALLING.
BYE! FEEL BETTER, KATE!

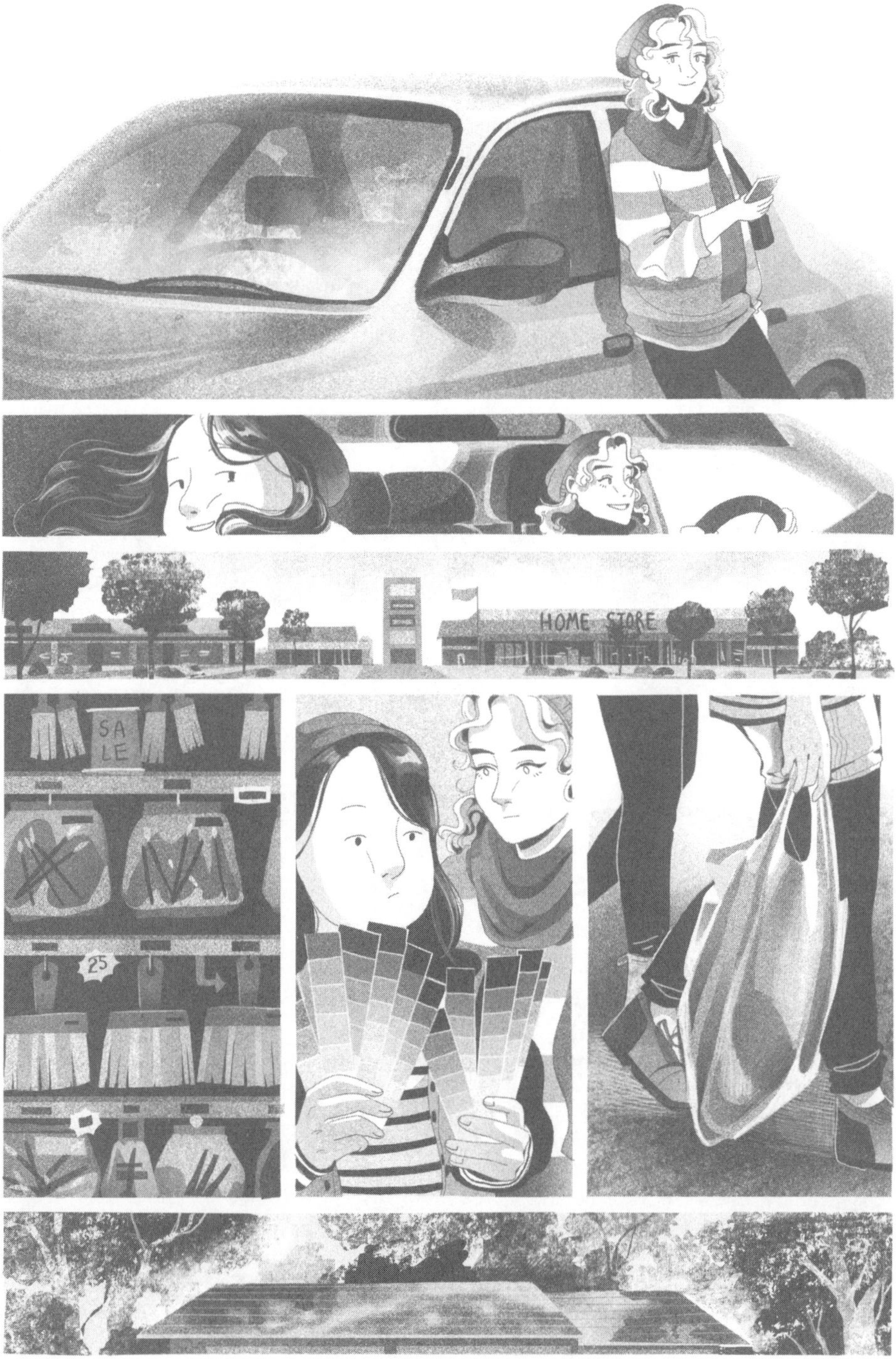
SA
LE
25
HOME STORE

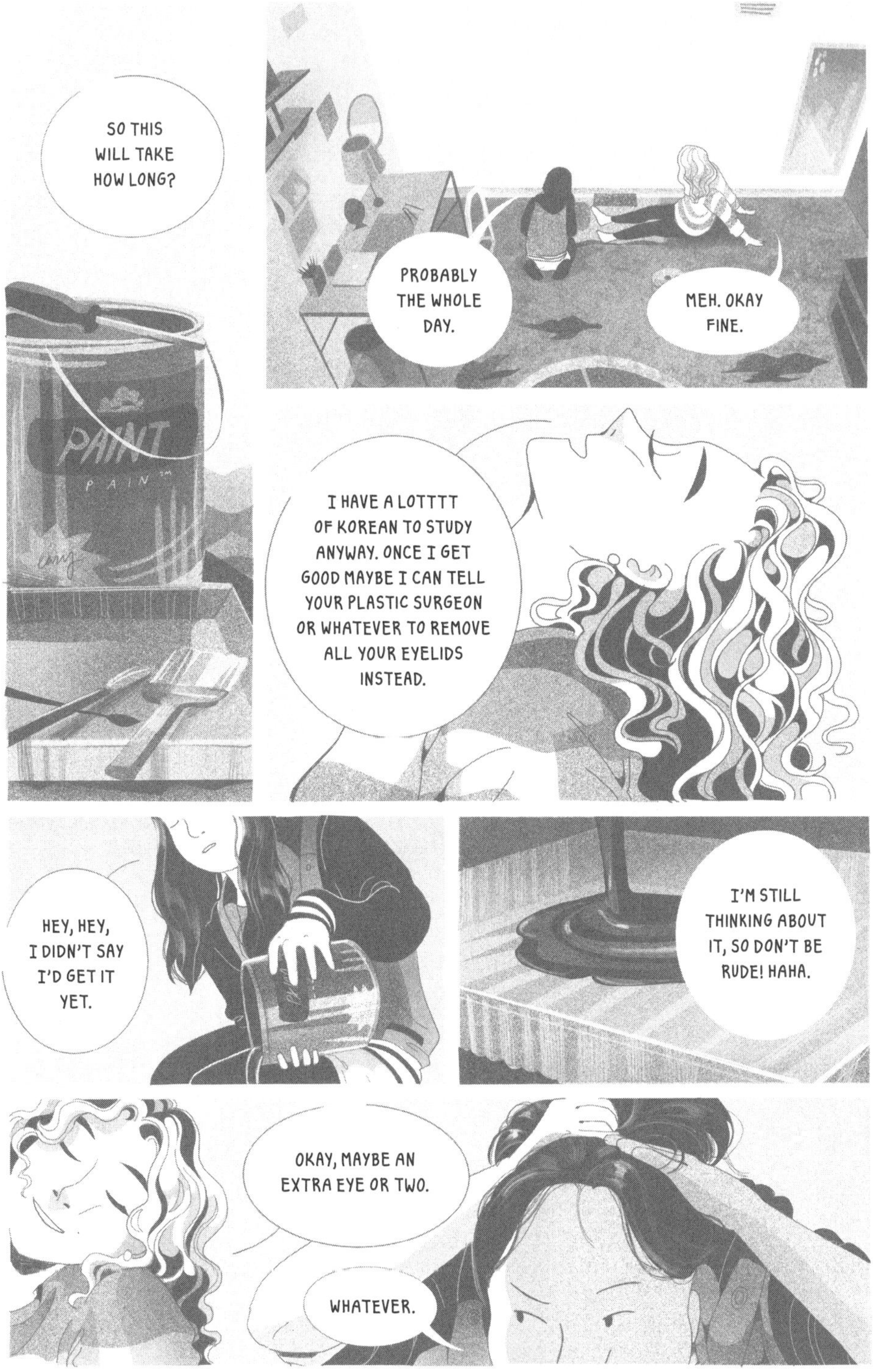
SO THIS WILL TAKE HOW LONG?
PROBABLY THE WHOLE DAY.
MEH. OKAY FINE.
PAINT
I HAVE A LOTTTT OF KOREAN TO STUDY ANYWAY. ONCE I GET GOOD MAYBE I CAN TELL YOUR PLASTIC SURGEON OR WHATEVER TO REMOVE ALL YOUR EYELIDS INSTEAD.
HEY, HEY, I DIDN'T SAY I'D GET IT YET.
I'M STILL THINKING ABOUT IT, SO DON'T BE RUDE! HAHA.
OKAY, MAYBE AN EXTRA EYE OR TWO.
WHATEVER.

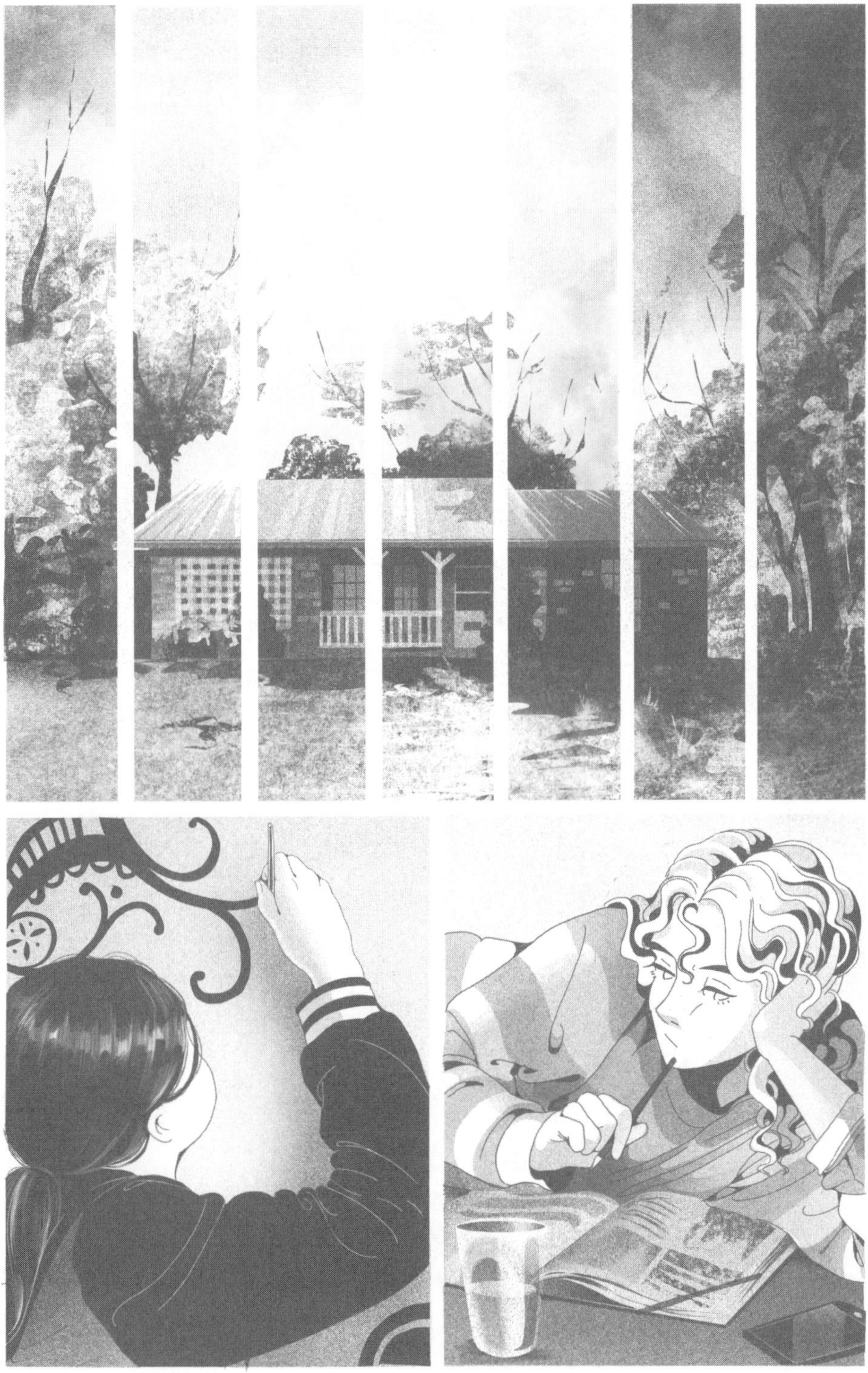

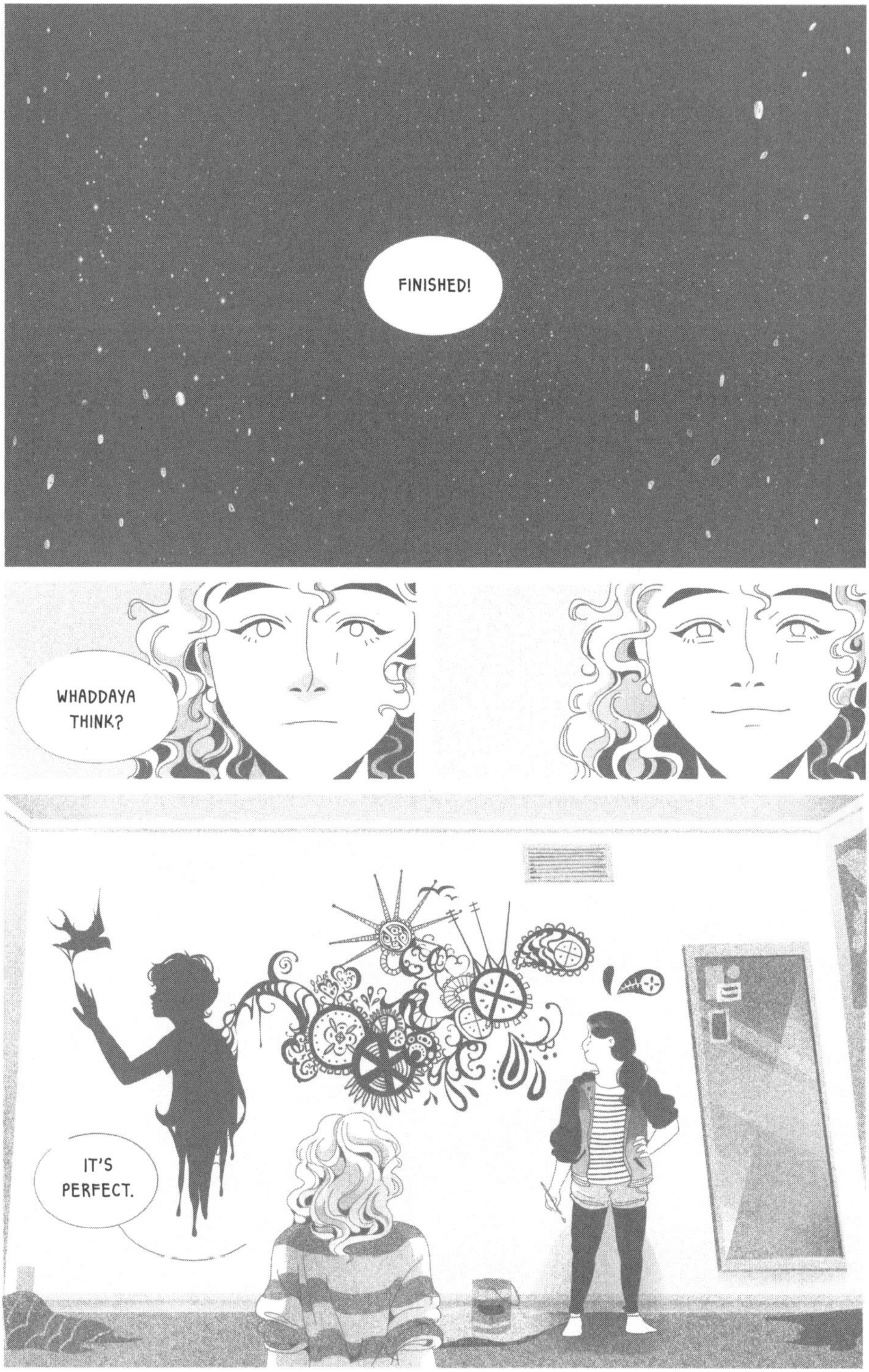
FINISHED!
WHADDAYA THINK?
IT'S PERFECT.

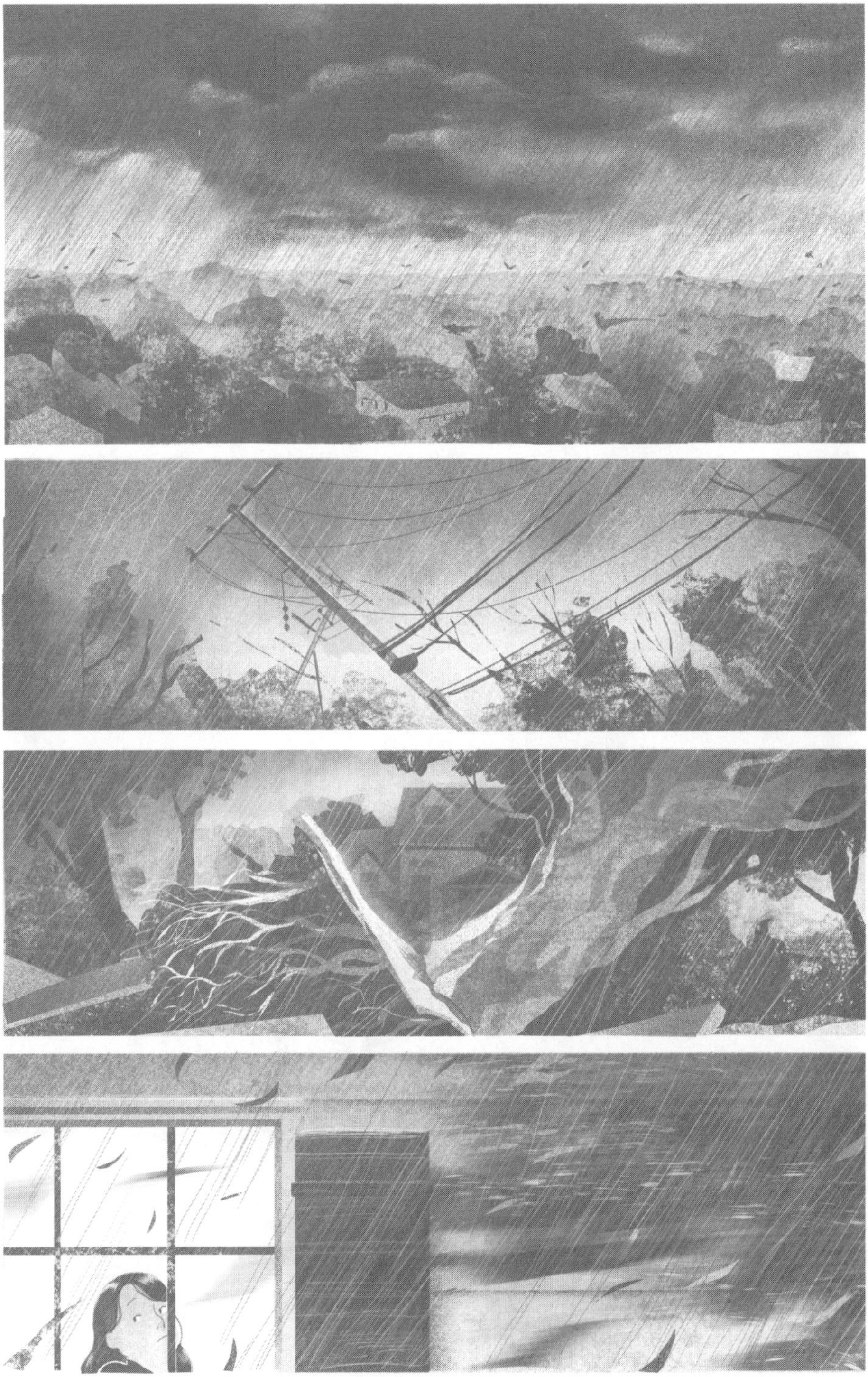

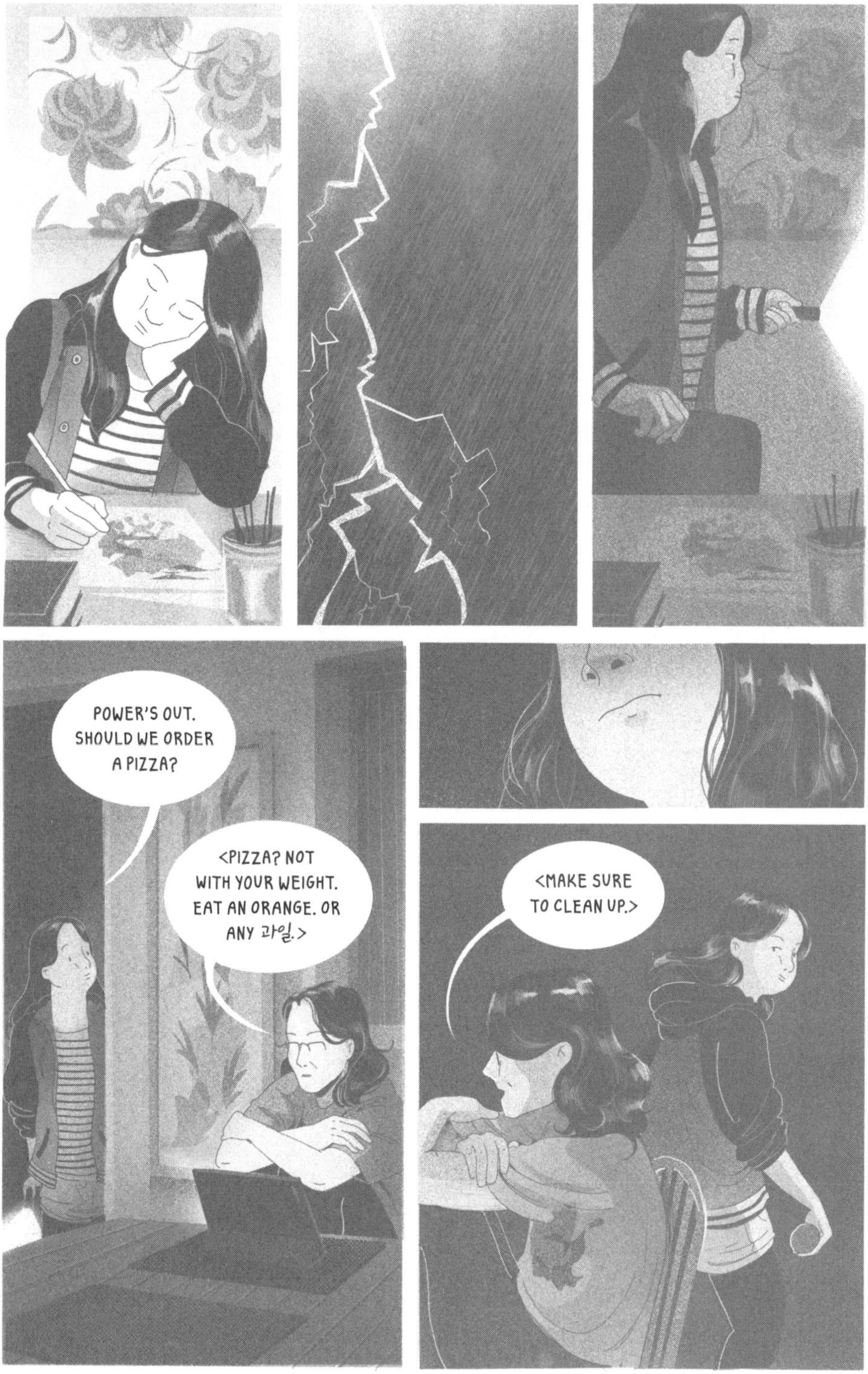
POWER'S OUT. SHOULD WE ORDER A PIZZA?
<PIZZA? NOT WITH YOUR WEIGHT. EAT AN ORANGE. OR ANY 과일.>
<MAKE SURE TO CLEAN UP.>

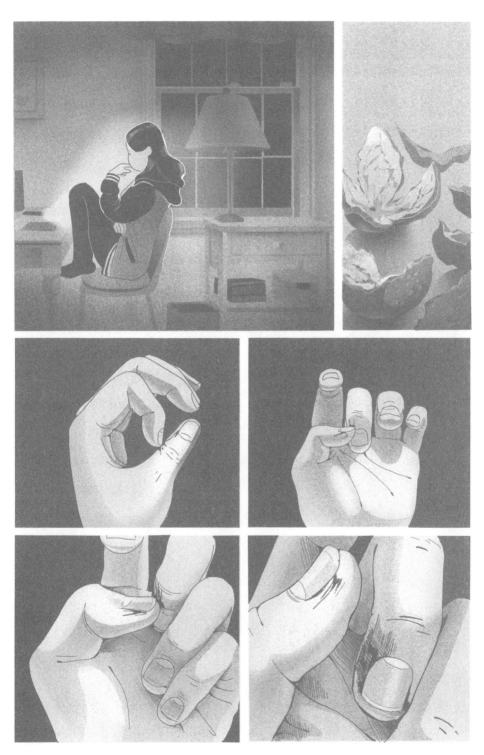

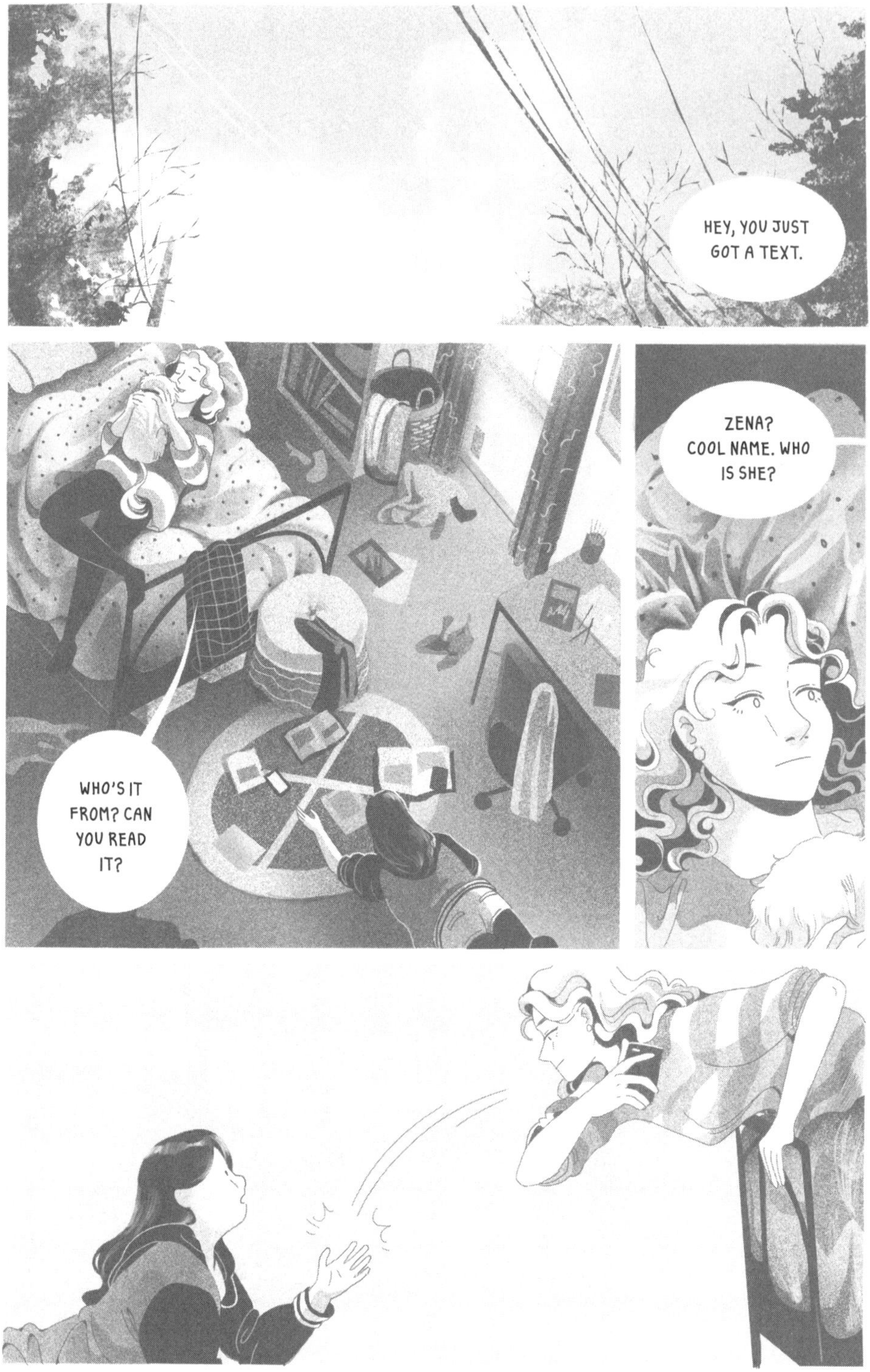
HEY, YOU JUST GOT A TEXT.
WHO'S IT FROM? CAN YOU READ IT?
ZENA? COOL NAME. WHO IS SHE?

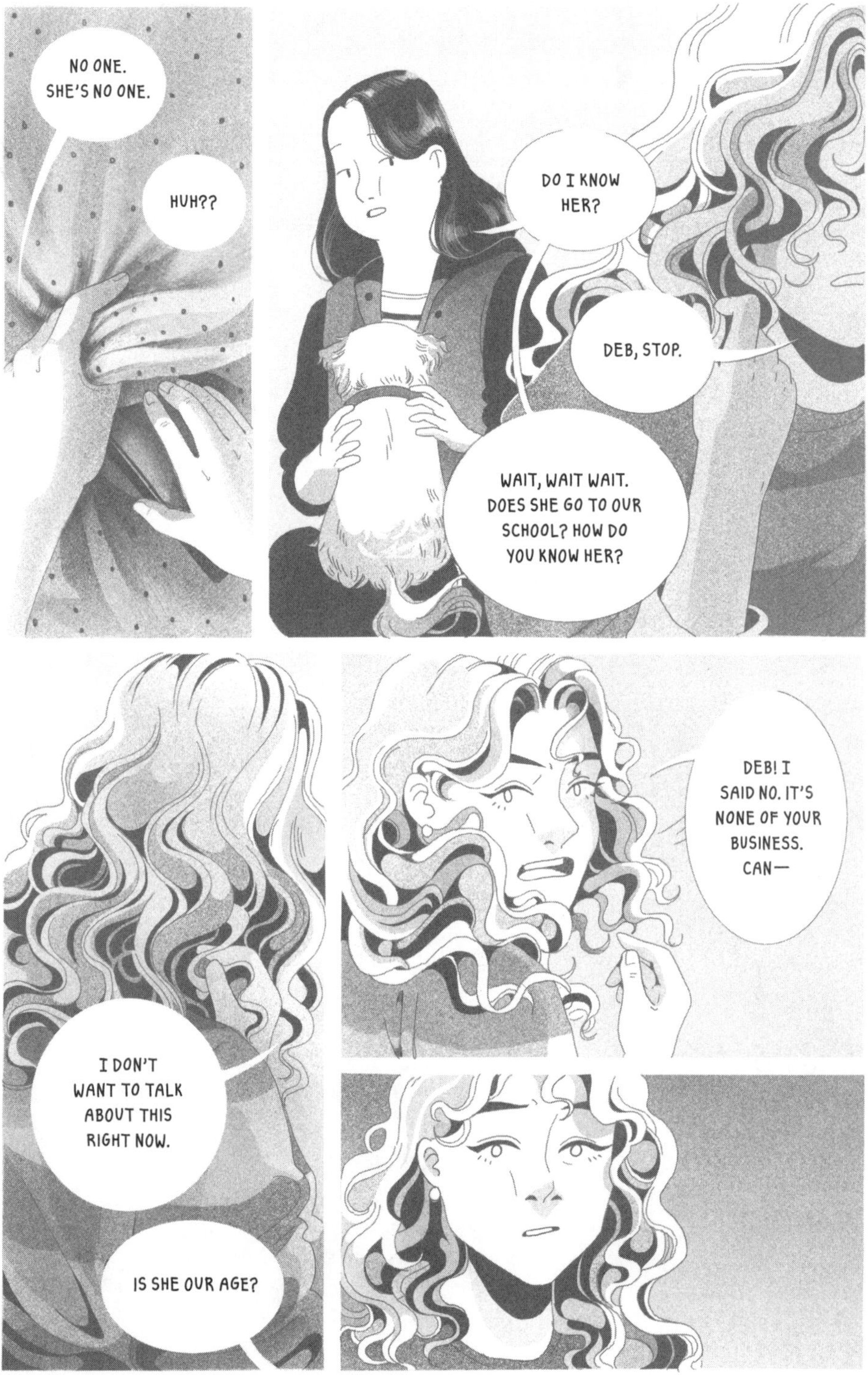
NO ONE. SHE'S NO ONE.
HUH??
DO I KNOW HER?
DEB, STOP.
WAIT, WAIT WAIT. DOES SHE GO TO OUR SCHOOL? HOW DO YOU KNOW HER?
DEB! I SAID NO. IT'S NONE OF YOUR BUSINESS. CAN—
I DON'T WANT TO TALK ABOUT THIS RIGHT NOW.
IS SHE OUR AGE?

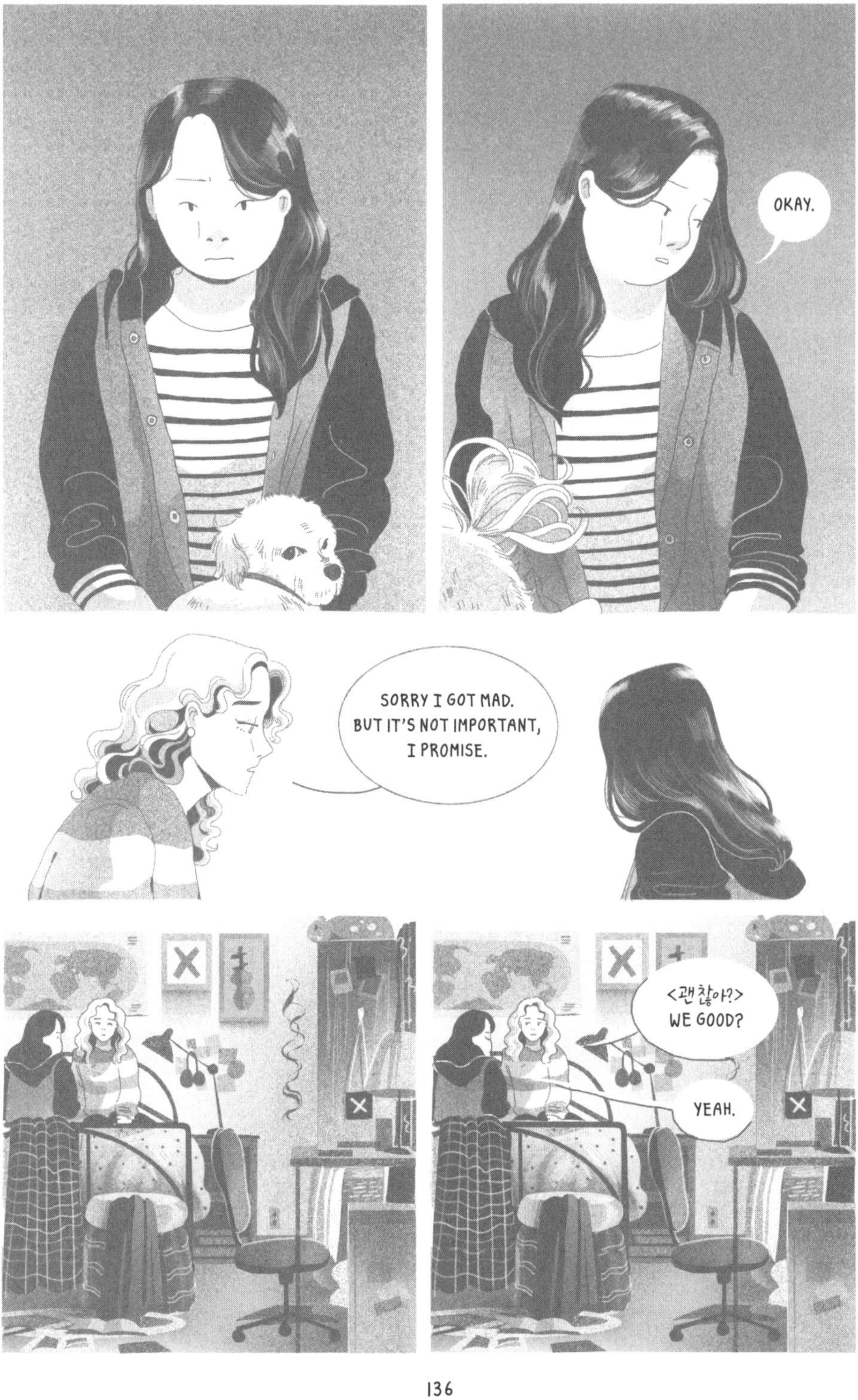
OKAY.
SORRY I GOT MAD. BUT IT'S NOT IMPORTANT, I PROMISE.
<괜찮아?> WE GOOD?
YEAH.

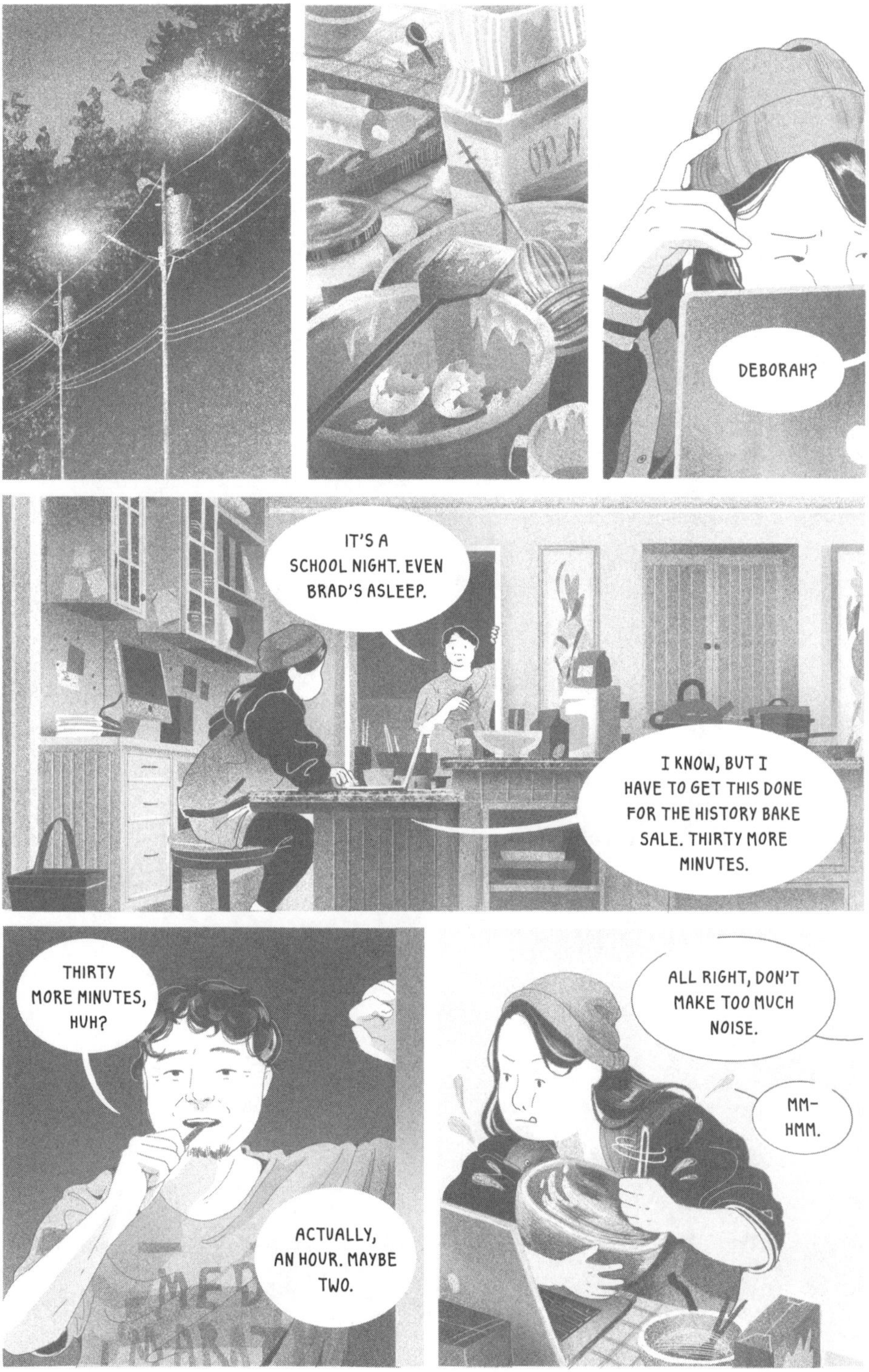
DEBORAH?
IT'S A SCHOOL NIGHT. EVEN BRAD'S ASLEEP.
I KNOW, BUT I HAVE TO GET THIS DONE FOR THE HISTORY BAKE SALE. THIRTY MORE MINUTES.
THIRTY MORE MINUTES, HUH?
ACTUALLY, AN HOUR. MAYBE TWO.
ALL RIGHT, DON'T MAKE TOO MUCH NOISE.
MM-HMM.

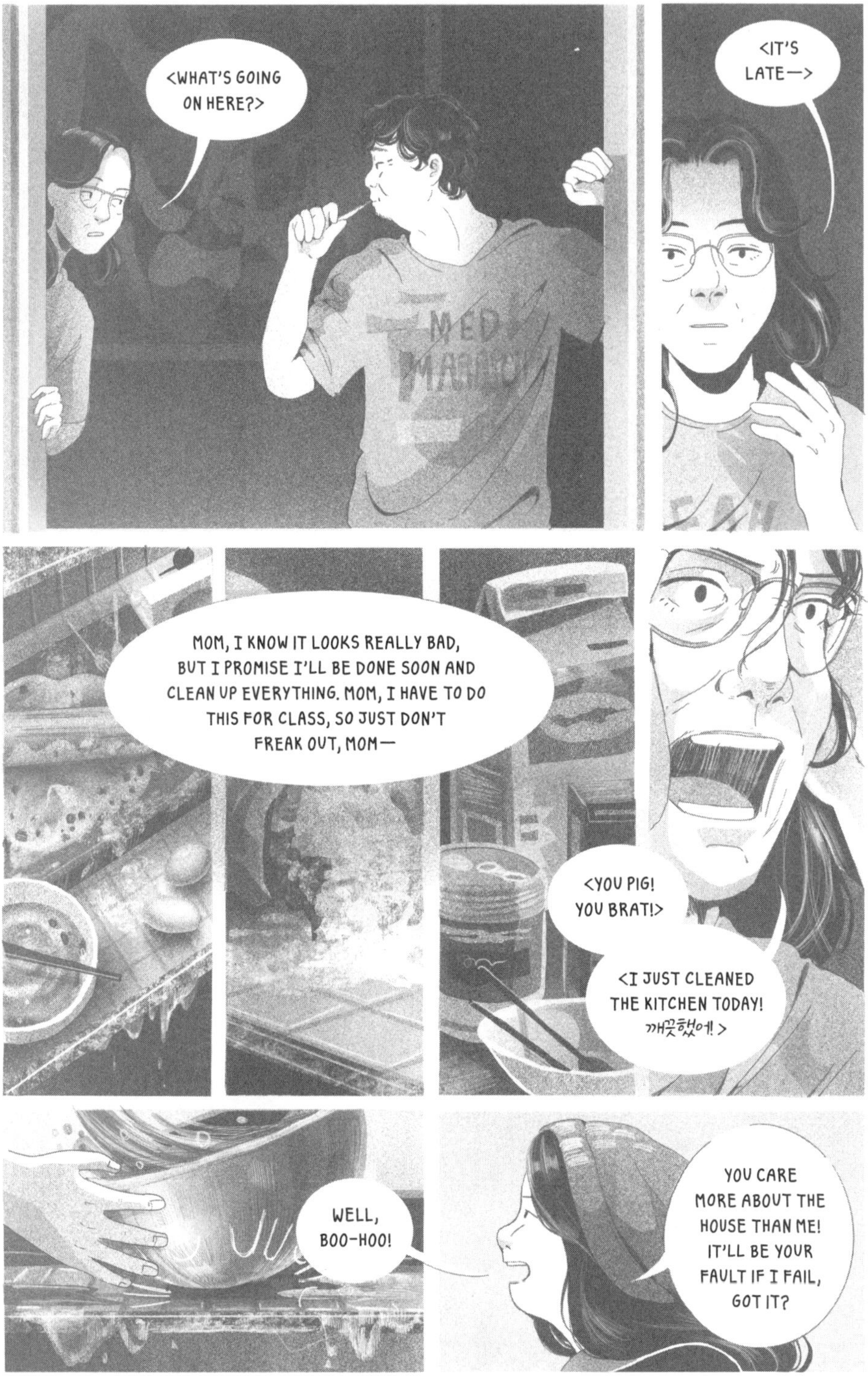
<WHAT'S GOING ON HERE?>
<IT'S LATE—>
MOM, I KNOW IT LOOKS REALLY BAD, BUT I PROMISE I'LL BE DONE SOON AND CLEAN UP EVERYTHING. MOM, I HAVE TO DO THIS FOR CLASS, SO JUST DON'T FREAK OUT, MOM—
<YOU PIG! YOU BRAT!>
<I JUST CLEANED THE KITCHEN TODAY! 깨끗했어! >
WELL, BOO-HOO!
YOU CARE MORE ABOUT THE HOUSE THAN ME! IT'LL BE YOUR FAULT IF I FAIL, GOT IT?

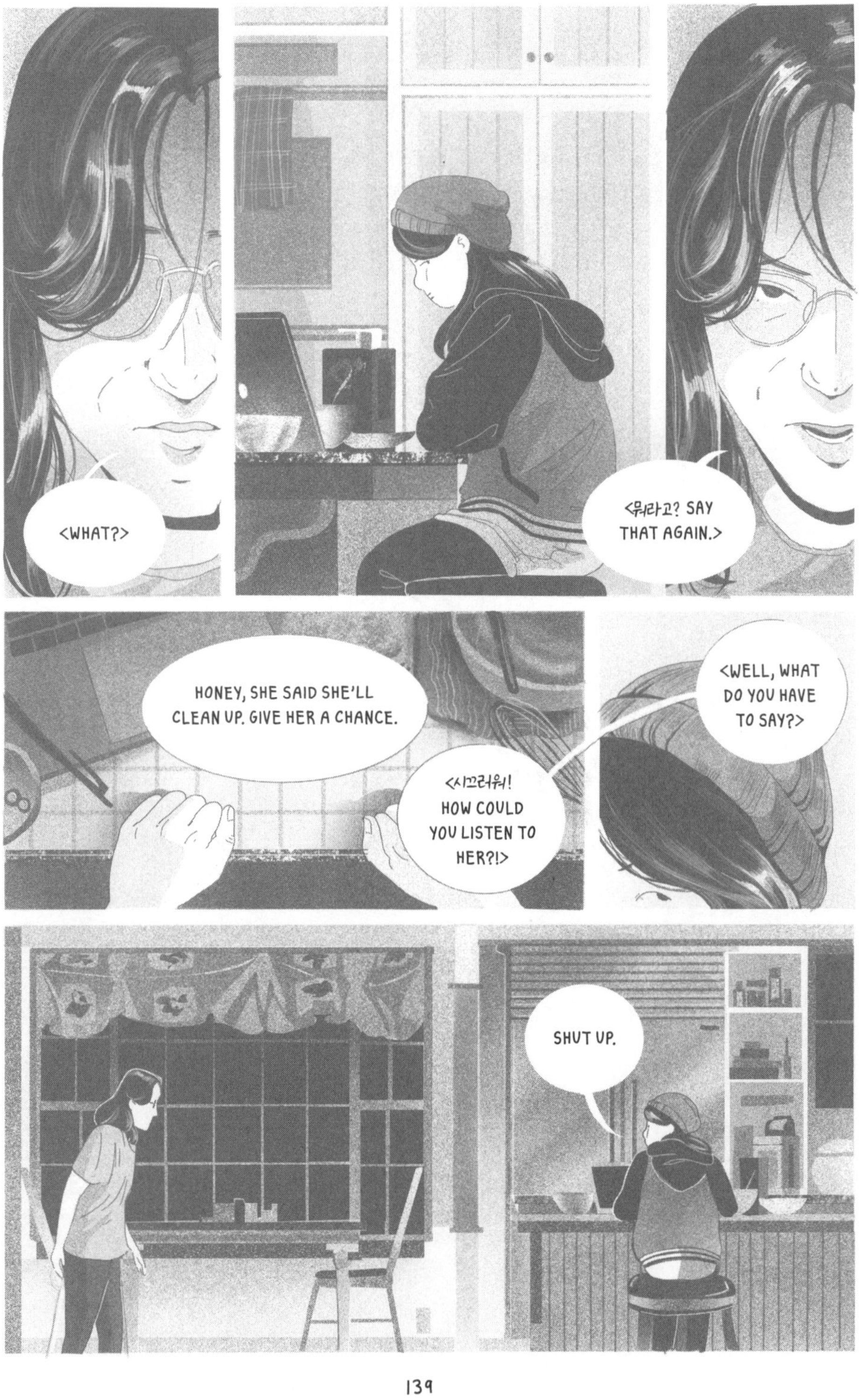
<WHAT?>
<뭐라고? SAY THAT AGAIN.>
HONEY, SHE SAID SHE'LL CLEAN UP. GIVE HER A CHANCE.
<시끄러워! HOW COULD YOU LISTEN TO HER?!>
<WELL, WHAT DO YOU HAVE TO SAY?>
SHUT UP.

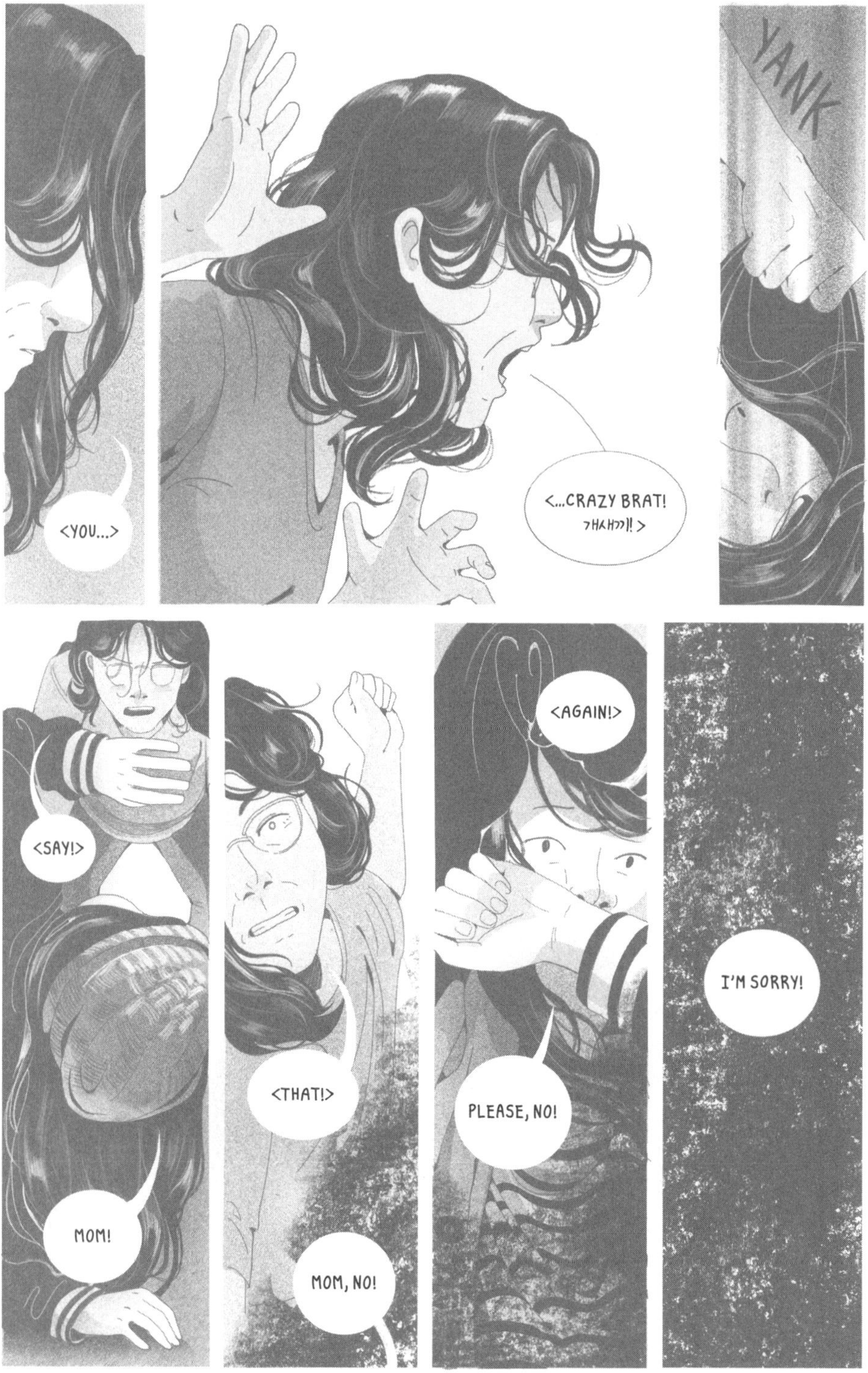

<YOU...>
<...CRAZY BRAT!
ㄱㅐㅅㅐㄲㅣ! >
YANK
<SAY!>
MOM!
<THAT!>
MOM, NO!
<AGAIN!>
PLEASE, NO!
I'M SORRY!

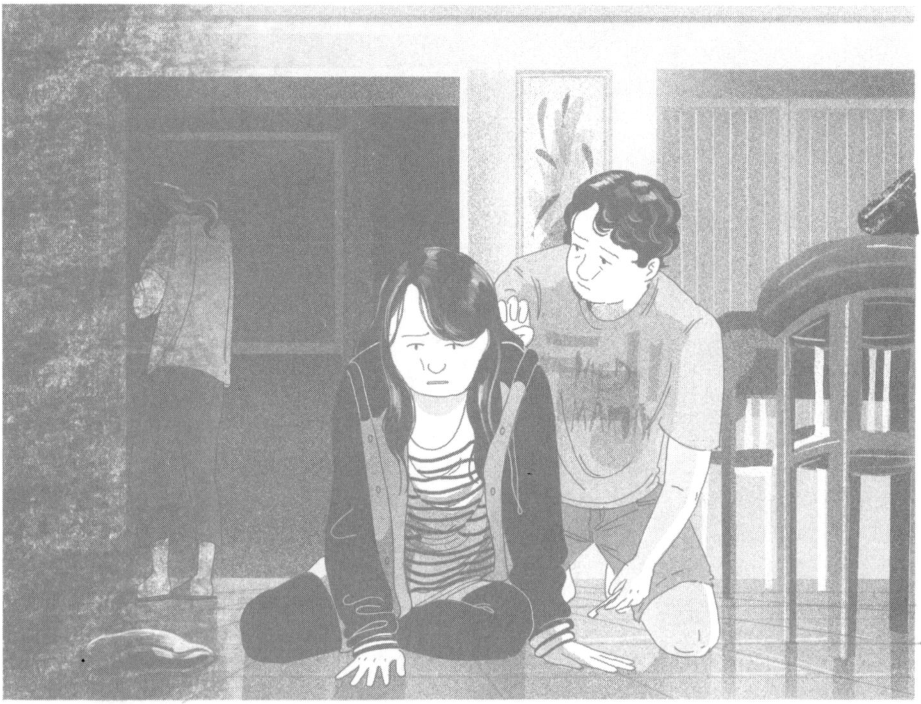

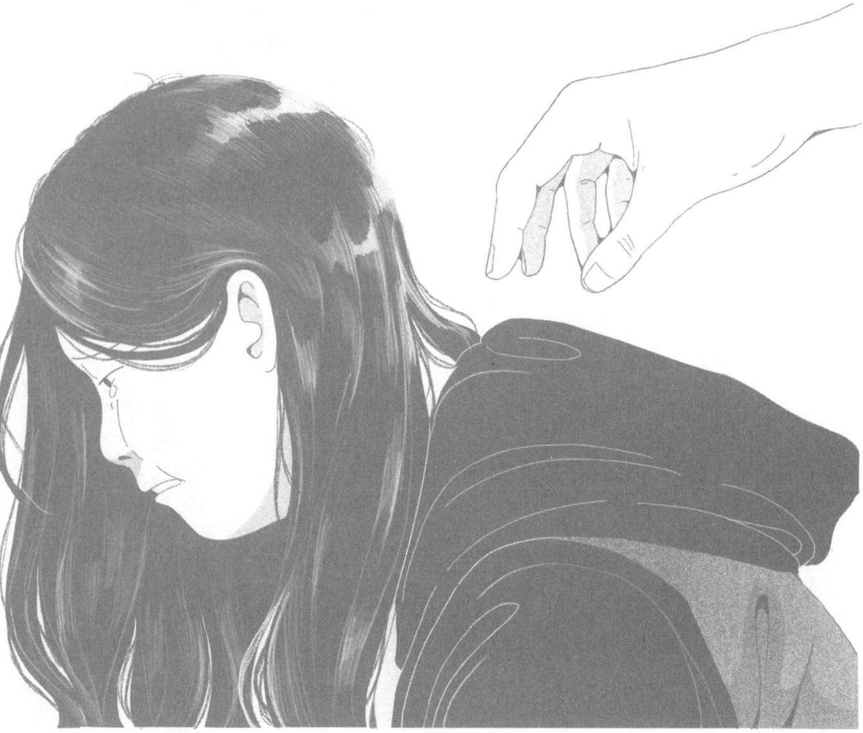

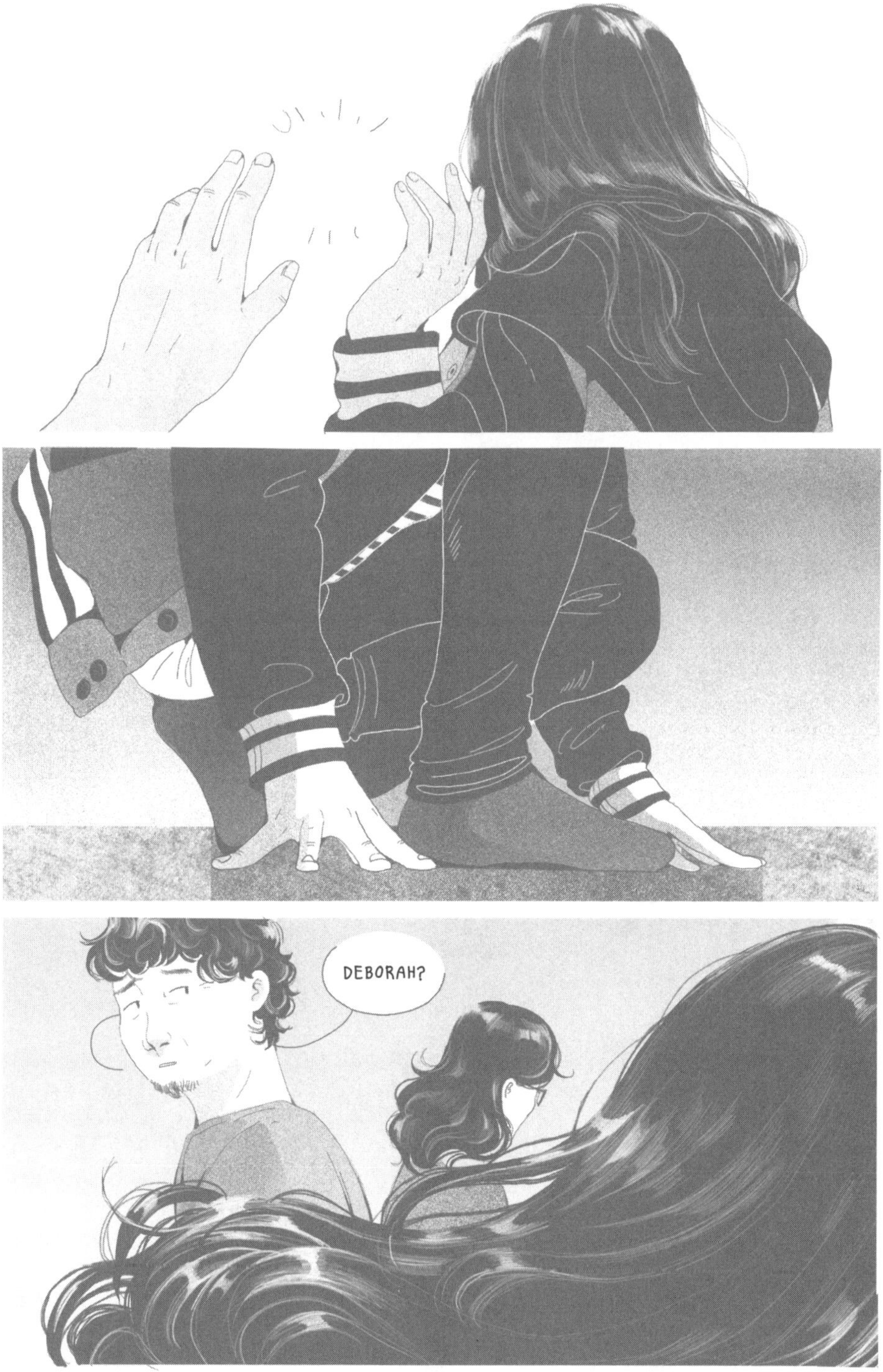
DEBORAH?

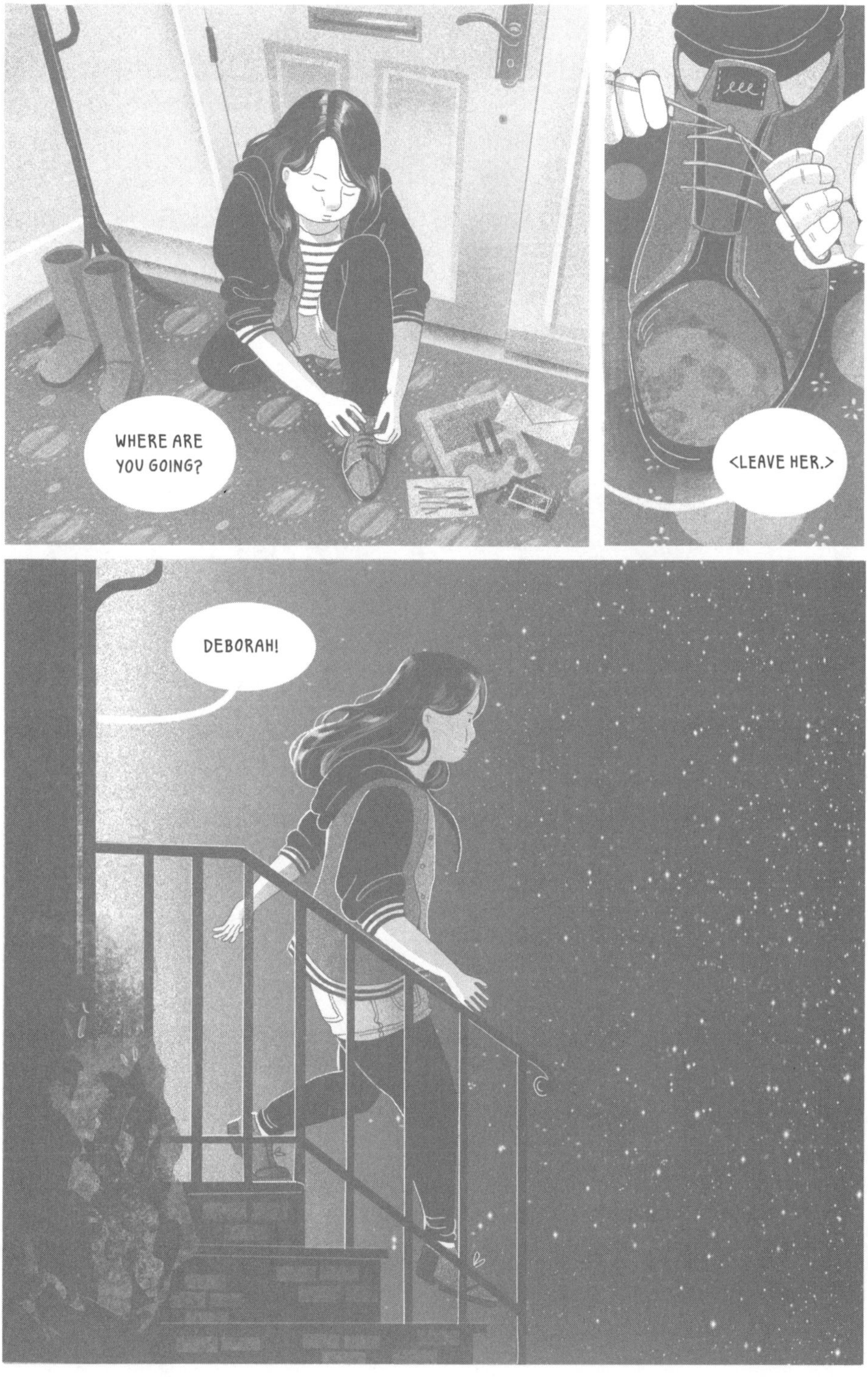
WHERE ARE YOU GOING?
<LEAVE HER.>
DEBORAH!

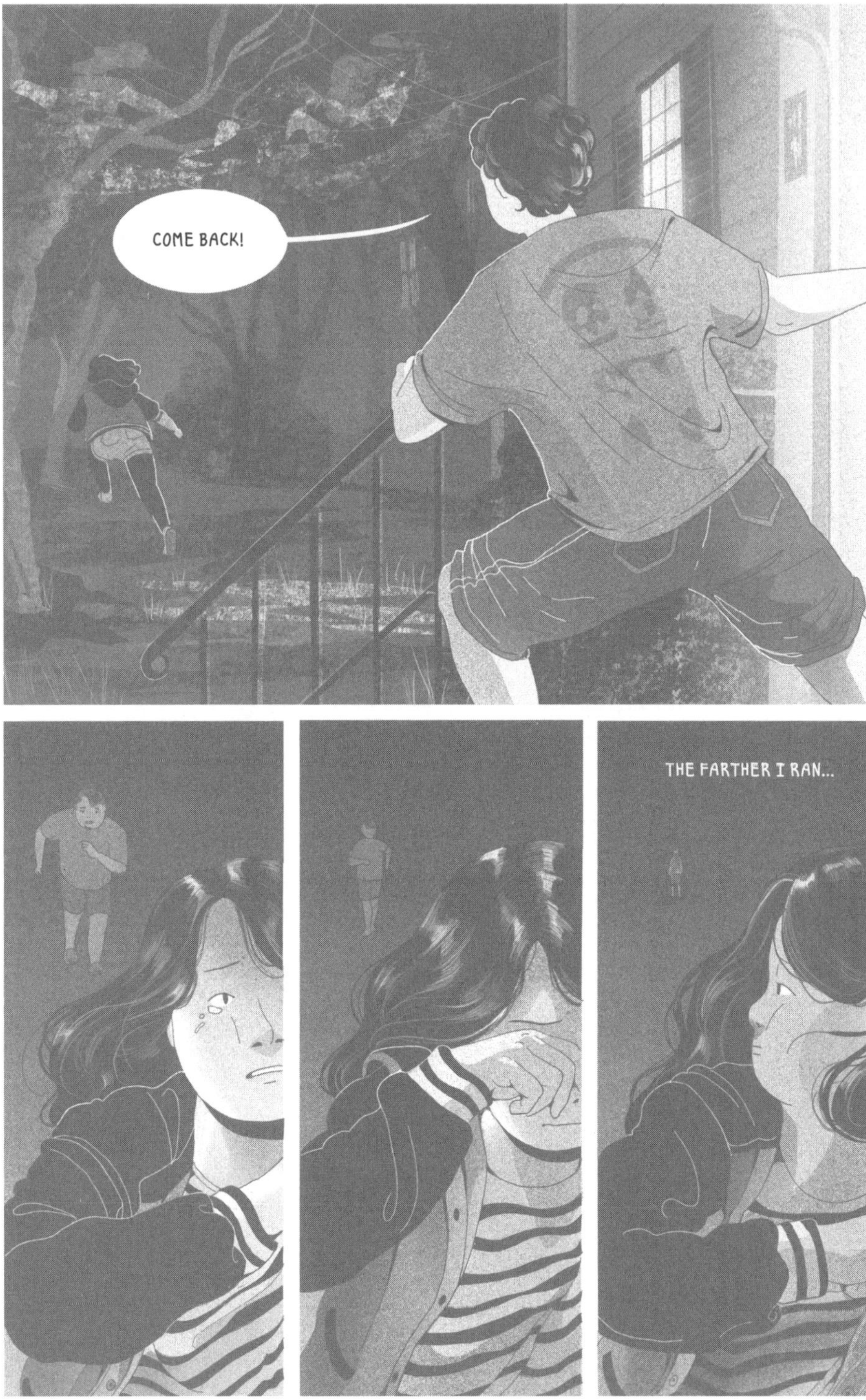
COME BACK!
THE FARTHER I RAN...

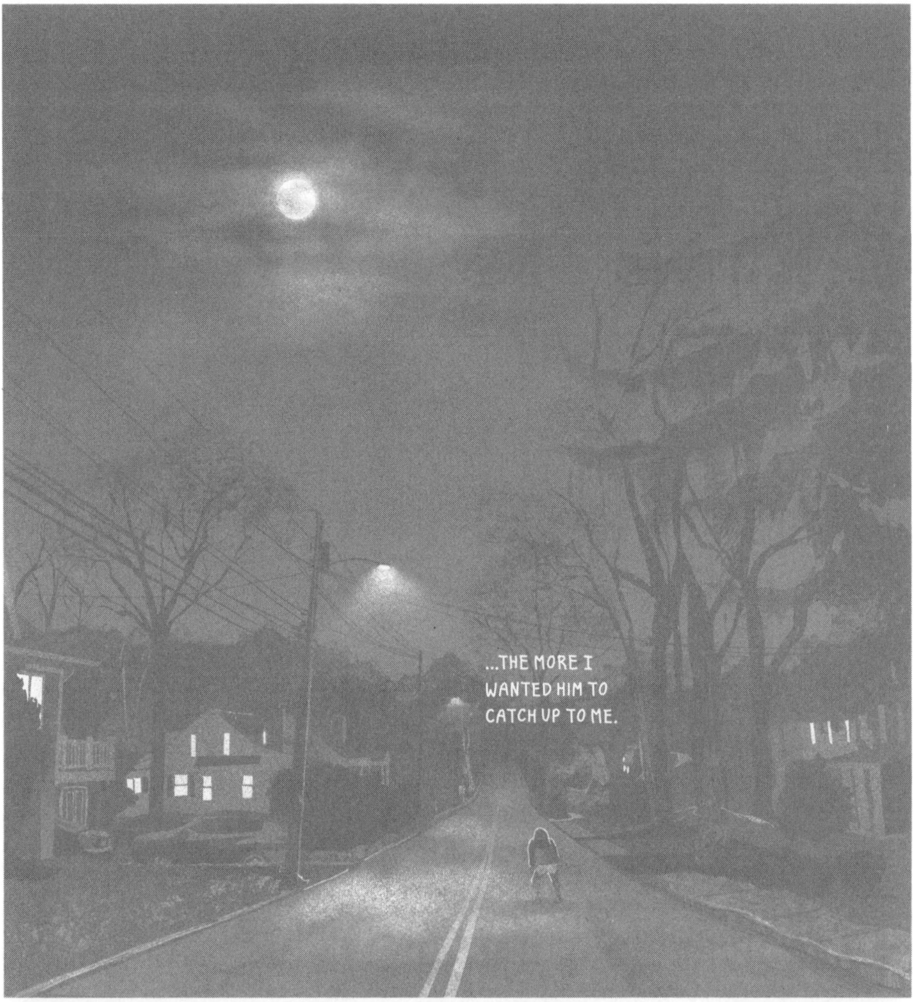
...THE MORE I
WANTED HIM TO
CATCH UP TO ME.

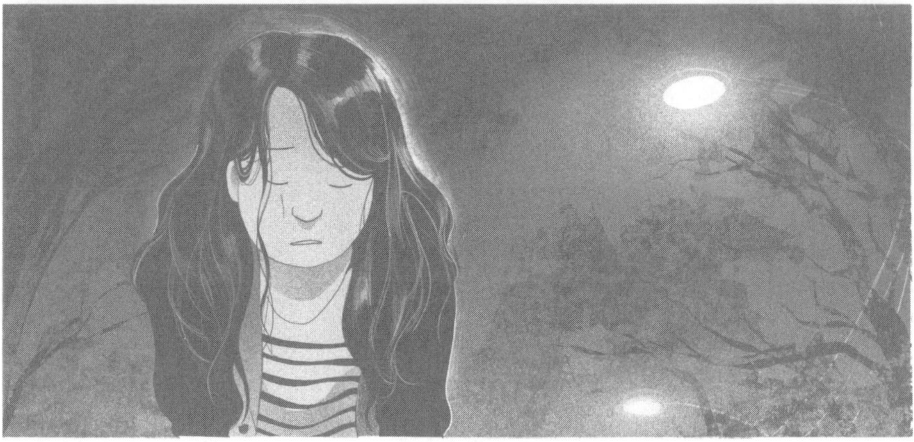

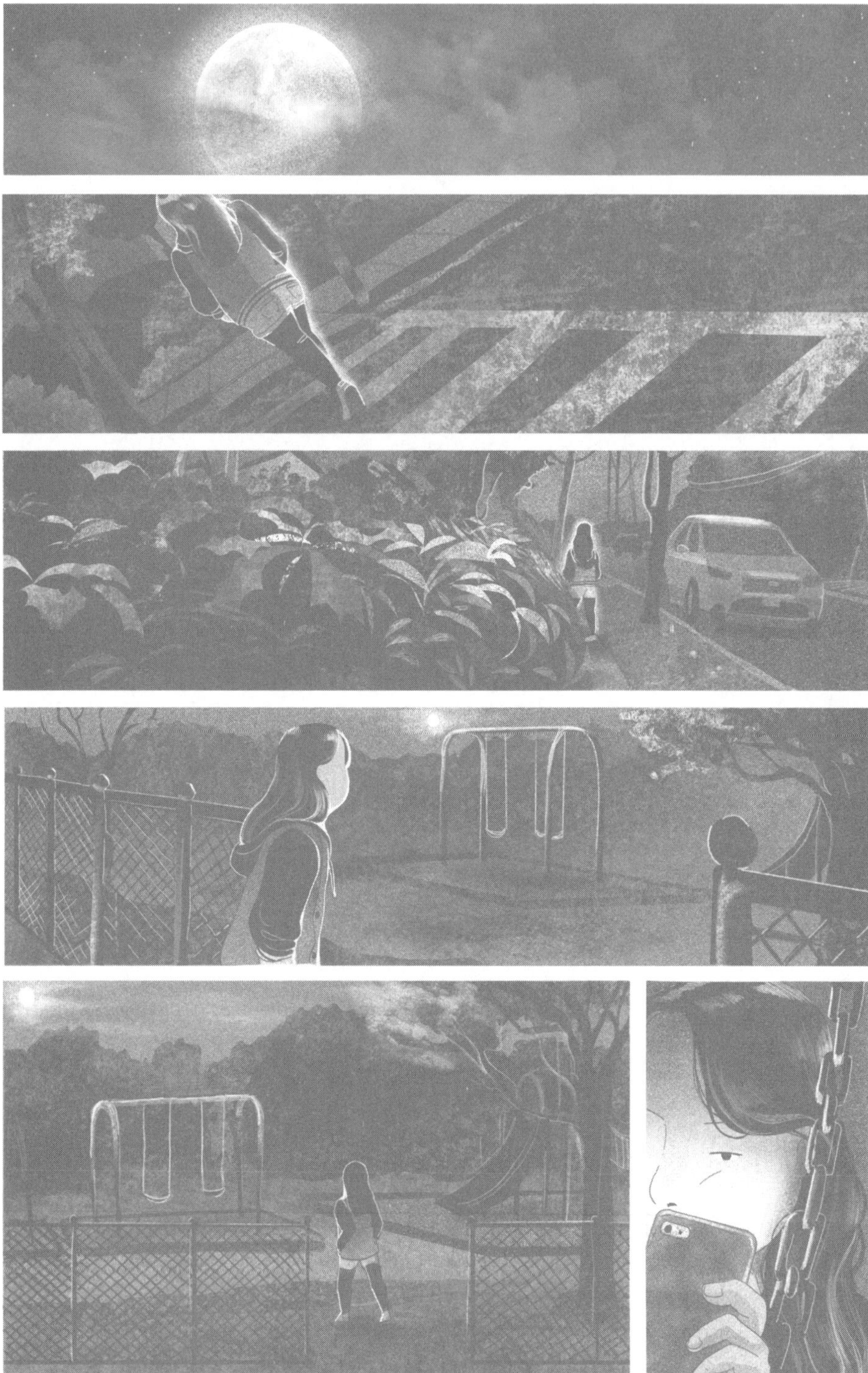

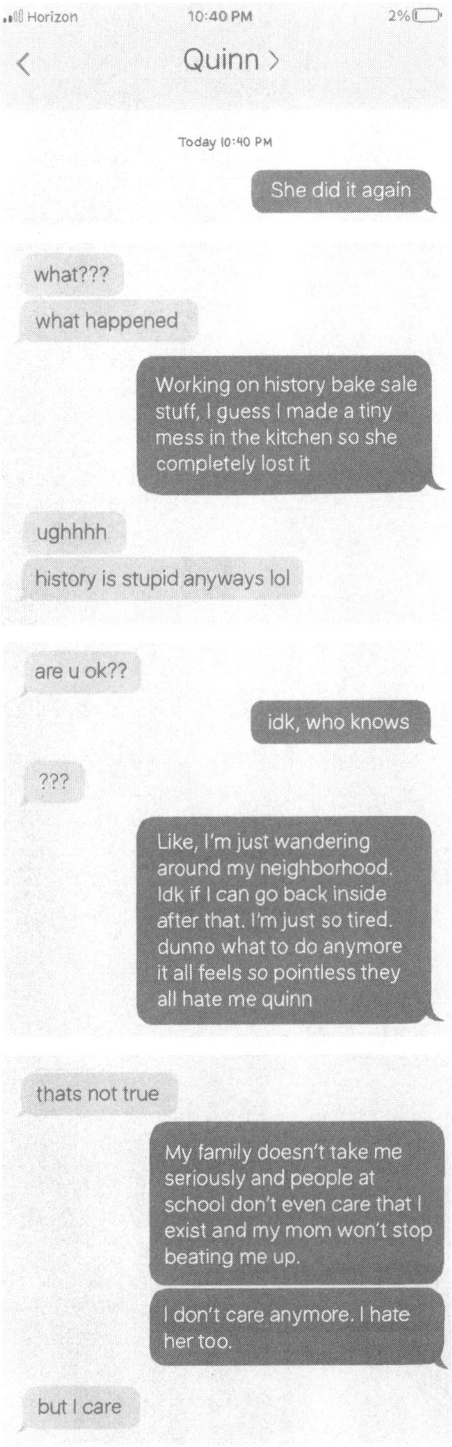
Horizon
10:40 PM
2%
Quinn >
Today 10:40 PM
She did it again
what???
what happened
Working on history bake sale stuff, I guess I made a tiny mess in the kitchen so she completely lost it
ughhhh
history is stupid anyways lol
are u ok??
idk, who knows
???
Like, I'm just wandering around my neighborhood. Idk if I can go back inside after that. I'm just so tired. dunno what to do anymore it all feels so pointless they all hate me quinn
thats not true
My family doesn't take me seriously and people at school don't even care that I exist and my mom won't stop beating me up.
I don't care anymore. I hate her too.
but I care

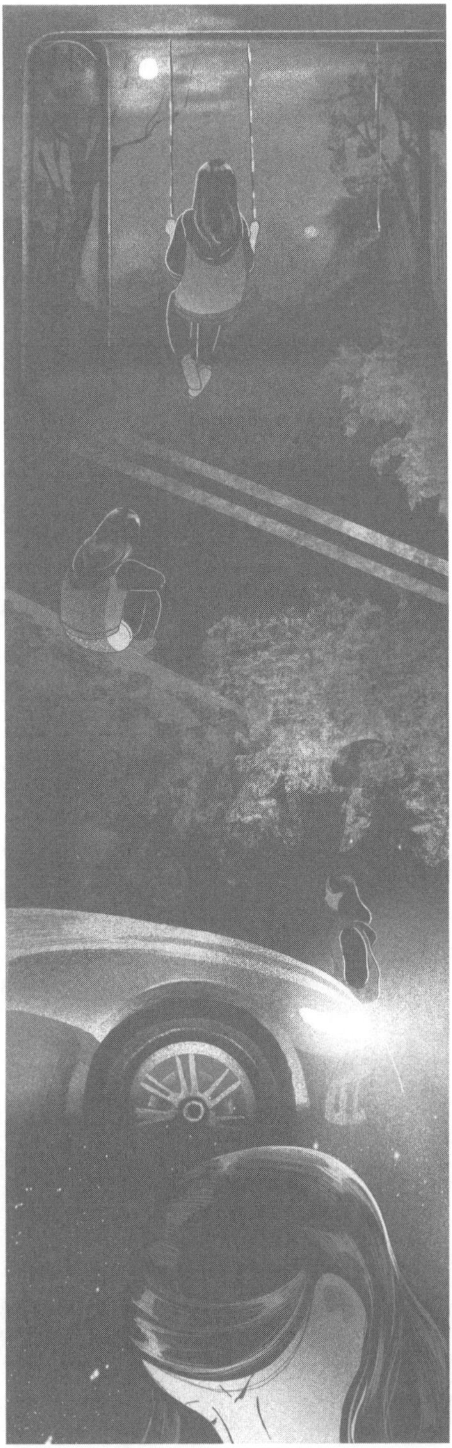

and I kno this sucks but pls
go back home, you have to
stay safe

idk

btw my phone is bout to die

deb where are you

stay where you are

im on my way

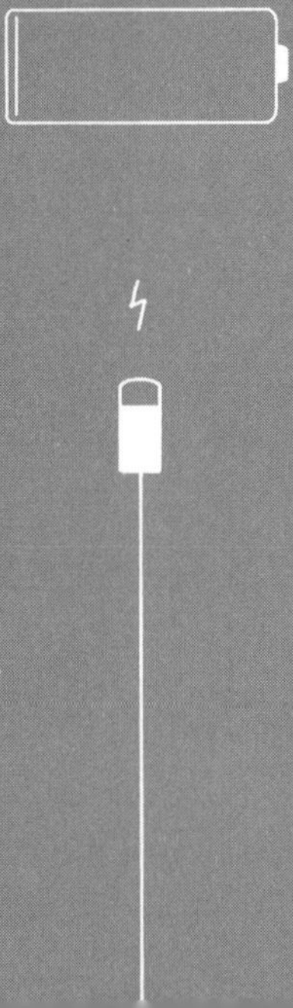

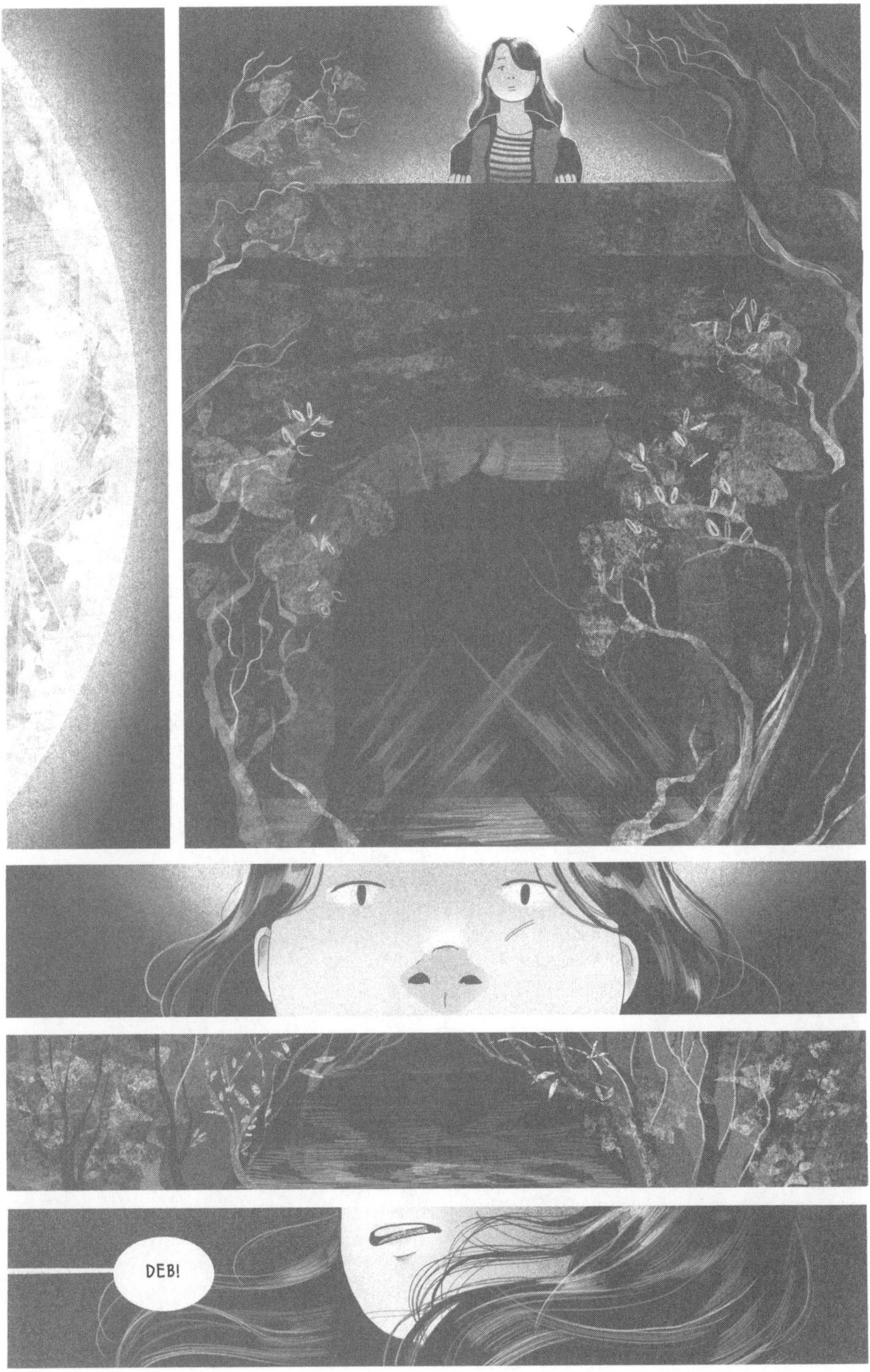
DEB!

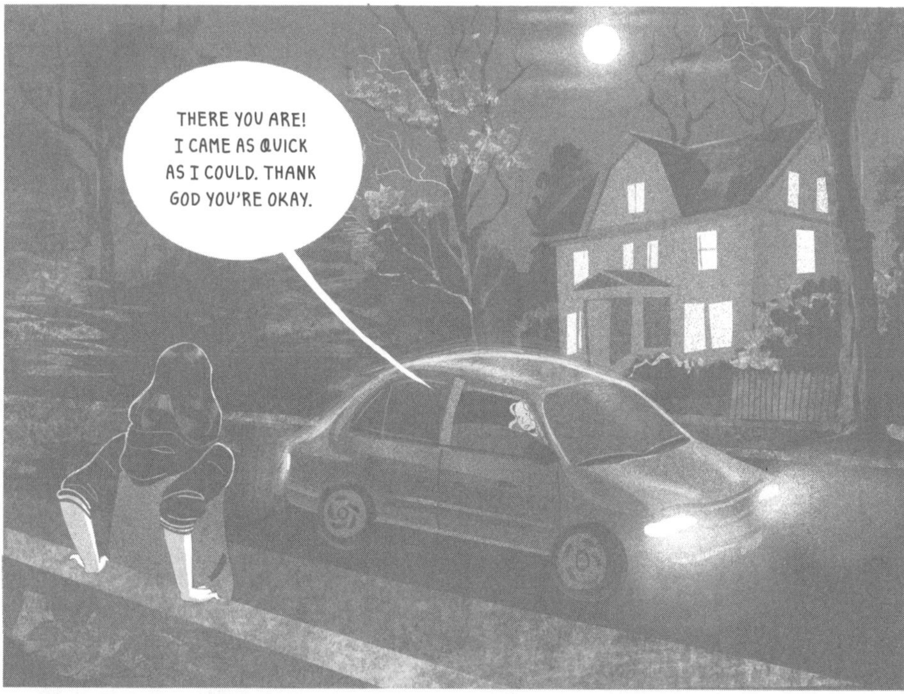
THERE YOU ARE! I CAME AS QUICK AS I COULD. THANK GOD YOU'RE OKAY.

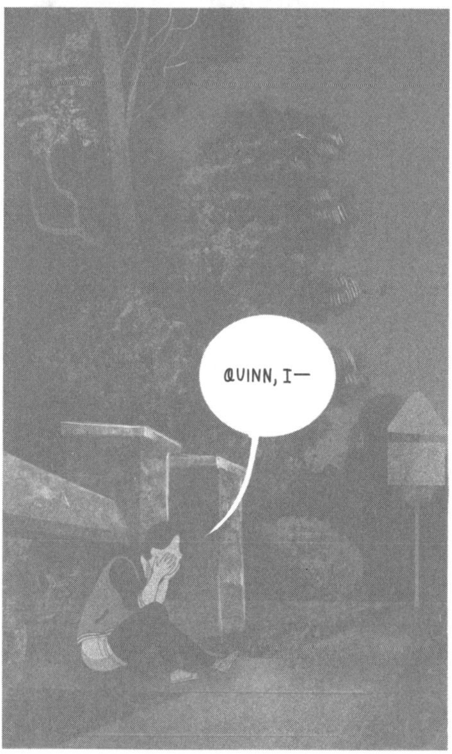
QUINN, I—

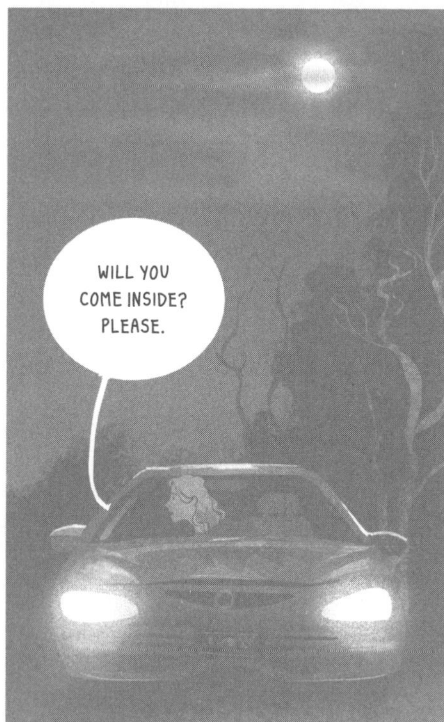
WILL YOU COME INSIDE? PLEASE.

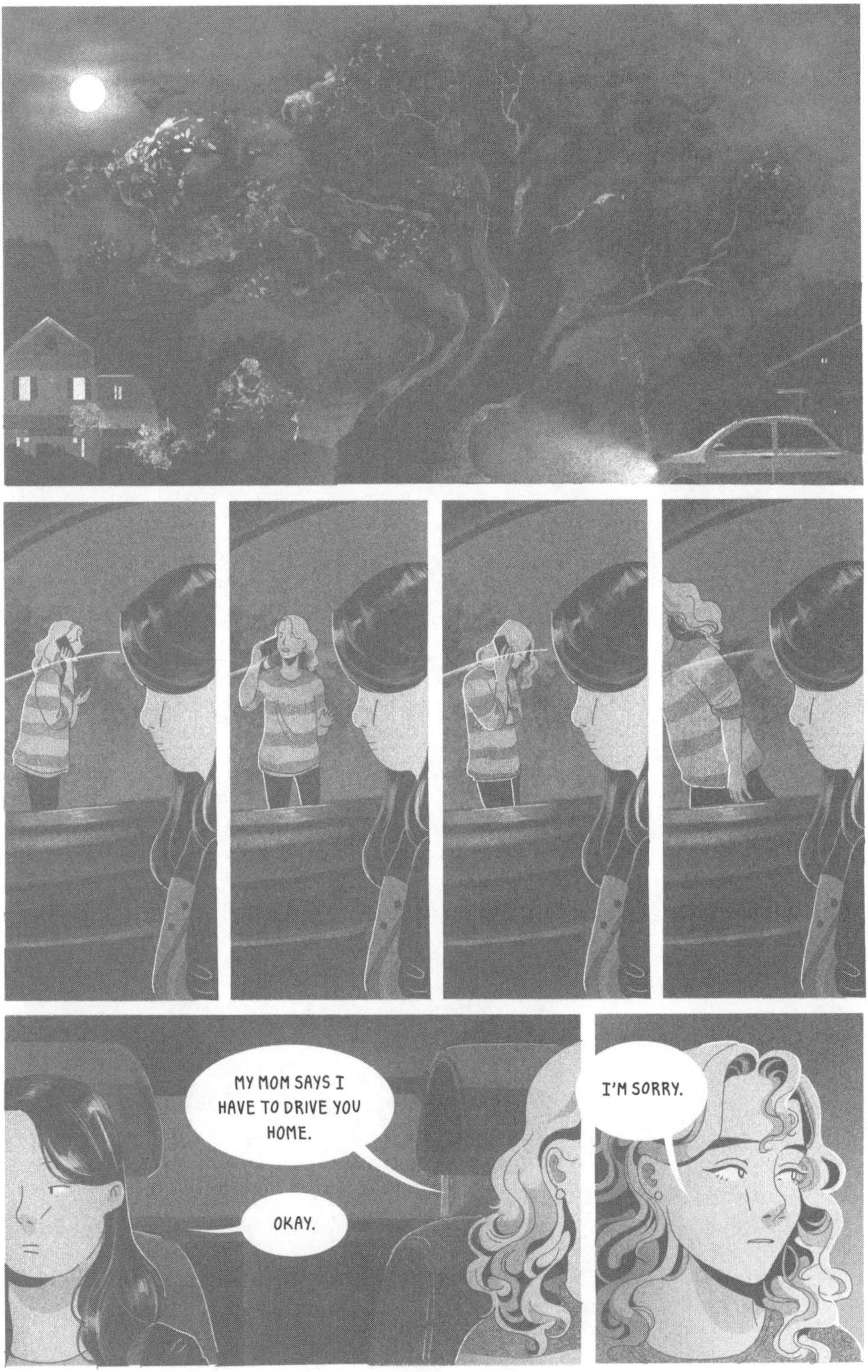
MY MOM SAYS I HAVE TO DRIVE YOU HOME.
OKAY.
I'M SORRY.

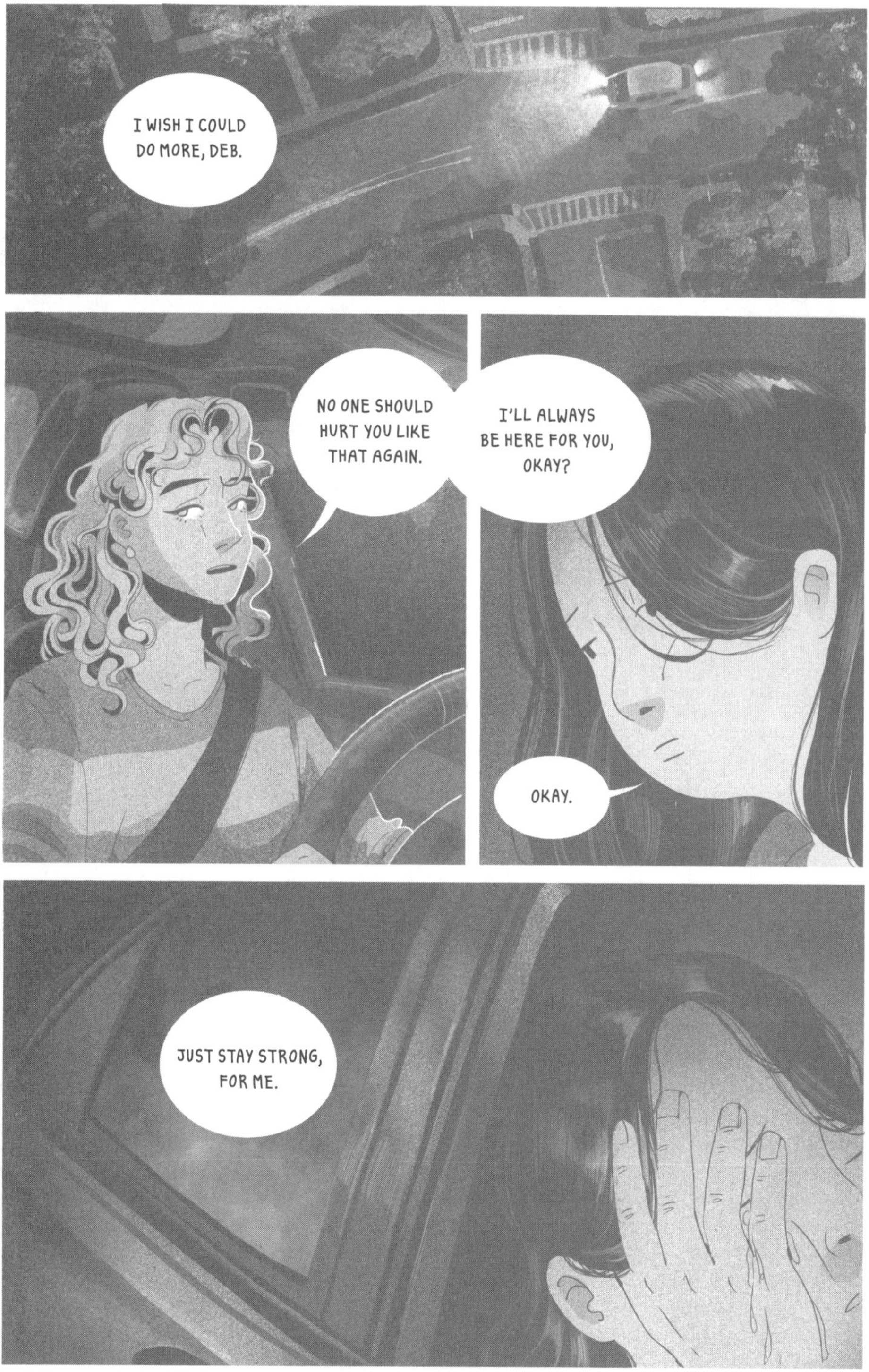
I WISH I COULD DO MORE, DEB.
NO ONE SHOULD HURT YOU LIKE THAT AGAIN.
I'LL ALWAYS BE HERE FOR YOU, OKAY?
OKAY.
JUST STAY STRONG, FOR ME.

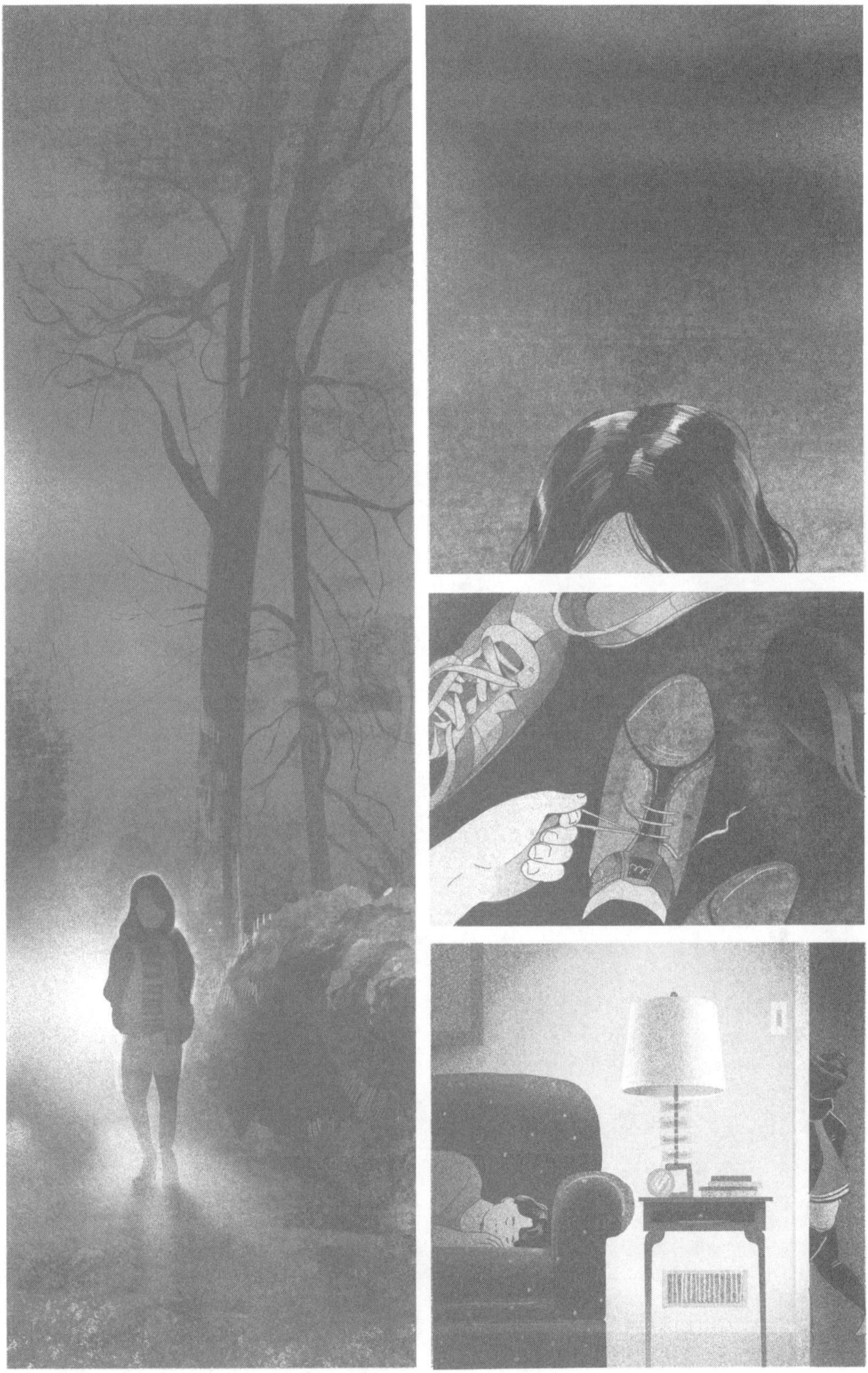

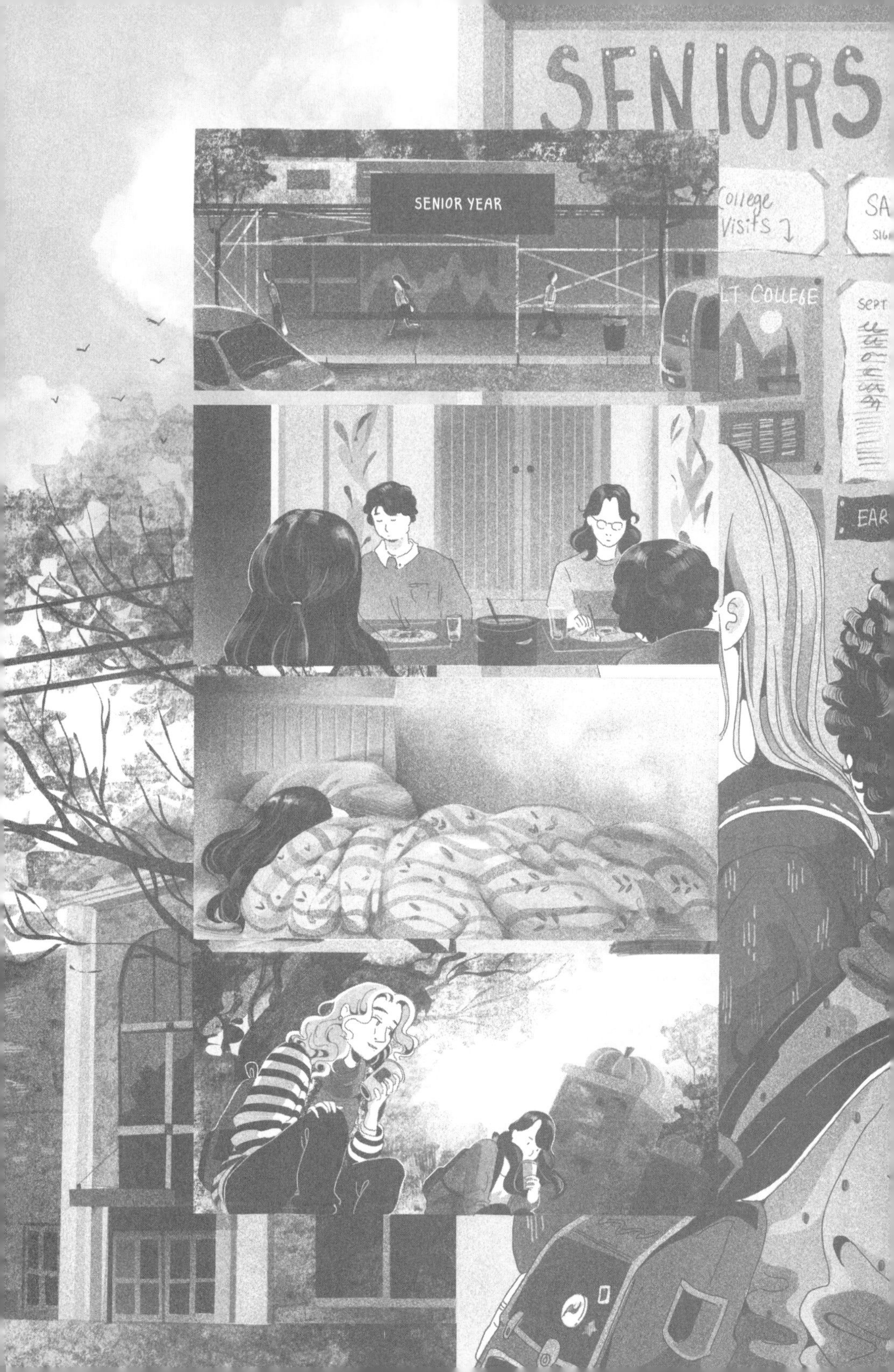
SENIORS
SENIOR YEAR
College Visits
LT COLLEGE
SEPT

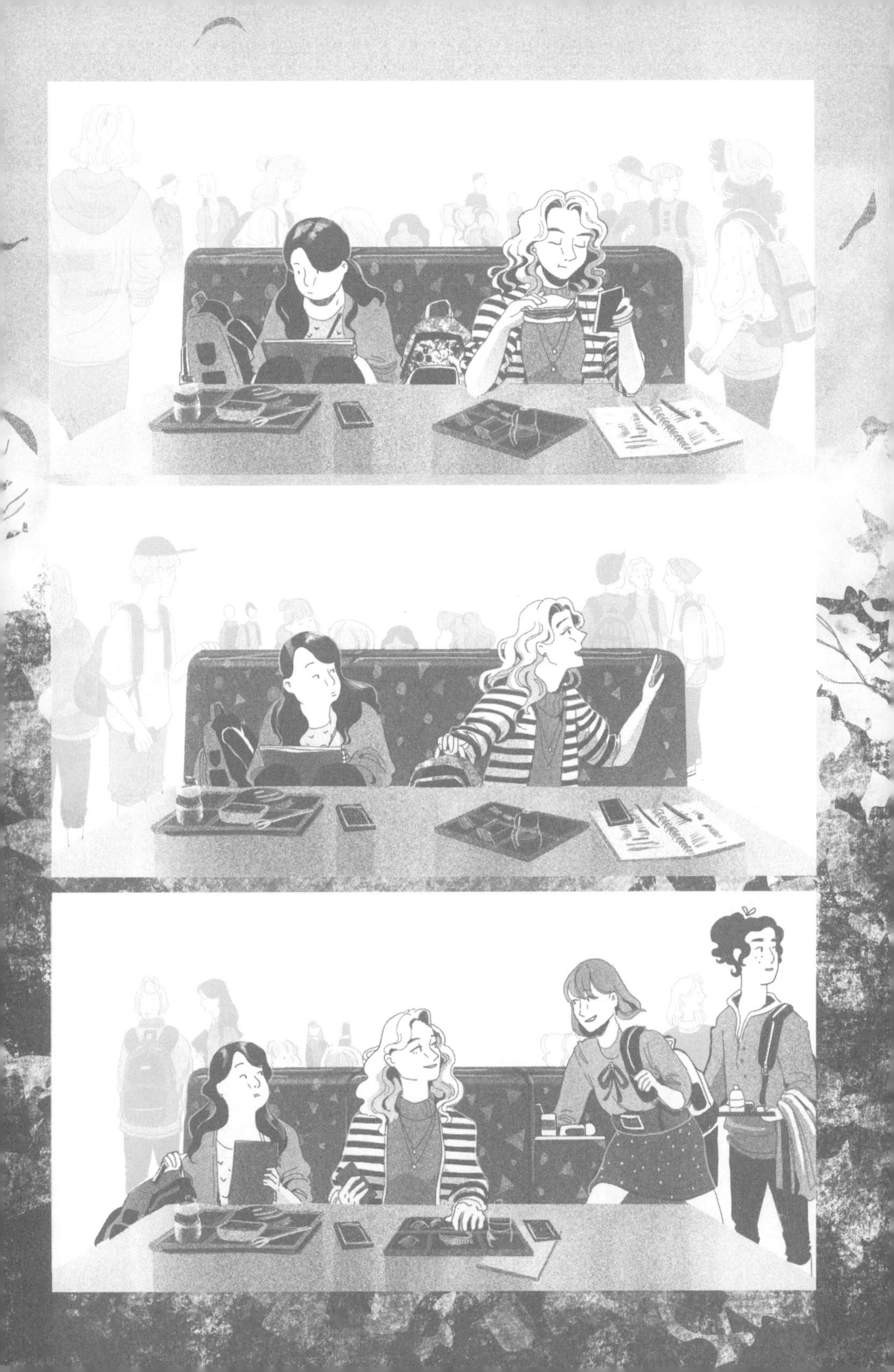

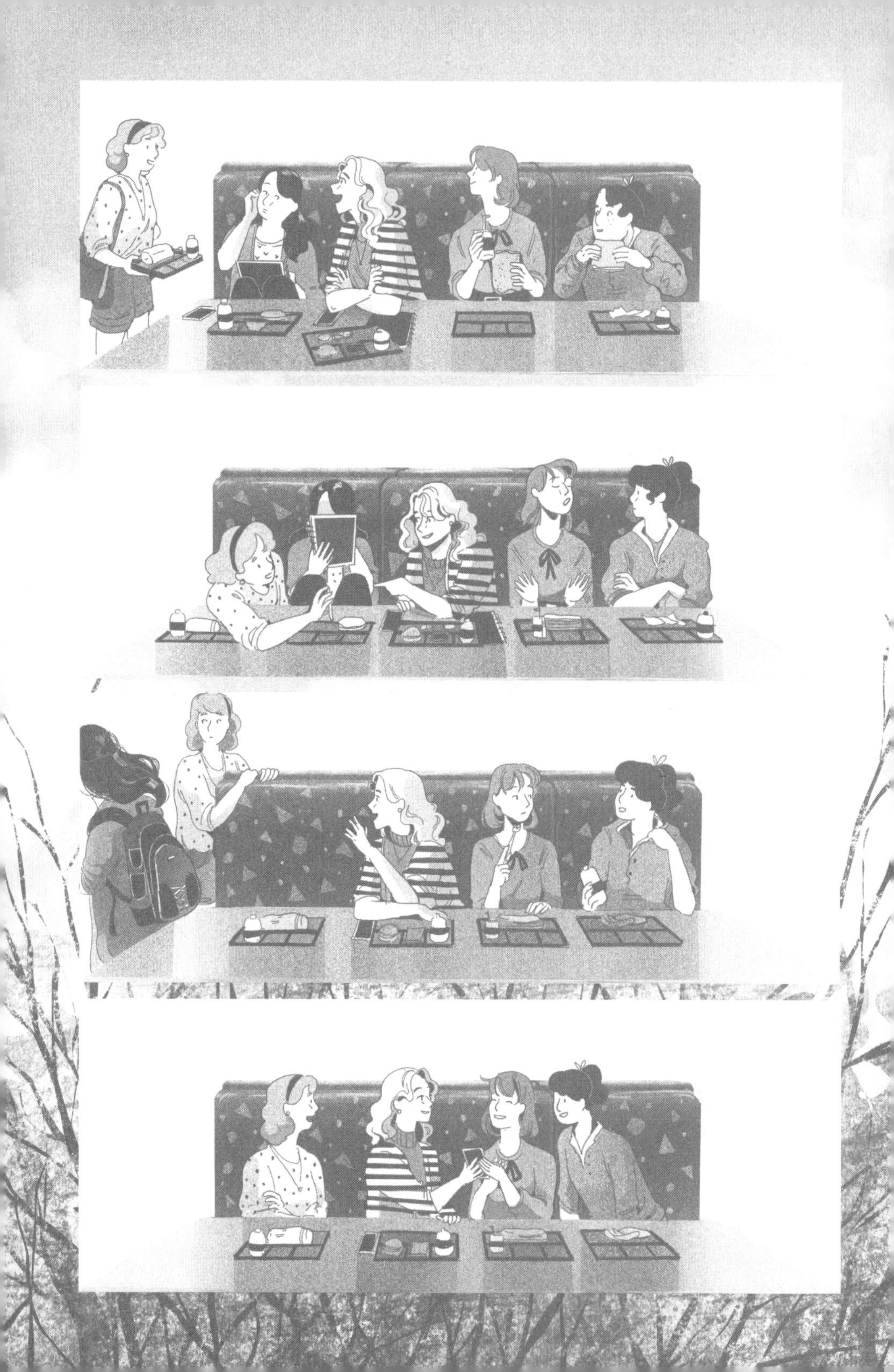

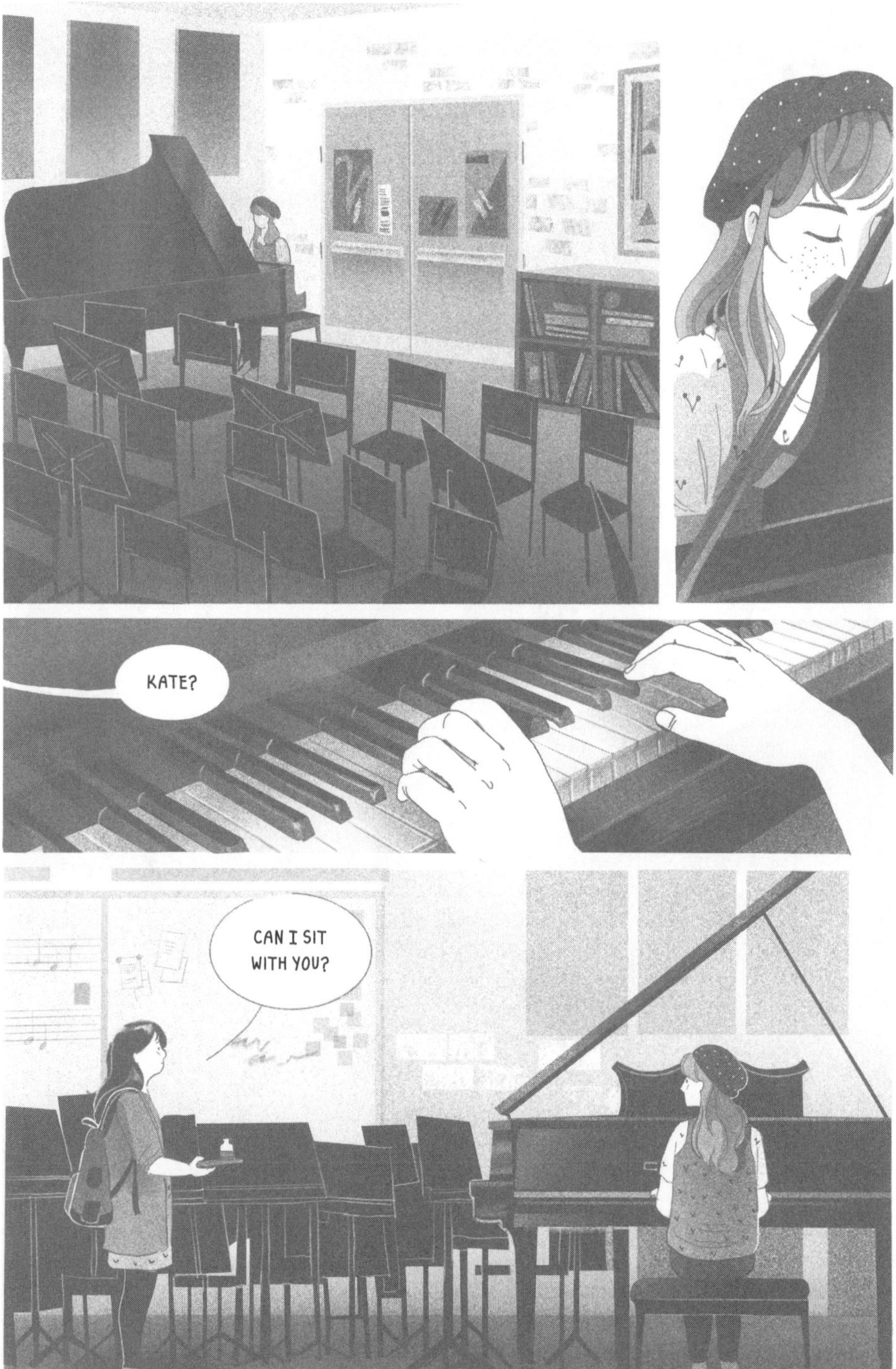
KATE?
CAN I SIT WITH YOU?

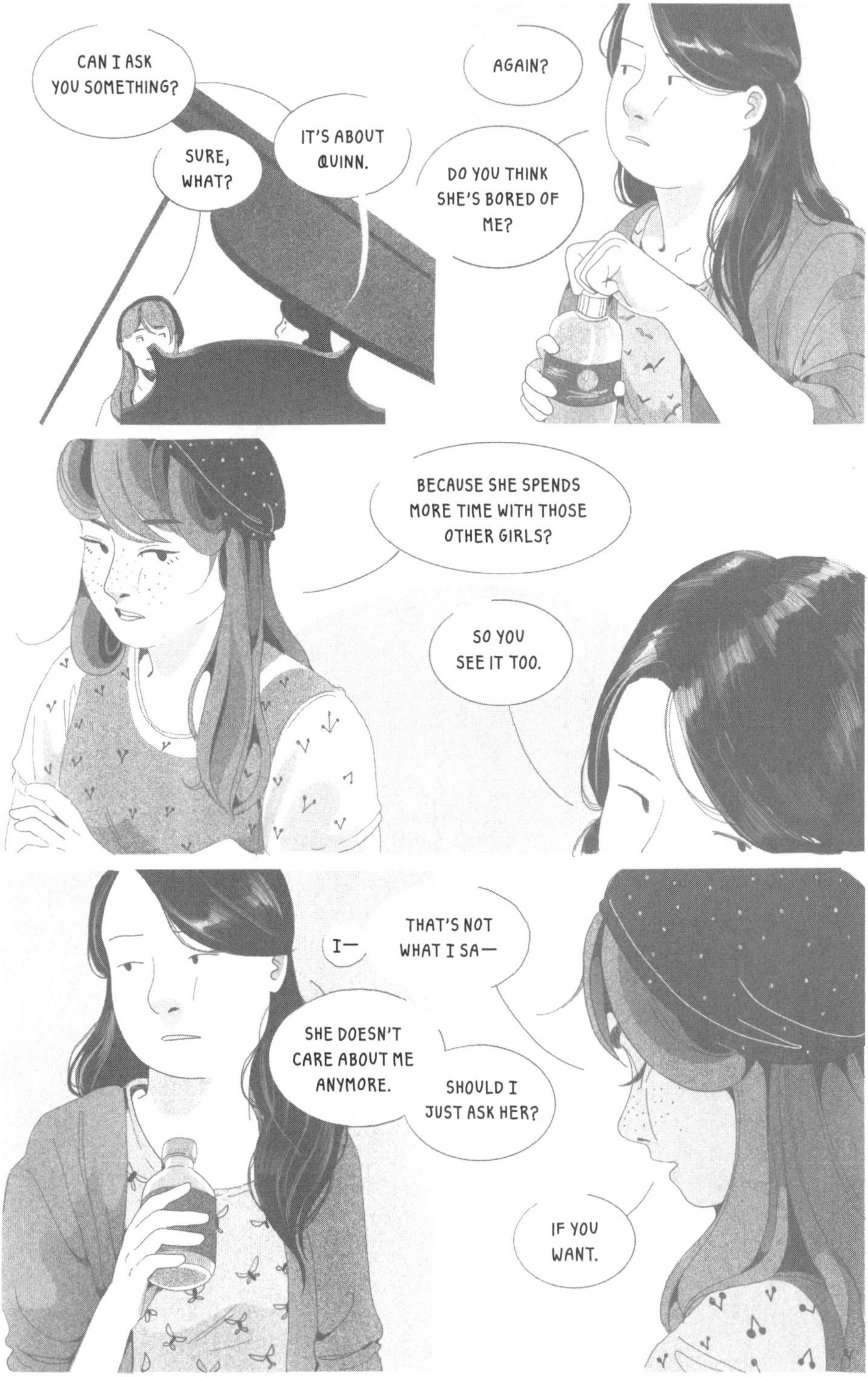
CAN I ASK YOU SOMETHING?
SURE, WHAT?
IT'S ABOUT QUINN.
AGAIN?
DO YOU THINK SHE'S BORED OF ME?
BECAUSE SHE SPENDS MORE TIME WITH THOSE OTHER GIRLS?
SO YOU SEE IT TOO.
I—
THAT'S NOT WHAT I SA—
SHE DOESN'T CARE ABOUT ME ANYMORE.
SHOULD I JUST ASK HER?
IF YOU WANT.

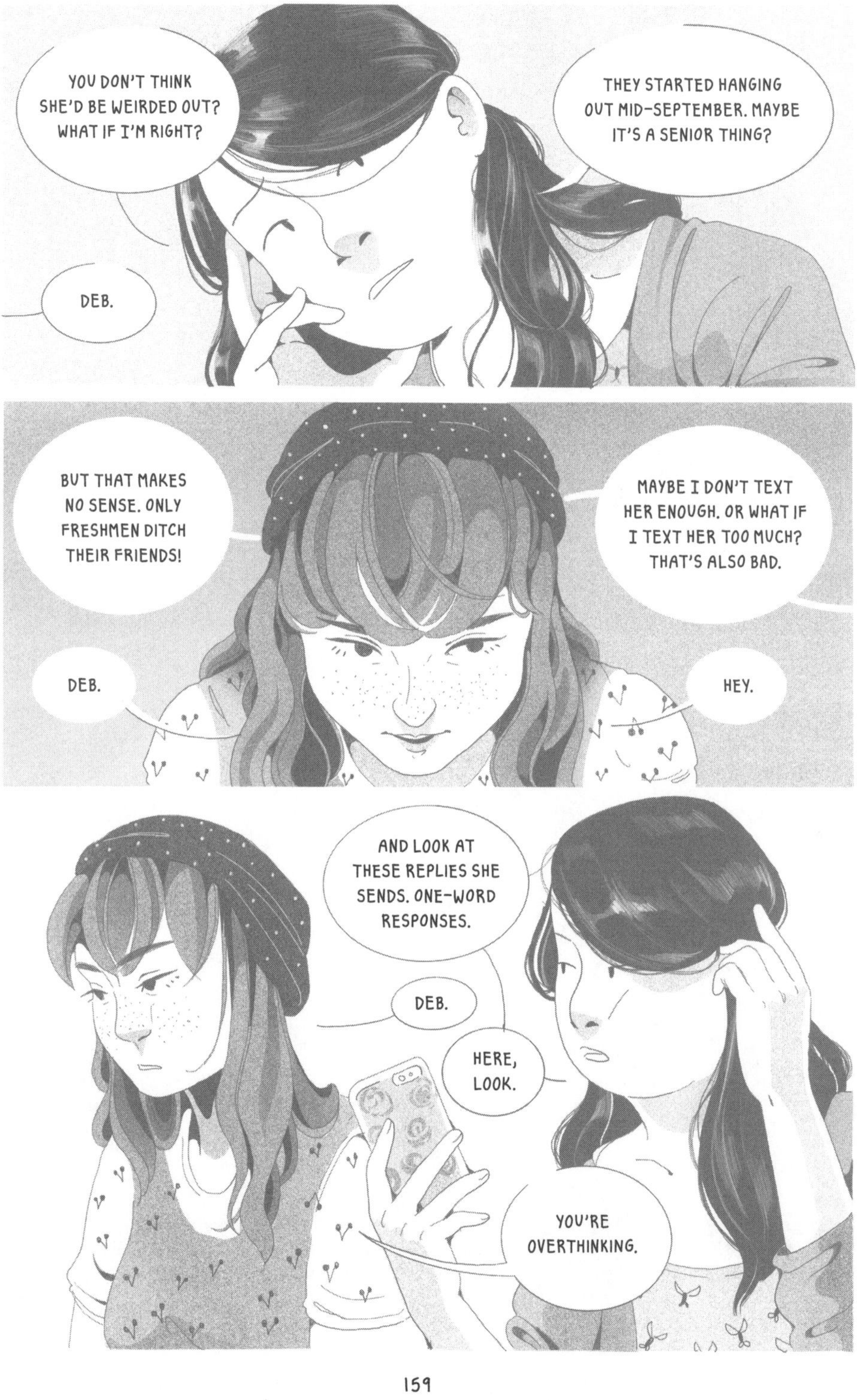
YOU DON'T THINK SHE'D BE WEIRDED OUT? WHAT IF I'M RIGHT?
THEY STARTED HANGING OUT MID-SEPTEMBER. MAYBE IT'S A SENIOR THING?
DEB.
BUT THAT MAKES NO SENSE. ONLY FRESHMEN DITCH THEIR FRIENDS!
MAYBE I DON'T TEXT HER ENOUGH. OR WHAT IF I TEXT HER TOO MUCH? THAT'S ALSO BAD.
DEB.
HEY.
AND LOOK AT THESE REPLIES SHE SENDS. ONE-WORD RESPONSES.
DEB.
HERE, LOOK.
YOU'RE OVERTHINKING.

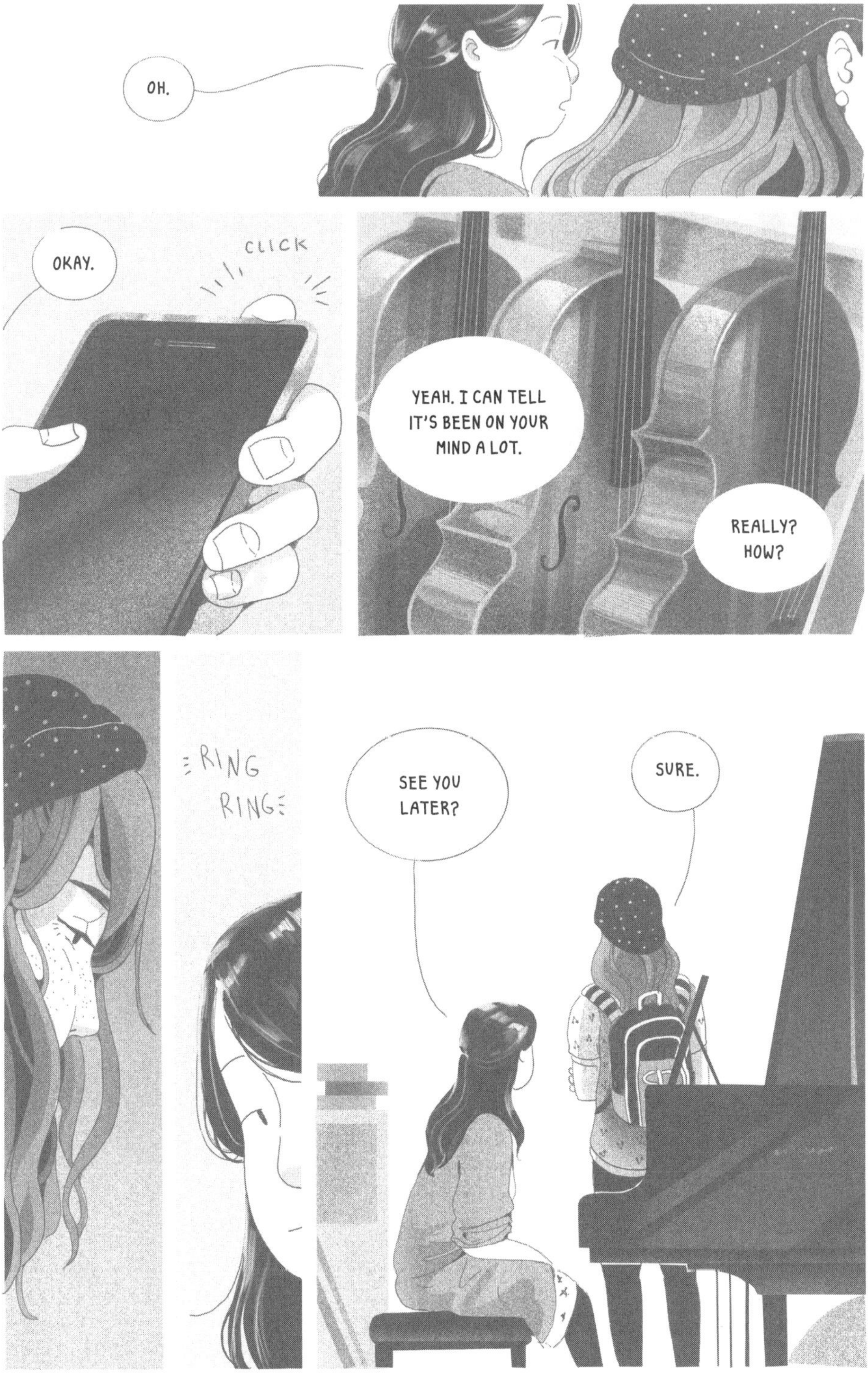
OH.
OKAY.
CLICK
YEAH. I CAN TELL IT'S BEEN ON YOUR MIND A LOT.
REALLY? HOW?
RING RING
SEE YOU LATER?
SURE.

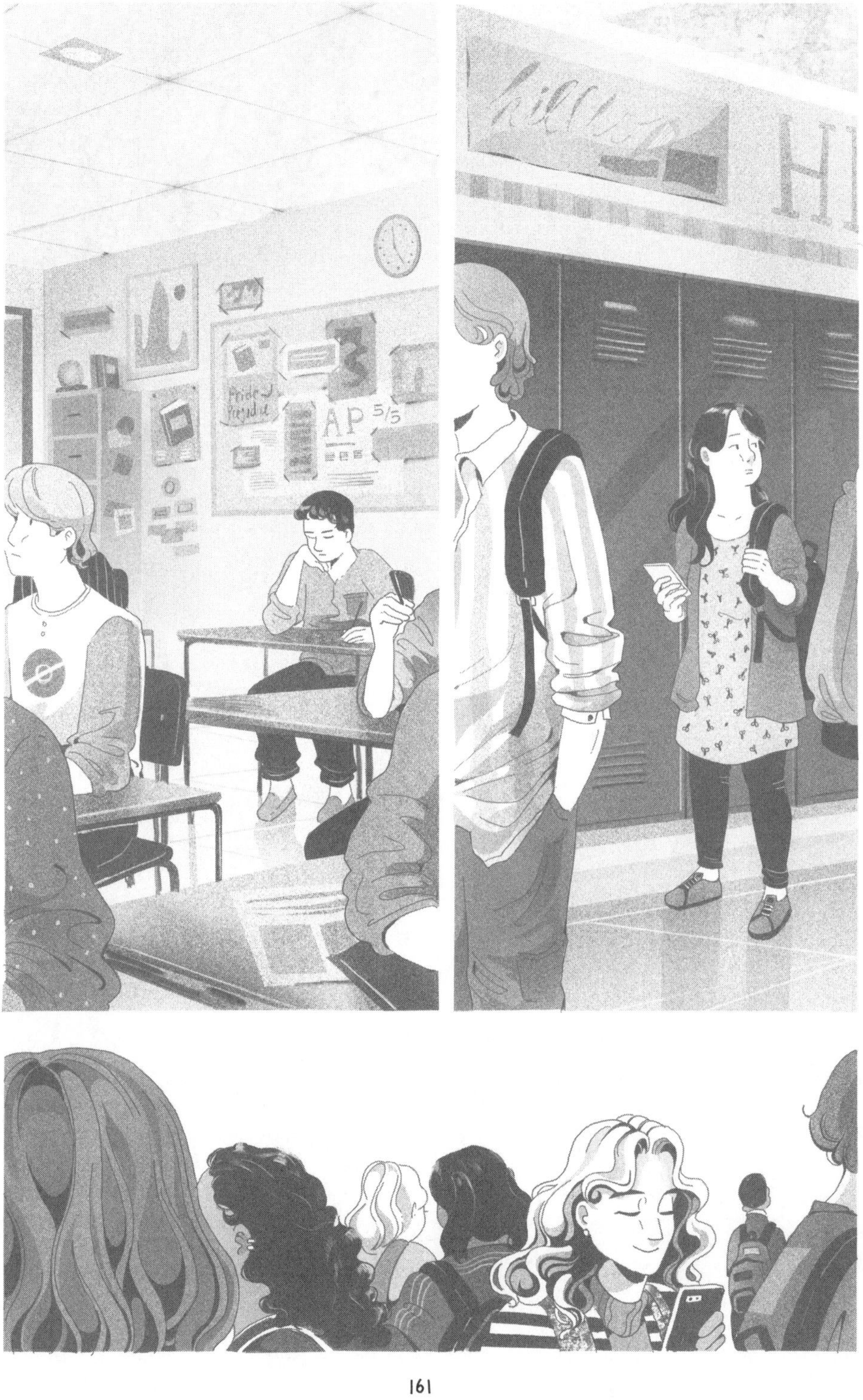
AP 5/5

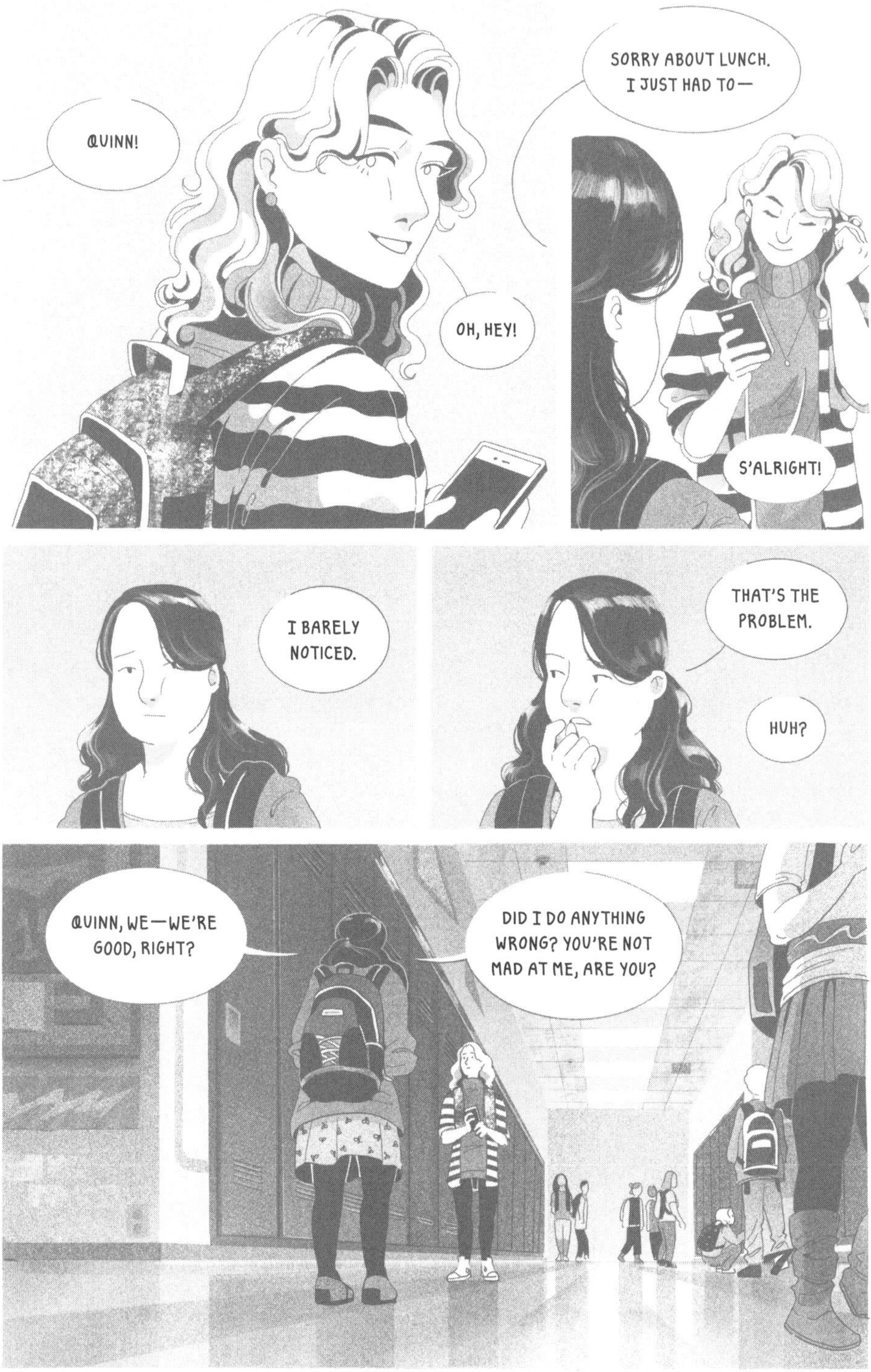
QUINN!
OH, HEY!
SORRY ABOUT LUNCH. I JUST HAD TO—
S'ALRIGHT!
I BARELY NOTICED.
THAT'S THE PROBLEM.
HUH?
QUINN, WE—WE'RE GOOD, RIGHT?
DID I DO ANYTHING WRONG? YOU'RE NOT MAD AT ME, ARE YOU?

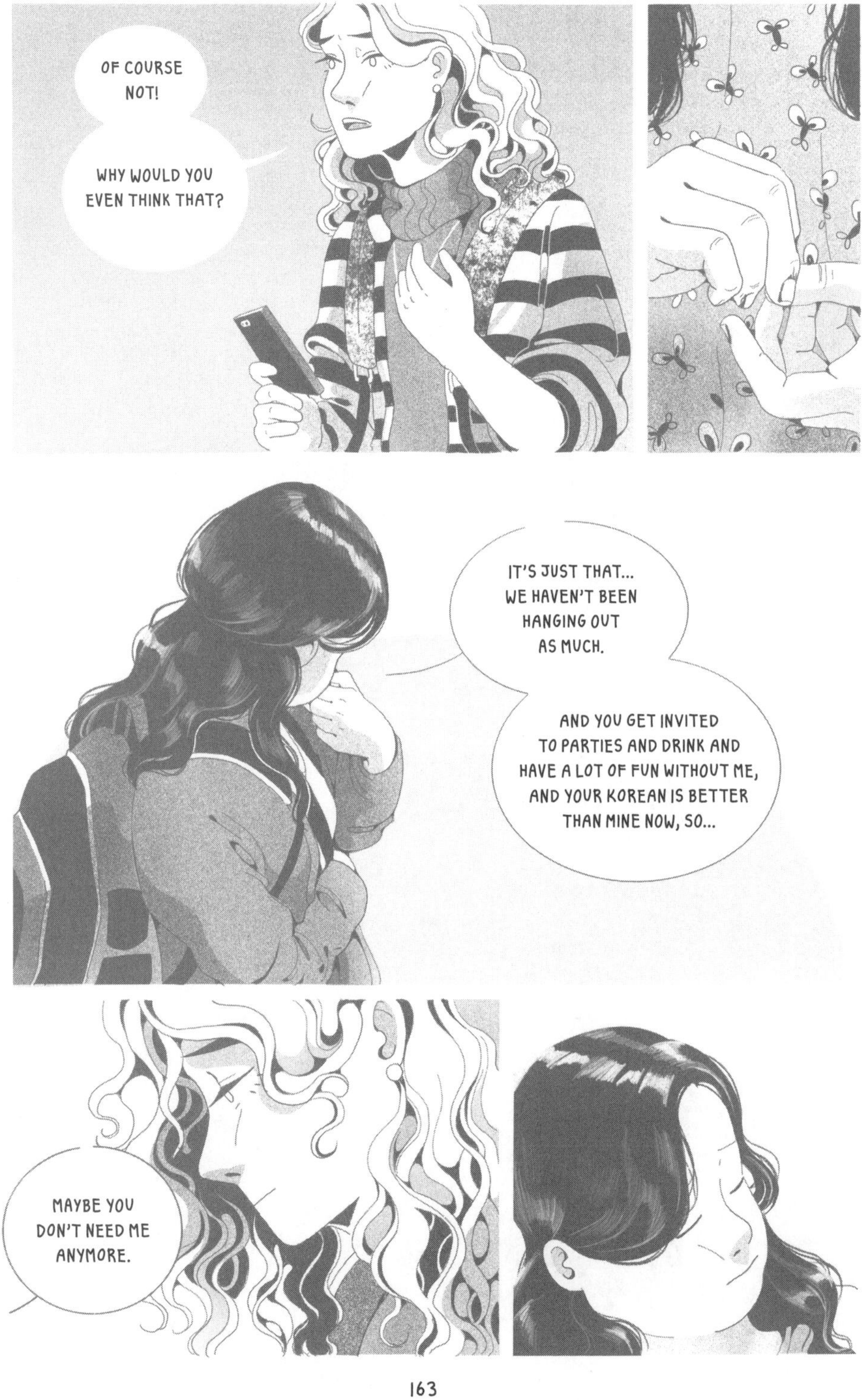
OF COURSE NOT!
WHY WOULD YOU EVEN THINK THAT?
IT'S JUST THAT... WE HAVEN'T BEEN HANGING OUT AS MUCH.
AND YOU GET INVITED TO PARTIES AND DRINK AND HAVE A LOT OF FUN WITHOUT ME, AND YOUR KOREAN IS BETTER THAN MINE NOW, SO...
MAYBE YOU DON'T NEED ME ANYMORE.

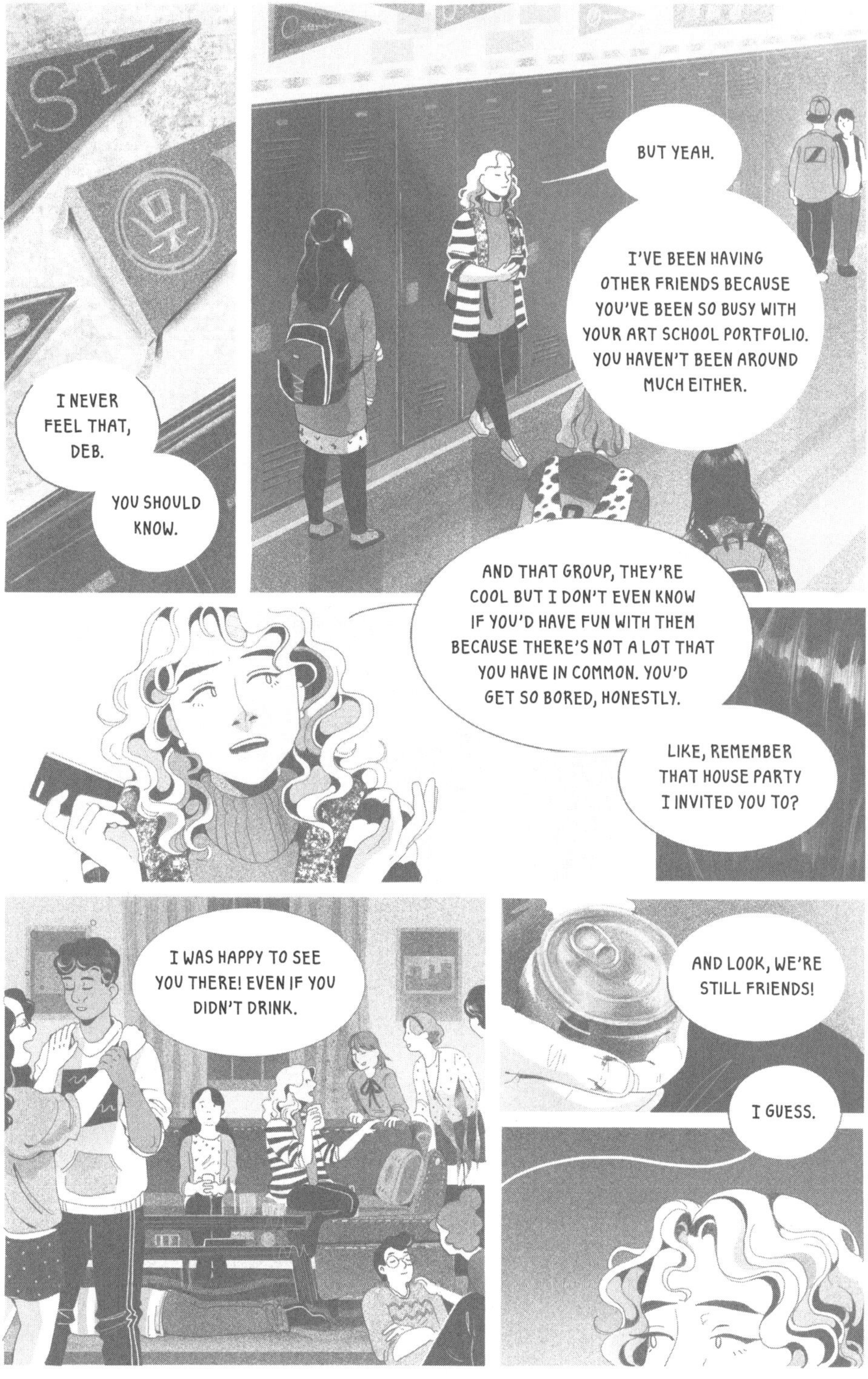
I NEVER FEEL THAT, DEB.
YOU SHOULD KNOW.
BUT YEAH.
I'VE BEEN HAVING OTHER FRIENDS BECAUSE YOU'VE BEEN SO BUSY WITH YOUR ART SCHOOL PORTFOLIO. YOU HAVEN'T BEEN AROUND MUCH EITHER.
AND THAT GROUP, THEY'RE COOL BUT I DON'T EVEN KNOW IF YOU'D HAVE FUN WITH THEM BECAUSE THERE'S NOT A LOT THAT YOU HAVE IN COMMON. YOU'D GET SO BORED, HONESTLY.
LIKE, REMEMBER THAT HOUSE PARTY I INVITED YOU TO?
I WAS HAPPY TO SEE YOU THERE! EVEN IF YOU DIDN'T DRINK.
AND LOOK, WE'RE STILL FRIENDS!
I GUESS.

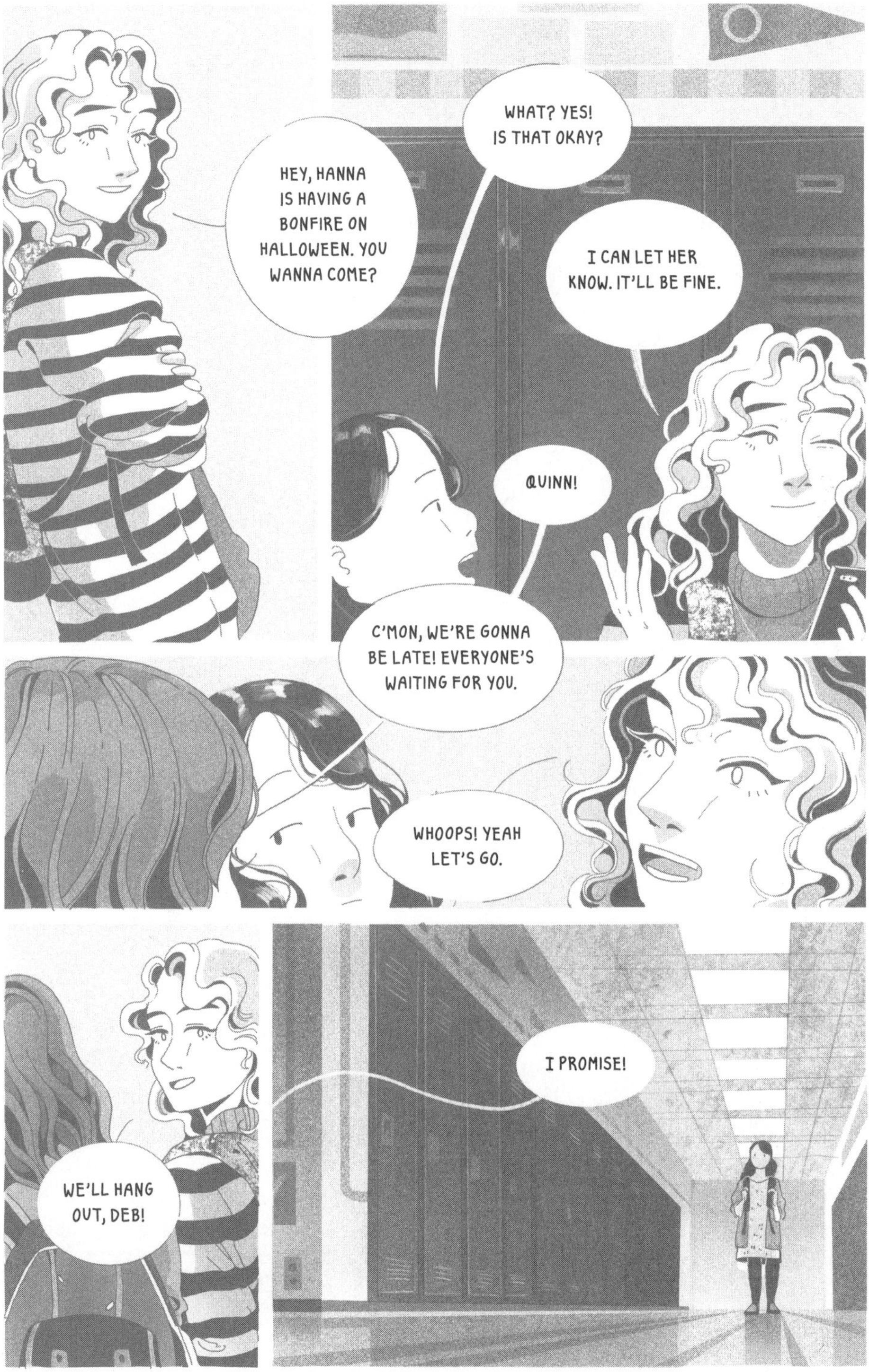
HEY, HANNA IS HAVING A BONFIRE ON HALLOWEEN. YOU WANNA COME?
WHAT? YES! IS THAT OKAY?
I CAN LET HER KNOW. IT'LL BE FINE.
QUINN!
C'MON, WE'RE GONNA BE LATE! EVERYONE'S WAITING FOR YOU.
WHOOPS! YEAH LET'S GO.
WE'LL HANG OUT, DEB!
I PROMISE!

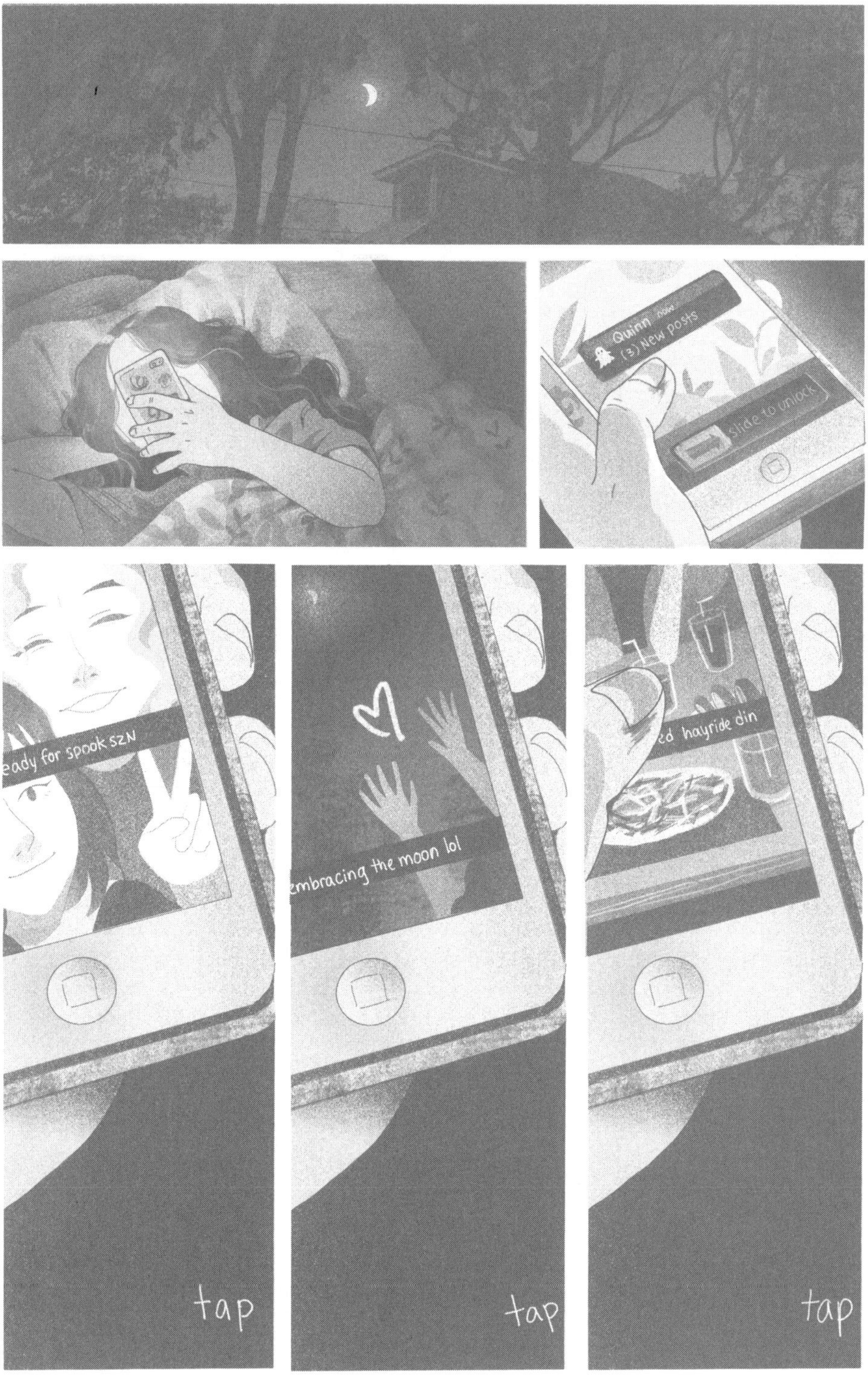

Quinn now
(3) New posts
slide to unlock
eady for spook szN
tap
embracing the moon lol
tap
ed hayride din
tap

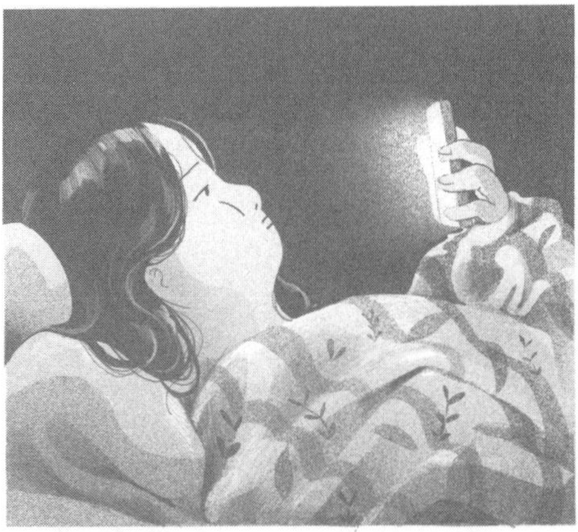
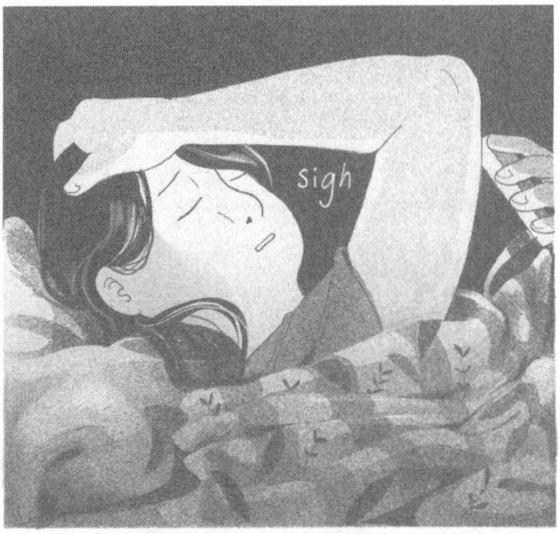
sigh
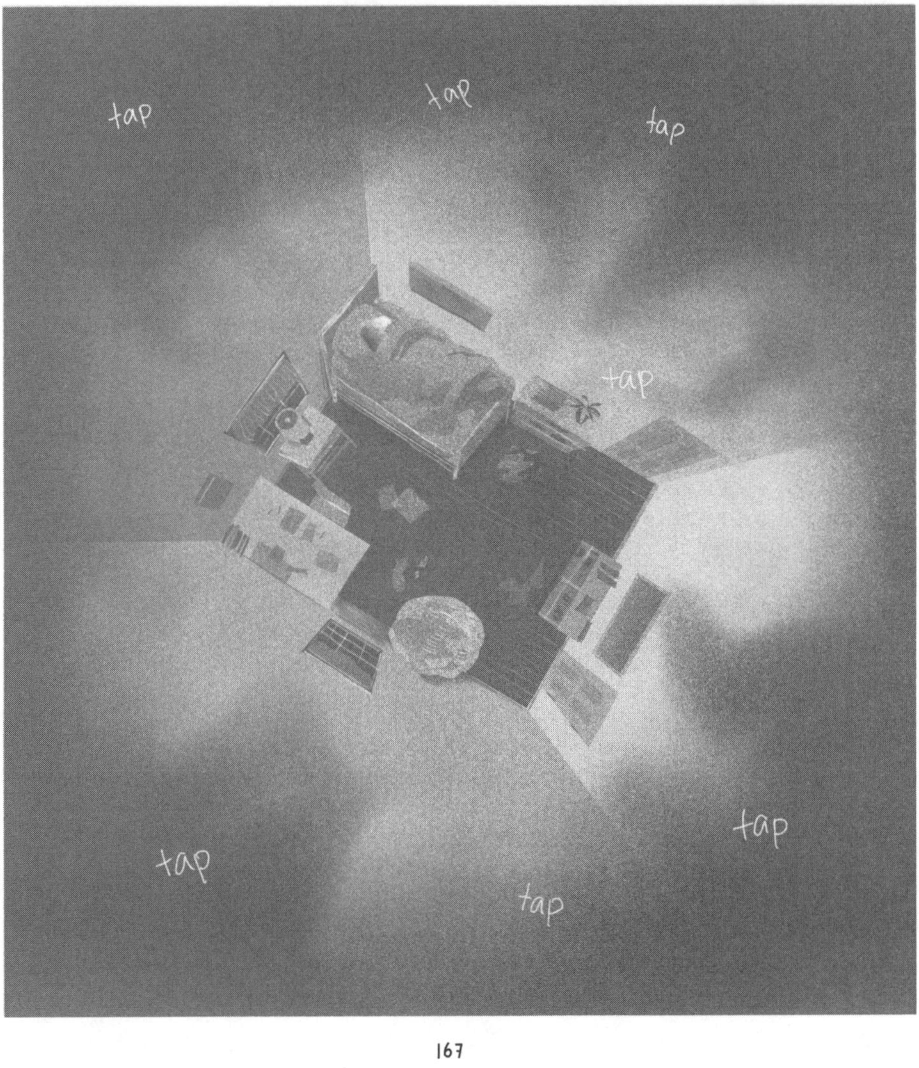
tap
tap
tap
tap
tap
tap
tap

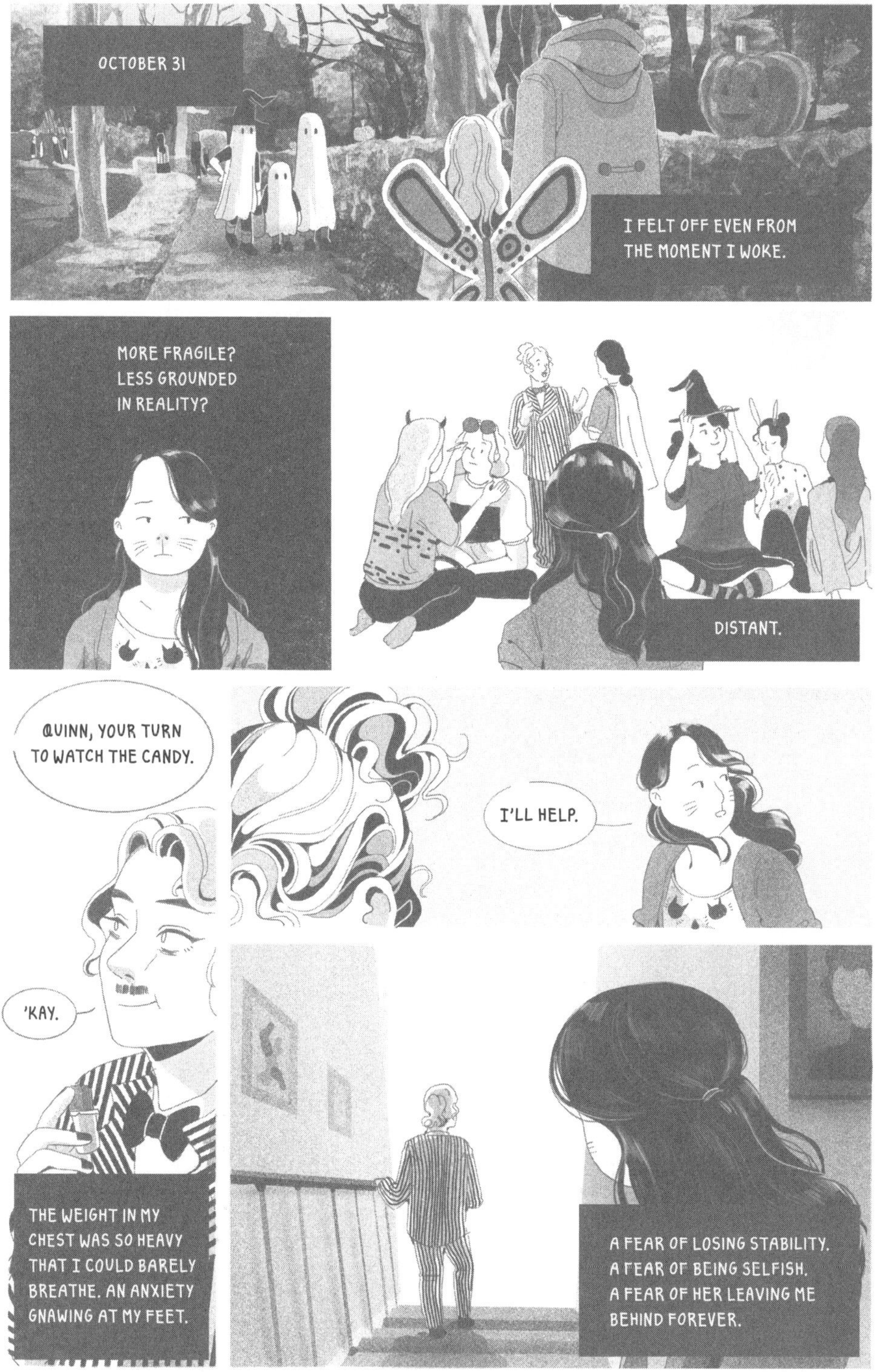
OCTOBER 31
I FELT OFF EVEN FROM THE MOMENT I WOKE.
MORE FRAGILE? LESS GROUNDED IN REALITY?
DISTANT.
QUINN, YOUR TURN TO WATCH THE CANDY.
I'LL HELP.
'KAY.
THE WEIGHT IN MY CHEST WAS SO HEAVY THAT I COULD BARELY BREATHE. AN ANXIETY GNAWING AT MY FEET.
A FEAR OF LOSING STABILITY.
A FEAR OF BEING SELFISH.
A FEAR OF HER LEAVING ME BEHIND FOREVER.

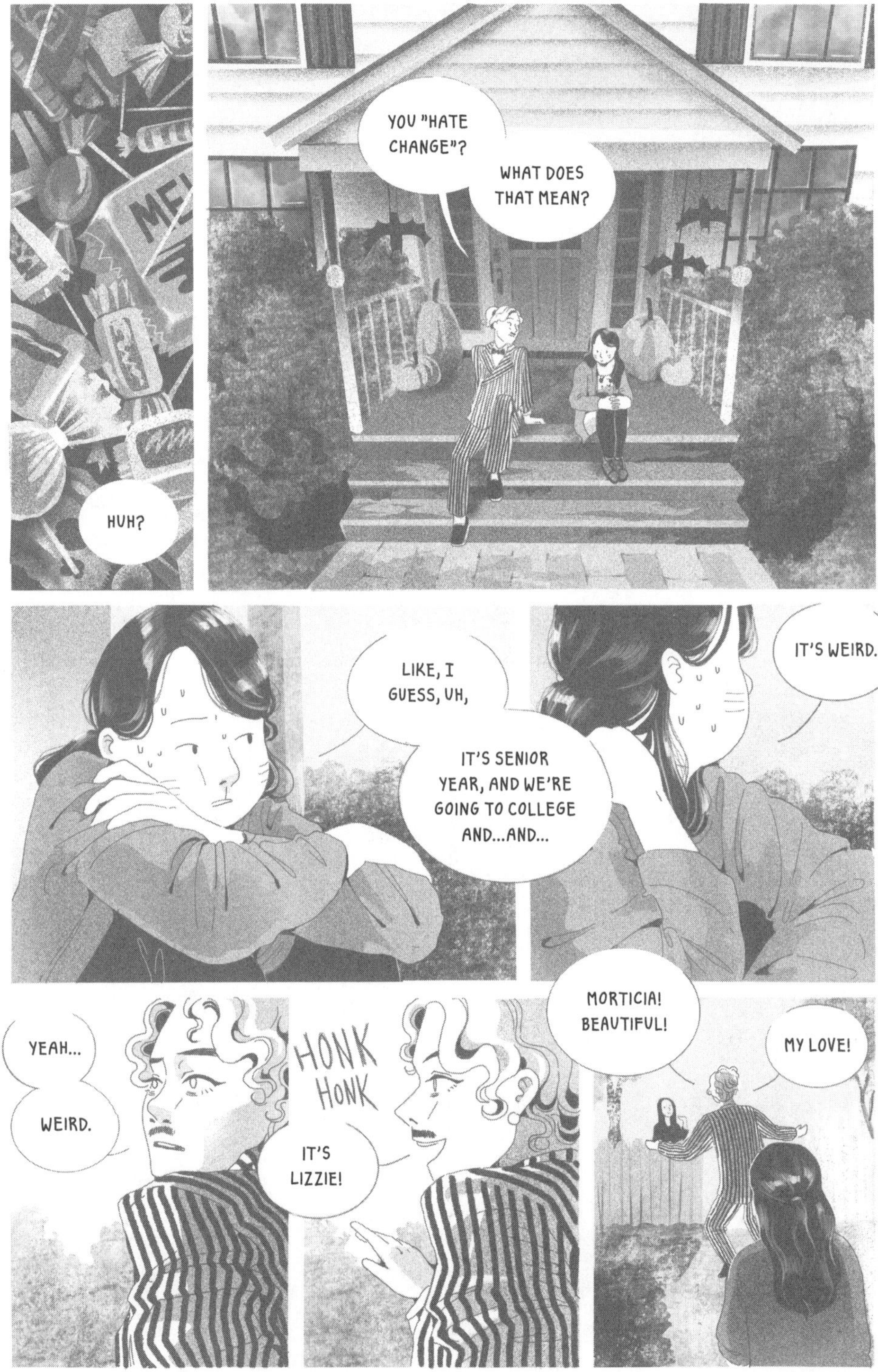
HUH?
YOU "HATE CHANGE"?
WHAT DOES THAT MEAN?
LIKE, I GUESS, UH,
IT'S SENIOR YEAR, AND WE'RE GOING TO COLLEGE AND...AND...
IT'S WEIRD.
YEAH...
WEIRD.
HONK HONK
IT'S LIZZIE!
MORTICIA! BEAUTIFUL!
MY LOVE!
MEL

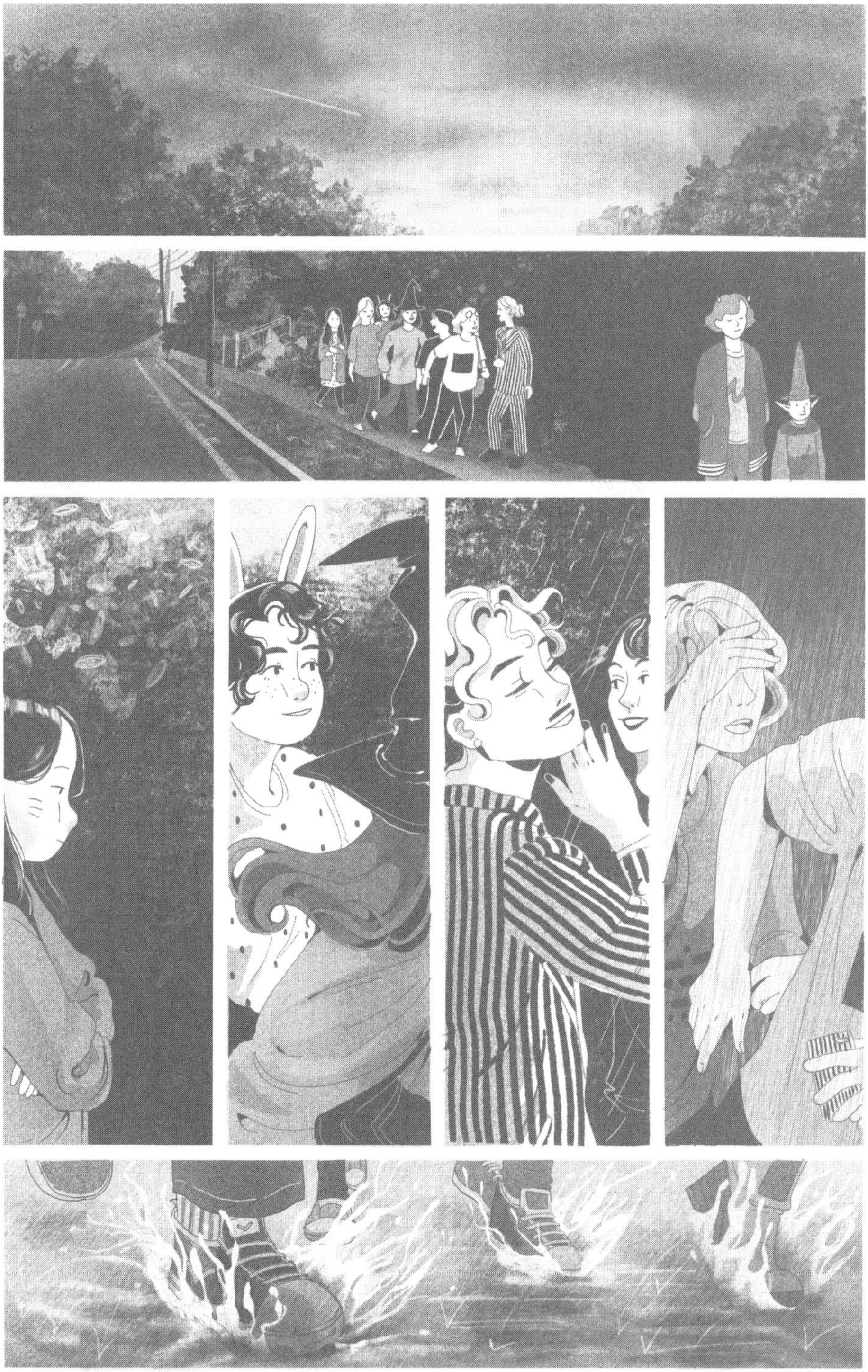

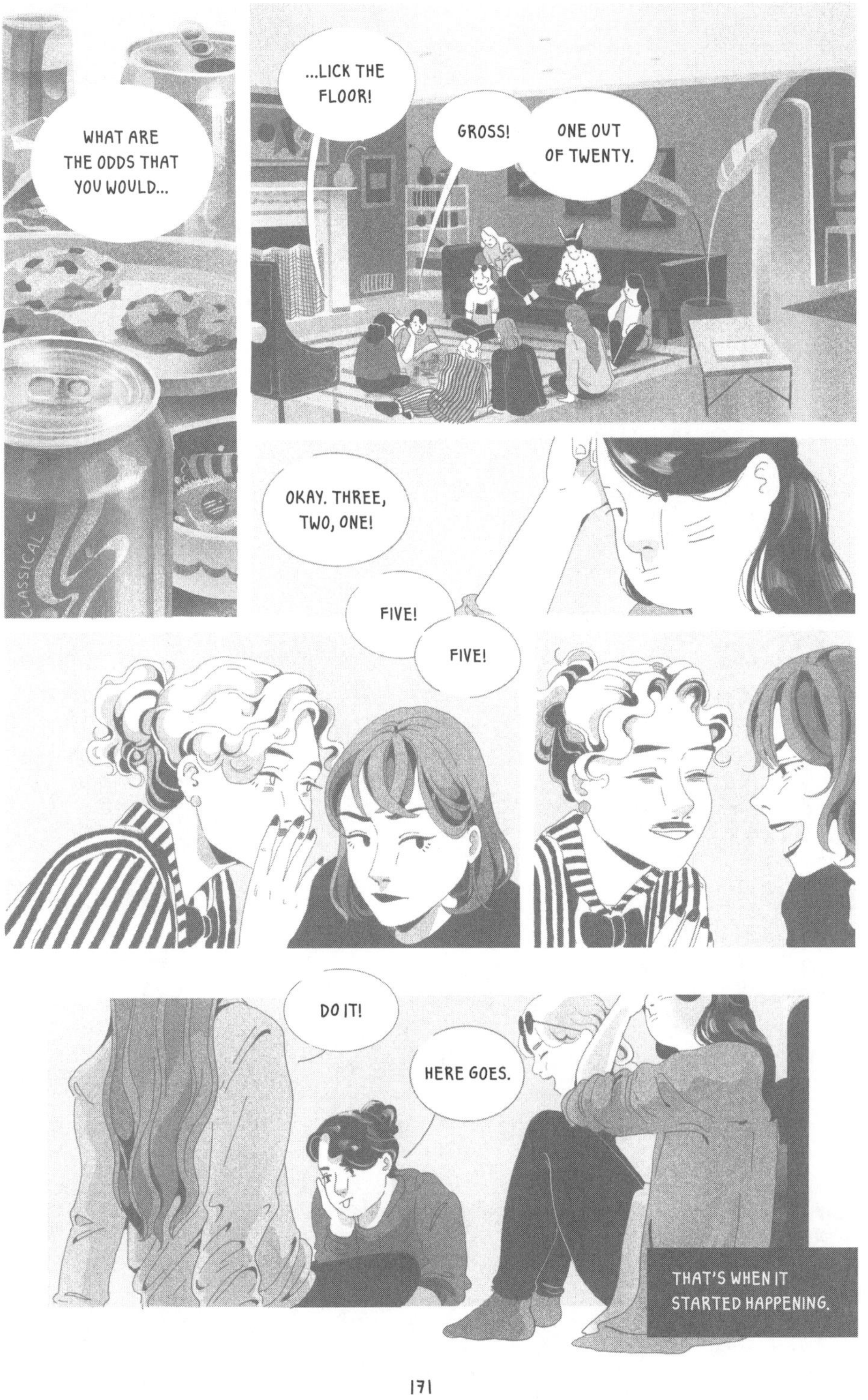
WHAT ARE THE ODDS THAT YOU WOULD...
CLASSICAL
...LICK THE FLOOR!
GROSS!
ONE OUT OF TWENTY.
OKAY. THREE, TWO, ONE!
FIVE!
FIVE!
DO IT!
HERE GOES.
THAT'S WHEN IT STARTED HAPPENING.

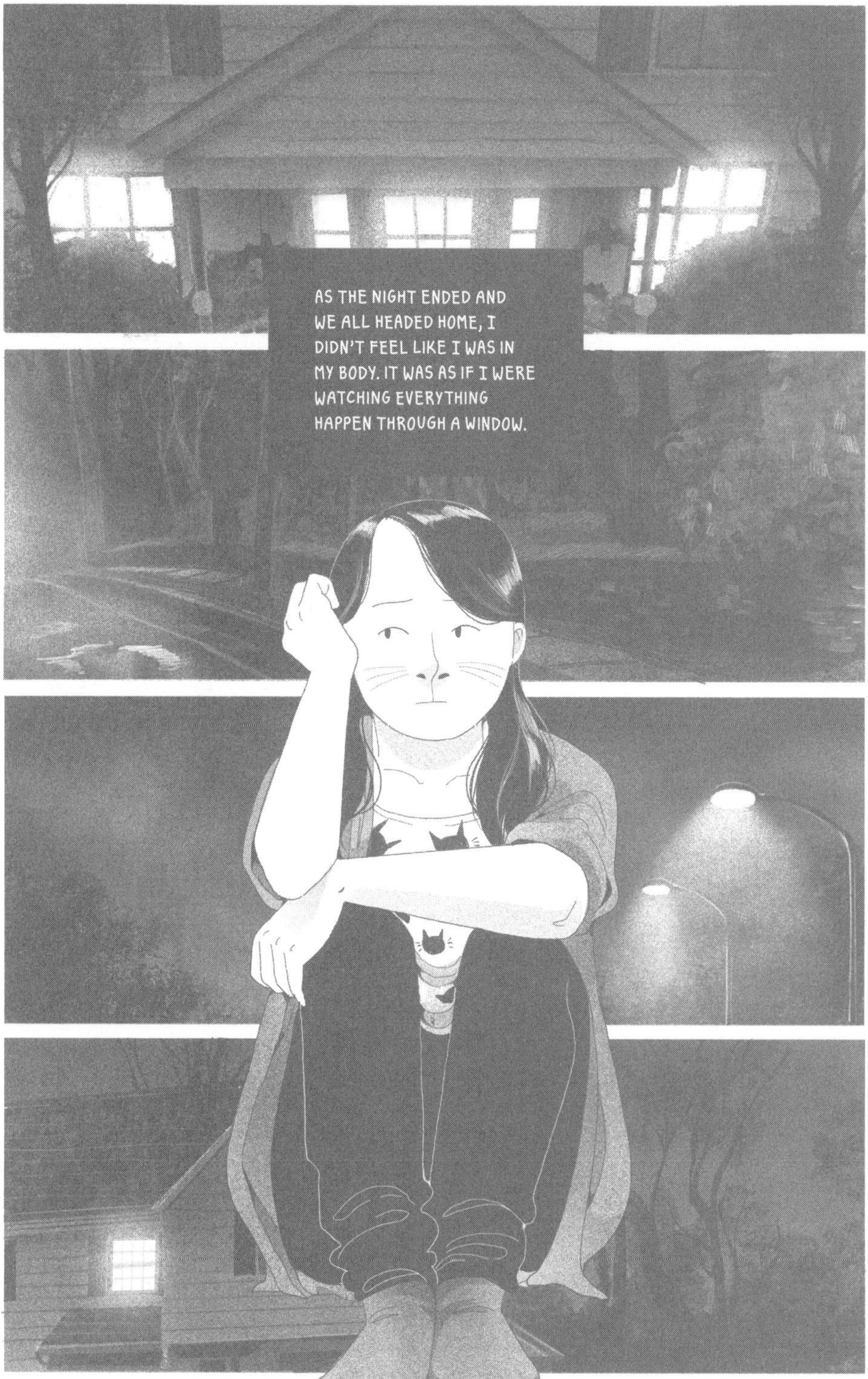
AS THE NIGHT ENDED AND WE ALL HEADED HOME, I DIDN'T FEEL LIKE I WAS IN MY BODY. IT WAS AS IF I WERE WATCHING EVERYTHING HAPPEN THROUGH A WINDOW.

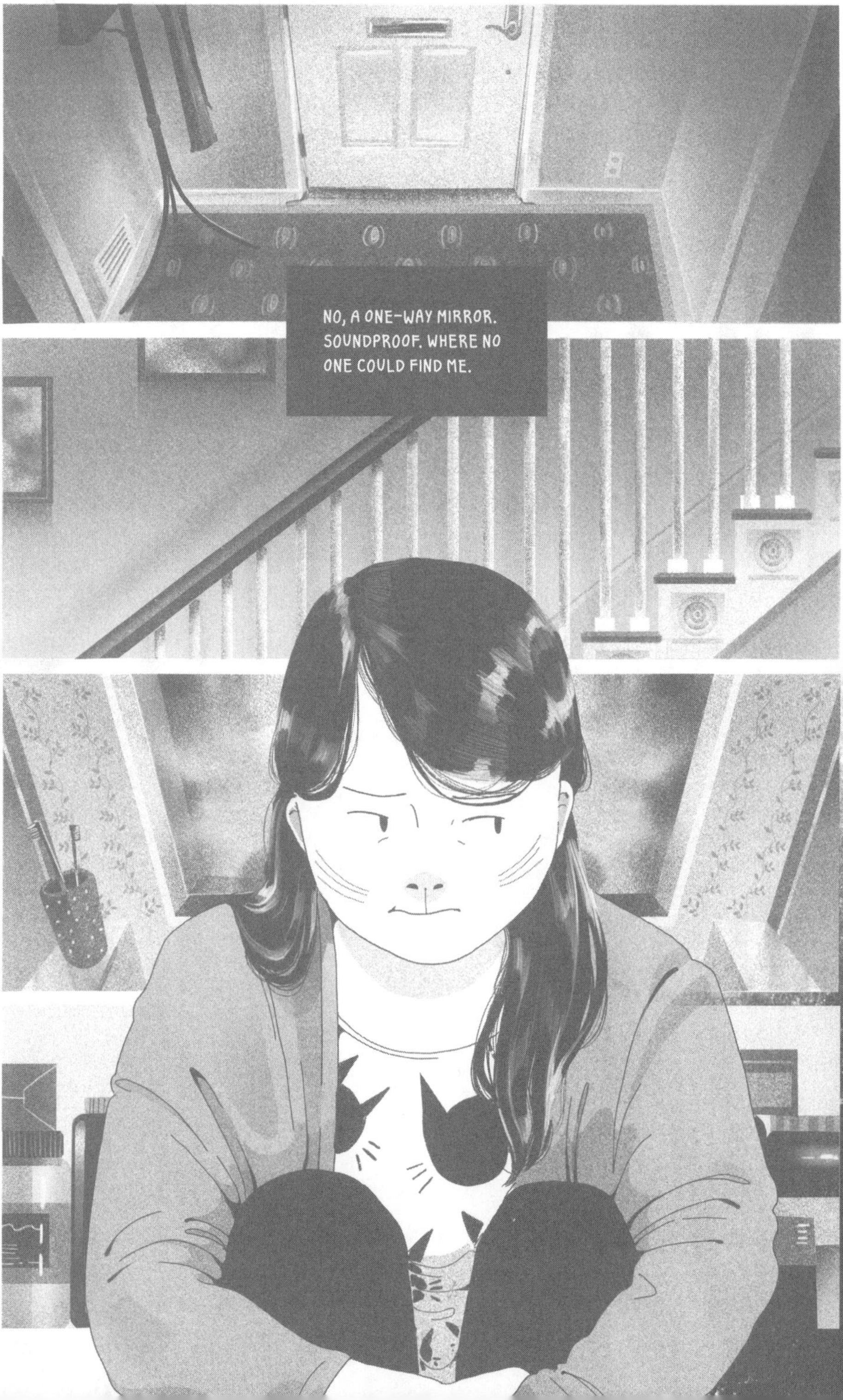
NO, A ONE-WAY MIRROR. SOUNDPROOF. WHERE NO ONE COULD FIND ME.

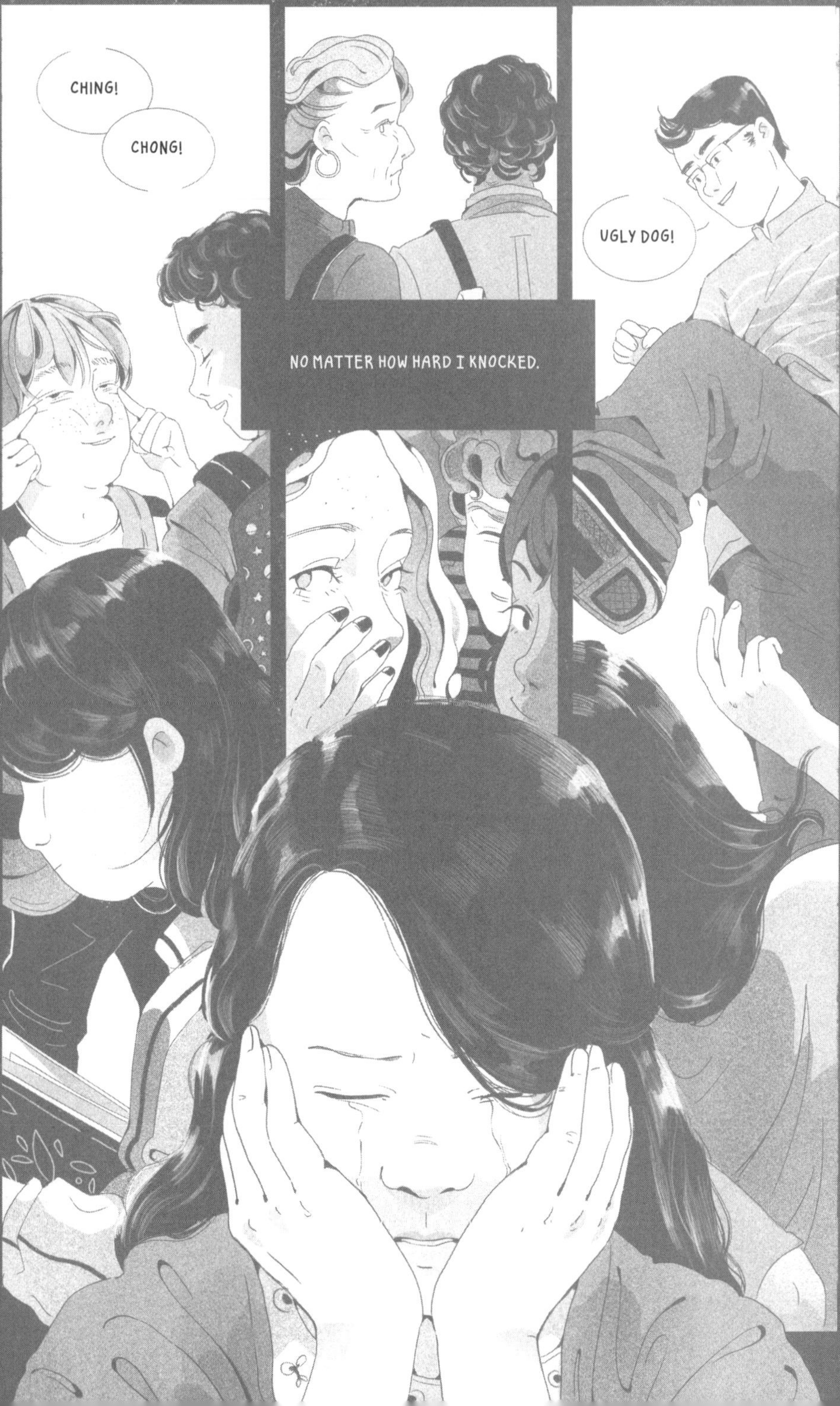
CHING!
CHONG!
UGLY DOG!
NO MATTER HOW HARD I KNOCKED.

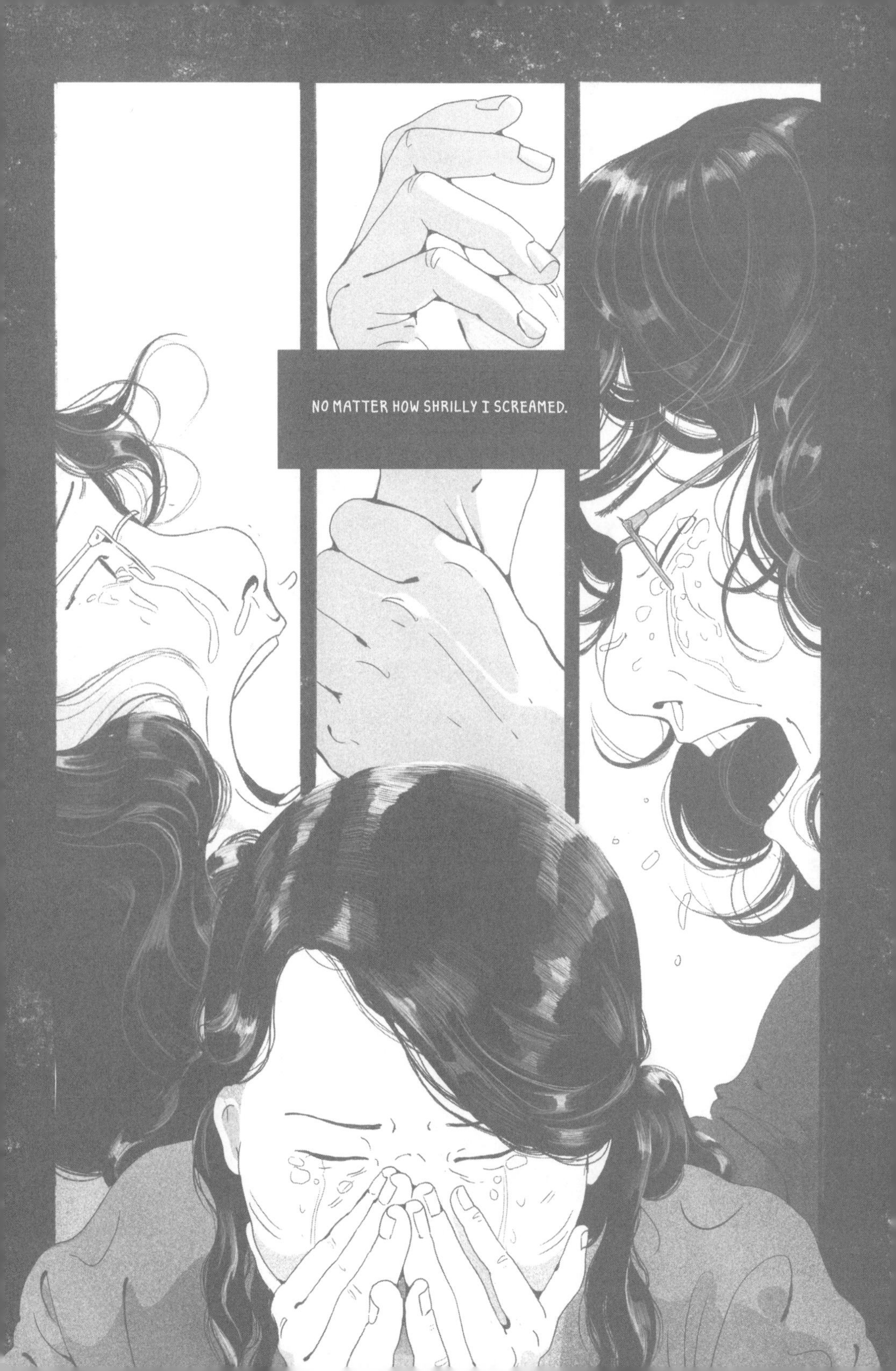
NO MATTER HOW SHRILLY I SCREAMED.

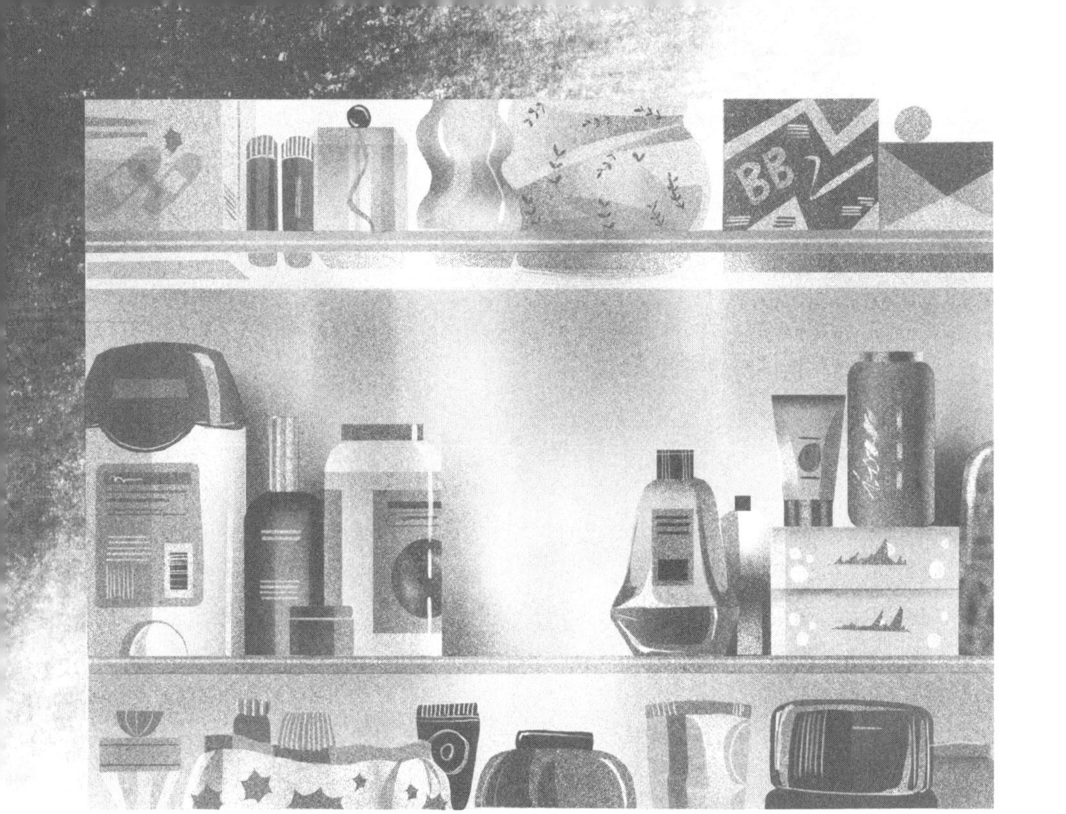
BB

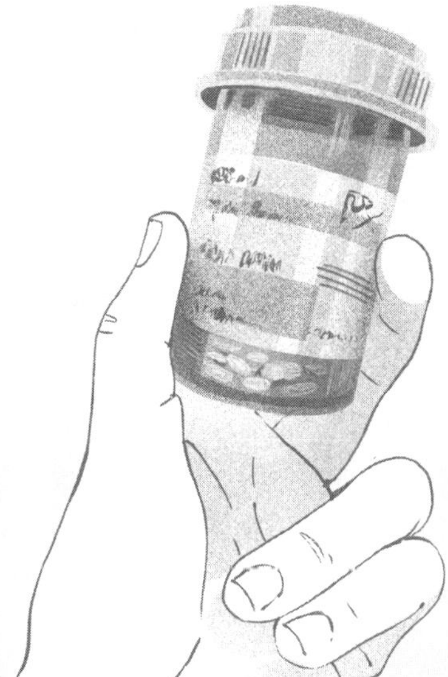

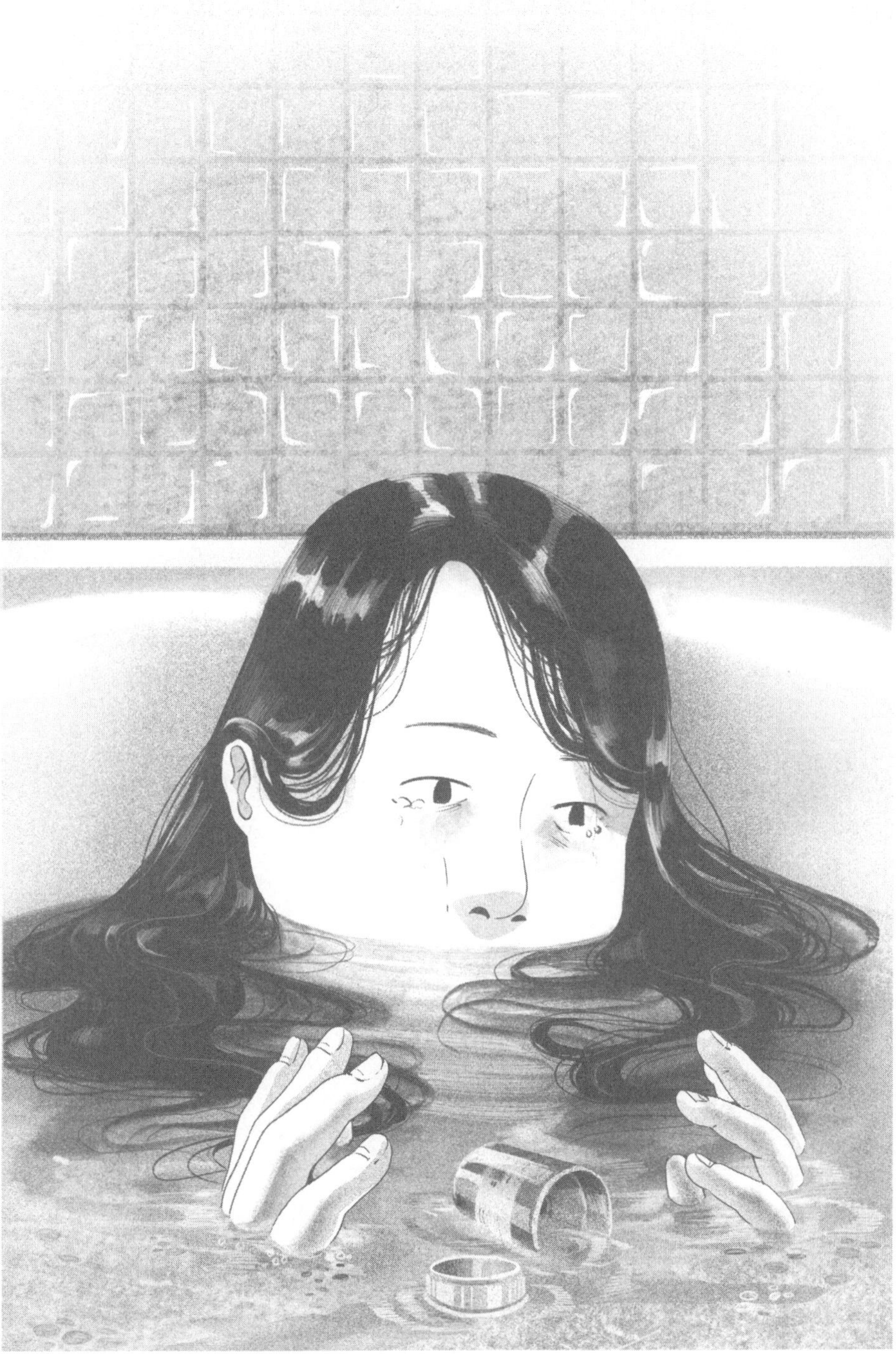

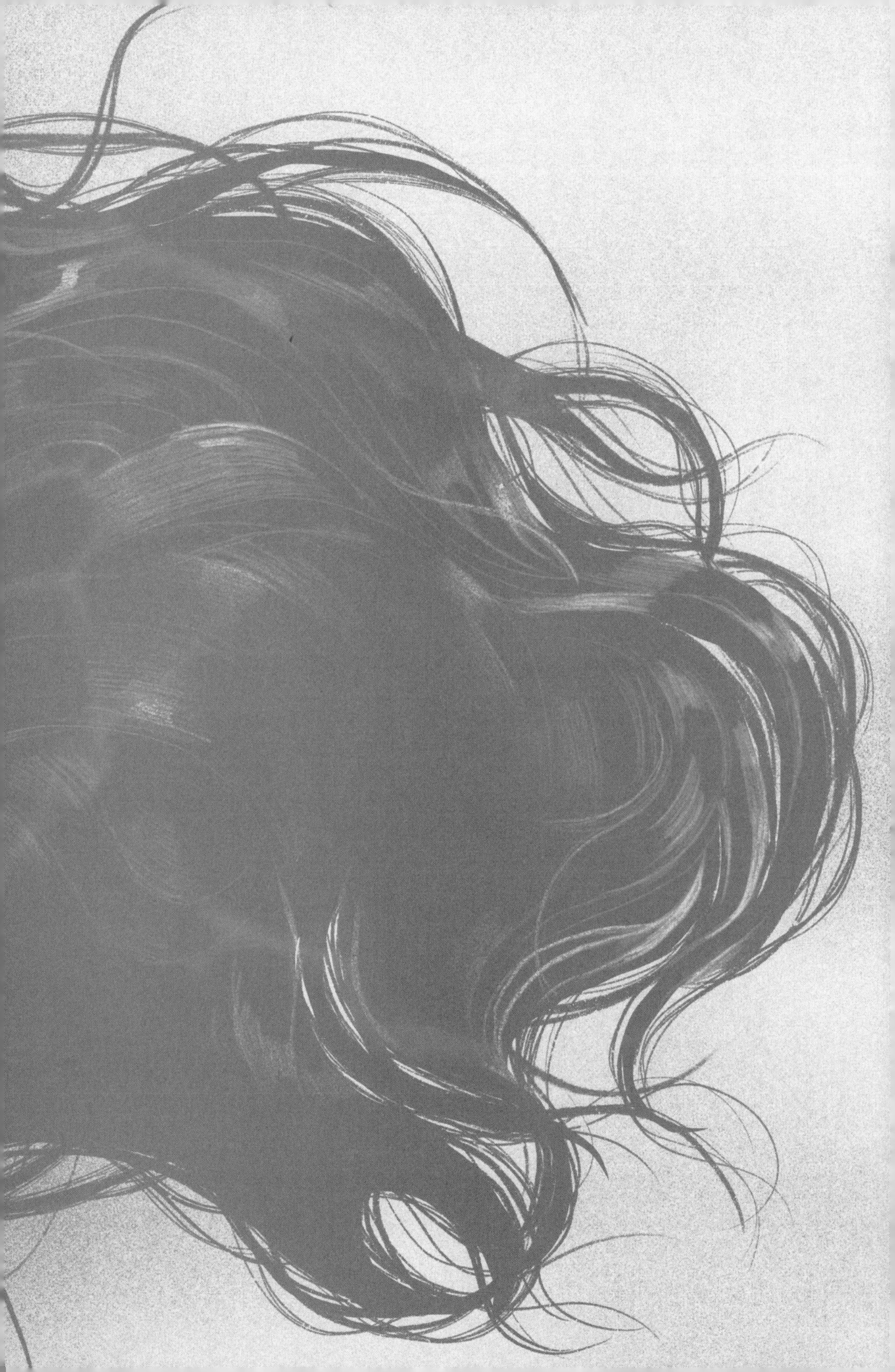

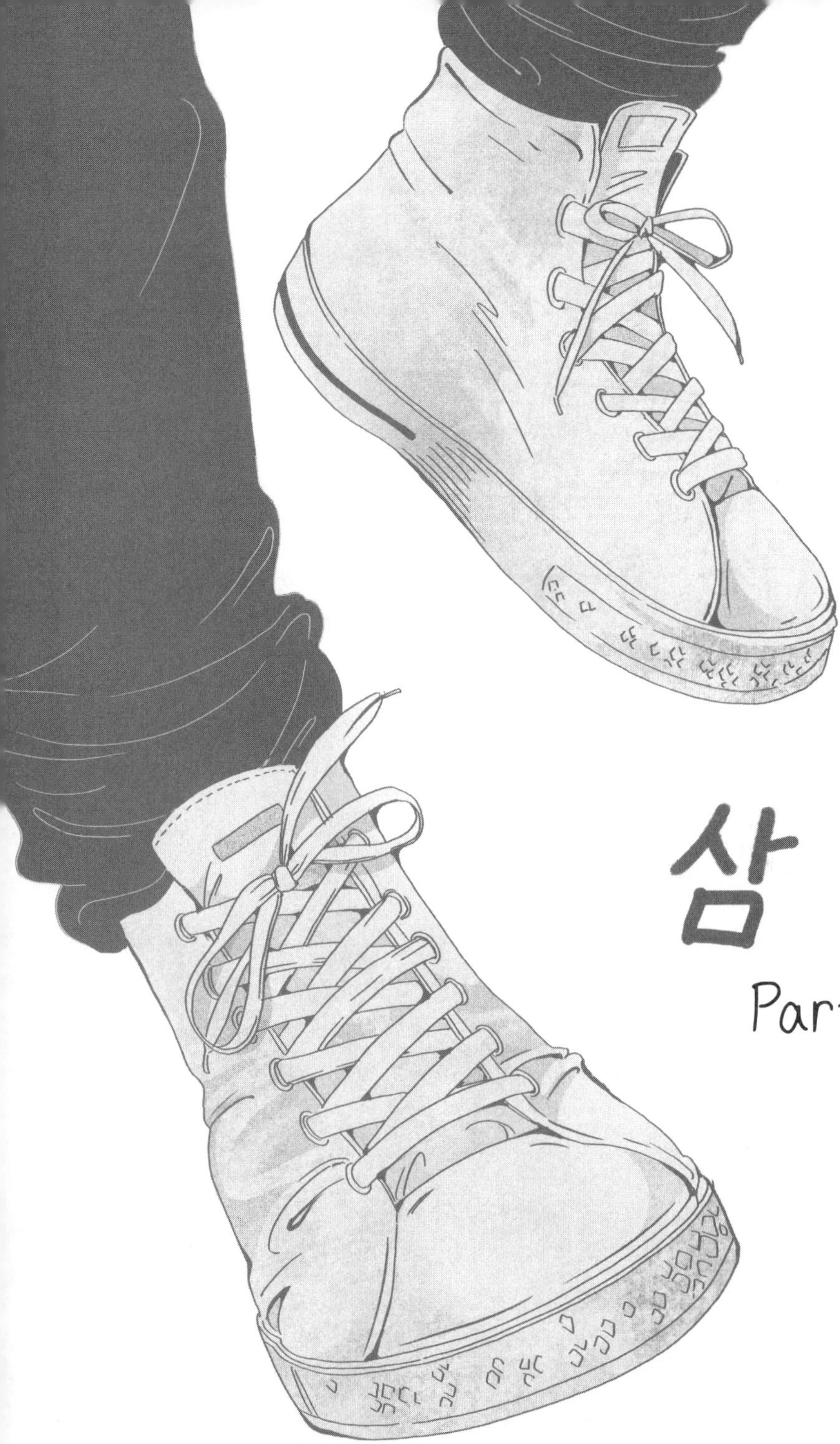

삼

Part 3

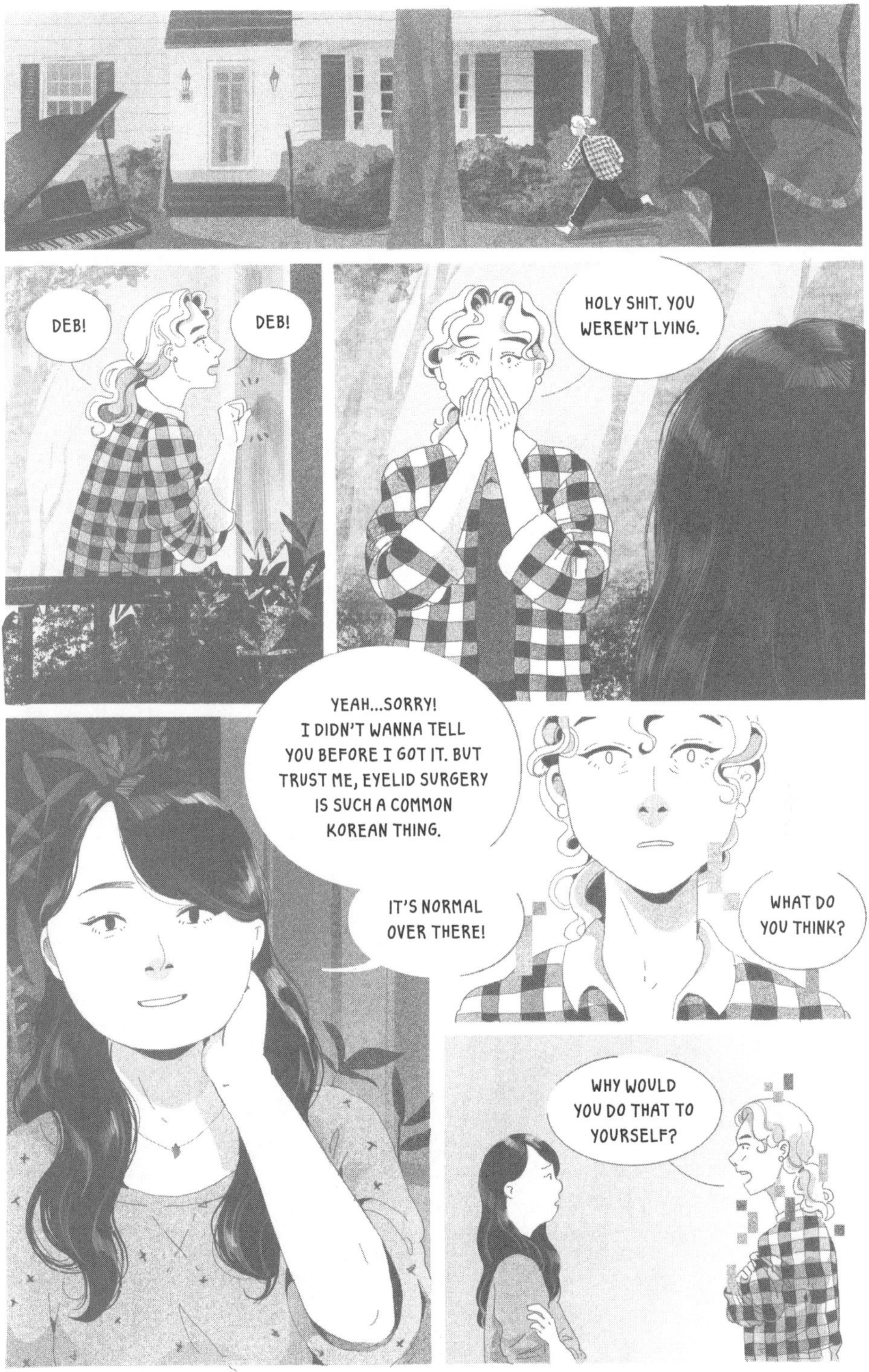

DEB!
DEB!
HOLY SHIT. YOU WEREN'T LYING.
YEAH...SORRY! I DIDN'T WANNA TELL YOU BEFORE I GOT IT. BUT TRUST ME, EYELID SURGERY IS SUCH A COMMON KOREAN THING.
IT'S NORMAL OVER THERE!
WHAT DO YOU THINK?
WHY WOULD YOU DO THAT TO YOURSELF?

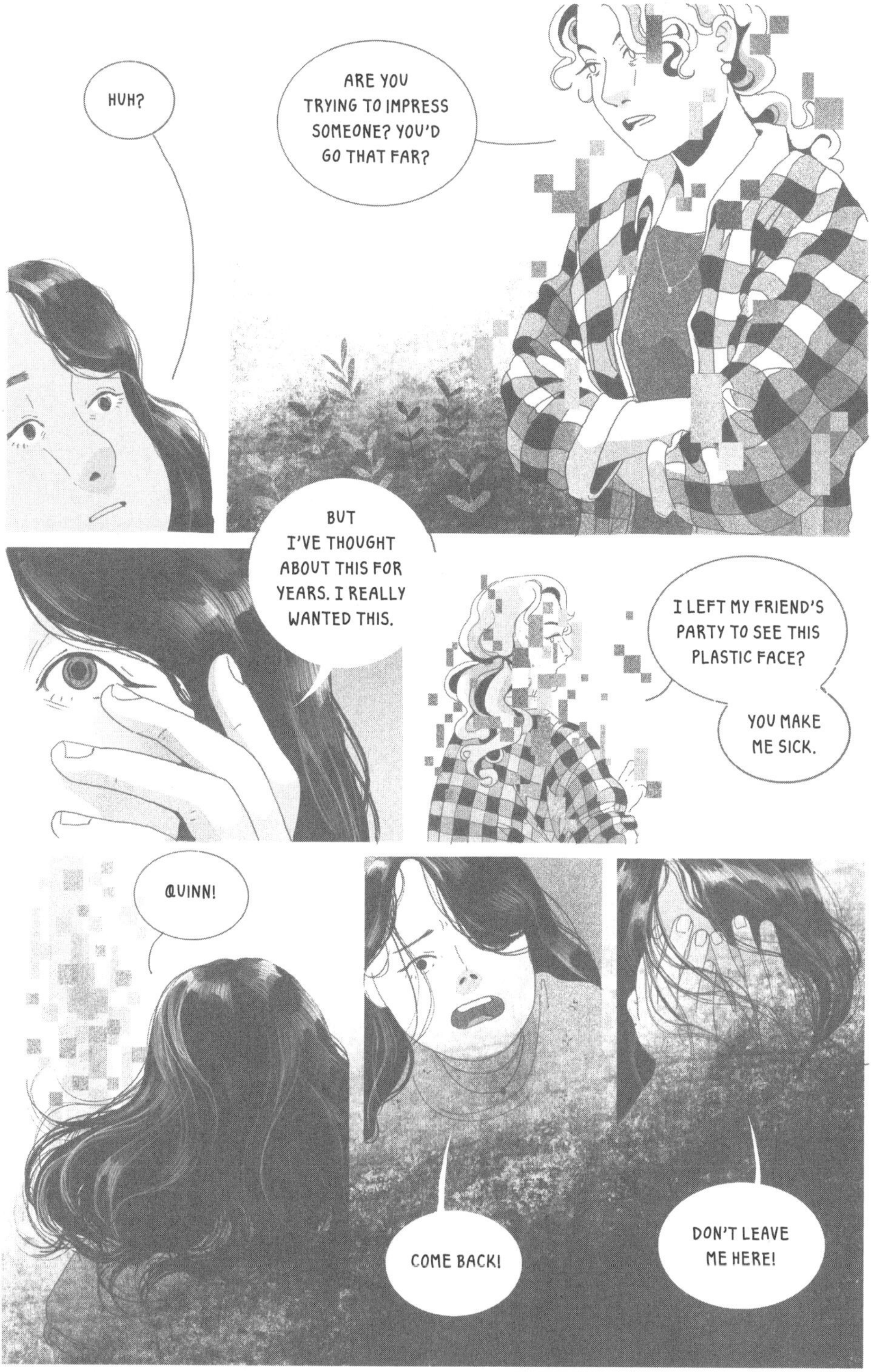
ARE YOU TRYING TO IMPRESS SOMEONE? YOU'D GO THAT FAR?
HUH?
BUT I'VE THOUGHT ABOUT THIS FOR YEARS. I REALLY WANTED THIS.
I LEFT MY FRIEND'S PARTY TO SEE THIS PLASTIC FACE?
YOU MAKE ME SICK.
QUINN!
COME BACK!
DON'T LEAVE ME HERE!

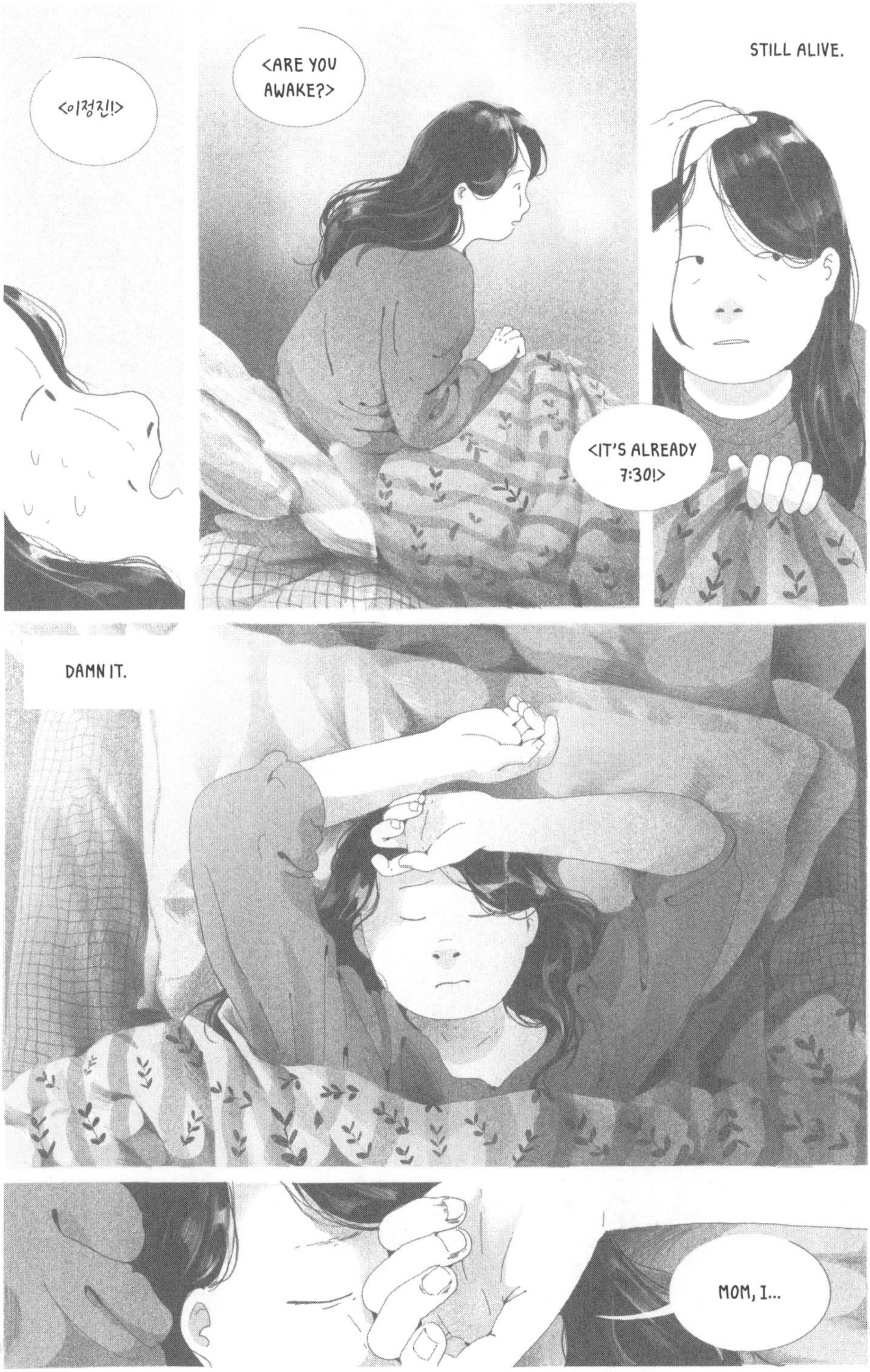
<이정진!>
<ARE YOU AWAKE?>
STILL ALIVE.
<IT'S ALREADY 7:30!>
DAMN IT.
MOM, I...

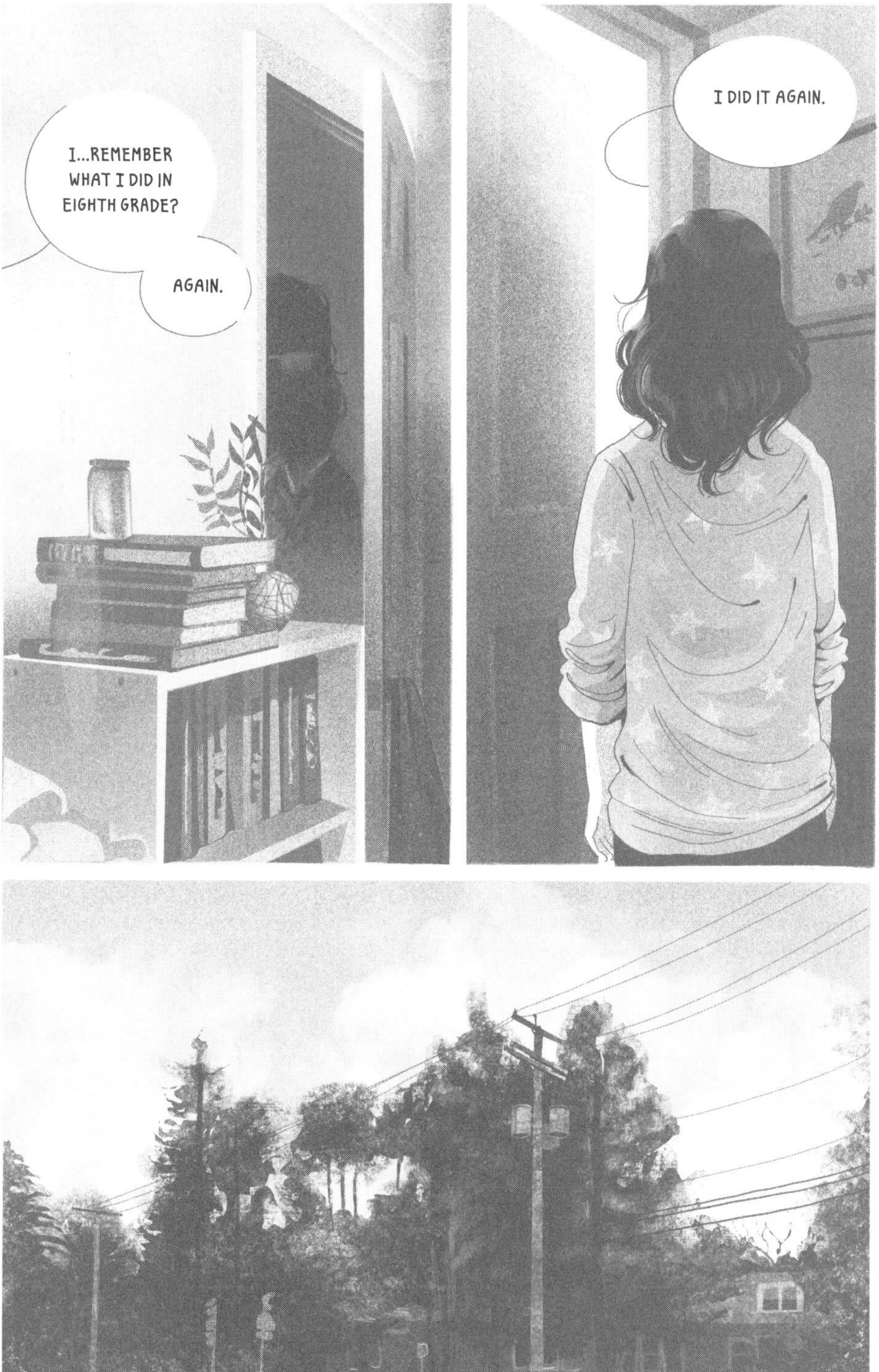
I...REMEMBER WHAT I DID IN EIGHTH GRADE?
AGAIN.
I DID IT AGAIN.

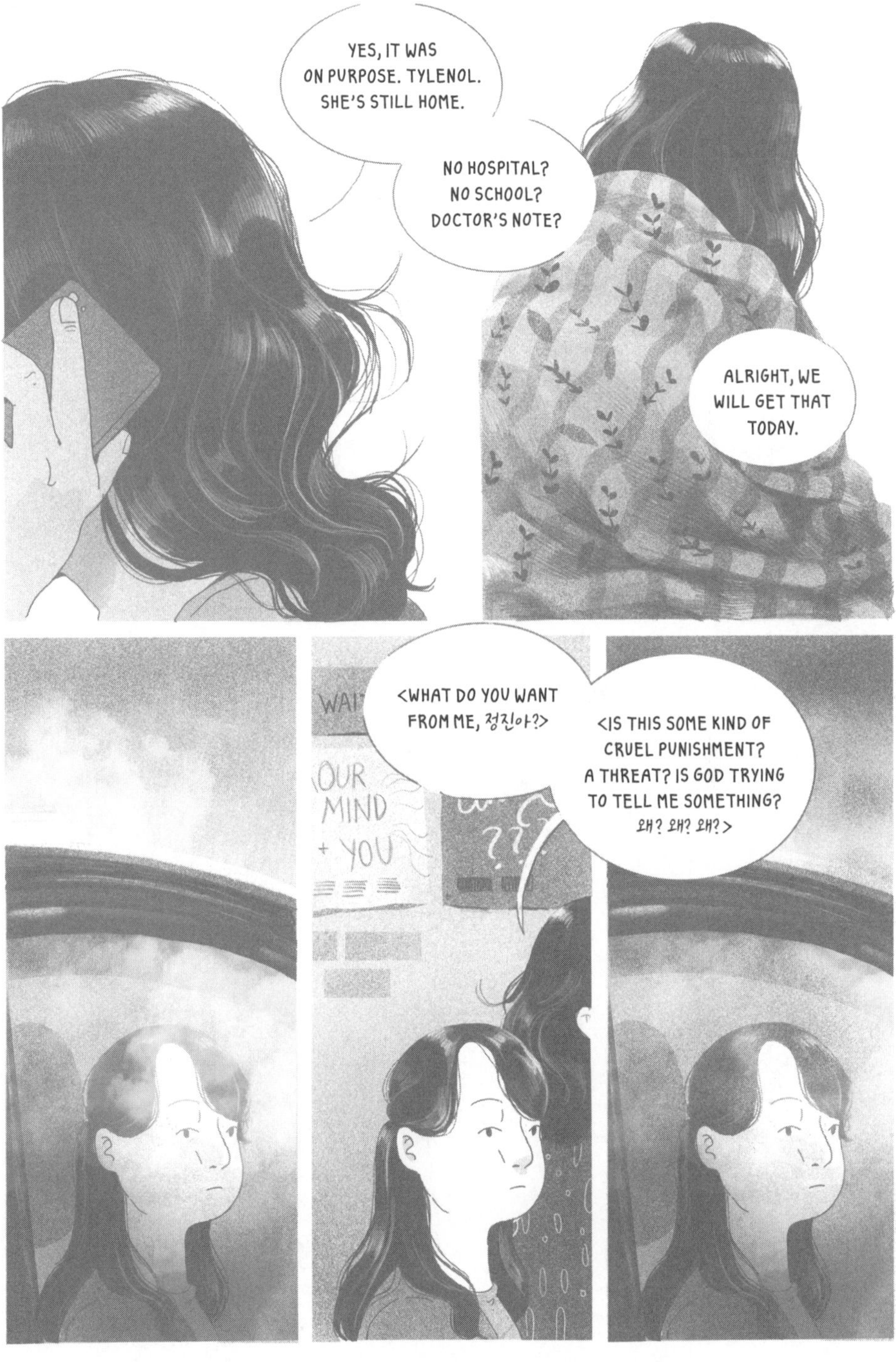
YES, IT WAS ON PURPOSE. TYLENOL. SHE'S STILL HOME.
NO HOSPITAL? NO SCHOOL? DOCTOR'S NOTE?
ALRIGHT, WE WILL GET THAT TODAY.
<WHAT DO YOU WANT FROM ME, 정진아?>
<IS THIS SOME KIND OF CRUEL PUNISHMENT? A THREAT? IS GOD TRYING TO TELL ME SOMETHING? 왜? 왜? 왜?>

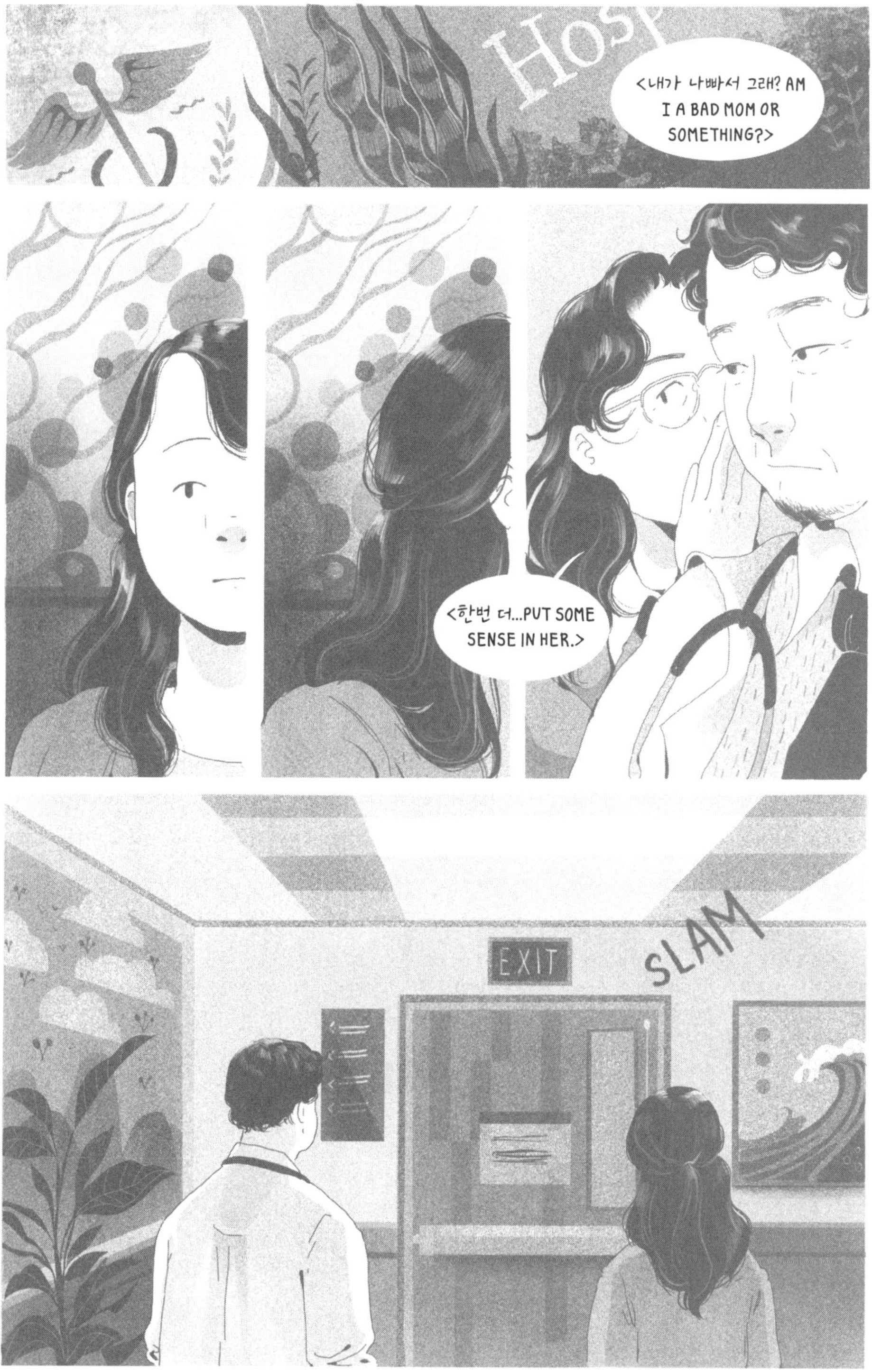
HOSP
<내가 나빠서 그래? AM I A BAD MOM OR SOMETHING?>
<한번 더...PUT SOME SENSE IN HER.>
EXIT
SLAM

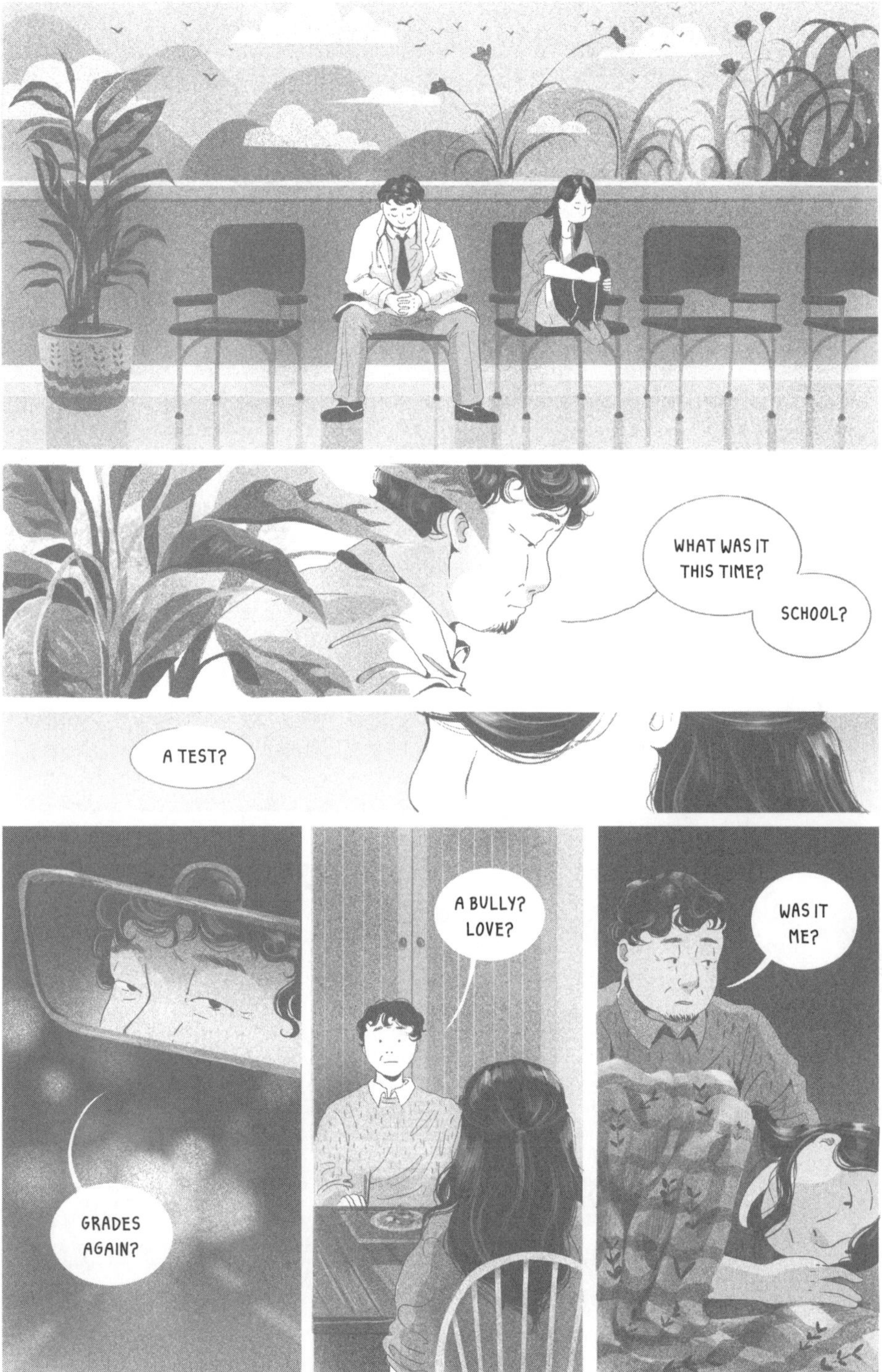
WHAT WAS IT THIS TIME?
SCHOOL?
A TEST?
GRADES AGAIN?
A BULLY? LOVE?
WAS IT ME?

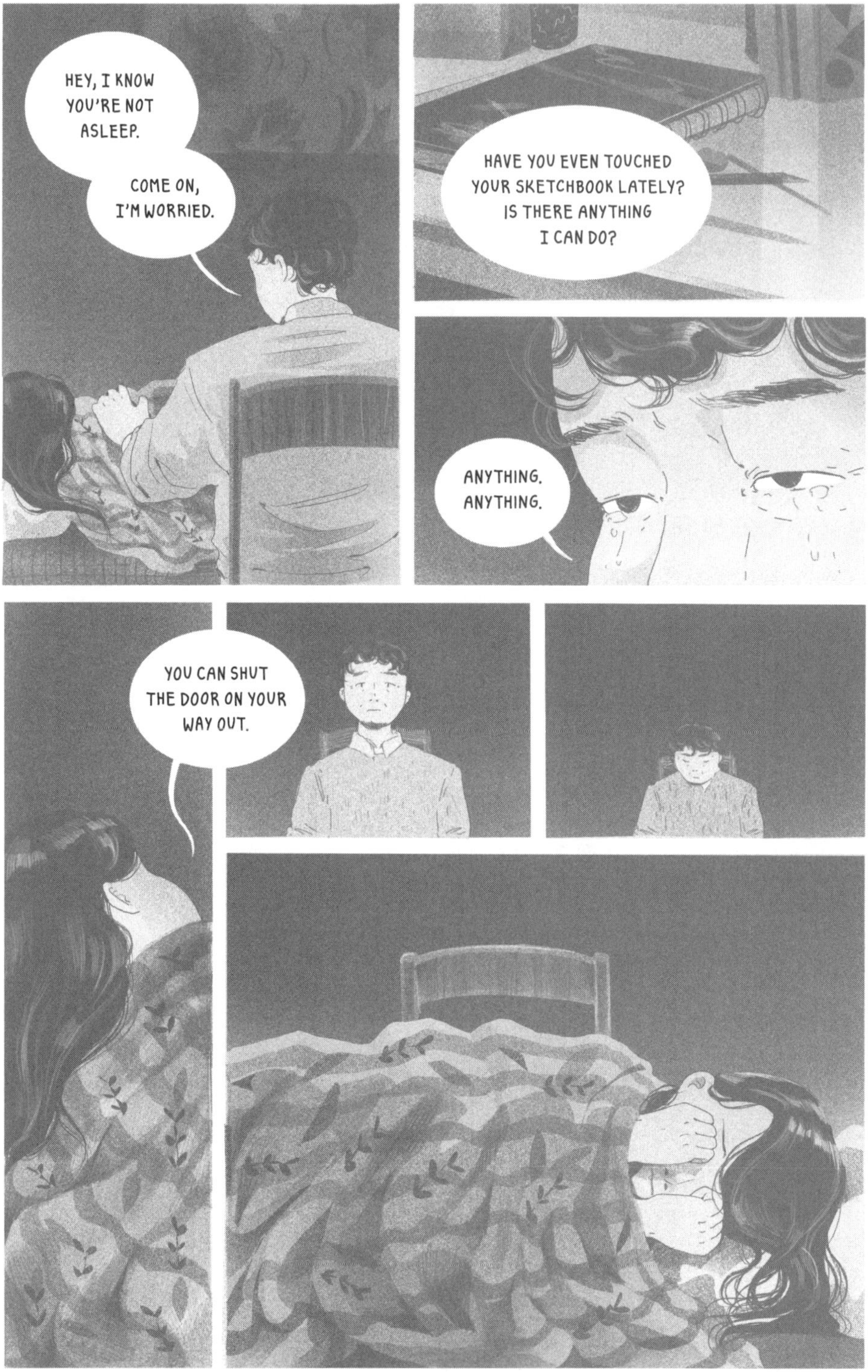
HEY, I KNOW YOU'RE NOT ASLEEP.
COME ON, I'M WORRIED.
HAVE YOU EVEN TOUCHED YOUR SKETCHBOOK LATELY? IS THERE ANYTHING I CAN DO?
ANYTHING. ANYTHING.
YOU CAN SHUT THE DOOR ON YOUR WAY OUT.

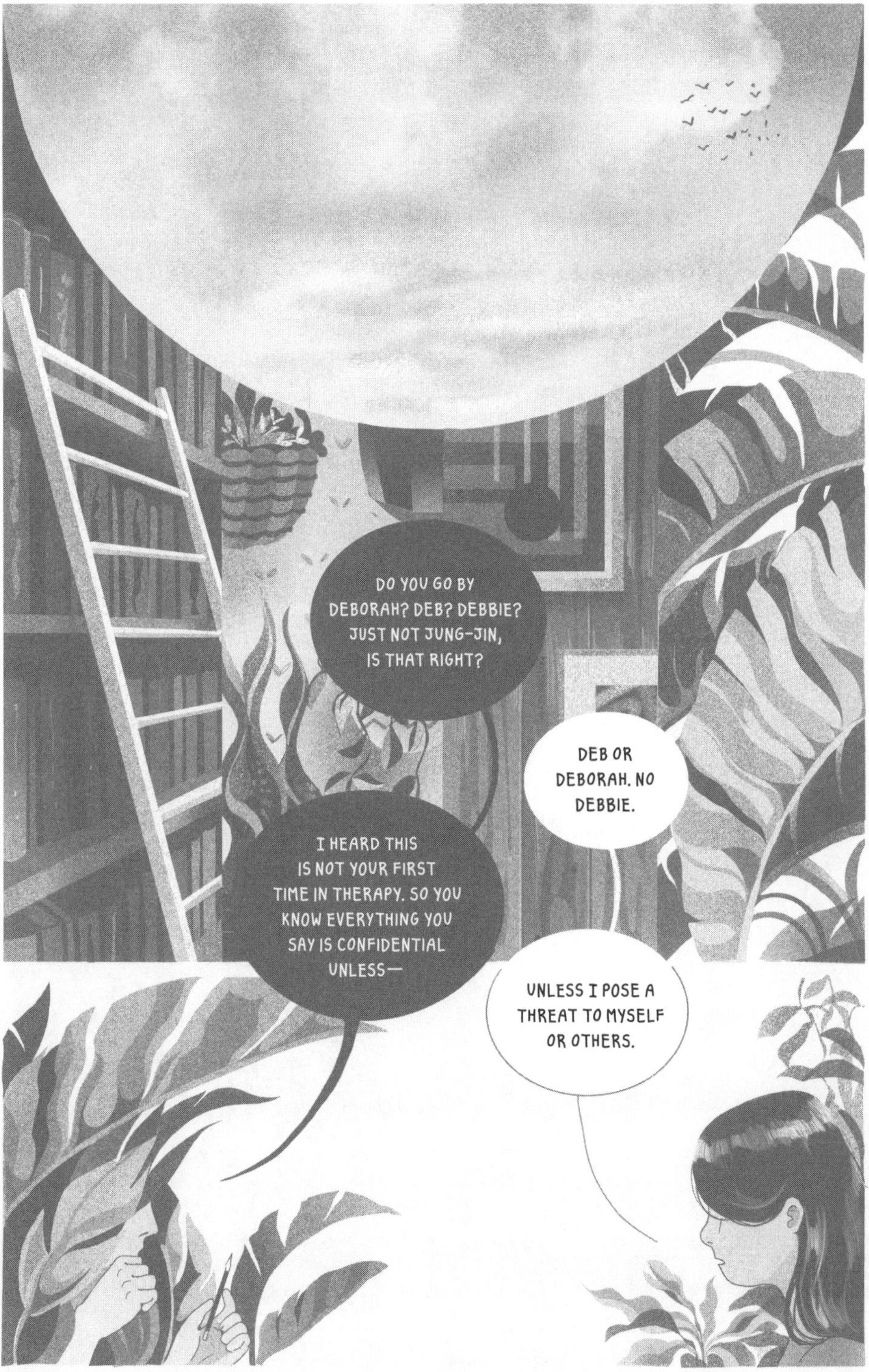
DO YOU GO BY DEBORAH? DEB? DEBBIE? JUST NOT JUNG-JIN, IS THAT RIGHT?
DEB OR DEBORAH. NO DEBBIE.
I HEARD THIS IS NOT YOUR FIRST TIME IN THERAPY. SO YOU KNOW EVERYTHING YOU SAY IS CONFIDENTIAL UNLESS—
UNLESS I POSE A THREAT TO MYSELF OR OTHERS.

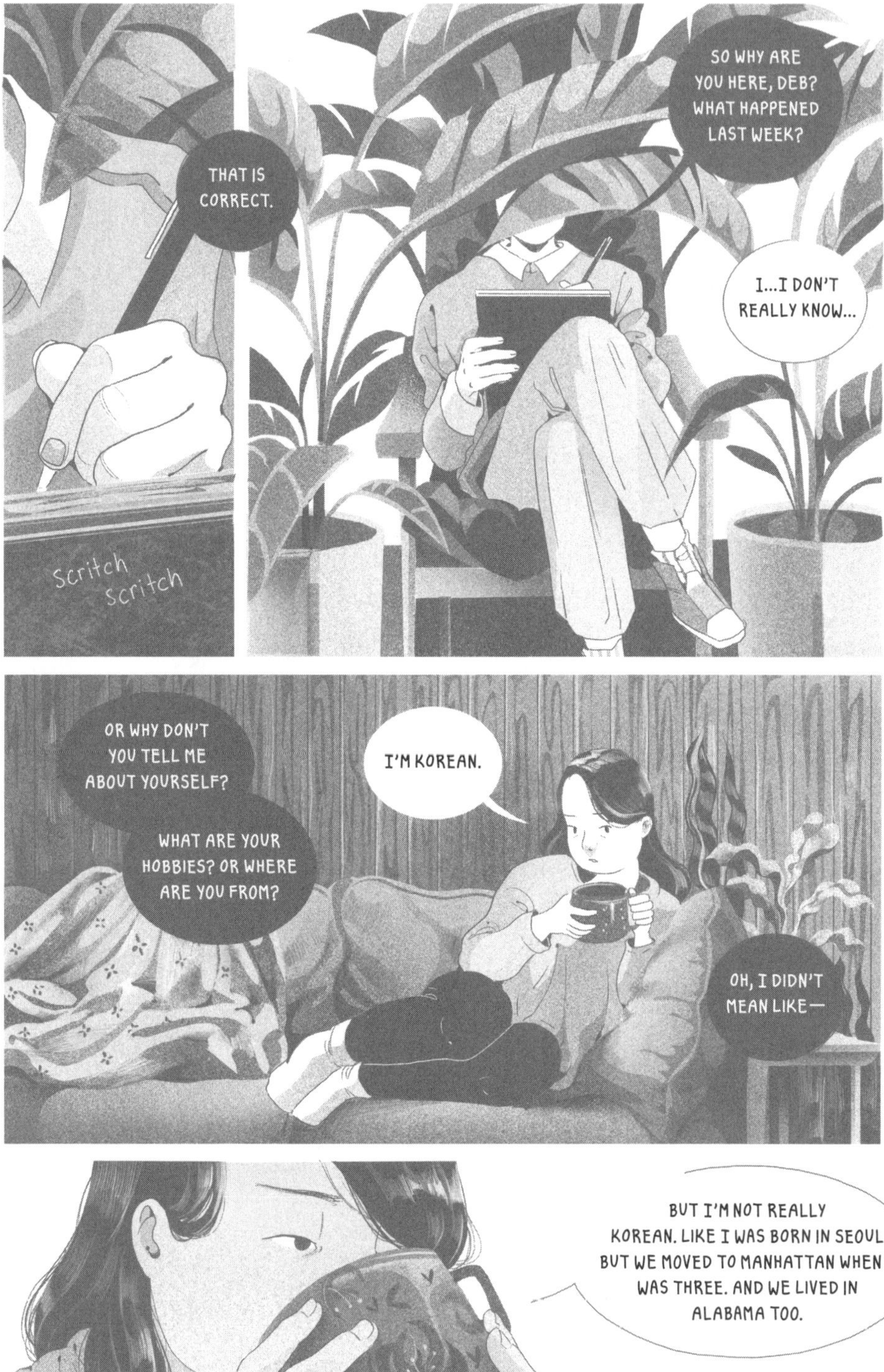
THAT IS CORRECT.
Scritch Scritch
SO WHY ARE YOU HERE, DEB? WHAT HAPPENED LAST WEEK?
I...I DON'T REALLY KNOW...
OR WHY DON'T YOU TELL ME ABOUT YOURSELF?
WHAT ARE YOUR HOBBIES? OR WHERE ARE YOU FROM?
I'M KOREAN.
OH, I DIDN'T MEAN LIKE—
BUT I'M NOT REALLY KOREAN. LIKE I WAS BORN IN SEOUL BUT WE MOVED TO MANHATTAN WHEN I WAS THREE. AND WE LIVED IN ALABAMA TOO.

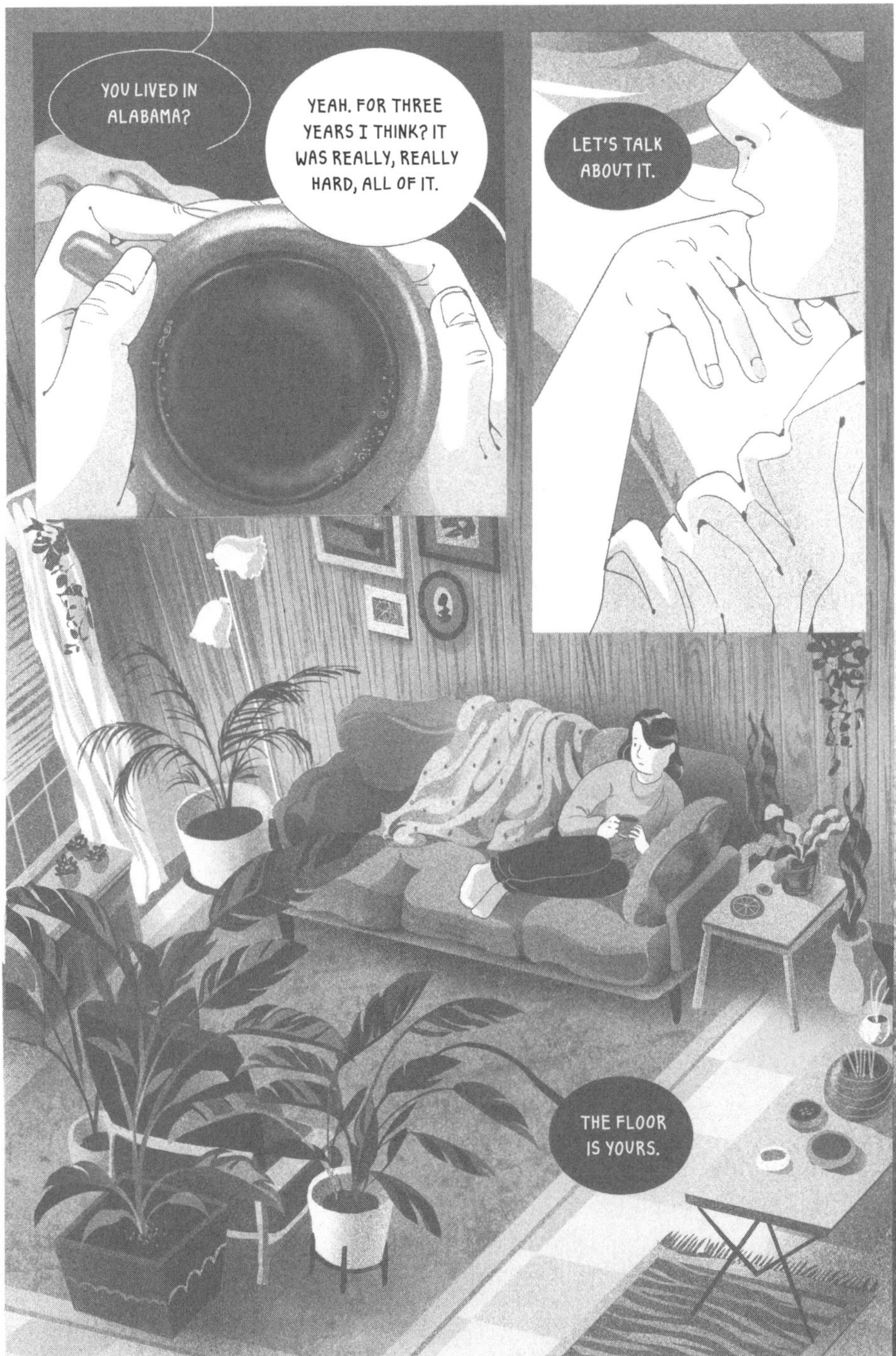
YOU LIVED IN ALABAMA?
YEAH. FOR THREE YEARS I THINK? IT WAS REALLY, REALLY HARD, ALL OF IT.
LET'S TALK ABOUT IT.
THE FLOOR IS YOURS.

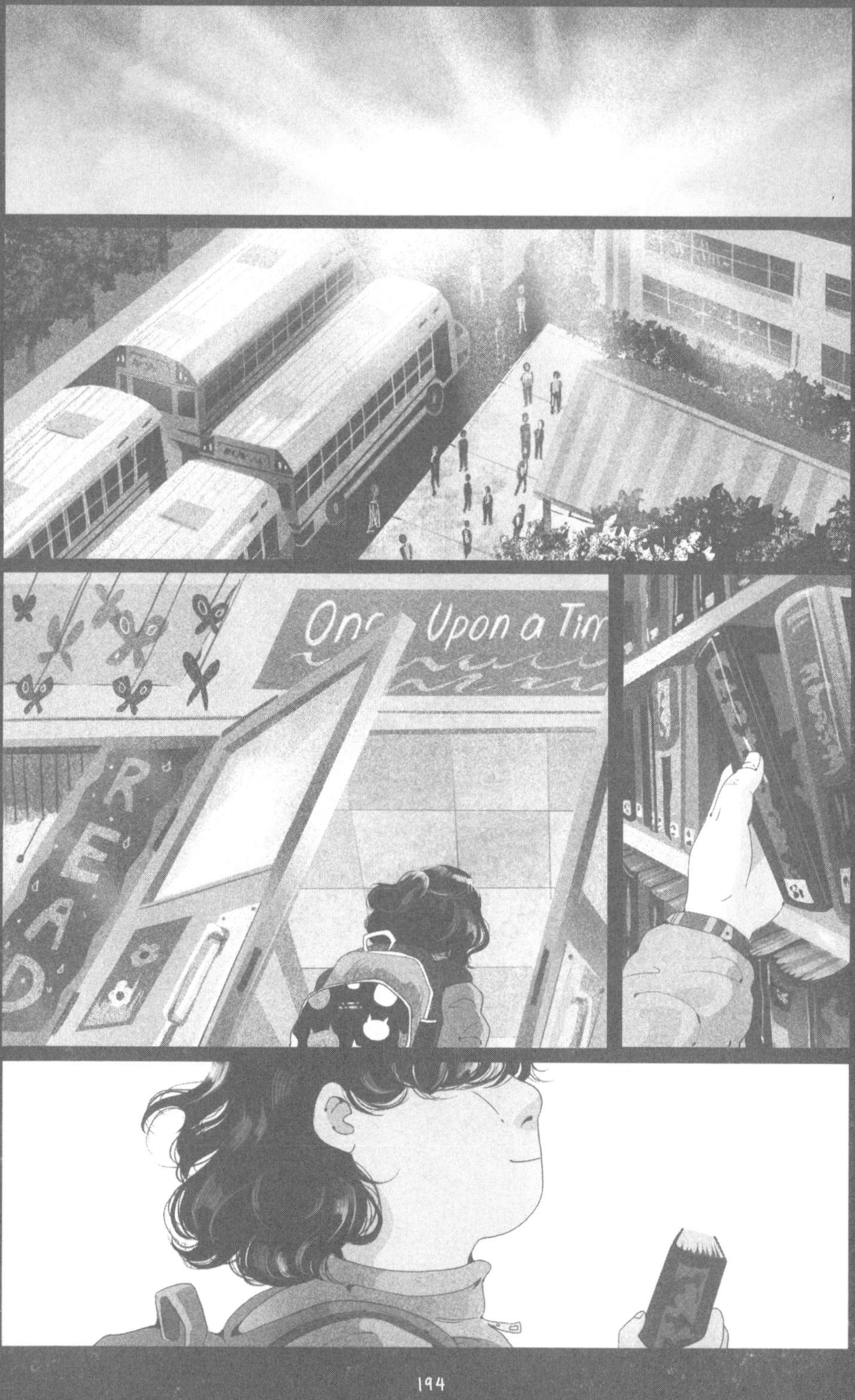
Onc Upon a Tim
READ

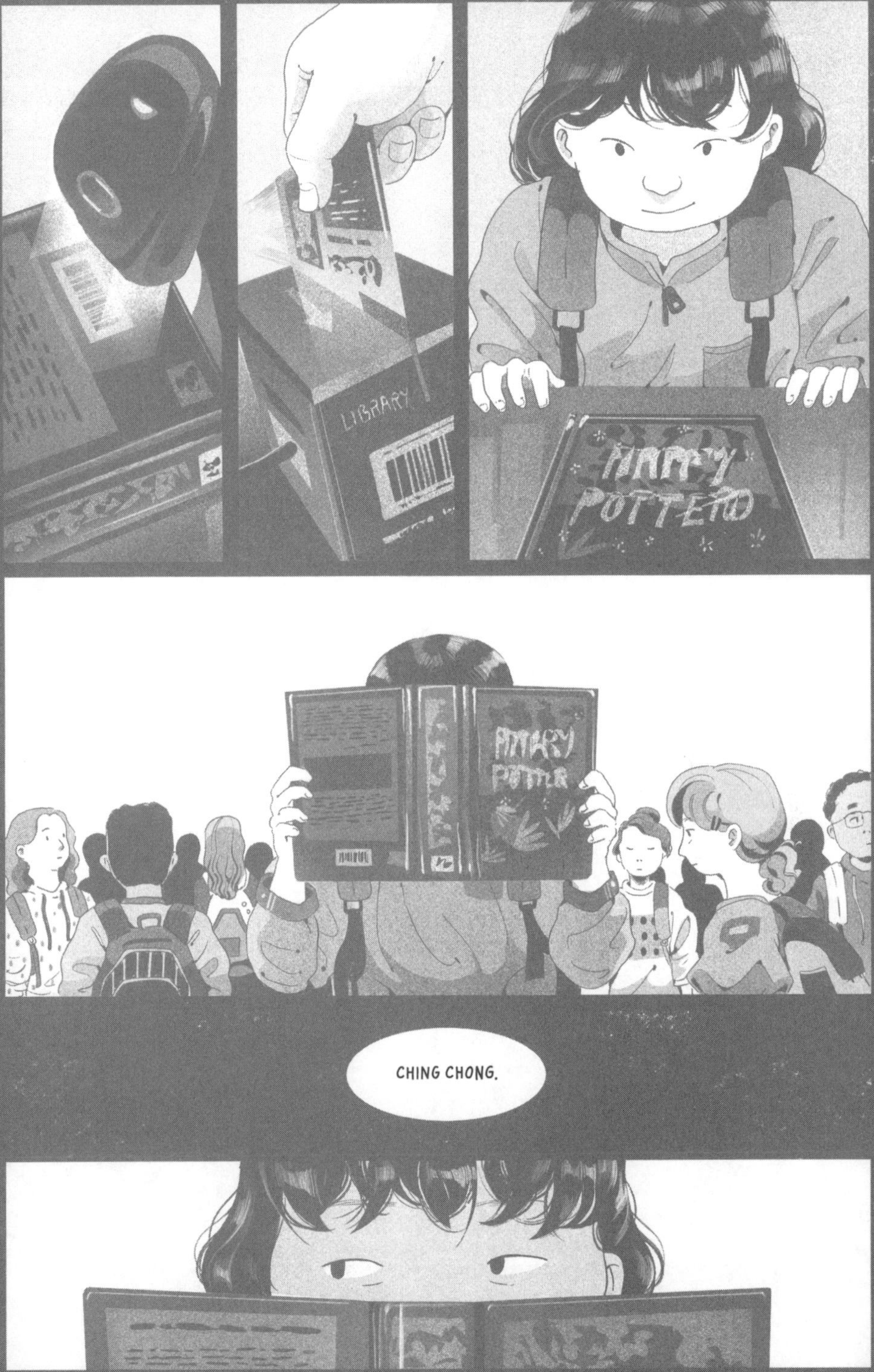
LIBRARY
CHING CHONG.

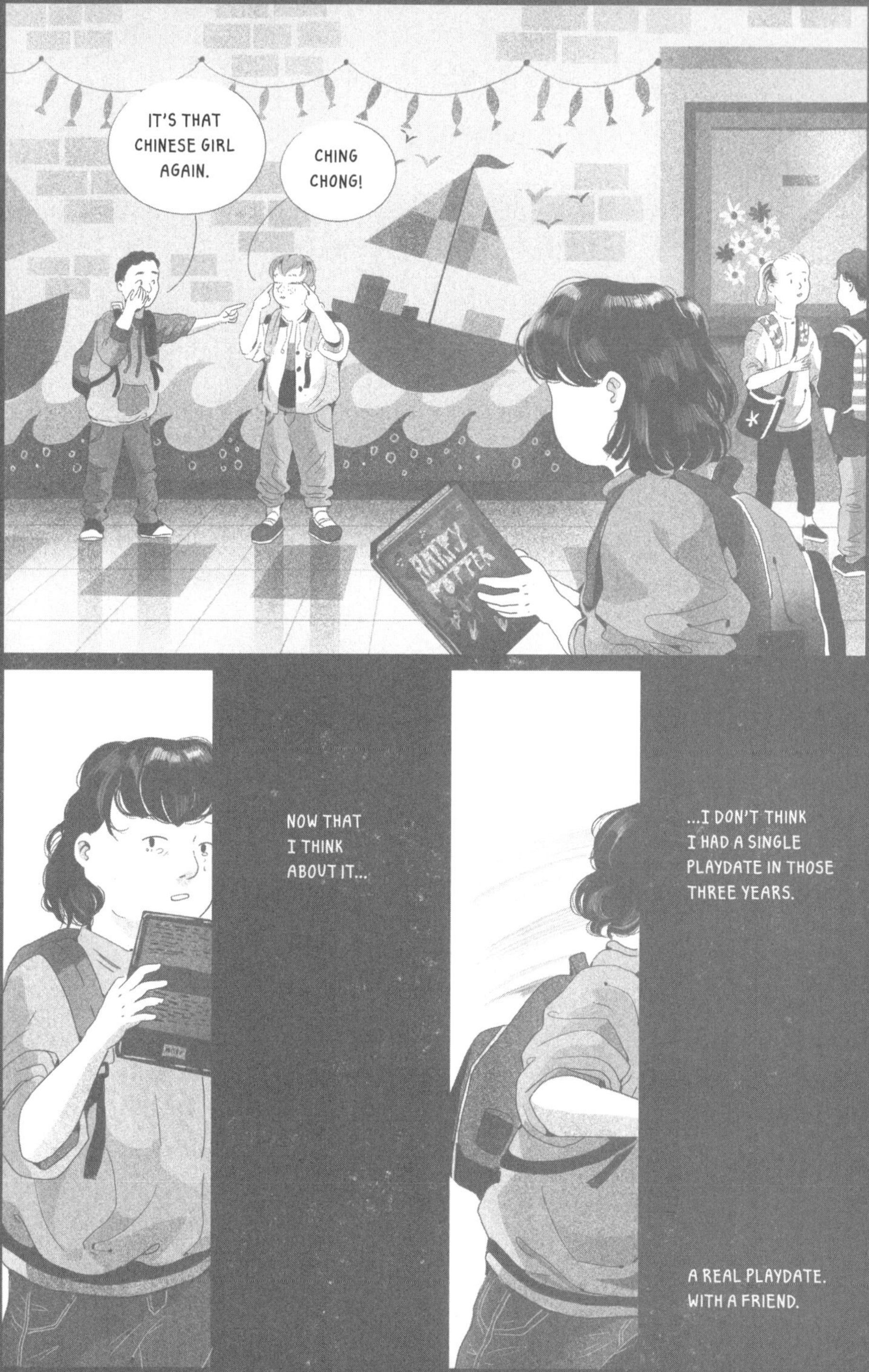
IT'S THAT CHINESE GIRL AGAIN.
CHING CHONG!
NOW THAT I THINK ABOUT IT...
...I DON'T THINK I HAD A SINGLE PLAYDATE IN THOSE THREE YEARS.
A REAL PLAYDATE. WITH A FRIEND.

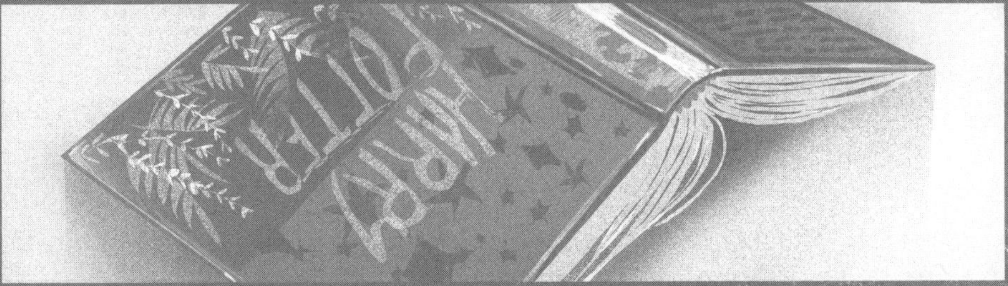

NEW JERSEY WAS DIFFERENT.

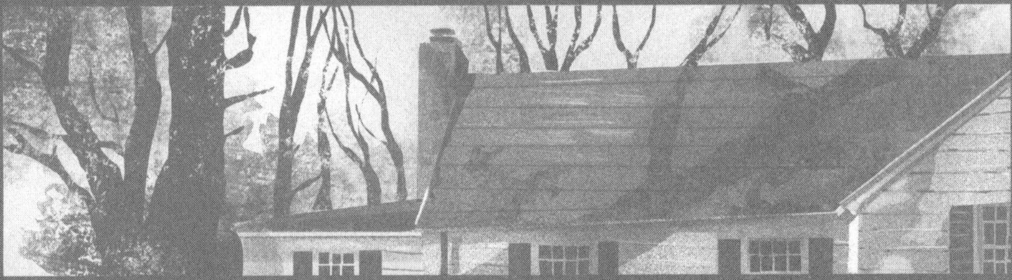

PEOPLE DON'T SAY ANYTHING TO YOUR FACE. BUT YOU CAN TELL THERE'S SOMETHING SINISTER ON THEIR MIND WHEN THEY ARE AROUND YOU, TALK TO YOU, LOOK AT YOU.

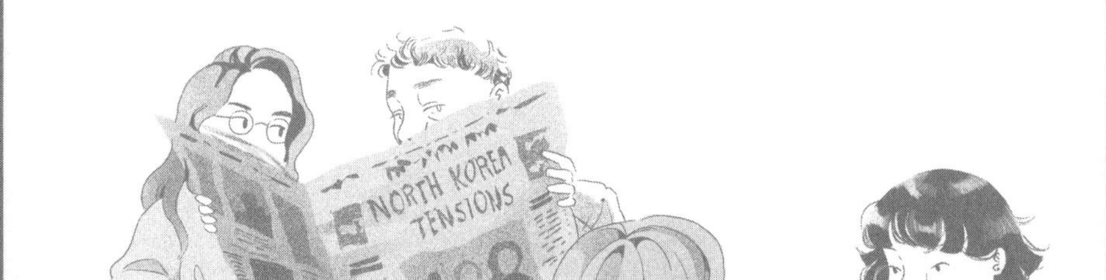
NORTH KOREA TENSIONS

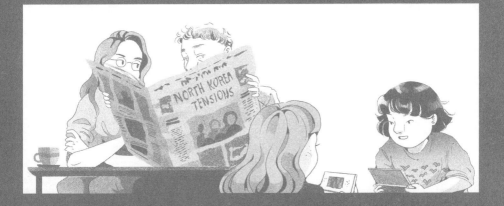

STRANGERS. TEACHERS. OTHER KIDS. THEIR PARENTS.

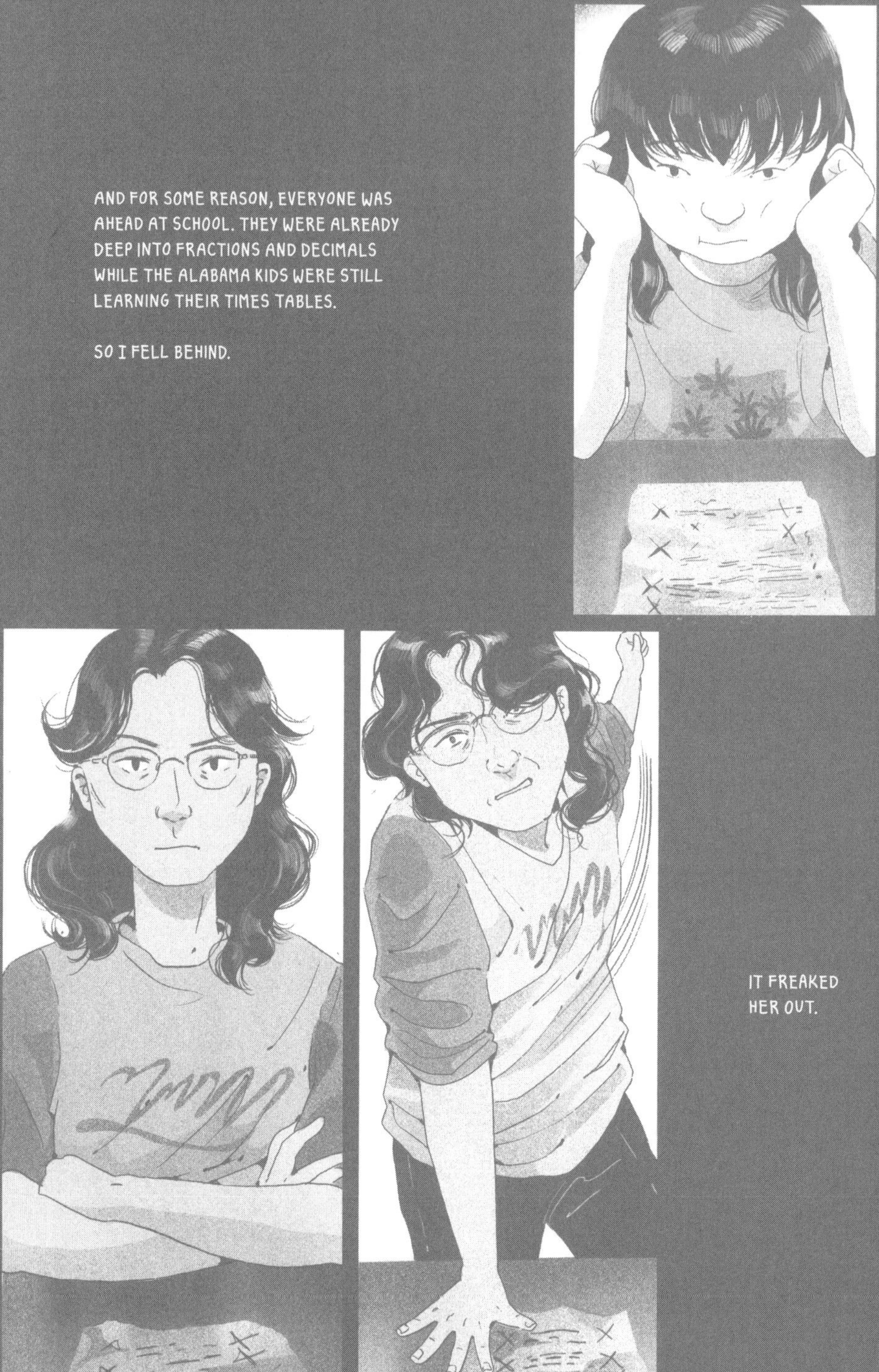
AND FOR SOME REASON, EVERYONE WAS AHEAD AT SCHOOL. THEY WERE ALREADY DEEP INTO FRACTIONS AND DECIMALS WHILE THE ALABAMA KIDS WERE STILL LEARNING THEIR TIMES TABLES.
SO I FELL BEHIND.
IT FREAKED HER OUT.

ALL MY FRIENDS WERE IN ORCHESTRA. BUT OUTSIDE OF THAT,

I HAD NO ONE.

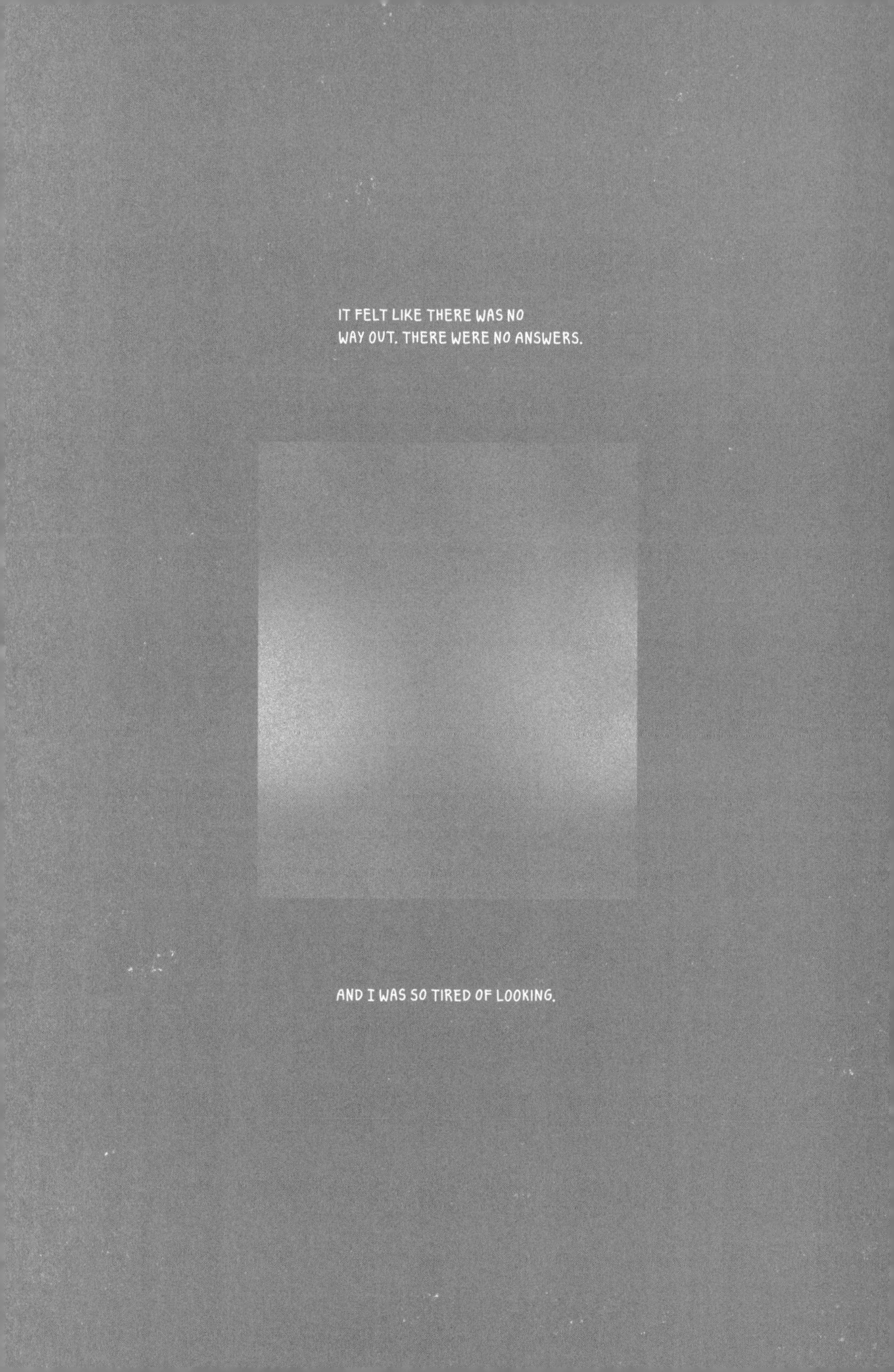
IT FELT LIKE THERE WAS NO WAY OUT. THERE WERE NO ANSWERS.
AND I WAS SO TIRED OF LOOKING.

THE FIRST TIME HAPPENED IN EIGHTH GRADE.

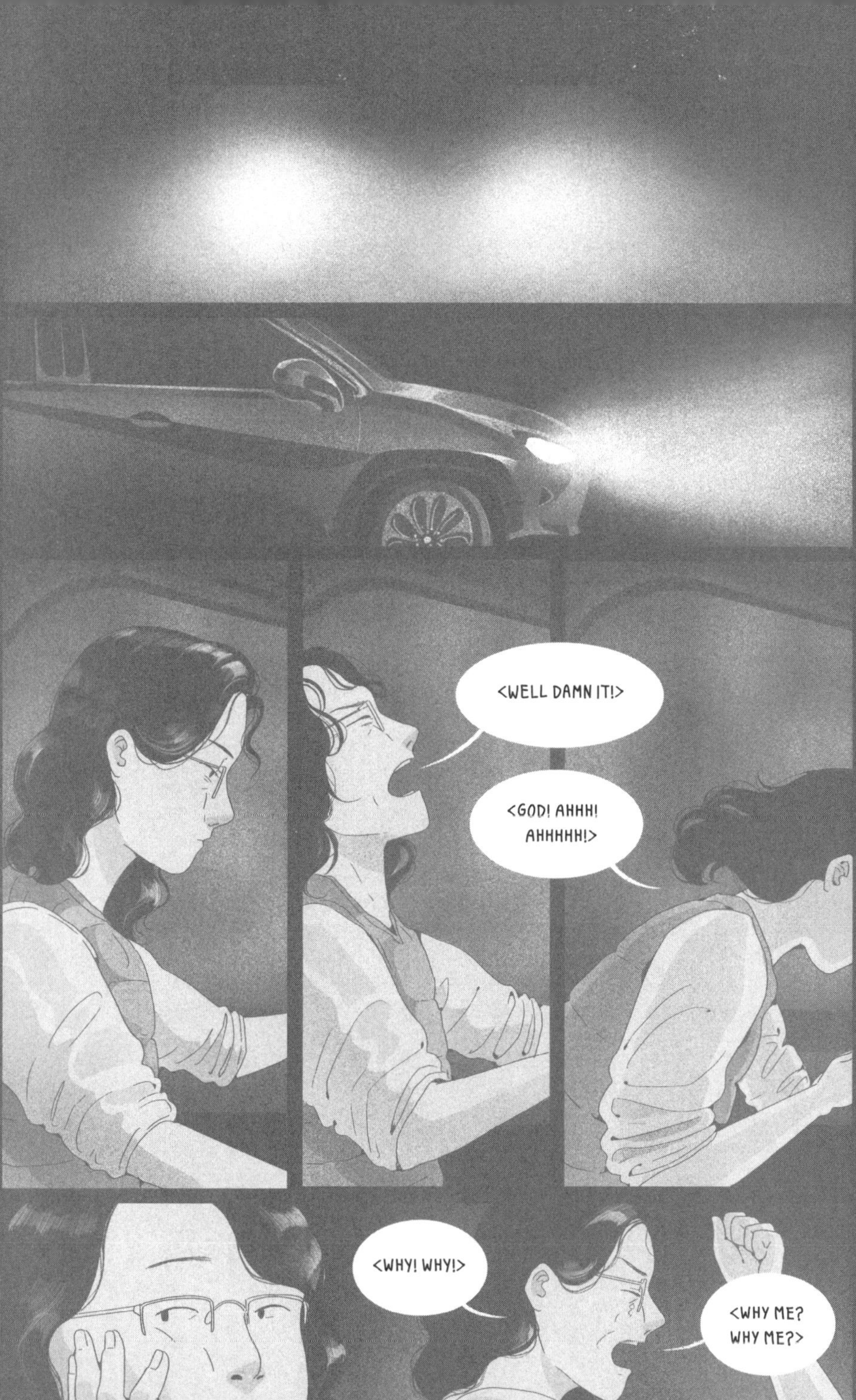
<WELL DAMN IT!>
<GOD! AHHH! AHHHHH!>
<WHY! WHY!>
<WHY ME? WHY ME?>

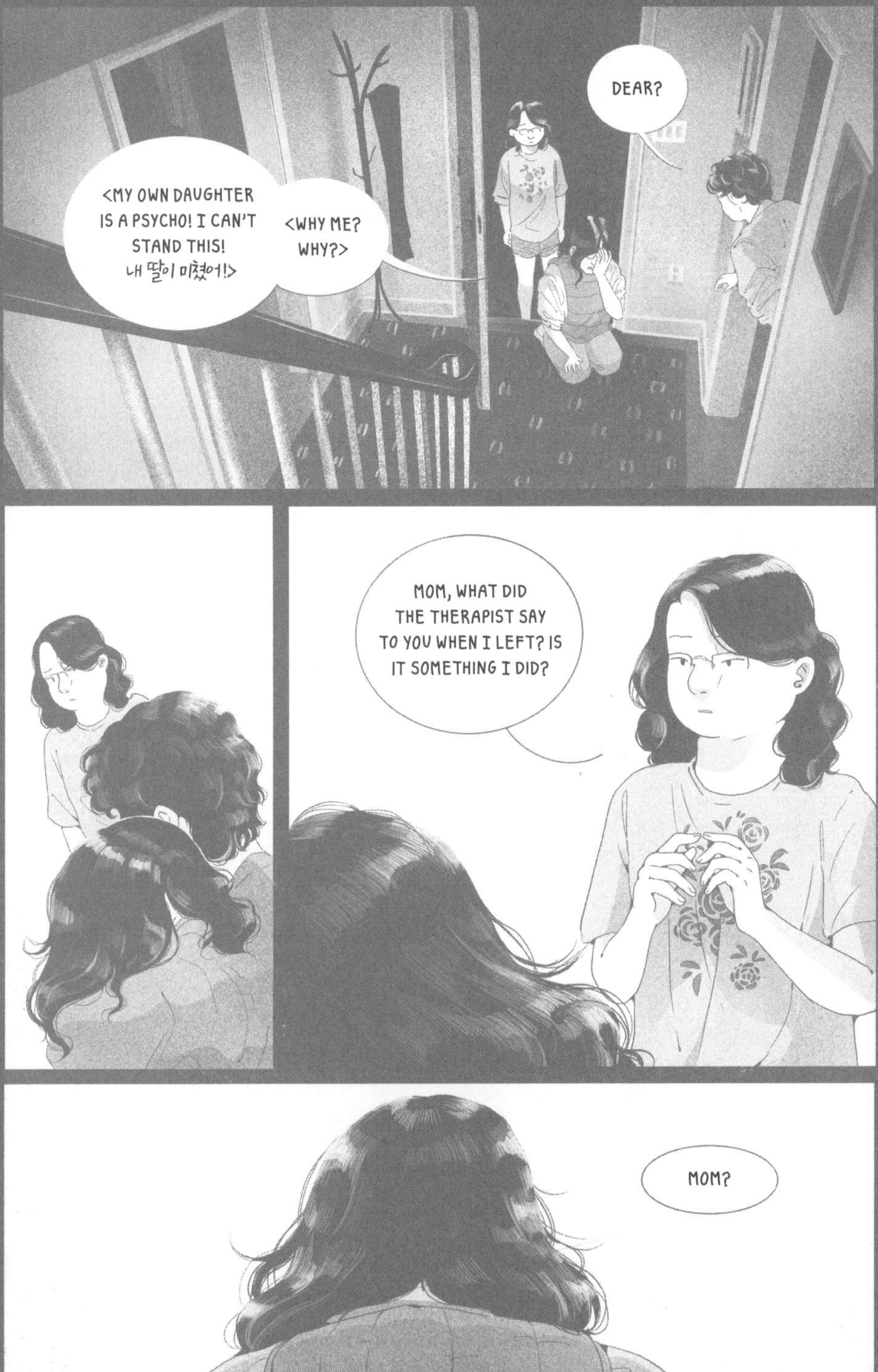
<MY OWN DAUGHTER IS A PSYCHO! I CAN'T STAND THIS! 내 딸이 미쳤어!>
<WHY ME? WHY?>
DEAR?
MOM, WHAT DID THE THERAPIST SAY TO YOU WHEN I LEFT? IS IT SOMETHING I DID?
MOM?

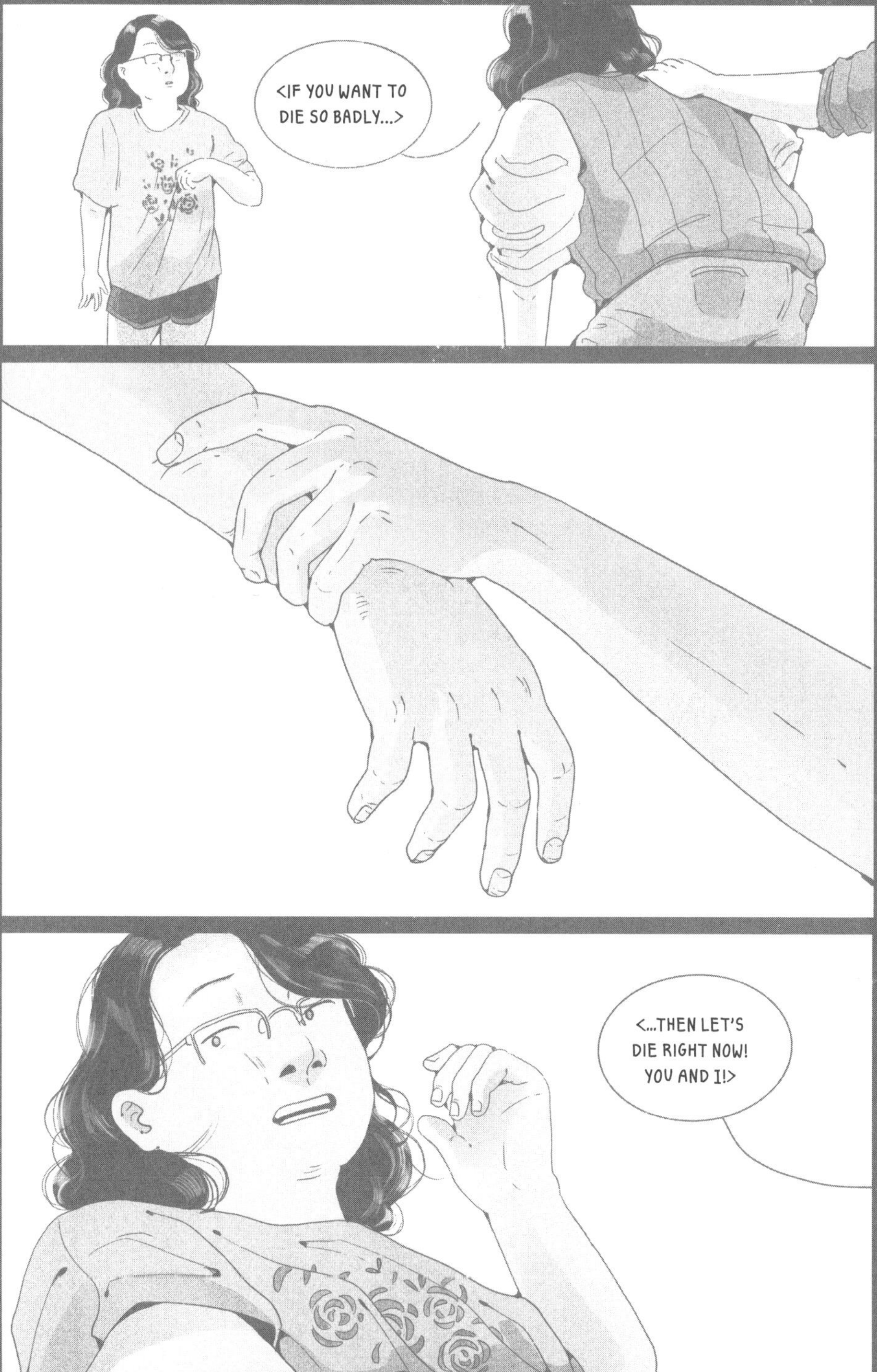
<IF YOU WANT TO DIE SO BADLY...>
<...THEN LET'S DIE RIGHT NOW! YOU AND I!>

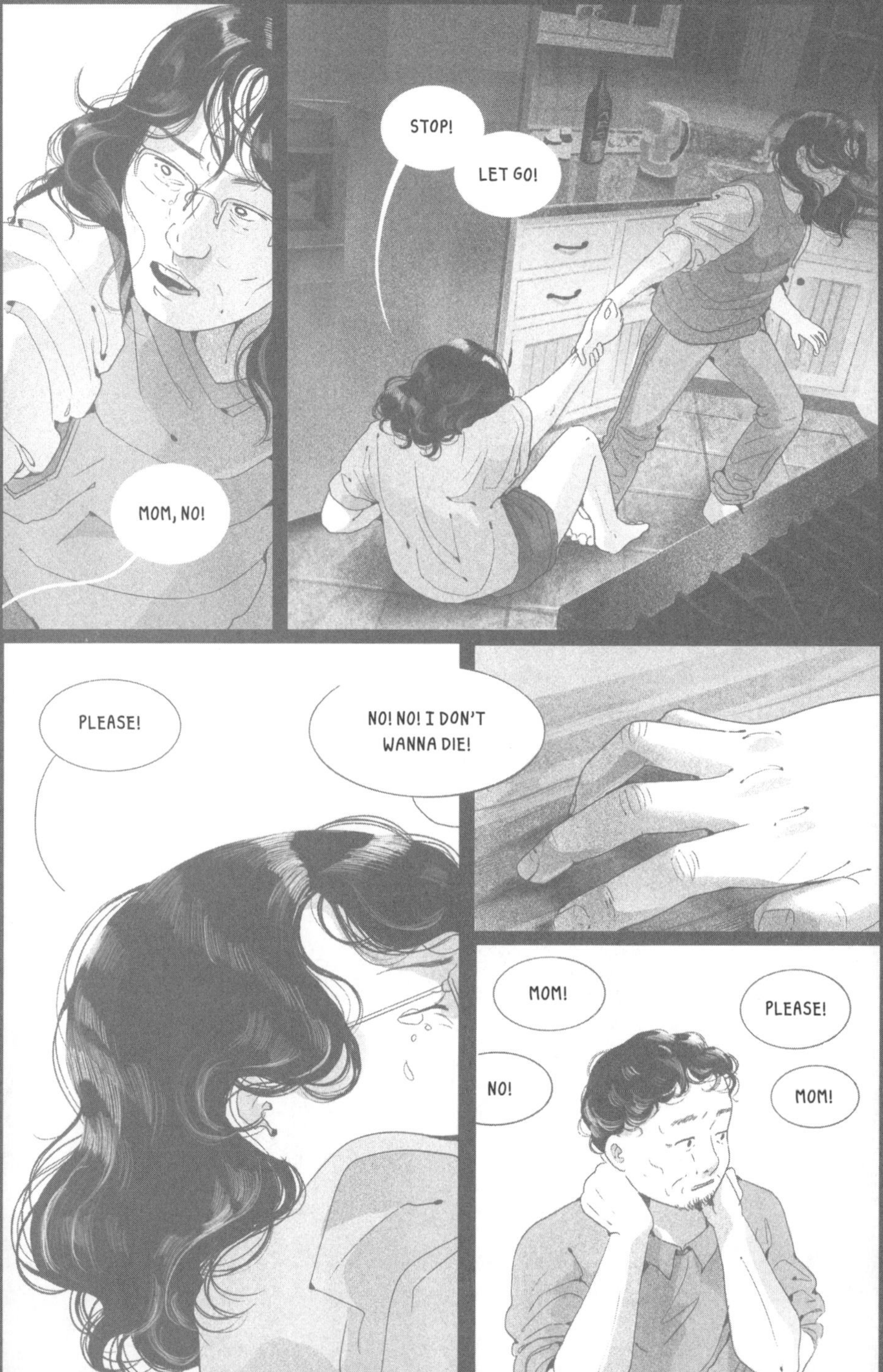
MOM, NO!
STOP!
LET GO!
PLEASE!
NO! NO! I DON'T WANNA DIE!
MOM!
PLEASE!
NO!
MOM!

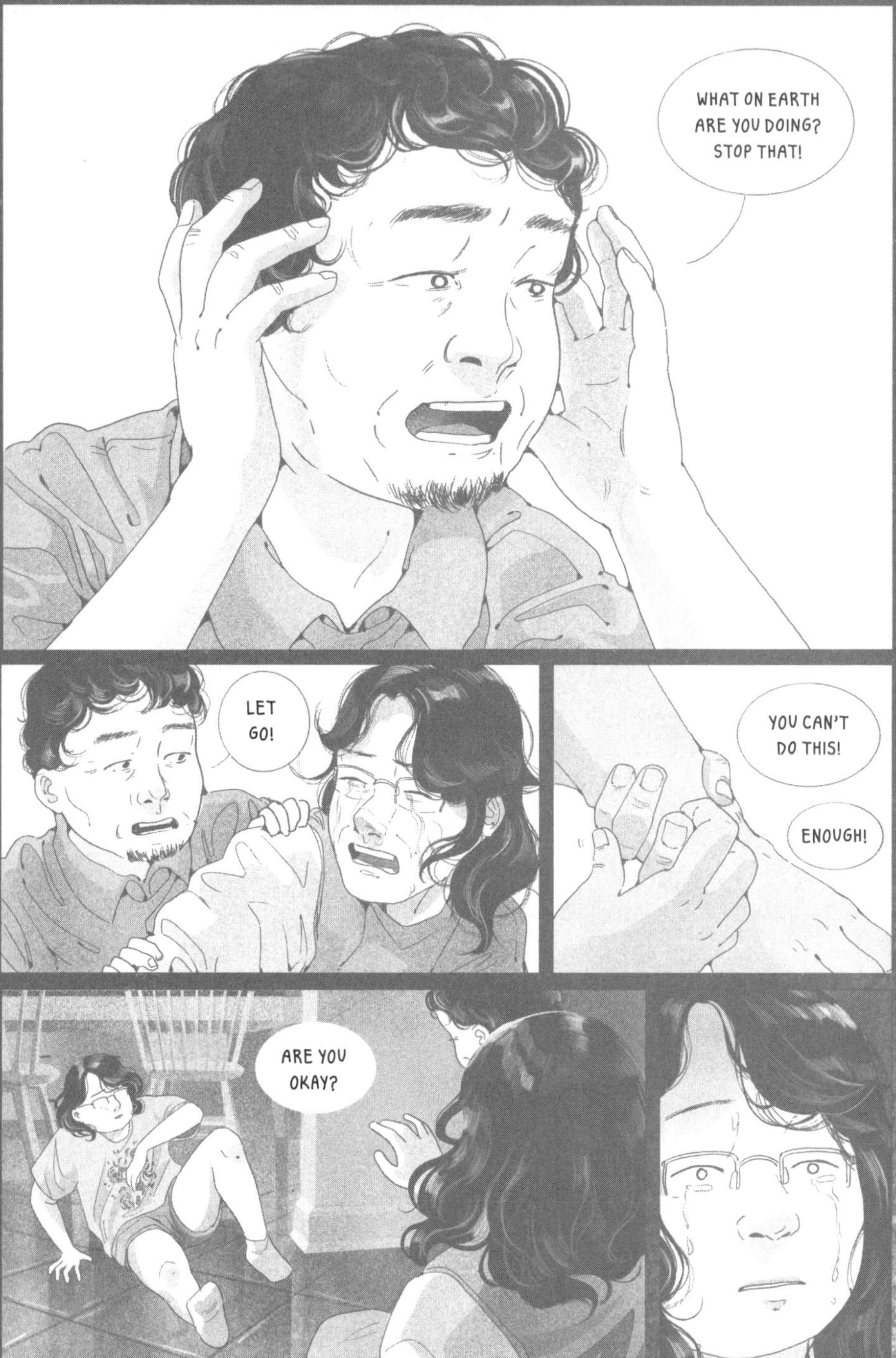

WHAT ON EARTH ARE YOU DOING? STOP THAT!
LET GO!
YOU CAN'T DO THIS!
ENOUGH!
ARE YOU OKAY?

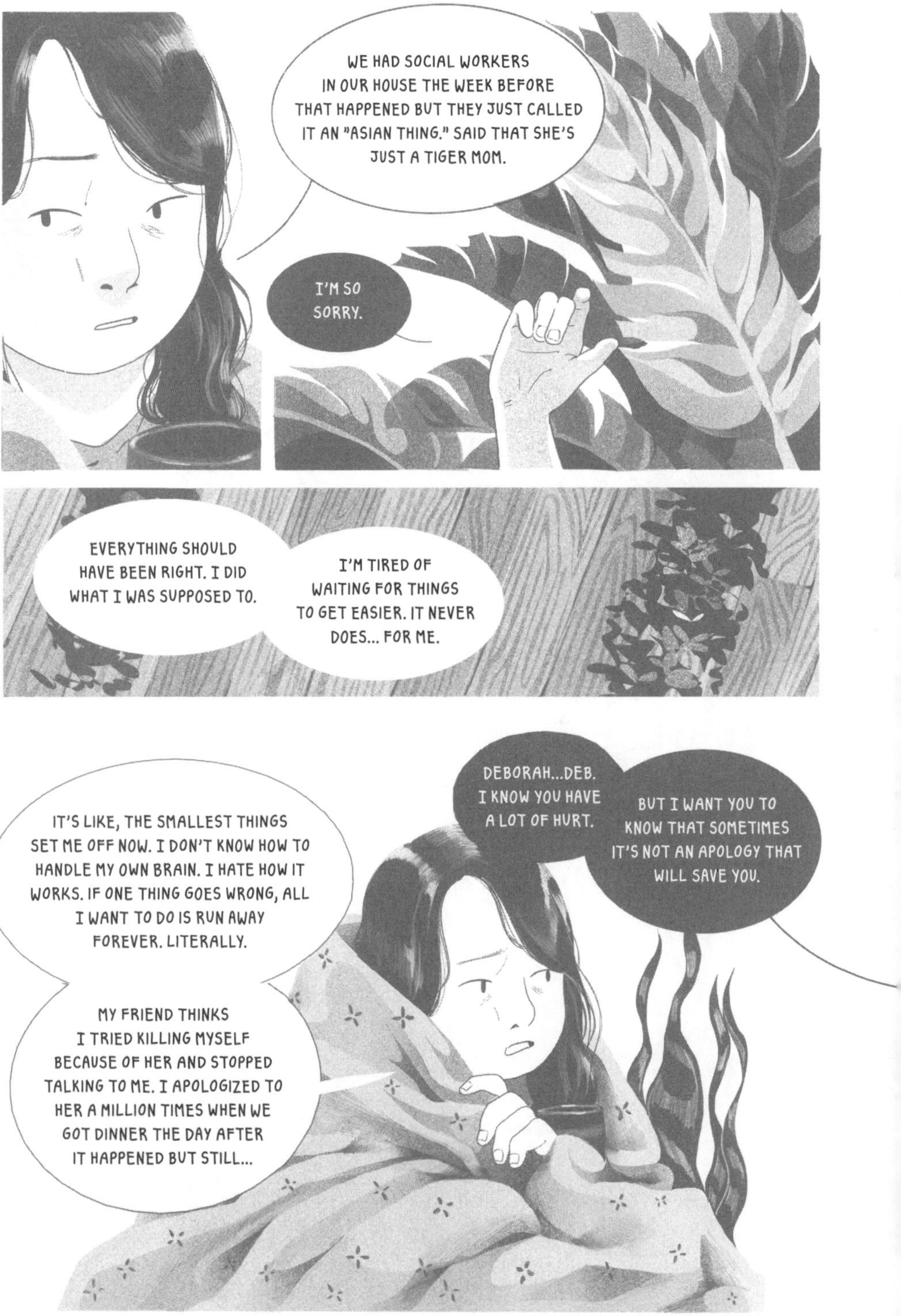
WE HAD SOCIAL WORKERS IN OUR HOUSE THE WEEK BEFORE THAT HAPPENED BUT THEY JUST CALLED IT AN "ASIAN THING." SAID THAT SHE'S JUST A TIGER MOM.
I'M SO SORRY.
EVERYTHING SHOULD HAVE BEEN RIGHT. I DID WHAT I WAS SUPPOSED TO.
I'M TIRED OF WAITING FOR THINGS TO GET EASIER. IT NEVER DOES... FOR ME.
IT'S LIKE, THE SMALLEST THINGS SET ME OFF NOW. I DON'T KNOW HOW TO HANDLE MY OWN BRAIN. I HATE HOW IT WORKS. IF ONE THING GOES WRONG, ALL I WANT TO DO IS RUN AWAY FOREVER. LITERALLY.
MY FRIEND THINKS I TRIED KILLING MYSELF BECAUSE OF HER AND STOPPED TALKING TO ME. I APOLOGIZED TO HER A MILLION TIMES WHEN WE GOT DINNER THE DAY AFTER IT HAPPENED BUT STILL...
DEBORAH...DEB. I KNOW YOU HAVE A LOT OF HURT.
BUT I WANT YOU TO KNOW THAT SOMETIMES IT'S NOT AN APOLOGY THAT WILL SAVE YOU.

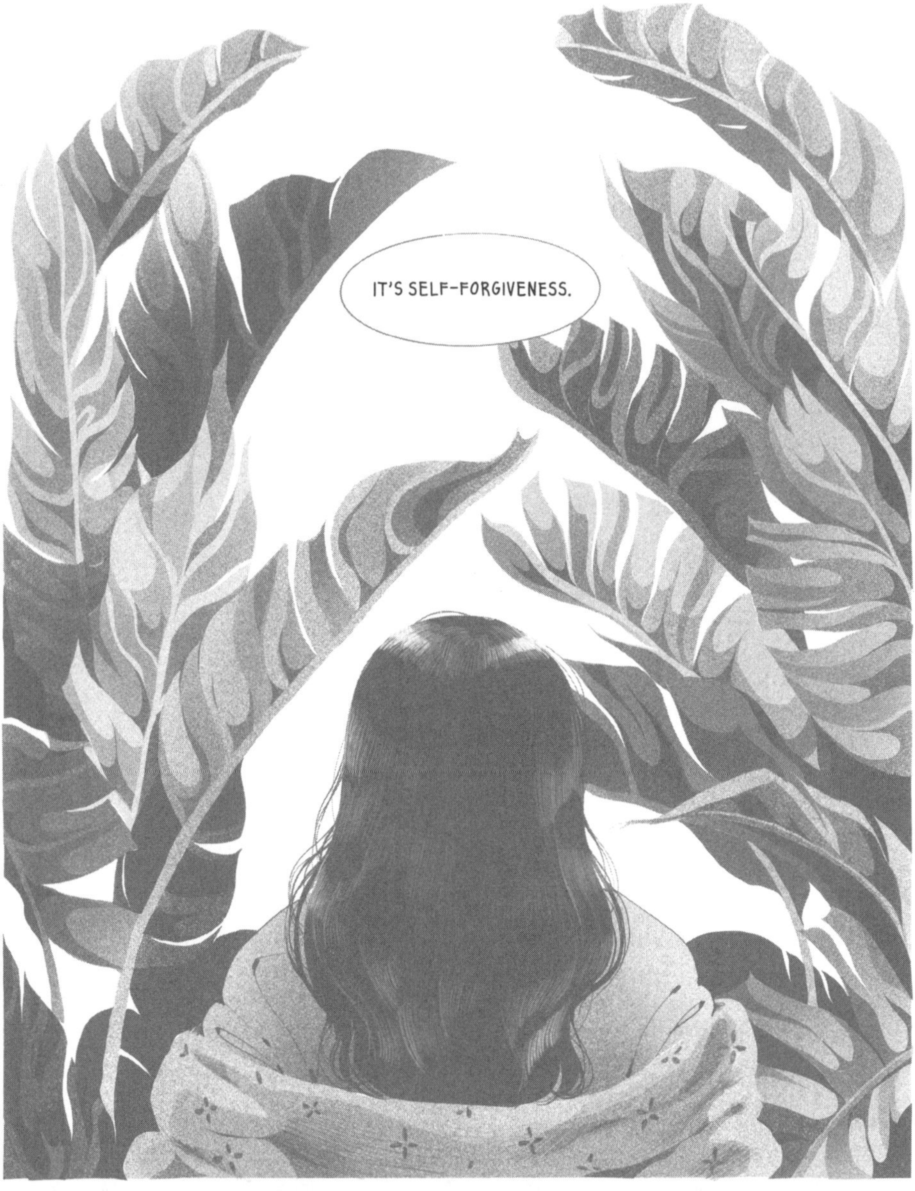
IT'S SELF-FORGIVENESS.

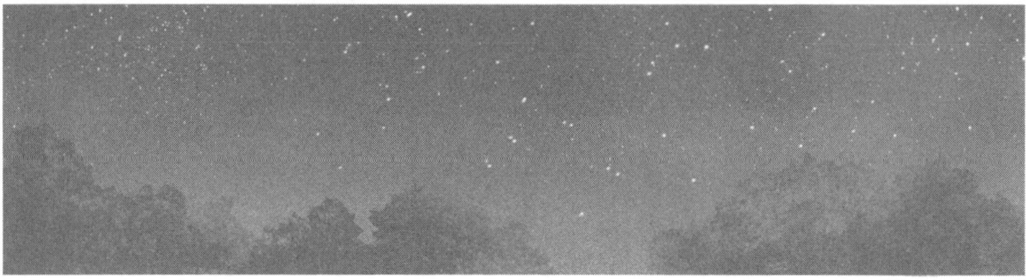

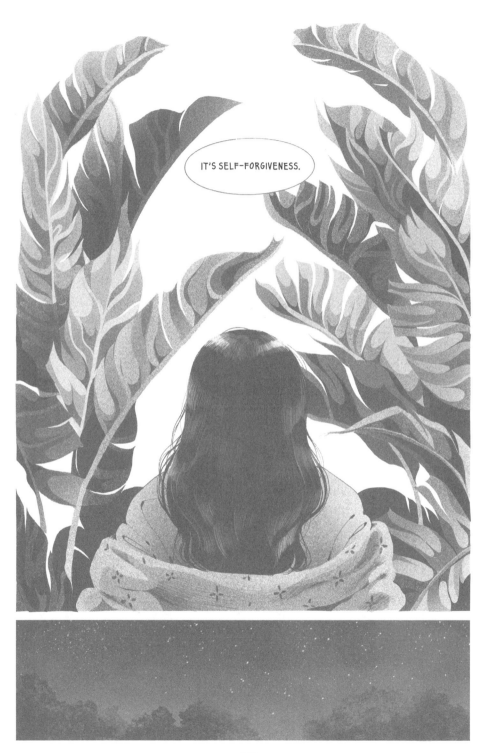

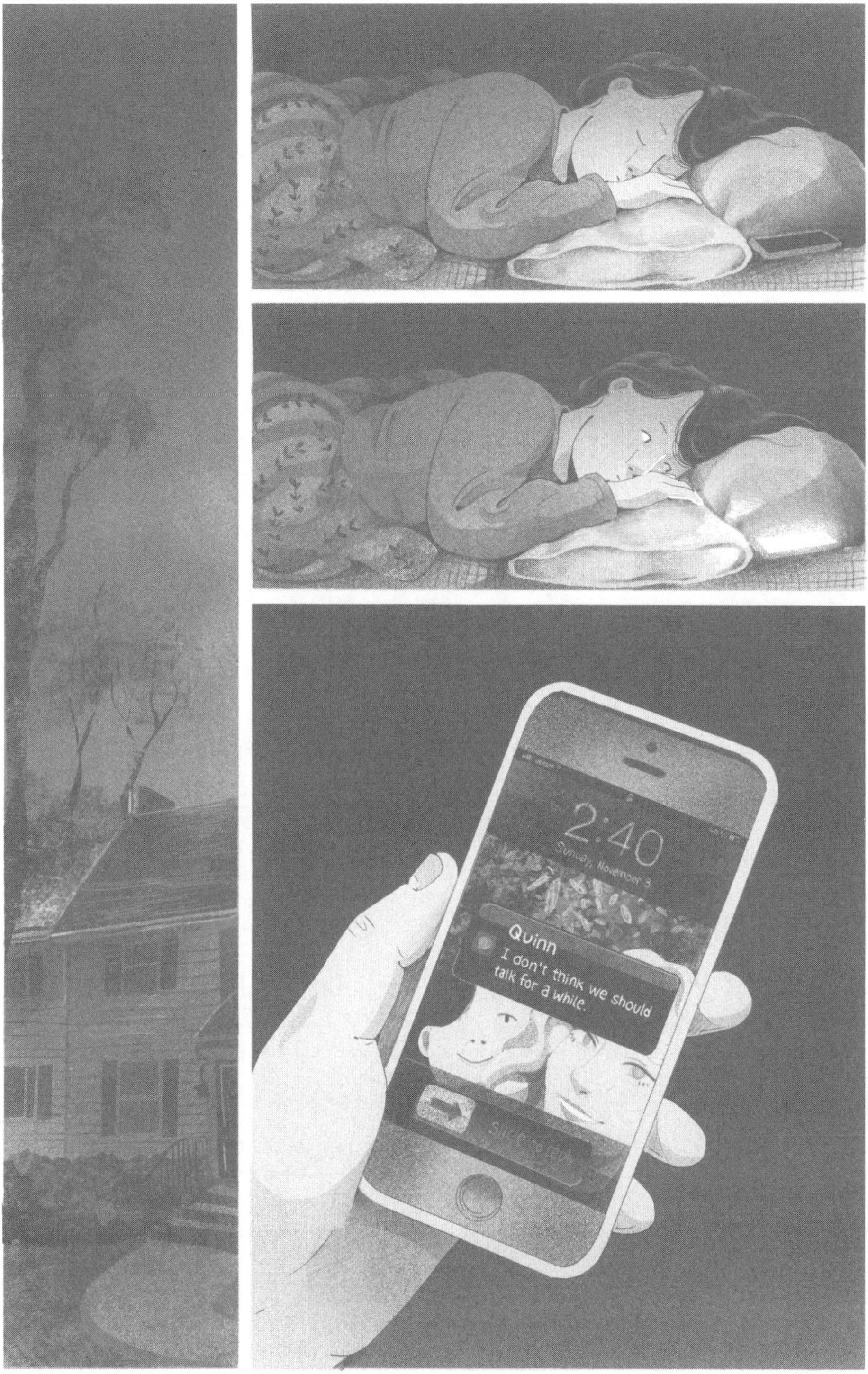
2:40
Sunday, November 3
Quinn
I don't think we should talk for a while.
Slide to unlock

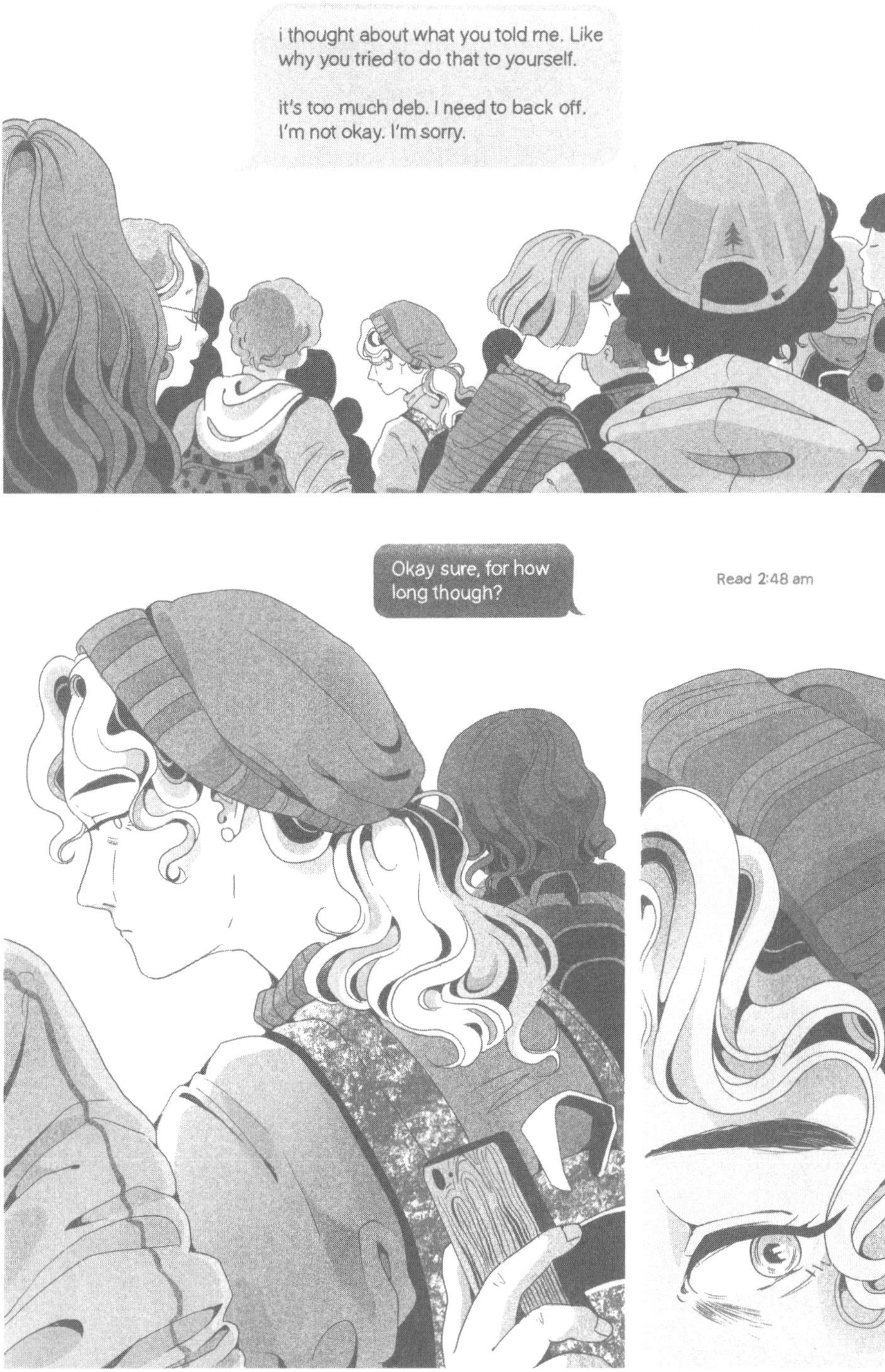
i thought about what you told me. Like why you tried to do that to yourself.
it's too much deb. I need to back off. I'm not okay. I'm sorry.
Okay sure, for how long though?
Read 2:48 am

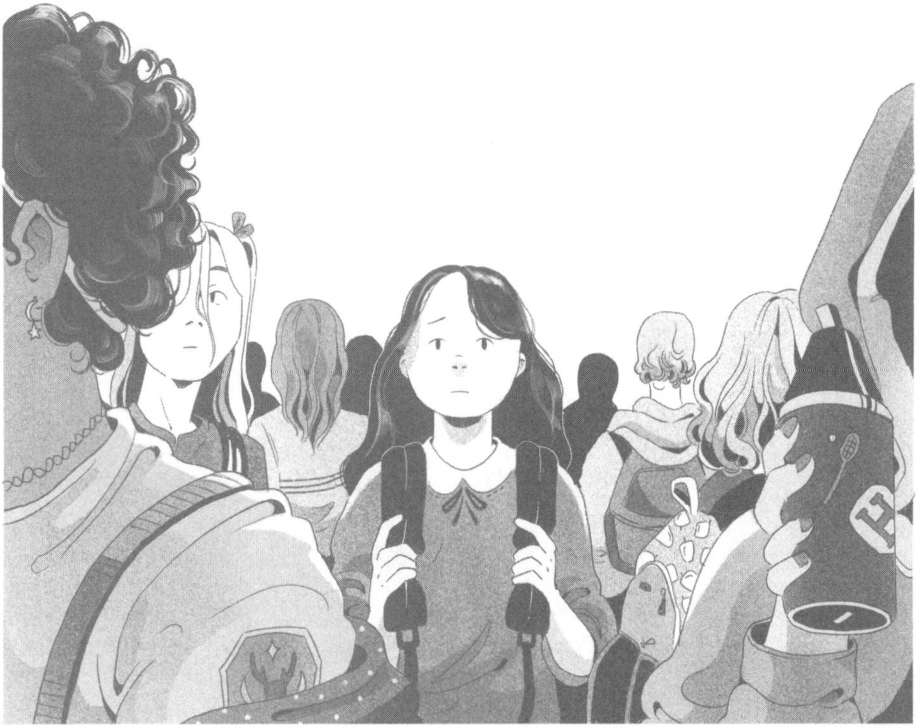

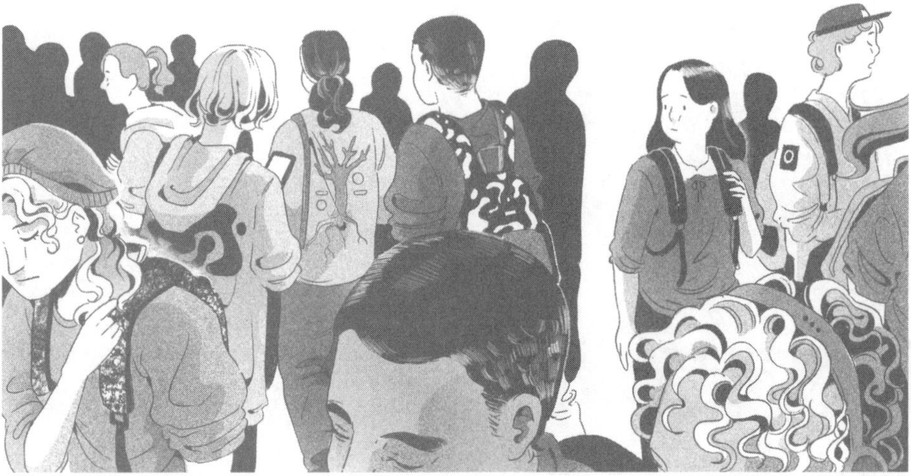

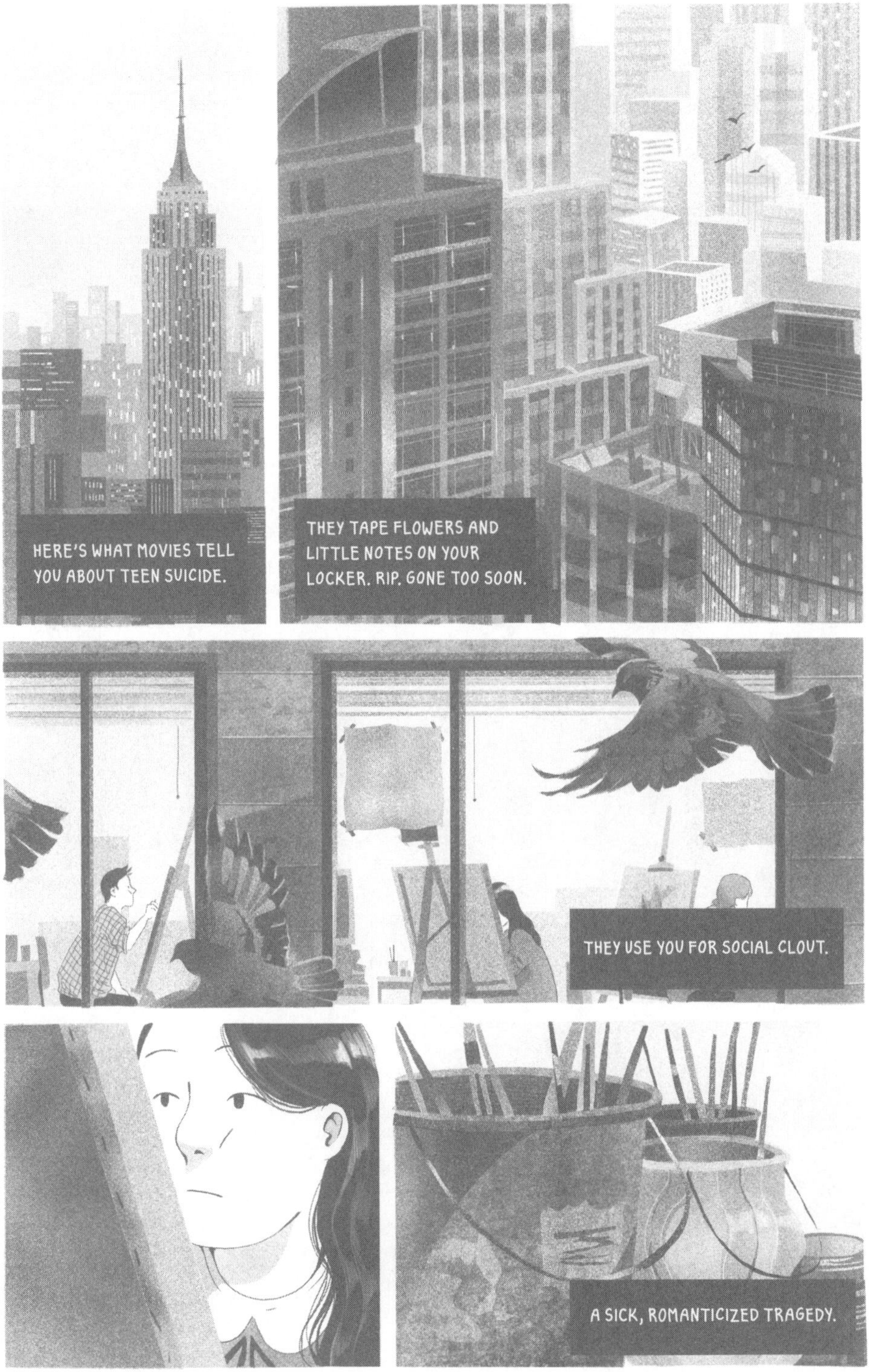
HERE'S WHAT MOVIES TELL YOU ABOUT TEEN SUICIDE.
THEY TAPE FLOWERS AND LITTLE NOTES ON YOUR LOCKER. RIP. GONE TOO SOON.
THEY USE YOU FOR SOCIAL CLOUT.
A SICK, ROMANTICIZED TRAGEDY.

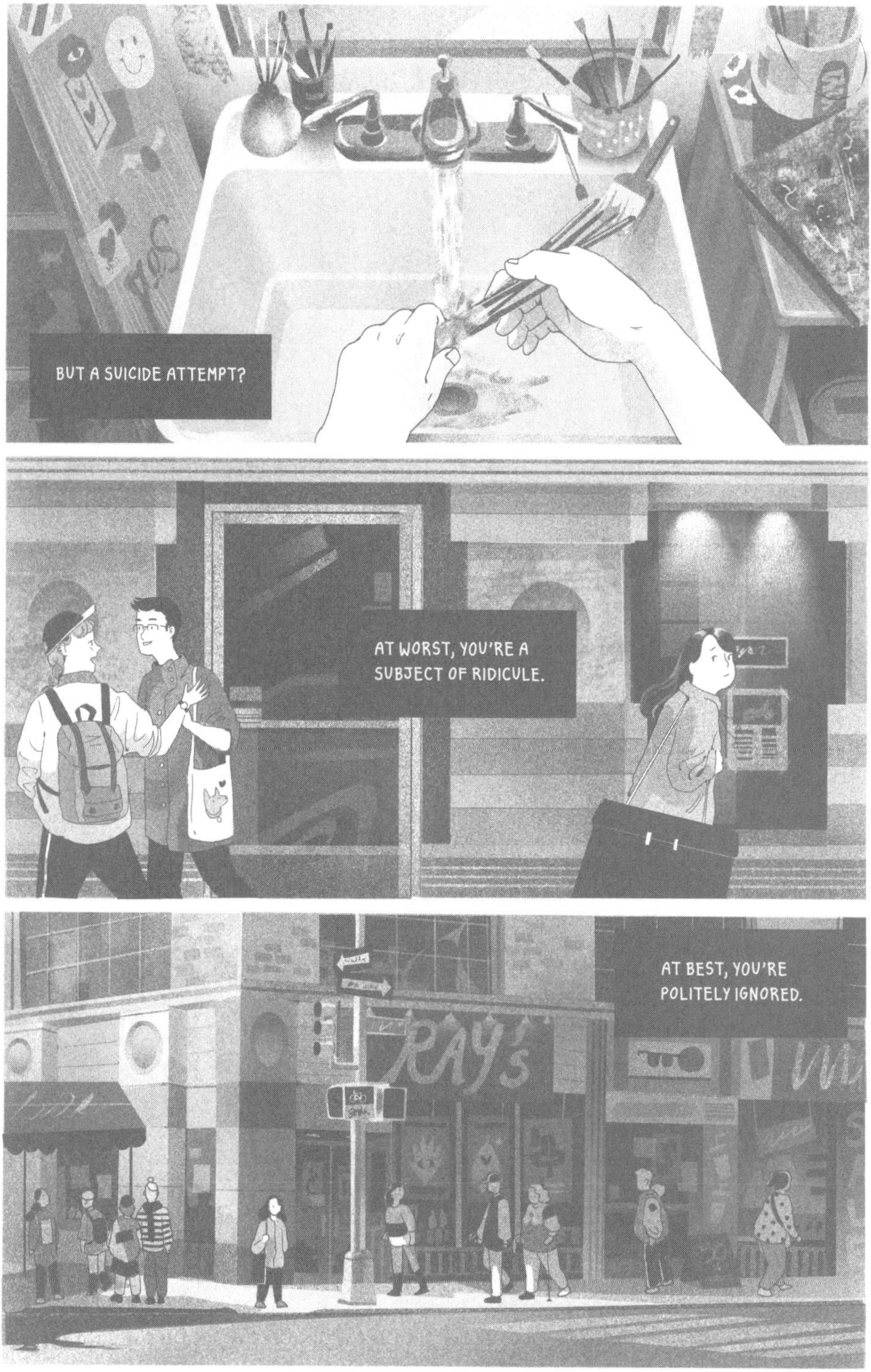
BUT A SUICIDE ATTEMPT?
AT WORST, YOU'RE A SUBJECT OF RIDICULE.
AT BEST, YOU'RE POLITELY IGNORED.
RAY'S

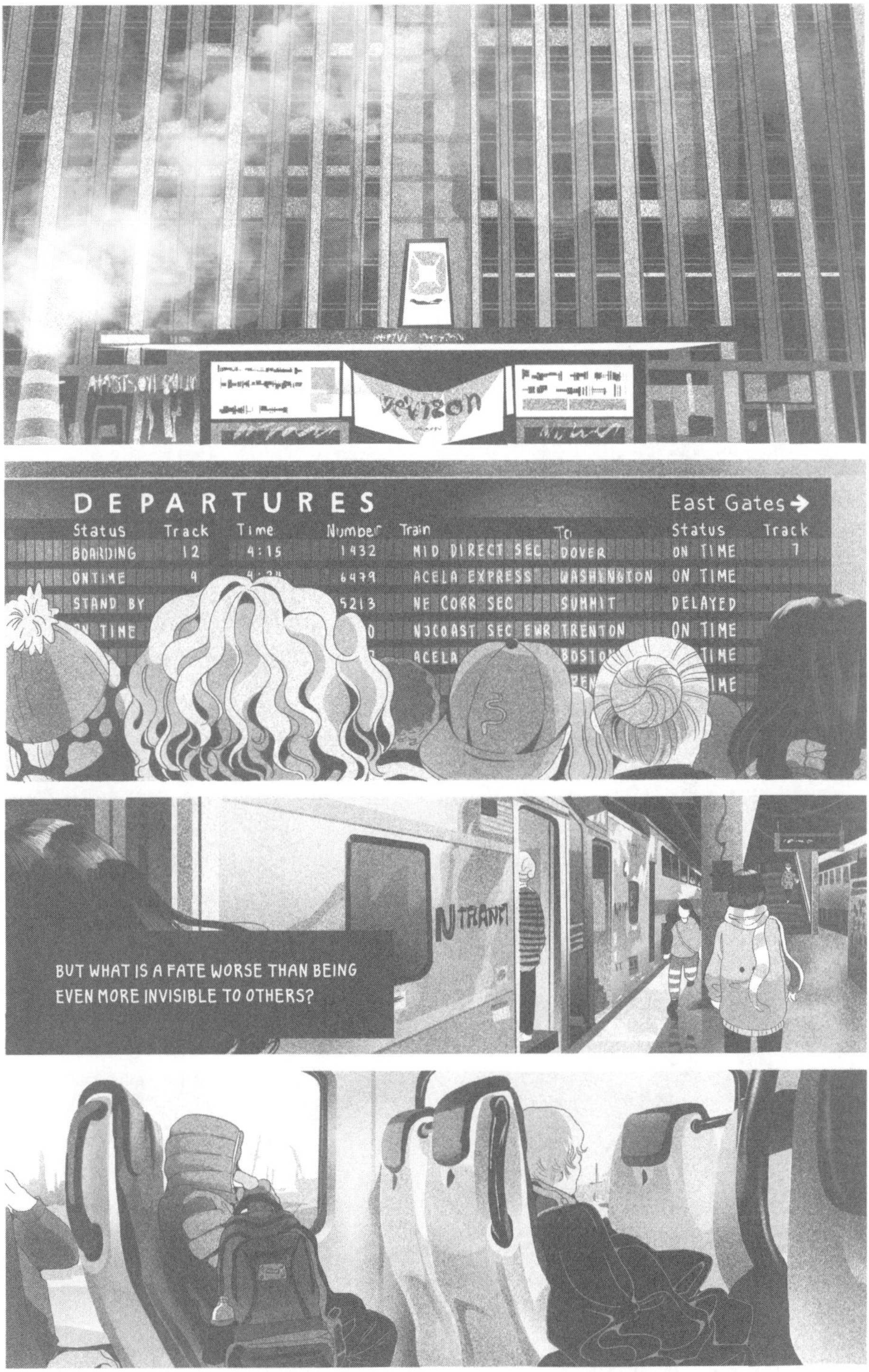
DEPARTURES
East Gates →
Status Track Time Number Train To Status Track
BOARDING 12 4:15 1432 MID DIRECT SEC DOVER ON TIME 7
ONTIME 9 6479 ACELA EXPRESS WASHINGTON ON TIME
STAND BY 5213 NE CORR SEC SUMMIT DELAYED
NJCOAST SEC EWR TRENTON ON TIME
BUT WHAT IS A FATE WORSE THAN BEING EVEN MORE INVISIBLE TO OTHERS?

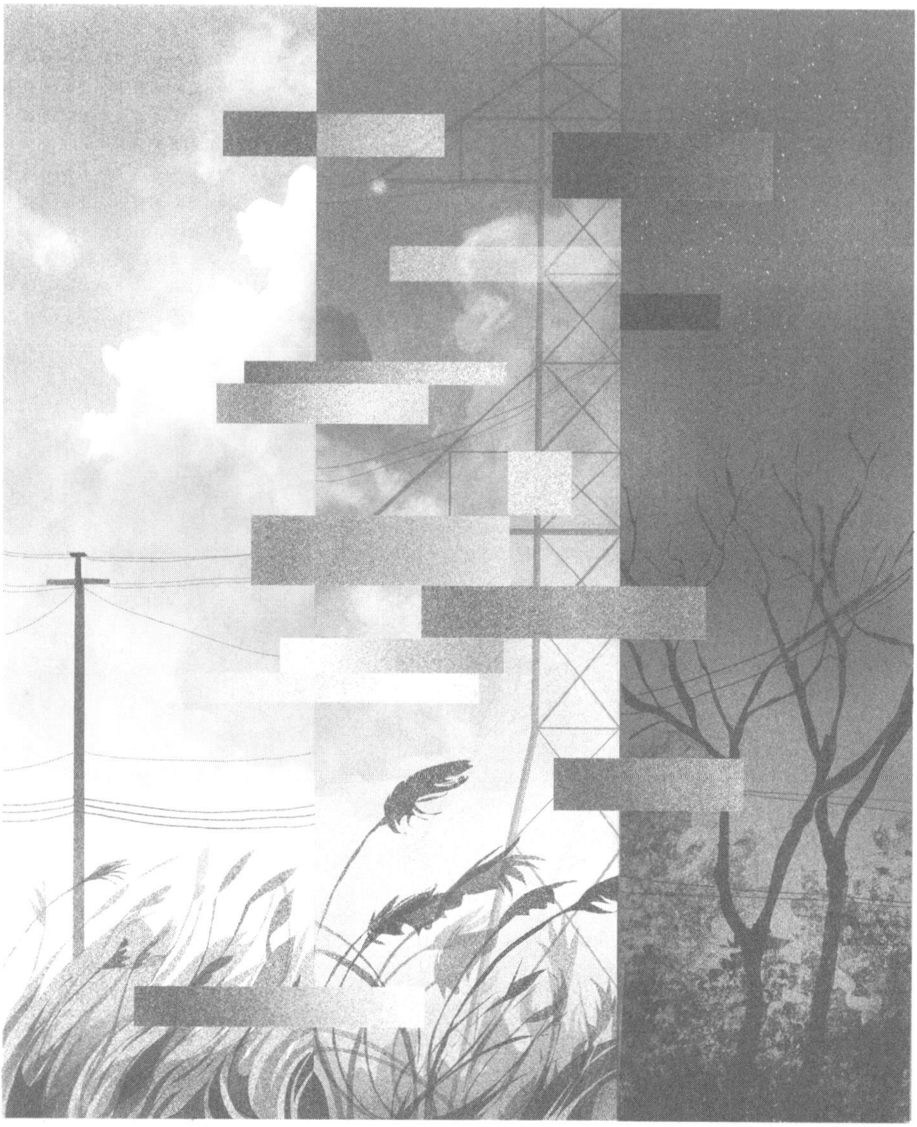

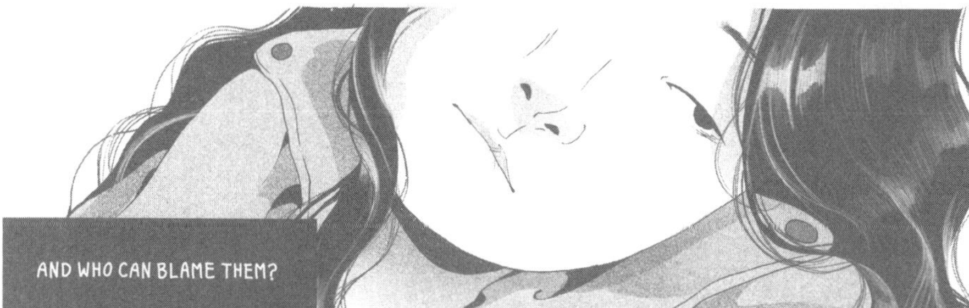
AND WHO CAN BLAME THEM?

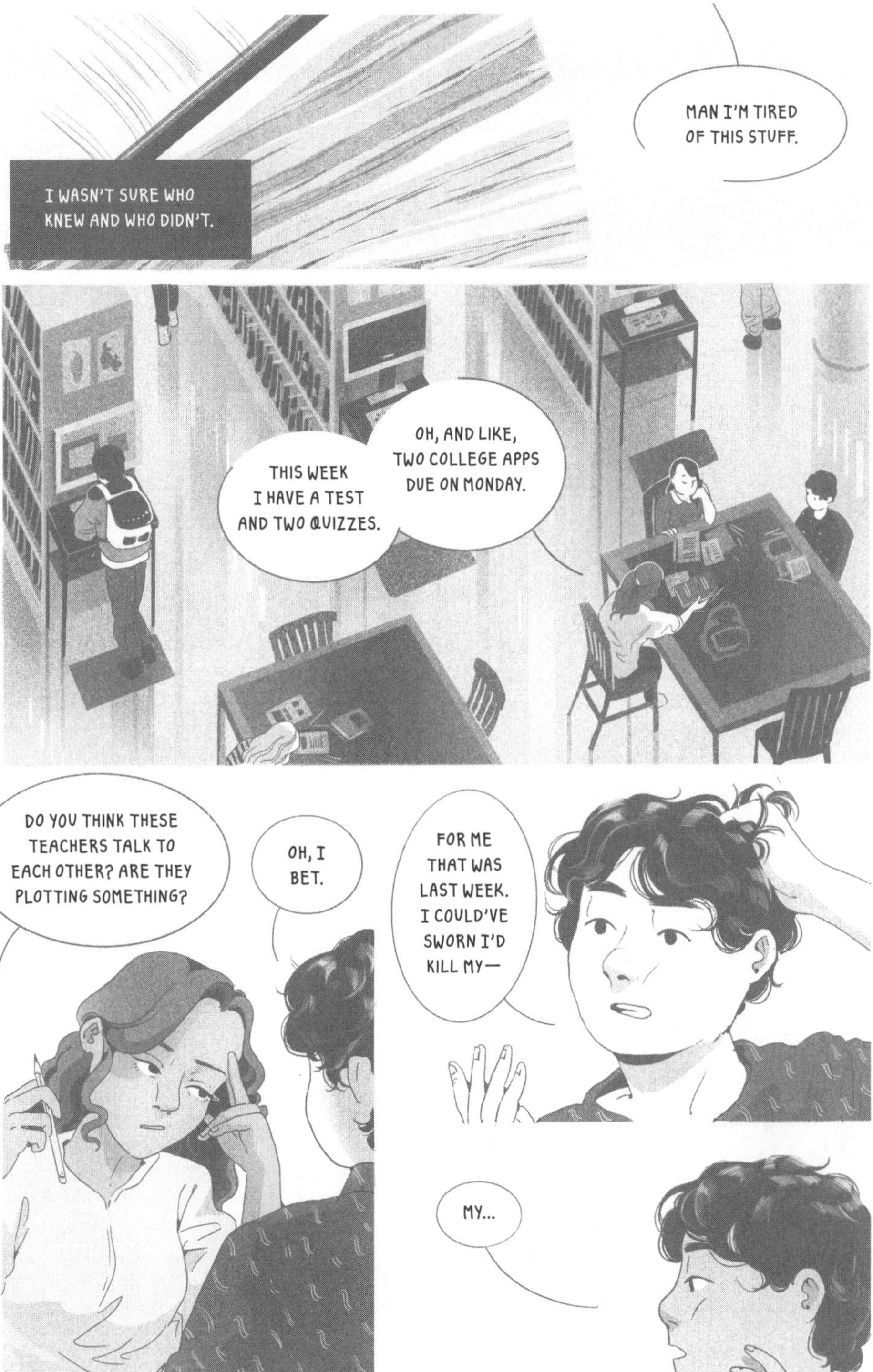
I WASN'T SURE WHO KNEW AND WHO DIDN'T.
MAN I'M TIRED OF THIS STUFF.
THIS WEEK I HAVE A TEST AND TWO QUIZZES.
OH, AND LIKE, TWO COLLEGE APPS DUE ON MONDAY.
DO YOU THINK THESE TEACHERS TALK TO EACH OTHER? ARE THEY PLOTTING SOMETHING?
OH, I BET.
FOR ME THAT WAS LAST WEEK. I COULD'VE SWORN I'D KILL MY—
MY...

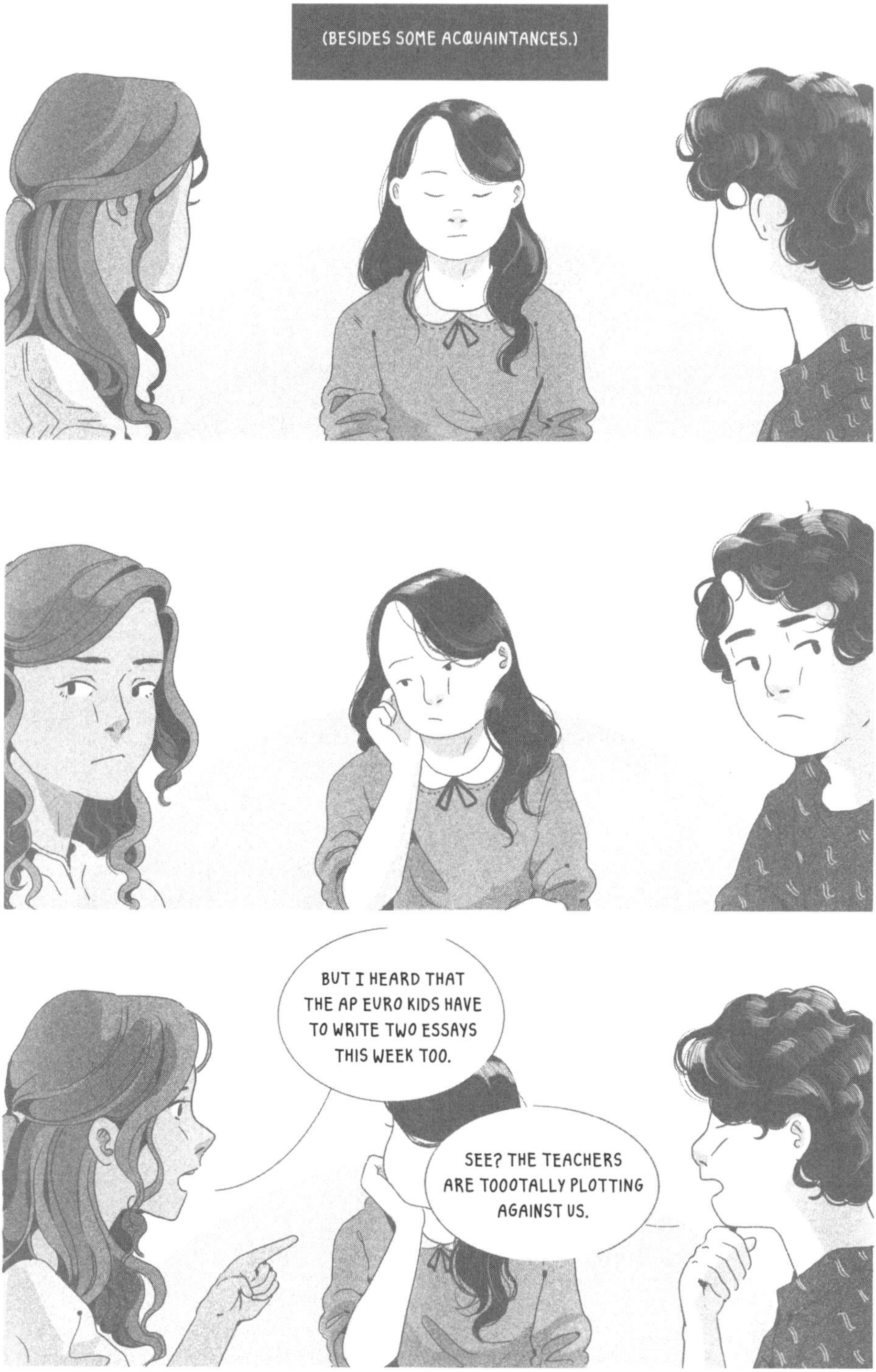
(BESIDES SOME ACQUAINTANCES.)
BUT I HEARD THAT THE AP EURO KIDS HAVE TO WRITE TWO ESSAYS THIS WEEK TOO.
SEE? THE TEACHERS ARE TOOOTALLY PLOTTING AGAINST US.

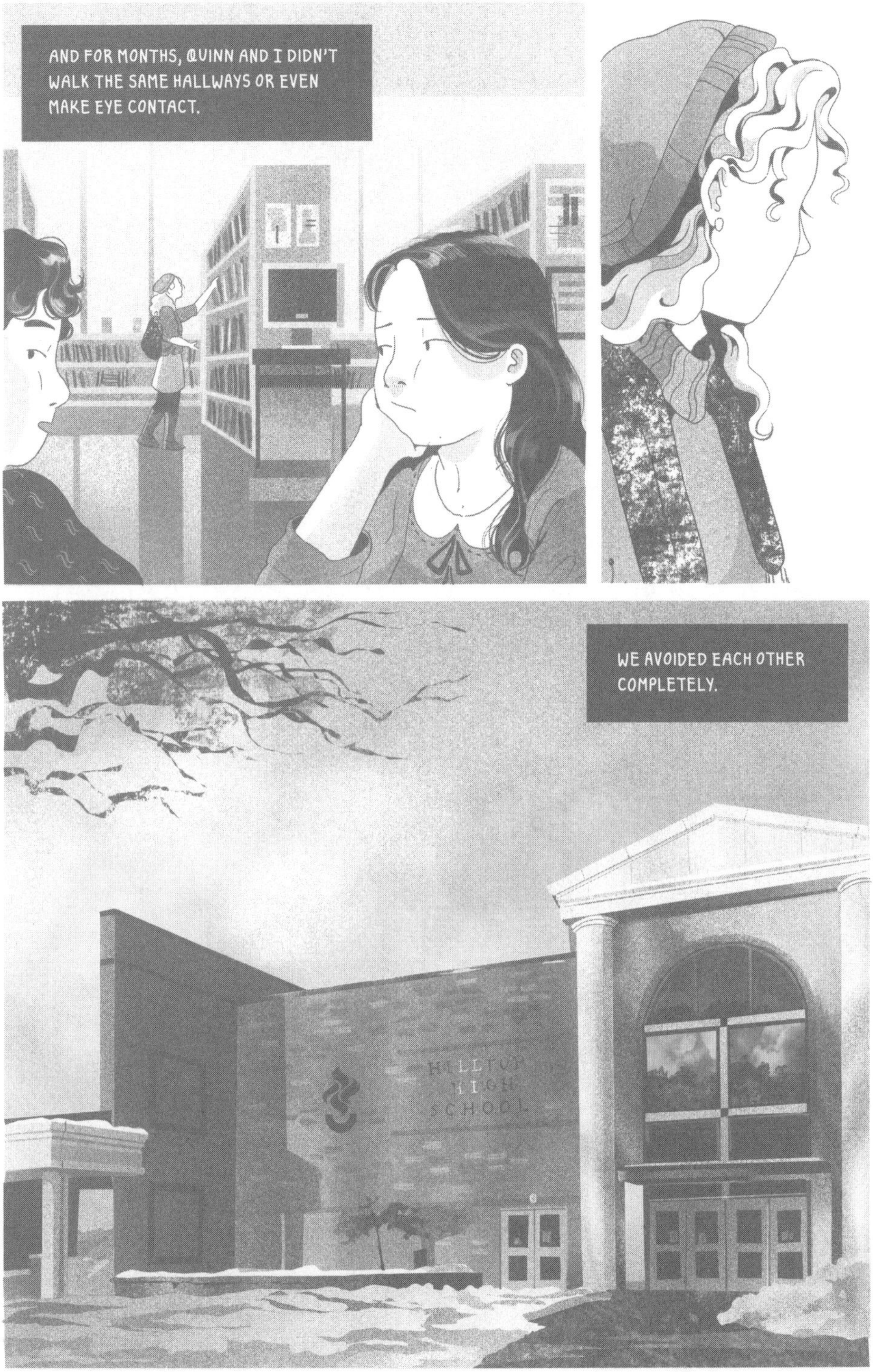
AND FOR MONTHS, QUINN AND I DIDN'T WALK THE SAME HALLWAYS OR EVEN MAKE EYE CONTACT.
WE AVOIDED EACH OTHER COMPLETELY.
HILLTOP HIGH SCHOOL

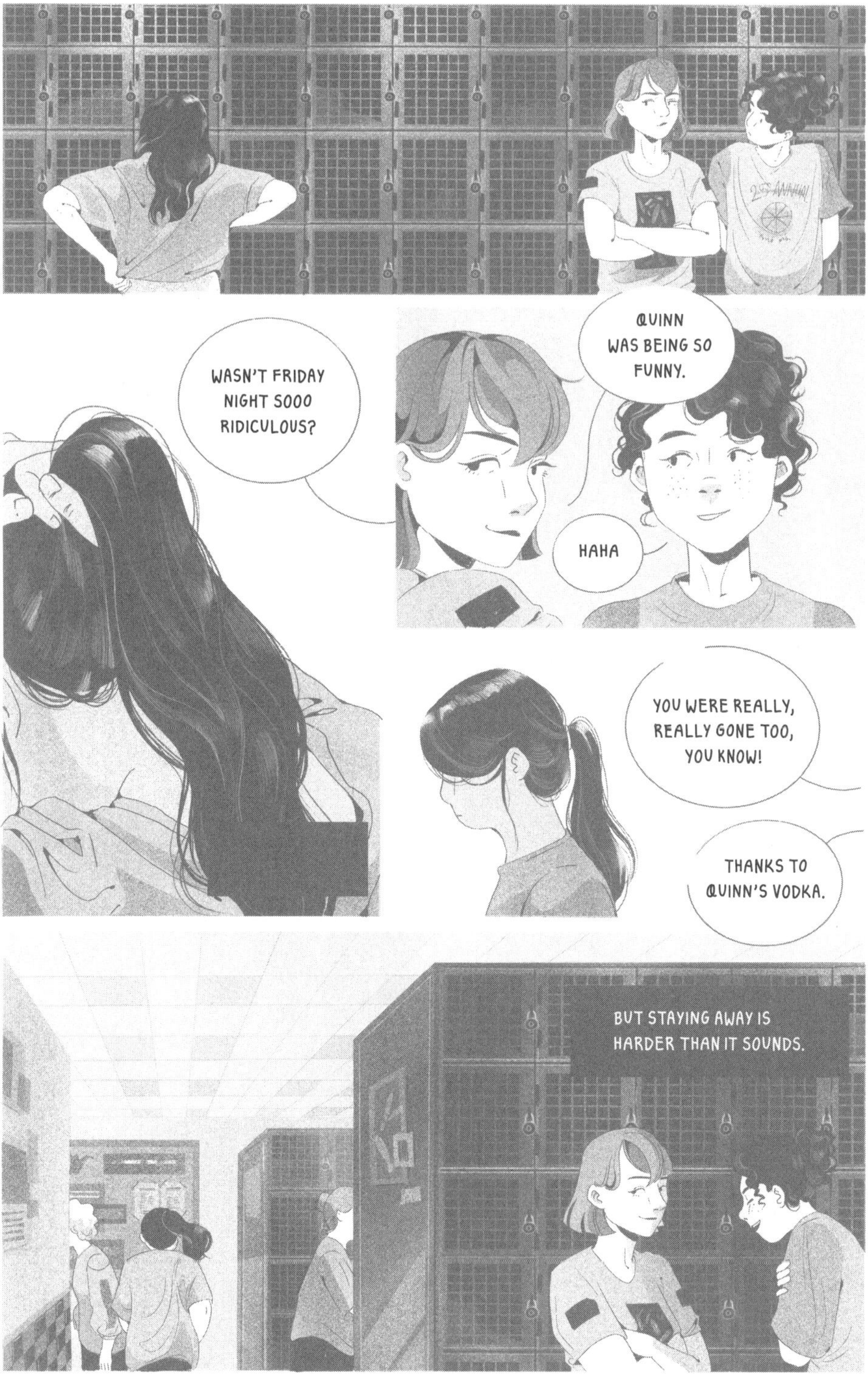
WASN'T FRIDAY NIGHT SOOO RIDICULOUS?
QUINN WAS BEING SO FUNNY.
HAHA
YOU WERE REALLY, REALLY GONE TOO, YOU KNOW!
THANKS TO QUINN'S VODKA.
BUT STAYING AWAY IS HARDER THAN IT SOUNDS.

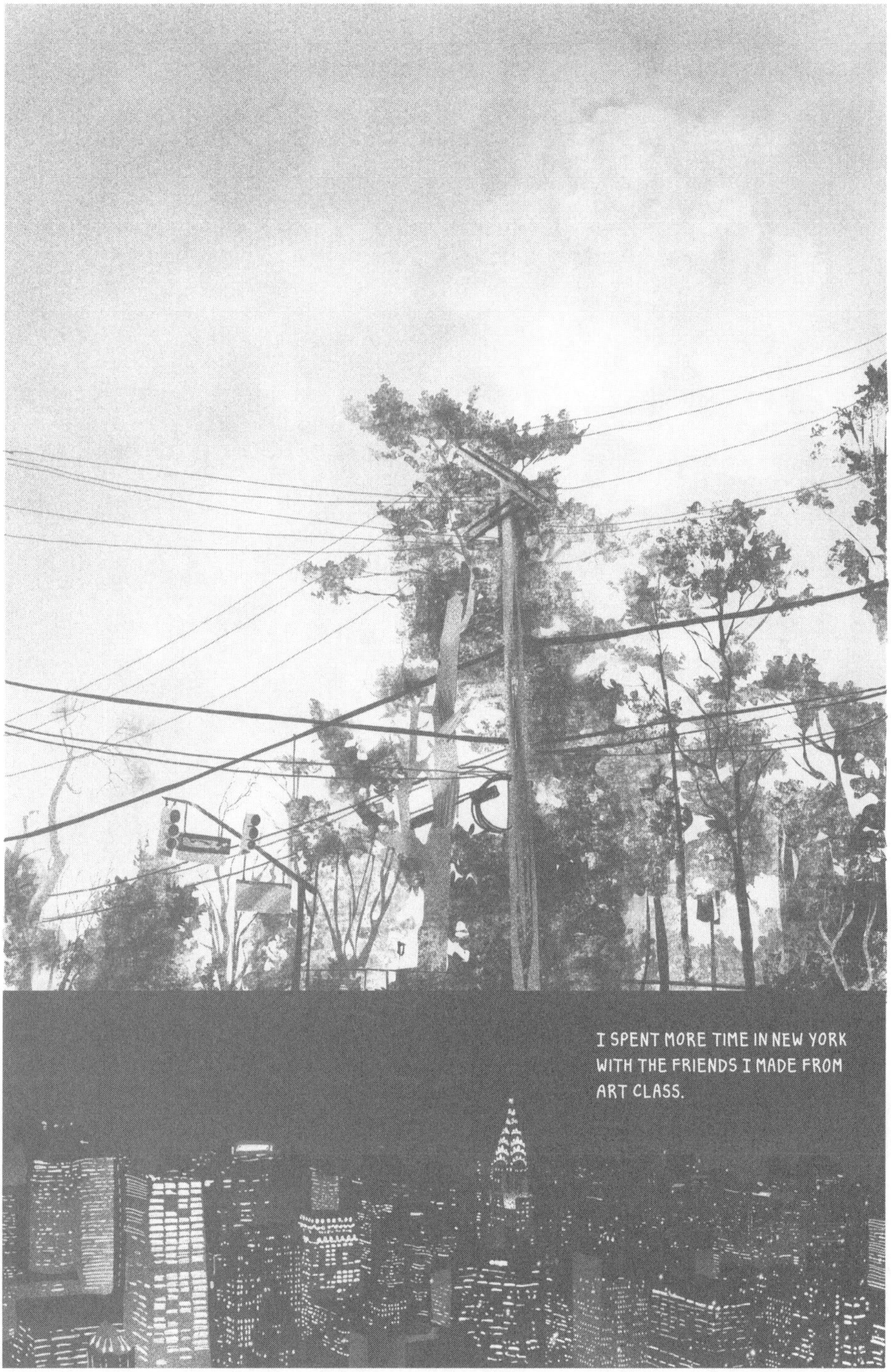
I SPENT MORE TIME IN NEW YORK WITH THE FRIENDS I MADE FROM ART CLASS.

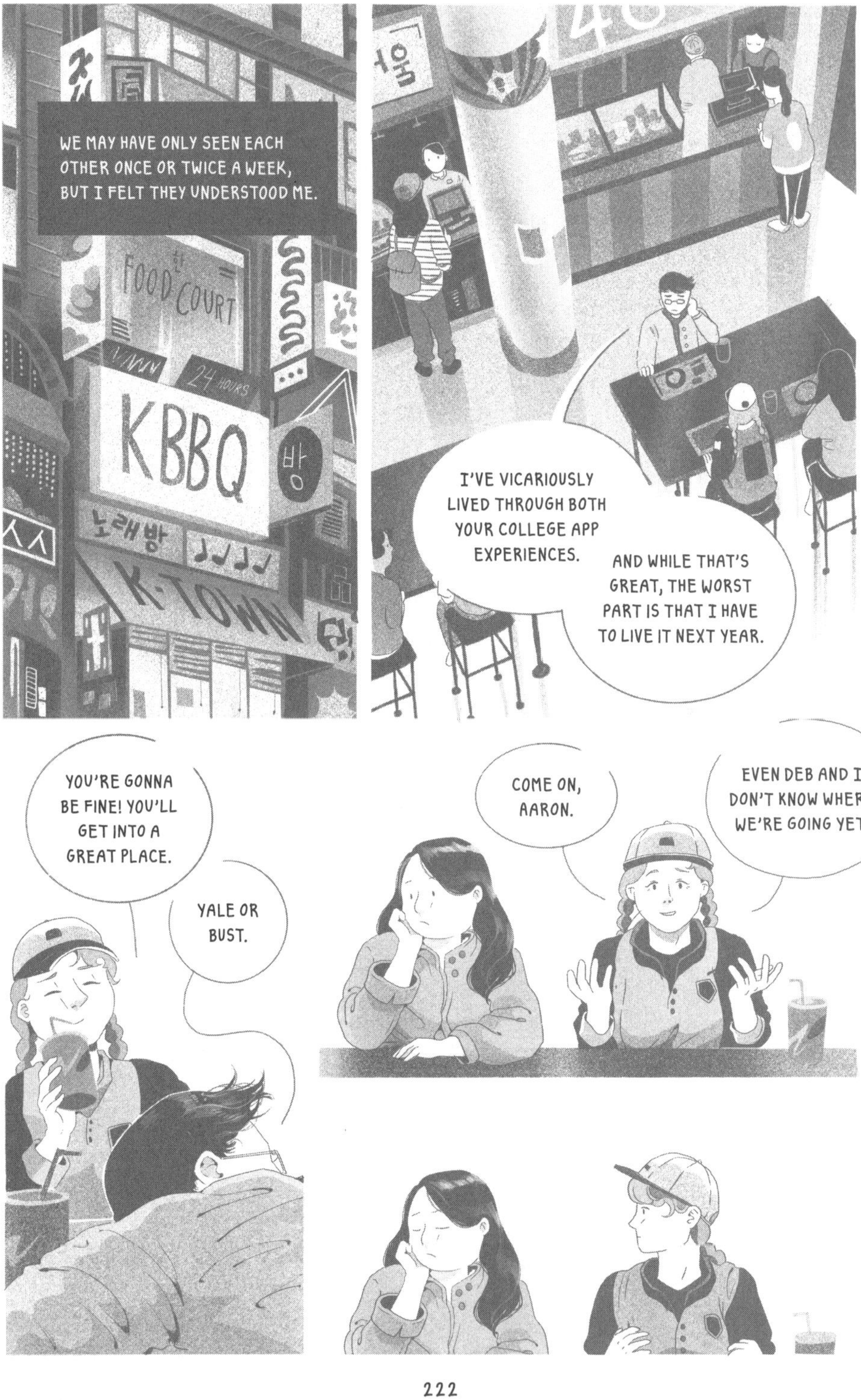

WE MAY HAVE ONLY SEEN EACH OTHER ONCE OR TWICE A WEEK, BUT I FELT THEY UNDERSTOOD ME.
FOOD COURT
24 HOURS
KBBQ
방
노래방
K-TOWN
I'VE VICARIOUSLY LIVED THROUGH BOTH YOUR COLLEGE APP EXPERIENCES.
AND WHILE THAT'S GREAT, THE WORST PART IS THAT I HAVE TO LIVE IT NEXT YEAR.
YOU'RE GONNA BE FINE! YOU'LL GET INTO A GREAT PLACE.
YALE OR BUST.
COME ON, AARON.
EVEN DEB AND I DON'T KNOW WHERE WE'RE GOING YET.

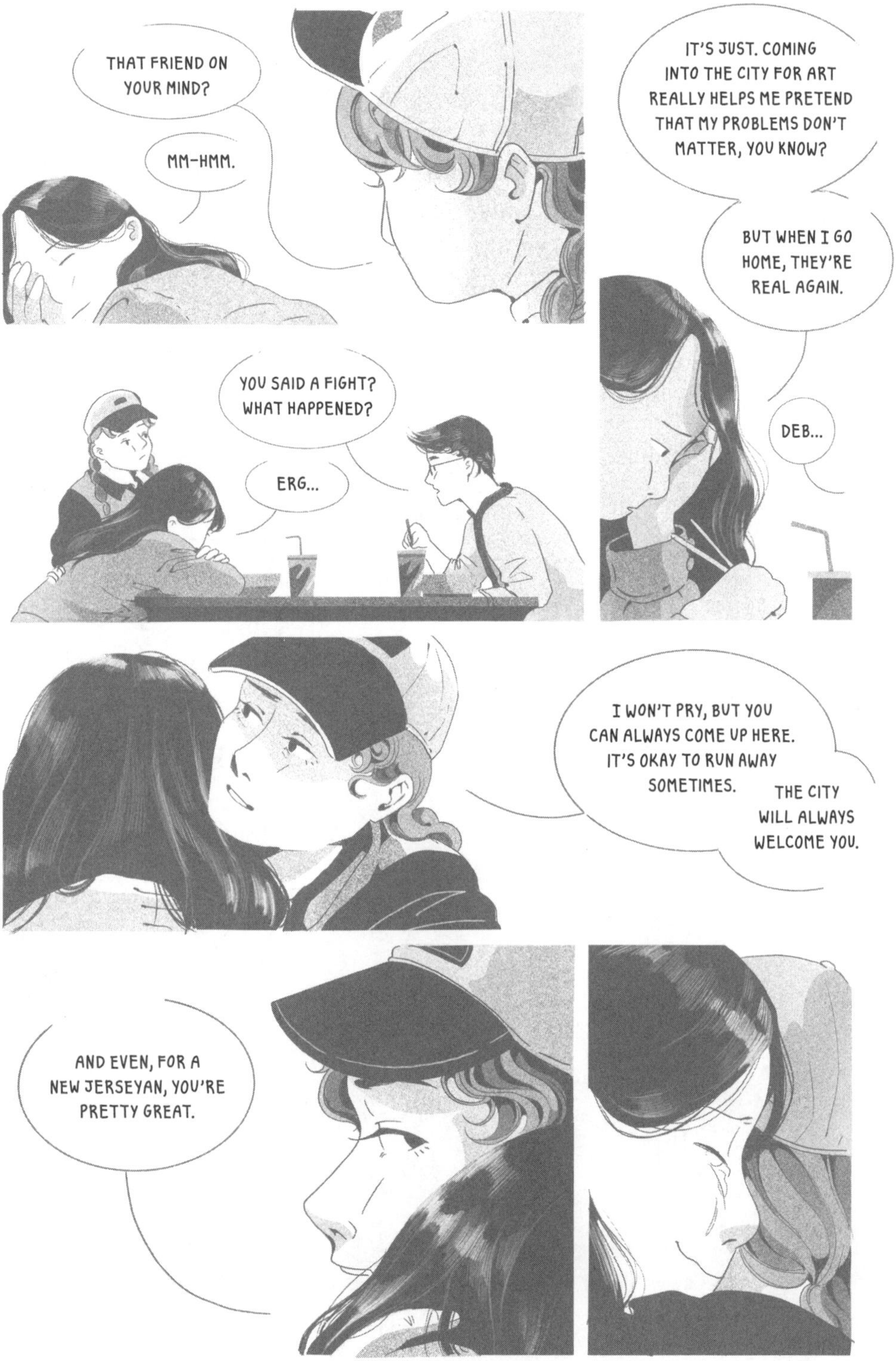
THAT FRIEND ON YOUR MIND?
MM-HMM.
IT'S JUST. COMING INTO THE CITY FOR ART REALLY HELPS ME PRETEND THAT MY PROBLEMS DON'T MATTER, YOU KNOW?
BUT WHEN I GO HOME, THEY'RE REAL AGAIN.
YOU SAID A FIGHT? WHAT HAPPENED?
ERG...
DEB...
I WON'T PRY, BUT YOU CAN ALWAYS COME UP HERE. IT'S OKAY TO RUN AWAY SOMETIMES.
THE CITY WILL ALWAYS WELCOME YOU.
AND EVEN, FOR A NEW JERSEYAN, YOU'RE PRETTY GREAT.

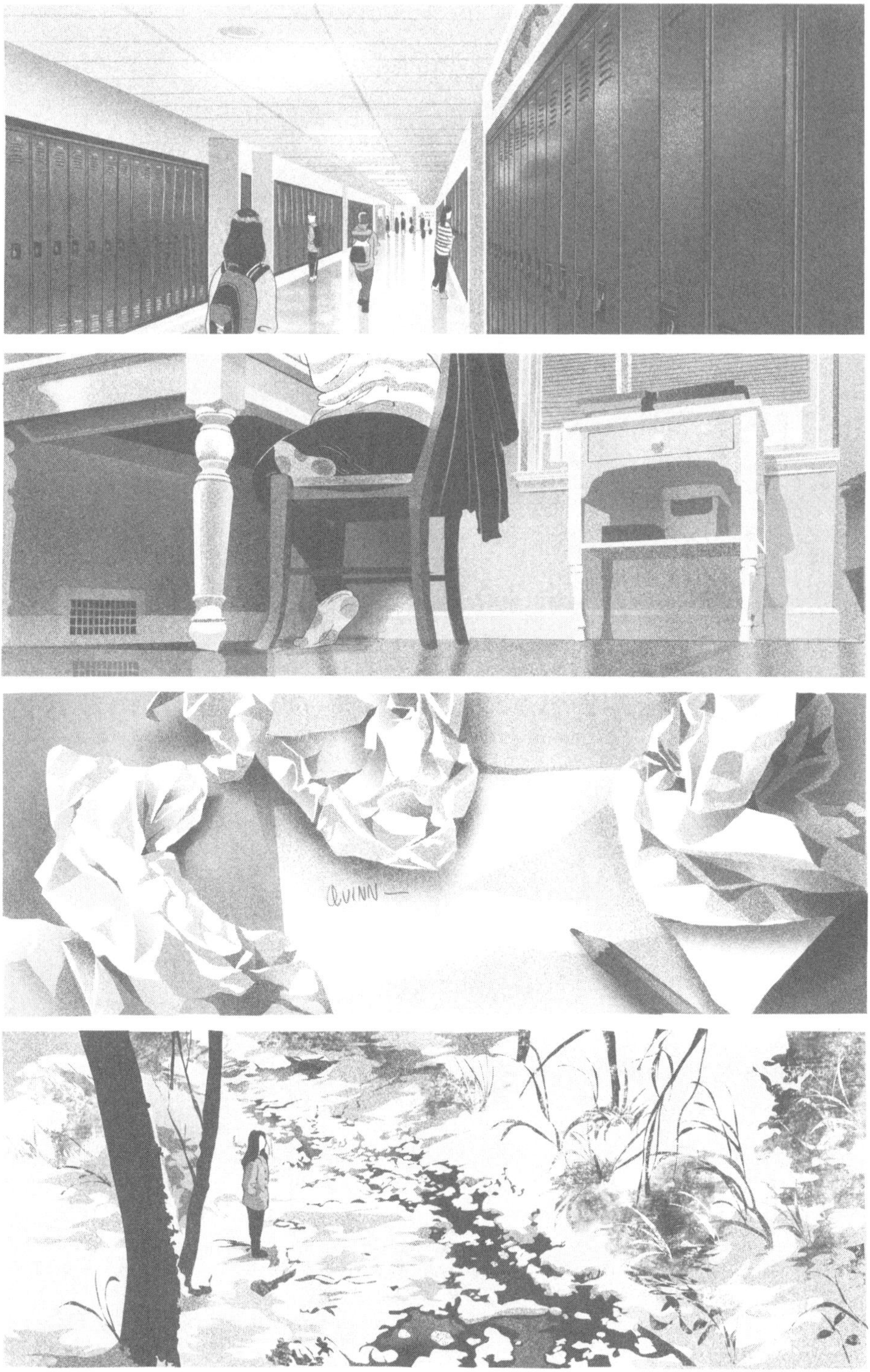
QUINN —

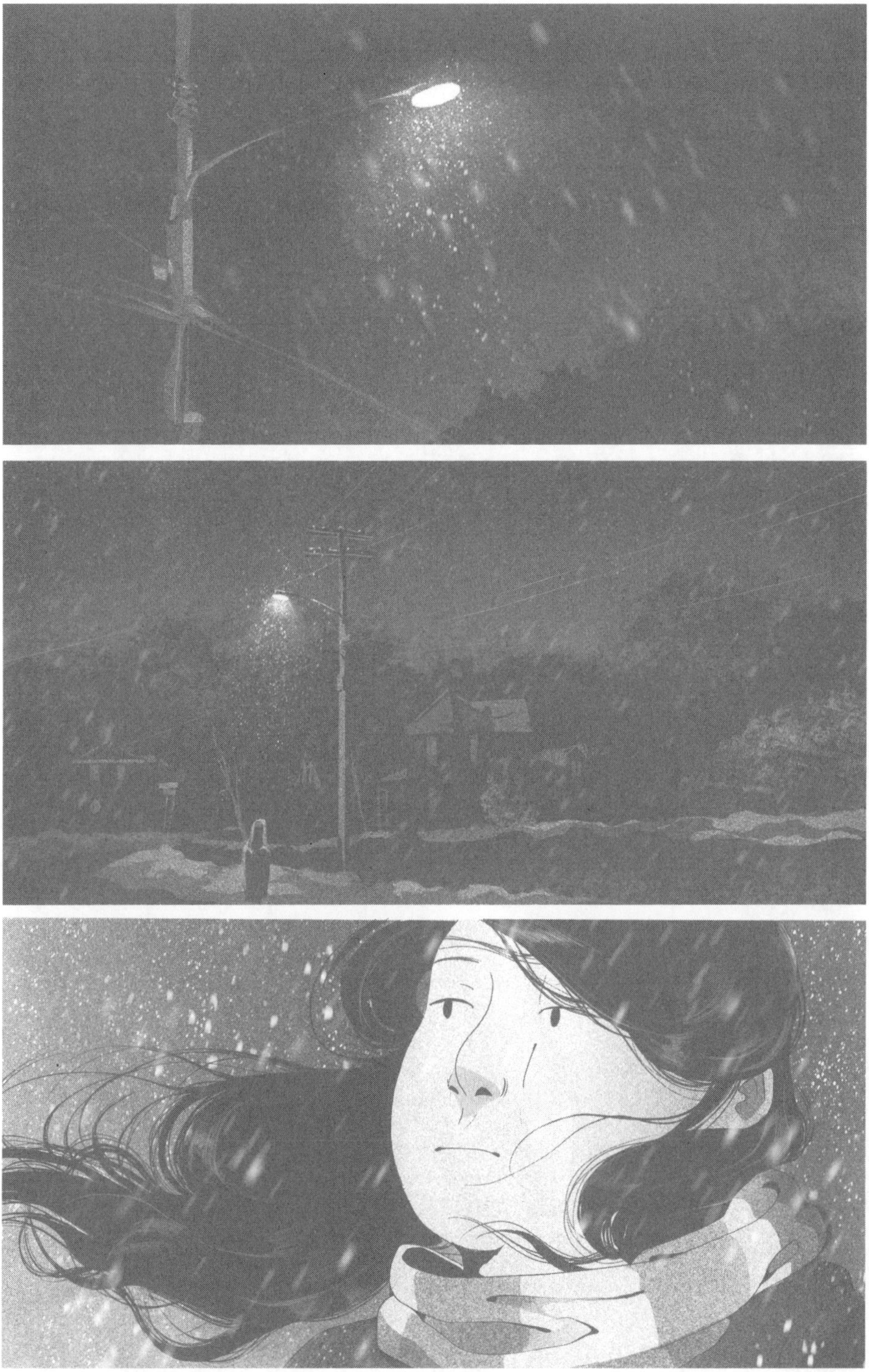

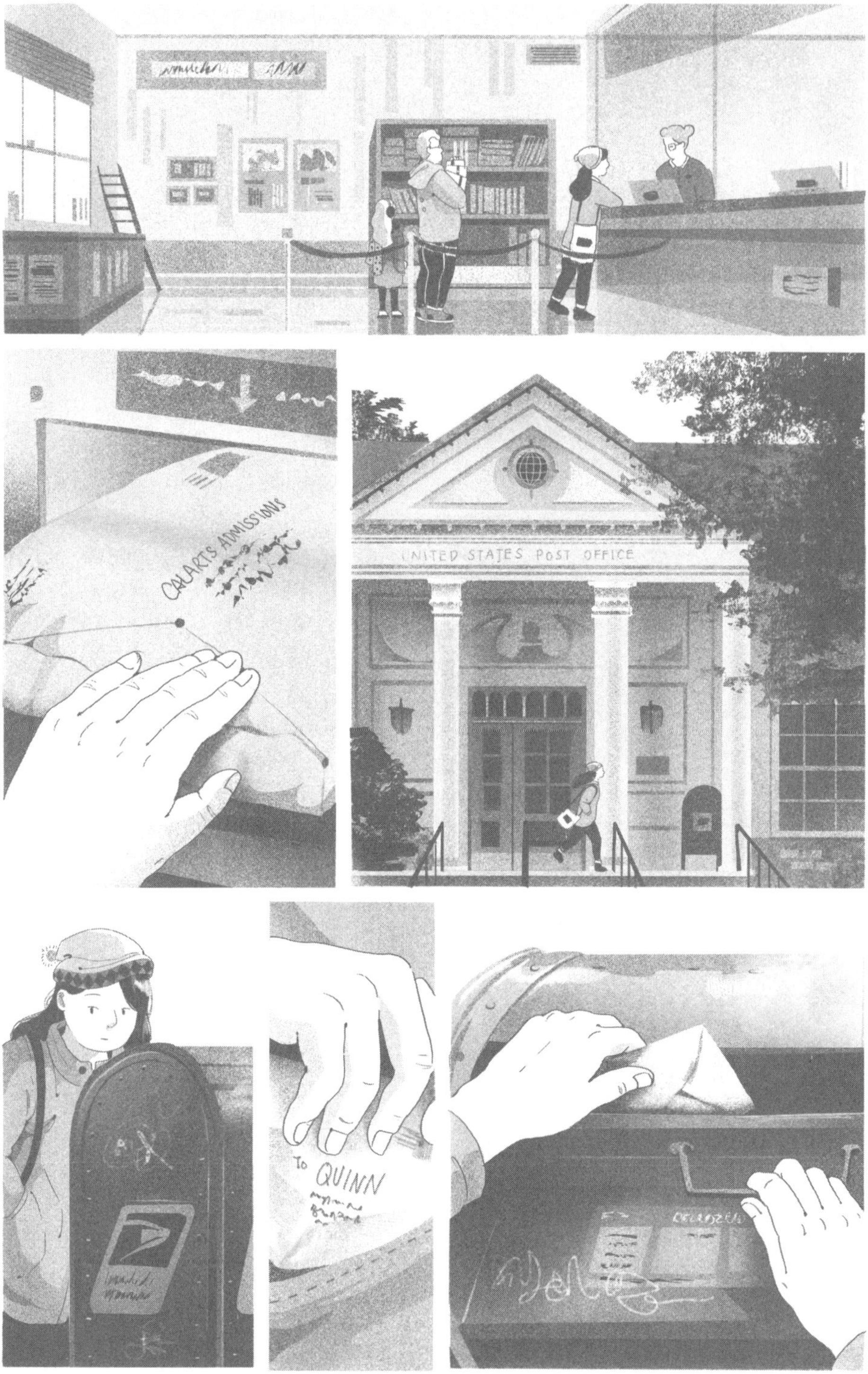
CALARTS ADMISSIONS
UNITED STATES POST OFFICE
TO QUINN

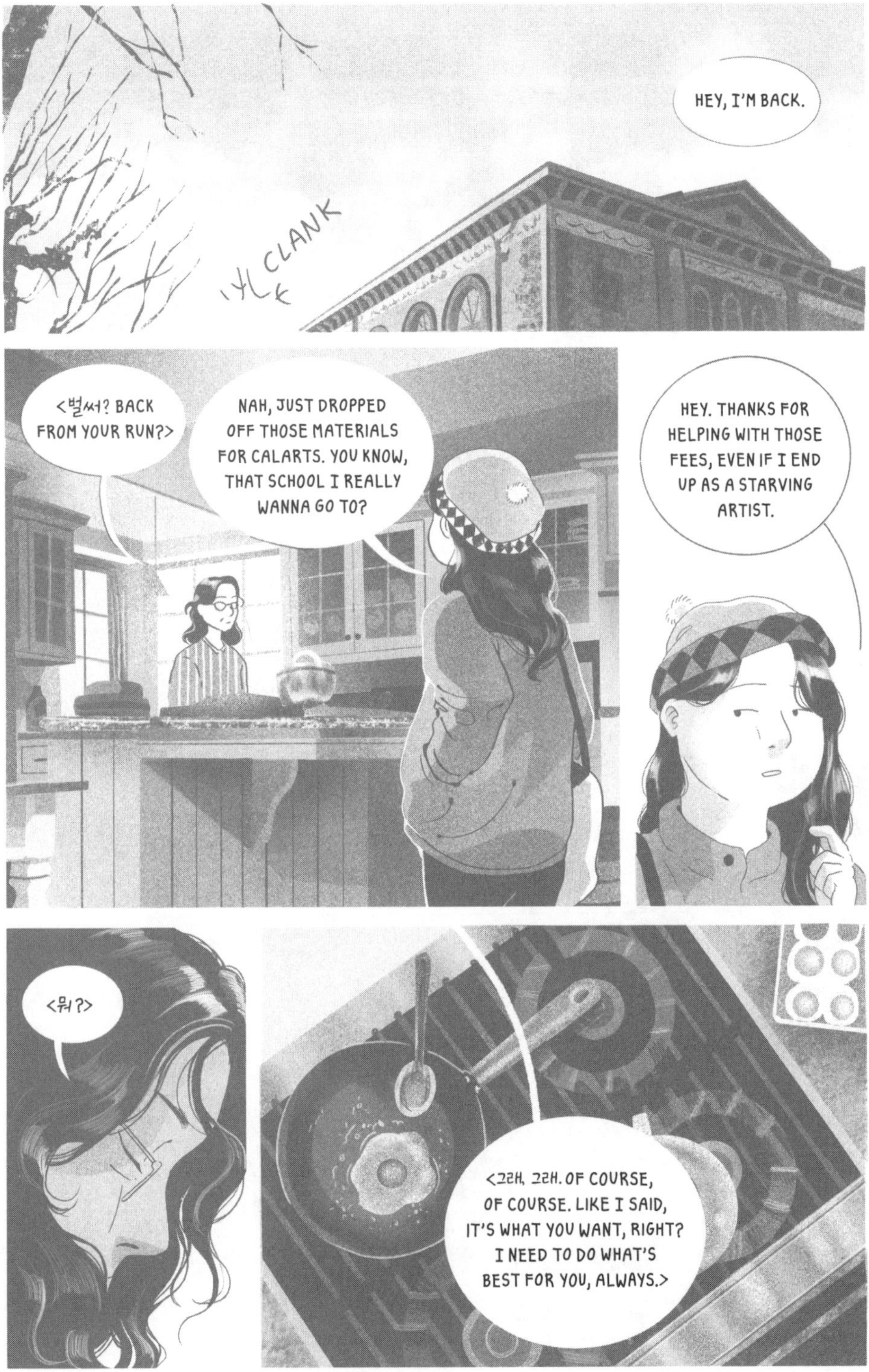
HEY, I'M BACK.
CLANK
<벌써? BACK FROM YOUR RUN?>
NAH, JUST DROPPED OFF THOSE MATERIALS FOR CALARTS. YOU KNOW, THAT SCHOOL I REALLY WANNA GO TO?
HEY. THANKS FOR HELPING WITH THOSE FEES, EVEN IF I END UP AS A STARVING ARTIST.
<뭐?>
<그래, 그래. OF COURSE, OF COURSE. LIKE I SAID, IT'S WHAT YOU WANT, RIGHT? I NEED TO DO WHAT'S BEST FOR YOU, ALWAYS.>

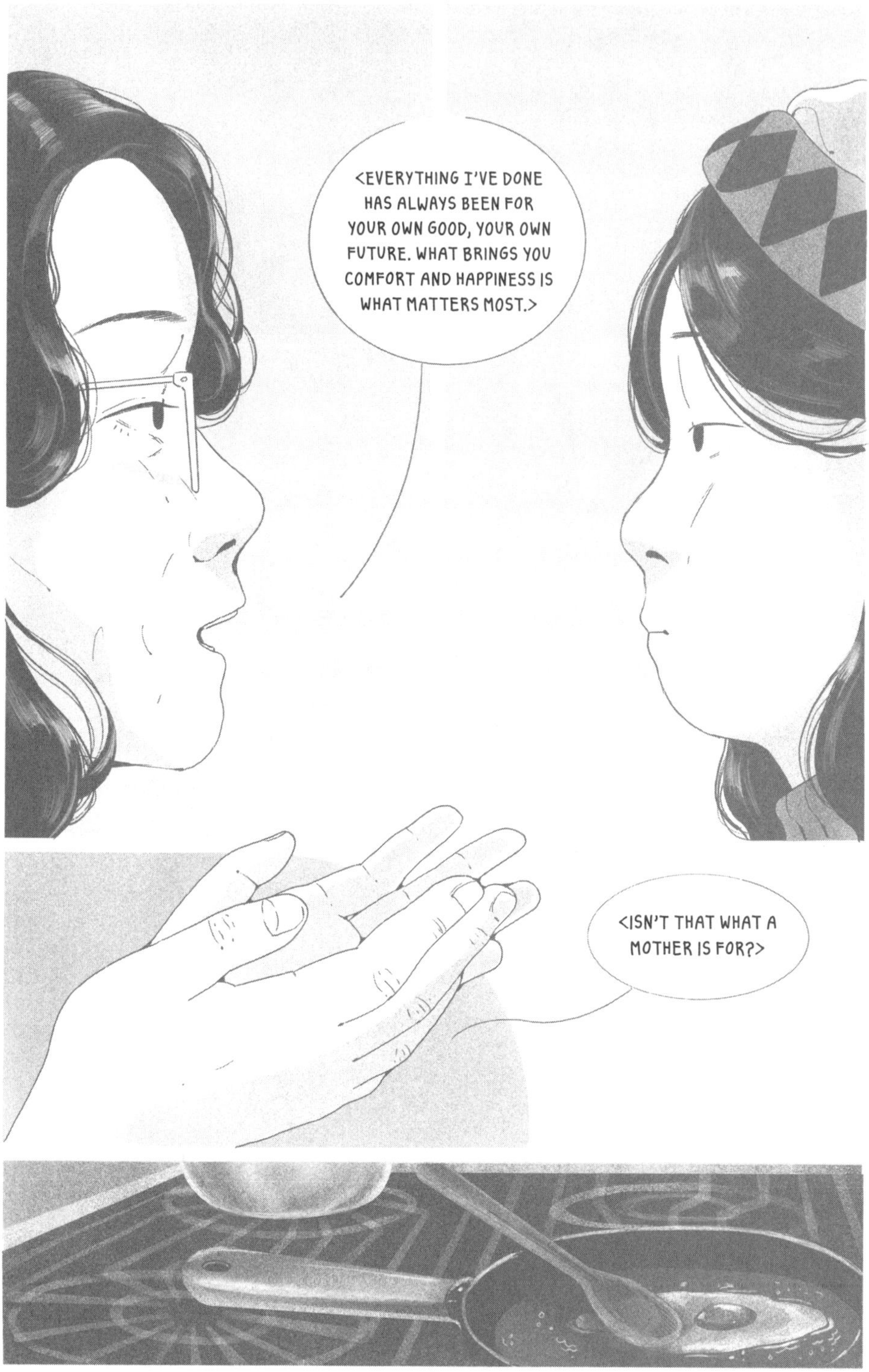
<EVERYTHING I'VE DONE HAS ALWAYS BEEN FOR YOUR OWN GOOD, YOUR OWN FUTURE. WHAT BRINGS YOU COMFORT AND HAPPINESS IS WHAT MATTERS MOST.>
<ISN'T THAT WHAT A MOTHER IS FOR?>

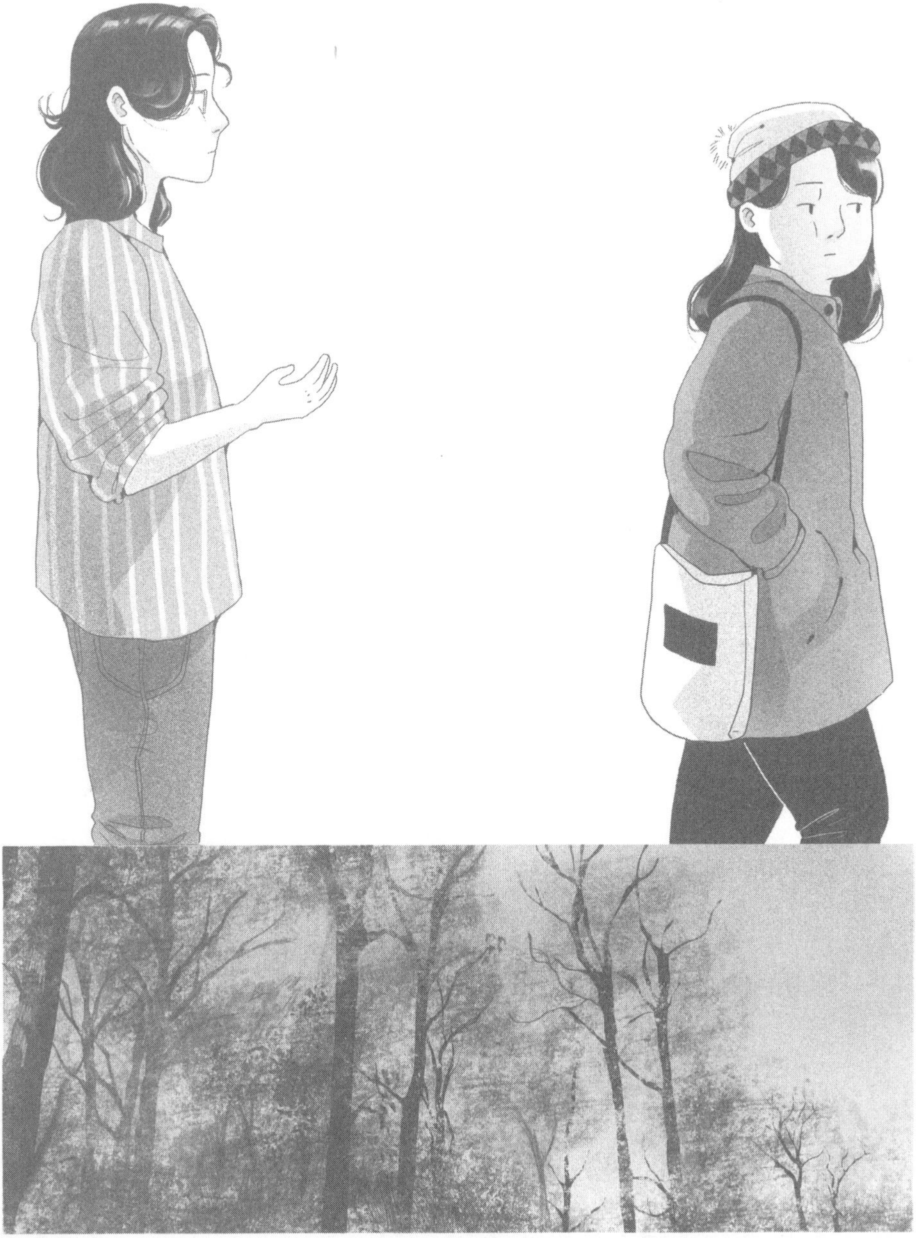

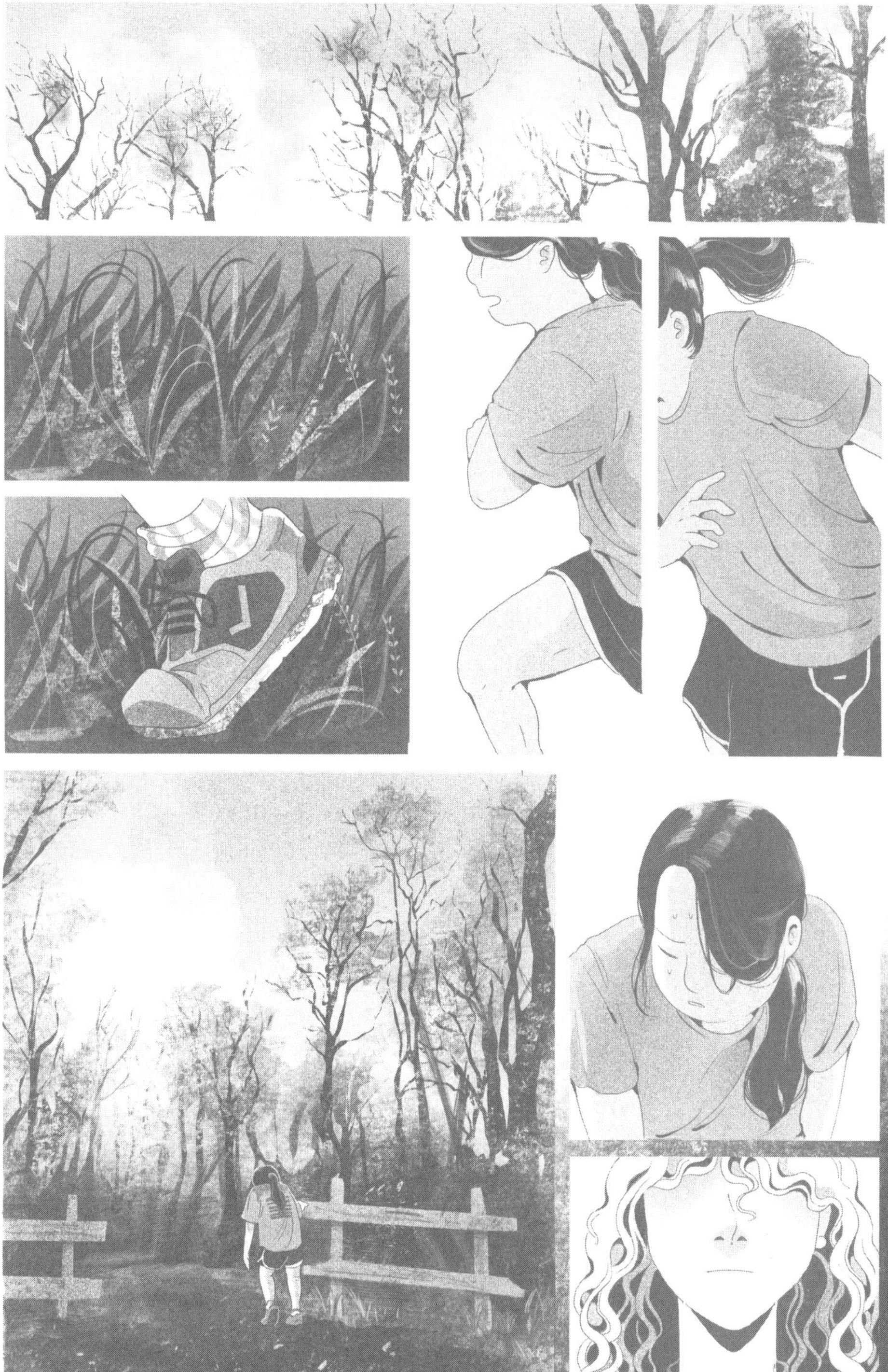

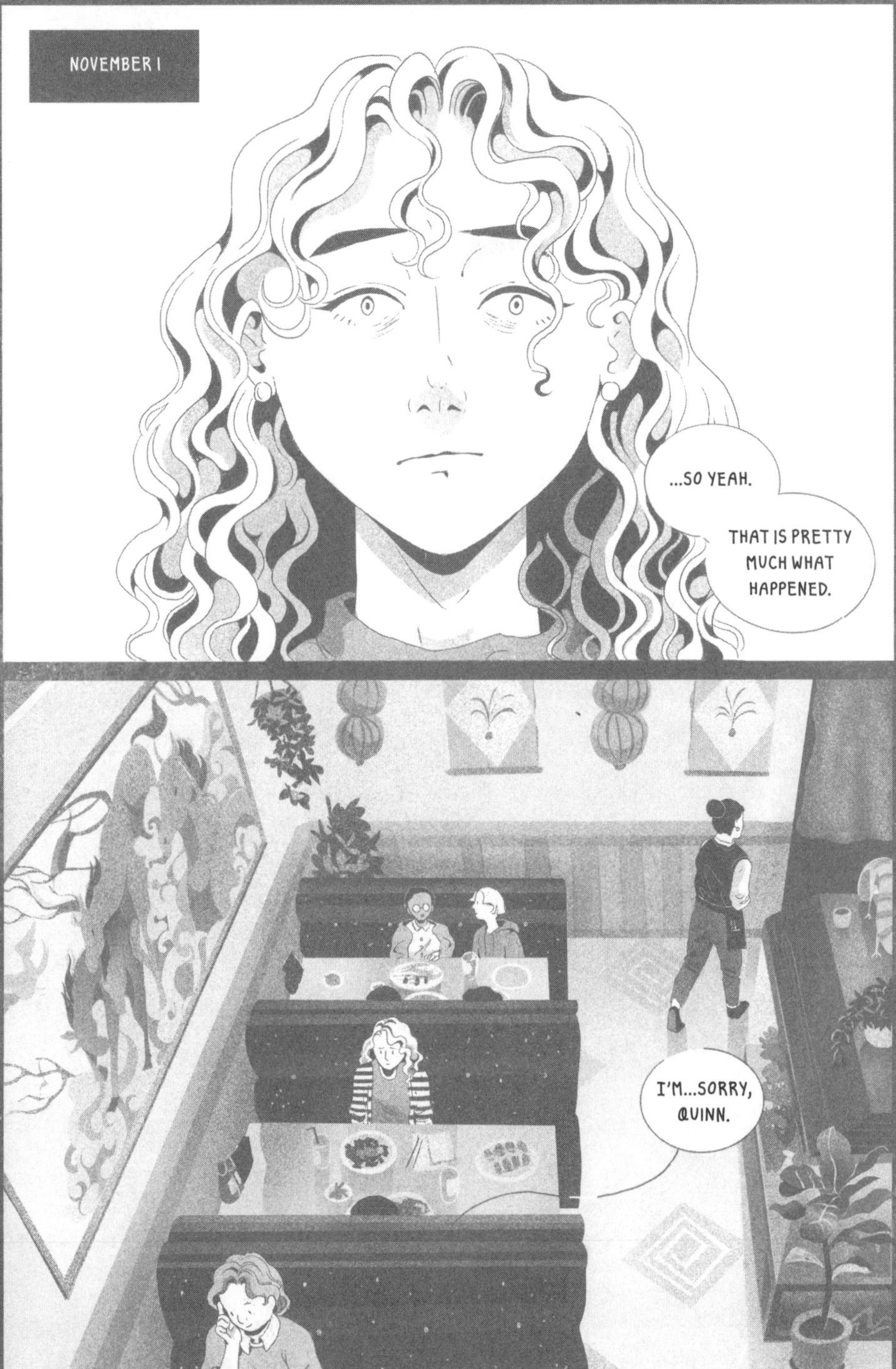
NOVEMBER 1
...SO YEAH.
THAT IS PRETTY MUCH WHAT HAPPENED.
I'M...SORRY, QUINN.

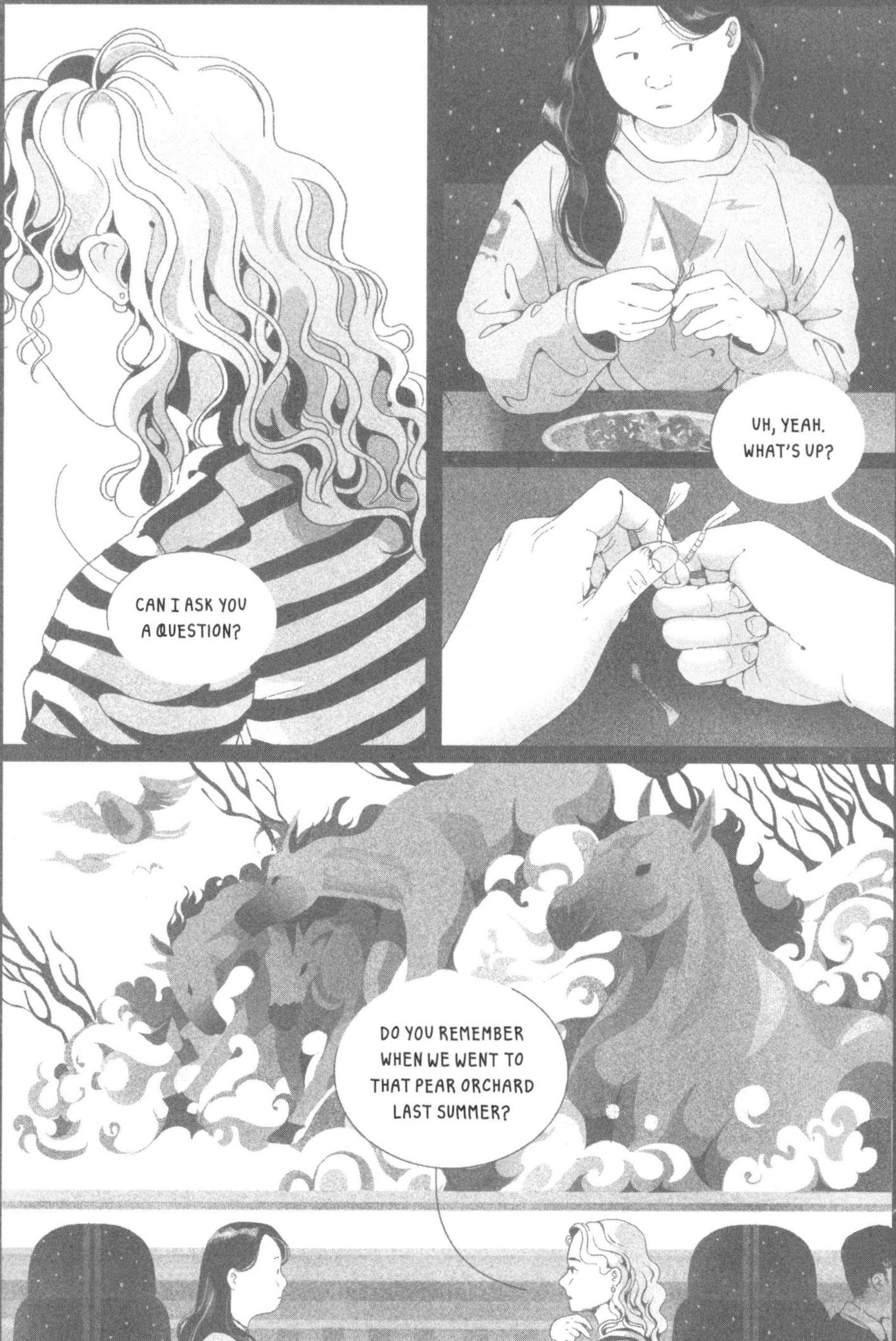
CAN I ASK YOU A QUESTION?
UH, YEAH. WHAT'S UP?
DO YOU REMEMBER WHEN WE WENT TO THAT PEAR ORCHARD LAST SUMMER?

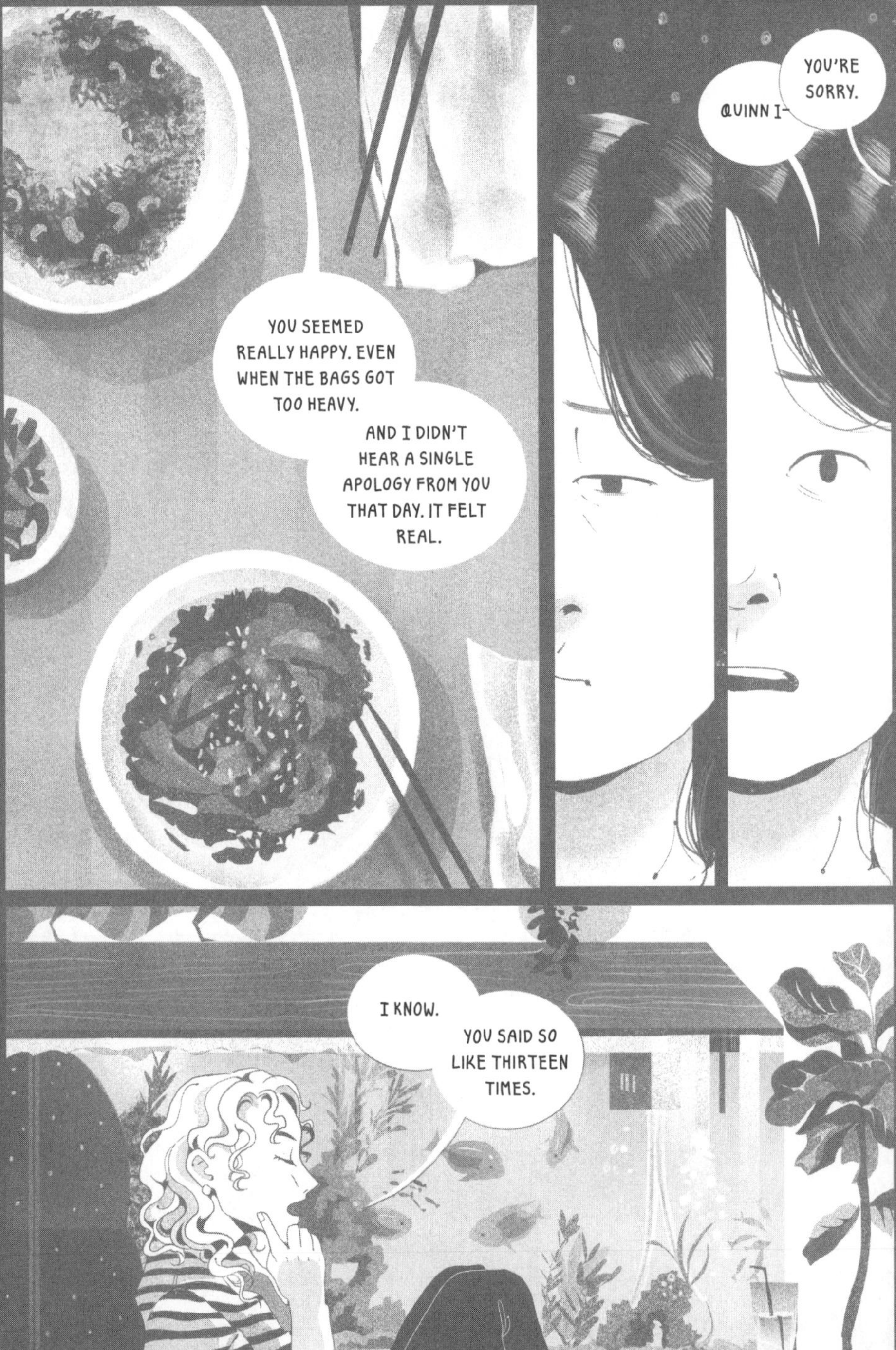
YOU SEEMED REALLY HAPPY. EVEN WHEN THE BAGS GOT TOO HEAVY.
AND I DIDN'T HEAR A SINGLE APOLOGY FROM YOU THAT DAY. IT FELT REAL.
QUINN I–
YOU'RE SORRY.
I KNOW.
YOU SAID SO LIKE THIRTEEN TIMES.

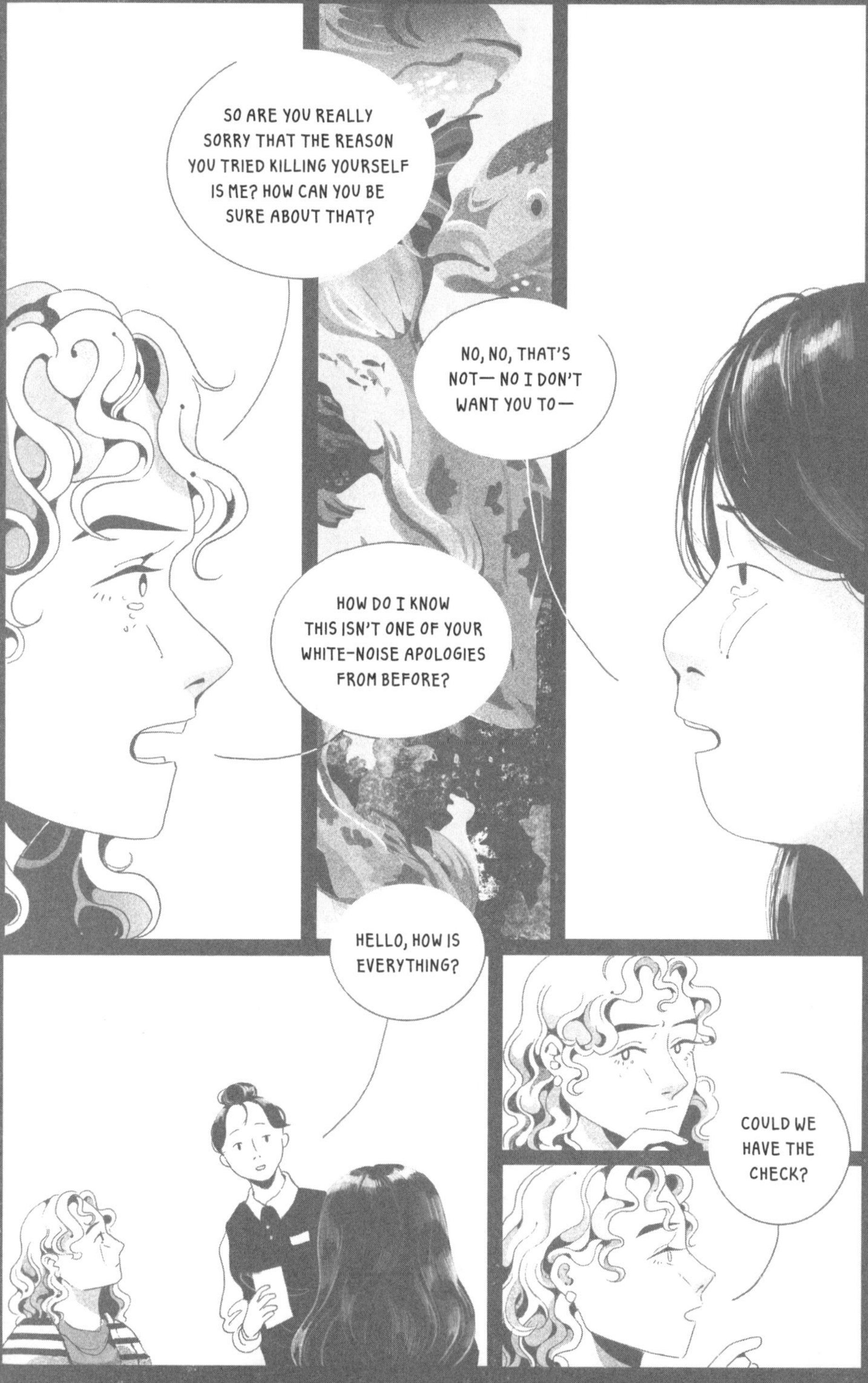
SO ARE YOU REALLY SORRY THAT THE REASON YOU TRIED KILLING YOURSELF IS ME? HOW CAN YOU BE SURE ABOUT THAT?
NO, NO, THAT'S NOT— NO I DON'T WANT YOU TO—
HOW DO I KNOW THIS ISN'T ONE OF YOUR WHITE-NOISE APOLOGIES FROM BEFORE?
HELLO, HOW IS EVERYTHING?
COULD WE HAVE THE CHECK?

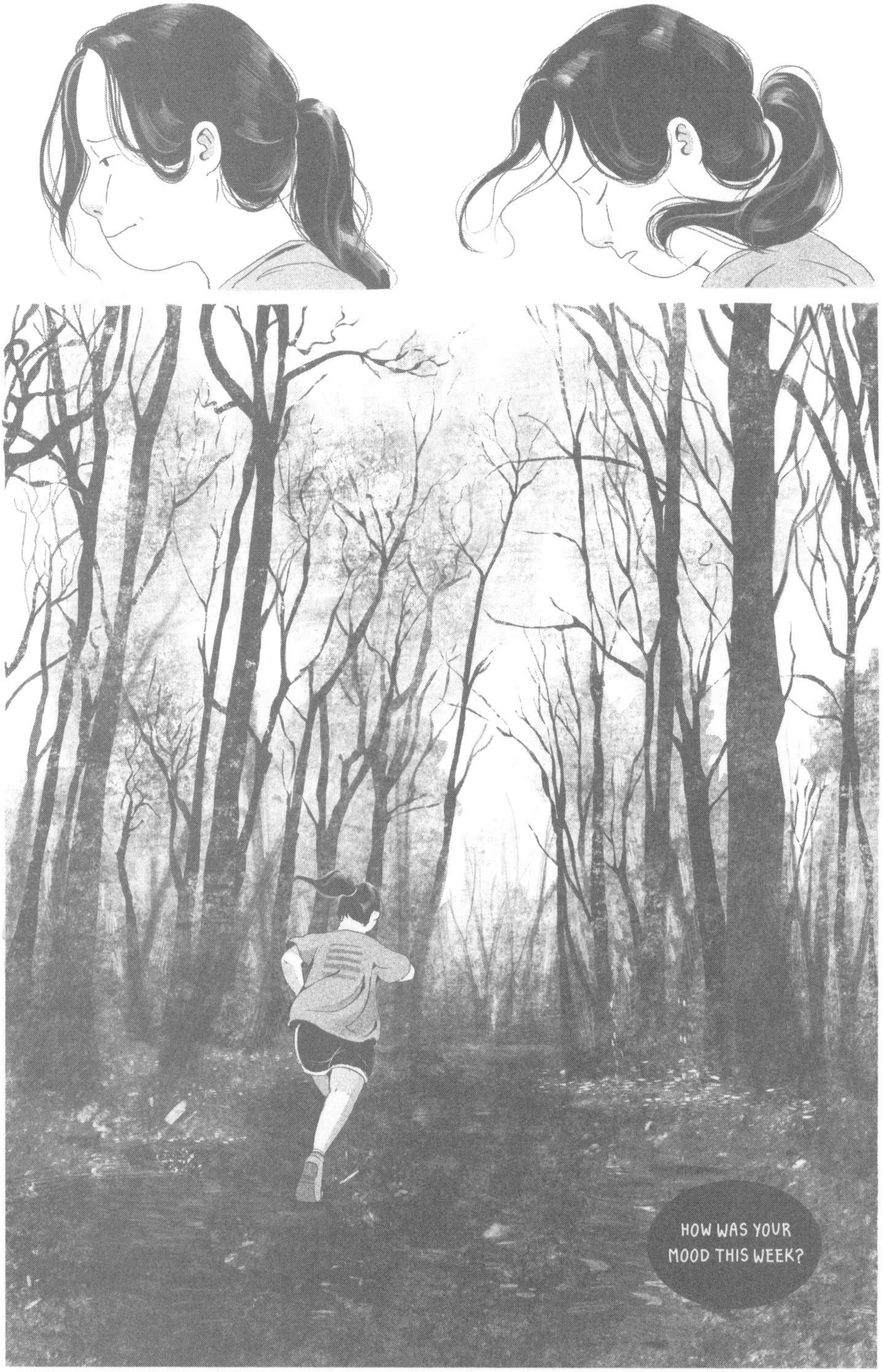
HOW WAS YOUR
MOOD THIS WEEK?

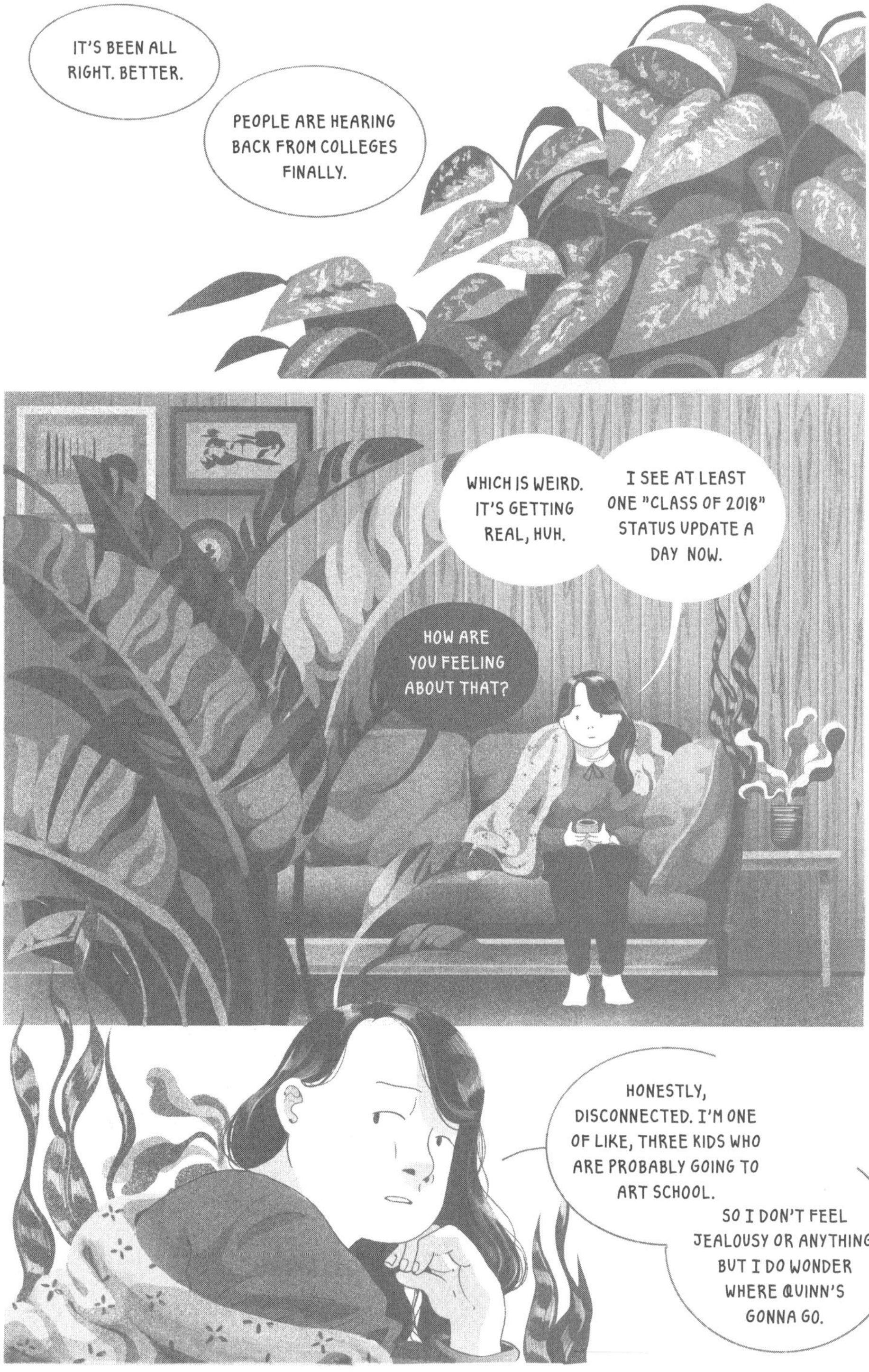
IT'S BEEN ALL RIGHT. BETTER.
PEOPLE ARE HEARING BACK FROM COLLEGES FINALLY.
WHICH IS WEIRD. IT'S GETTING REAL, HUH.
I SEE AT LEAST ONE "CLASS OF 2018" STATUS UPDATE A DAY NOW.
HOW ARE YOU FEELING ABOUT THAT?
HONESTLY, DISCONNECTED. I'M ONE OF LIKE, THREE KIDS WHO ARE PROBABLY GOING TO ART SCHOOL.
SO I DON'T FEEL JEALOUSY OR ANYTHING. BUT I DO WONDER WHERE QUINN'S GONNA GO.

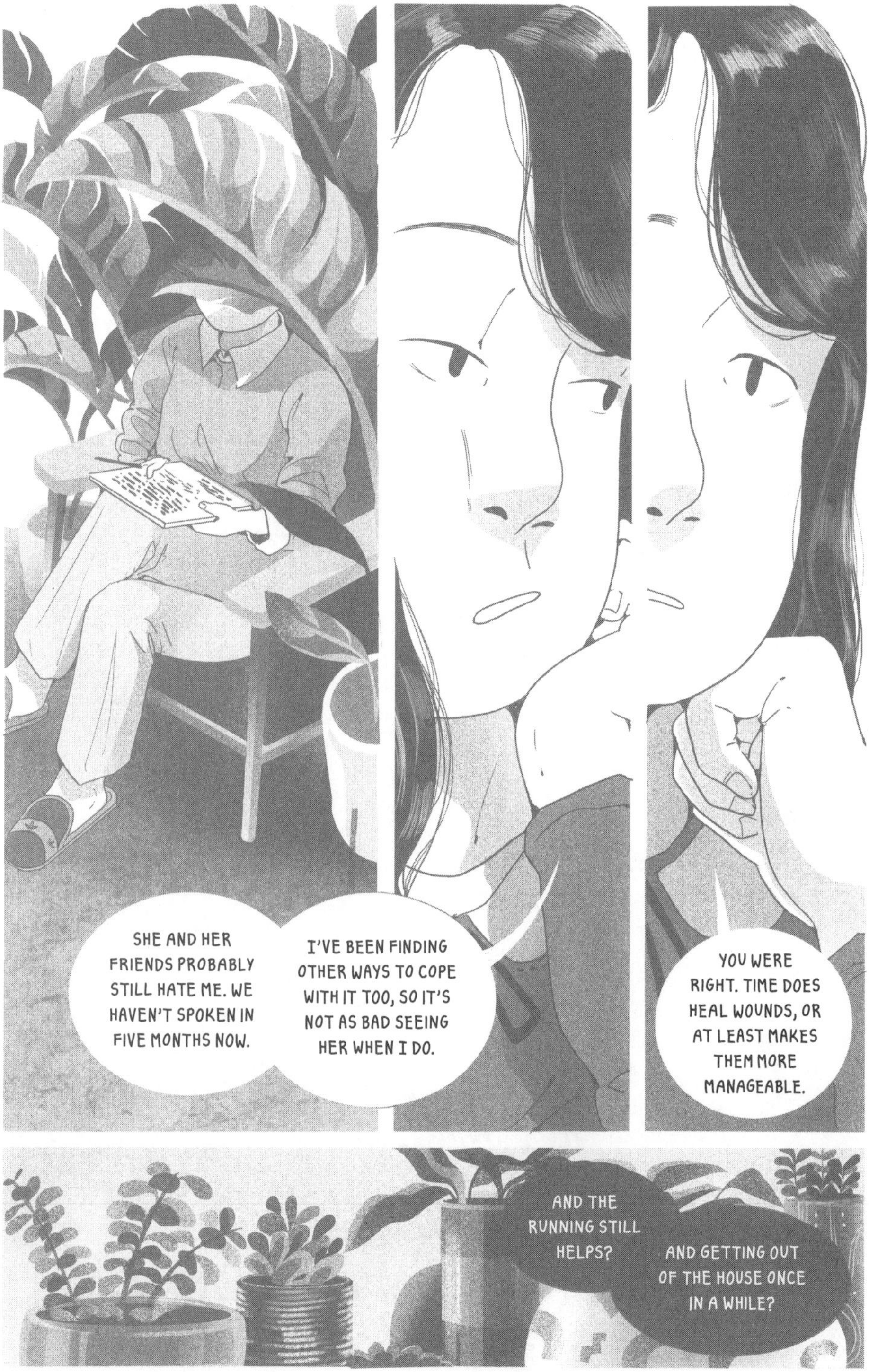
SHE AND HER FRIENDS PROBABLY STILL HATE ME. WE HAVEN'T SPOKEN IN FIVE MONTHS NOW.
I'VE BEEN FINDING OTHER WAYS TO COPE WITH IT TOO, SO IT'S NOT AS BAD SEEING HER WHEN I DO.
YOU WERE RIGHT. TIME DOES HEAL WOUNDS, OR AT LEAST MAKES THEM MORE MANAGEABLE.
AND THE RUNNING STILL HELPS?
AND GETTING OUT OF THE HOUSE ONCE IN A WHILE?

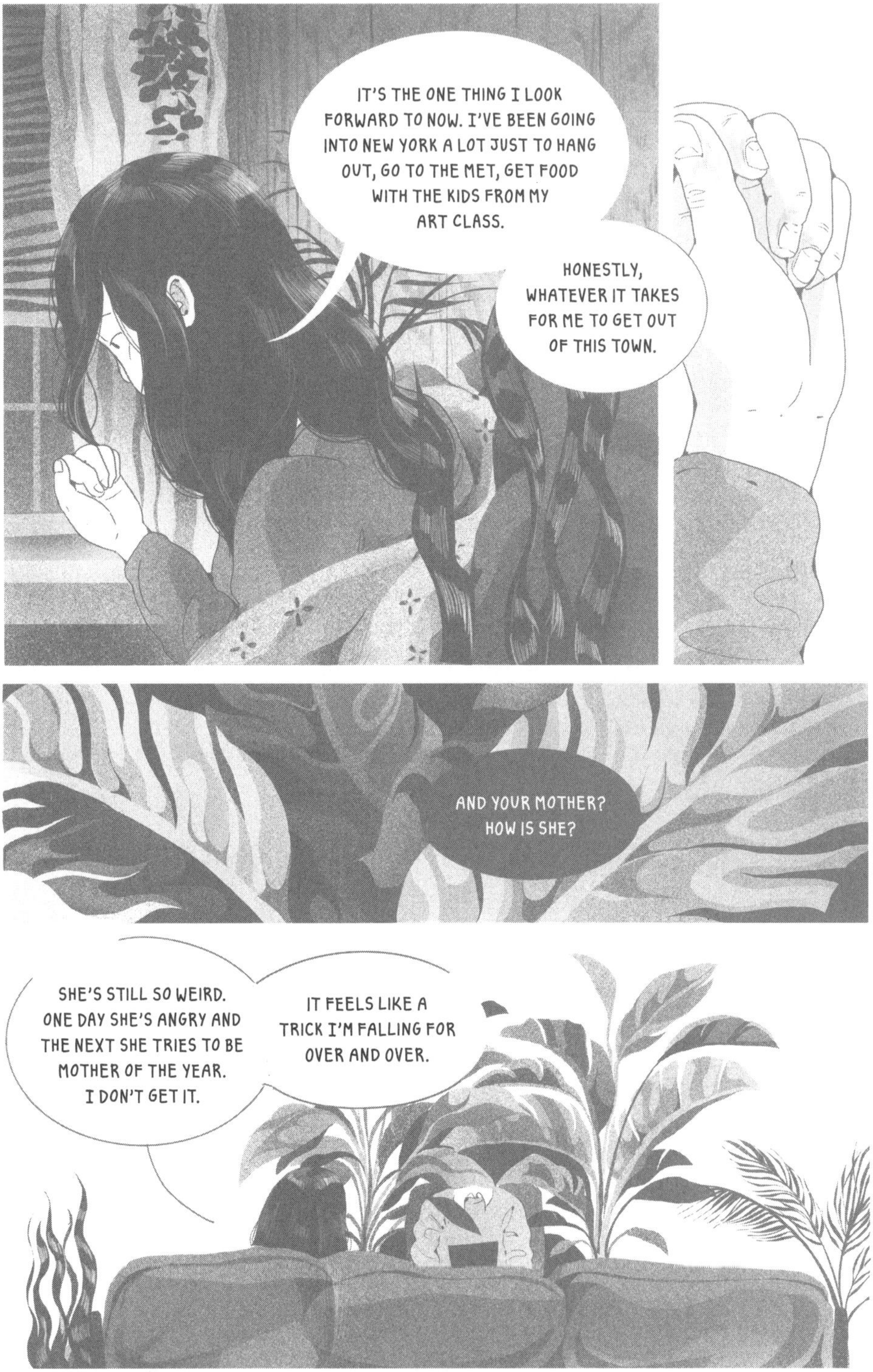
IT'S THE ONE THING I LOOK FORWARD TO NOW. I'VE BEEN GOING INTO NEW YORK A LOT JUST TO HANG OUT, GO TO THE MET, GET FOOD WITH THE KIDS FROM MY ART CLASS.
HONESTLY, WHATEVER IT TAKES FOR ME TO GET OUT OF THIS TOWN.
AND YOUR MOTHER? HOW IS SHE?
SHE'S STILL SO WEIRD. ONE DAY SHE'S ANGRY AND THE NEXT SHE TRIES TO BE MOTHER OF THE YEAR. I DON'T GET IT.
IT FEELS LIKE A TRICK I'M FALLING FOR OVER AND OVER.

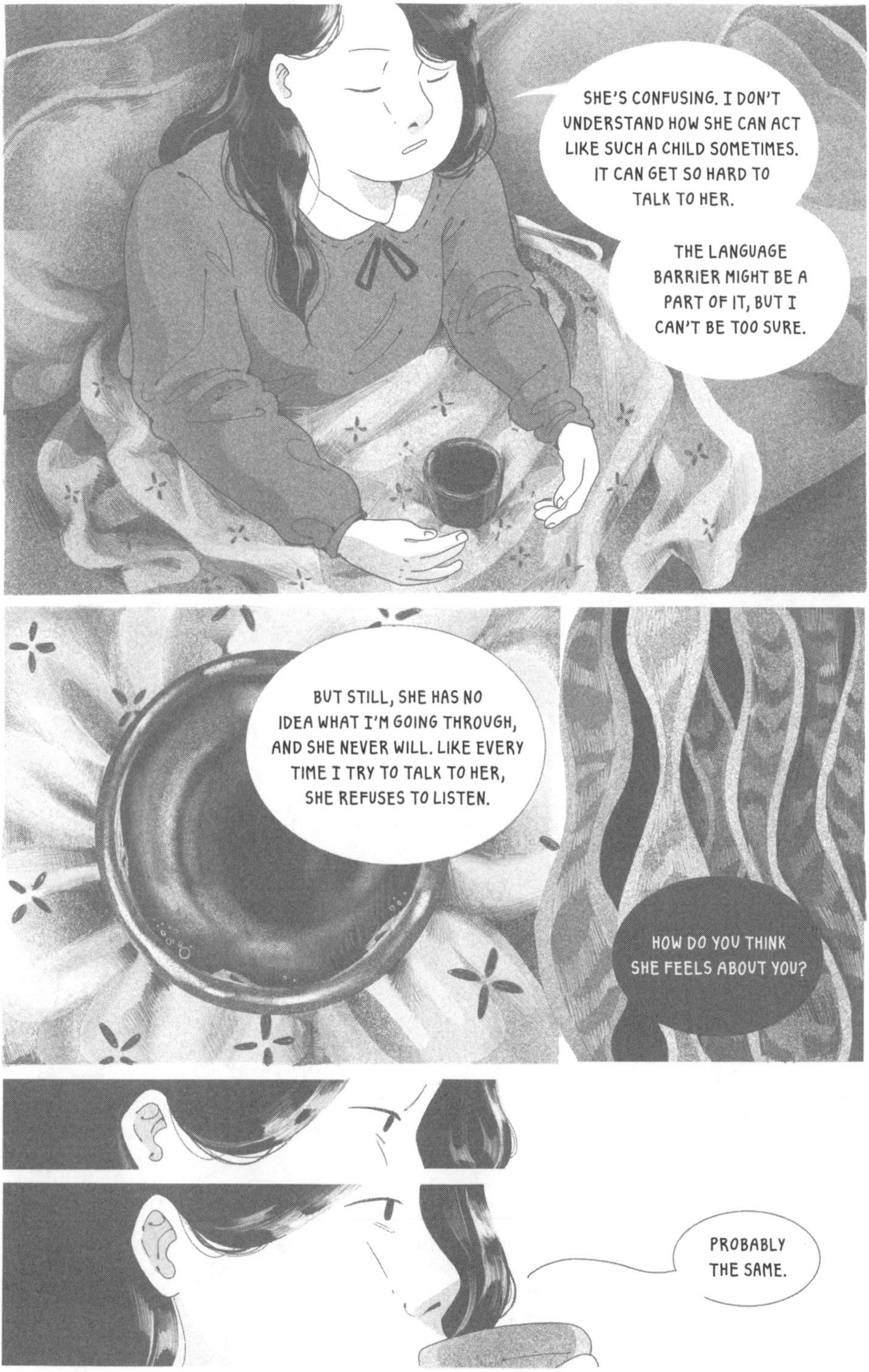
SHE'S CONFUSING. I DON'T UNDERSTAND HOW SHE CAN ACT LIKE SUCH A CHILD SOMETIMES. IT CAN GET SO HARD TO TALK TO HER.
THE LANGUAGE BARRIER MIGHT BE A PART OF IT, BUT I CAN'T BE TOO SURE.
BUT STILL, SHE HAS NO IDEA WHAT I'M GOING THROUGH, AND SHE NEVER WILL. LIKE EVERY TIME I TRY TO TALK TO HER, SHE REFUSES TO LISTEN.
HOW DO YOU THINK SHE FEELS ABOUT YOU?
PROBABLY THE SAME.

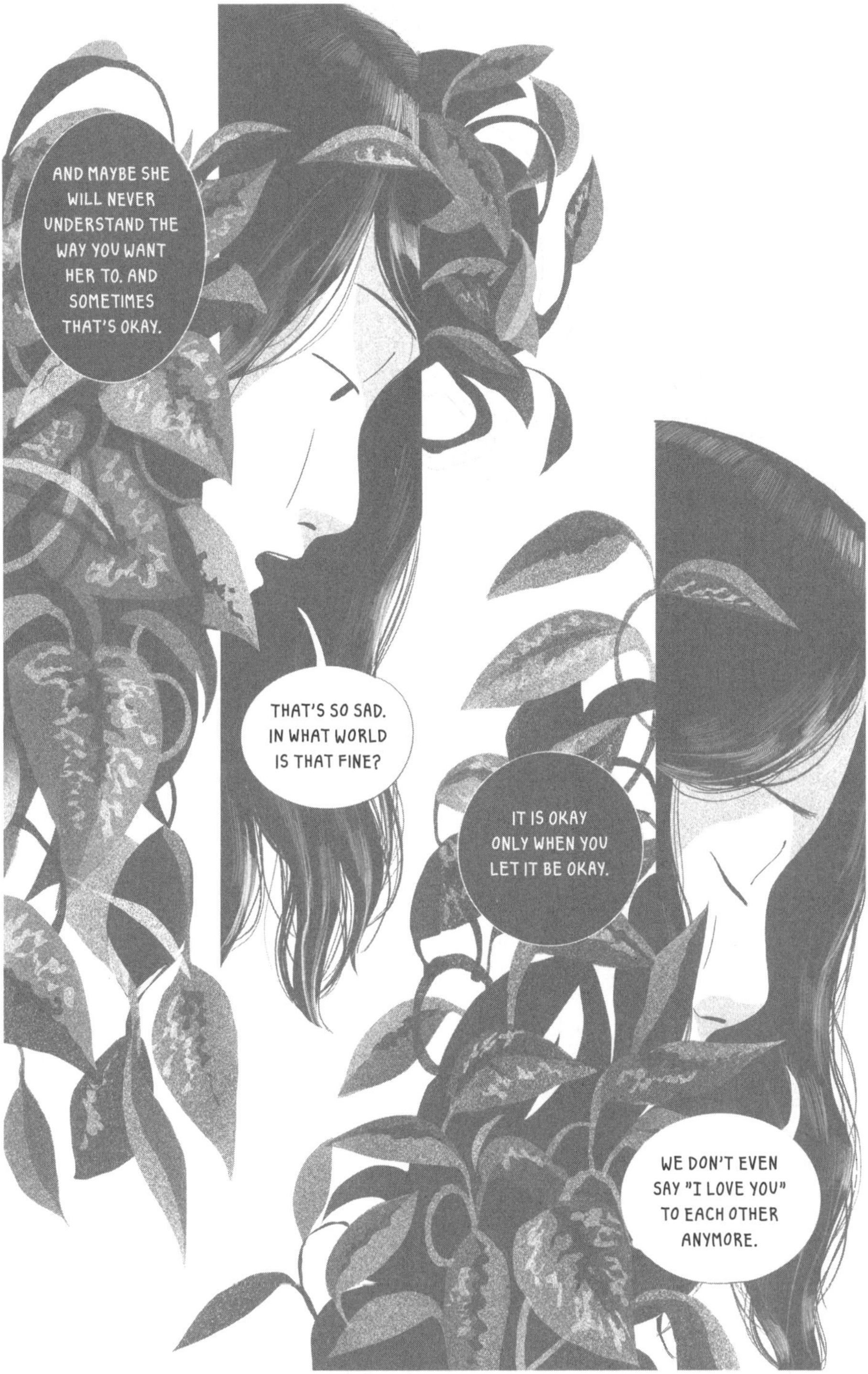
AND MAYBE SHE WILL NEVER UNDERSTAND THE WAY YOU WANT HER TO. AND SOMETIMES THAT'S OKAY.
THAT'S SO SAD. IN WHAT WORLD IS THAT FINE?
IT IS OKAY ONLY WHEN YOU LET IT BE OKAY.
WE DON'T EVEN SAY "I LOVE YOU" TO EACH OTHER ANYMORE.

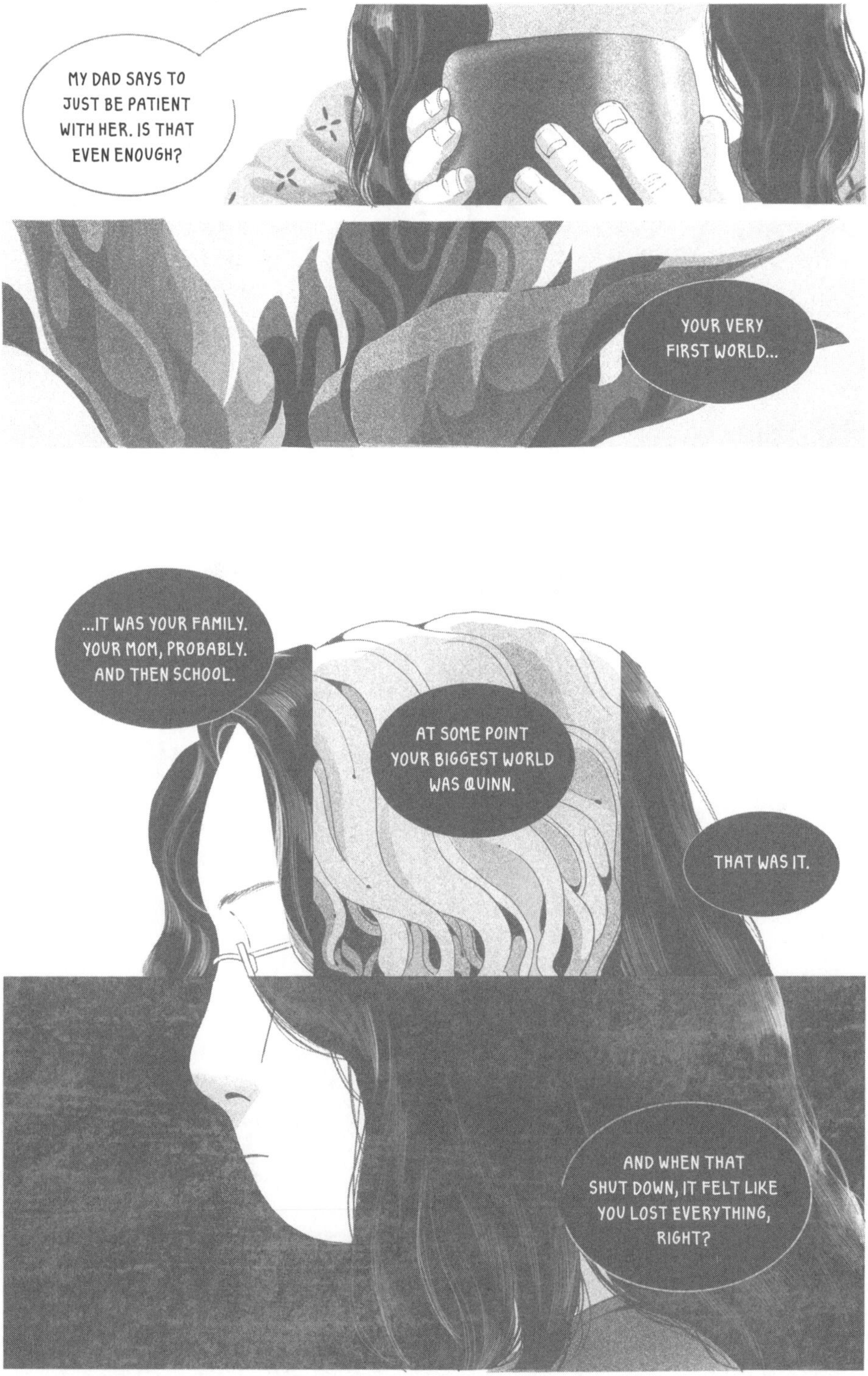
MY DAD SAYS TO JUST BE PATIENT WITH HER. IS THAT EVEN ENOUGH?
YOUR VERY FIRST WORLD...
...IT WAS YOUR FAMILY. YOUR MOM, PROBABLY. AND THEN SCHOOL.
AT SOME POINT YOUR BIGGEST WORLD WAS QUINN.
THAT WAS IT.
AND WHEN THAT SHUT DOWN, IT FELT LIKE YOU LOST EVERYTHING, RIGHT?

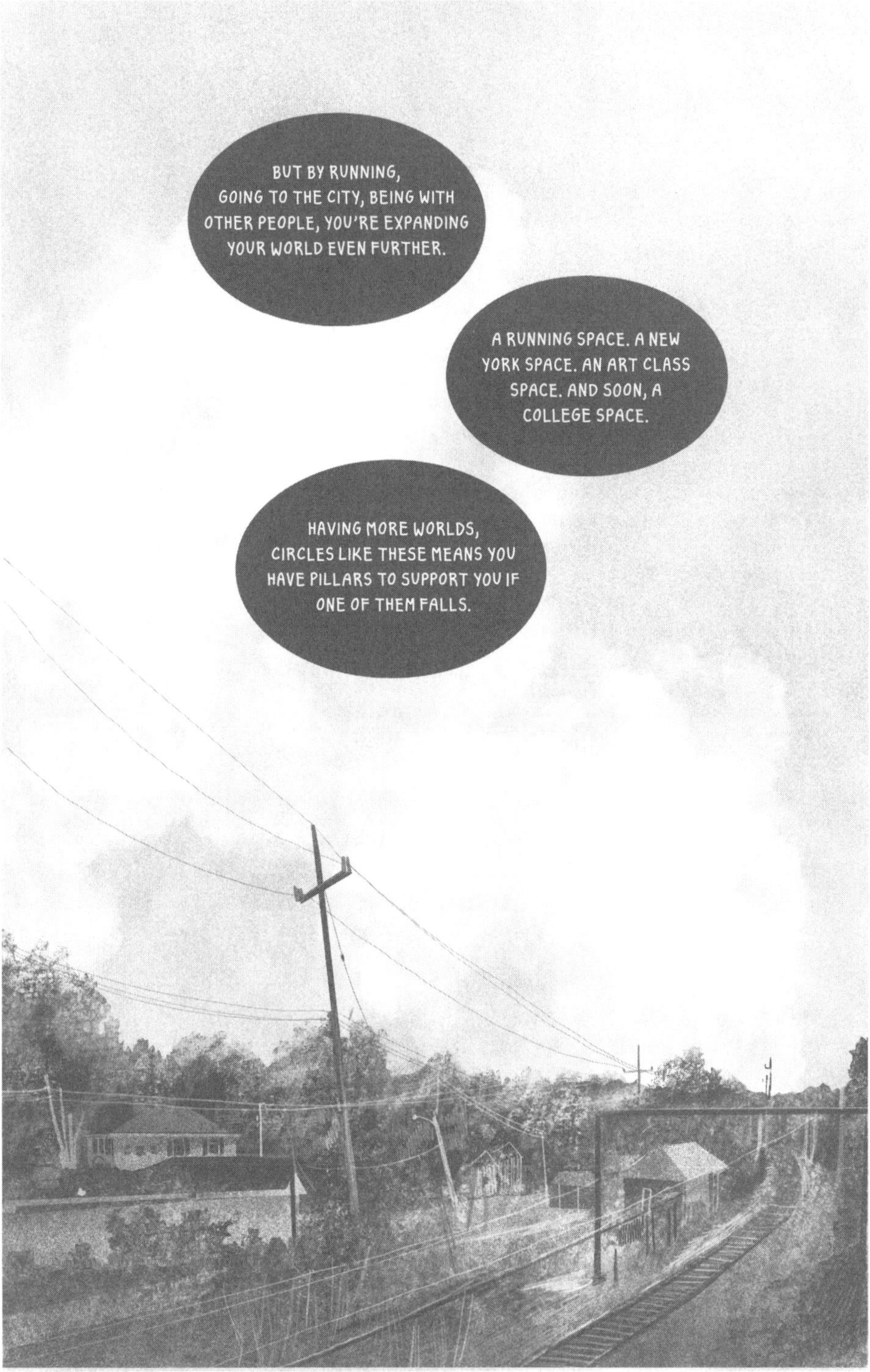
BUT BY RUNNING, GOING TO THE CITY, BEING WITH OTHER PEOPLE, YOU'RE EXPANDING YOUR WORLD EVEN FURTHER.
A RUNNING SPACE. A NEW YORK SPACE. AN ART CLASS SPACE. AND SOON, A COLLEGE SPACE.
HAVING MORE WORLDS, CIRCLES LIKE THESE MEANS YOU HAVE PILLARS TO SUPPORT YOU IF ONE OF THEM FALLS.

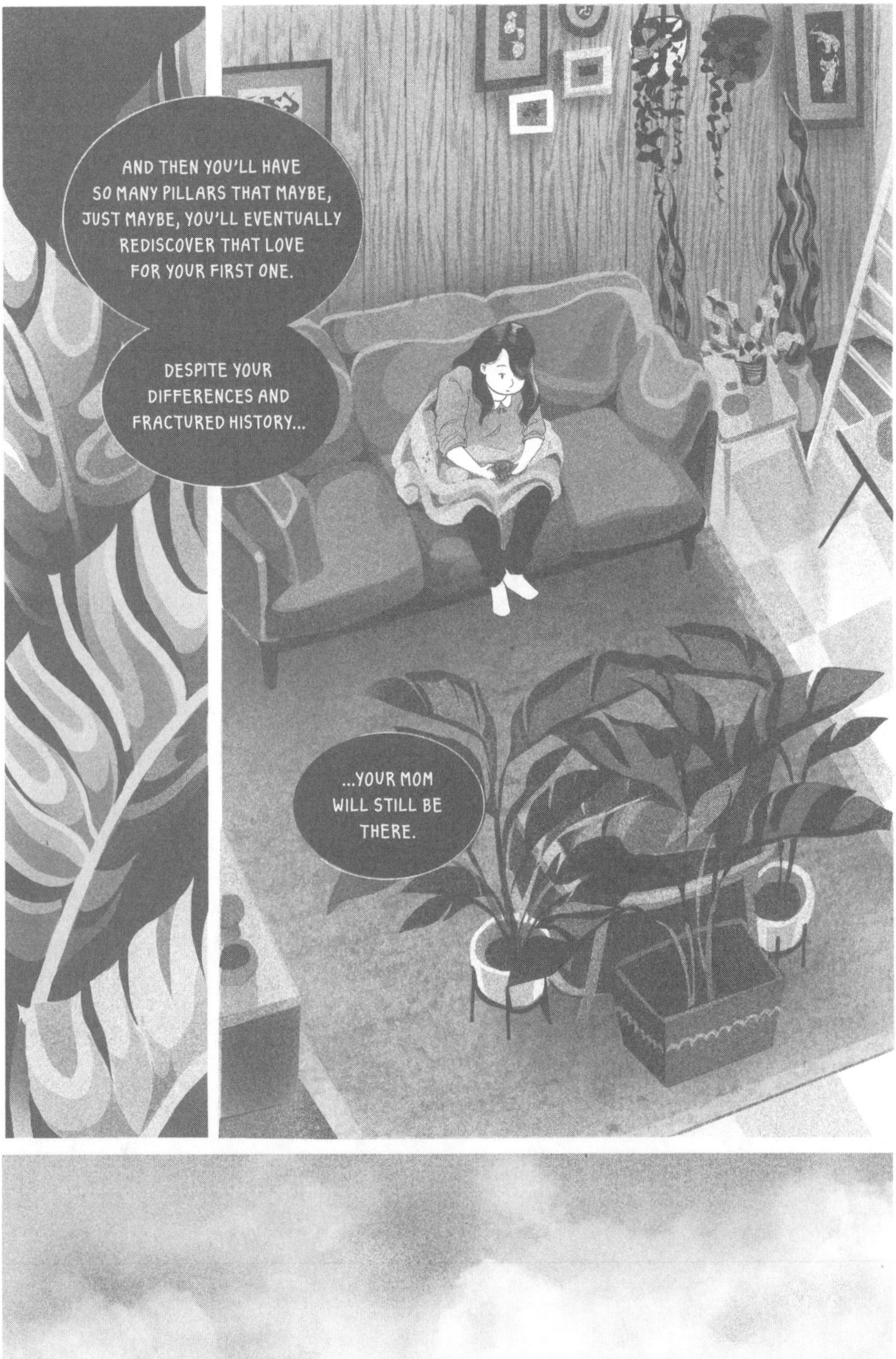
AND THEN YOU'LL HAVE SO MANY PILLARS THAT MAYBE, JUST MAYBE, YOU'LL EVENTUALLY REDISCOVER THAT LOVE FOR YOUR FIRST ONE.
DESPITE YOUR DIFFERENCES AND FRACTURED HISTORY...
...YOUR MOM WILL STILL BE THERE.

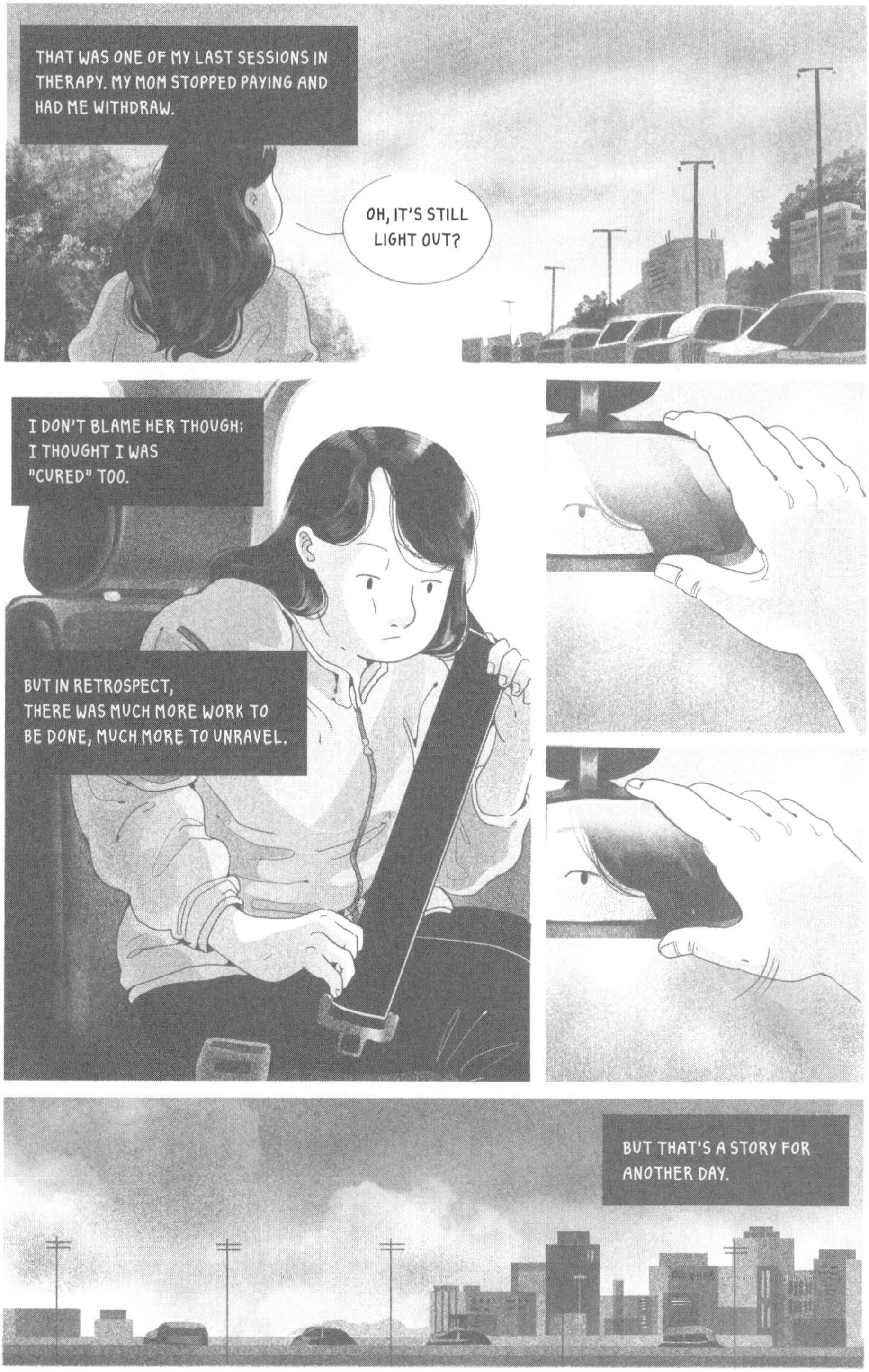
THAT WAS ONE OF MY LAST SESSIONS IN THERAPY. MY MOM STOPPED PAYING AND HAD ME WITHDRAW.
OH, IT'S STILL LIGHT OUT?
I DON'T BLAME HER THOUGH; I THOUGHT I WAS "CURED" TOO.
BUT IN RETROSPECT, THERE WAS MUCH MORE WORK TO BE DONE, MUCH MORE TO UNRAVEL.
BUT THAT'S A STORY FOR ANOTHER DAY.

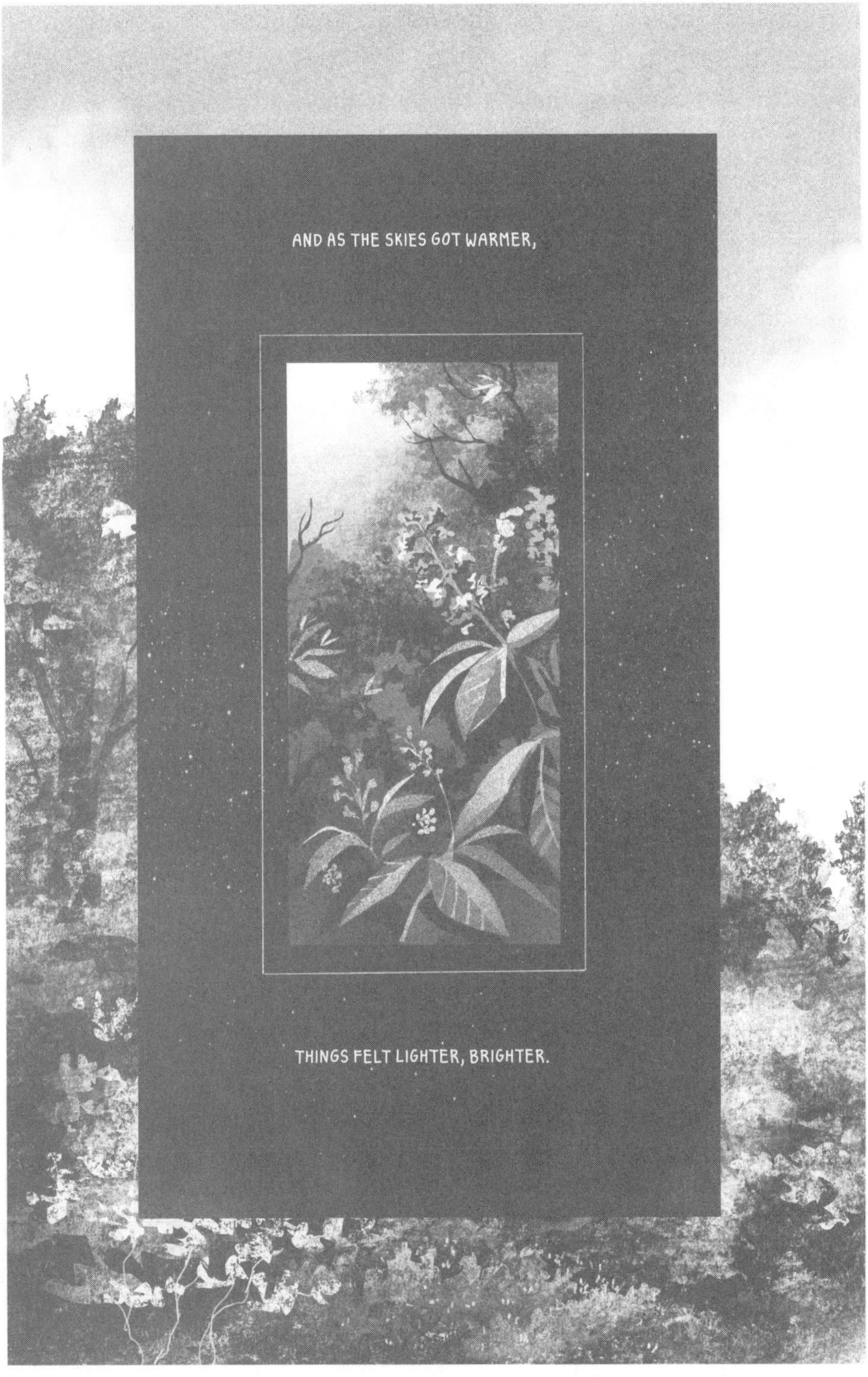
AND AS THE SKIES GOT WARMER,
THINGS FELT LIGHTER, BRIGHTER.

you for your application to New
University, but we cannot give you a
or the Class of 2018. Unfortunately
as a very difficult decision.

Accepted
Students
Day: 4/12/14

Congratul

CLAS
OF 20

Congratu

FUTURES BECOME CLEARER.

ng in
eposit

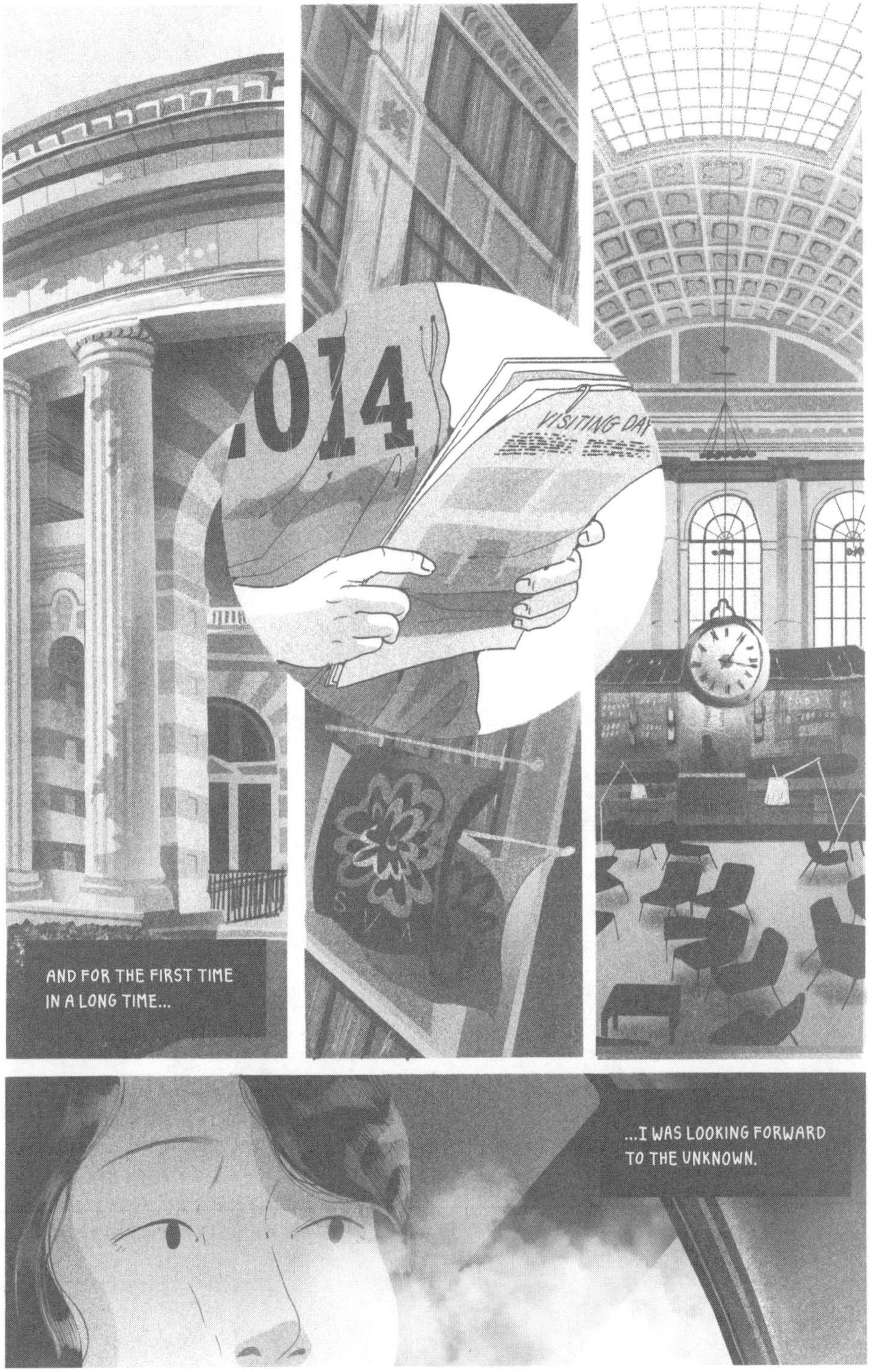
AND FOR THE FIRST TIME
IN A LONG TIME...
...I WAS LOOKING FORWARD
TO THE UNKNOWN.

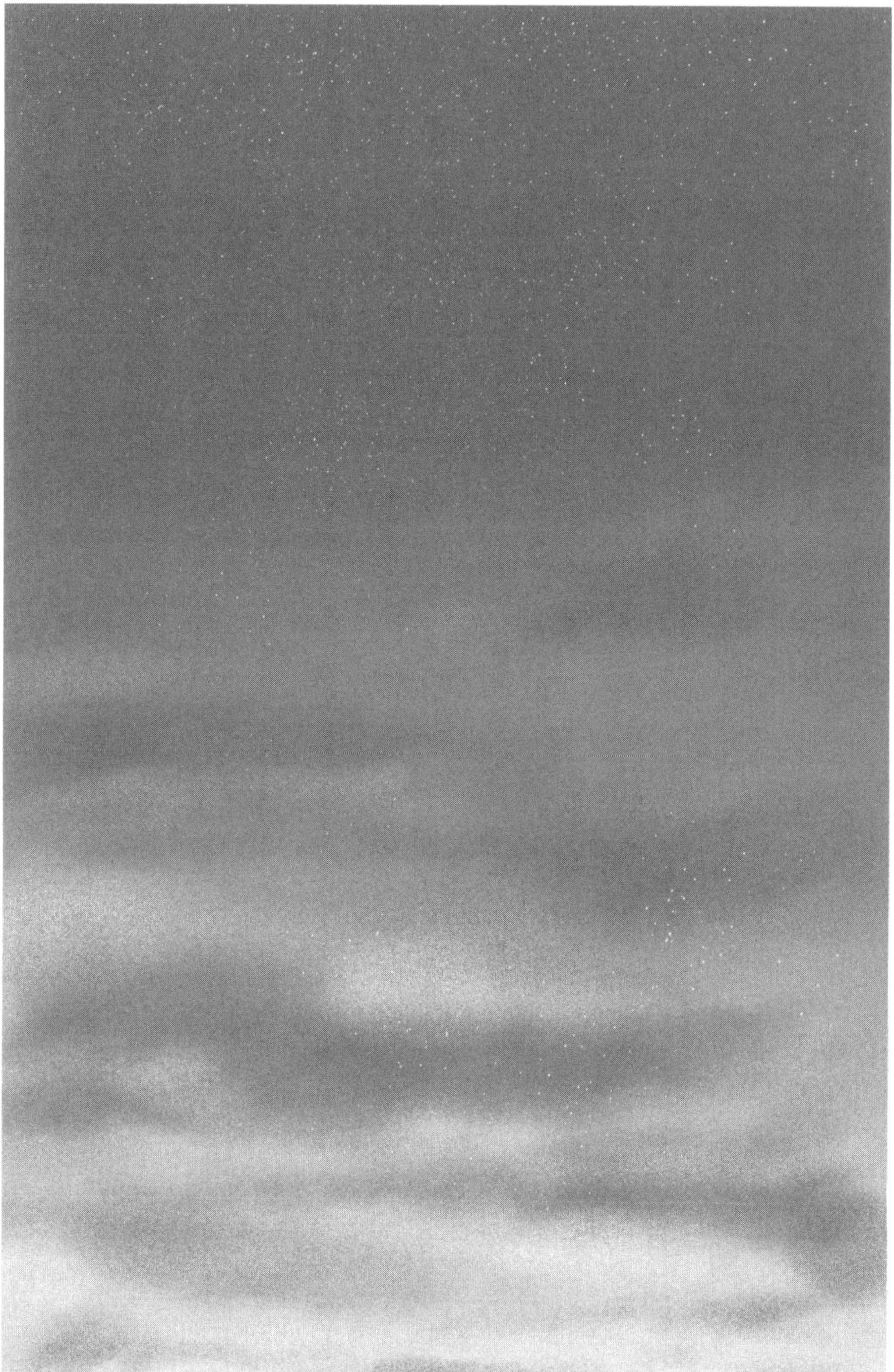

사
Part 4

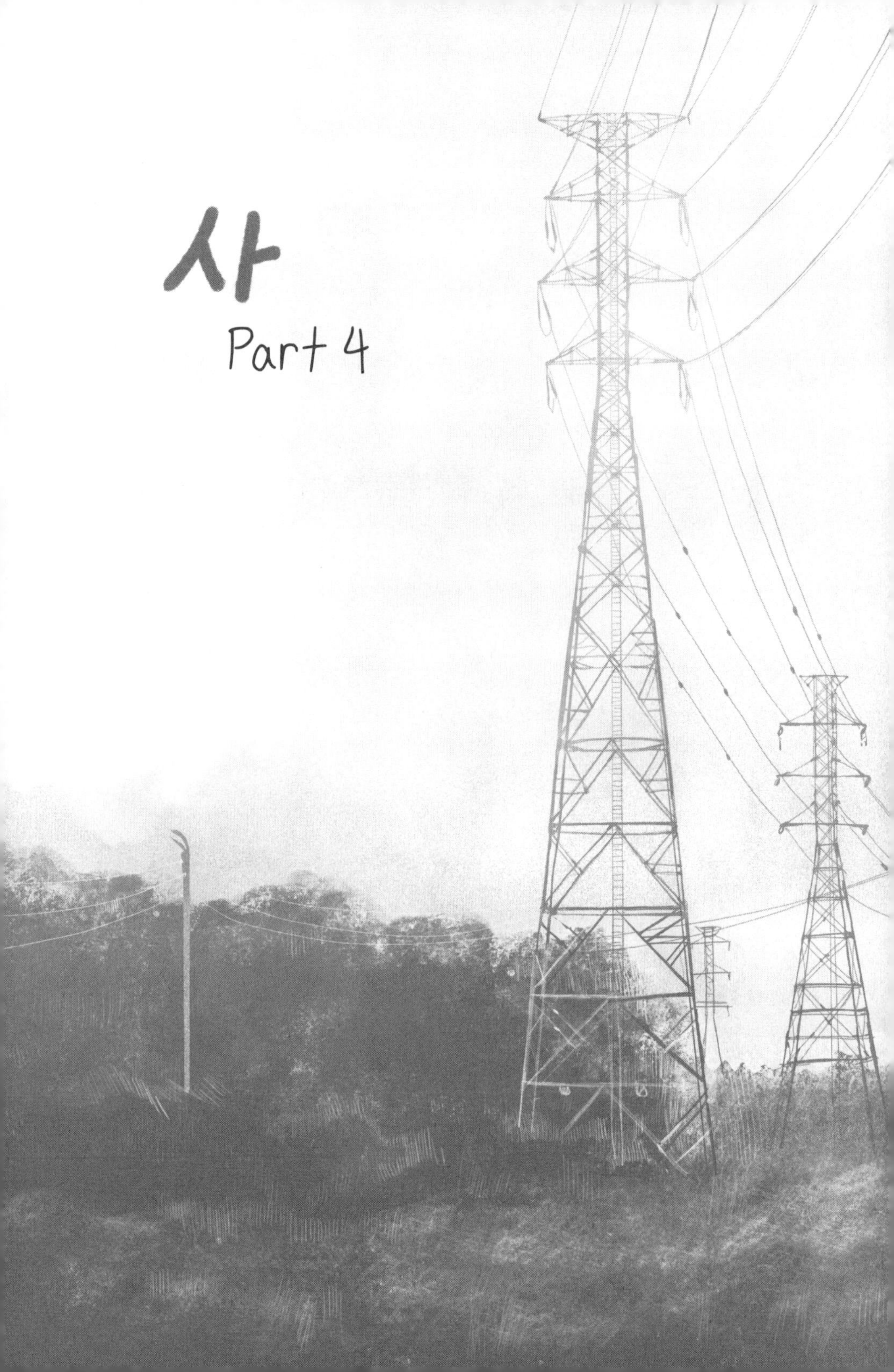

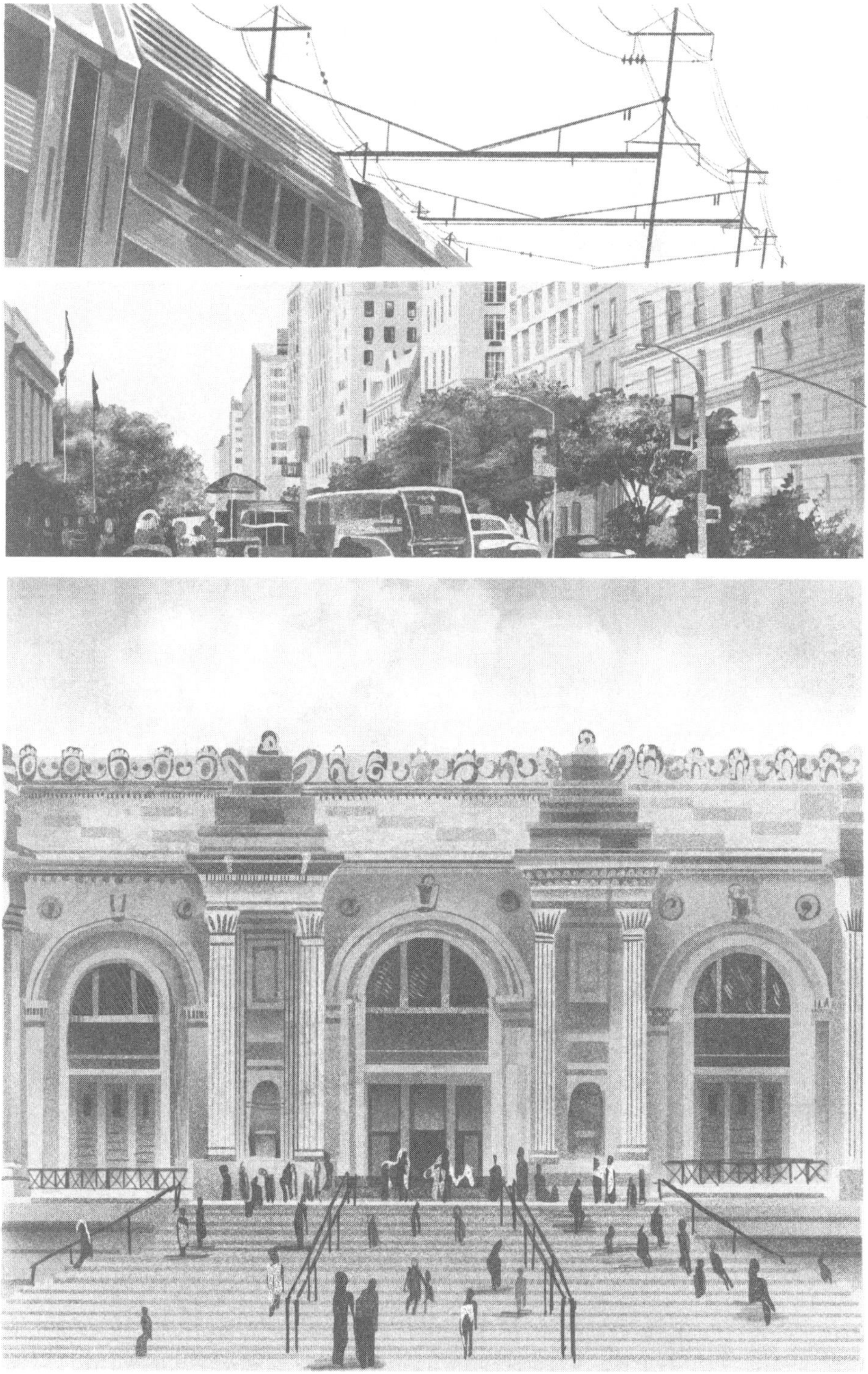

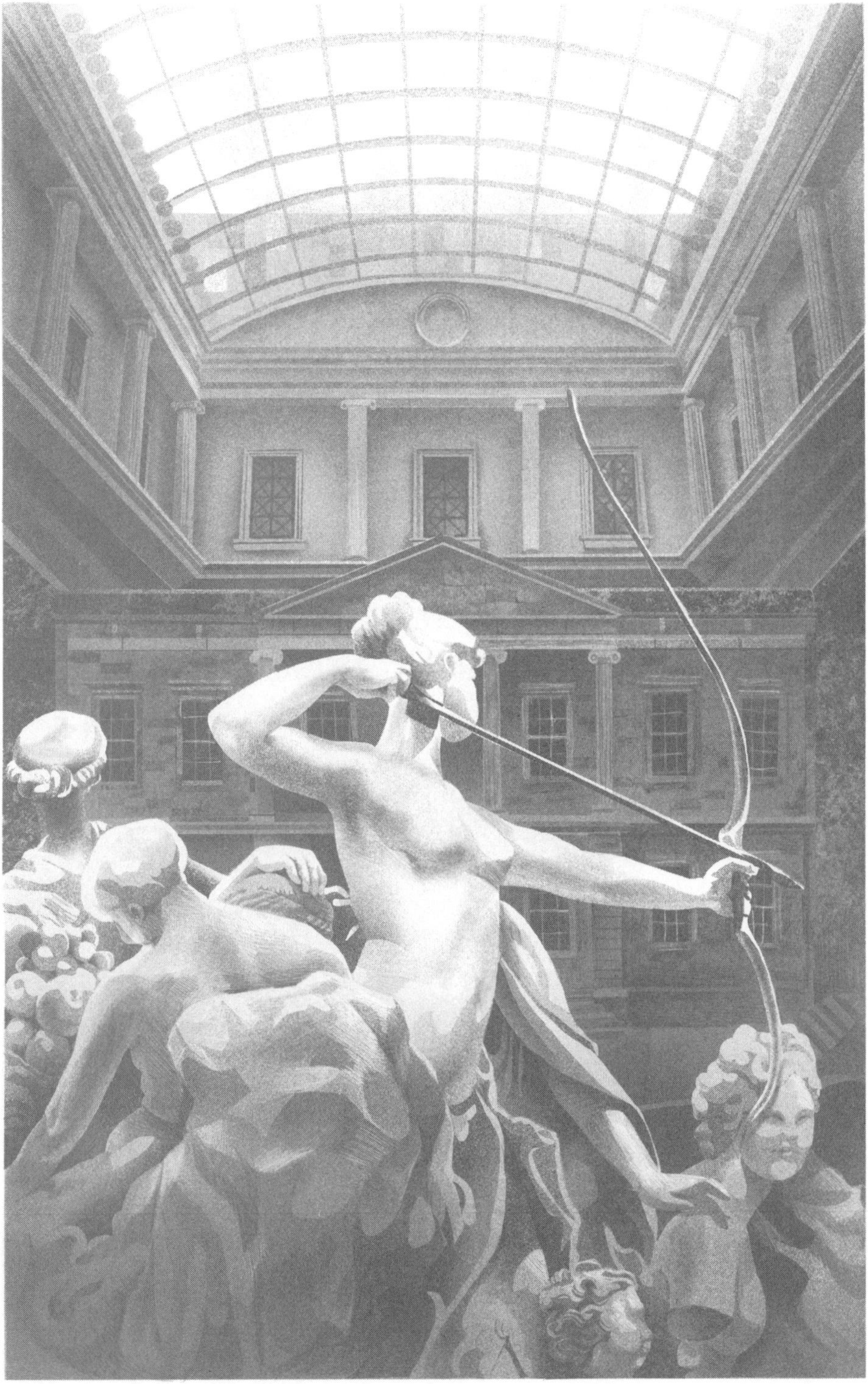

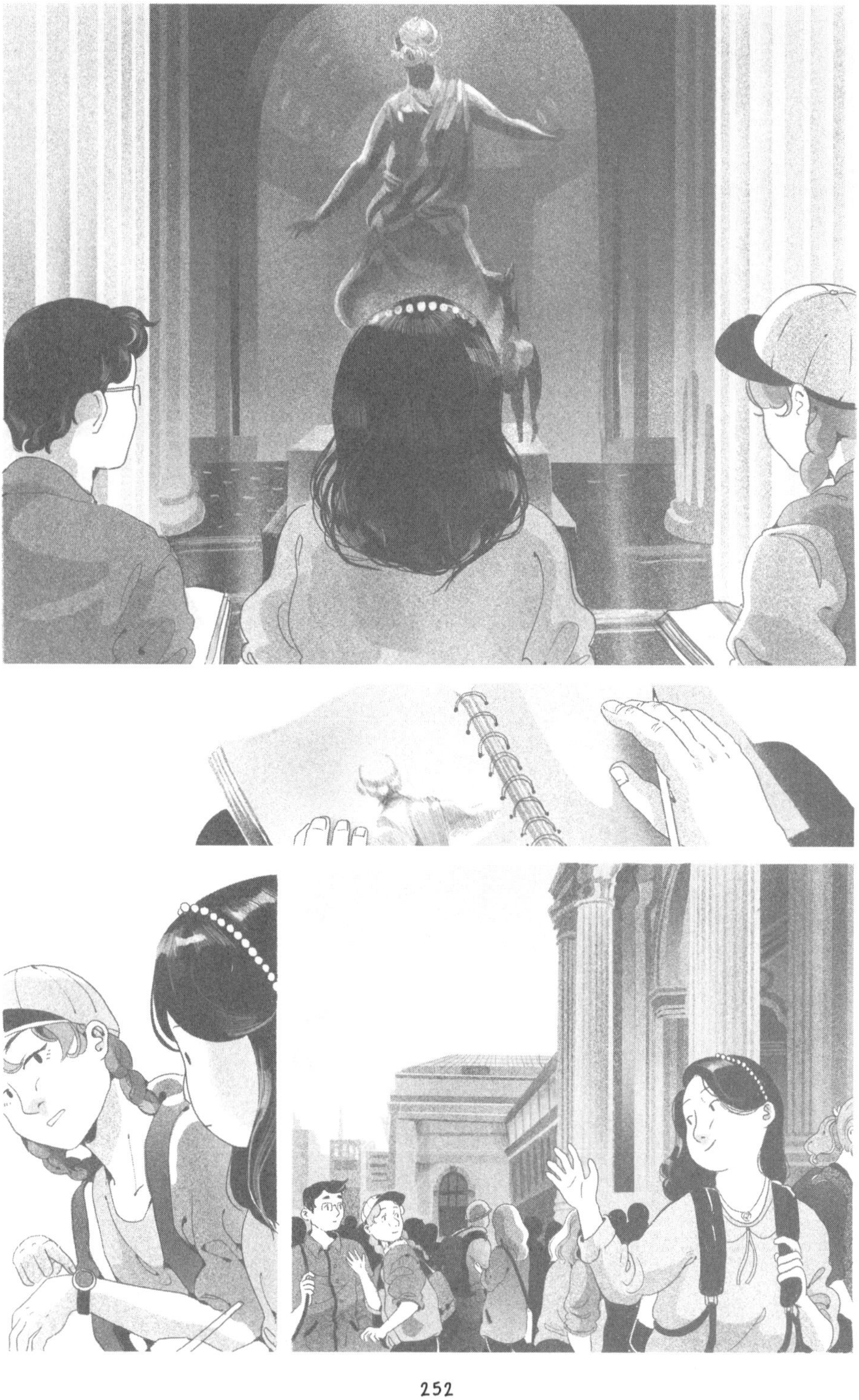

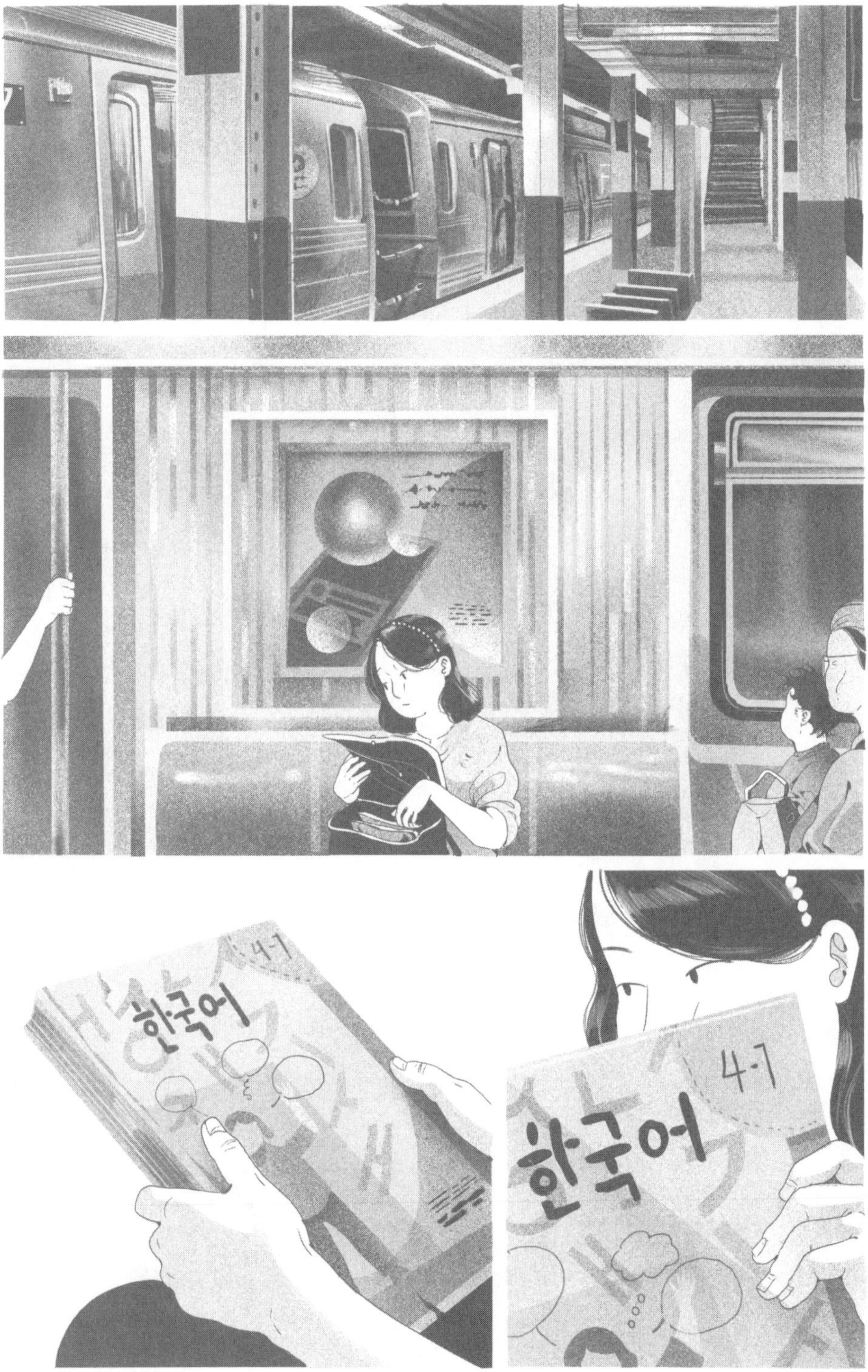
4-1
한국어
4-1
한국어

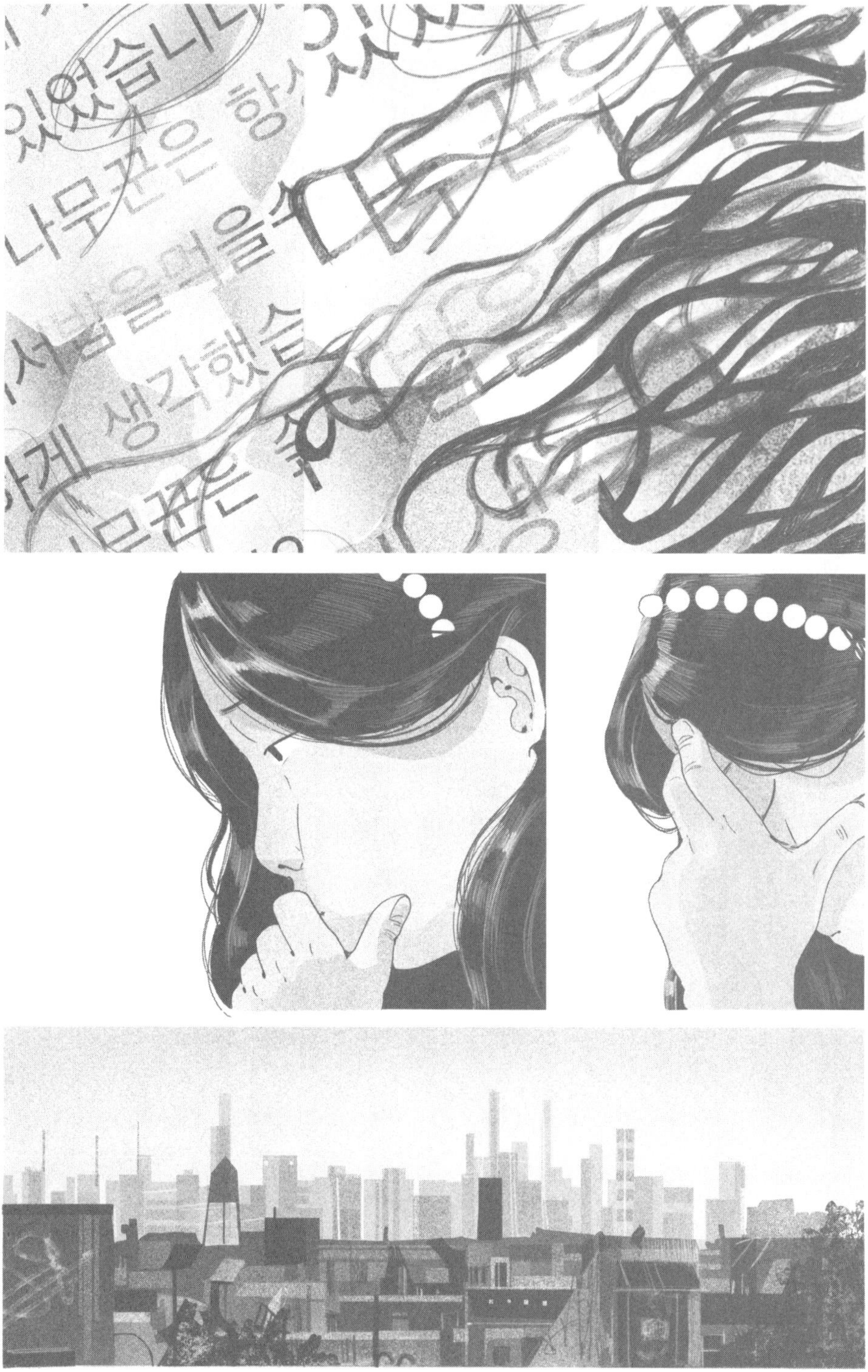
있었습니
나무꾼은 항
나무꾼을
생각했습
나무꾼은

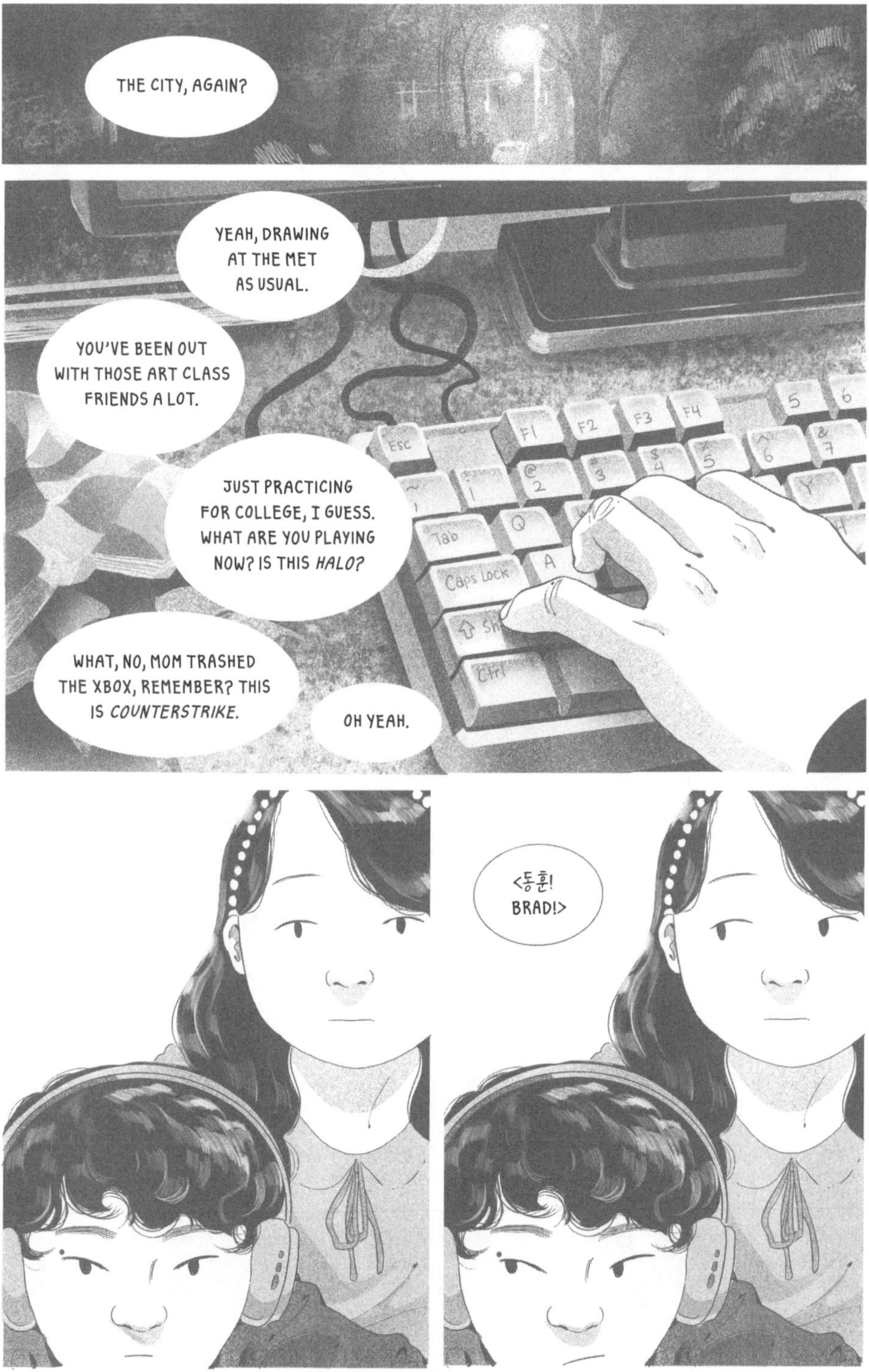
THE CITY, AGAIN?
YEAH, DRAWING AT THE MET AS USUAL.
YOU'VE BEEN OUT WITH THOSE ART CLASS FRIENDS A LOT.
JUST PRACTICING FOR COLLEGE, I GUESS. WHAT ARE YOU PLAYING NOW? IS THIS *HALO?*
WHAT, NO, MOM TRASHED THE XBOX, REMEMBER? THIS IS *COUNTERSTRIKE.*
OH YEAH.
<동훈! BRAD!>

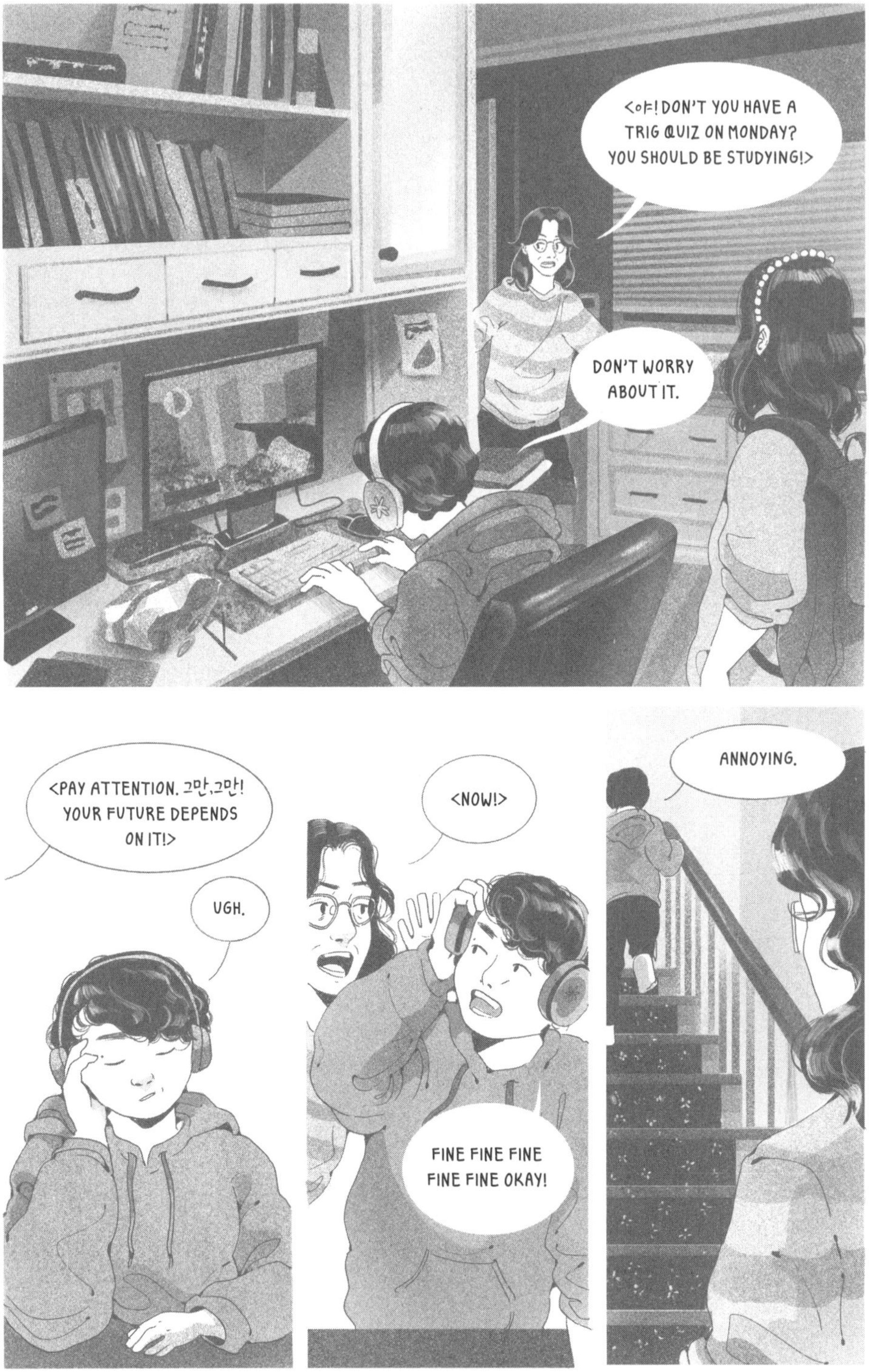
<야! DON'T YOU HAVE A TRIG QUIZ ON MONDAY? YOU SHOULD BE STUDYING!>
DON'T WORRY ABOUT IT.
<PAY ATTENTION. 그만,그만! YOUR FUTURE DEPENDS ON IT!>
UGH.
<NOW!>
FINE FINE FINE FINE FINE OKAY!
ANNOYING.

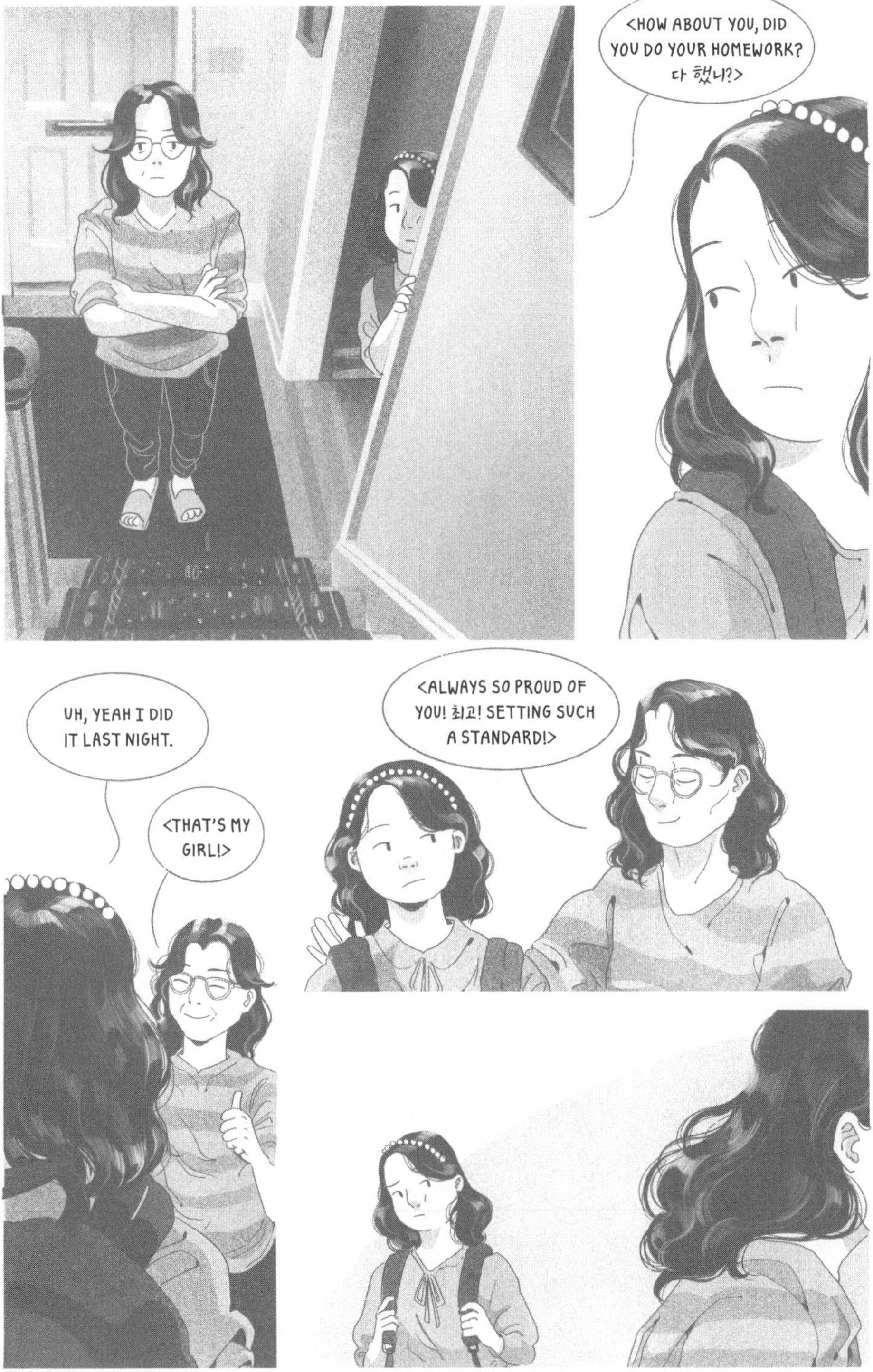
<HOW ABOUT YOU, DID YOU DO YOUR HOMEWORK? 다 했니?>
UH, YEAH I DID IT LAST NIGHT.
<THAT'S MY GIRL!>
<ALWAYS SO PROUD OF YOU! 최고! SETTING SUCH A STANDARD!>

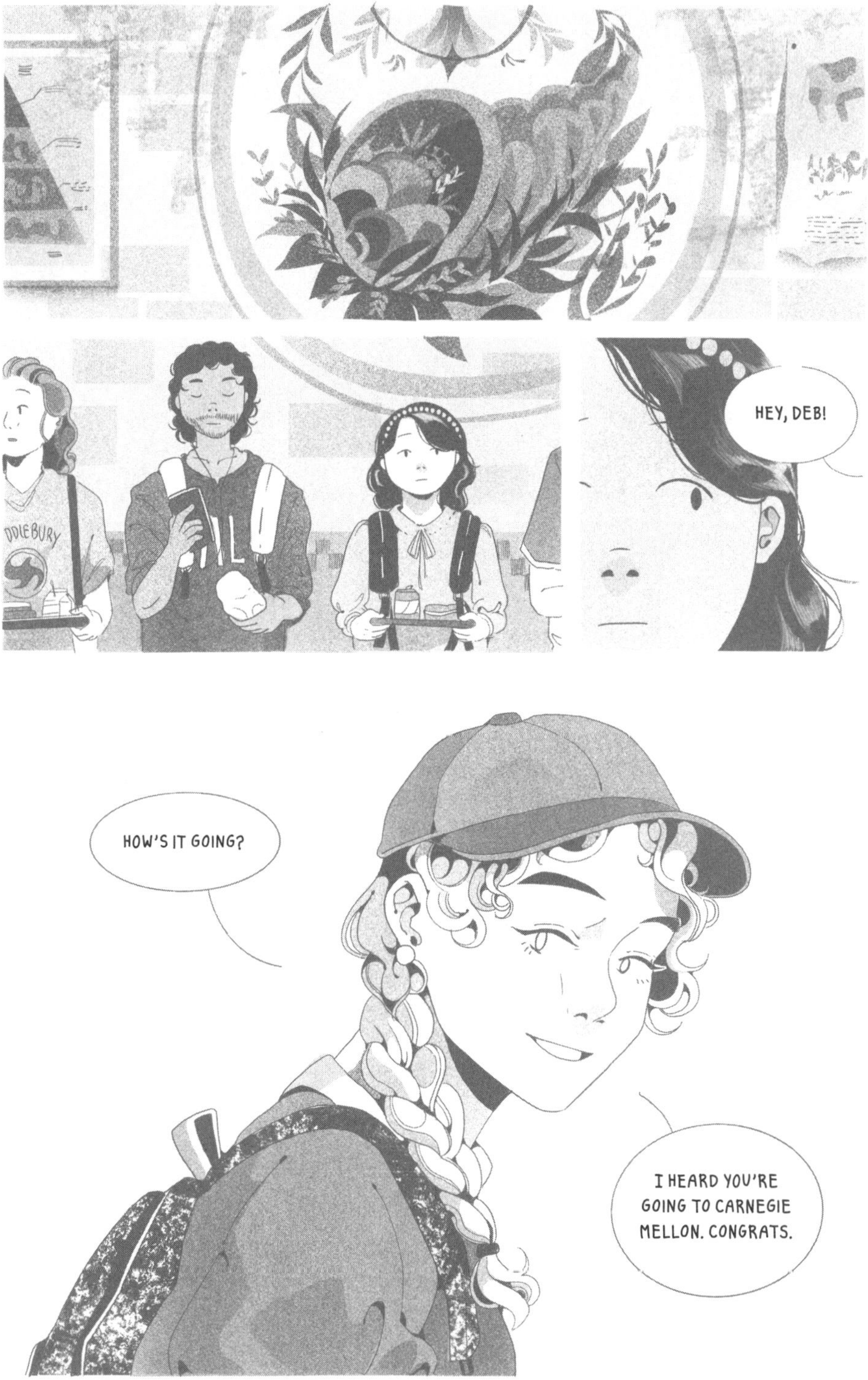
HEY, DEB!
HOW'S IT GOING?
I HEARD YOU'RE GOING TO CARNEGIE MELLON. CONGRATS.

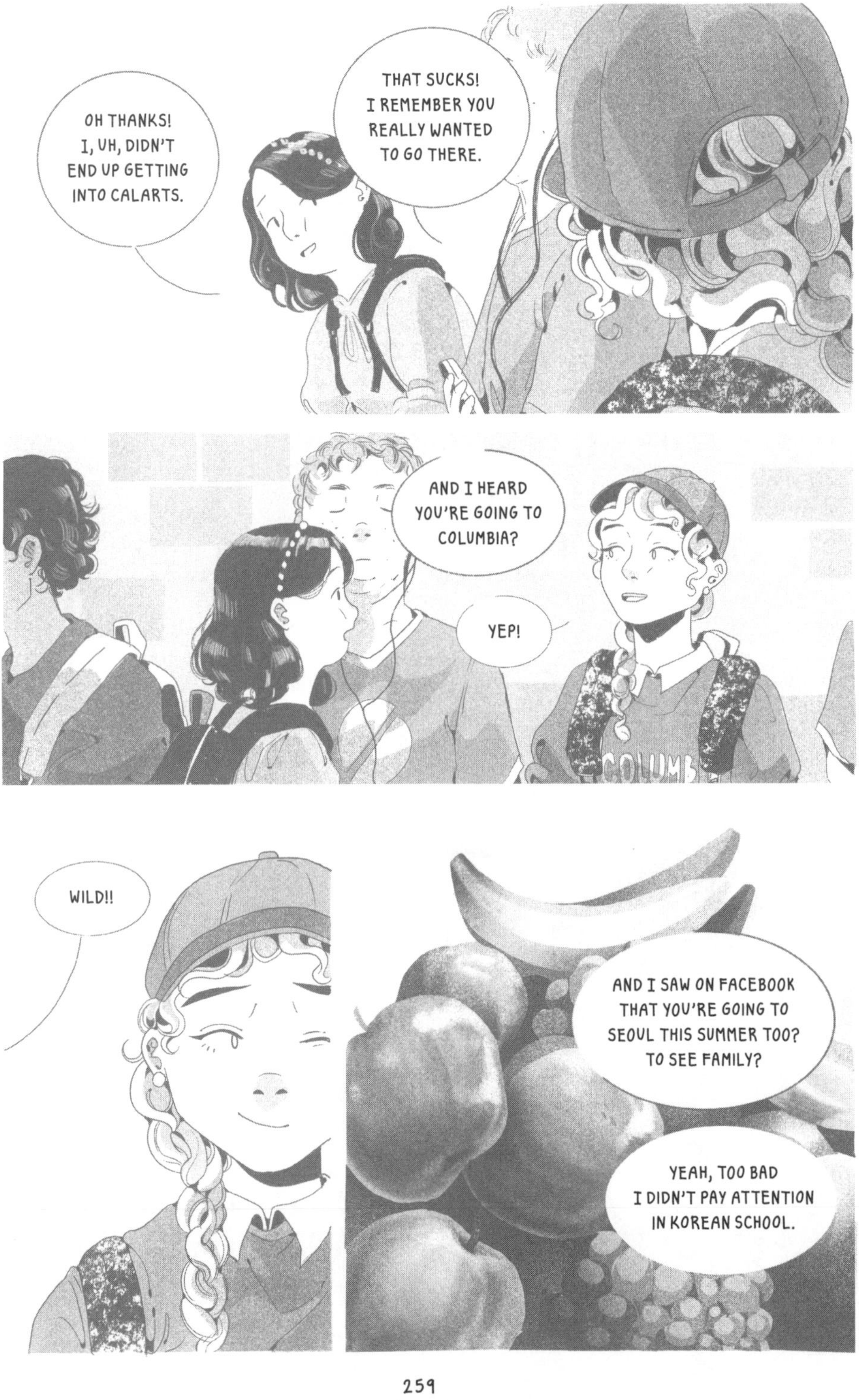
OH THANKS! I, UH, DIDN'T END UP GETTING INTO CALARTS.
THAT SUCKS! I REMEMBER YOU REALLY WANTED TO GO THERE.
AND I HEARD YOU'RE GOING TO COLUMBIA?
YEP!
WILD!!
AND I SAW ON FACEBOOK THAT YOU'RE GOING TO SEOUL THIS SUMMER TOO? TO SEE FAMILY?
YEAH, TOO BAD I DIDN'T PAY ATTENTION IN KOREAN SCHOOL.

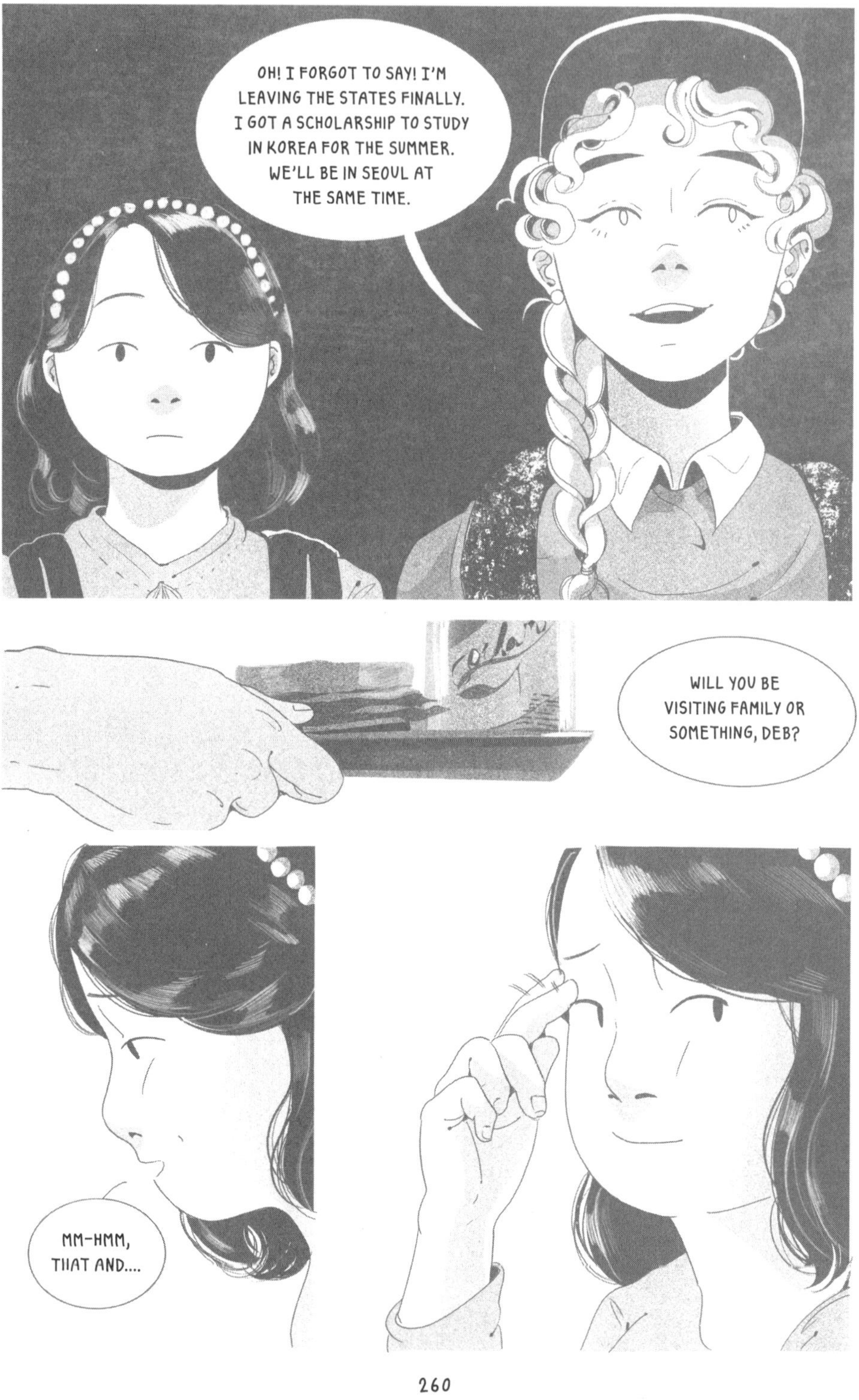
OH! I FORGOT TO SAY! I'M LEAVING THE STATES FINALLY. I GOT A SCHOLARSHIP TO STUDY IN KOREA FOR THE SUMMER. WE'LL BE IN SEOUL AT THE SAME TIME.
WILL YOU BE VISITING FAMILY OR SOMETHING, DEB?
MM-HMM, THAT AND....

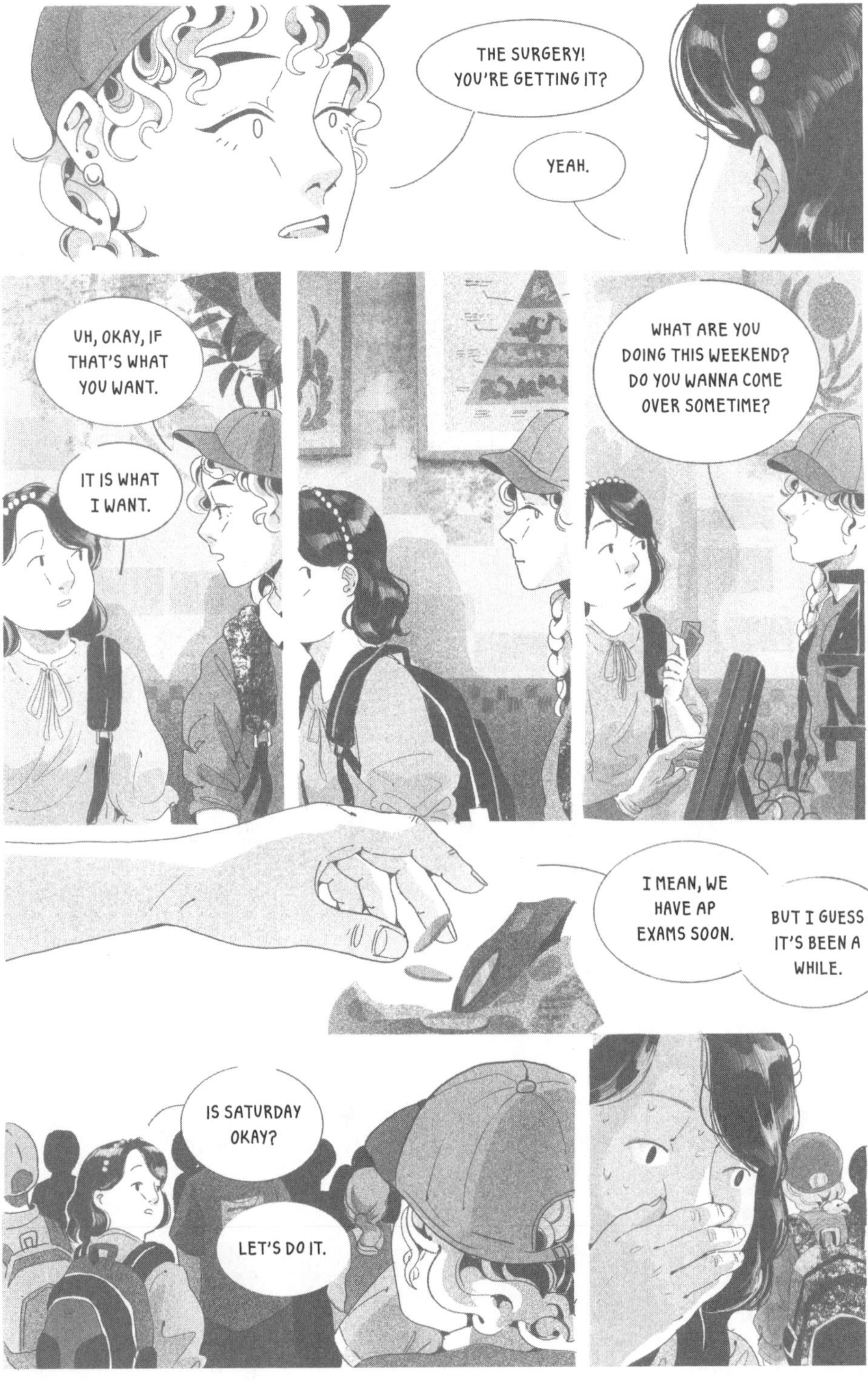
THE SURGERY! YOU'RE GETTING IT?
YEAH.
UH, OKAY, IF THAT'S WHAT YOU WANT.
IT IS WHAT I WANT.
WHAT ARE YOU DOING THIS WEEKEND? DO YOU WANNA COME OVER SOMETIME?
I MEAN, WE HAVE AP EXAMS SOON.
BUT I GUESS IT'S BEEN A WHILE.
IS SATURDAY OKAY?
LET'S DO IT.

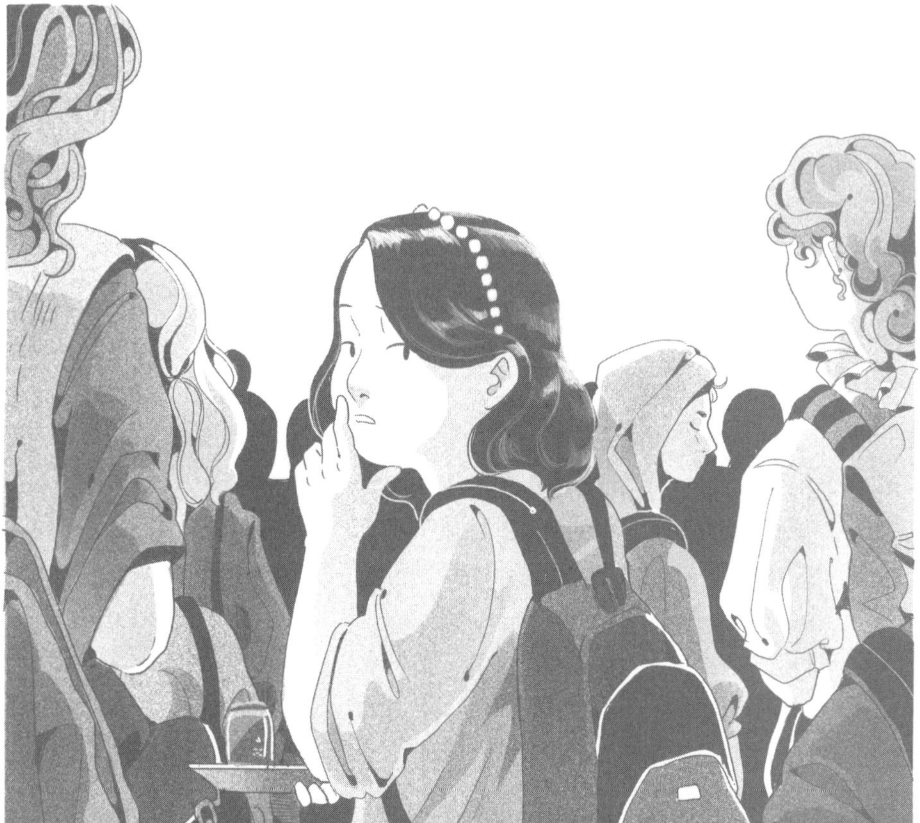

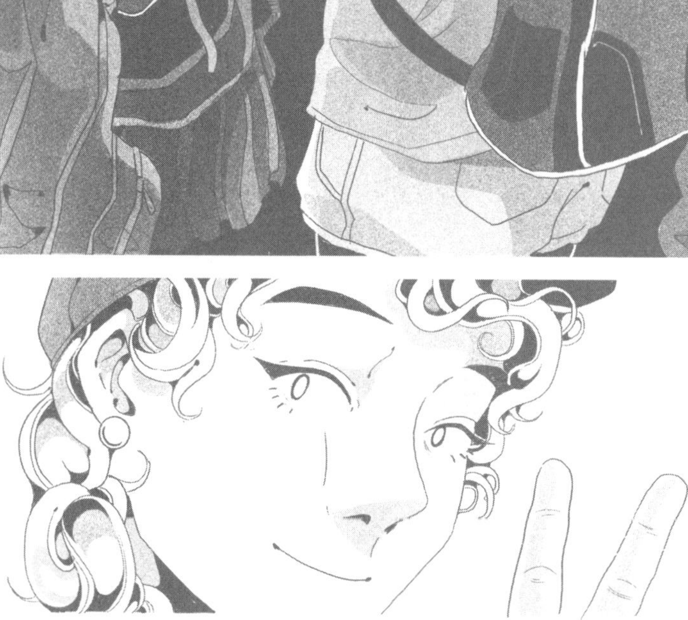

BREATHE IN.

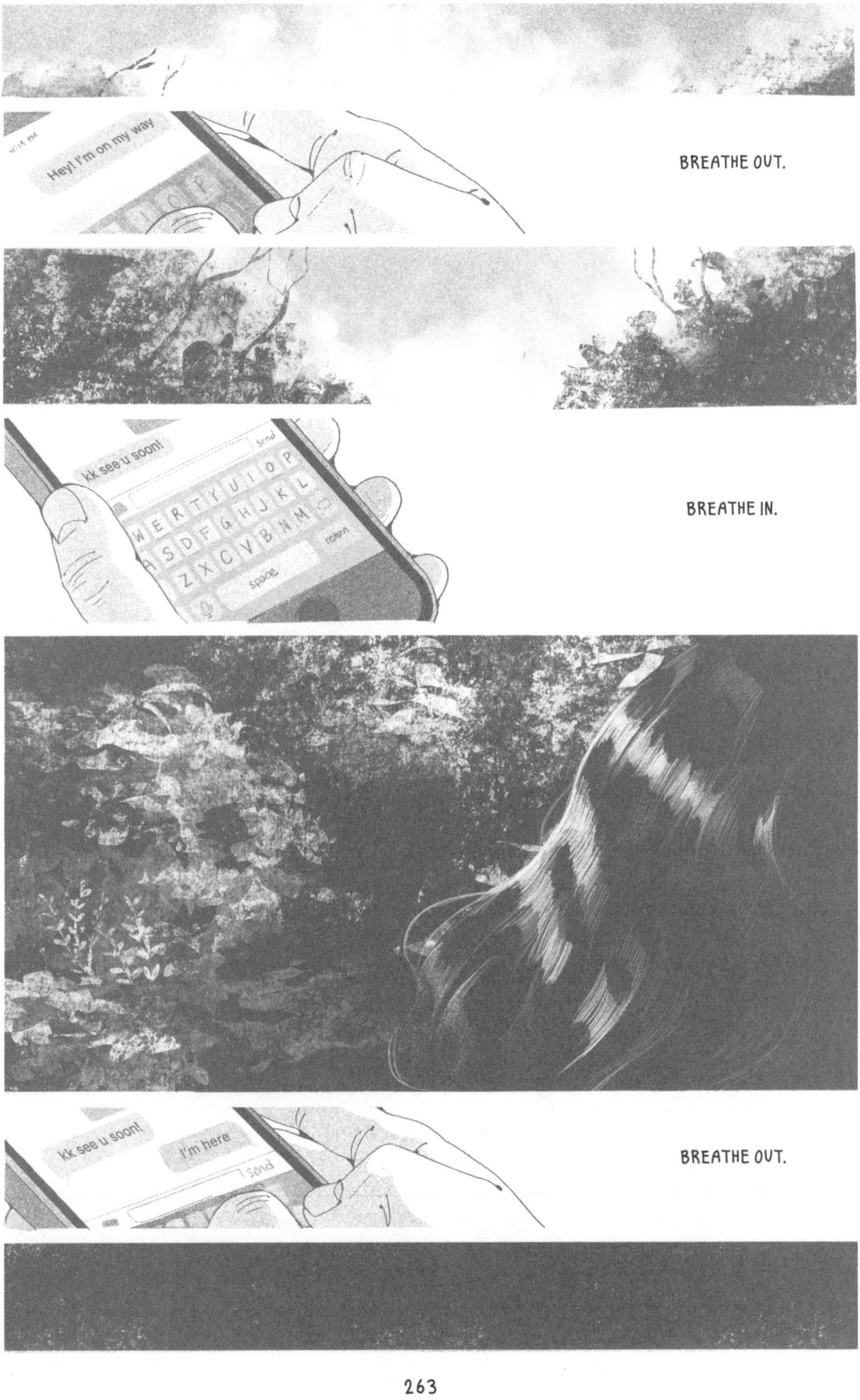
Hey! I'm on my way
BREATHE OUT.
kk see u soon!
BREATHE IN.
kk see u soon!
I'm here
BREATHE OUT.

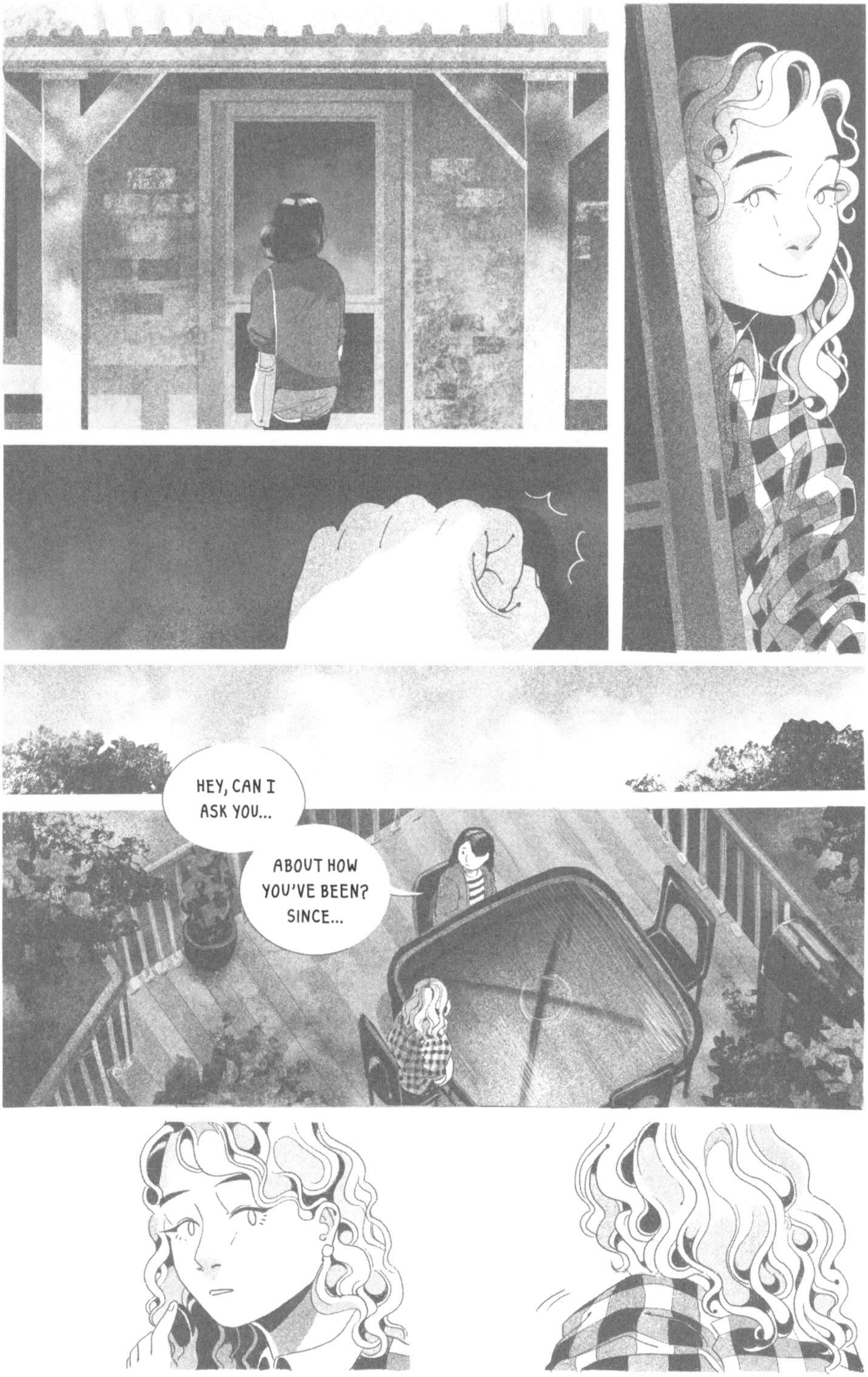
HEY, CAN I ASK YOU...
ABOUT HOW YOU'VE BEEN? SINCE...

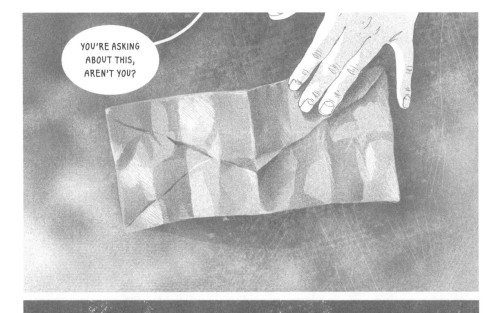

YOU'RE ASKING ABOUT THIS, AREN'T YOU?

YOU BET I GOT IT. TOOK A WHILE FOR YOU TO ASK, DON'T YOU THINK?

YOU'VE GOTTEN SO STIFF AND CALLOUS AND THE LETTER SHOWS. NO MATTER HOW MUCH I READ THIS, ALL THE ASKS FOR FORGIVENESS FEEL SO COLD AND UNFEELING.

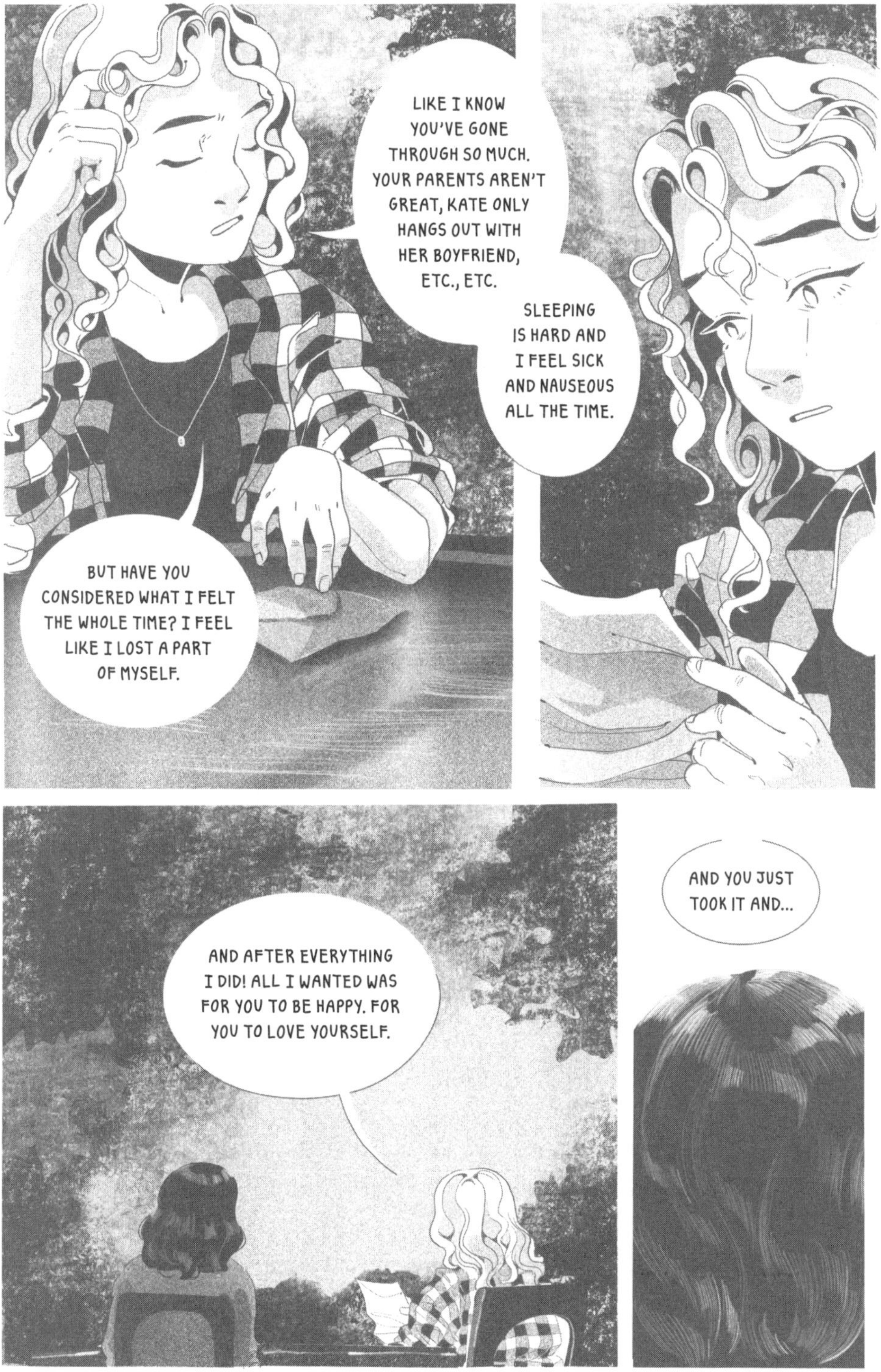
LIKE I KNOW YOU'VE GONE THROUGH SO MUCH. YOUR PARENTS AREN'T GREAT, KATE ONLY HANGS OUT WITH HER BOYFRIEND, ETC., ETC.
SLEEPING IS HARD AND I FEEL SICK AND NAUSEOUS ALL THE TIME.
BUT HAVE YOU CONSIDERED WHAT I FELT THE WHOLE TIME? I FEEL LIKE I LOST A PART OF MYSELF.
AND AFTER EVERYTHING I DID! ALL I WANTED WAS FOR YOU TO BE HAPPY. FOR YOU TO LOVE YOURSELF.
AND YOU JUST TOOK IT AND...

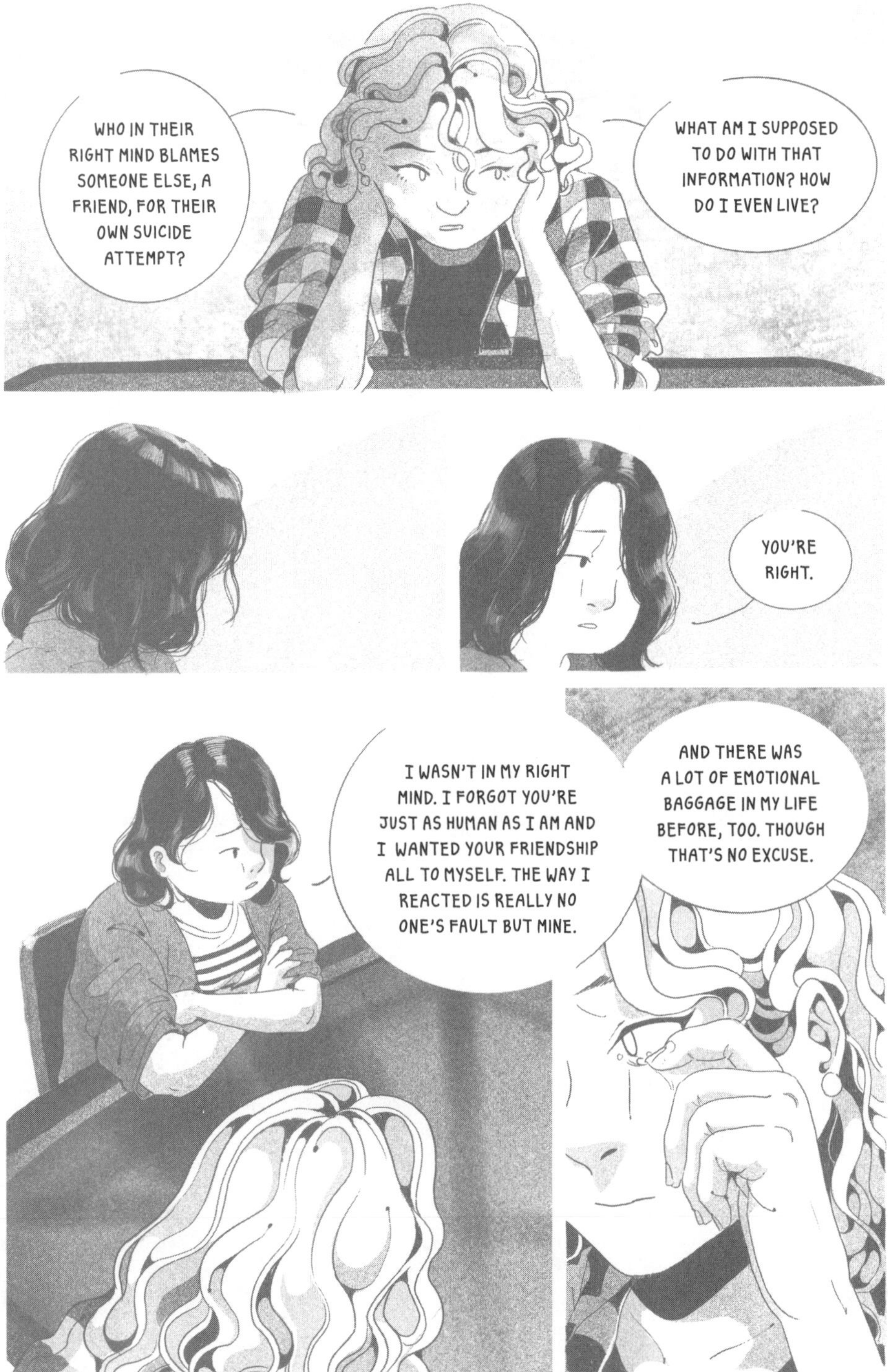
WHO IN THEIR RIGHT MIND BLAMES SOMEONE ELSE, A FRIEND, FOR THEIR OWN SUICIDE ATTEMPT?
WHAT AM I SUPPOSED TO DO WITH THAT INFORMATION? HOW DO I EVEN LIVE?
YOU'RE RIGHT.
I WASN'T IN MY RIGHT MIND. I FORGOT YOU'RE JUST AS HUMAN AS I AM AND I WANTED YOUR FRIENDSHIP ALL TO MYSELF. THE WAY I REACTED IS REALLY NO ONE'S FAULT BUT MINE.
AND THERE WAS A LOT OF EMOTIONAL BAGGAGE IN MY LIFE BEFORE, TOO. THOUGH THAT'S NO EXCUSE.

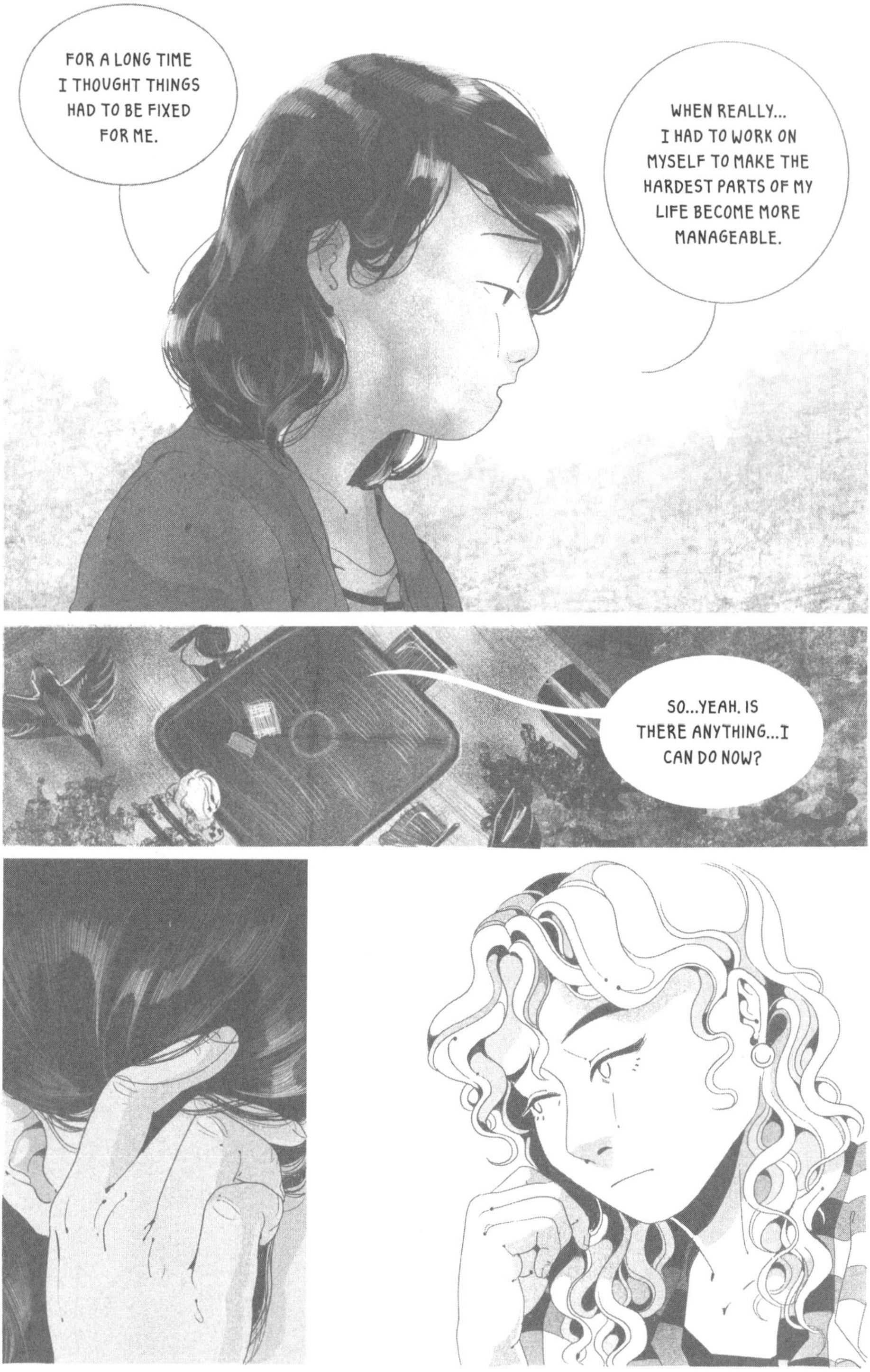
FOR A LONG TIME I THOUGHT THINGS HAD TO BE FIXED FOR ME.
WHEN REALLY... I HAD TO WORK ON MYSELF TO MAKE THE HARDEST PARTS OF MY LIFE BECOME MORE MANAGEABLE.
SO...YEAH. IS THERE ANYTHING...I CAN DO NOW?

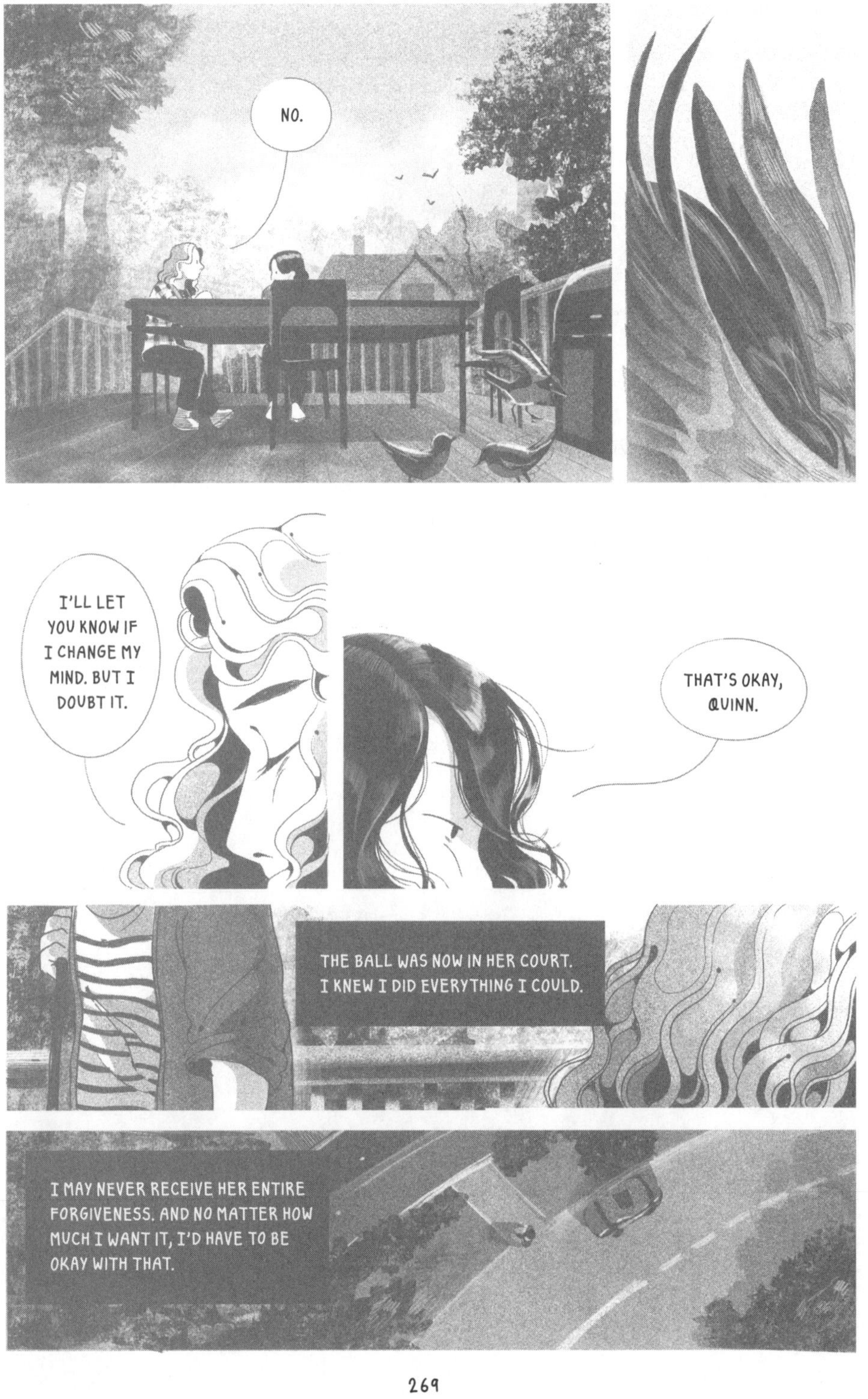
NO.
I'LL LET YOU KNOW IF I CHANGE MY MIND. BUT I DOUBT IT.
THAT'S OKAY, QUINN.
THE BALL WAS NOW IN HER COURT. I KNEW I DID EVERYTHING I COULD.
I MAY NEVER RECEIVE HER ENTIRE FORGIVENESS. AND NO MATTER HOW MUCH I WANT IT, I'D HAVE TO BE OKAY WITH THAT.

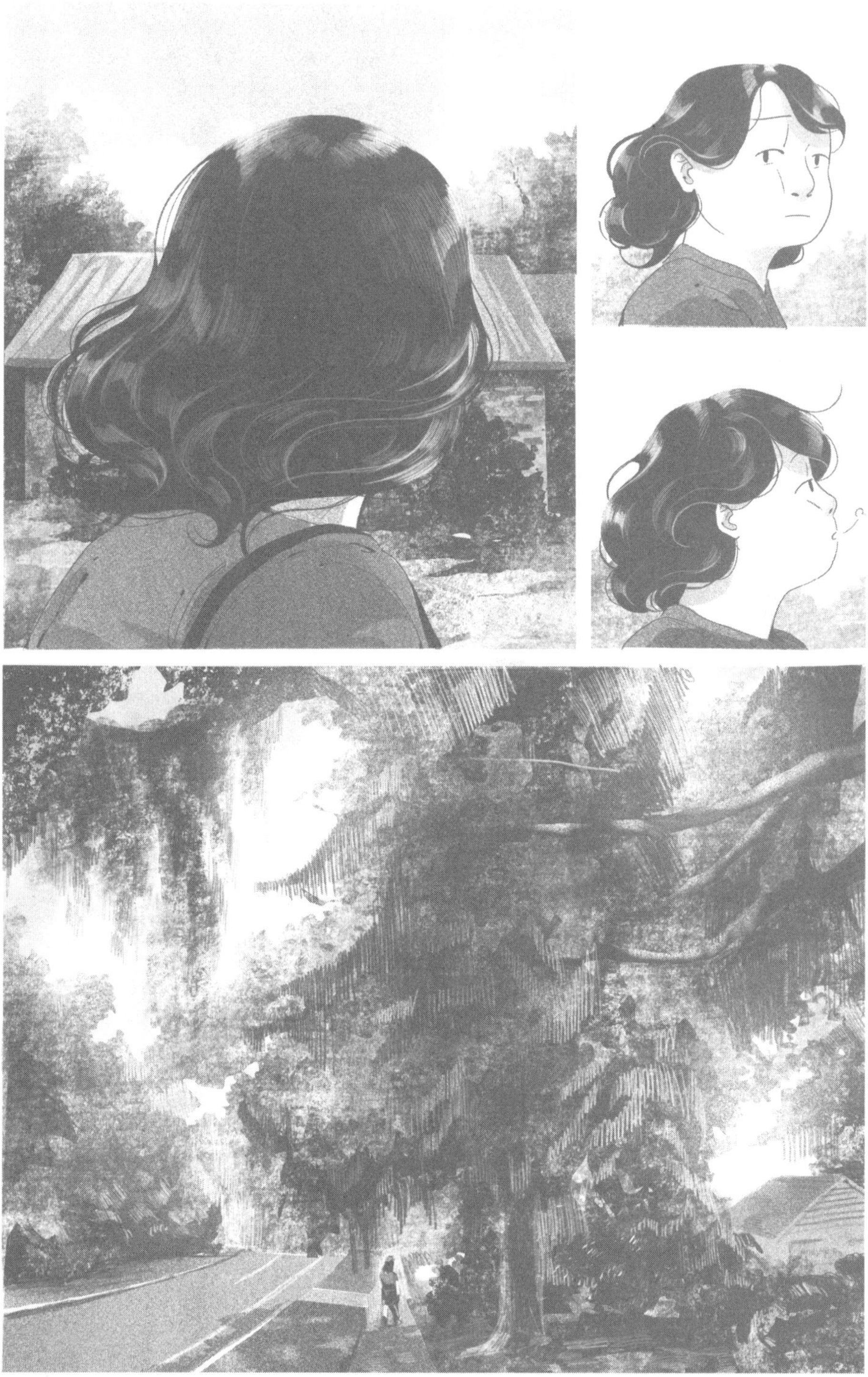

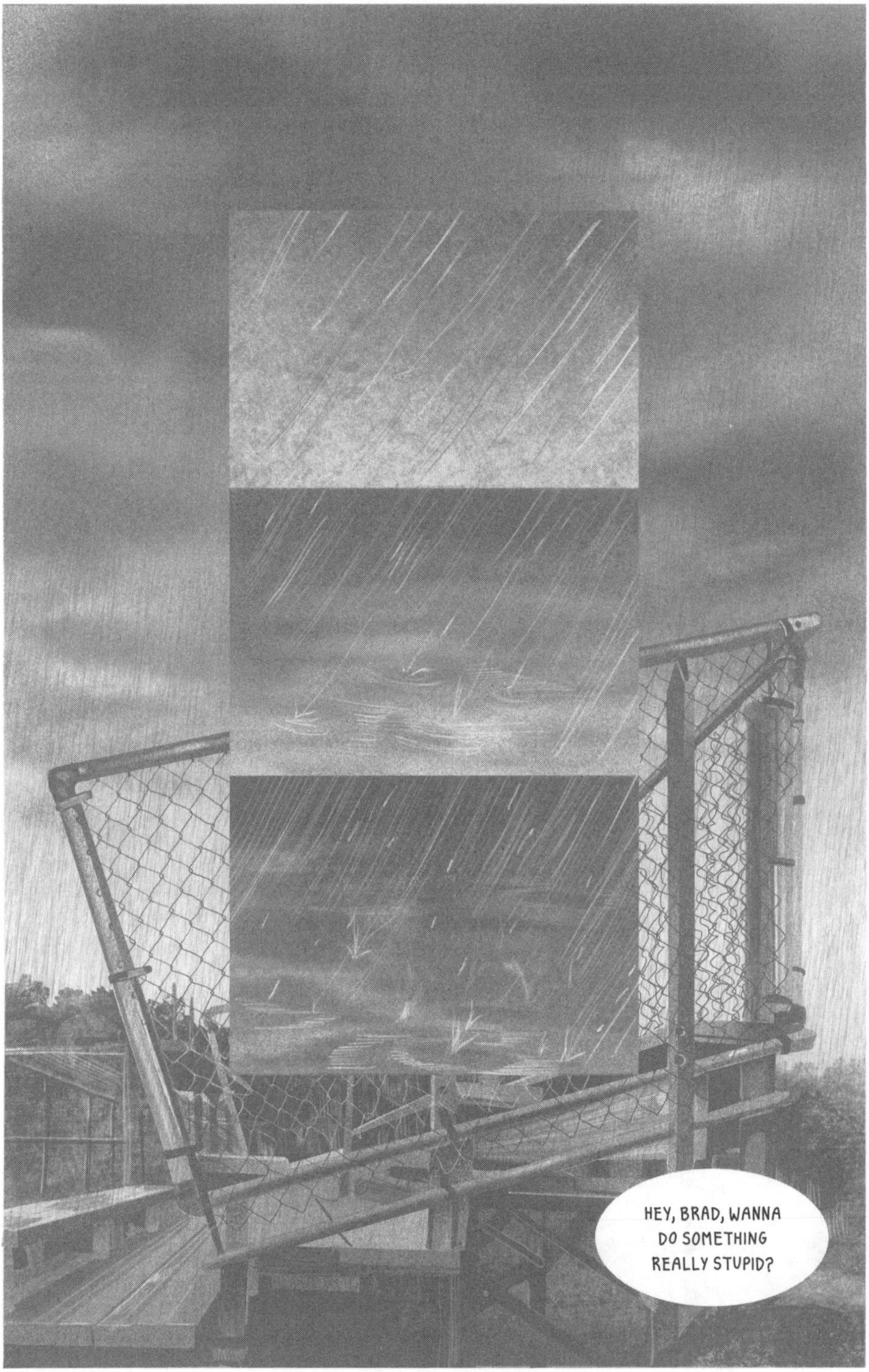
HEY, BRAD, WANNA DO SOMETHING REALLY STUPID?

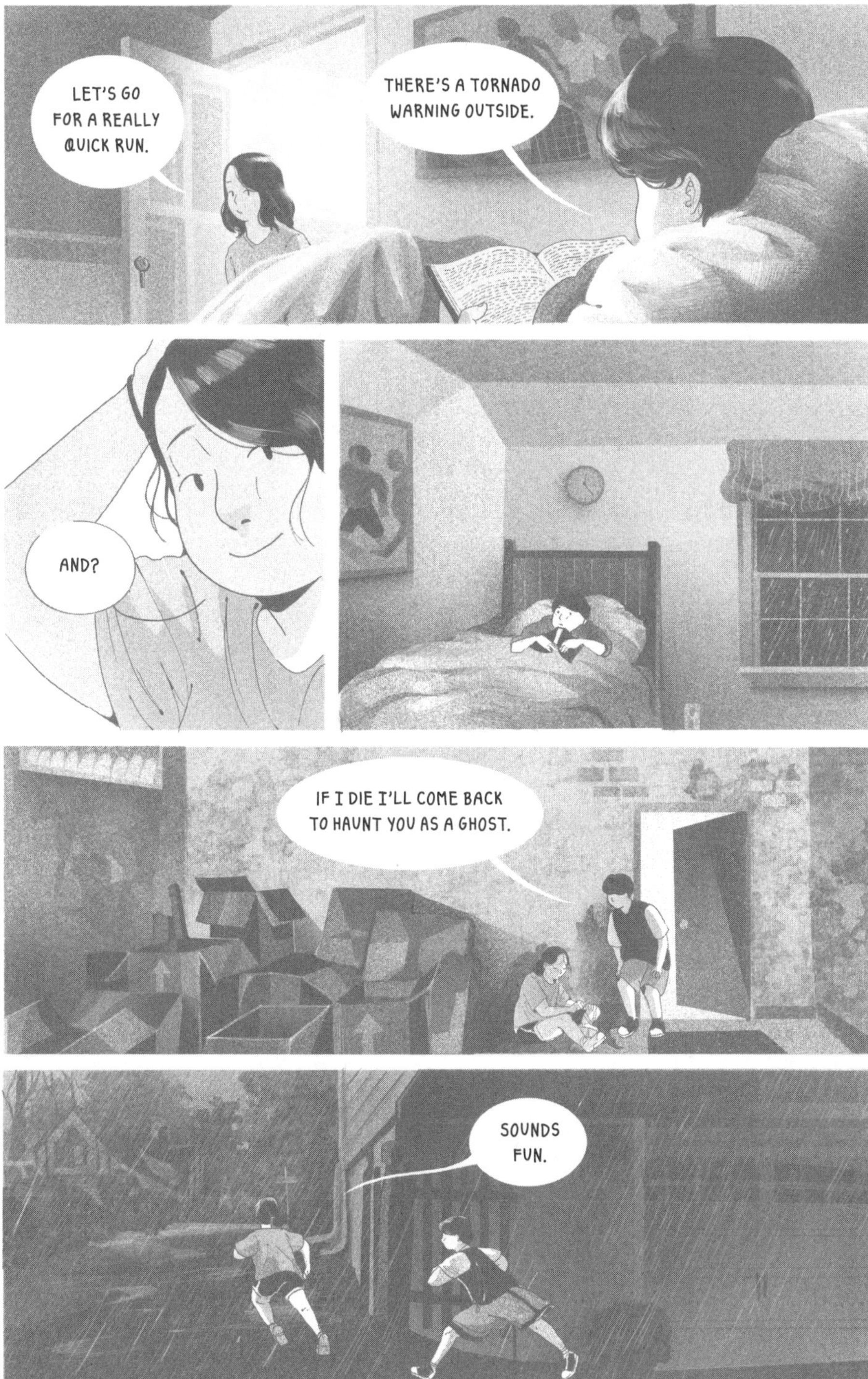
LET'S GO FOR A REALLY QUICK RUN.
THERE'S A TORNADO WARNING OUTSIDE.
AND?
IF I DIE I'LL COME BACK TO HAUNT YOU AS A GHOST.
SOUNDS FUN.

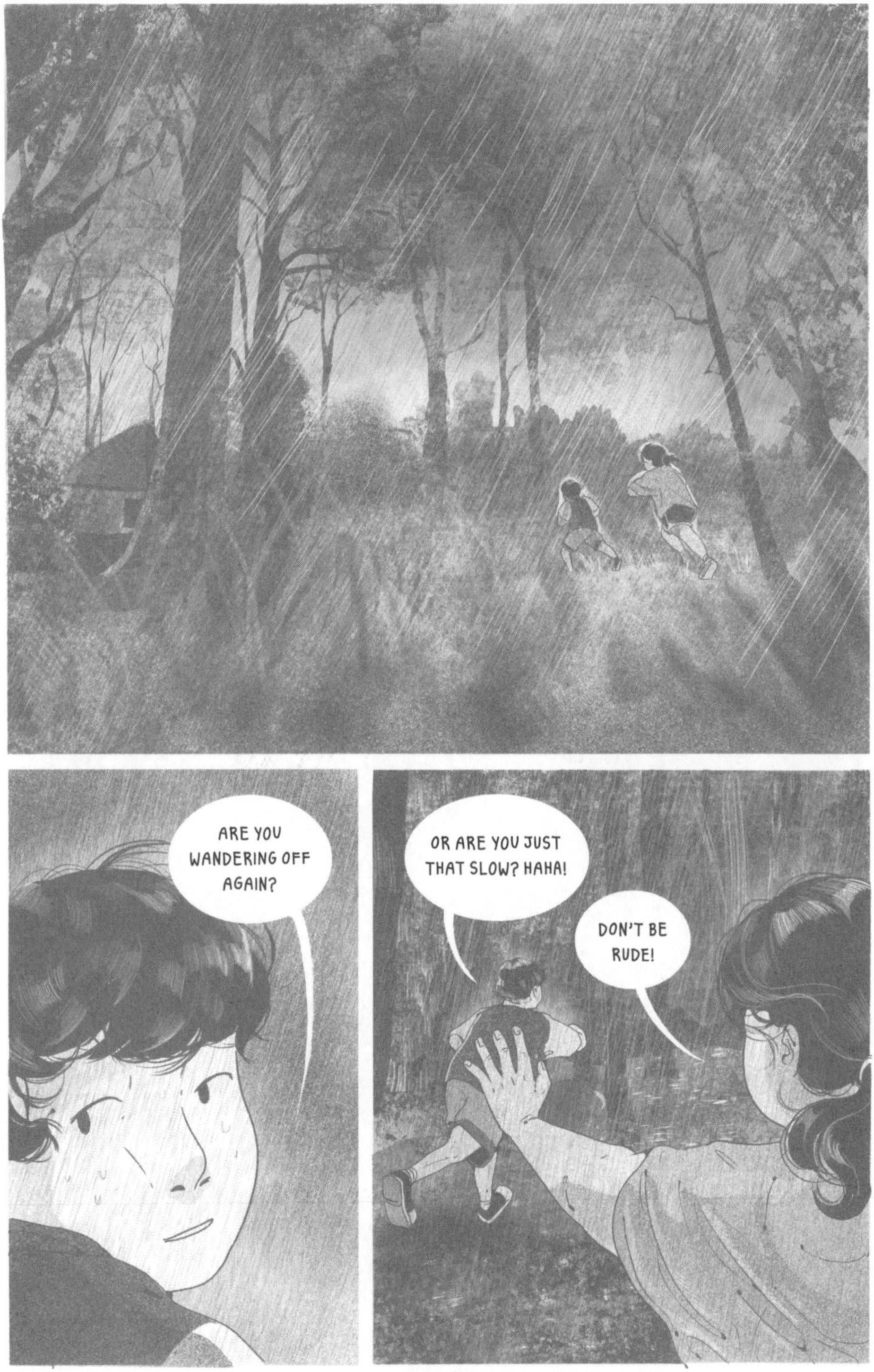
ARE YOU WANDERING OFF AGAIN?
OR ARE YOU JUST THAT SLOW? HAHA!
DON'T BE RUDE!

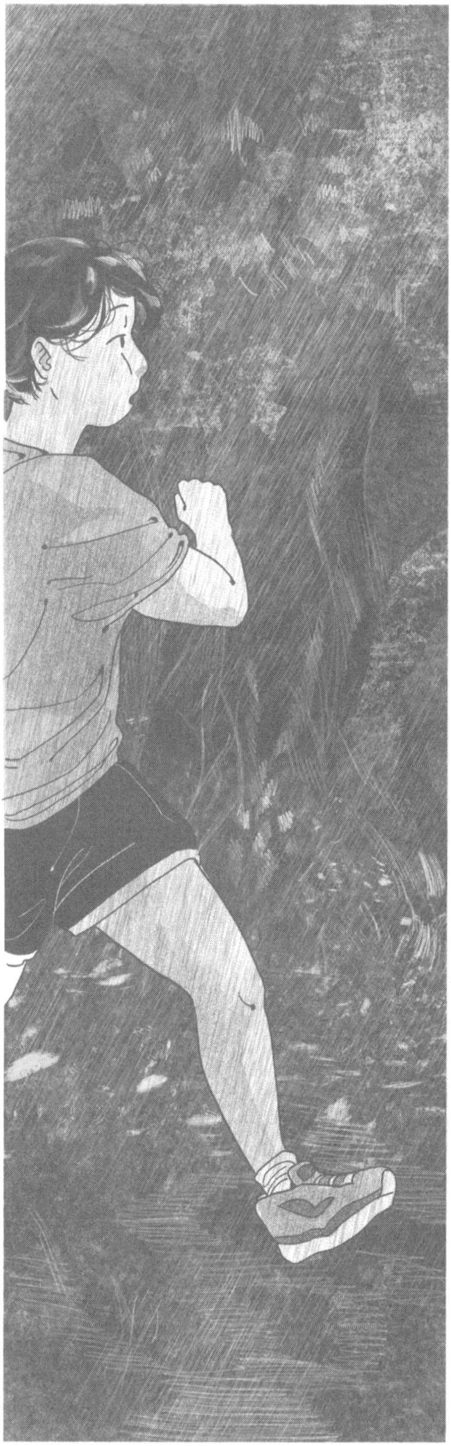
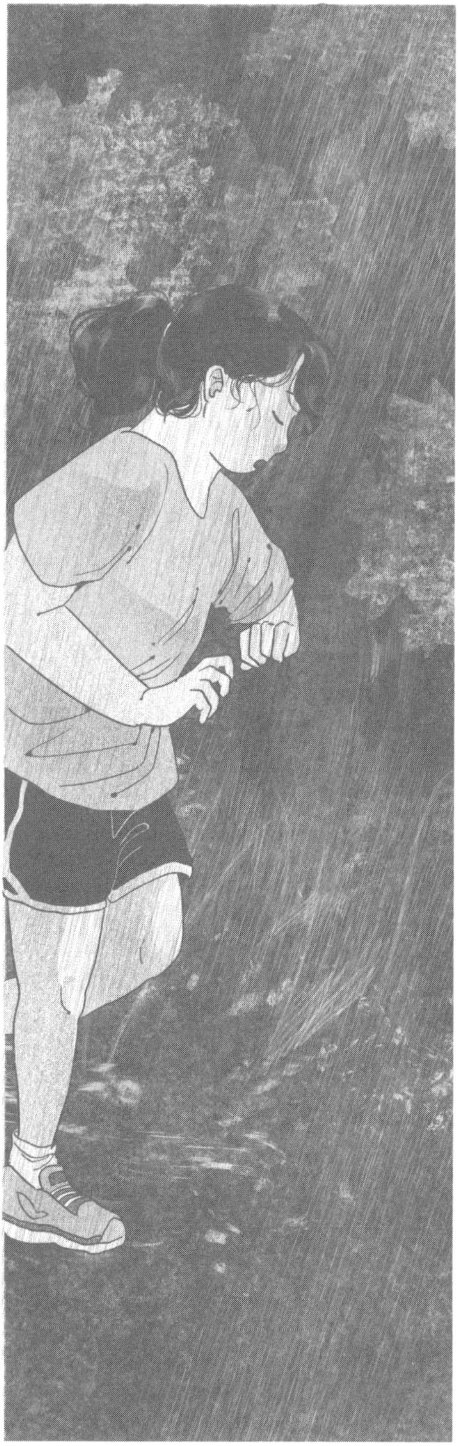

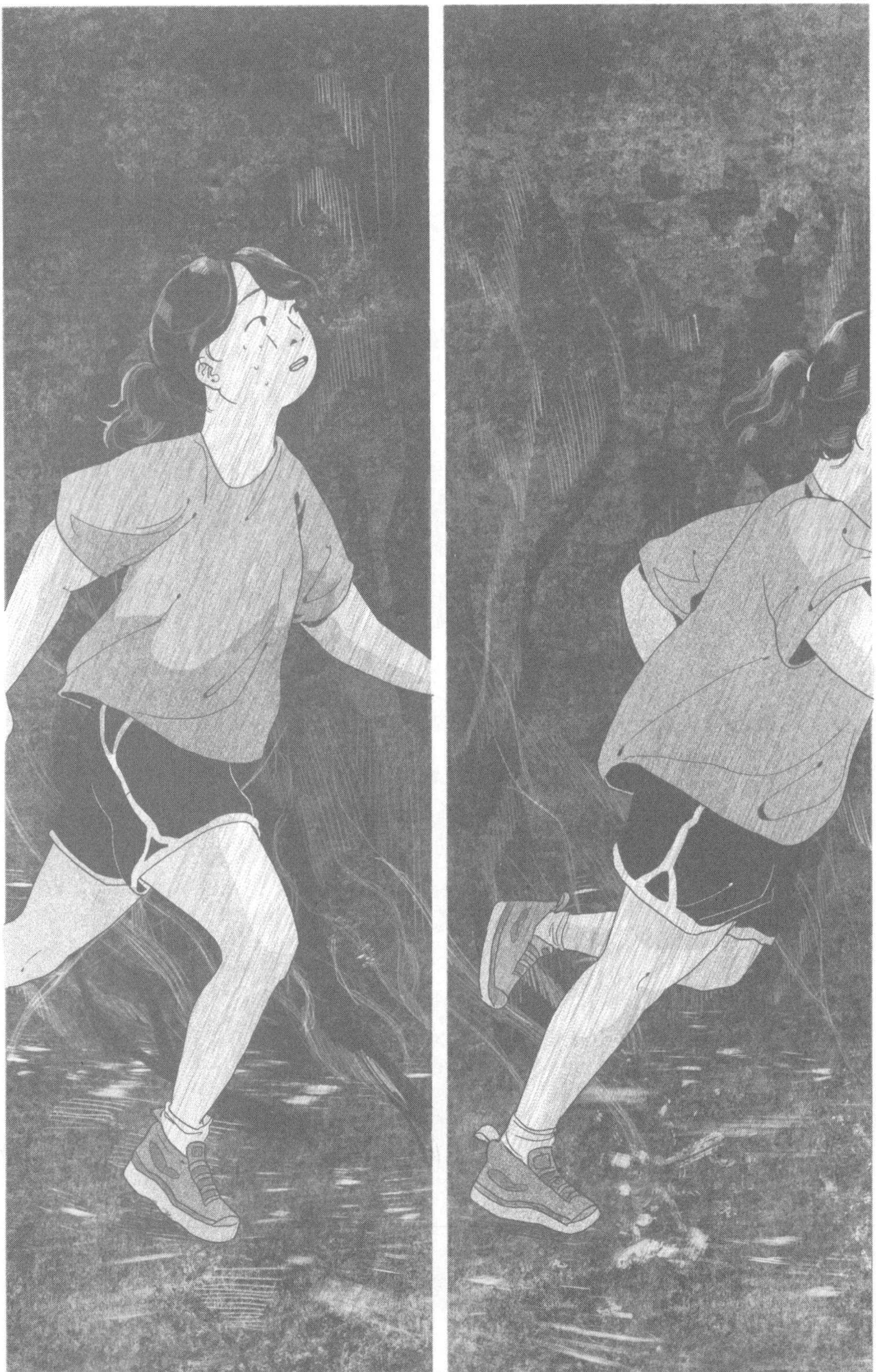

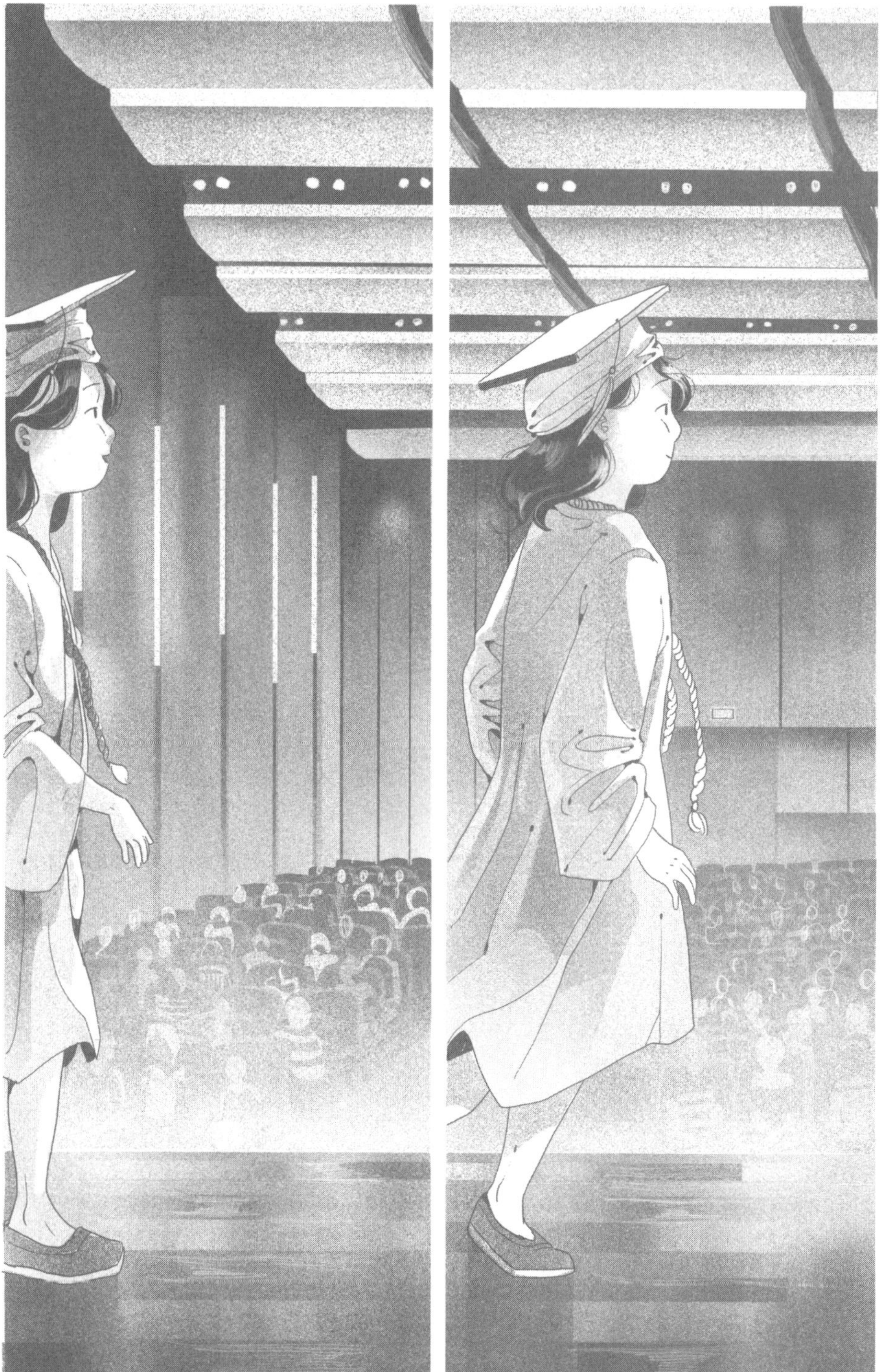

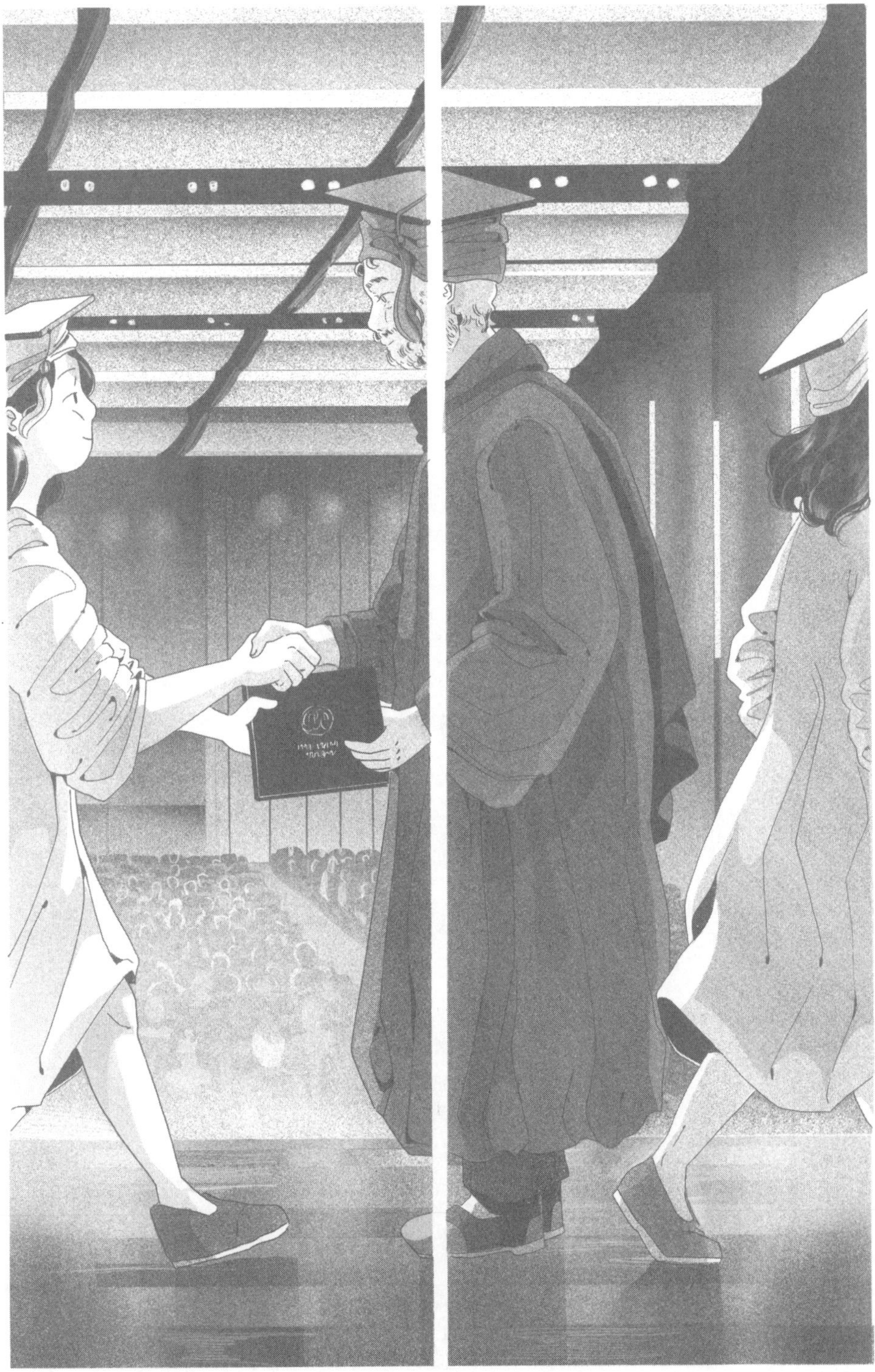

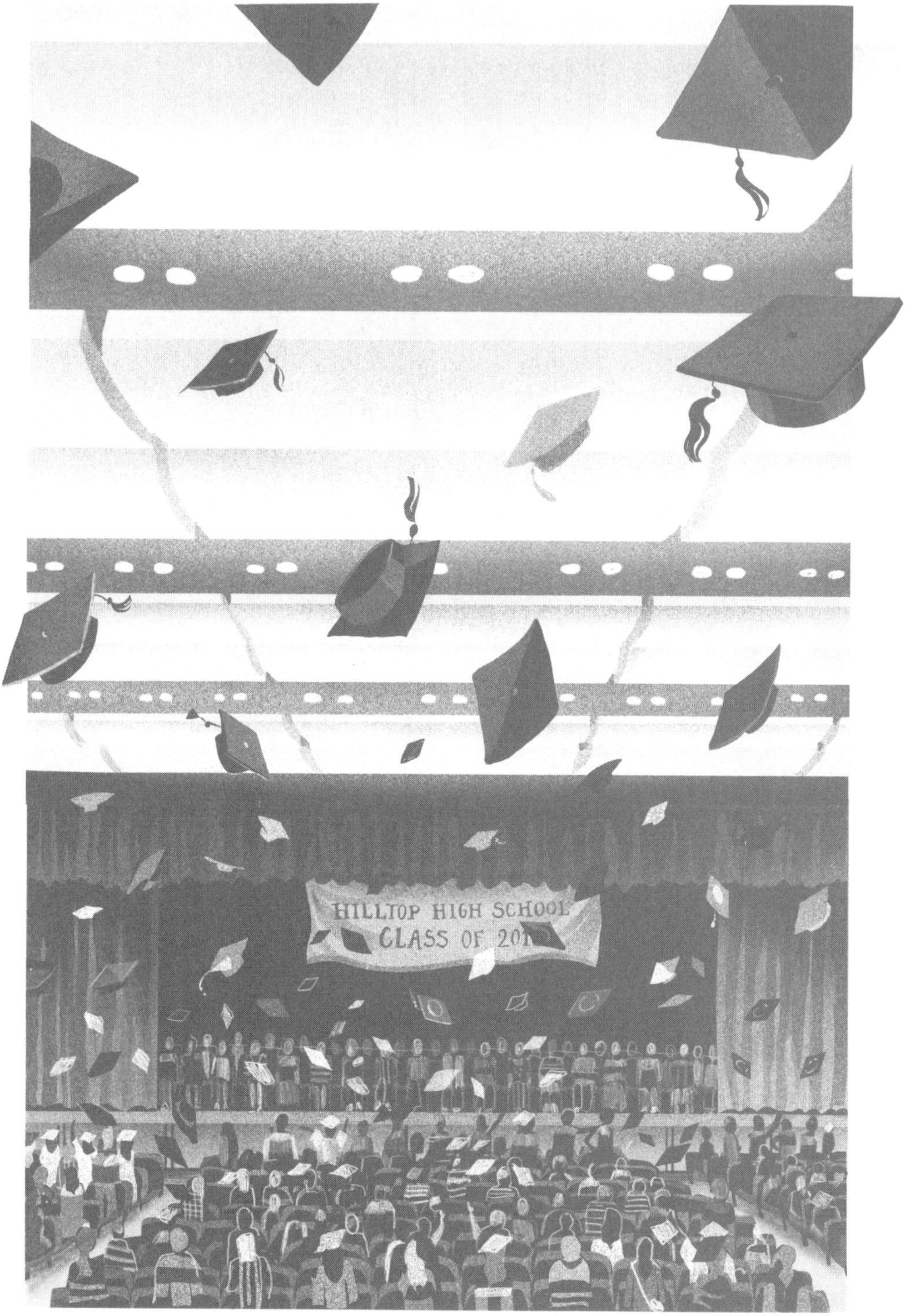
HILLTOP HIGH SCHOOL
CLASS OF 201

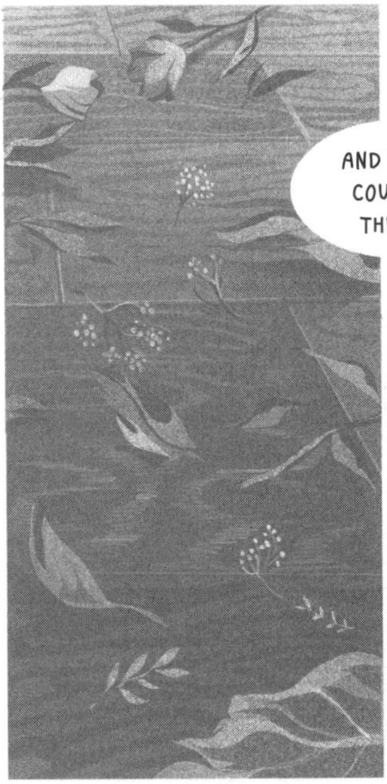
AND WHEN I COUNT TO THREE...

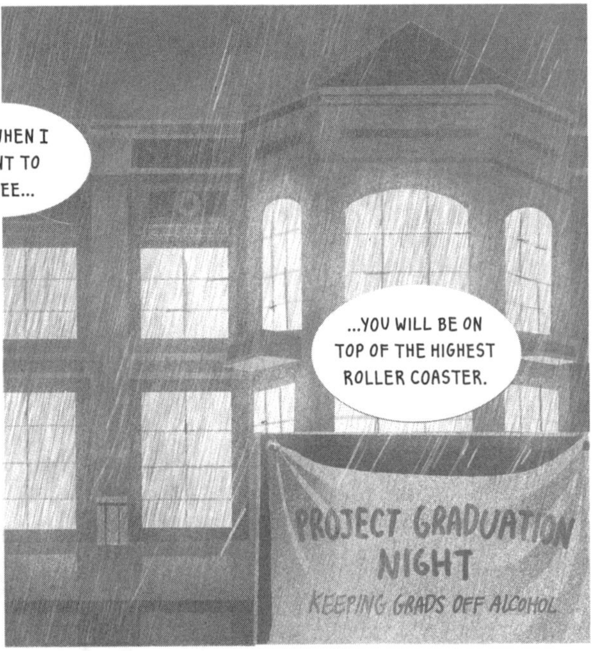
...YOU WILL BE ON TOP OF THE HIGHEST ROLLER COASTER.
PROJECT GRADUATION NIGHT
KEEPING GRADS OFF ALCOHOL

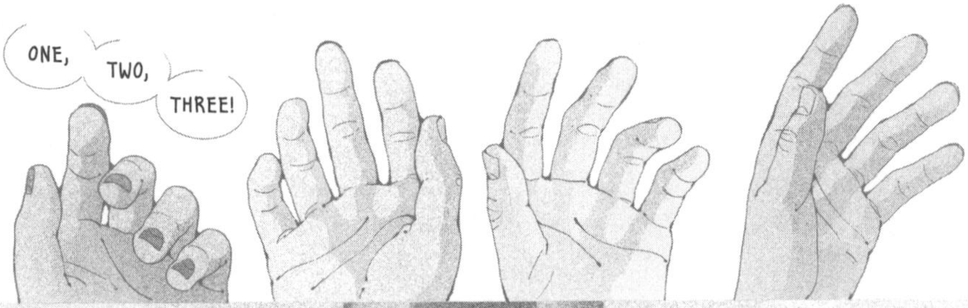
ONE,
TWO,
THREE!

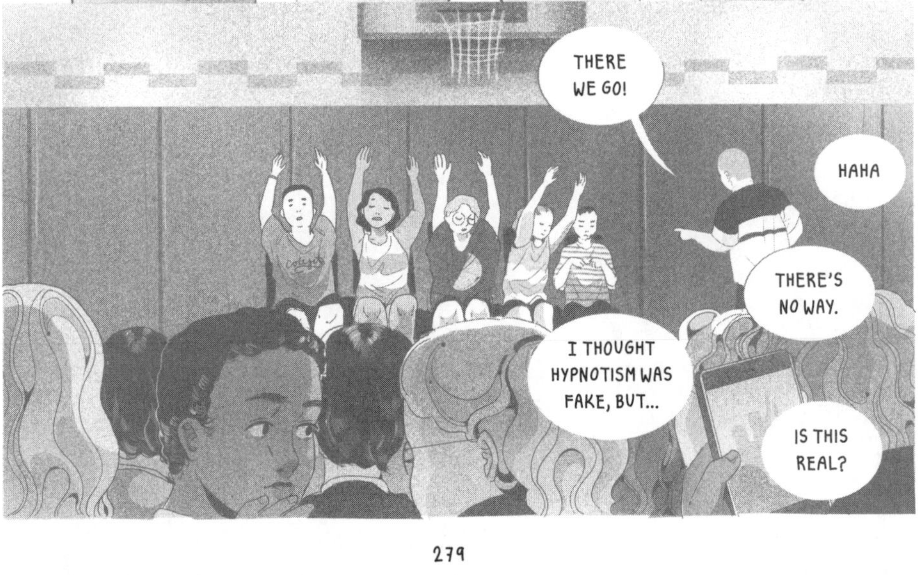
THERE WE GO!
HAHA
THERE'S NO WAY.
I THOUGHT HYPNOTISM WAS FAKE, BUT...
IS THIS REAL?

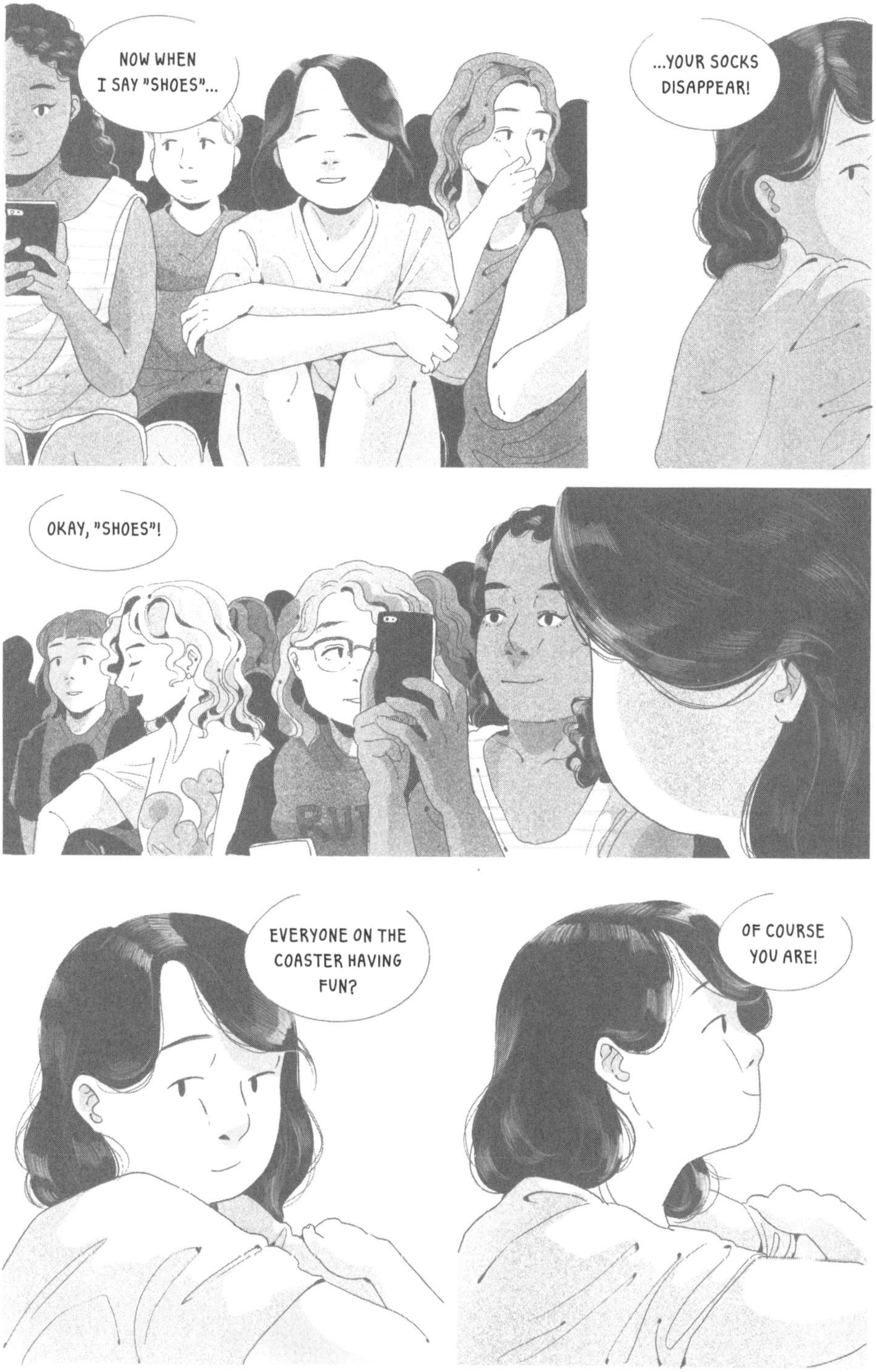
NOW WHEN I SAY "SHOES"...
...YOUR SOCKS DISAPPEAR!
OKAY, "SHOES"!
EVERYONE ON THE COASTER HAVING FUN?
OF COURSE YOU ARE!

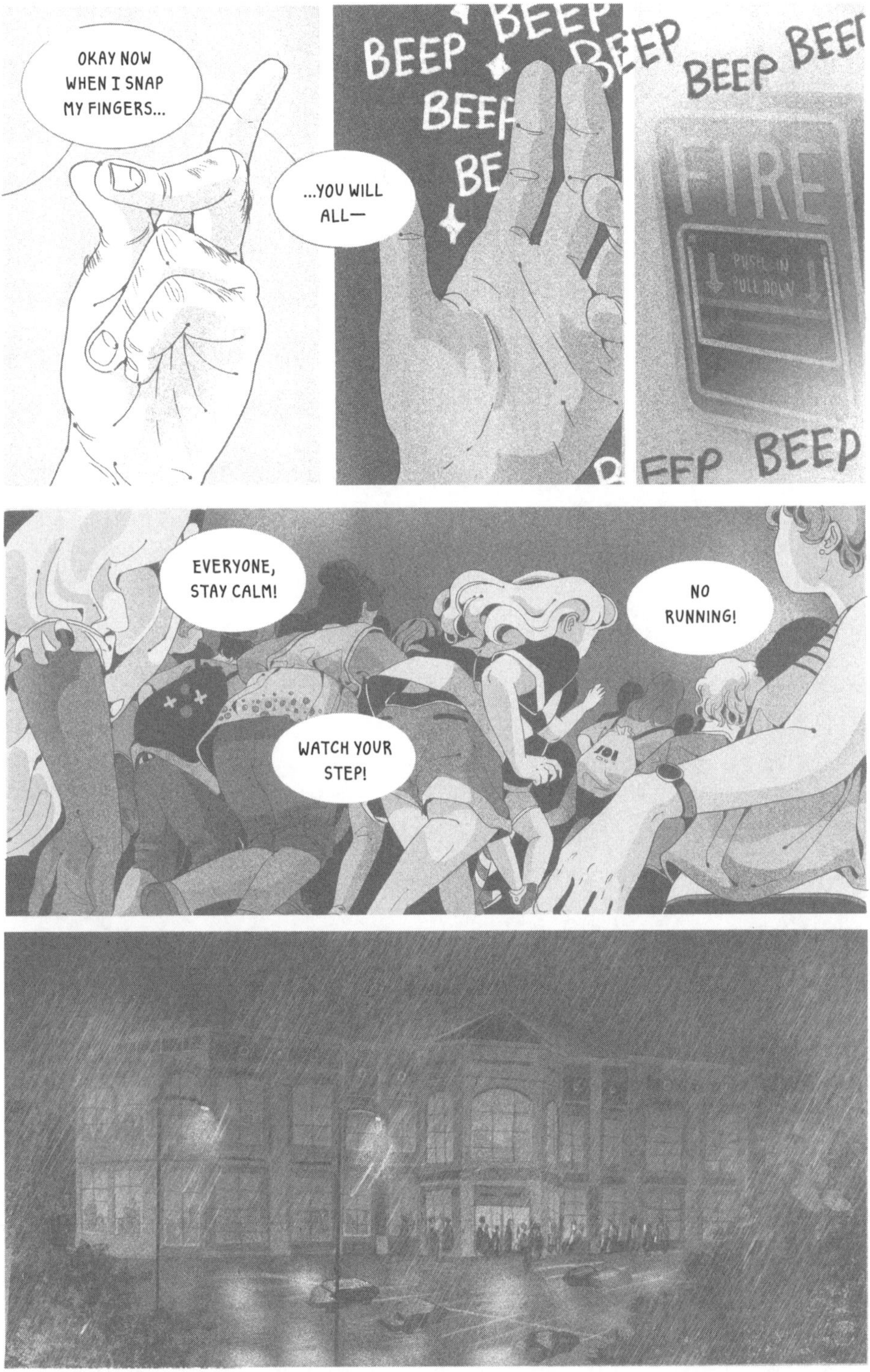
OKAY NOW WHEN I SNAP MY FINGERS...
...YOU WILL ALL—
BEEP BEEP BEEP BEEP
BEEP BEEP
FIRE
PUSH IN PULL DOWN
BEEP
EVERYONE, STAY CALM!
NO RUNNING!
WATCH YOUR STEP!

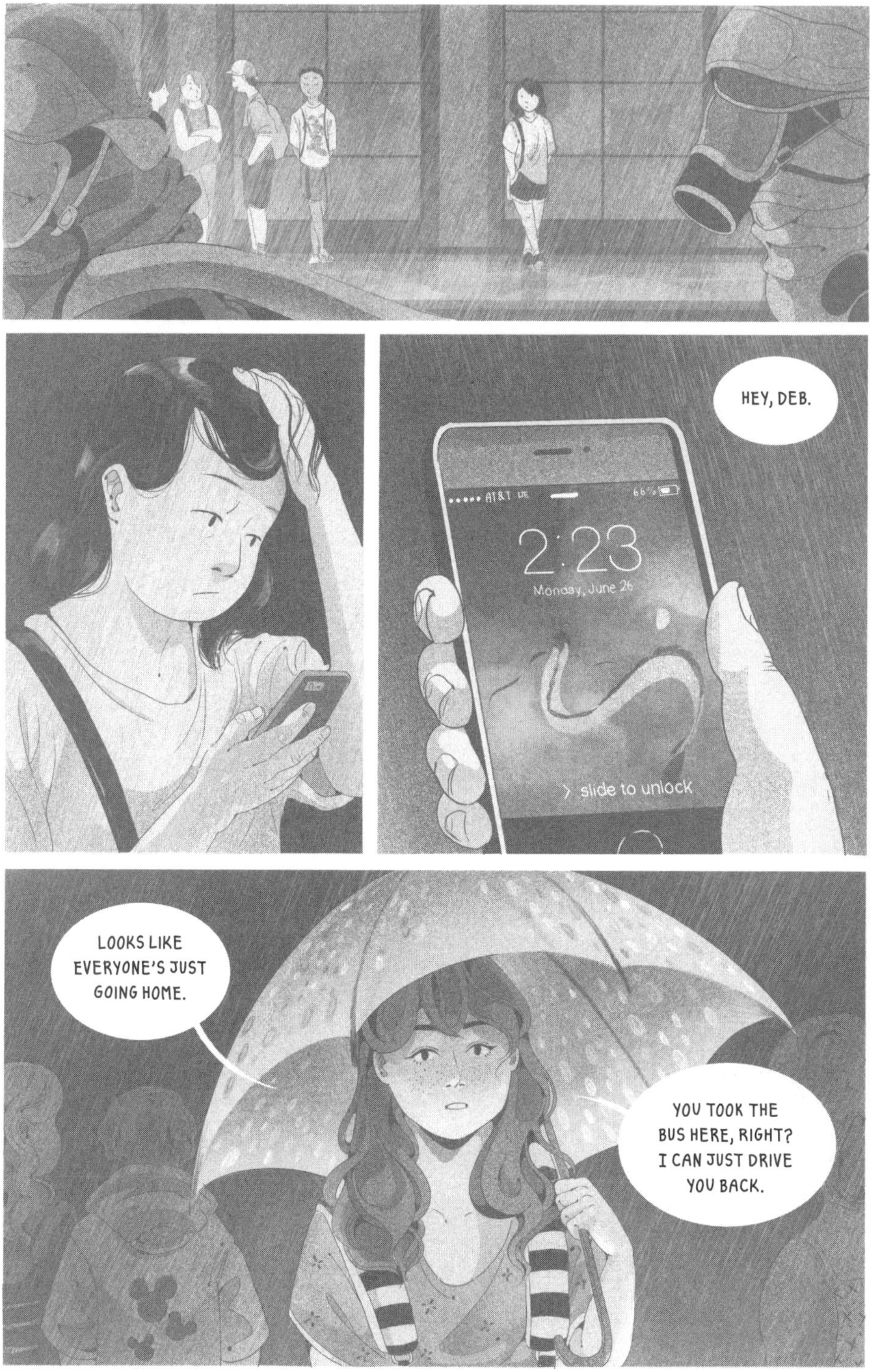
HEY, DEB.
AT&T LTE
66%
2:23
Monday, June 26
slide to unlock
LOOKS LIKE EVERYONE'S JUST GOING HOME.
YOU TOOK THE BUS HERE, RIGHT? I CAN JUST DRIVE YOU BACK.

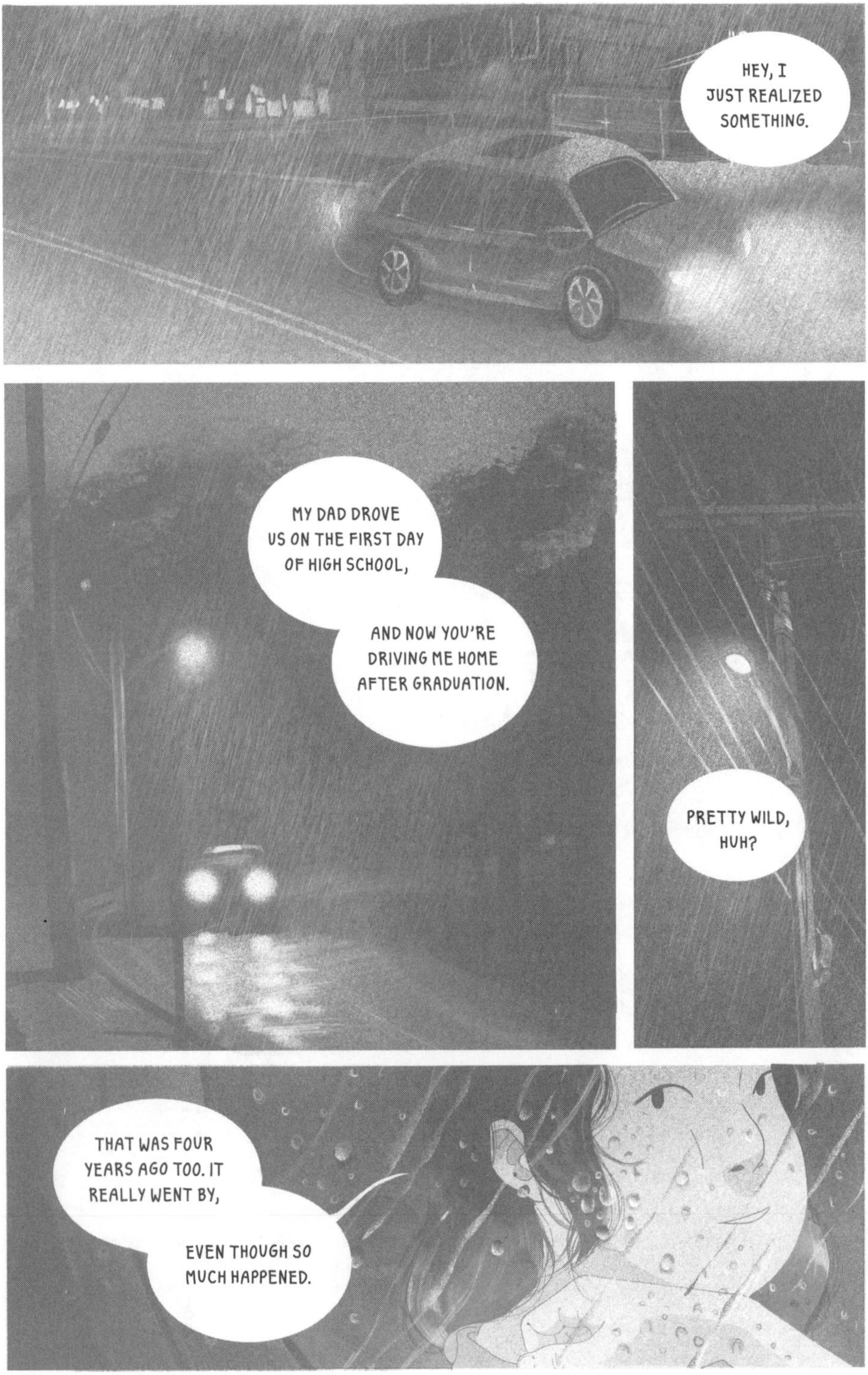
HEY, I JUST REALIZED SOMETHING.
MY DAD DROVE US ON THE FIRST DAY OF HIGH SCHOOL,
AND NOW YOU'RE DRIVING ME HOME AFTER GRADUATION.
PRETTY WILD, HUH?
THAT WAS FOUR YEARS AGO TOO. IT REALLY WENT BY,
EVEN THOUGH SO MUCH HAPPENED.

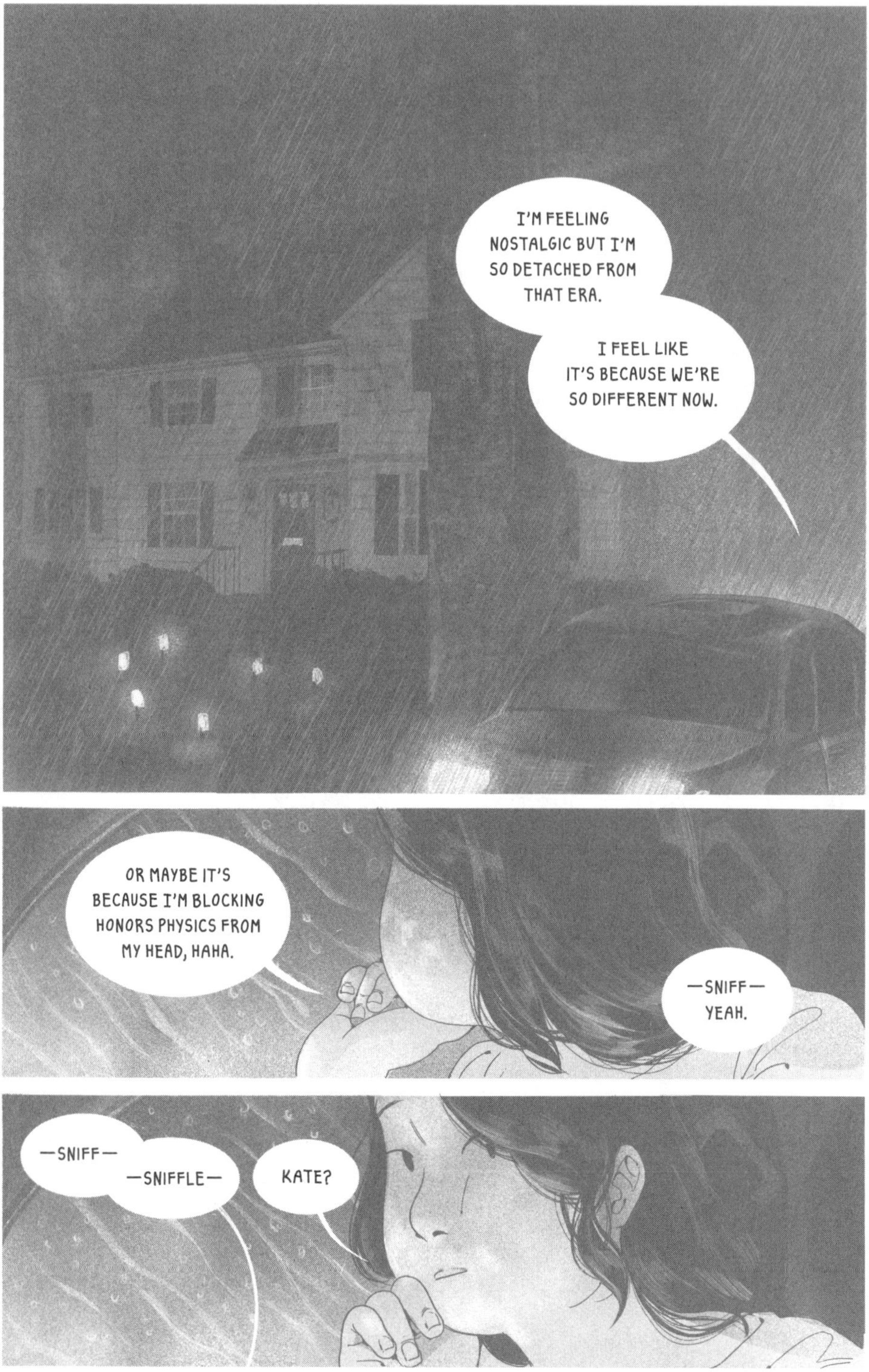
I'M FEELING NOSTALGIC BUT I'M SO DETACHED FROM THAT ERA.
I FEEL LIKE IT'S BECAUSE WE'RE SO DIFFERENT NOW.
OR MAYBE IT'S BECAUSE I'M BLOCKING HONORS PHYSICS FROM MY HEAD, HAHA.
—SNIFF— YEAH.
—SNIFF—
—SNIFFLE—
KATE?

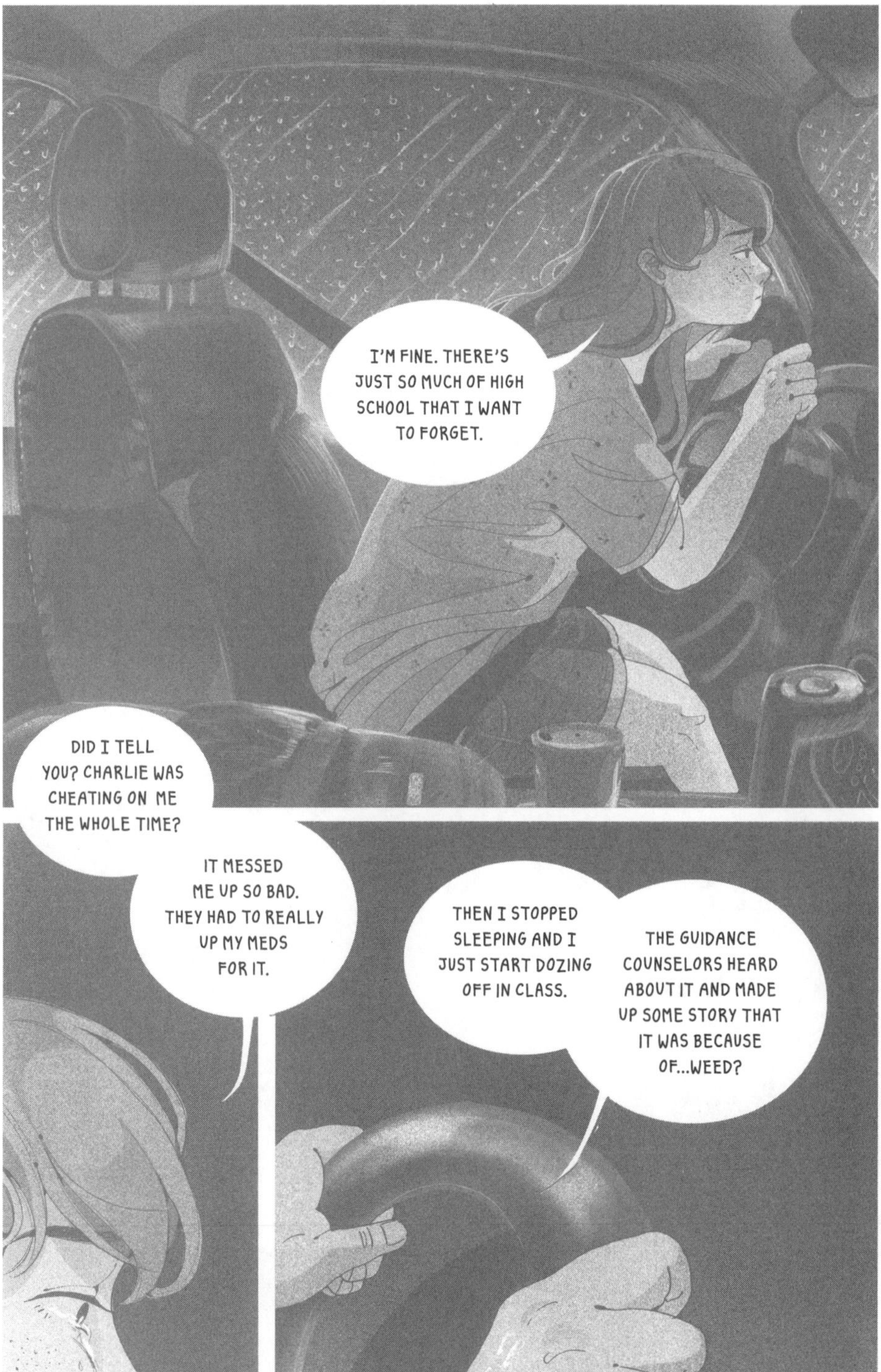

I'M FINE. THERE'S JUST SO MUCH OF HIGH SCHOOL THAT I WANT TO FORGET.
DID I TELL YOU? CHARLIE WAS CHEATING ON ME THE WHOLE TIME?
IT MESSED ME UP SO BAD. THEY HAD TO REALLY UP MY MEDS FOR IT.
THEN I STOPPED SLEEPING AND I JUST START DOZING OFF IN CLASS.
THE GUIDANCE COUNSELORS HEARD ABOUT IT AND MADE UP SOME STORY THAT IT WAS BECAUSE OF...WEED?

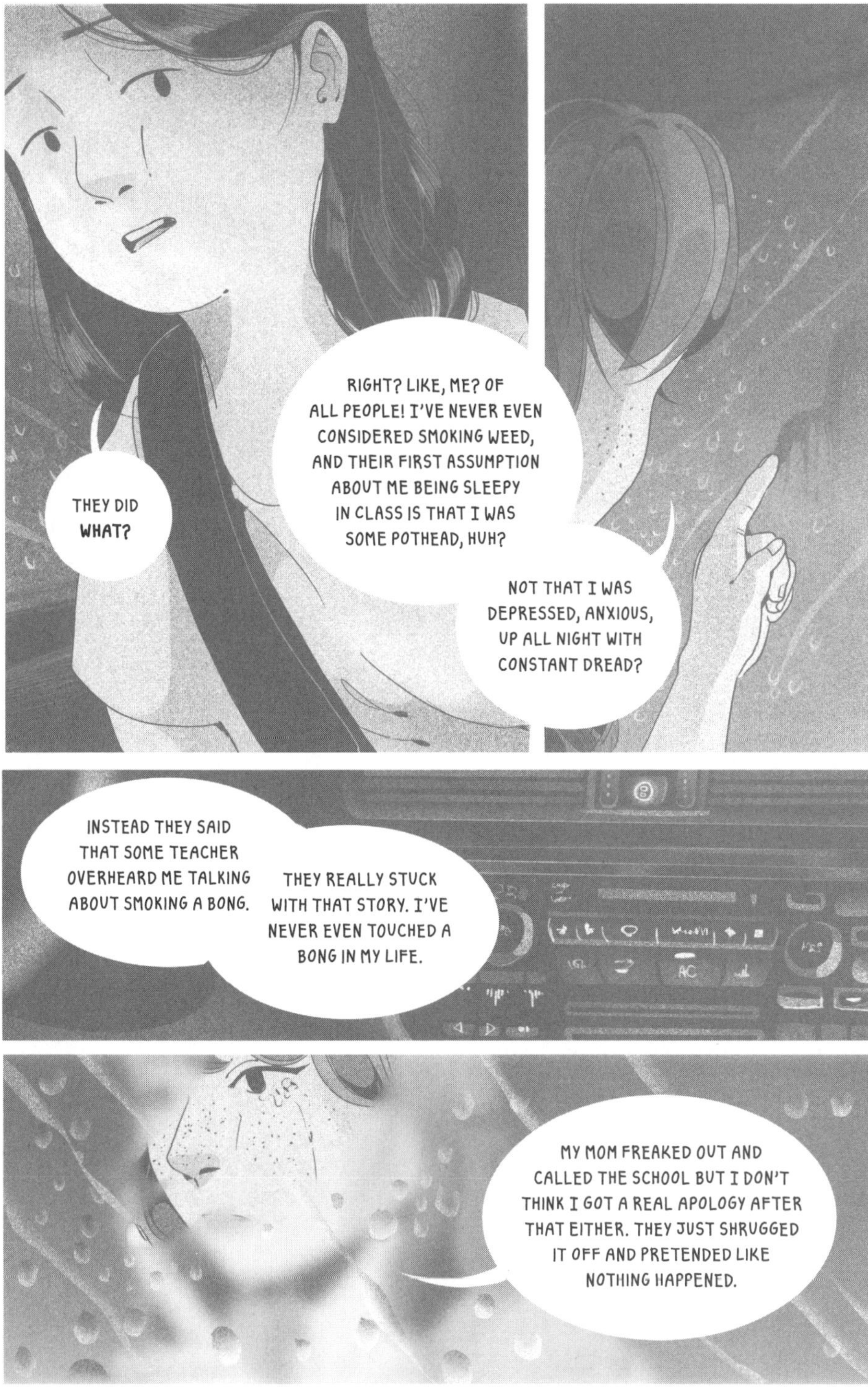

THEY DID WHAT?
RIGHT? LIKE, ME? OF ALL PEOPLE! I'VE NEVER EVEN CONSIDERED SMOKING WEED, AND THEIR FIRST ASSUMPTION ABOUT ME BEING SLEEPY IN CLASS IS THAT I WAS SOME POTHEAD, HUH?
NOT THAT I WAS DEPRESSED, ANXIOUS, UP ALL NIGHT WITH CONSTANT DREAD?
INSTEAD THEY SAID THAT SOME TEACHER OVERHEARD ME TALKING ABOUT SMOKING A BONG.
THEY REALLY STUCK WITH THAT STORY. I'VE NEVER EVEN TOUCHED A BONG IN MY LIFE.
AC
MY MOM FREAKED OUT AND CALLED THE SCHOOL BUT I DON'T THINK I GOT A REAL APOLOGY AFTER THAT EITHER. THEY JUST SHRUGGED IT OFF AND PRETENDED LIKE NOTHING HAPPENED.

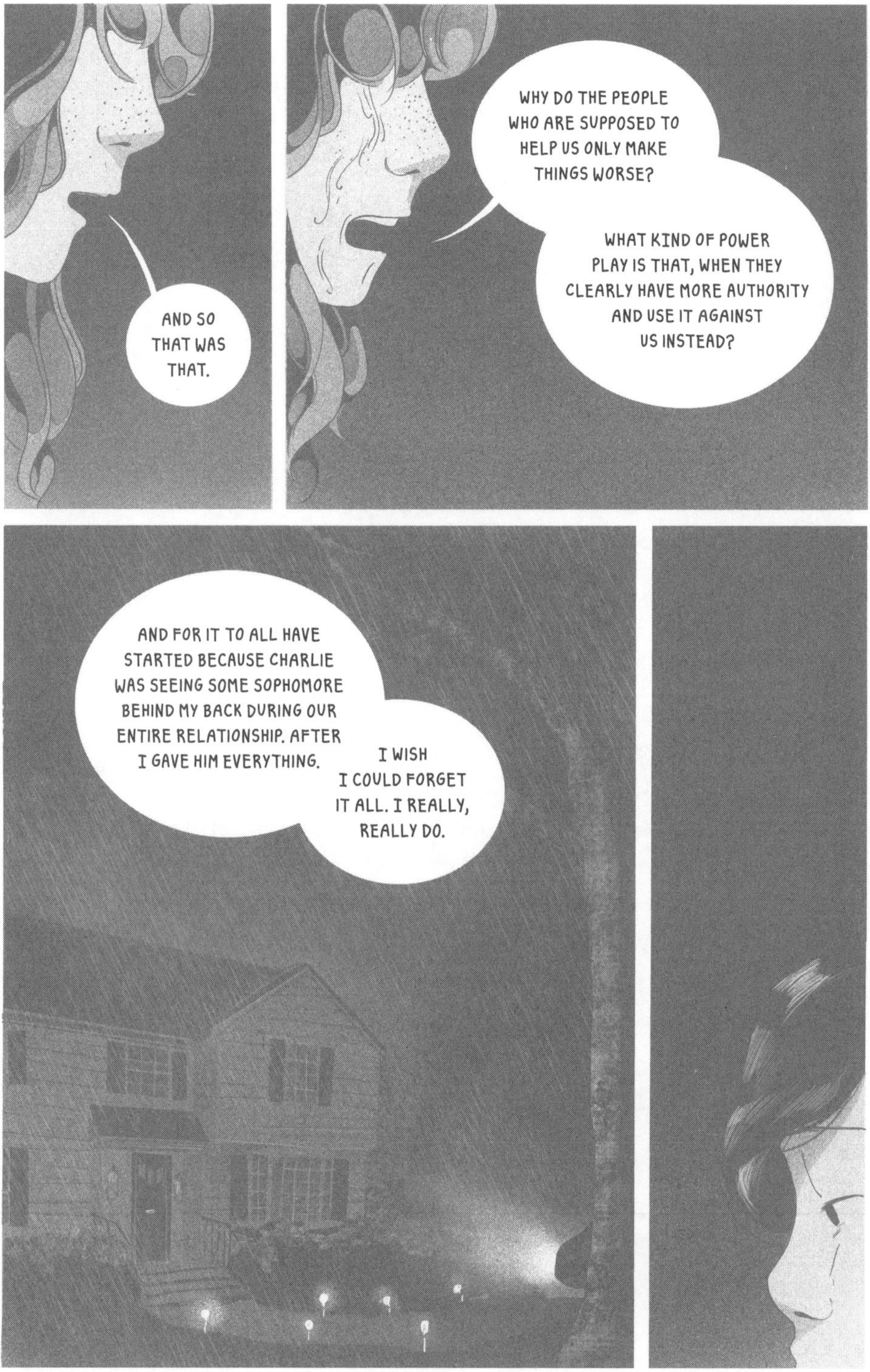
AND SO THAT WAS THAT.
WHY DO THE PEOPLE WHO ARE SUPPOSED TO HELP US ONLY MAKE THINGS WORSE?
WHAT KIND OF POWER PLAY IS THAT, WHEN THEY CLEARLY HAVE MORE AUTHORITY AND USE IT AGAINST US INSTEAD?
AND FOR IT TO ALL HAVE STARTED BECAUSE CHARLIE WAS SEEING SOME SOPHOMORE BEHIND MY BACK DURING OUR ENTIRE RELATIONSHIP. AFTER I GAVE HIM EVERYTHING.
I WISH I COULD FORGET IT ALL. I REALLY, REALLY DO.

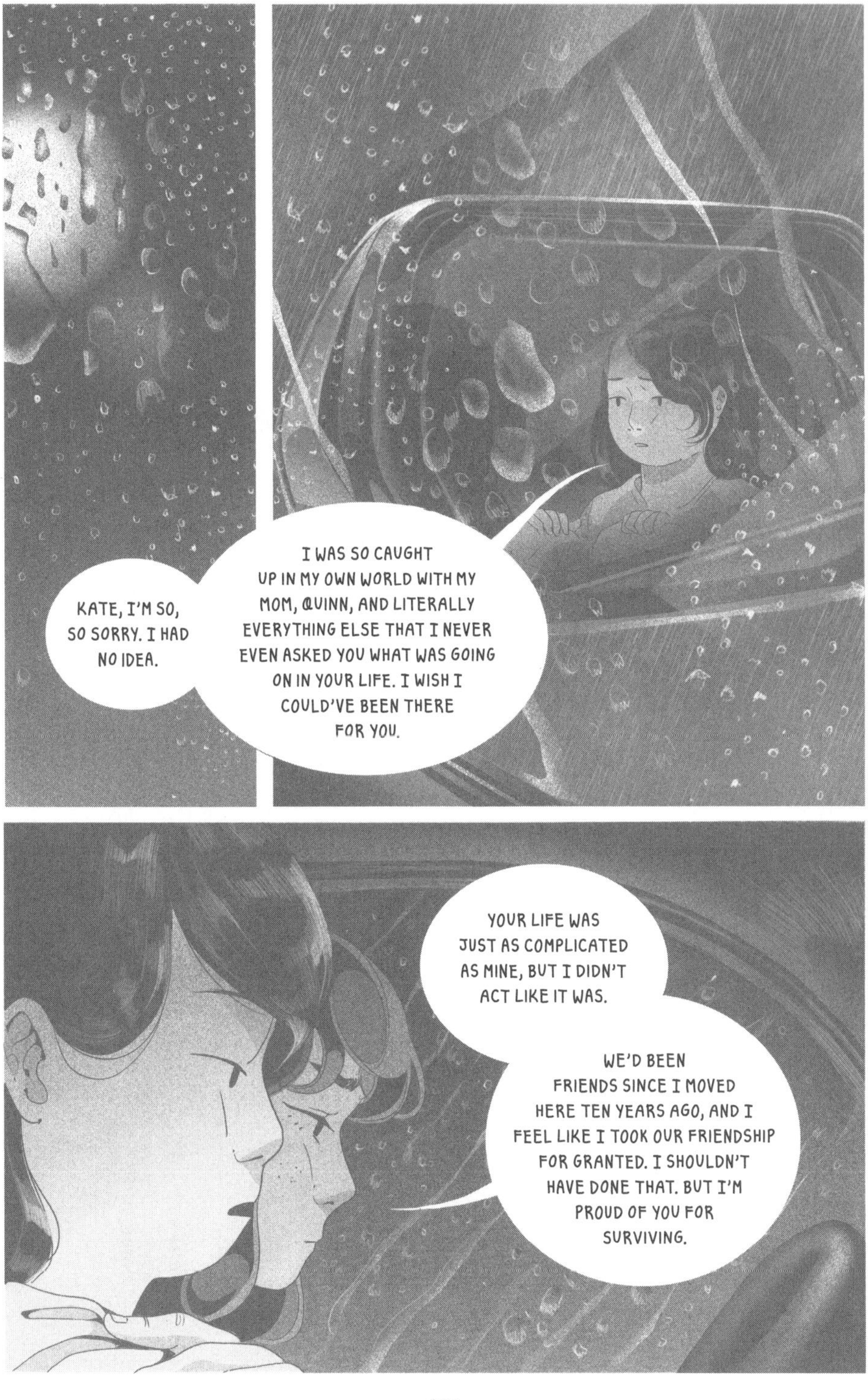
KATE, I'M SO, SO SORRY. I HAD NO IDEA.
I WAS SO CAUGHT UP IN MY OWN WORLD WITH MY MOM, QUINN, AND LITERALLY EVERYTHING ELSE THAT I NEVER EVEN ASKED YOU WHAT WAS GOING ON IN YOUR LIFE. I WISH I COULD'VE BEEN THERE FOR YOU.
YOUR LIFE WAS JUST AS COMPLICATED AS MINE, BUT I DIDN'T ACT LIKE IT WAS.
WE'D BEEN FRIENDS SINCE I MOVED HERE TEN YEARS AGO, AND I FEEL LIKE I TOOK OUR FRIENDSHIP FOR GRANTED. I SHOULDN'T HAVE DONE THAT. BUT I'M PROUD OF YOU FOR SURVIVING.

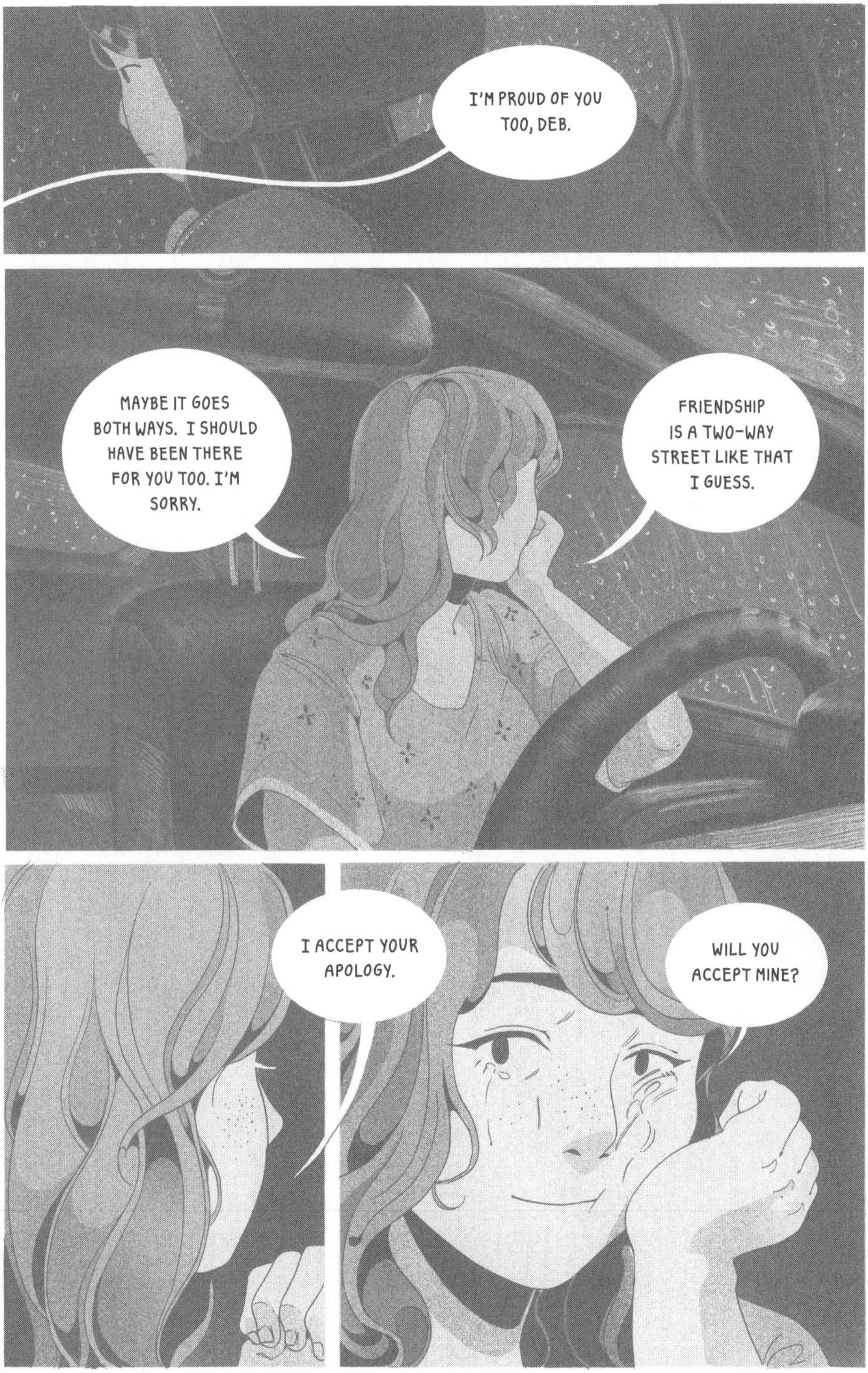
I'M PROUD OF YOU TOO, DEB.
MAYBE IT GOES BOTH WAYS. I SHOULD HAVE BEEN THERE FOR YOU TOO. I'M SORRY.
FRIENDSHIP IS A TWO-WAY STREET LIKE THAT I GUESS.
I ACCEPT YOUR APOLOGY.
WILL YOU ACCEPT MINE?

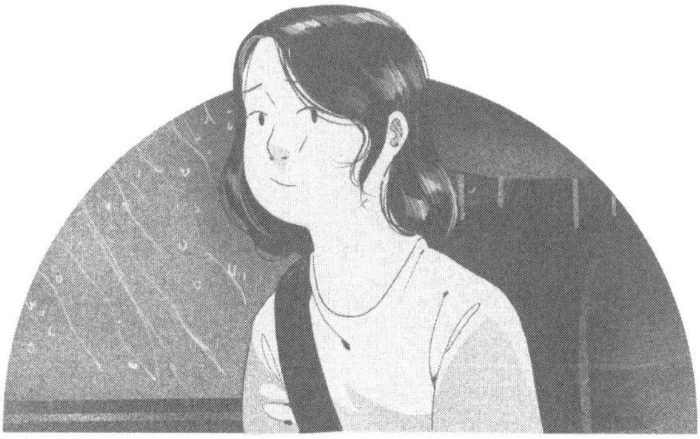

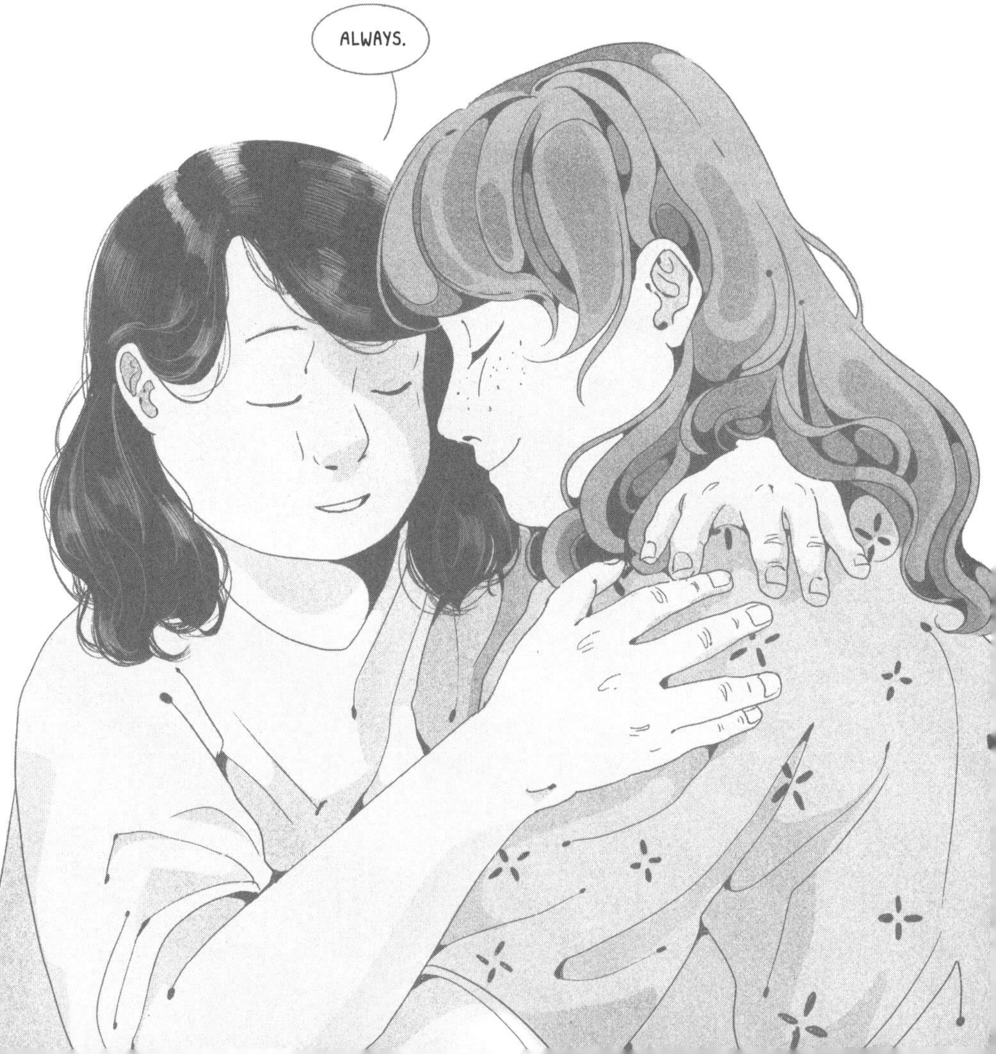
ALWAYS.

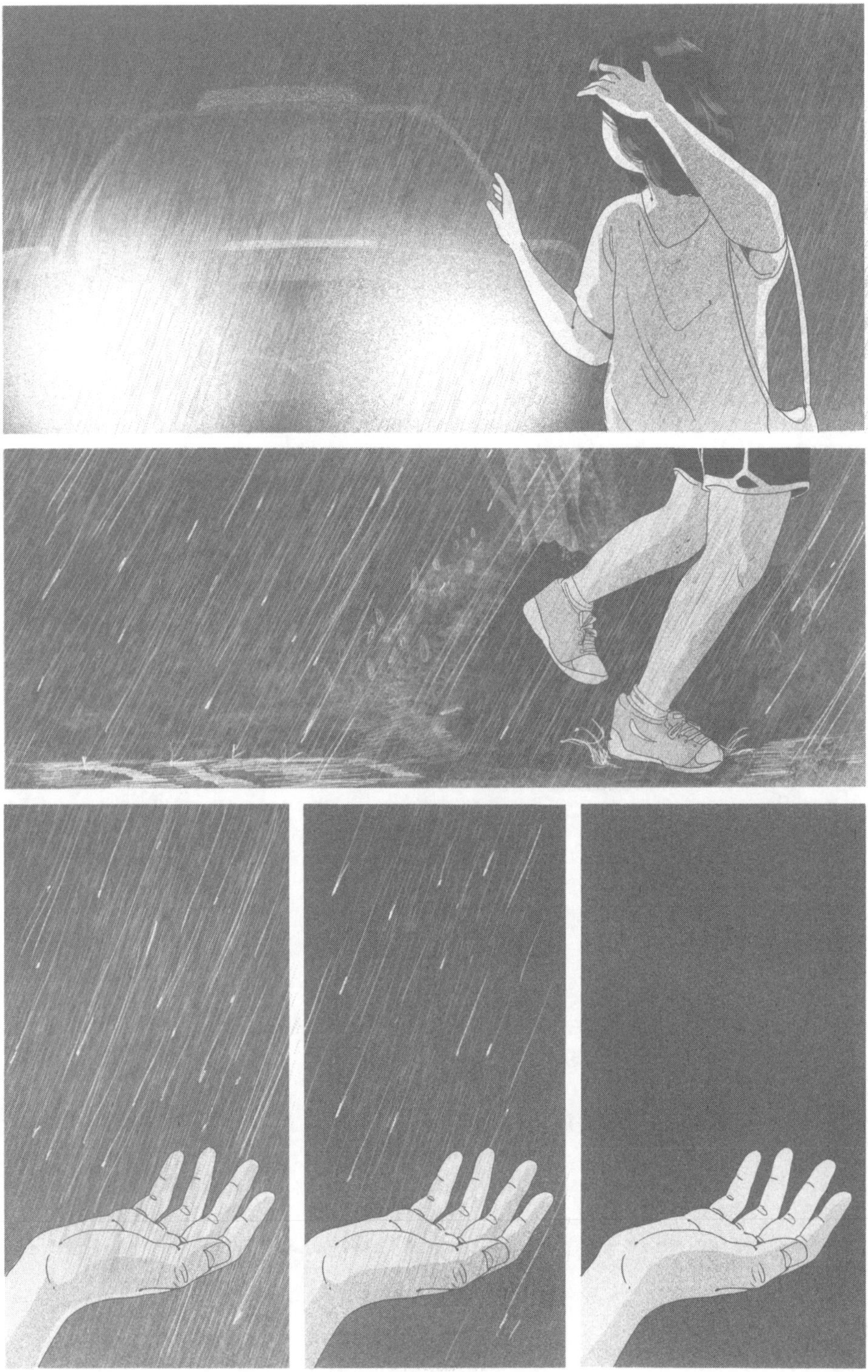

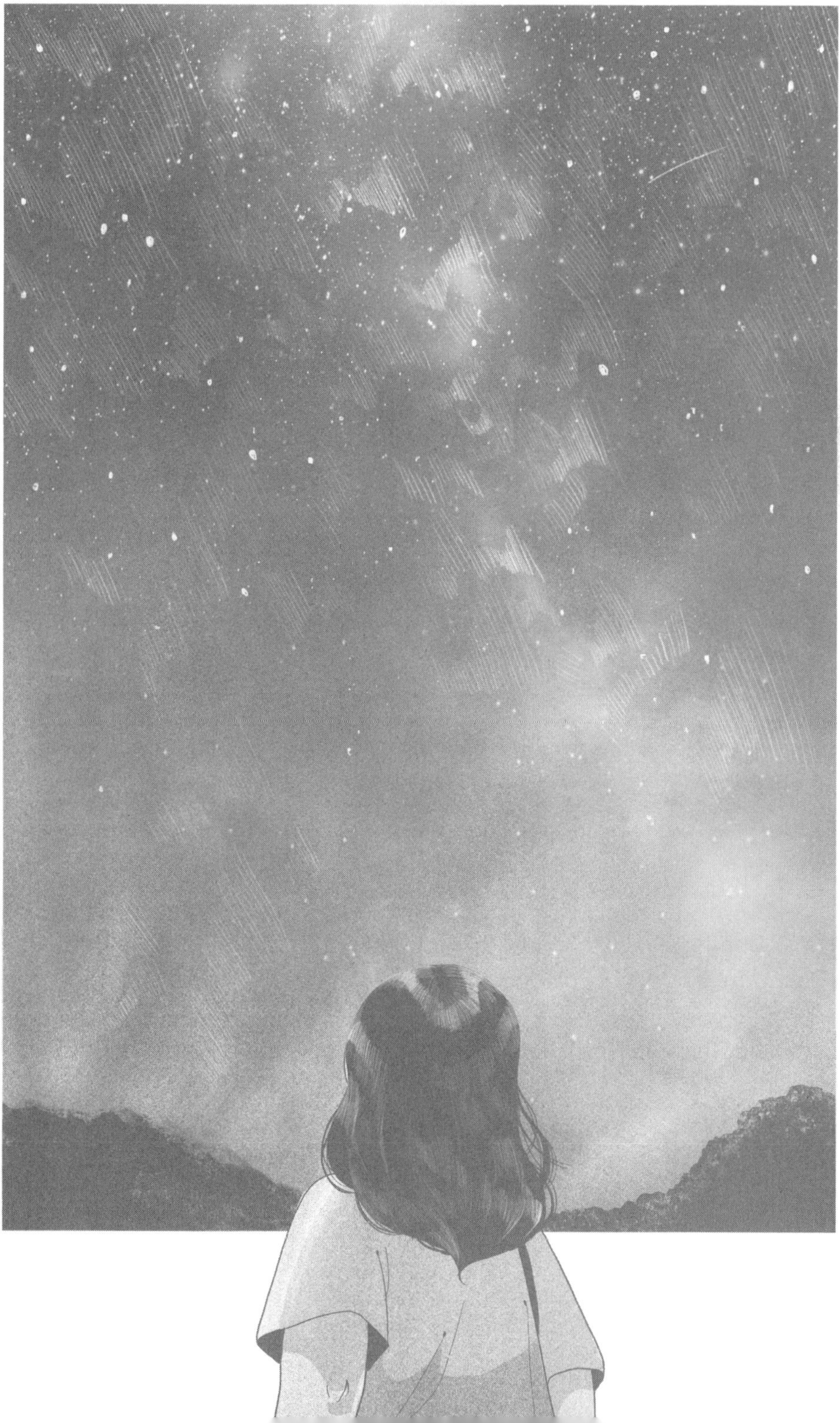

오

Part 5

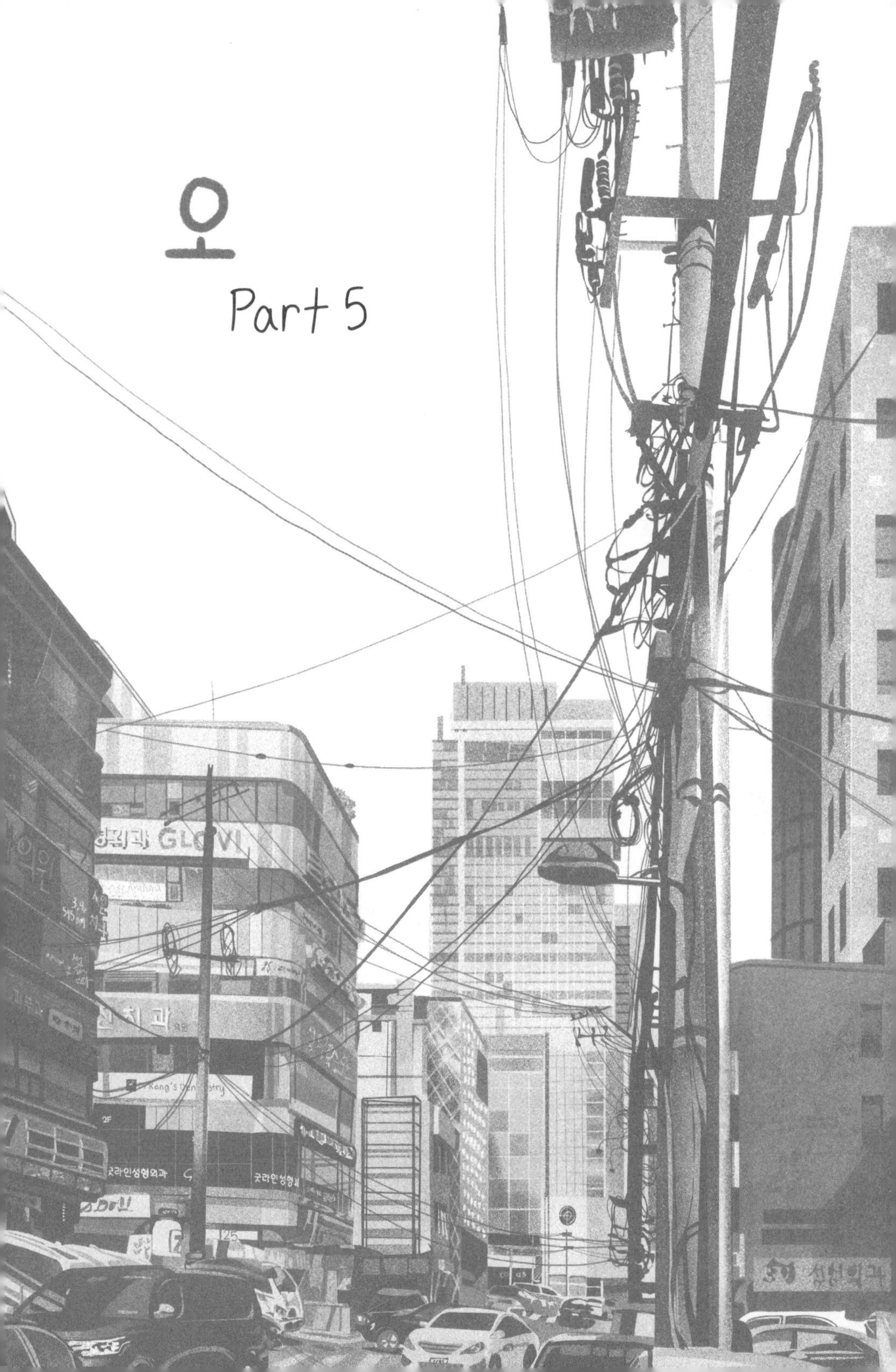
GLOVI

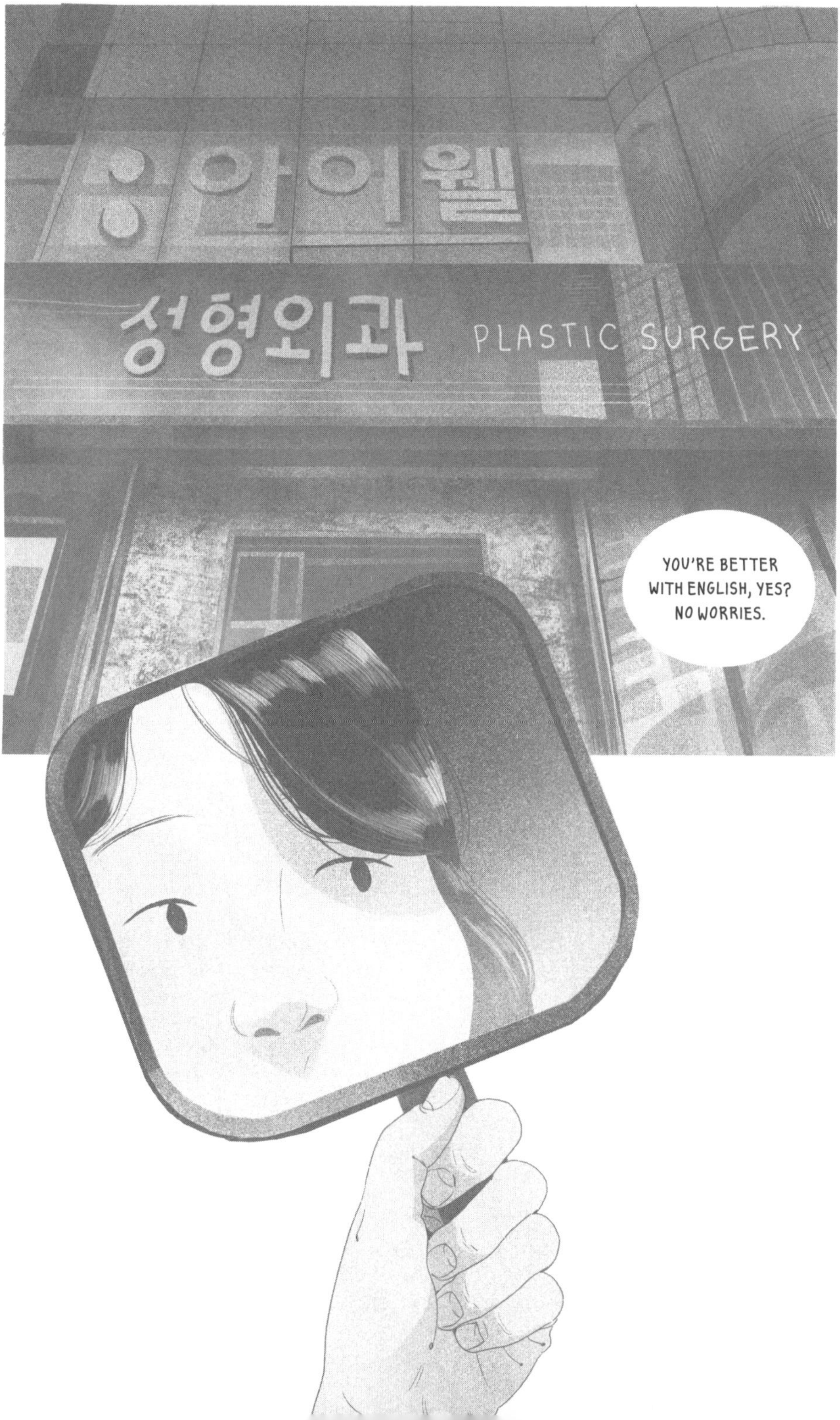

아이웰
성형외과 PLASTIC SURGERY
YOU'RE BETTER WITH ENGLISH, YES? NO WORRIES.

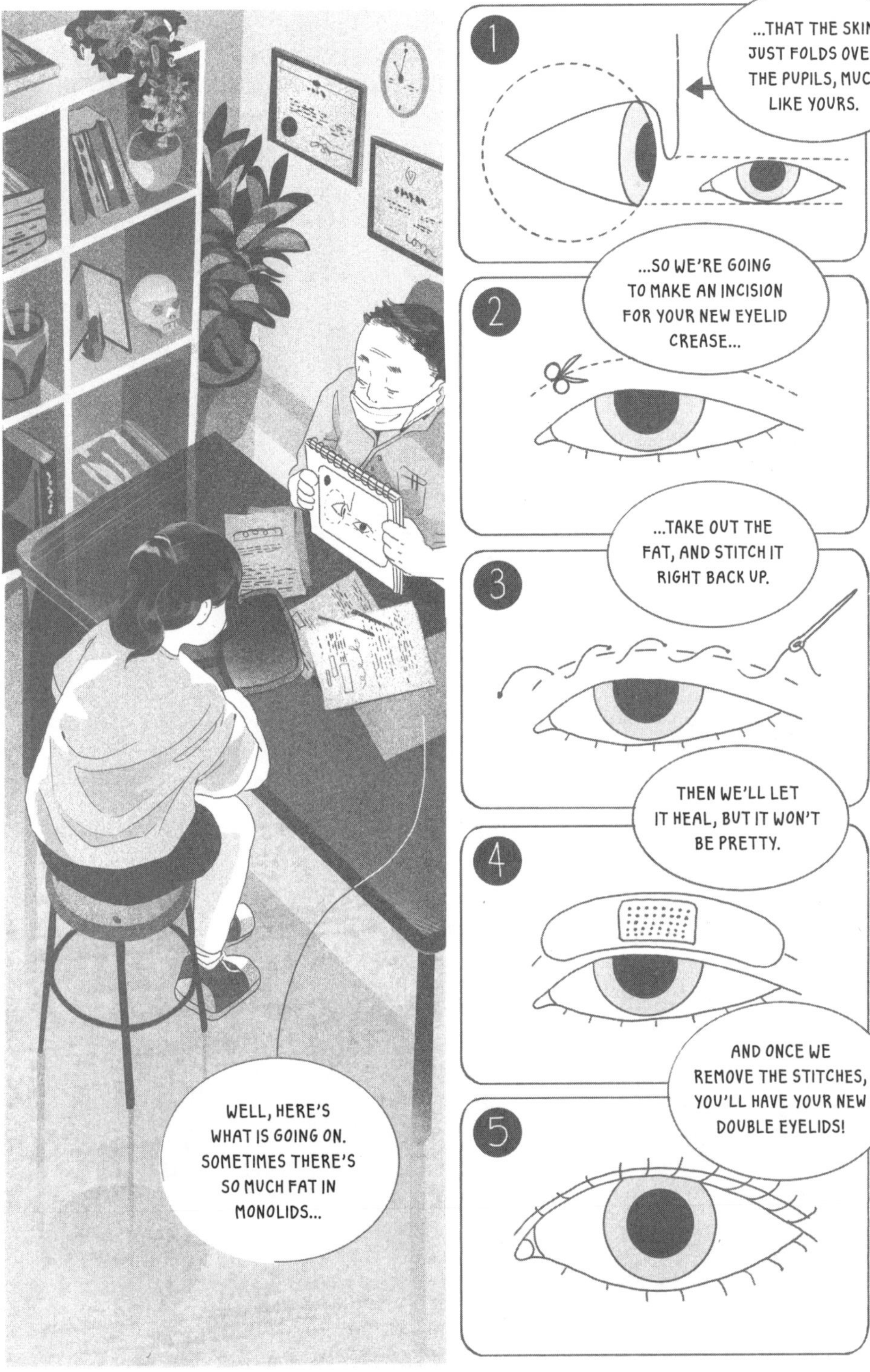

WELL, HERE'S WHAT IS GOING ON. SOMETIMES THERE'S SO MUCH FAT IN MONOLIDS...
1
...THAT THE SKIN JUST FOLDS OVER THE PUPILS, MUCH LIKE YOURS.
2
...SO WE'RE GOING TO MAKE AN INCISION FOR YOUR NEW EYELID CREASE...
3
...TAKE OUT THE FAT, AND STITCH IT RIGHT BACK UP.
4
THEN WE'LL LET IT HEAL, BUT IT WON'T BE PRETTY.
5
AND ONCE WE REMOVE THE STITCHES, YOU'LL HAVE YOUR NEW DOUBLE EYELIDS!

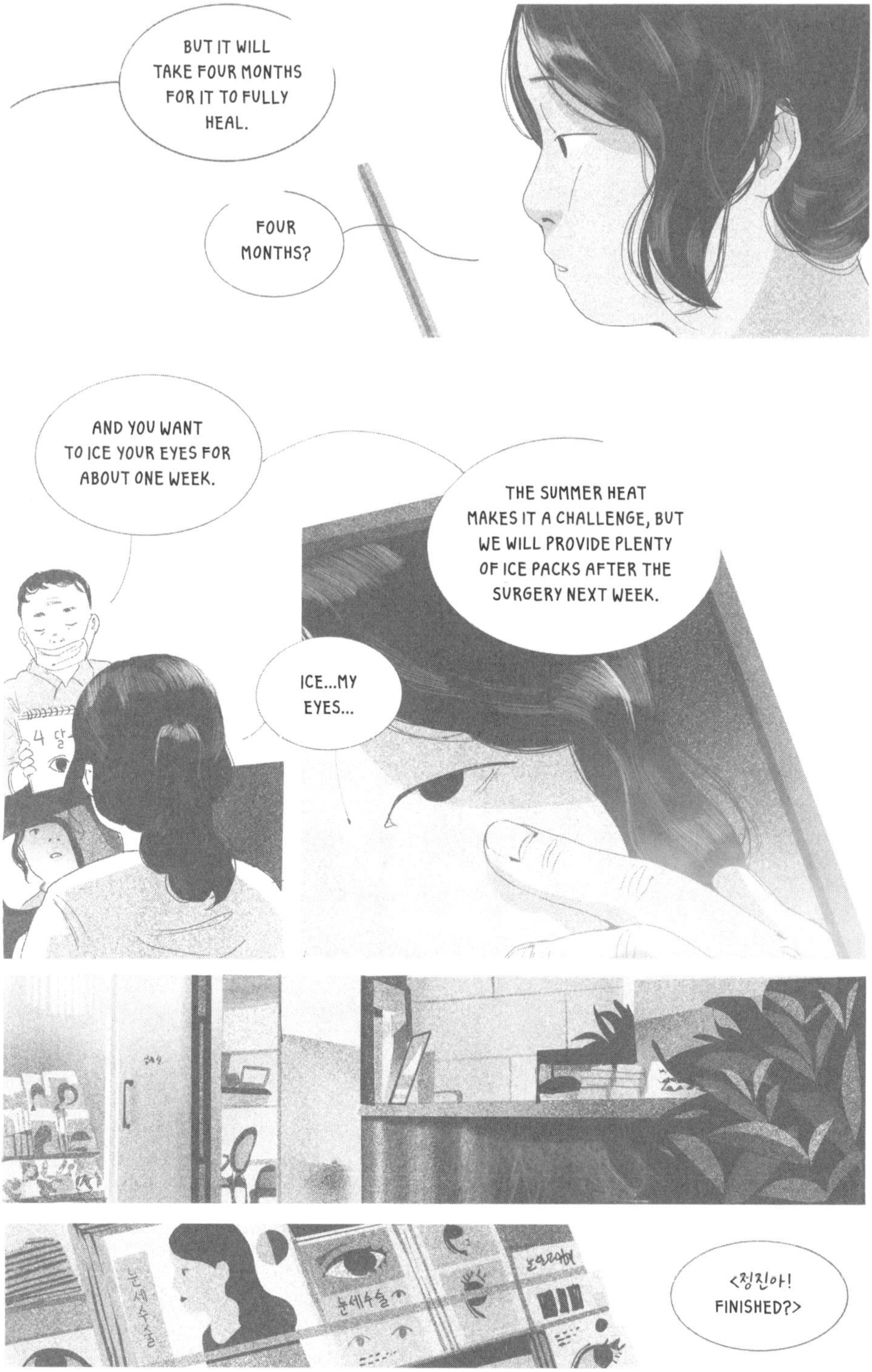
BUT IT WILL TAKE FOUR MONTHS FOR IT TO FULLY HEAL.
FOUR MONTHS?
AND YOU WANT TO ICE YOUR EYES FOR ABOUT ONE WEEK.
THE SUMMER HEAT MAKES IT A CHALLENGE, BUT WE WILL PROVIDE PLENTY OF ICE PACKS AFTER THE SURGERY NEXT WEEK.
ICE...MY EYES...
<정진아! FINISHED?>

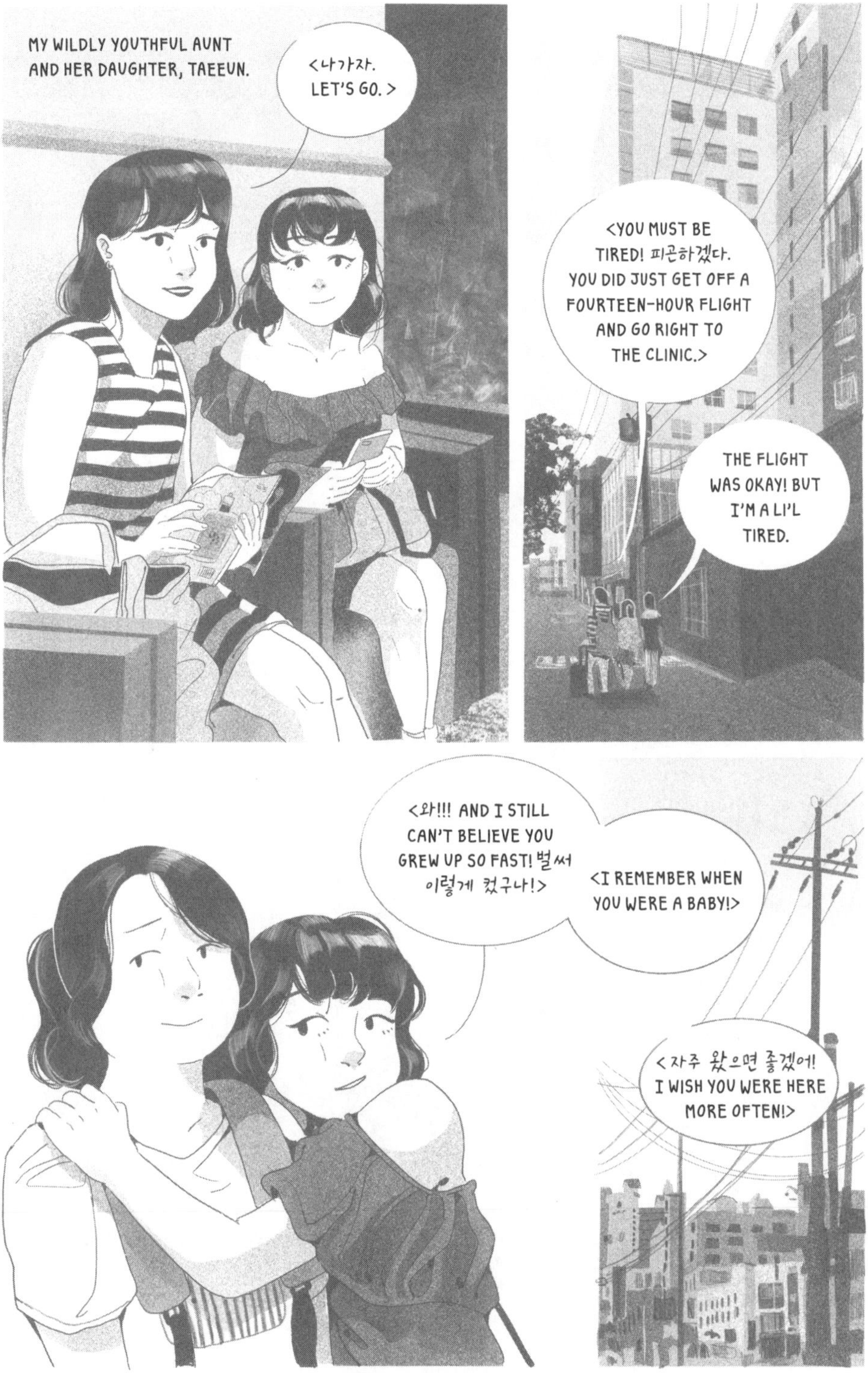
MY WILDLY YOUTHFUL AUNT AND HER DAUGHTER, TAEEUN.
<나가자. LET'S GO.>
<YOU MUST BE TIRED! 피곤하겠다. YOU DID JUST GET OFF A FOURTEEN-HOUR FLIGHT AND GO RIGHT TO THE CLINIC.>
THE FLIGHT WAS OKAY! BUT I'M A LI'L TIRED.
<와!!! AND I STILL CAN'T BELIEVE YOU GREW UP SO FAST! 벌써 이렇게 컸구나!>
<I REMEMBER WHEN YOU WERE A BABY!>
<자주 왔으면 좋겠어! I WISH YOU WERE HERE MORE OFTEN!>

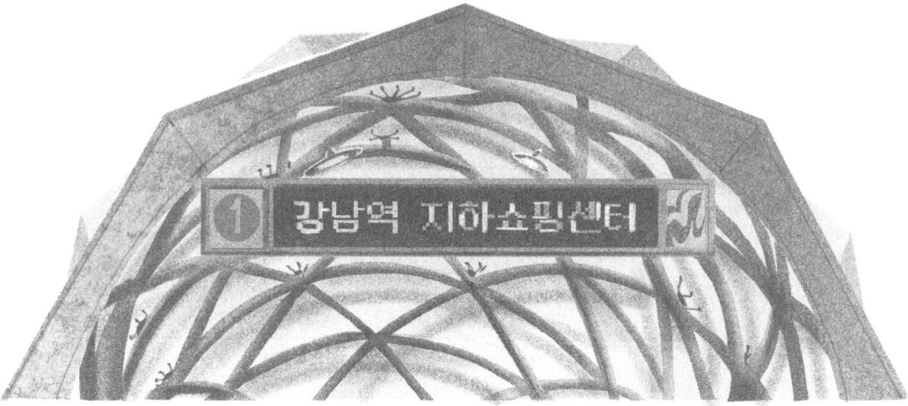
1
강남역 지하쇼핑센터

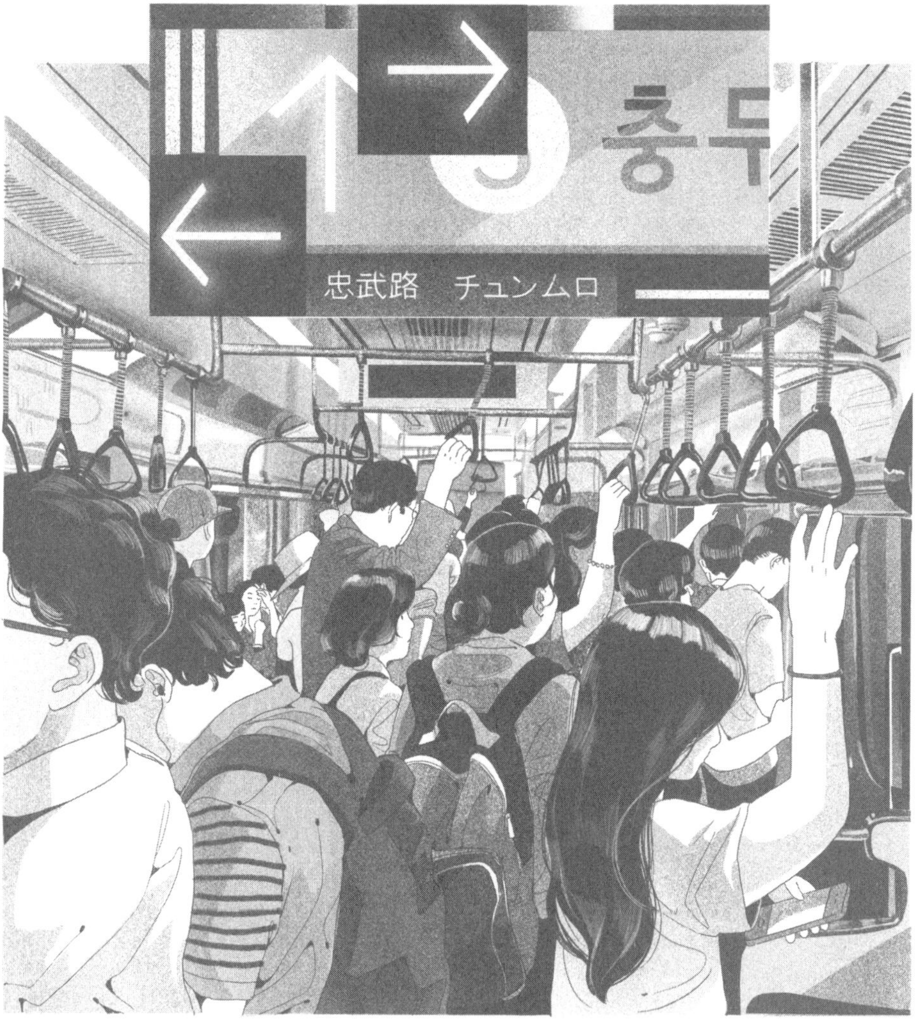
충무
忠武路　チュンムロ

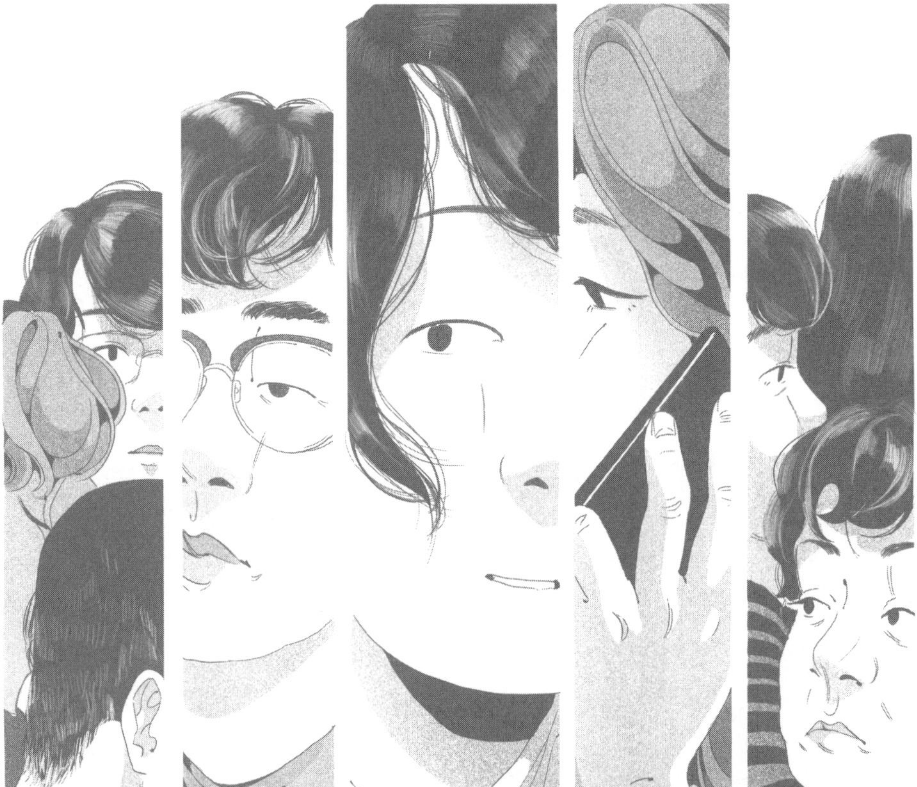

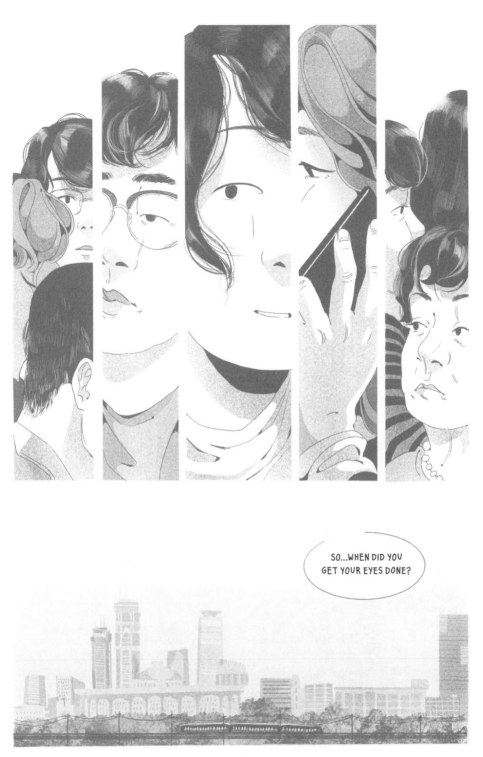

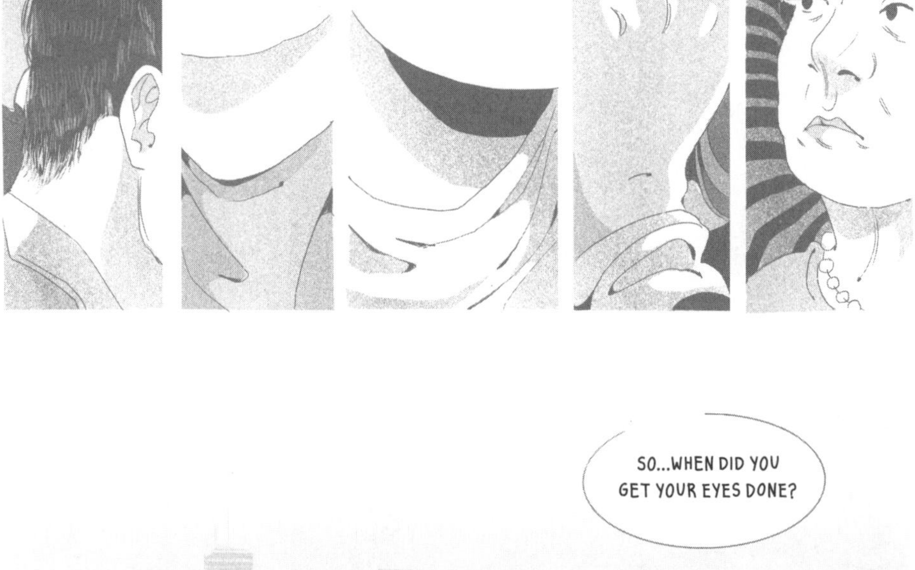
SO...WHEN DID YOU GET YOUR EYES DONE?

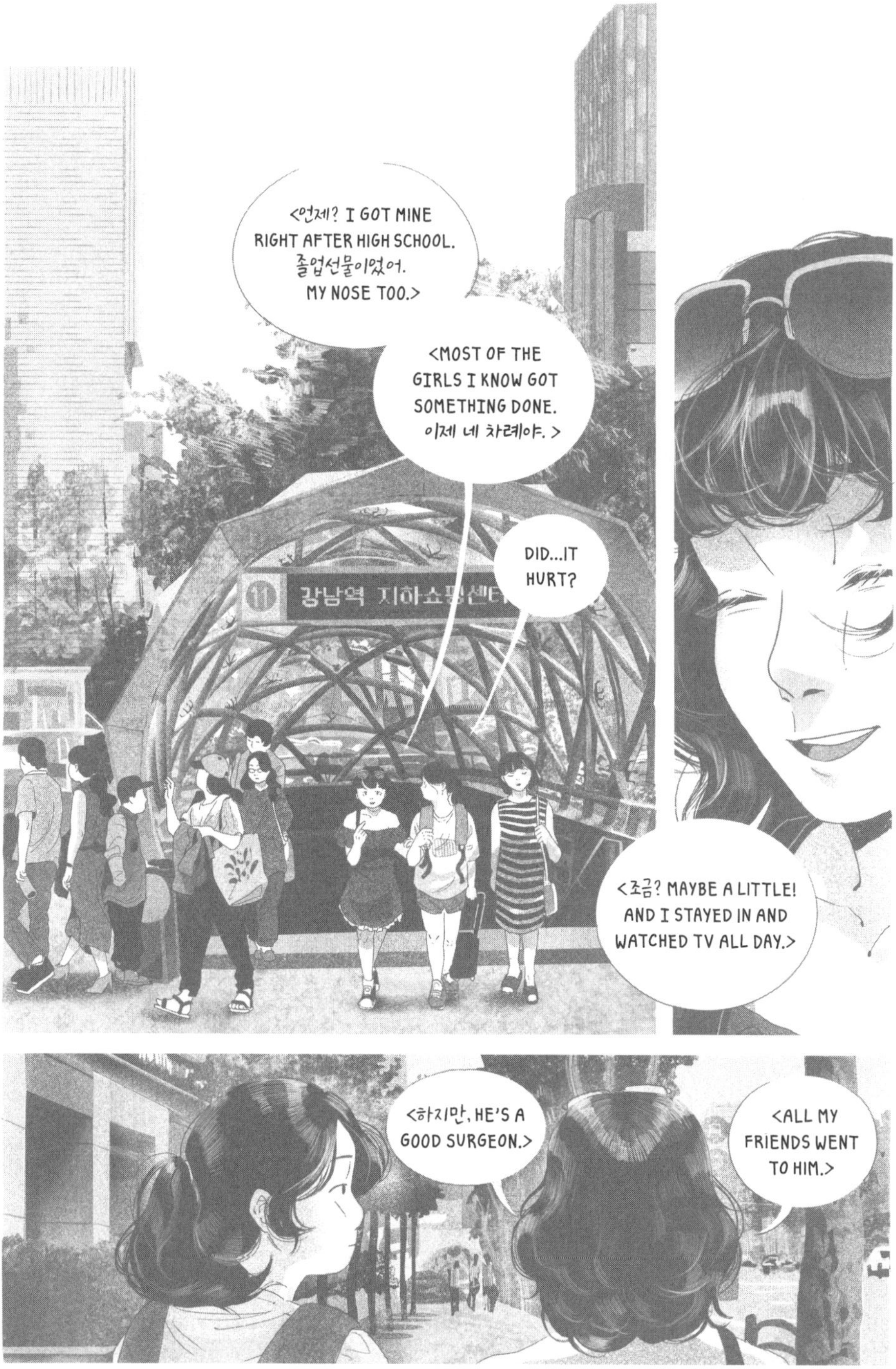
<언제? I GOT MINE RIGHT AFTER HIGH SCHOOL. 졸업선물이었어. MY NOSE TOO.>
<MOST OF THE GIRLS I KNOW GOT SOMETHING DONE. 이제 네 차례야.>
DID...IT HURT?
강남역 지하쇼핑센터
<조금? MAYBE A LITTLE! AND I STAYED IN AND WATCHED TV ALL DAY.>
<하지만, HE'S A GOOD SURGEON.>
<ALL MY FRIENDS WENT TO HIM.>

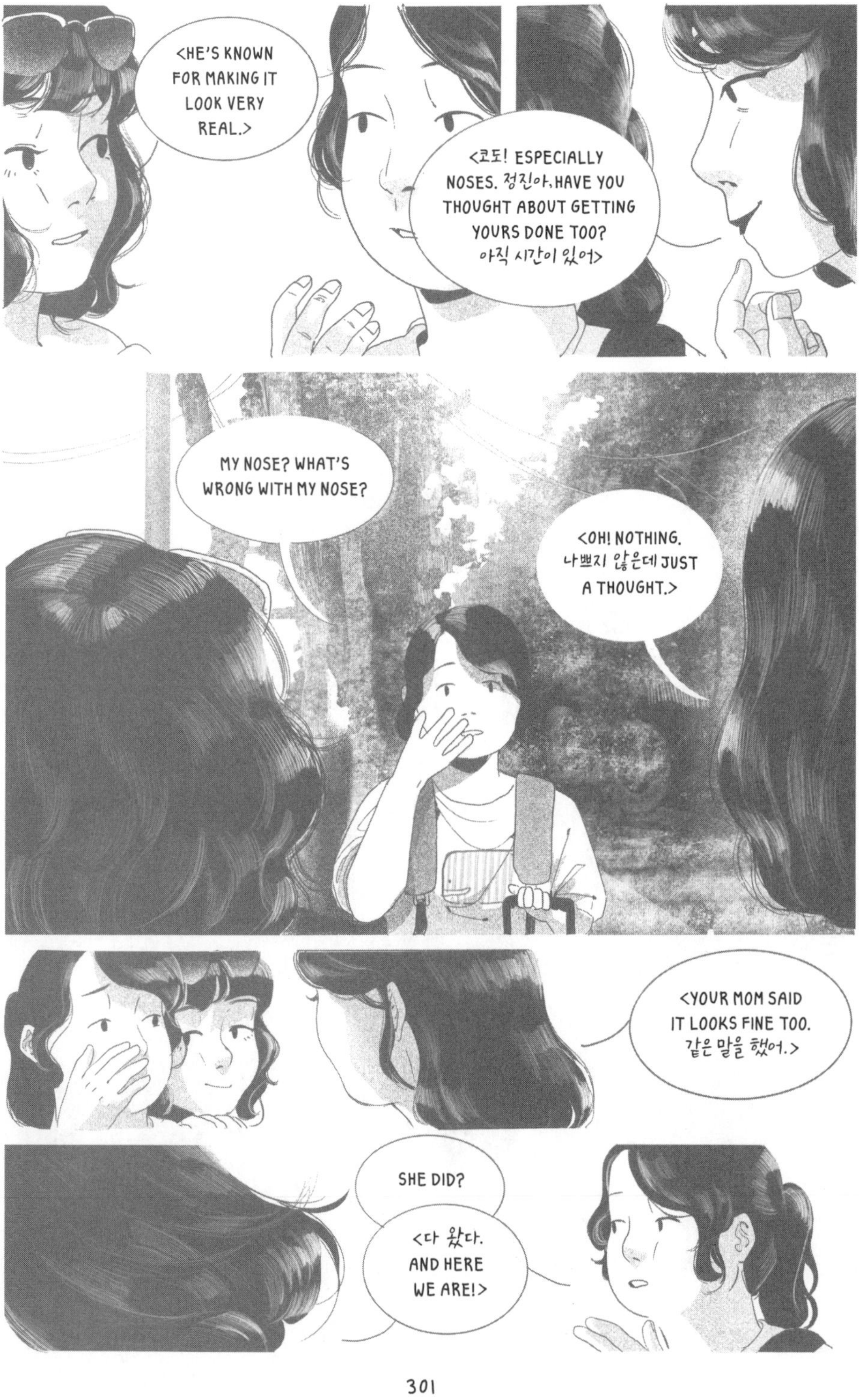

<HE'S KNOWN FOR MAKING IT LOOK VERY REAL.>
<코도! ESPECIALLY NOSES. 정진아, HAVE YOU THOUGHT ABOUT GETTING YOURS DONE TOO? 아직 시간이 있어>
MY NOSE? WHAT'S WRONG WITH MY NOSE?
<OH! NOTHING. 나쁘지 않은데 JUST A THOUGHT.>
<YOUR MOM SAID IT LOOKS FINE TOO. 같은 말을 했어.>
SHE DID?
<다 왔다. AND HERE WE ARE!>

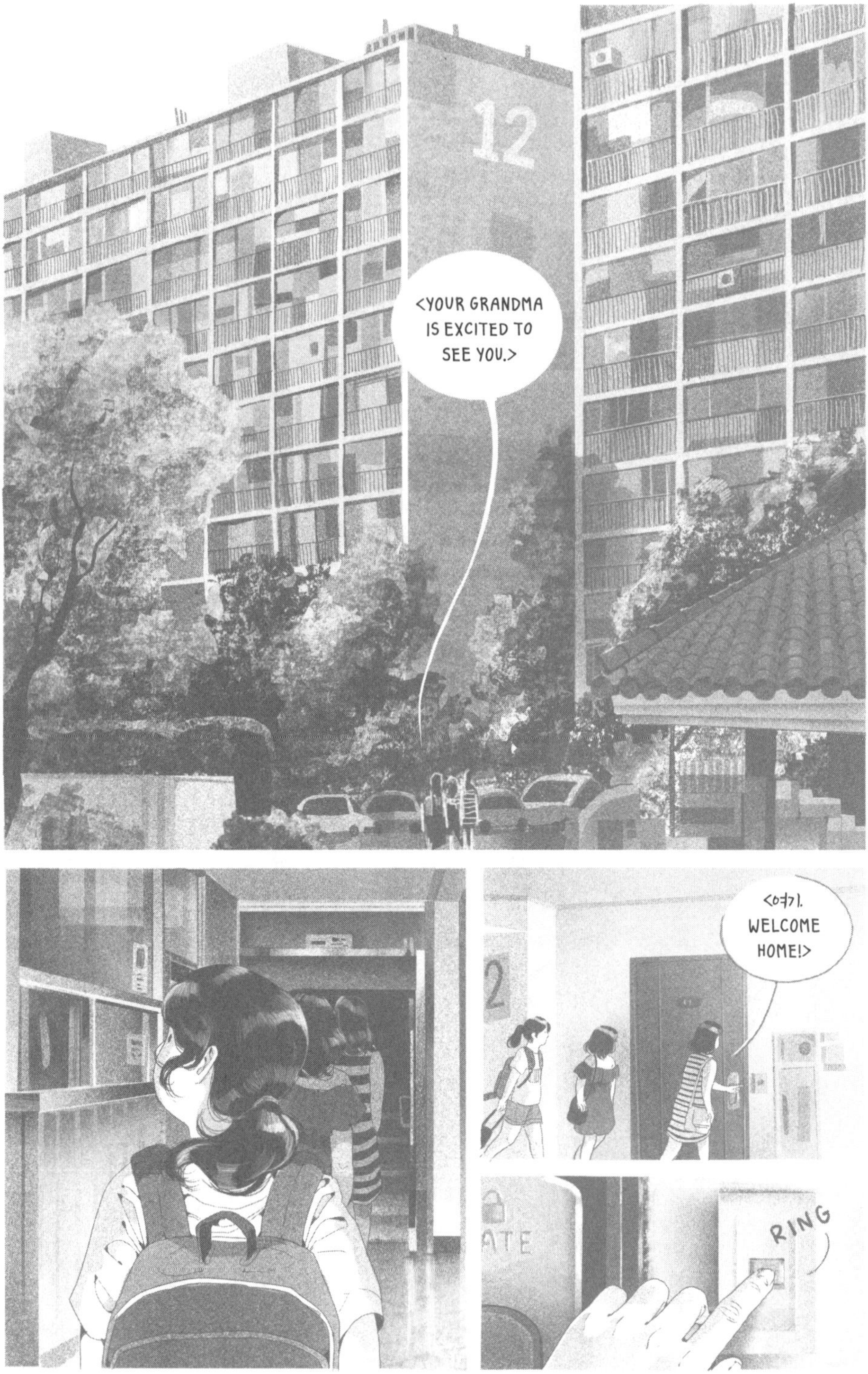
<YOUR GRANDMA IS EXCITED TO SEE YOU.>
<여기. WELCOME HOME!>
RING

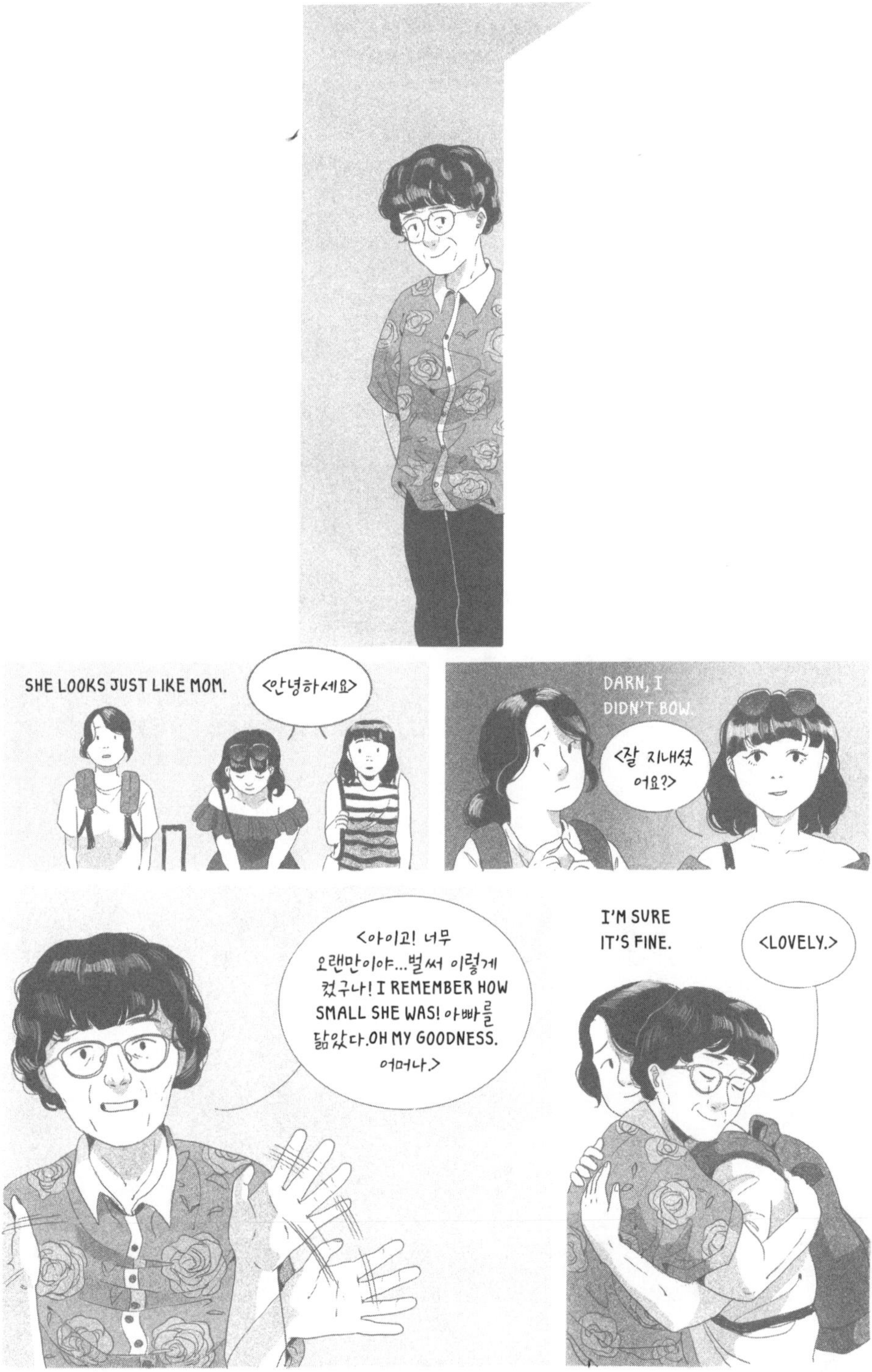
SHE LOOKS JUST LIKE MOM.
<안녕하세요>
DARN, I DIDN'T BOW.
<잘 지내셨어요?>
<아이고! 너무 오랜만이야...벌써 이렇게 컸구나! I REMEMBER HOW SMALL SHE WAS! 아빠를 닮았다.OH MY GOODNESS. 어머나.>
I'M SURE IT'S FINE.
<LOVELY.>

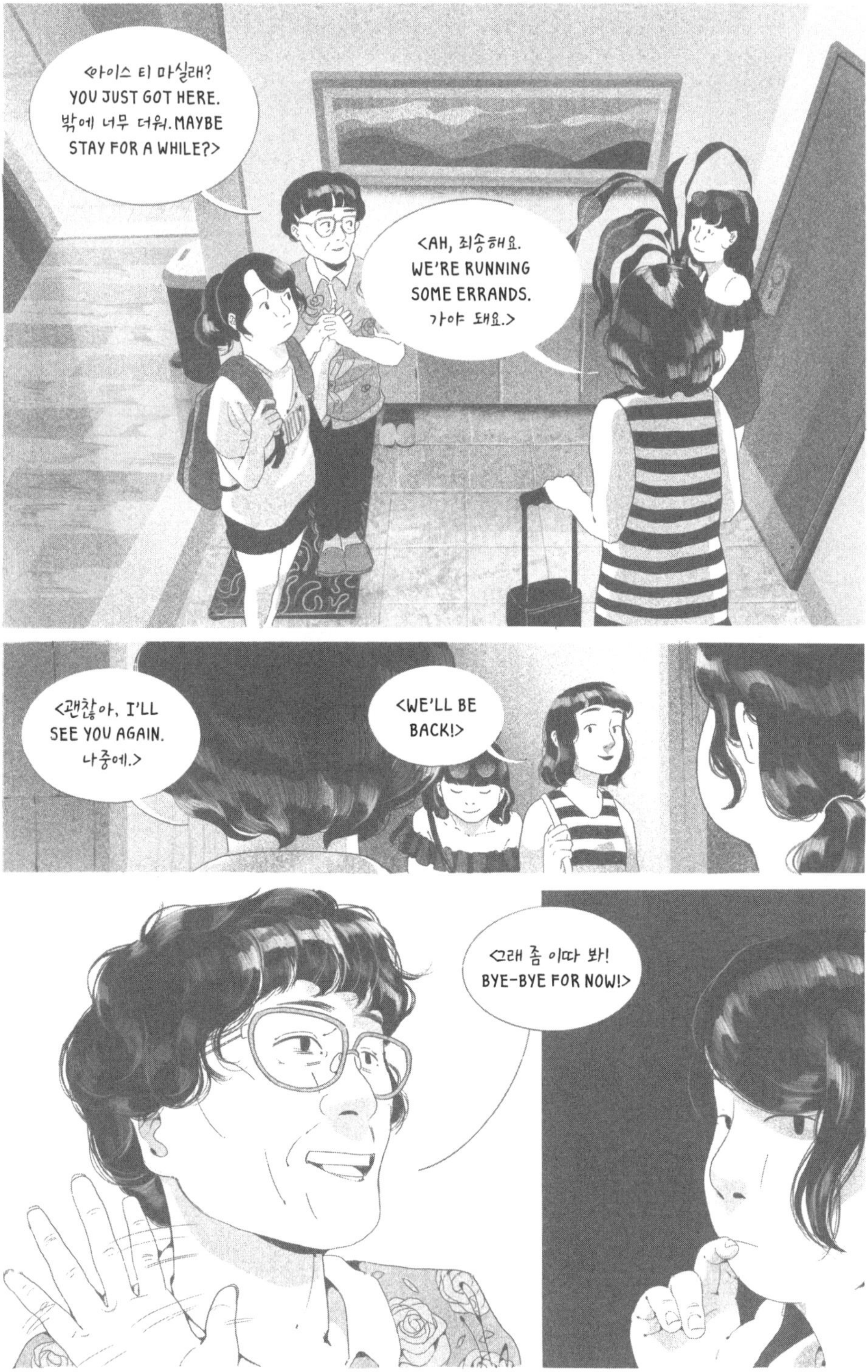
<아이스 티 마실래? YOU JUST GOT HERE. 밖에 너무 더워. MAYBE STAY FOR A WHILE?>
<AH, 죄송해요. WE'RE RUNNING SOME ERRANDS. 가야 돼요.>
<괜찮아, I'LL SEE YOU AGAIN. 나중에.>
<WE'LL BE BACK!>
<그래 좀 이따 봐! BYE-BYE FOR NOW!>

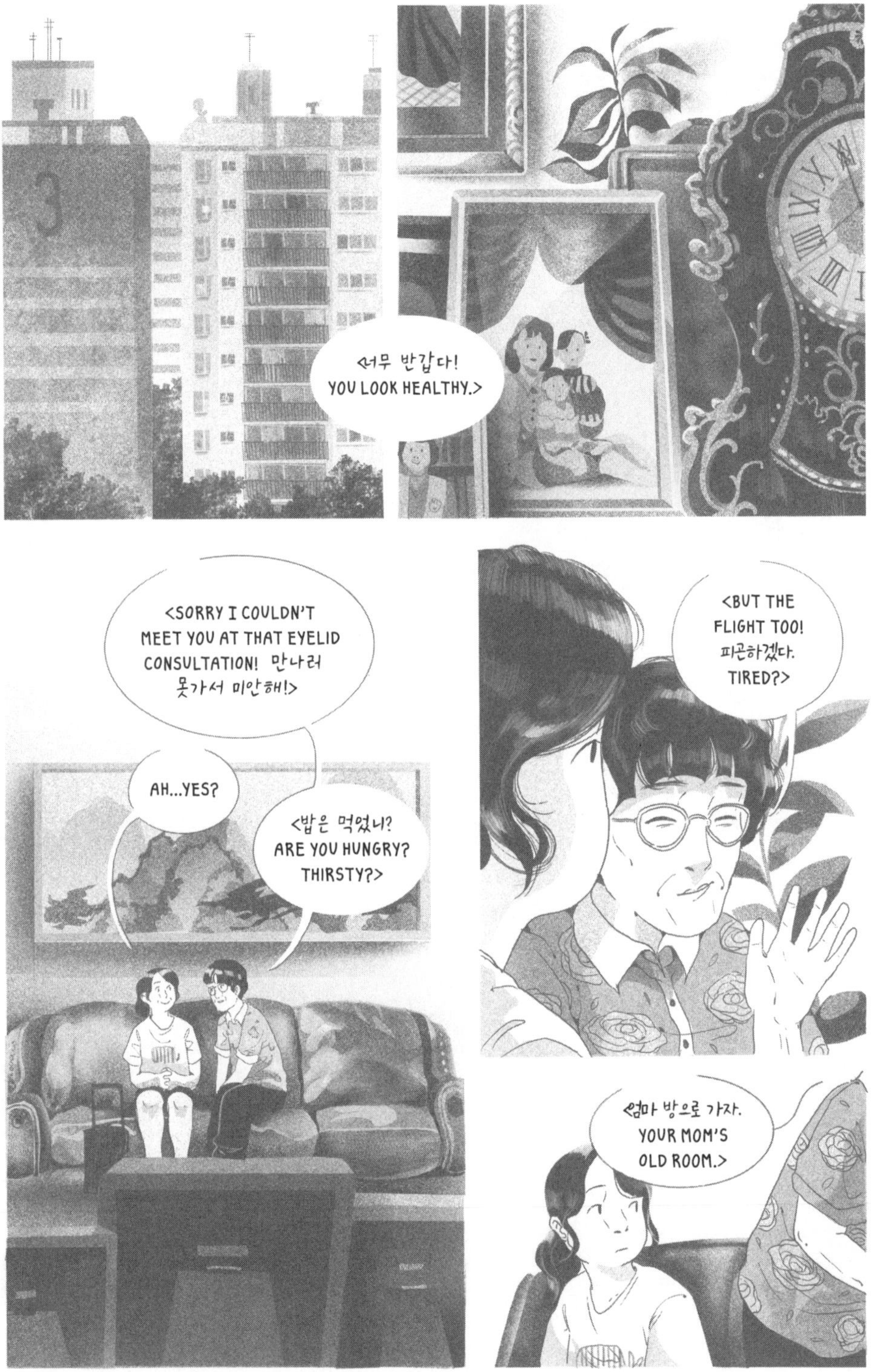
<너무 반갑다! YOU LOOK HEALTHY.>
<SORRY I COULDN'T MEET YOU AT THAT EYELID CONSULTATION! 만나러 못가서 미안해!>
AH...YES?
<밥은 먹었니? ARE YOU HUNGRY? THIRSTY?>
<BUT THE FLIGHT TOO! 피곤하겠다. TIRED?>
<엄마 방으로 가자. YOUR MOM'S OLD ROOM.>

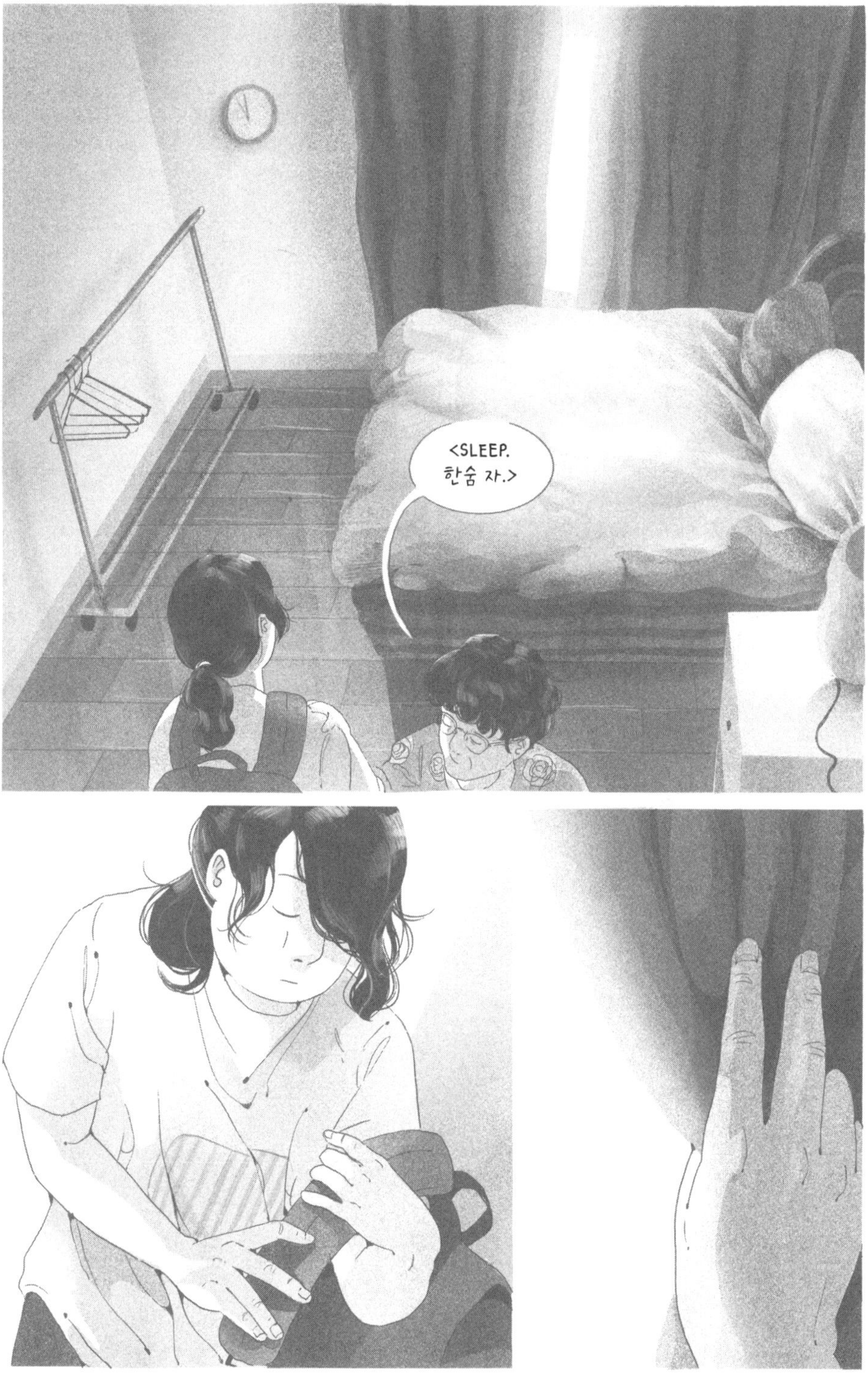
<SLEEP. 한숨 자.>

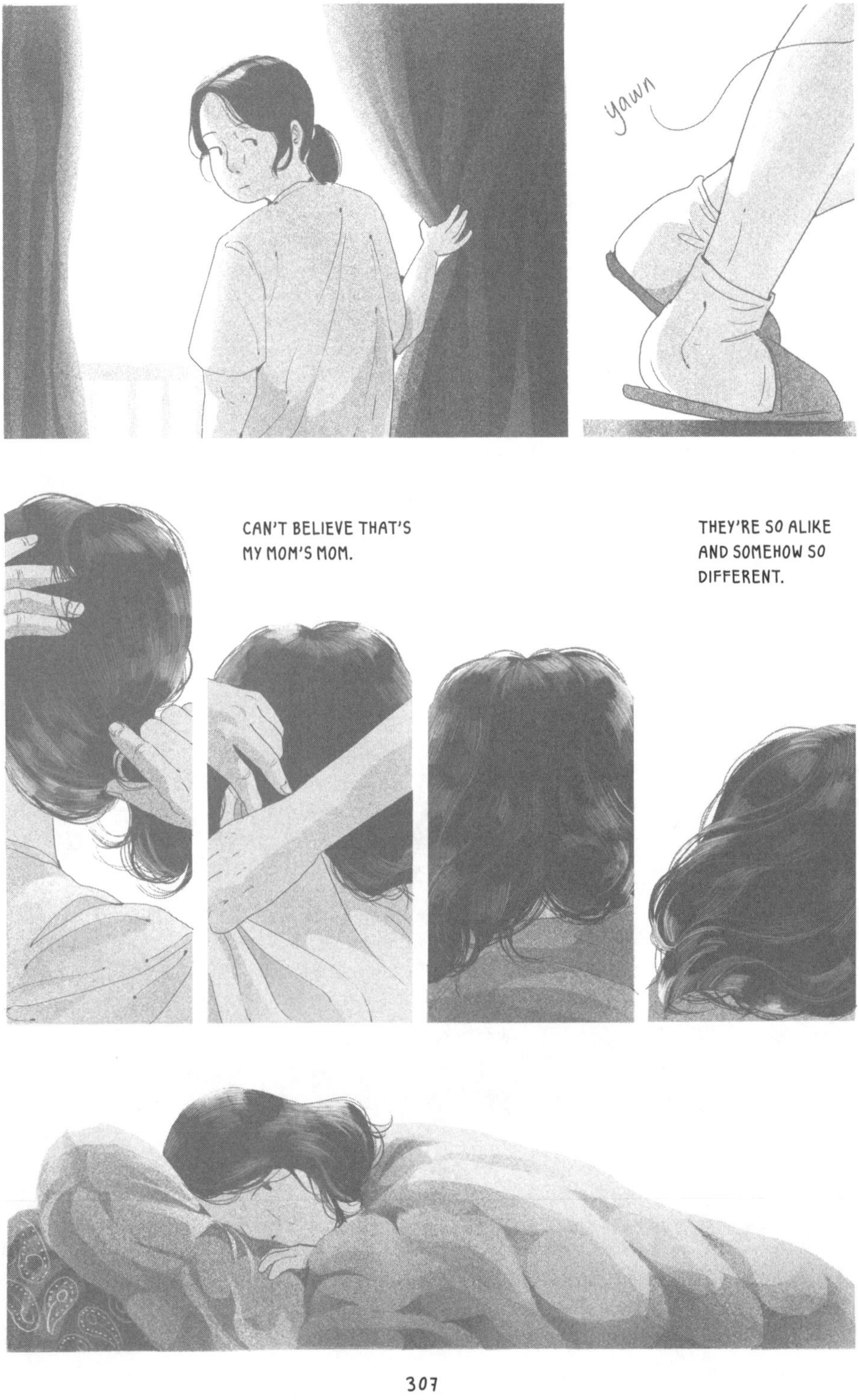
yawn
CAN'T BELIEVE THAT'S MY MOM'S MOM.
THEY'RE SO ALIKE AND SOMEHOW SO DIFFERENT.

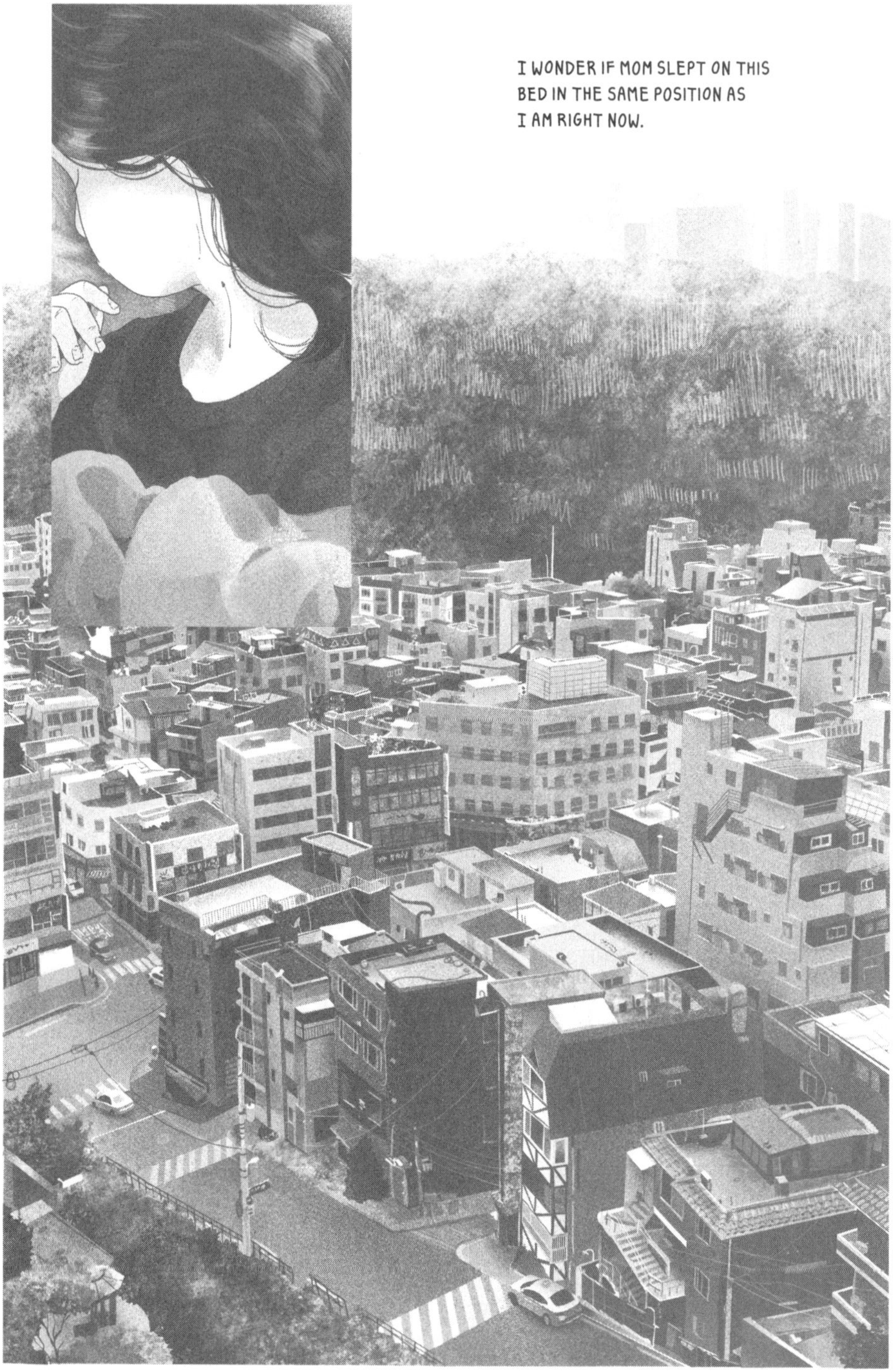
I WONDER IF MOM SLEPT ON THIS BED IN THE SAME POSITION AS I AM RIGHT NOW.

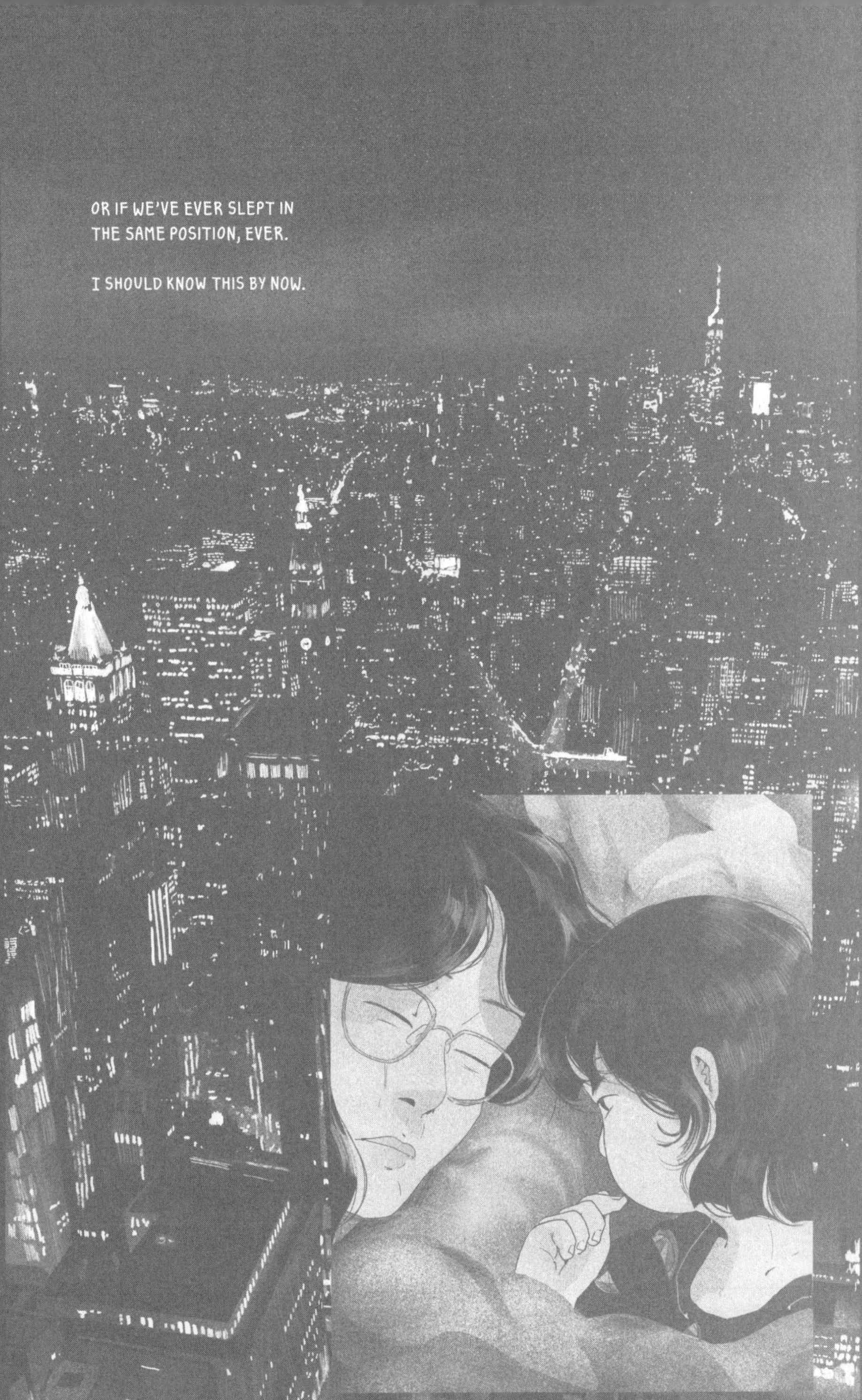
OR IF WE'VE EVER SLEPT IN
THE SAME POSITION, EVER.
I SHOULD KNOW THIS BY NOW.

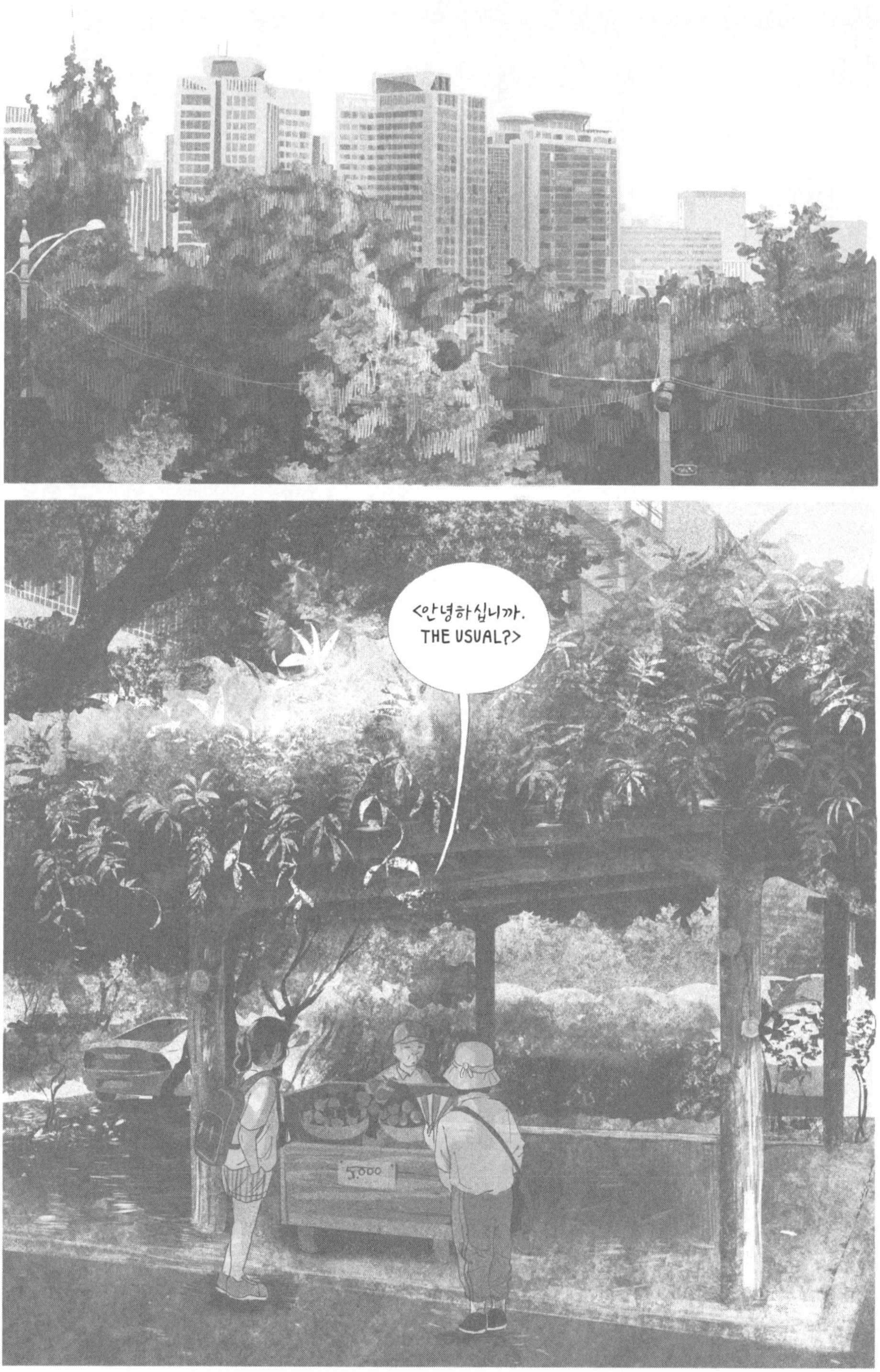
<안녕하십니까.
THE USUAL?>
5,000

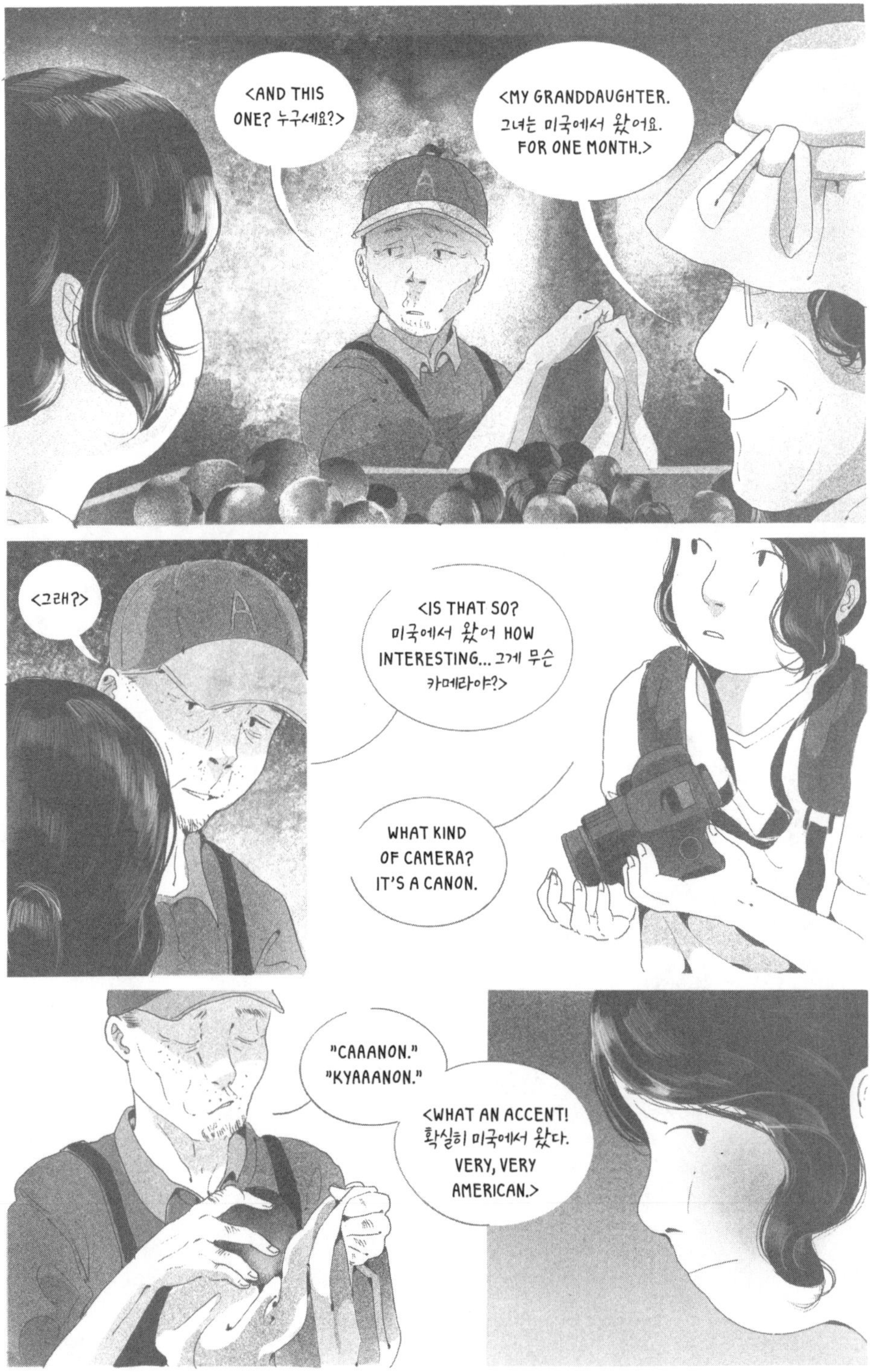
<AND THIS ONE? 누구세요?>
<MY GRANDDAUGHTER. 그녀는 미국에서 왔어요. FOR ONE MONTH.>
<그래?>
<IS THAT SO? 미국에서 왔어 HOW INTERESTING... 그게 무슨 카메라야?>
WHAT KIND OF CAMERA? IT'S A CANON.
"CAAANON." "KYAAANON."
<WHAT AN ACCENT! 확실히 미국에서 왔다. VERY, VERY AMERICAN.>

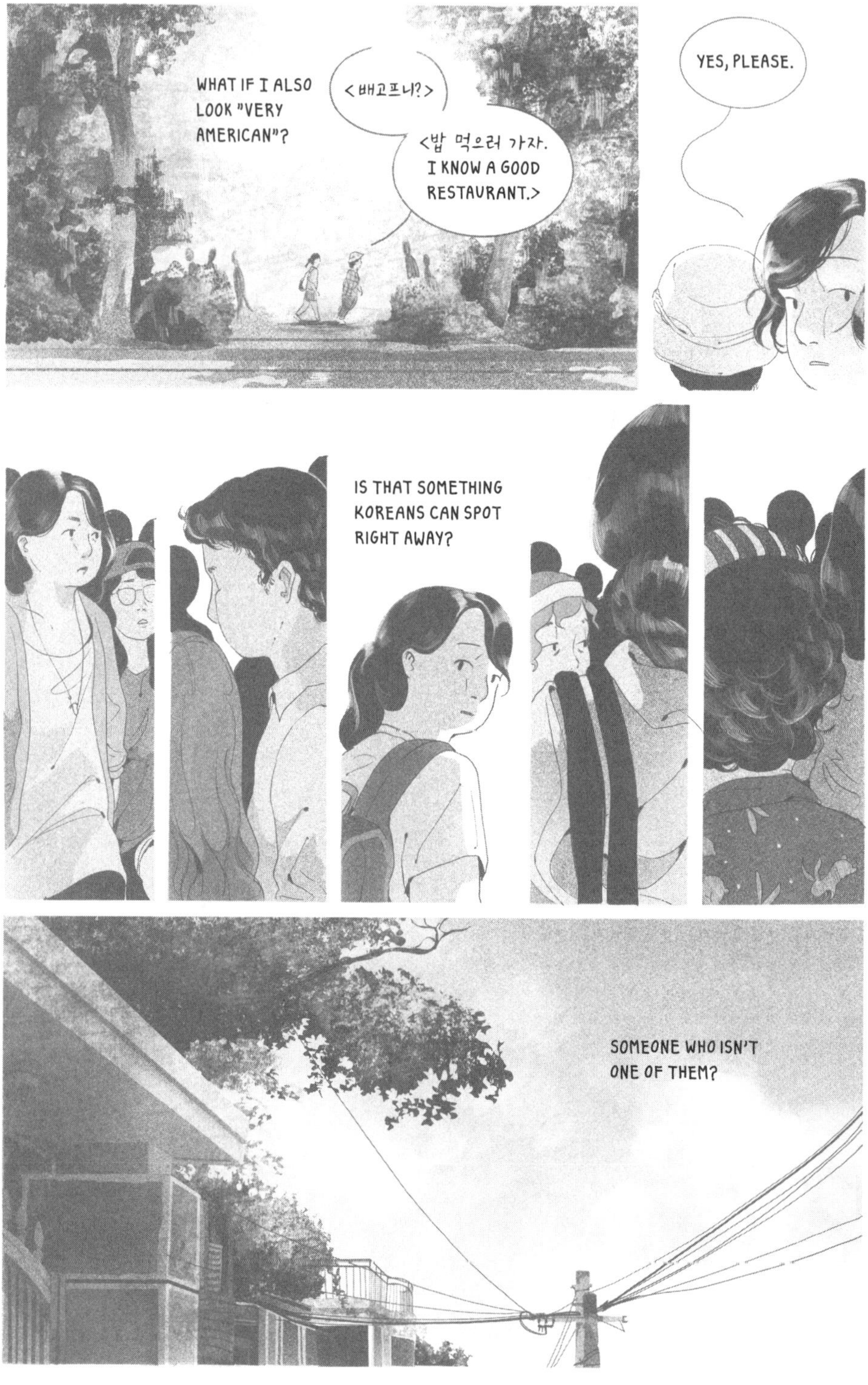
WHAT IF I ALSO LOOK "VERY AMERICAN"?
<배고프니?>
<밥 먹으러 가자. I KNOW A GOOD RESTAURANT.>
YES, PLEASE.
IS THAT SOMETHING KOREANS CAN SPOT RIGHT AWAY?
SOMEONE WHO ISN'T ONE OF THEM?

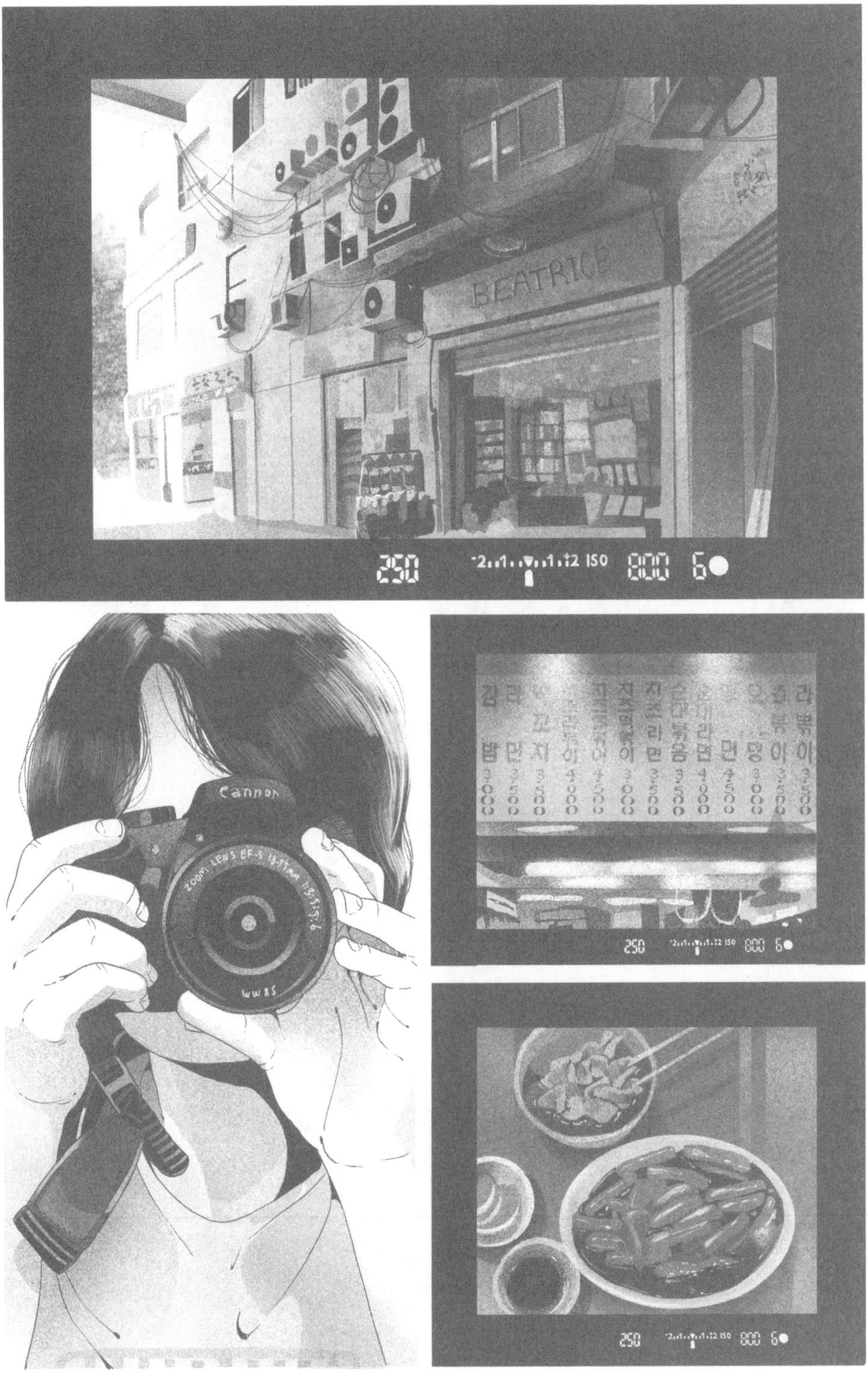
BEATRICE
250 800 6
Cannon
250 800 6
250 800 6

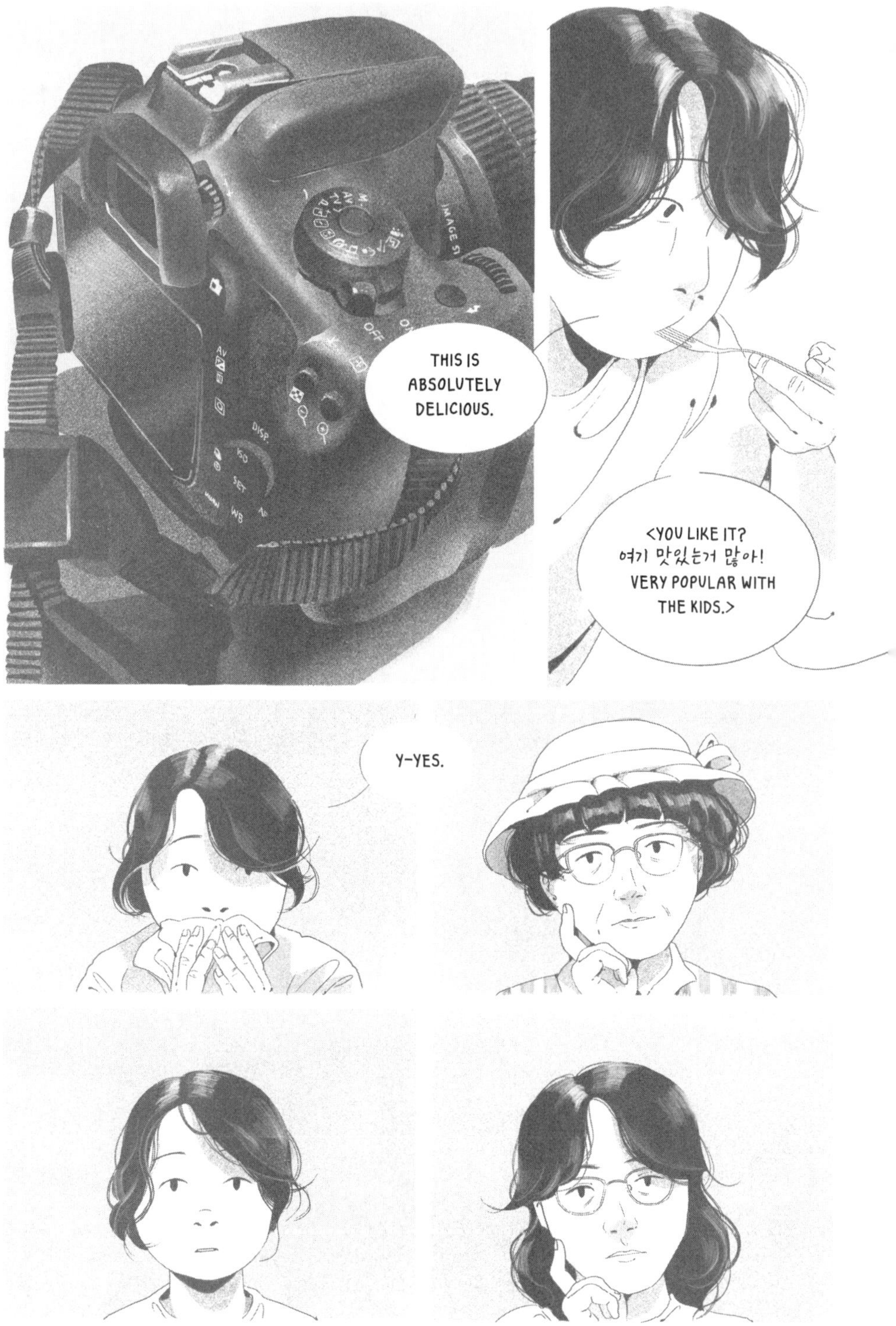
THIS IS ABSOLUTELY DELICIOUS.
<YOU LIKE IT? 여기 맛있는거 많아! VERY POPULAR WITH THE KIDS.>
Y-YES.

ANOTHER LULL IN THE CONVERSATION.

SHE KEEPS HER DISTANCE TOO.
IS SHE SAD OR SOMETHING?

WELL I HAVEN'T BEEN HERE FOR
A DECADE. A LOT HAS PROBABLY CHANGED
SINCE THEN. HELL, I FORGOT HOW TO
SPEAK MY FIRST LANGUAGE.

I REALLY WONDER WHAT'S ON HER
MIND RIGHT NOW. MAYBE ABOUT HOW
WELL SHE KNEW ME WHEN I WAS
A BABY, BUT NOW I'M RETURNING
TO HER JUST A STRANGER. IS SHE
SEARCHING FOR PARTS OF MY MOM IN
ME? CAN SHE EVEN FIND ANY? AM
I WHAT SHE EXPECTED? IS SHE
DISAPPOINTED? OR...

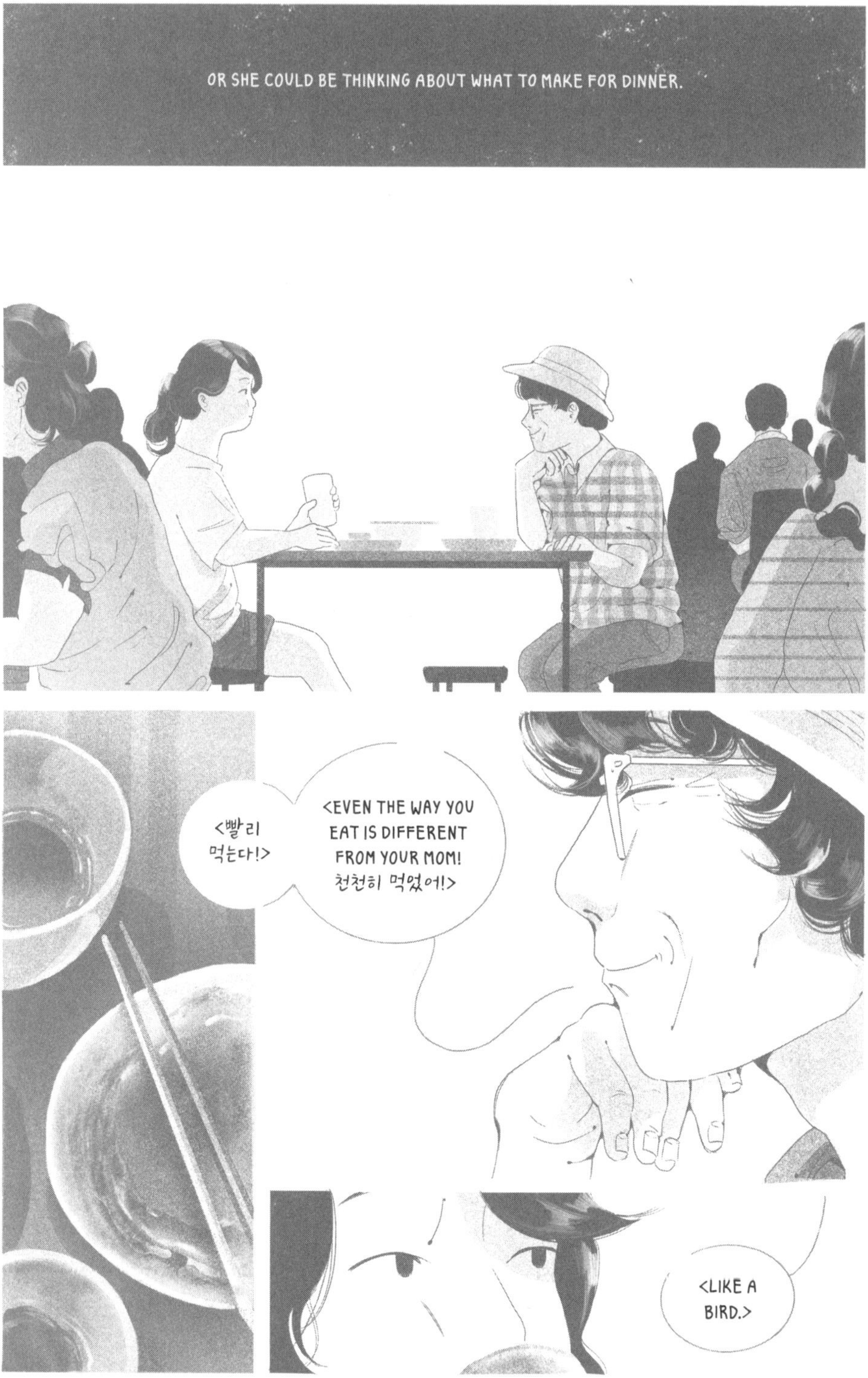
OR SHE COULD BE THINKING ABOUT WHAT TO MAKE FOR DINNER.
<빨리 먹는다!>
<EVEN THE WAY YOU EAT IS DIFFERENT FROM YOUR MOM! 천천히 먹었어!>
<LIKE A BIRD.>

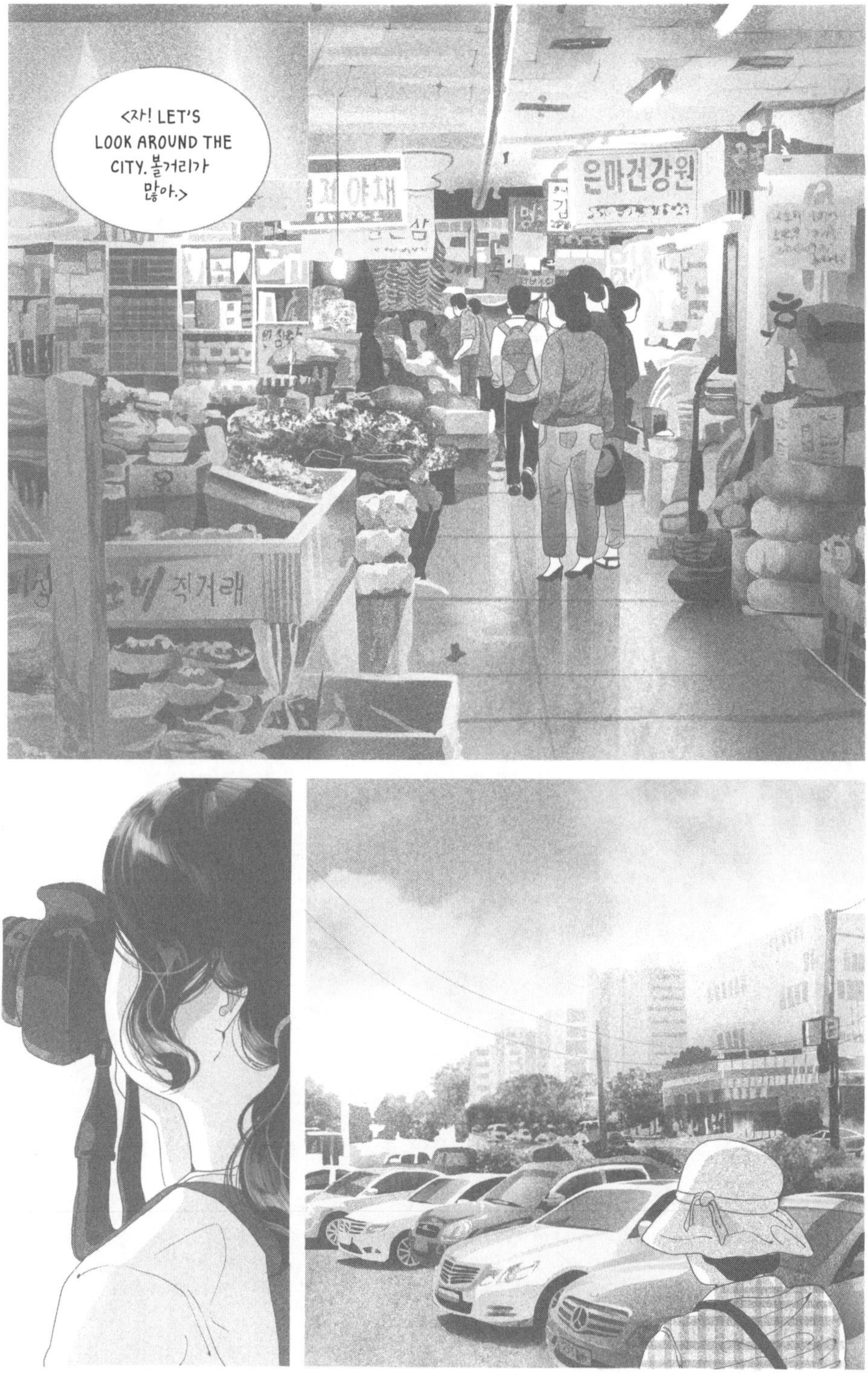
<자! LET'S LOOK AROUND THE CITY. 볼거리가 많아.>
은마건강원

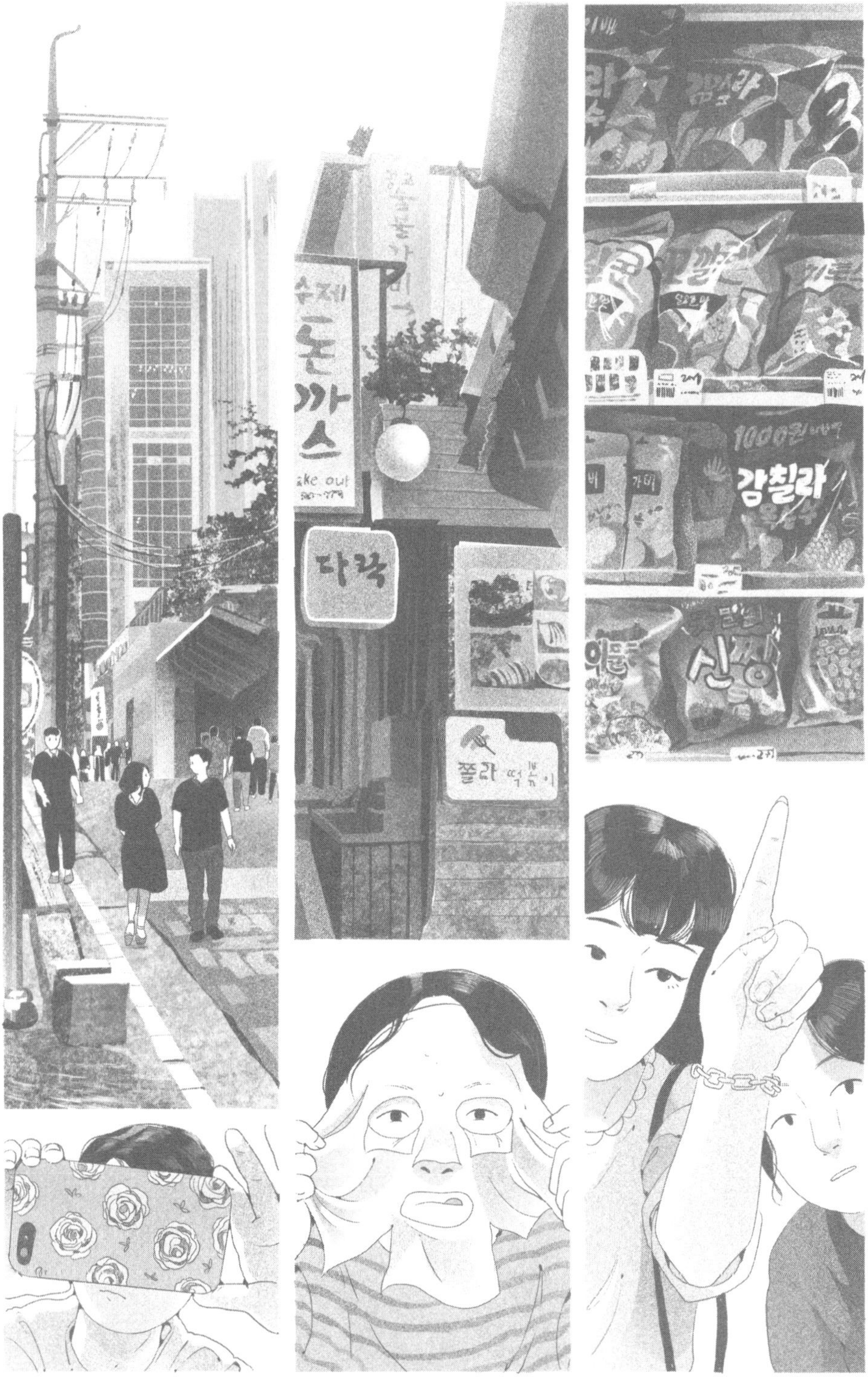
돈까스
ake out
다락
쫄라
감칠라
신짱

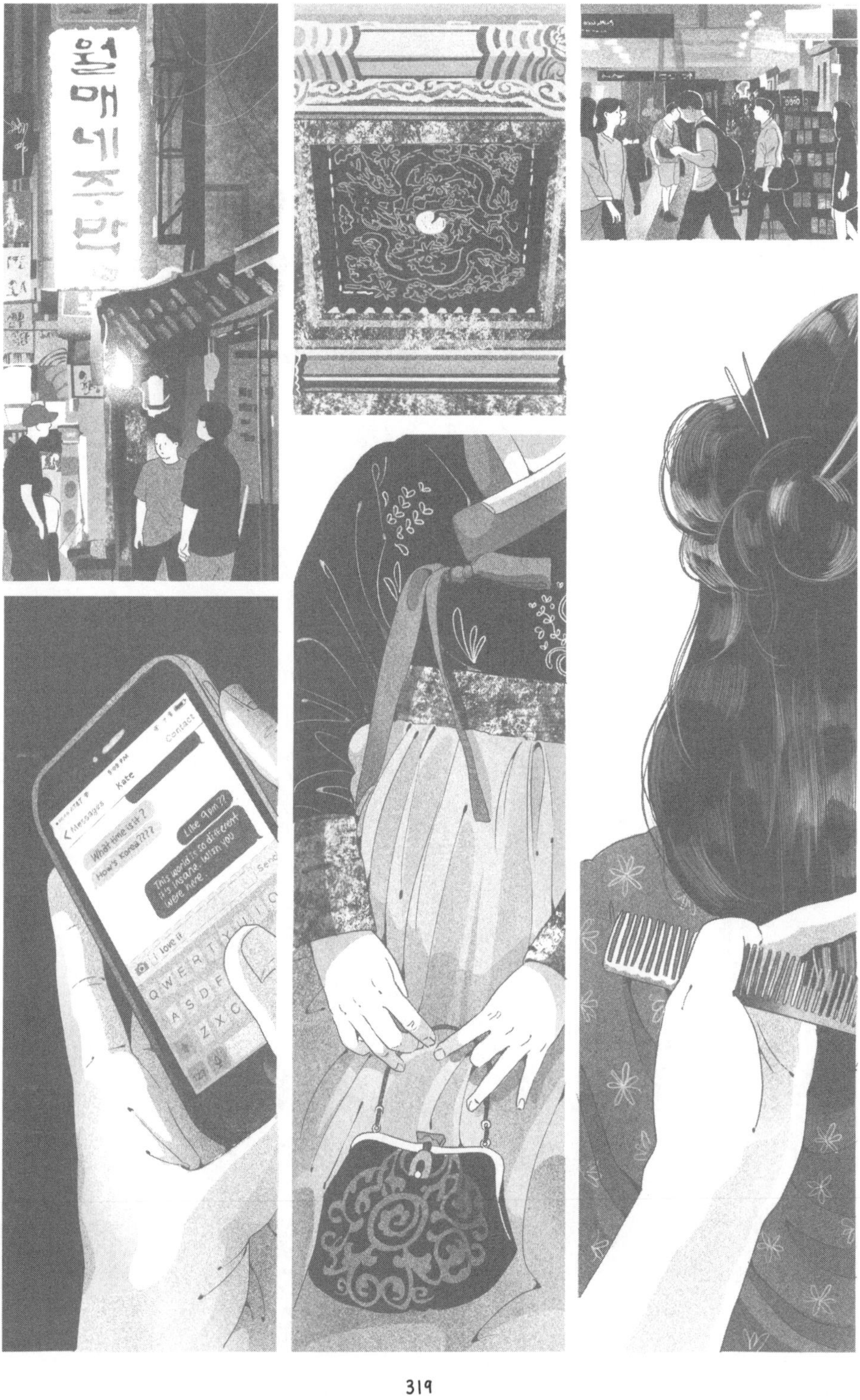
월매네주막
Messages
Kate
Contact
What time is it?
How's Korea????
Like 9pm??
This world is so different it's insane. Wish you were here.
I love it
Send

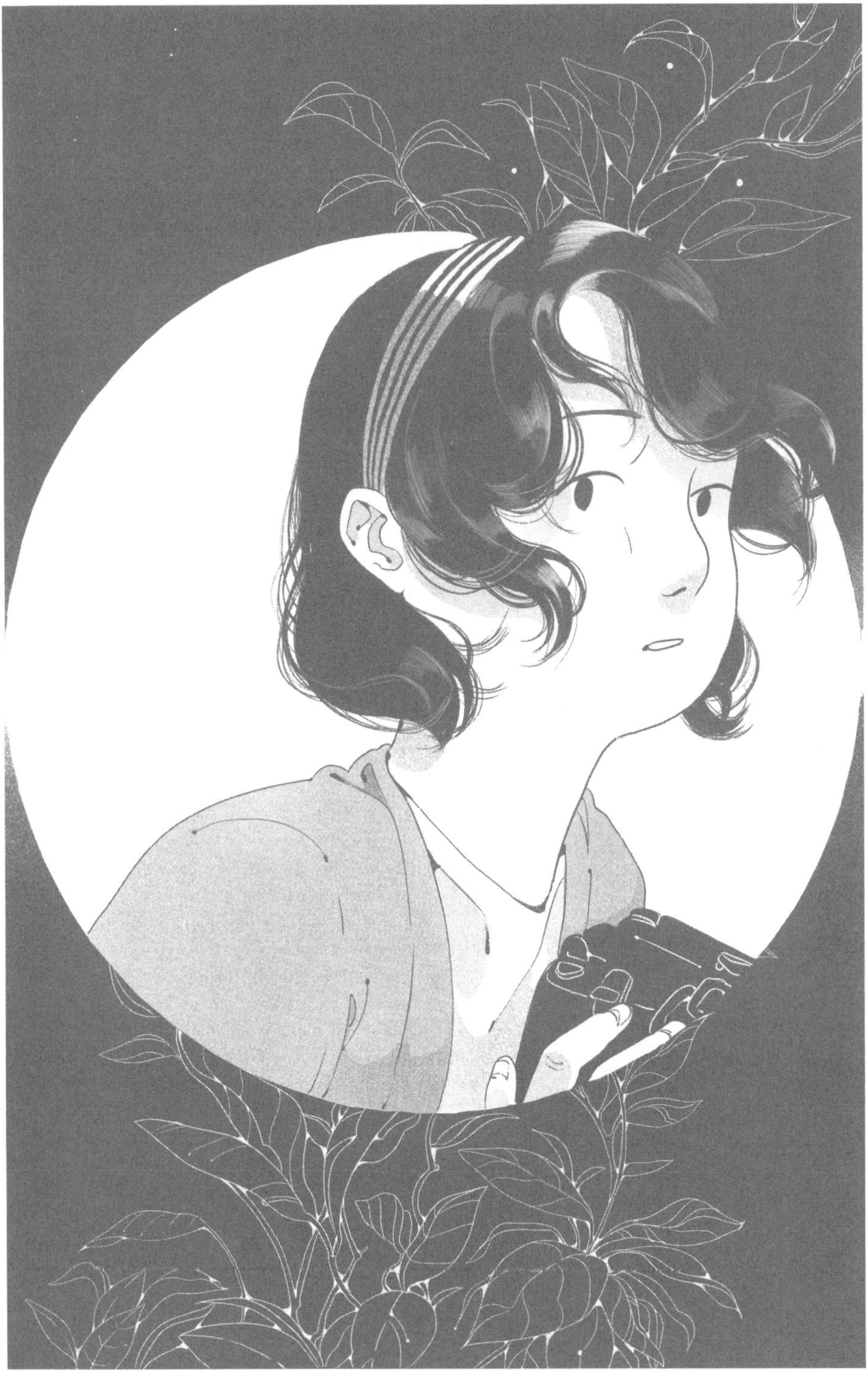

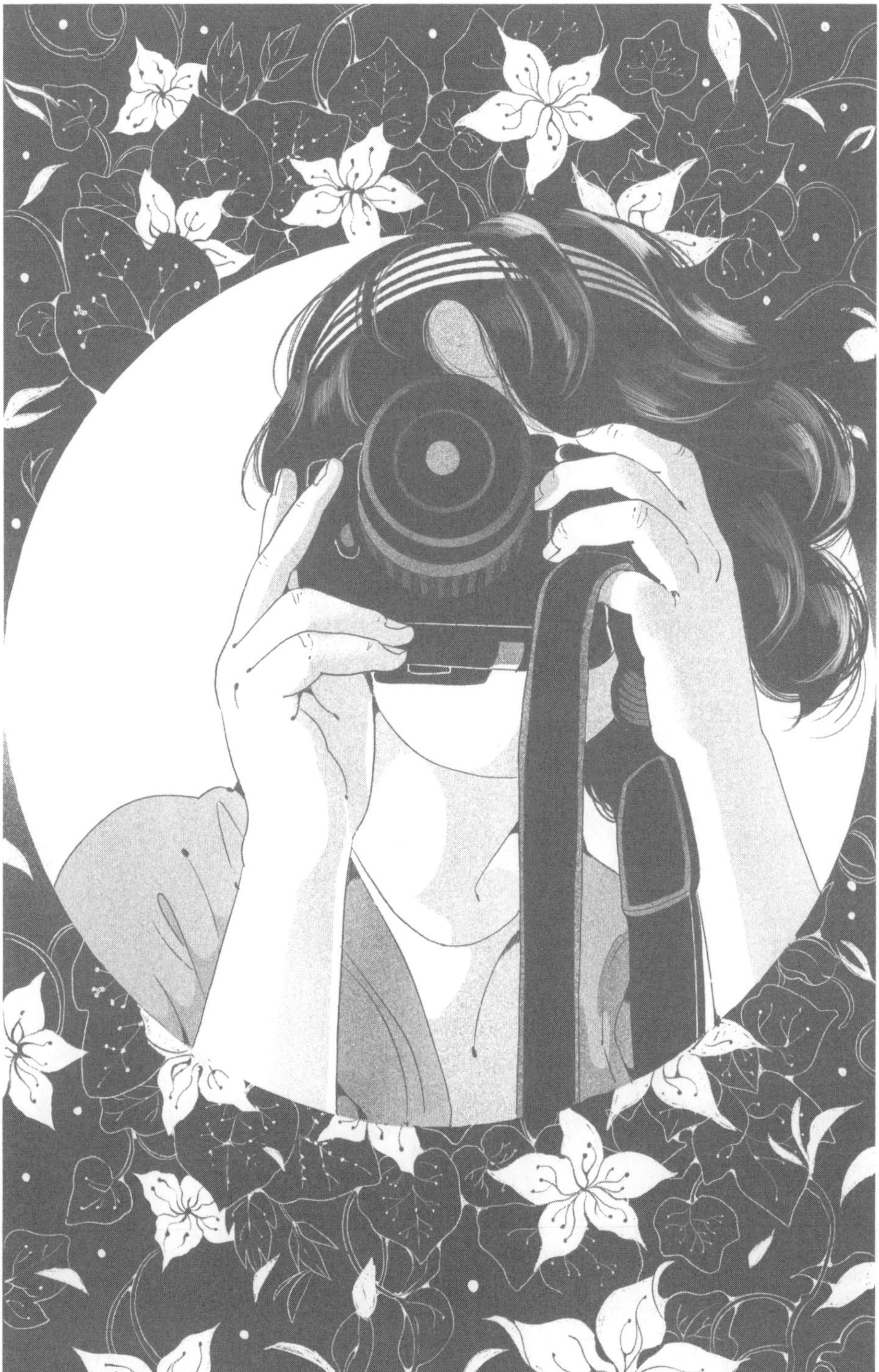

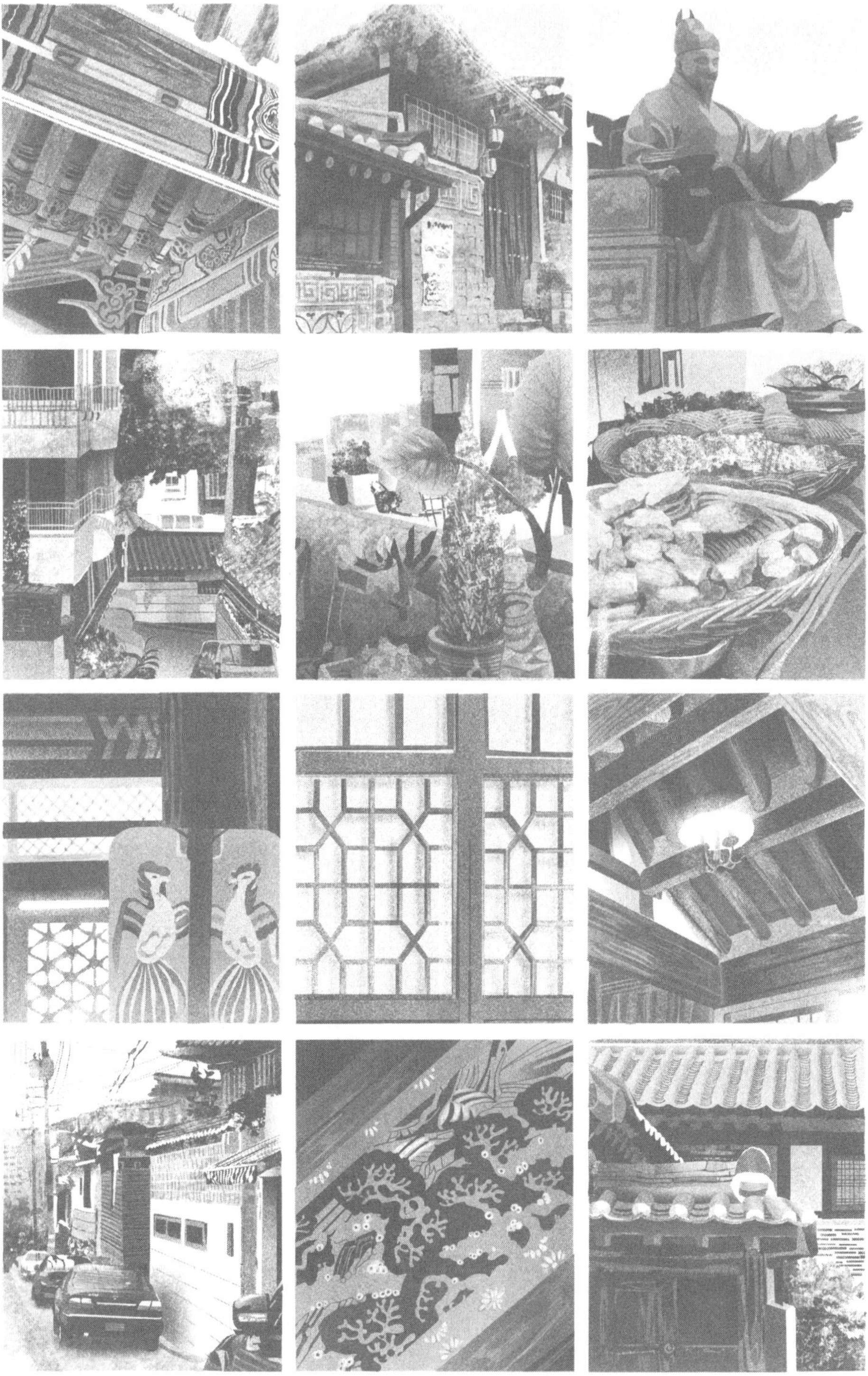

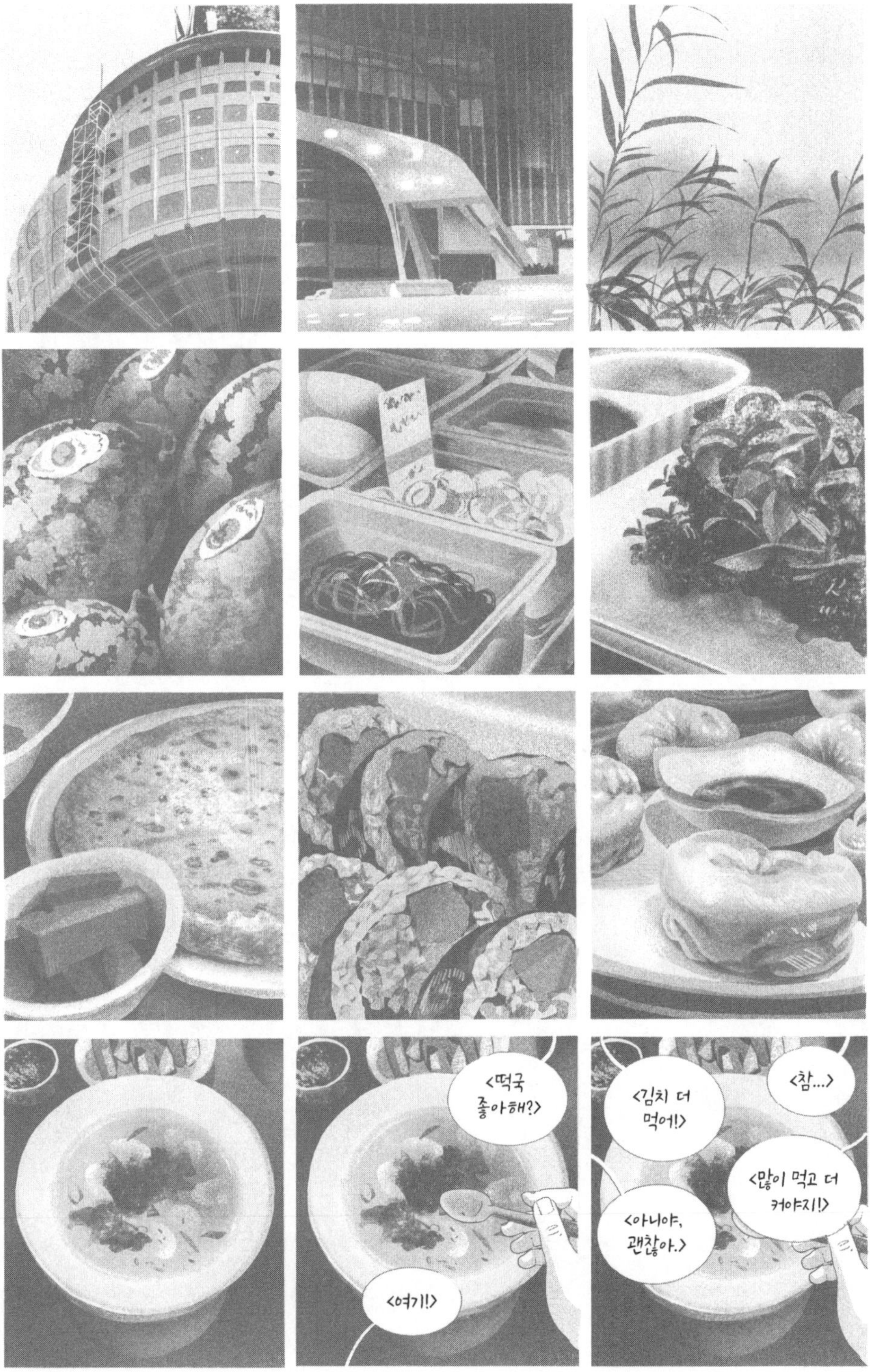
<떡국 좋아해?>
<여기!>
<김치 더 먹어!>
<참...>
<많이 먹고 더 커야지!>
<아니야, 괜찮아.>

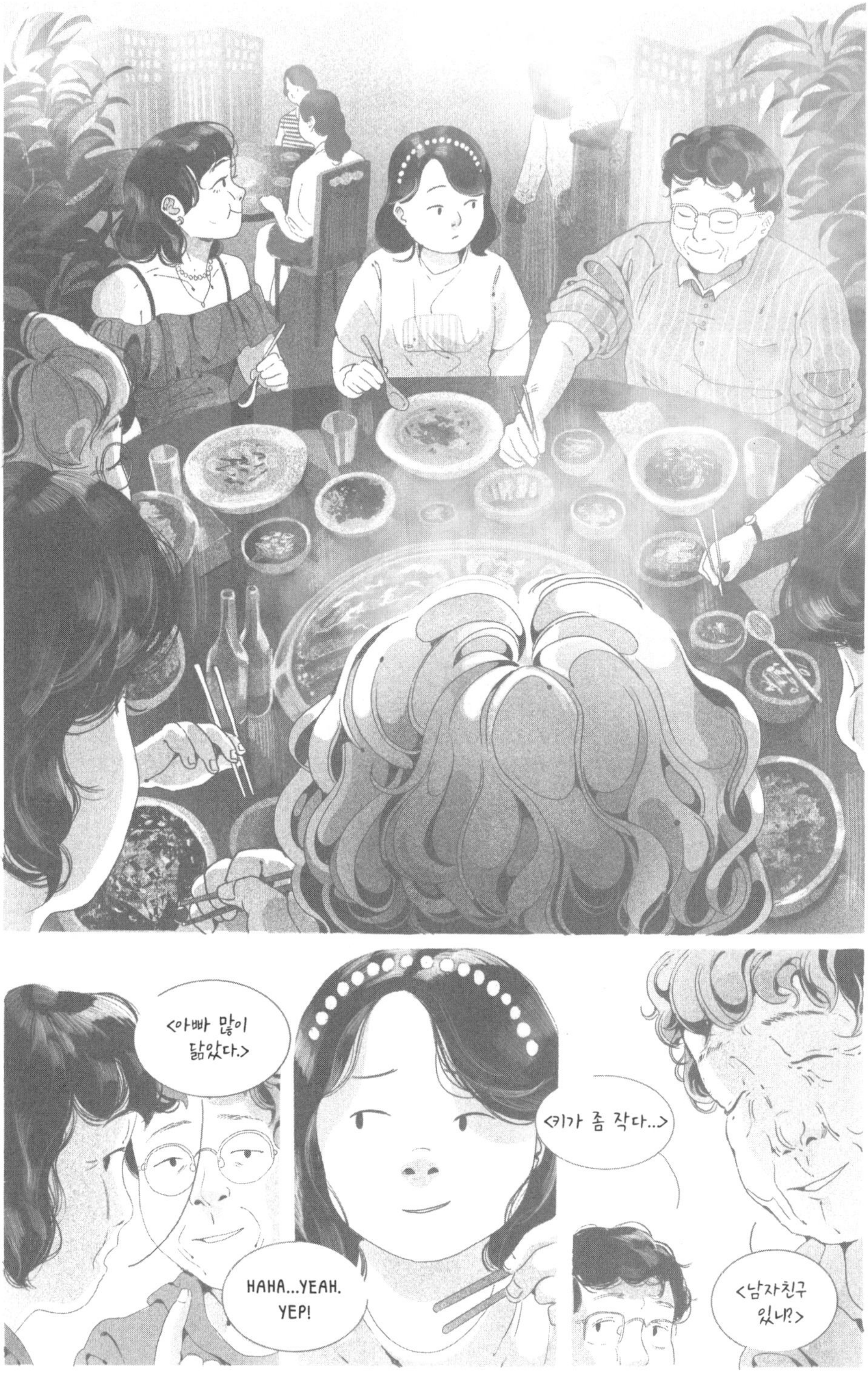
<아빠 많이 닮았다.>
HAHA...YEAH. YEP!
<키가 좀 작다..>
<남자친구 있나?>

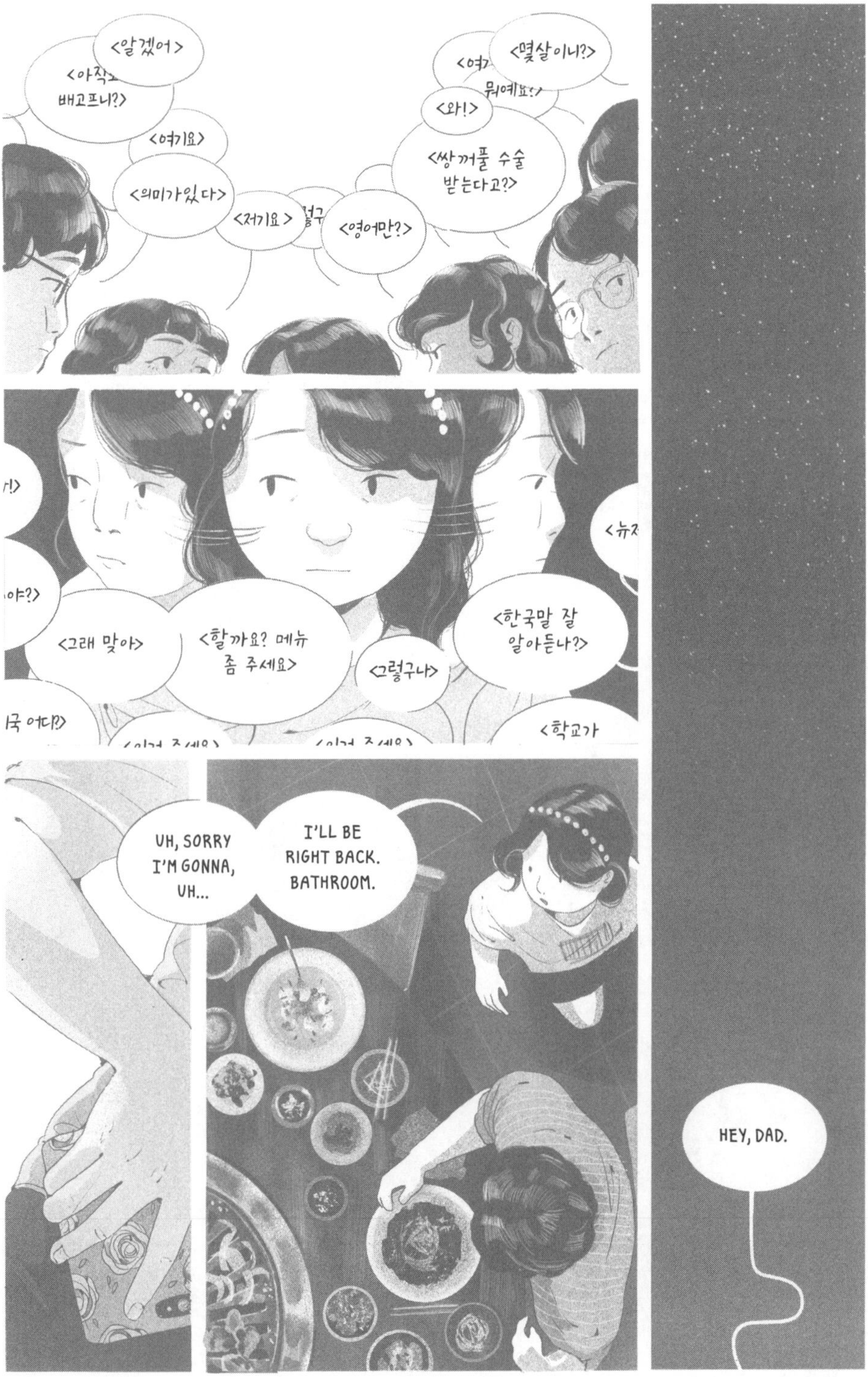
<알겠어>
<여기요>
<의미가있다>
<저기요>
<영어만?>
<와!>
<쌍꺼풀 수술 받는다고?>
<몇살이니?>
<그래 맞아>
<할까요? 메뉴 좀 주세요>
<그렇구나>
<한국말 잘 알아듣나?>
UH, SORRY I'M GONNA, UH...
I'LL BE RIGHT BACK. BATHROOM.
HEY, DAD.

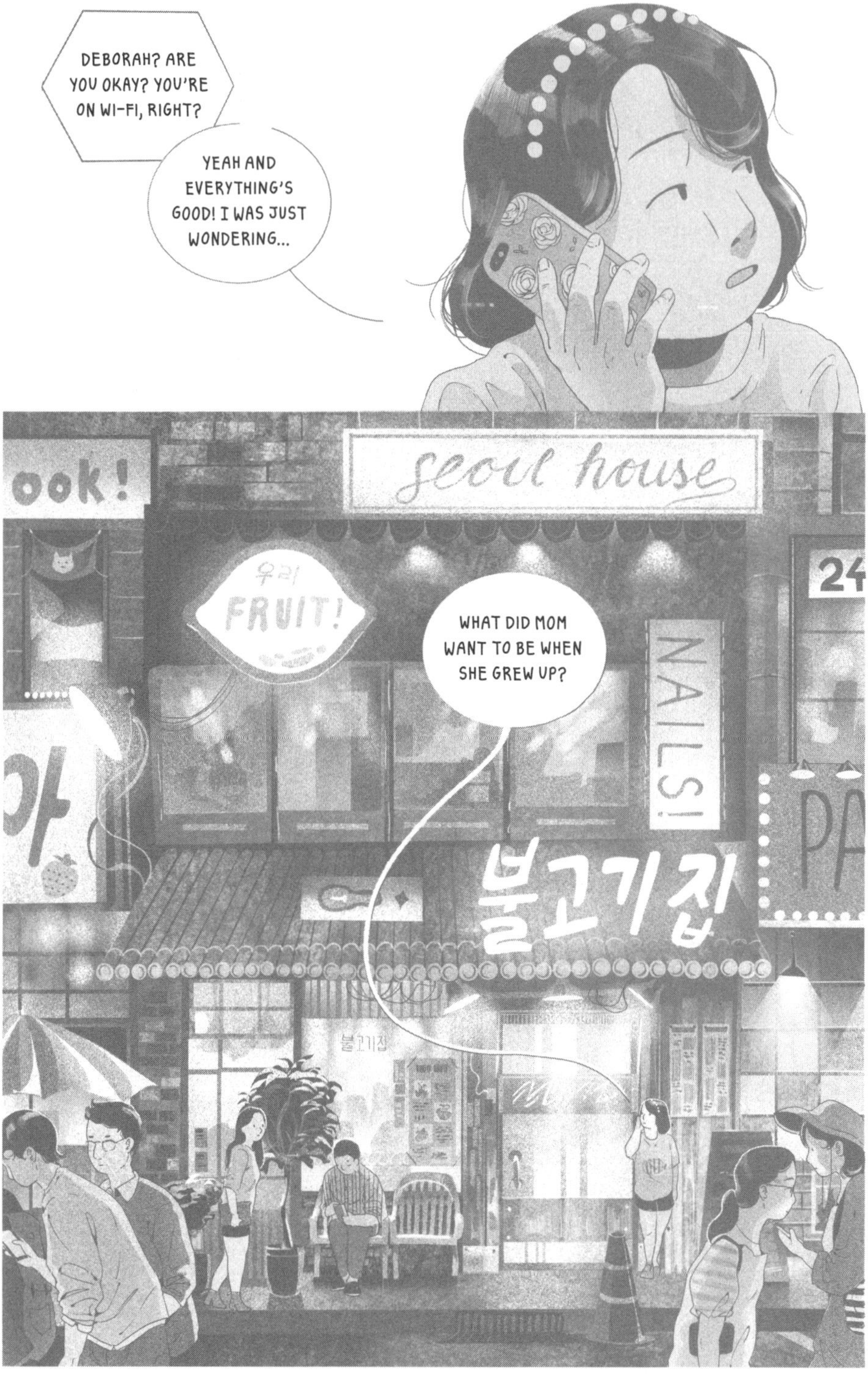
DEBORAH? ARE YOU OKAY? YOU'RE ON WI-FI, RIGHT?
YEAH AND EVERYTHING'S GOOD! I WAS JUST WONDERING...
ook!
seoul house
우리
FRUIT!
24
WHAT DID MOM WANT TO BE WHEN SHE GREW UP?
NAILS!
아
불고기집

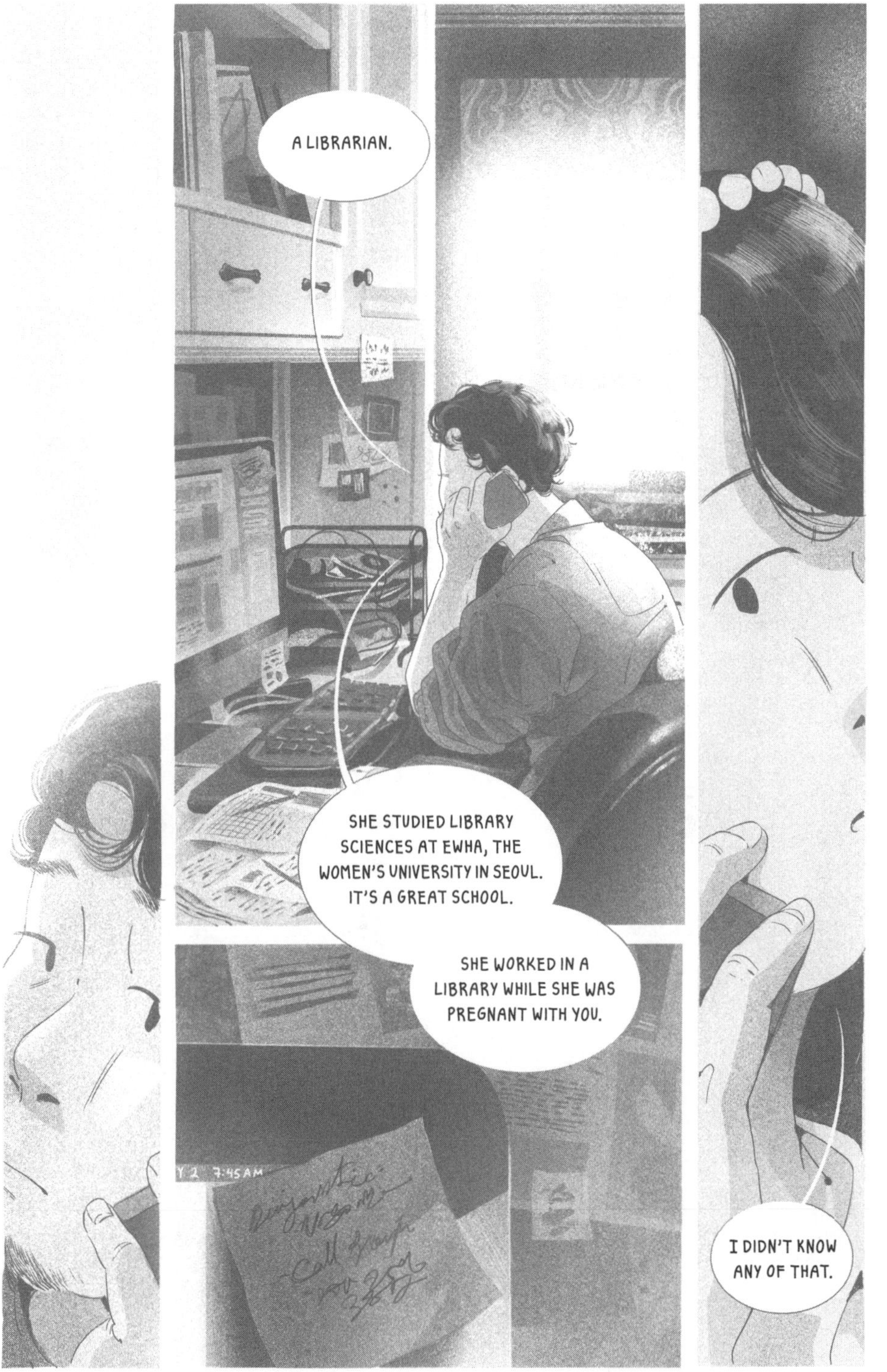
A LIBRARIAN.
SHE STUDIED LIBRARY SCIENCES AT EWHA, THE WOMEN'S UNIVERSITY IN SEOUL. IT'S A GREAT SCHOOL.
SHE WORKED IN A LIBRARY WHILE SHE WAS PREGNANT WITH YOU.
I DIDN'T KNOW ANY OF THAT.

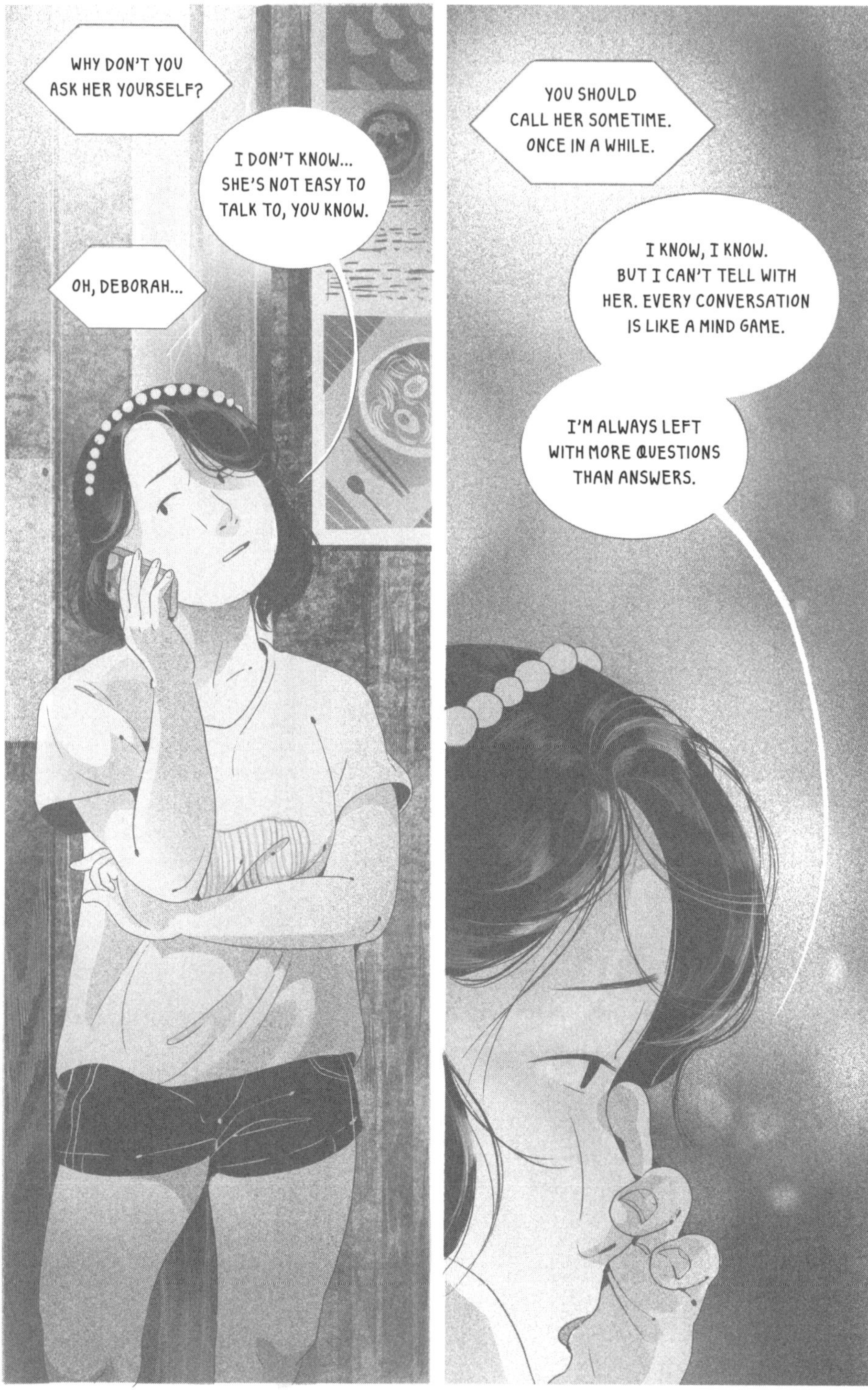
WHY DON'T YOU ASK HER YOURSELF?
I DON'T KNOW... SHE'S NOT EASY TO TALK TO, YOU KNOW.
OH, DEBORAH...
YOU SHOULD CALL HER SOMETIME. ONCE IN A WHILE.
I KNOW, I KNOW. BUT I CAN'T TELL WITH HER. EVERY CONVERSATION IS LIKE A MIND GAME.
I'M ALWAYS LEFT WITH MORE QUESTIONS THAN ANSWERS.

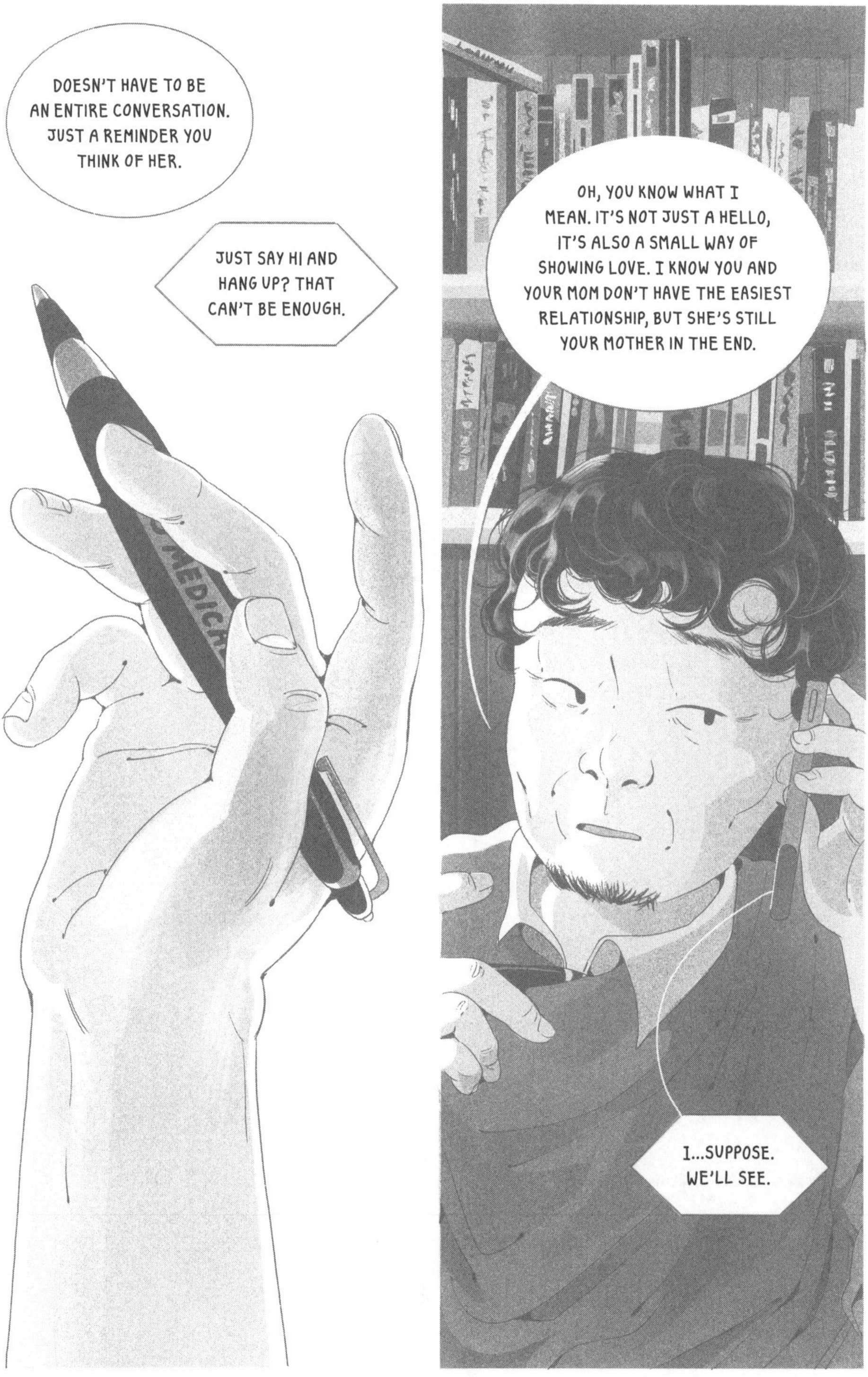
DOESN'T HAVE TO BE AN ENTIRE CONVERSATION. JUST A REMINDER YOU THINK OF HER.
JUST SAY HI AND HANG UP? THAT CAN'T BE ENOUGH.
OH, YOU KNOW WHAT I MEAN. IT'S NOT JUST A HELLO, IT'S ALSO A SMALL WAY OF SHOWING LOVE. I KNOW YOU AND YOUR MOM DON'T HAVE THE EASIEST RELATIONSHIP, BUT SHE'S STILL YOUR MOTHER IN THE END.
I...SUPPOSE. WE'LL SEE.

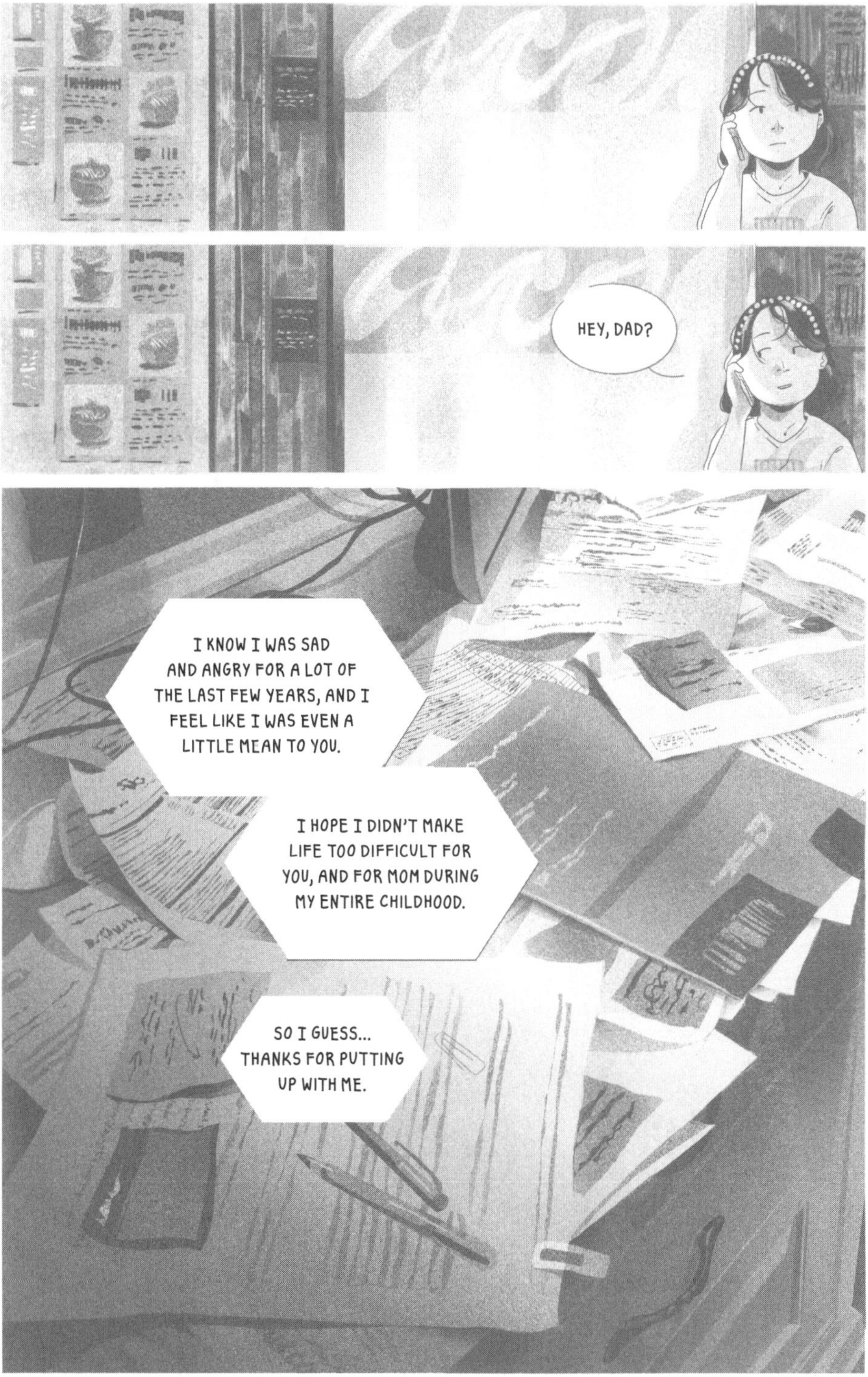
HEY, DAD?
I KNOW I WAS SAD AND ANGRY FOR A LOT OF THE LAST FEW YEARS, AND I FEEL LIKE I WAS EVEN A LITTLE MEAN TO YOU.
I HOPE I DIDN'T MAKE LIFE TOO DIFFICULT FOR YOU, AND FOR MOM DURING MY ENTIRE CHILDHOOD.
SO I GUESS... THANKS FOR PUTTING UP WITH ME.

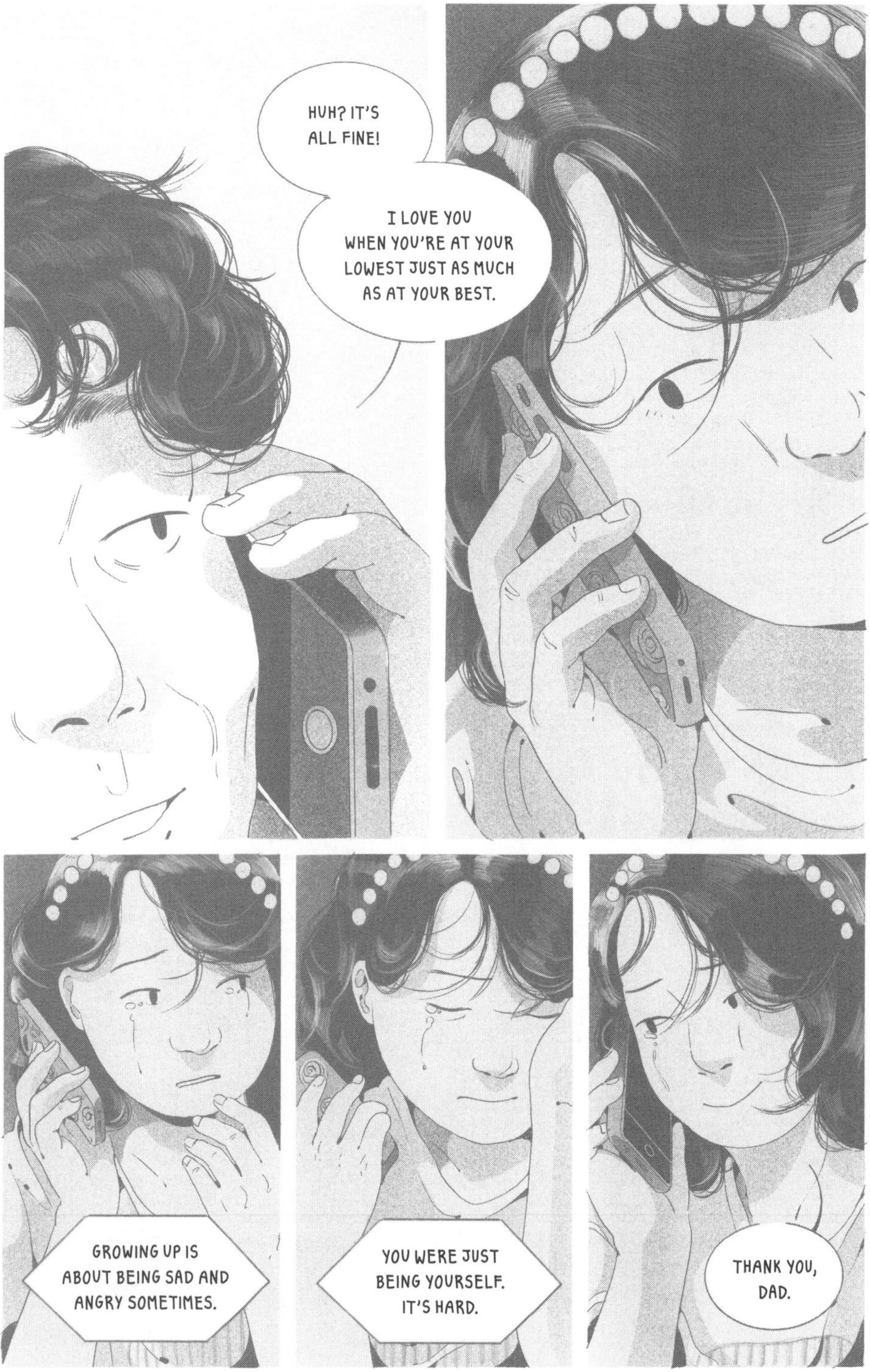
HUH? IT'S ALL FINE!
I LOVE YOU WHEN YOU'RE AT YOUR LOWEST JUST AS MUCH AS AT YOUR BEST.
GROWING UP IS ABOUT BEING SAD AND ANGRY SOMETIMES.
YOU WERE JUST BEING YOURSELF. IT'S HARD.
THANK YOU, DAD.

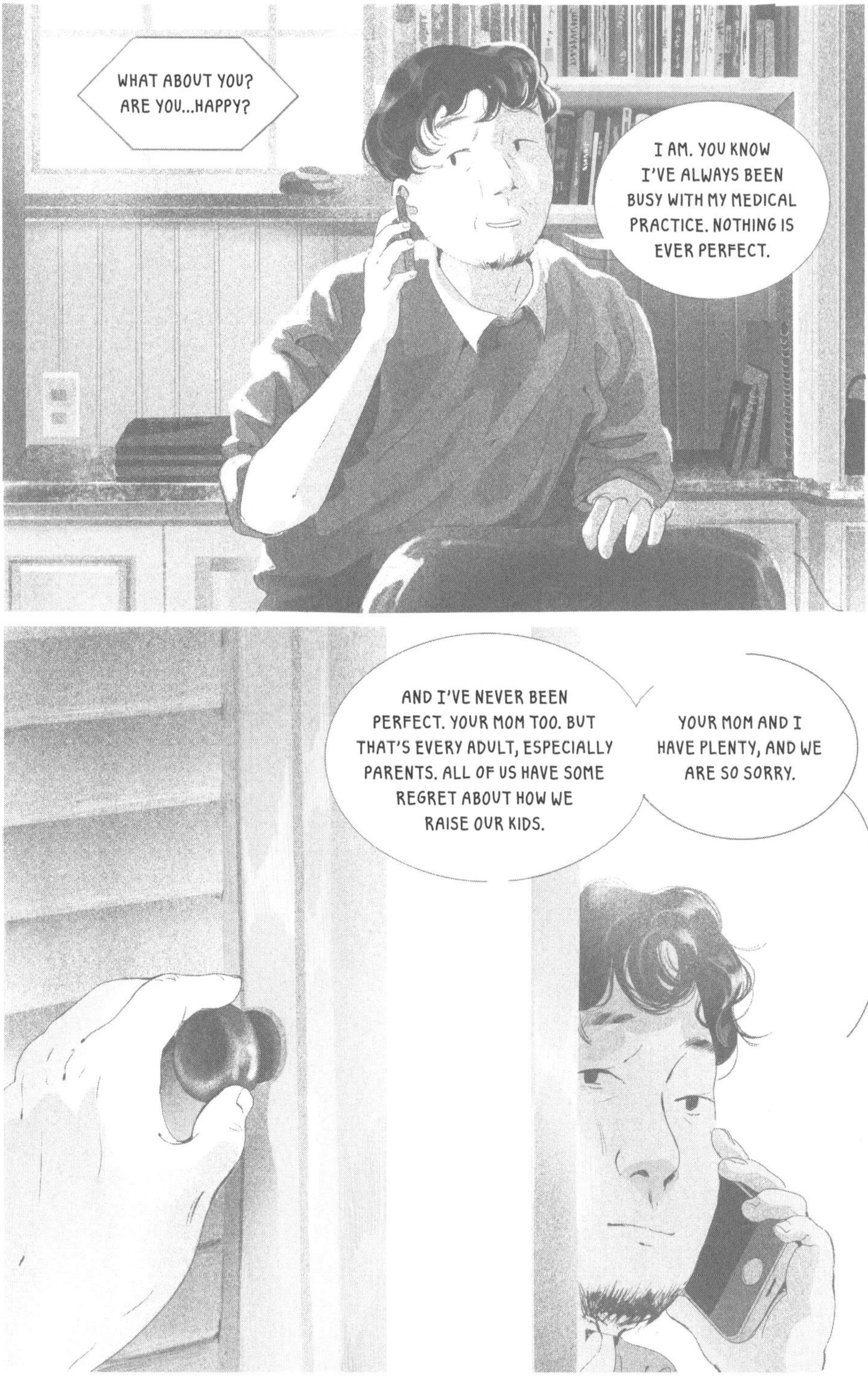
WHAT ABOUT YOU? ARE YOU...HAPPY?
I AM. YOU KNOW I'VE ALWAYS BEEN BUSY WITH MY MEDICAL PRACTICE. NOTHING IS EVER PERFECT.
AND I'VE NEVER BEEN PERFECT. YOUR MOM TOO. BUT THAT'S EVERY ADULT, ESPECIALLY PARENTS. ALL OF US HAVE SOME REGRET ABOUT HOW WE RAISE OUR KIDS.
YOUR MOM AND I HAVE PLENTY, AND WE ARE SO SORRY.

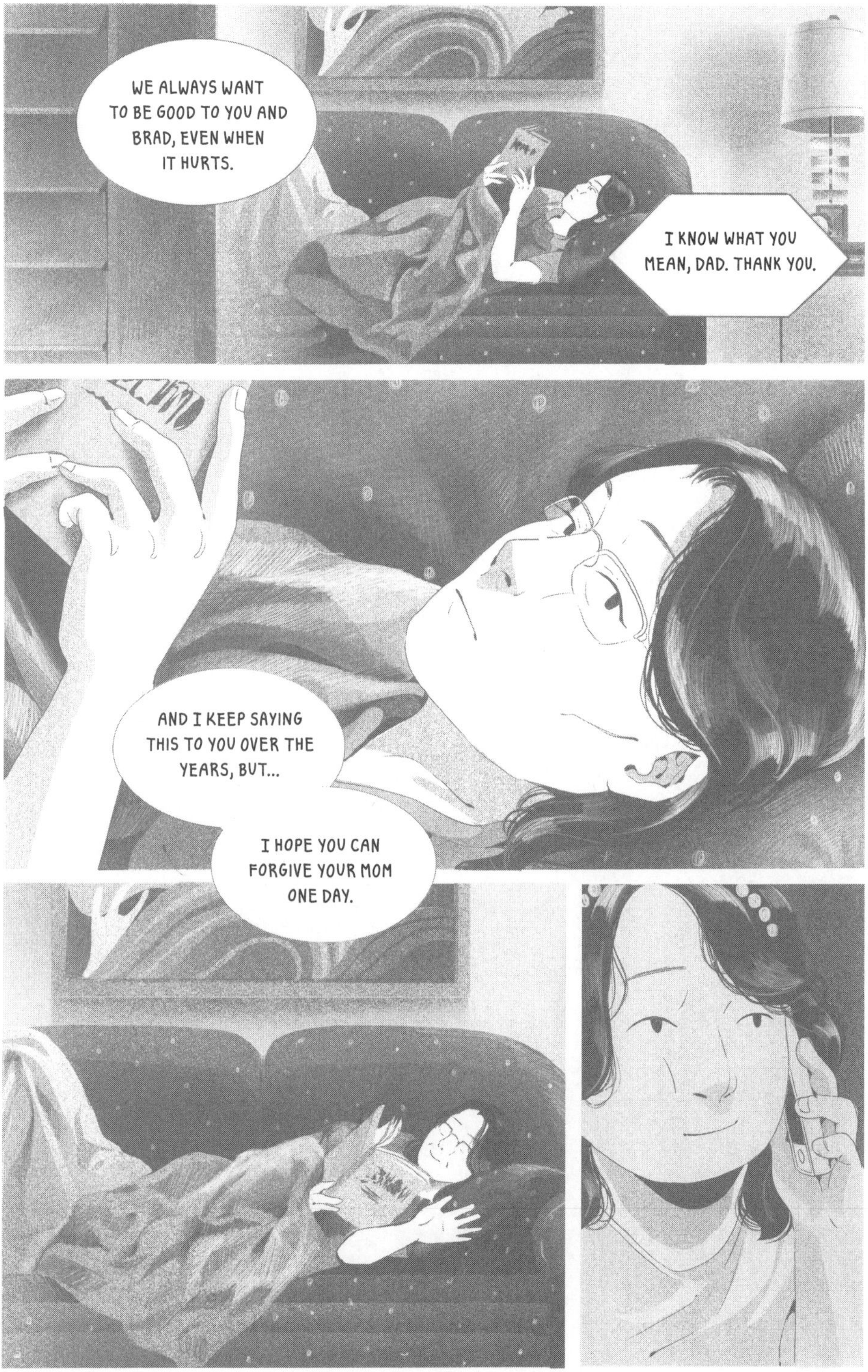
WE ALWAYS WANT TO BE GOOD TO YOU AND BRAD, EVEN WHEN IT HURTS.
I KNOW WHAT YOU MEAN, DAD. THANK YOU.
AND I KEEP SAYING THIS TO YOU OVER THE YEARS, BUT...
I HOPE YOU CAN FORGIVE YOUR MOM ONE DAY.

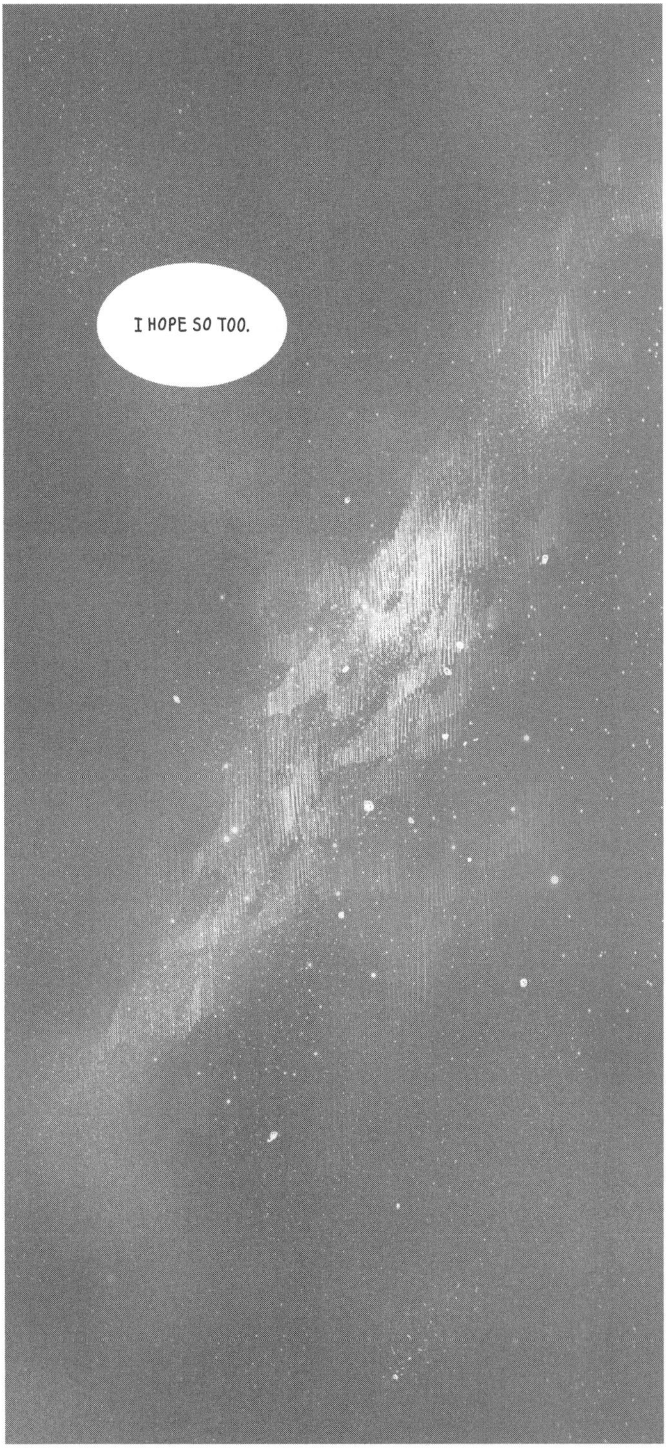
I HOPE SO TOO.

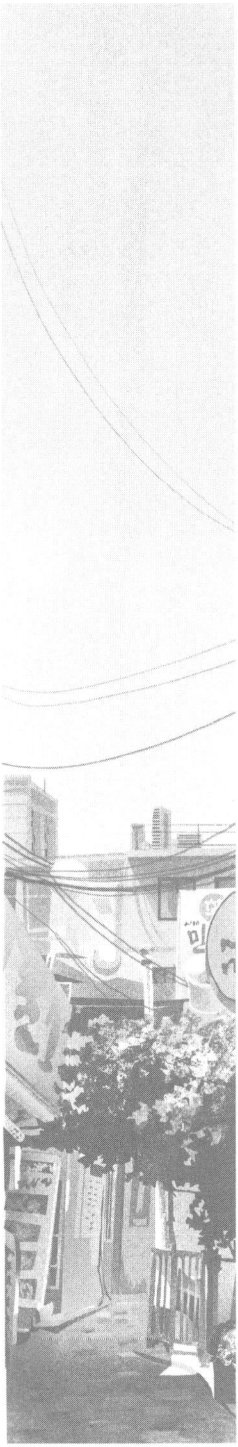

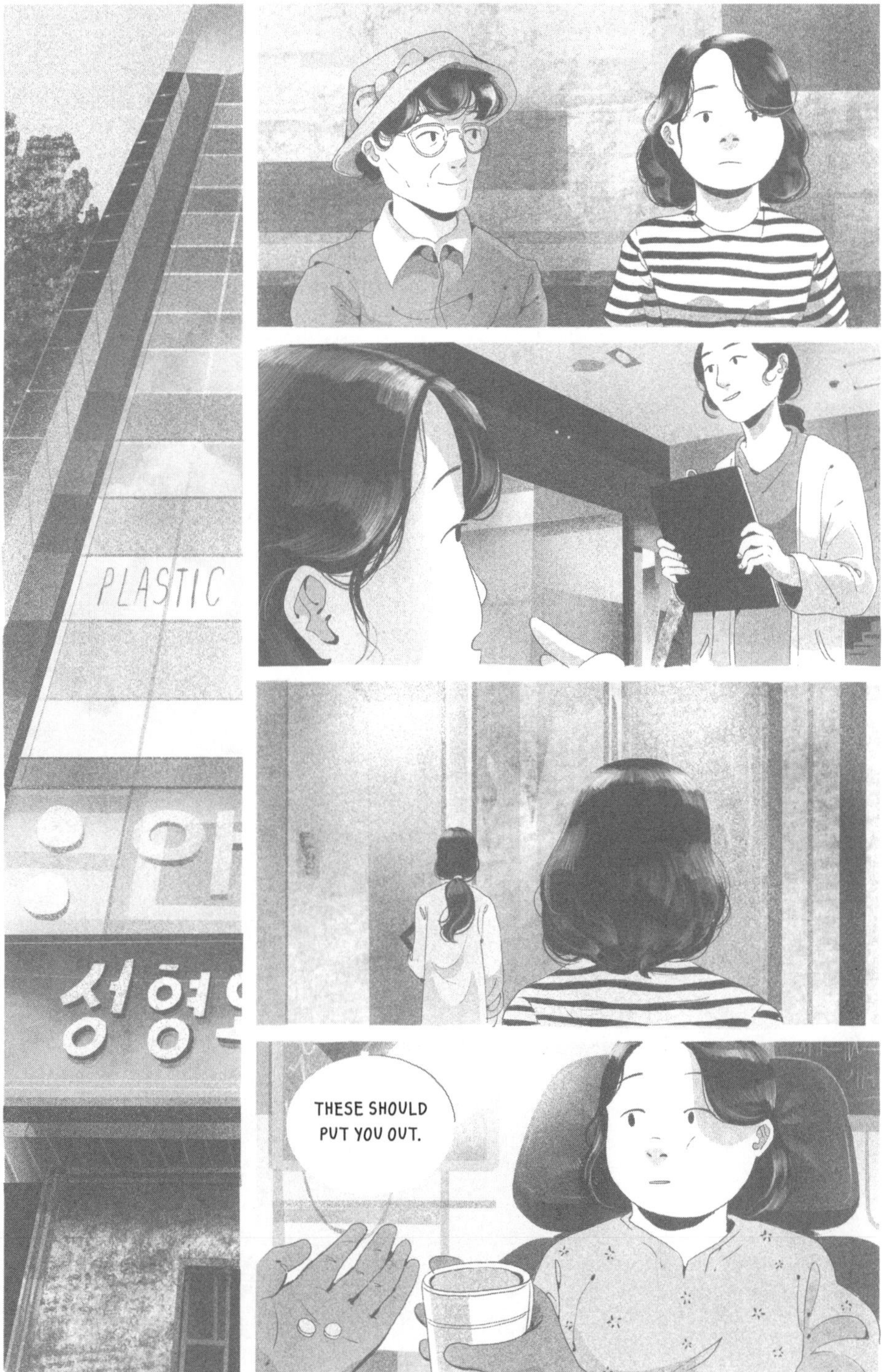
PLASTIC
성형
THESE SHOULD PUT YOU OUT.

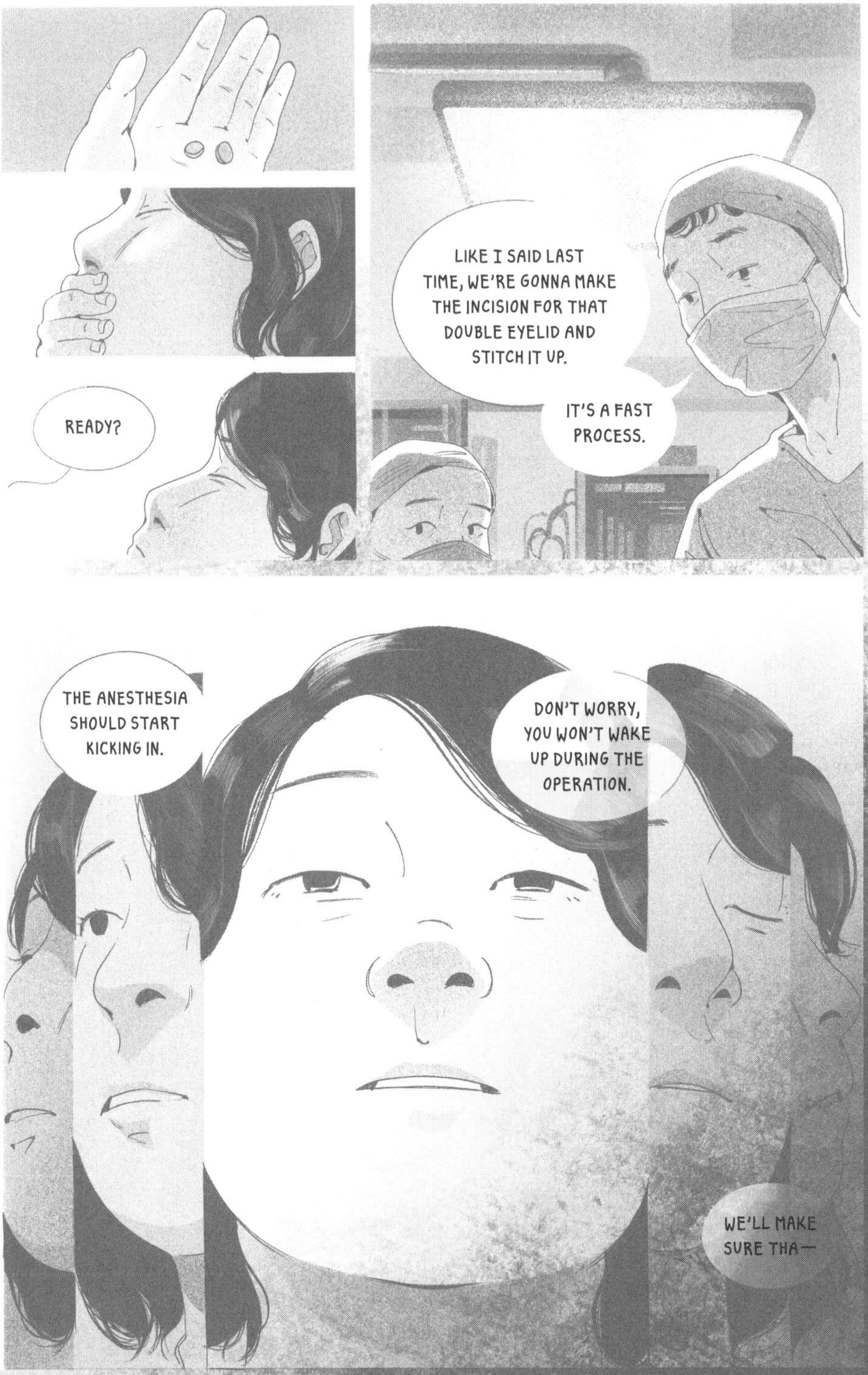
LIKE I SAID LAST TIME, WE'RE GONNA MAKE THE INCISION FOR THAT DOUBLE EYELID AND STITCH IT UP.
IT'S A FAST PROCESS.
READY?
THE ANESTHESIA SHOULD START KICKING IN.
DON'T WORRY, YOU WON'T WAKE UP DURING THE OPERATION.
WE'LL MAKE SURE THA—

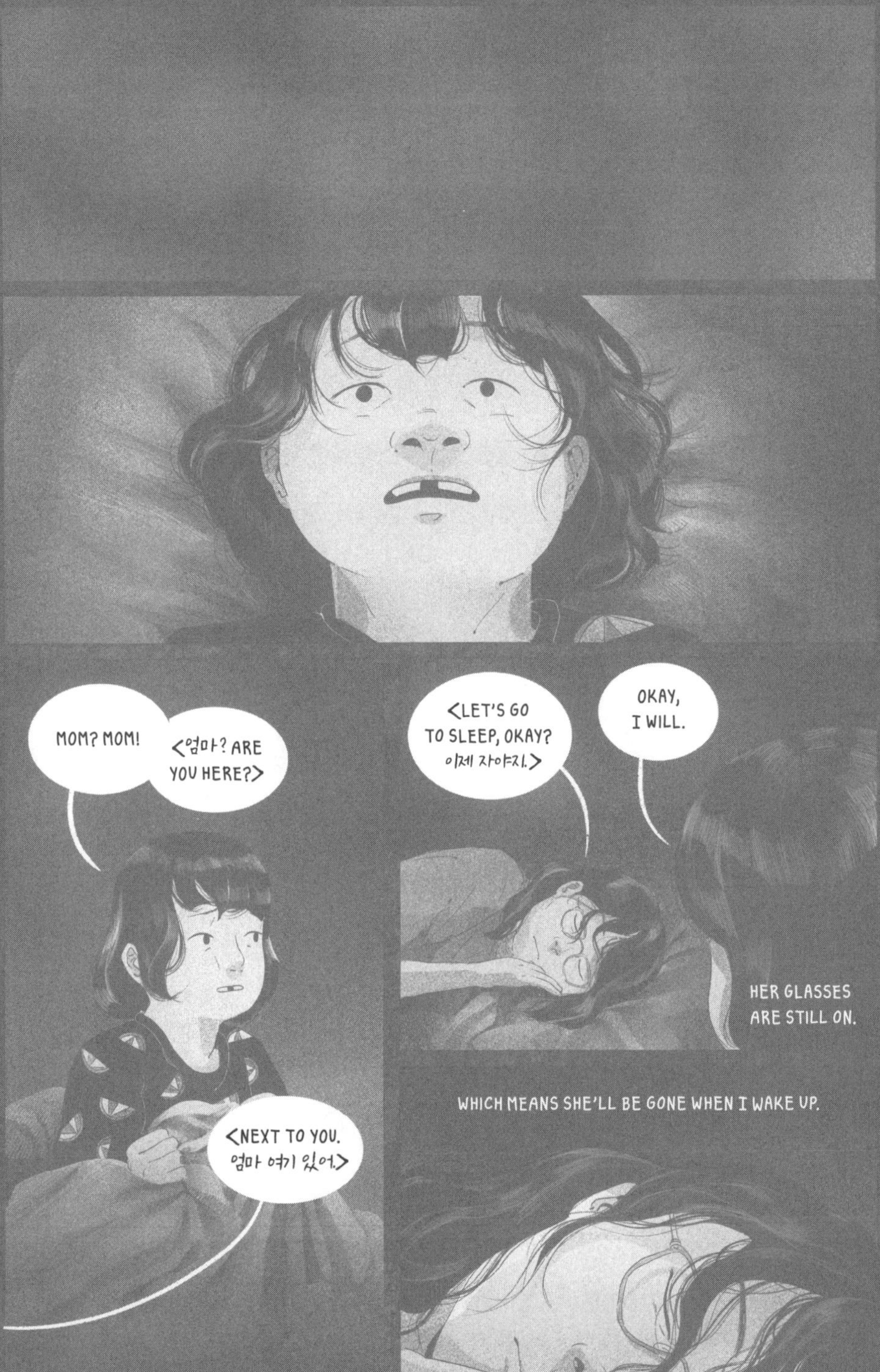
MOM? MOM!
<엄마? ARE YOU HERE?>
<NEXT TO YOU. 엄마 여기 있어.>
<LET'S GO TO SLEEP, OKAY? 이제 자야지.>
OKAY, I WILL.
HER GLASSES ARE STILL ON.
WHICH MEANS SHE'LL BE GONE WHEN I WAKE UP.

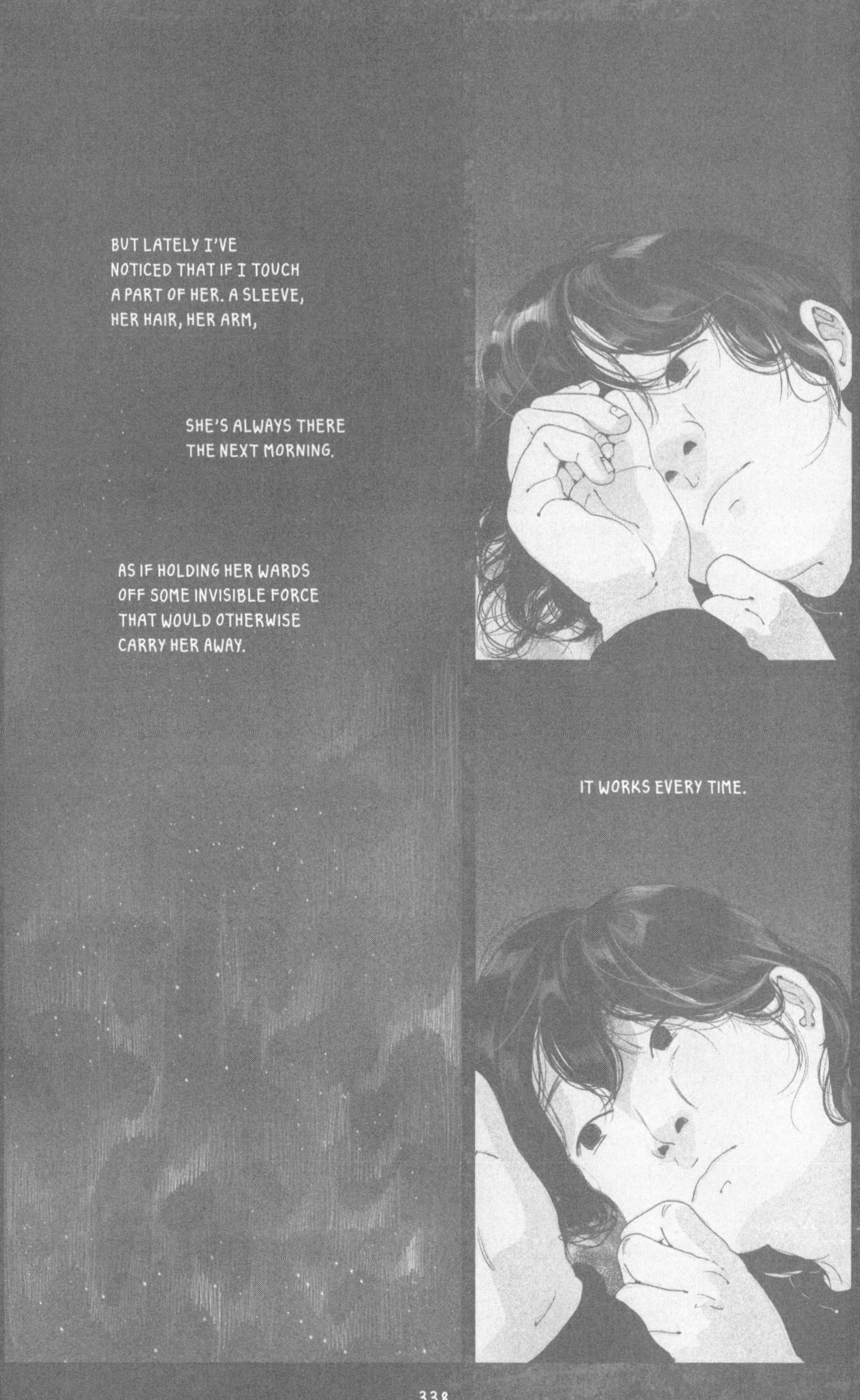
BUT LATELY I'VE NOTICED THAT IF I TOUCH A PART OF HER. A SLEEVE, HER HAIR, HER ARM,
SHE'S ALWAYS THERE THE NEXT MORNING.
AS IF HOLDING HER WARDS OFF SOME INVISIBLE FORCE THAT WOULD OTHERWISE CARRY HER AWAY.
IT WORKS EVERY TIME.

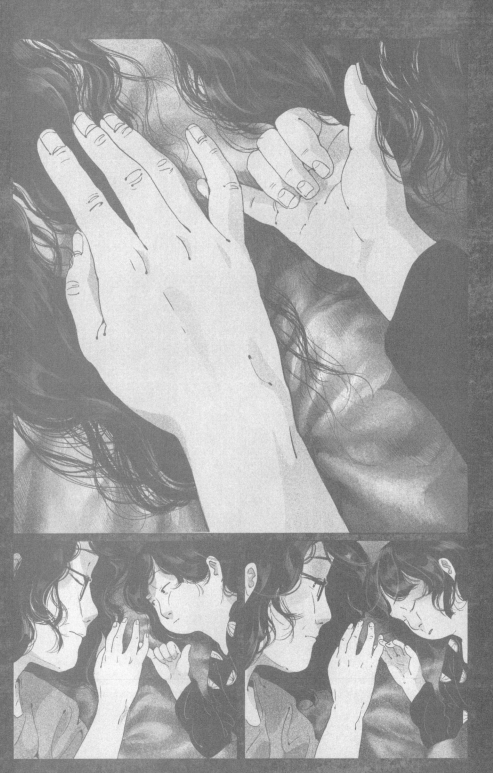

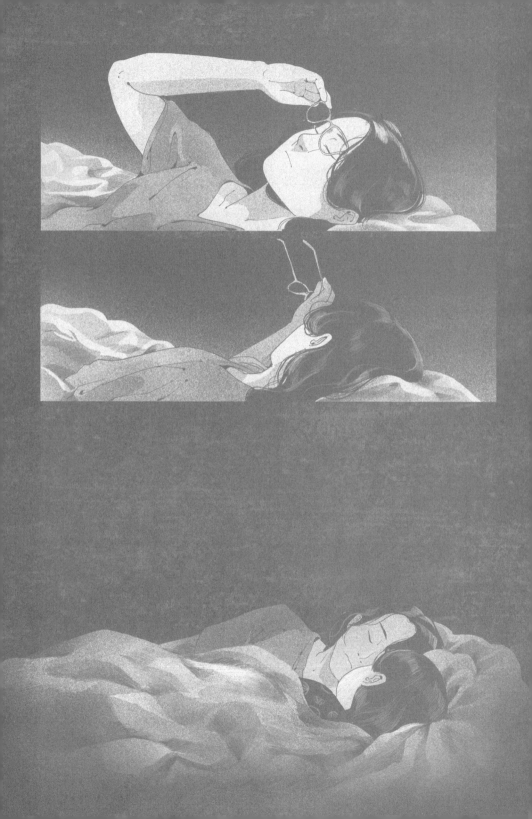